Authors

James L. Kinneavy, the Jane and Roland Blumberg Centennial Professor of English at The University of Texas at Austin, directed the development and writing of the composition strand in the program. He is the author of *A Theory of Discourse* and coauthor of *Writing in the Liberal Arts Tradition.* Professor Kinneavy is a leader in the field of rhetoric and composition and a respected educator whose teaching experience spans all levels—elementary, secondary, and college. He has continually been concerned with teaching writing to high school students.

John E. Warriner developed the organizational structure for the Handbook of Grammar, Usage, and Mechanics in the book. He coauthored the *English Workshop* series, was general editor of the *Composition: Models and Exercises* series, and editor of *Short Stories: Characters in Conflict.* He taught English for thirty-two years in junior and senior high school and college.

Writers and Editors

Ellen Ashdown has a Ph.D. in English from the University of Florida. She has taught composition and literature at the college level. She is a professional writer of educational materials and has published articles and reviews on education and art.

Norbert Elliot has a Ph.D. in English from the University of Tennessee. A Professor of English at New Jersey Institute of Technology, he is a specialist in test development and writing assessment.

Mary Hix has an M.A. in English from Wake Forest University. She has taught freshman composition courses. She is a professional writer and editor of educational materials in language arts.

Madeline Travers-Hovland has a Master of Arts in Teaching from Harvard University. She has taught English in elementary and secondary schools and has been an elementary school librarian. She is a professional writer of educational materials in literature and composition.

Alice M. Sohn has a Ph.D. in English Education from Florida State University. She has taught English in middle school, secondary school, and college. She has been a writer and editor of educational materials in language arts for seventeen years.

Patricia Street was an honors student in English Expression at Brown University. A professional writer for thirty years and a writer/editor of educational materials in language arts for ten years, she is currently compiling a reference book for writers.

Acknowledgments

We wish to thank the following teachers, who participated in field testing of pre-publication materials for this series:

Susan Almand-Myers
Meadow Park
Intermediate School
Beaverton, Oregon

Theresa L. Bagwell
Naylor Middle School
Tucson, Arizona

Ruth Bird
Freeport High School
Sarver, Pennsylvania

Joan M. Brooks
Central Junior High
School
Guymon, Oklahoma

Candice C. Bush
J. D. Smith Junior High
School
N. Las Vegas, Nevada

Mary Jane Childs
Moore West Junior High
School
Oklahoma City,
Oklahoma

Brian Christensen
Valley High School
West Des Moines, Iowa

Lenise Christopher
Western High School
Las Vegas, Nevada

Mary Ann Crawford
Ruskin Senior High
School
Kansas City, Missouri

Linda Dancy
Greenwood Lakes
Middle School
Lake Mary, Florida

Elaine A. Espindle
Peabody Veterans
Memorial High
School
Peabody, Massachusetts

Joan Justice
North Middle School
O'Fallon, Missouri

Beverly Kahwaty
Pueblo High School
Tucson, Arizona

Lamont Leon
Van Buren Junior High
School
Tampa, Florida

Susan Lusch
Fort Zumwalt South
High School
St. Peters, Missouri

Michele K. Lyall
Rhodes Junior High
School
Mesa, Arizona

Belinda Manard
McKinley Senior High
School
Canton, Ohio

Nathan Masterson
Peabody Veterans
Memorial High School
Peabody, Massachusetts

Marianne Mayer
Swope Middle School
Reno, Nevada

Penne Parker
Greenwood Lakes
Middle School
Lake Mary, Florida

Amy Ribble
Gretna Junior-Senior
High School
Gretna, Nebraska

Kathleen R. St. Clair
Western High School
Las Vegas, Nevada

Carla Sankovich
Billinghurst Middle School
Reno, Nevada

Sheila Shaffer
Cholla Middle School
Phoenix, Arizona

Joann Smith
Lehman Junior High
School
Canton, Ohio

Margie Stevens
Raytown Middle School
Raytown, Missouri

Mary Webster
Central Junior High
School
Guymon, Oklahoma

Susan M. Yentz
Oviedo High School
Oviedo, Florida

We wish to thank the following teachers, who contributed student papers for the Revised Edition of *Elements of Writing, First Course.*

Peter J. Caron
Cumberland Middle School
Cumberland,
Rhode Island

Judy Newby
Hillsboro Middle School
Hillsboro, Ohio

Merry Anne Hilty
Heskett Middle School
Bedford Heights, Ohio

Susan Gordon
Randolph Middle School
Randolph, New Jersey

Contents in Brief

Table of Contents

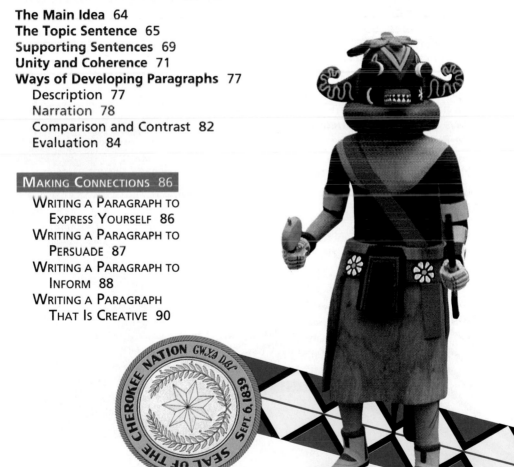

▶ CHAPTER 3 LEARNING ABOUT COMPOSITIONS 92

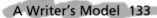

The Granger Collection, New York.

PART TWO   HANDBOOK

▶ CHAPTER *18* THE CLAUSE   514

► CHAPTER **19** KINDS OF SENTENCE STRUCTURE 532

Simple, Compound, and Complex Sentences

▶ CHAPTER 22 USING PRONOUNS CORRECTLY 604

Nominative and Objective Case Forms

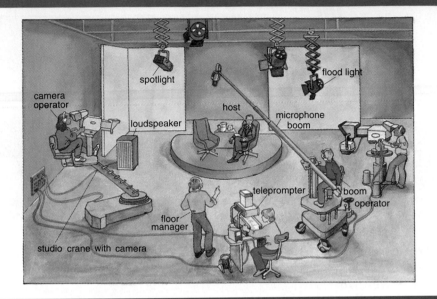

> CHAPTER 23 **USING MODIFIERS CORRECTLY** 627

Comparison and Placement

CHAPTER 28 SPELLING

Improving Your Spelling

CHAPTER 29 CORRECTING COMMON ERRORS

Key Language Skills Review

PART THREE RESOURCES

Models

Fiction

Arna Bontemps, *Chariot in the Sky: A Story of the Jubilee Singers*

Judith Ortiz Cofer, "An Hour with Abuelo"

Eugenia W. Collier, "Marigolds"

Mona Gardner, "The Dinner Party"

"Green Dragon Pond," a Bai folk tale

Rudyard Kipling, "Rikki-tikki-tavi"

Barry Lopez, "Coyote Places the Stars"

Gary Paulsen, *Hatchet*

Marjorie Kinnan Rawlings, *The Yearling*

Mari Sandoz, "Winter Thunder"

George Shannon, "A Drink for Crow," *Stories to Solve*

Virginia Driving Hawk Sneve, "The Medicine Bag"

Gary Soto, "The Jacket"

Joyce Carol Thomas, *Water Girl*

Yoshiko Uchida, *A Jar of Dreams*

Dorothy West, "The Richer, the Poorer"

Nonfiction

Wallace H. Black Elk and William S. Lyon, *Black Elk: The Sacred Ways of a Lakota*

Dan Carlinsky, "Kites"

"A Doll Made to Order," *Newsweek*

Lonnie Dyer, "Kachinas: Sacred Drama of the Hopis"

Delia Ephron, "How to Eat Like a Child"

Anne Frank, *The Diary of a Young Girl*

Ernesto Galarza, *Barrio Boy*

Anthony Glass, *Journal of an Indian Trader*

Whitney Hair, "Cures from the Jungle," *Ranger Rick*

Fred Johnson, *Meet-a-Cheetah*

Marjorie Lamb, "One Day a Month, Go Without Meat," *2 Minutes a Day for a Greener Planet*

Gary Larson, *The PreHistory of the Far Side*

John G. Neihardt, *Black Elk Speaks*

Dudley Randall, "Questions and Answers"

Sally Ride with Susan Okie, "Weightless in Space," *To Space and Back*

Carson I. A. Ritchie, *Insects, The Creeping Conquerors and Human History*

Louise L. Sherman, "A Review of Lois Lowry's *Number the Stars*"

Monica Sone, *Nisei Daughter*

Jesse Stuart, "What America Means to Me"

James P. Terzian and Kathryn Cramer, *Mighty Hard Road*

"Ubuhlali and Unmaka—Beaded Necklaces and Bangles," *African Crafts*

Greg Walz-Chojnacki, "The Spaceport Mermaids," *Odyssey*

Eudora Welty, *One Writer's Beginnings*

Eliot Wigginton, *I Wish I Could Give My Son a Wild Raccoon*

Poetry

Matsuo Bashō, *Haiku*

Ted Hughes, "My Aunt"

PART ONE

WRITING

CALLING THE SIGNALS

James L. Kinneavy

The quarterback looks up at the game clock. Nine seconds to go. An anxious buzz fills the stands as the fans desperately hope for a last-minute miracle. "22!" the quarterback calls out, quickly glancing around to make sure that the team is in place. "Red—44—Hup!" The defensive line digs in, pawing the ground like a herd of raging bulls. A running back moves quickly across the field behind the line. "Hup! Hup!" the quarterback yells. He takes the ball from the center. Helmets and pads crash as both teams struggle for precious ground.

The quarterback set the play in motion. But he was just the instrument. Where did it all really begin? Who was really **calling the signals**?

The Signal

Callers

Long before football season opened, players and coaches labored over the hundreds of pages that make up the team's playbook. The big play didn't begin on the field. Someone planned it. Someone wrote it down. And then—at long last—the players put all that writing into action on the playing field.

It's this way with almost everything that happens in life—from the very simplest things to the most complicated. Writers call many of the signals.

Movie actors and TV stars act out what someone else has first written. Singers sing notes and lyrics that are scored on paper. Scientists record the results of their experiments on paper. Politicians are elected because they make convincing speeches—speeches that are often written by someone else. And the laws they help pass after they're elected are all written down. Even most of the world's religions are based on the written word.

Is writing calling your signals? Probably. Have you ever bought anything after seeing it advertised? Somebody wrote the words that persuaded you. How did you learn that new computer game? Did you read the instructions? Somebody wrote them. Have you ever tried out for a sport? Somebody wrote the announcement about the time and place of the tryouts. Somebody wrote the words you're reading now!

Writers are people with power. They call the signals.

What's the Power?

All *writers* share the same power—the power of communication. They all have something to say (a *subject*), someone to say it to (an *audience*), and a way to say it (a *language*). You can have this power of communication, too. Try to think of communication as a triangle. Language—both written and spoken—is at the center.

How Do Writers Communicate?

The Writing Process

Powerful communicators know that planning is the key to good writing. Planning helps writers develop their ideas and then communicate them in a way that readers will understand and enjoy. Planning is an important part of a *writing process* that includes some basic steps, or stages. In one way or another, all writers use these basic steps.

Prewriting	Thinking and planning—coming up with a subject to write about, a purpose, and an audience; gathering ideas and details, making a plan for presenting ideas and details
Writing	Writing a first draft—using sentences and paragraphs to get ideas across; following a plan for presenting ideas
Evaluating and Revising	Reading over the draft to see what changes are needed; making changes to improve the draft
Proofreading and Publishing	Looking for and fixing mistakes; writing or printing out a final copy; sharing it with an audience

Why Do Writers Write?

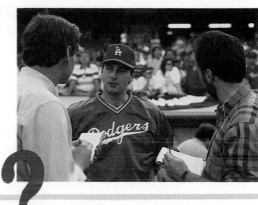

The Aims of Writing

Writers almost always have some purpose in mind for writing. They know what they want to accomplish before they start. All writing has one or more of four basic *aims*, or purposes. These are to inform, to persuade, to express yourself, and to be creative.

To Inform	Writers may give facts and other kinds of information, or they may explain something.
To Persuade	Writers sometimes try to persuade other people. They want readers to think about something differently or to take action.
To Express Themselves	Often, writers write just to express their own feelings and thoughts.
To Be Creative	Writers may also write to be creative. They create stories, poems, songs, and plays.

On the next few pages are four models about a boy named Arturo and his *abuelo*, or grandfather, who is also named Arturo. Notice how the different aim of each model shapes what the writers say and how they say it.

PERSUASIVE WRITING

To the Editor:

I want to tell you and the readers of the <u>Central Middle School Gazette</u> about something that might make all of you think about your grandparents, older relatives, or older neighbors a little differently.

The other day I went to see my grandfather at a nursing home in Brooklyn and discovered some things that really surprised me. I found out that he likes to write and loves words, just like me. He's writing an autobiography titled <u>Así es la vida,</u> which means "that's the way life is" in Spanish. He also writes poetry and reads it to the other people who live at the home.

I never would have known these things about him if I hadn't taken the time to visit him. I'm really glad that I'm getting to know him better.

To everybody reading this, I'd just like to say: Take some time to talk with older people and try to learn more about their lives and the things that interest them. You'll probably find out something surprising, too.

Arturo G.

READER'S RESPONSE

1. For what purpose has Arturo written this letter to his school newspaper? What does he want his readers to do?
2. What example does Arturo use to support his opinion? Do you think the example is convincing? Why or why not?

EXPRESSIVE WRITING

I'm very glad that little Arturo came to see today, even though I'm sure his mother talked into it. He only stayed for an hour, but he d seem to be in much of a hurry to leave when time was up.

... Arturo is not so little a

I'm very glad that little Arturo came to see me today, even though I'm sure his mother talked him into it. He only stayed for an hour, but he didn't seem to be in much of a hurry to leave when the time was up.

I guess that my Arturo is not so little anymore. Now that he is becoming a young man, I think he's old enough to understand that there's a little more to his old grandfather than he knew about when he was a child. That's why I read to him from Así es la vida. I know that he would appreciate it because his mother has told me that he loves to read and to write, as I do.

I hope that when Arturo grows up, he'll still think about me and tell his children what his abuelo was really like.

Arturo used to come to see me only a couple of times a year, along with the rest of the grandchildren. I have a feeling he may want to visit me a little more often now. Maybe I'll read him some of my poetry next time.

READER'S RESPONSE

1. Who is writing this journal entry? What are his thoughts and feelings about Arturo's visit?
2. What kind of person do you think Arturo's *abuelo* is? Why do you think so?

INFORMATIVE WRITING

Poetry Reading a Big Hit at Nursing Home

Visitors to Brooklyn's Golden Years nursing home may not realize that it houses some talented poets, but Golden Years residents who have attended the home's weekly poetry reading know better.

The poetry reading is a chance for residents of the home to share their original poetry with each other. It's becoming a popular activity.

One poet-resident, Arturo Benítez—a regular favorite at the reading—takes time each day to prepare poems he plans to share, penciling them into a red hardback notebook. He says he writes at least one new poem a week.

It's enthusiasm like his that seems to have made the reading such a big hit.

"For some crazy reason, people seem to like to hear me read my poetry," he says with a laugh. "I guess I like to hear other folks read their poetry, too."

READER'S RESPONSE

1. For what purpose do you think this newspaper article was written? What is the writer's opinion about the poetry reading at Golden Years?
2. What details has the writer added to this article to make it more interesting to readers? Who is the intended audience for the article?

AN HOUR WITH ABUELO

by Judith Ortiz Cofer

"Just one hour, *una hora*, is all I'm asking of you, son." My grandfather is in a nursing home in Brooklyn, and my mother wants me to spend some time with him, since the doctors say that he doesn't have too long to go now. *I* don't have much time left of my summer vacation, and there's a stack of books next to my bed I've got to read if I'm going to get into the AP English class I want. I'm going stupid in some of my classes, and Mr. Williams, the principal at Central, said that if I passed some reading tests, he'd let me move up.

Besides, I hate the place, the old people's home, especially the way it smells like industrial-strength ammonia and other stuff I won't mention, since it turns my stomach. And really the abuelo always has a lot of relatives visiting him, so I've gotten out of going out there except at Christmas, when a whole van-load of grandchildren are herded over there to give him gifts and a hug. We all make it quick and spend the rest of the time in the recreation area, where they play checkers and stuff with some of the old people's games, and I catch up on back issues of *Modern Maturity*. I'm not picky, I'll read almost anything.

Anyway, after my mother nags me for about a week, I let her drive me to Golden Years. She drops me off in front. She wants me to go in alone and have a "good time" talking to Abuelo. I tell her to be back in one hour or I'll take the bus back to Paterson. She squeezes my hand and says, *"Gracias, hijo,"* in a choked-up voice like I'm doing her a big favor.

I get depressed the minute I walk into the place. They line up the old people in wheelchairs in the hallway as if they were

about to be raced to the finish line by orderlies who don't even look at them when they push them here and there. I walk fast to room 10, Abuelo's "suite." He is sitting up in his bed writing with a pencil in one of those old-fashioned black hardback notebooks. It has the outline of the island of Puerto Rico on it. I slide into the hard vinyl chair by his bed. He sort of smiles and the lines on his face get deeper, but he doesn't say anything. Since I'm supposed to talk to him, I say, "What are you doing, Abuelo, writing the story of your life?"

It's supposed to be a joke, but he answers, "Sí, how did you know, Arturo?"

His name is Arturo too. I was named after him. I don't really know my grandfather. His children, including my mother, came to New York and New Jersey (where I was born) and he stayed on the Island until my grandmother died. Then he got sick, and since nobody could leave their jobs to go take care of him, they brought him to this nursing home in Brooklyn. I see him a couple of times a year, but he's always surrounded by his sons and daughters. My mother tells me that Don Arturo had once been a teacher back in Puerto Rico, but had lost his job after the war. Then he became a farmer. She's always saying in a sad voice, "Ay, bendito! What a waste of a fine mind." Then she usually shrugs her shoulders and says, "*Así es la vida.*" That's the way life is. It sometimes makes me mad that the adults I know just accept whatever is thrown at them because "that's the way things are." Not for me. I go after what I want.

Anyway, Abuelo is looking at me like he was trying to see into my head, but he doesn't say anything. Since I like stories, I decide I may as well ask him if he'll read me what he wrote.

I look at my watch: I've already used up twenty minutes of the hour I promised my mother.

Abuelo starts talking in his slow way. He speaks what my mother calls book English. He taught himself from a dictionary, and his words sound stiff, like he's sounding them out in his head before he says them. With his children he speaks Spanish, and that funny book English with us grandchildren. I'm surprised that he's still so sharp, because his body is shrinking like a crumpled-up brown paper sack with some bones in it. But I can see from looking into his eyes that the light is still on in there.

"It is a short story, Arturo. The story of my life. It will not take very much time to read it."

"I have time, Abuelo." I'm a little embarrassed that he saw me looking at my watch.

"Yes, hijo. You have spoken the truth. La verdad. You have much time."

Abuelo reads: "'I loved words from the beginning of my life. In the *campo* where I was born one of seven sons, there were few books. My mother read them to us over and over: the Bible, the stories of Spanish conquistadors and of pirates that she had read as a child and brought with her from the city of Mayagüez; that was before she married my father, a coffee bean farmer; and she taught us words from the newspaper that a boy on a horse brought every week to her. She taught each of us how to write on a slate with chalks that she ordered by mail every year. We used those chalks until they were so small that you lost them between your fingers.

"'I always wanted to be a writer and a teacher. With my heart and my soul I knew that I wanted to be around books all of my life. And so against the wishes of my father, who wanted all his sons to help him on the land, she sent me to high school in

14

Mayagüez. For four years I boarded with a couple she knew. I paid my rent in labor, and I ate vegetables I grew myself. I wore my clothes until they were thin as parchment. But I graduated at the top of my class! My whole family came to see me that day. My mother brought me a beautiful *guayabera,* a white shirt made of the finest cotton and embroidered by her own hands. I was a happy young man.

"'In those days you could teach in a country school with a high school diploma. So I went back to my mountain village and got a job teaching all grades in a little classroom built by the parents of my students.

"'I had books sent to me by the government. I felt like a rich man although the pay was very small. I had books. All the books I wanted! I taught my students how to read poetry and plays, and how to write them. We made up songs and put on shows for the parents. It was a beautiful time for me.

"'Then the war came, and the American President said that all Puerto Rican men would be drafted. I wrote to our governor and explained that I was the only teacher in the mountain vil-

lage. I told him that the children would go back to the fields and grow up ignorant if I could not teach them their letters. I said that I thought I was a better teacher than a soldier. The governor did not answer my letter. I went into the U.S. Army.

"'I told my sergeant that I could be a teacher in the army. I could teach all the farm boys their letters so that they could read the instructions on the ammunition boxes and not blow themselves up. The sergeant said I was too smart for my own good, and gave me a job cleaning latrines. He said to me there is reading material for you there, scholar. Read the writing on the walls. I spent the war mopping floors and cleaning toilets.

"'When I came back to the Island, things had changed. You had to have a college degree to teach school, even the lower grades. My parents were sick, two of my brothers had been killed in the war, the others had stayed in Nueva York. I was the only one left to help the old people. I became a farmer. I married a good woman who gave me many good children. I taught them all how to read and write before they started school.'"

Abuelo then puts the notebook down on his lap and closes his eyes.

"*Así es la vida* is the title of my book," he says in a whisper, almost to himself. Maybe he's forgotten that I'm there.

For a long time he doesn't say anything else. I think that he's sleeping, but then I see that he's watching me through half-closed lids, maybe waiting for my opinion of his writing. I'm trying to think of something nice to say. I liked it and all, but not the title. And I think that he could've been a teacher if he had wanted to bad enough. Nobody is going to stop me from doing what I want with my life. I'm not going to let la vida get in my way. I want to discuss this with him, but the words are not coming into my head in Spanish just yet. I'm about to ask him why he didn't keep fighting to make his dream come true, when an old lady in hot-pink running shoes sort of appears at the door.

She is wearing a pink jogging outfit too. The world's oldest marathoner, I say to myself. She calls out to my grandfather in a flirty voice, "Yoo-hoo, Arturo, remember what day this is? It's poetry-reading day in the rec room! You promised us you'd read your new one today."

I see my abuelo perking up almost immediately. He points to his wheelchair, which is hanging like a huge metal bat in the open closet. He makes it obvious that he wants me to get it. I put it together, and with Mrs. Pink Running Shoes's help, we get him in it. Then he says in a strong deep voice I hardly recognize, "Arturo, get that notebook from the table, please."

I hand him another map-of-the-Island notebook—this one is red. On it in big letters it says, *POEMAS DE ARTURO*.

I start to push him toward the rec room, but he shakes his finger at me.

"Arturo, look at your watch now. I believe your time is over." He gives me a wicked smile.

Then with her pushing the wheelchair—maybe a little too fast—they roll down the hall. He is already reading from his notebook, and she's making bird noises. I look at my watch and the hour *is* up, to the minute. I can't help but think that my abuelo has been timing *me*. It cracks me up. I walk slowly down the hall toward the exit sign. I want my mother to have to wait a little. I don't want her to think that I'm in a hurry or anything.

READER'S RESPONSE

1. Do you think that Arturo will come back and visit his grandfather again? Why?
2. What details does the writer include that make the characters in this story seem realistic?

Writing and Thinking Activities

1. Get together with two or three other students. Then discuss these questions about the four models you've just read.
   a. Which model mostly tells the writer's thoughts and feelings?
   b. Which one tries to convince its reader to do something? What does the writer want the reader to do?
   c. Which one gives readers news or information by using facts and interesting details?
   d. Which model mostly tells readers a story? In what parts of this model does the writer show the most creativity?

2. When you communicate with other people, what are your aims? During two hours of a typical day, keep track of each time you use language. Think about the times you write, read, speak, and listen. How often is your aim to inform? to persuade? to express yourself? to be creative? Share what you found out with two or three classmates. What aims do each of you most often have?

3. Which type of writing do you think is used most often? Is it informative, persuasive, self-expressive, or creative? Pick out a magazine or newspaper to bring to class. Work with some other students to find examples of all four types of writing. Then decide which one is used most. Do some publications have just one type of writing?

4. What is creative writing? To be creative is the main purpose of writing that creates literature, such as novels, short stories, poems, and plays. But isn't all writing creative in some way? What about letters, book reports, and newspaper articles? Would you call them creative? Find some examples of writing that is creative, even though the basic purpose or aim is informative, persuasive, or self-expressive.

1 WRITING AND THINKING

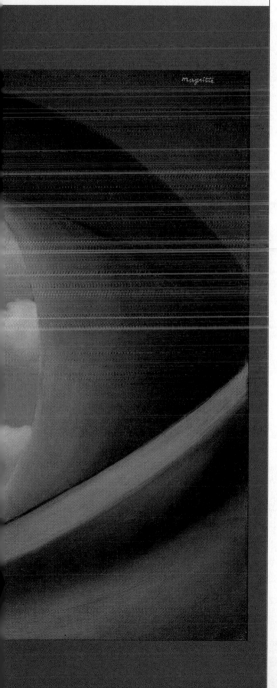

Looking at the Process

Did you ever stop and think about what happens when you write? You actually go through an amazing **process.** It begins with thoughts and feelings that grow in your brain until they finally flow out as written words on paper.

Writing and You. Do you find that it's sometimes easy to write, but at other times the words just won't cooperate? Is your brain brimming with ideas? Or is it often hard to think of something to write about? Professional writers have the same problems. Sometimes they can't come up with a good idea. The words just won't come out right. What is the hardest part of writing for you?

As You Read. As you read what editor Dudley Randall says about writing poetry, see if you think his advice applies to other kinds of writing besides poetry.

René Magritte, *The False Mirror (Le Faux Miroir)* (1928). Oil on canvas, 21 1/4 × 31 7/8" (54 × 80.9 cm). The Museum of Modern Art, New York. Purchase. © 1996 Museum of Modern Art, New York. © 1996 Charly Herscovici/Artists Rights Society (ARS), N.Y.

Q & A
Questions Answers

The following questions are asked frequently in letters from beginning poets to Broadside Press.

by Dudley Randall

The answers are by Dudley Randall, Broadside Press editor.

1 Q. I am a fifteen-year-old high school student and have been writing poetry for one year. How do I go about having a book published?

A. How fortunate that you became a poet so early! You have many years of writing ahead of you, so it's not necessary to rush into the permanence of book format. Some poets, Robert Hayden among them, published books very young, and now they don't want their juvenile publications to be seen. I asked Hayden for permission to reprint a poem from his first book, *Heartshape in the Dust,* and he said, "No, *no,* No, NO, *NO!* I wrote those poems in my apprentice years, when I was learning to write, and I don't want any of them reprinted."

This period of learning how to write, discovering new poets, experimenting with new forms, can be one of your most enjoyable. Don't terminate it prematurely. Read, read, read. And write, write, write.

Don't try for book publication until you have published extensively in magazines and newspapers. Mari Evans was well-known for her contributions to magazines and anthologies before she published her first book. Such publication will be an indication that many different editors have found your work acceptable. Then publishers, perhaps, will have seen your poems somewhere, and will be more willing to risk from $500 to $10,000 on a first book by you, than on a book by an unknown poet.

All the poems you sent me were in rimed couplets, which are only one of many forms and which have their limitations. Master the scores of other forms which you will find in Karl Shapiro's *A Prosody Handbook* or in any handbook on writing poetry. Also, learn correct spelling and grammar. When you have learned the rules, you can break them, if you have good reasons to.

After you have done these things, you can start sending your poems to magazines. Choose publications where the competition is not too tough, like your local newspaper, your school newspaper or yearbook, literary magazine, or your church bulletin. After mastering spelling, grammar, and forms, you will be ready to be published, but try ephemeral publications first, not the permanence of books, which you may regret later. Have fun!

"This period of learning how to write, discovering new poets, experimenting with new forms, can be one of your most enjoyable."

2
Q. I have a teacher who reads and criticizes my poems. He says they are full of clichés. What can I do?

A. One of the best ways to learn to write is to have your work read and criticized by a competent person. You must develop a thick skin to criticism, and the ability to evaluate it objectively and apply it to your work to make it better. Praise only flatters your ego, but searching criticism exposes your flaws and points out what you must do to write better.

Clichés are expressions which have been worked to death and have lost their freshness, surprise, and power, like "right on," "pigs," "Queen of the Nile," "Amerikkka," "sweet as a rose." Perhaps the reason you use clichés is that you have not read enough to observe their repetition. Read more widely and develop the knack of spotting over-used expressions and eliminate them from your writing.

READER'S RESPONSE

1. In his first answer, Randall advises the fifteen-year-old poet, "Read, read, read. And write, write, write." How much reading do you do? What kinds of reading do you enjoy most?
2. Randall says that criticism helps you learn to write better. How do you feel when someone criticizes your writing? How do you think you can learn to be a better writer?
3. Clichés are hard to overcome. List some familiar clichés ("tough as nails," "fresh as a daisy," and so on). Then see if you can think of a fresh way to express each idea. You can work with a partner or several classmates.

LOOKING AHEAD

In this chapter you'll practice a general approach or process that applies to all types of writing. As you work through the chapter, remember that

- careful thinking is part of writing
- the planning that you do before you write is crucial
- the writing process can be adapted to fit your own writing style

smooth as silk

green as grass

Aim—The "Why" of Writing

People write because they have something to say, someone to say it to, and a purpose for saying it. That's the general *why* for communicating. But what are the specific purposes people have for writing?

Maybe you think there are many, many purposes for writing. But there are really only a few.

WHY PEOPLE WRITE	
To express themselves	To get to know themselves better; to find meaning in their lives
To share information	To give information other people need or want; to share special knowledge
To persuade	To convince other people to do something or believe something
To create literature	To be creative; to say something in a unique way

Everything people write has one of these four purposes—sometimes more than one at the same time. For example, a writer may want to share information *and* to persuade, to express himself or herself *and* to create literature.

Like all the other writers in the world, you'll be writing for at least one of these four purposes.

Process—The "How" of Writing

Writing is a skill that improves with practice. It's also part of a *process*, a series of steps that lead to an end result. The following diagram shows the steps that usually take place in the writing process. But every writer is different. You may spend less time prewriting than the person sitting next to you. And that person may spend much more time revising than you do. As you review the writing process, notice how every stage requires thinking. Writing and thinking happen together whenever you write.

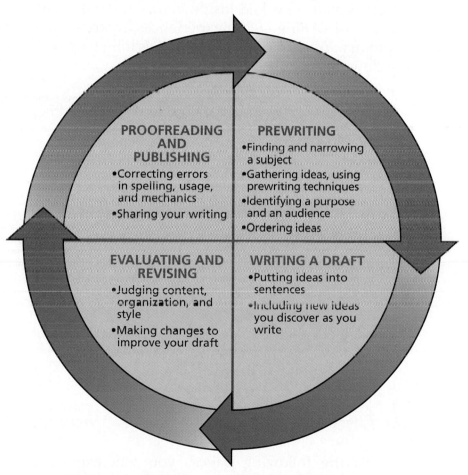

PROOFREADING AND PUBLISHING
•Correcting errors in spelling, usage, and mechanics
•Sharing your writing

PREWRITING
•Finding and narrowing a subject
•Gathering ideas, using prewriting techniques
•Identifying a purpose and an audience
•Ordering ideas

EVALUATING AND REVISING
•Judging content, organization, and style
•Making changes to improve your draft

WRITING A DRAFT
•Putting ideas into sentences
•Including new ideas you discover as you write

Unlike a chiseler working in stone, you can make changes easily when you write. At any point in the writing process, you can go back to an earlier stage or even start all over again. Suppose you're writing a committee report about a food drive your scout troop will sponsor. As you write your first draft, you may realize you don't know enough about the kinds of food you need to collect. So you go back to prewriting to gather more information.

Finding Ideas for Writing

Have you ever complained, "I can't think of anything to write about"? Locked inside your mind are thousands of ideas for writing—your experiences, interests, and observations. You can unlock ideas for writing by practicing the following prewriting techniques.

PREWRITING TECHNIQUES		
Writer's Journal	Keeping a record of personal experiences, observations, and ideas	Page 27
Freewriting	Writing for a few minutes about whatever comes to mind	Page 28
Brainstorming ·	Listing all ideas as quickly as you think of them	Page 29
Clustering	Brainstorming ideas and using circles and lines to show connections	Page 31
Asking Questions	Asking the *5W–How?* and "What if?" questions	Page 33
Reading and Listening with a Focus	Reading and listening to find specific information	Page 35

In the following pages, you will experiment with different prewriting techniques. Some will probably feel more comfortable and work better for you than others. And you'll often use more than one prewriting technique at a time.

COMPUTER NOTE: If you store your prewriting notes and drafts in separate files on a diskette, you won't have to worry about carrying around or losing paper notes.

Writer's Journal

In your *writer's journal* you'll write about things that happen and things that interest you. Journal entries can be very short or go on for several pages. You can include "Things I Like"—a special section of quotations, articles, and cartoons. Soon your journal will become a good sourcebook for writing ideas.

- For your writer's journal, use a special notebook or folder. Set aside a time to write every day.
- Forget about grammar, spelling, and punctuation at this stage. Just get your thoughts down on paper.
- Encourage your imagination. Write about dreams and daydreams. Try creating songs, poems, or stories. If you enjoy drawing, include pictures and cartoons.

HERE'S HOW

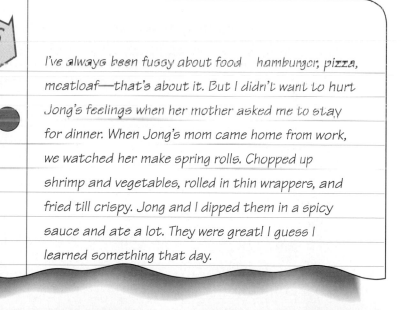

I've always been fussy about food   hamburger, pizza, meatloaf—that's about it. But I didn't want to hurt Jong's feelings when her mother asked me to stay for dinner. When Jong's mom came home from work, we watched her make spring rolls. Chopped up shrimp and vegetables, rolled in thin wrappers, and fried till crispy. Jong and I dipped them in a spicy sauce and ate a lot. They were great! I guess I learned something that day.

EXERCISE 1 ▶   **Keeping a Writer's Journal**

Ten years from now, what will you remember about your life? Your ideas, feelings, and experiences are worth recording. Write a journal entry that you can share with your classmates. Write about something important that happened yesterday or something you're looking forward to.

Freewriting

Freewriting is writing down whatever ideas pop into your head about a subject. Set a time limit of three to five minutes, and go!

- Write about something that's important to you.
- Write whatever your subject makes you think of or remember. Don't worry about complete sentences, spelling, or punctuation.
- If you get stuck, write anything. Don't let your pen or pencil stop, just continue writing down all your ideas. Keep writing until the time is up.

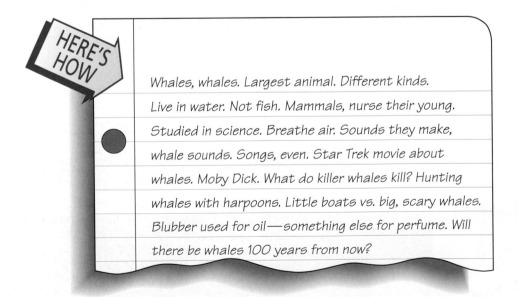

HERE'S HOW

Whales, whales. Largest animal. Different kinds.

Live in water. Not fish. Mammals, nurse their young.

Studied in science. Breathe air. Sounds they make, whale sounds. Songs, even. Star Trek movie about whales. Moby Dick. What do killer whales kill? Hunting whales with harpoons. Little boats vs. big, scary whales. Blubber used for oil—something else for perfume. Will there be whales 100 years from now?

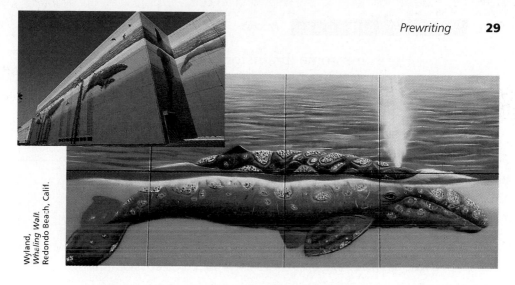

Wyland,
Whaling Wall.
Redondo Beach, Calif.

Focused freewriting, or *looping,* helps you narrow your topic and gather details. Choose a word or phrase from freewriting you've already done. (You might choose "hunting whales," for example.) Then freewrite for several minutes on this limited topic.

EXERCISE 2 ▶ **Using Freewriting**

Where do you go to have fun? Where do you go when you want to think? Where do you feel most at home? Think of a place that's special to you. How would you describe the place and your feelings about it? Freewrite in your journal for three minutes about the place. Or freewrite about another topic that's important to you.

Brainstorming

You can *brainstorm* alone, but it's more fun with a partner or a group. Then you can bounce ideas off each other.

- Write a subject—any subject—at the top of a piece of paper or on a chalkboard.
- Write down every single thought about the subject that comes to mind. Don't stop to judge ideas. (You can do that later.)
- Keep going until you run out of ideas.

Here are some brainstorming notes on the subject "shopping mall." Notice that the list includes some silly ideas that will be thrown out later.

Shopping Mall	
place to meet friends	non-shopping mall, don't
spend most of Saturday there	shop much
people watching, make up	walk around—talk
stories	record stores, video games
shopping mall on Mars?	some adults grouchy with us
underwater shopping mall?	everyone who's anyone
saw a movie star at the mall	great food—yogurt bar,
	potato bar

EXERCISE 3   **Using Brainstorming**

Brainstorming is more fun in a group. Team up with two or three classmates for a brainstorming session on one of the following subjects or on one of your own. Brainstorm as long a list of ideas as you can.

1. UFOs
2. fears
3. rock groups

4. video games
5. community problems
6. heroes

Clustering

Clustering is sometimes called *webbing* or may be called *making connections.* When you make a cluster diagram, you break a topic into its smaller parts.

- Write your subject in the center of your paper and circle it.
- Around the subject, write related ideas as you think of them. Circle these ideas, and draw lines to connect them with the subject.
- An idea may make you think of other ideas. Connect these with circles and lines, too.

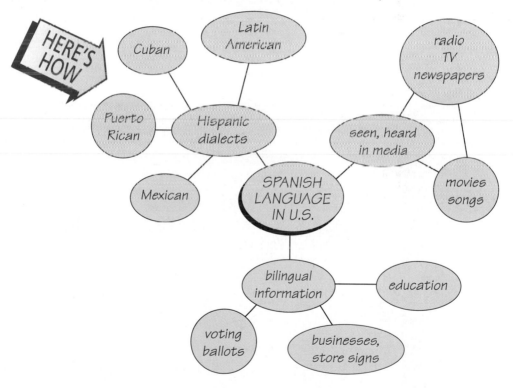

EXERCISE 4 ▶ **Using Clustering**

Make a cluster diagram for a subject you didn't use from Exercise 3 (page 30), or pick a subject of your own. Use circles and lines to show how ideas are connected.

CRITICAL THINKING

Observing with Your Five Senses

While you're awake, you receive steady input from each of your five senses (sight, hearing, smell, taste, touch). Most of the time you ignore these *sensory details.* But as a writer you need to *observe* the world around you with all five senses alert and ready to receive information.

Here are a writer's notes on a Cuban American New Year's Eve celebration.

HERE'S HOW

SIGHT:	dark night; brightly lit house; about thirty family members and friends; children playing; men tending the back-yard barbecue
SOUND:	record player; singing; people talking, telling jokes, laughter; children's shouts; TV in living room
SMELL:	slow-roasting pig; spicy smells; freshly ground coffee
TASTE:	crisp barbecued pork; black beans and rice; yucca; fried plantains; guava pastries; bitter orange
TOUCH:	warm night; breezes through open win-dows; embroidered tablecloth; paper plates and plastic forks and knives

CRITICAL THINKING EXERCISE:
Observing Sensory Details

Imagine yourself as a supercomputer designed to record every sensory detail. You're collecting details for a description that will go into a time capsule to be opened in the year 3000. Collect details for all five senses as you observe one of the following.

1. a basketball or football game
2. a pizza parlor or other restaurant
3. the school cafeteria
4. a dance
5. a birthday party
6. a city street or highway

Asking Questions

Practice asking yourself two different kinds of questions. One kind helps you find facts. The other kind exercises your imagination.

5W-How? Questions. News reporters track down information by asking the ***5W-How? questions:*** *Who? What? Where? When? Why?* and *How?* For some topics, some question words won't apply. And with other topics, you may think of several good questions for a question word.

Here are some questions one writer asked when preparing to write a school newspaper article about new automobile designs.

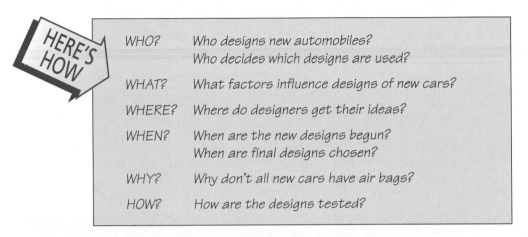

WHO?	*Who designs new automobiles?*
	Who decides which designs are used?
WHAT?	*What factors influence designs of new cars?*
WHERE?	*Where do designers get their ideas?*
WHEN?	*When are the new designs begun?*
	When are final designs chosen?
WHY?	*Why don't all new cars have air bags?*
HOW?	*How are the designs tested?*

HERE'S HOW

"What if?" Questions.   What if you could become invisible? What if you could fly? *"What if?" questions* will help you find ideas for creative writing. The following are some "What if?" questions you might ask to spark your imagination.

- *What if I could change one thing in my life?* (What if I were a genius? What if I lived on a ranch?)
- *What if some common thing did not exist?* (What if there were no telephones? What if Earth had no water?)
- *What if one situation in the world could be changed?* (What if everyone lived forever? What if everyone spoke the same language?)

EXERCISE 5 ▶ Asking the *5W-How?* Questions

As a reporter for your local newspaper, you have been assigned to write an article about a popular music group that's coming to town. Choose a real group, and make a list of *5W-How?* questions that you'd like to ask the musicians.

EXERCISE 6 ▶ Asking "What if?" Questions

You and a partner are planning a short story for your class magazine. Brainstorm as many "What if?" questions as you can. (This is the way movie producers get their ideas: What if a family went on a vacation and left their son home alone?) Then write a brief plot outline for your story.

EXAMPLES   What if the person on TV could hear what you say?
What if two of your classmates were actually aliens from another planet?

Reading and Listening with a Focus

Suppose you're writing about what America was like before Columbus arrived. How can you find out? For a topic you can't observe directly, find information by reading and listening with a focus—with something specific in mind.

Reading.   Reading sources include items such as books, magazines, newspapers, and pamphlets. Here are some techniques you can use to find specific information.

- Check a book's table of contents and index. Go directly to the pages on your topic.
- Don't read everything. Skim the text quickly. Look only for information on your topic. Don't forget to check photos and captions, too.
- When you find information on your topic, read carefully. Take notes on main ideas and important details.

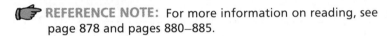 **REFERENCE NOTE:** For more information on reading, see page 878 and pages 880–885.

Listening.   Some people learn better by listening than by reading. You can gather information on a specific topic by listening to speeches, interviews, radio and TV programs, audiotapes, and videotapes. You can use the following techniques whenever you listen for information.

- Get ready ahead of time by thinking of questions on your topic.
- Listen for main ideas and important details. Take notes to help you remember.

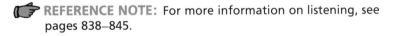 REFERENCE NOTE: For more information on listening, see pages 838–845.

EXERCISE 7 ▶ **Practicing Reading and Listening**

Look through a TV program listing for this week (most newspapers publish a daily guide), and make a list of all the nature programs. (Nature programs are about subjects such as plants, animals, weather, astronomy, earth sciences, oceanography, and geology.) Choose one program on your list, and watch it. Jot down at least five facts you learn from watching the program.

Prewriting

Thinking About Purpose and Audience

Purpose.　Before you write, always ask yourself, *"Why am I writing?"* This chart shows the basic *purposes* for writing and some forms you might use for each purpose.

MAIN PURPOSE	FORMS OF WRITING
To express your feelings	Journal entry, letter, personal essay
To explain or inform	Science or history report, news story, biography, autobiography, travel essay
To persuade	Persuasive essay, letter to the editor, advertisement, political speech
To be creative	Short story, poem, play

Audience.　You also need to identify your *audience,* or readers. Think about how you'll adapt your writing to a specific audience. Ask yourself these questions:

- What do my readers already know about my topic?
- What will I need to explain? What will they find most interesting?
- What kinds of words and sentences (simple or more difficult and complex) should I use?

Perhaps your hobby is collecting arrowheads. If you're writing a letter to a relative in Juneau, Alaska, your cousin may have no idea what arrowheads are. You'll need to explain what they look like, how they're made, and where they're found. You'll probably use the kind of vocabulary

and language that you would use if you were speaking directly to your cousin.

Depending on who you are, your audience will vary. As a student, you often write for teachers. If you were in business, you might write an annual report for the company or a newsletter to employees. Remember to consider your audience before you write, and to adjust your writing accordingly.

E X E R C I S E 8 ▶   **Thinking About Purpose and Audience**

You're writing a science report about active volcanoes in Hawaii. Your purpose is to inform, and your readers are your classmates. Which of these statements belong in your report? Which ones don't?

1. Two active volcanoes in Hawaii Volcanoes National Park are Mauna Loa and Kilauea.
2. The town of Volcano, Hawaii, where many scientists live, is built right next to an active volcano.
3. I'm really afraid to even think about volcanoes ever since I saw a late-night movie about a killer volcano.
4. Mount Vesuvius in Italy is a steep-sided, symmetrical composite volcano.
5. When volcanoes erupt, they can cause a lot of damage.

 *Prewriting*

Arranging Ideas

How you present your ideas is just as important as what you have to say. So after you find a topic and gather information about it, you need to plan the order of ideas. This chart shows four common ways of ordering, or arranging, information.

WAYS TO ORGANIZE IDEAS		
TYPE OF ORDER	DEFINITION	EXAMPLES
Chronological	Describe events in the order they happen.	Story, narrative poem, explanation of a process, history, biography, play
Spatial	Describe objects according to location (near to far, left to right, and so on).	Description, directions, explanation
Importance	Give details from least to most important or the reverse.	Persuasive writing, description, explanation, evaluative writing
Logical	Group related details together.	Definition, classification

 REFERENCE NOTE: For more information on arranging ideas, see pages 74–75.

CRITICAL THINKING
Arranging Ideas

Your topic, purpose, and details will give you a clue about which order to use. For example, you're writing a description of Skylab, the U.S. space station launched in 1973. Your purpose is to inform; your audience is your classmates. You've collected information about each room. So you decide to use spatial order, moving from one end of the space station to the other end.

In the following story of a mongoose fighting a cobra named Nagaina, a natural order is chronological. What happens first? What happens last?

> Rikki-tikki was bounding all round Nagaina, keeping just out of reach of her stroke, his little eyes like hot coals. Nagaina gathered herself together, and flung out at him. Rikki-tikki jumped up and backward. Again and again and again she struck, and each time her head came with a whack on the matting of the veranda and she gathered herself together like a watch spring. Then Rikki-tikki danced in a circle to get behind her, and Nagaina spun around to keep her head to his head, so that the rustle of her tail on the matting sounded like dry leaves blown along by the wind.
>
> Rudyard Kipling, "Rikki-tikki-tavi"

CRITICAL THINKING EXERCISE:
Choosing an Order for Ideas

For each of the following writing situations, think about the kinds of details you would use. Then choose an appropriate order for those details. Look at the chart on page 39, Ways to Organize Ideas, for a description of each of the types of order.

1. In a letter to a pen pal, you describe what your room looks like.
2. You are writing a letter to the editor of the local newspaper. To persuade readers to approve a new park tax, you give three reasons why your town needs more parks.
3. You enjoy creative writing. For your little sister's birthday present, you plan to write an adventure story about dragons.
4. For an English assignment, you are going to review a new book that you have just read, telling whether you think it's worth recommending to your classmates.

Using Visuals to Organize Ideas

Visuals—such as charts, graphs, maps, sequence chains, time lines, drawings, or diagrams—can turn messy, disorganized prewriting notes into neat packages of ideas and details. Charts and sequence chains can help you organize your ideas.

Charts.   Think about the details you have gathered, and look for ways to group ideas. Then decide on the headings that will cover most of your information. Write your details under those headings. In the following chart, for example, one writer gives three types of information about the Ojibwas and the Seminoles.

	OJIBWAS 1600s	SEMINOLES 1700s
WHERE THEY LIVED	Around the Great Lakes	Florida
KIND OF HOUSE	Wigwam	Open-sided houses on stilts
SOURCES OF FOOD	Hunted, fished, farmed, and gathered wild plants	Hunted, fished, and farmed

Seminole War Chief

Ojibwa warrior

Sequence Chains.   A *sequence chain* organizes events in chronological order. You can use a sequence chain to show the main events in a story or the steps in a process. The following is a sequence chain for a short story.

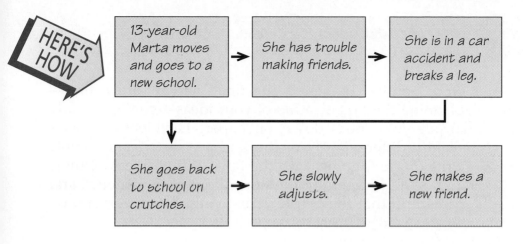

EXERCISE 9 ▸ **Making a Chart**

How can you show a comparison of two countries? Make a chart to organize the following notes about the United States and China. What headings will you use?

> The United States has a total area of 3,600,000 square miles.
> It has more than 250,000,000 people.
> Its form of government is a republic.
> China has a population of more than 1,100,000,000 people.
> It is governed by a communist regime.
> It has a total area of more than 3,690,000 square miles.

EXERCISE 10 ▸ **Making a Sequence Chain**

Create a sequence chain for one of these assignments. (Do one or the other, not both.)

1. Show the main events in a story. You can create a plot for a short story, or show the events in a story that you have read or in a movie or TV show that you have seen.
2. Show the stages in the writing process. Use the information in the pie-shaped diagram on page 25.

Writing a First Draft

Once you've completed the final step in prewriting—planning the organization of your ideas—you'll be ready to put your ideas down on paper. Each person has a slightly different way of drafting a paper. Some people write quickly, going with the flow of their ideas. Others draft slowly, carefully thinking about each sentence and paragraph that they write. Trust your own style, and do whatever works best for you.

- Use your prewriting plans to guide you as you write your first draft.
- As you write, you may come up with new ideas. Include these ideas in your draft.
- Don't worry about spelling and grammar errors. You can correct them later.

WRITING NOTE In writing, *voice* is the way the words sound. As you put your ideas into sentences and paragraphs, try to express your ideas simply and naturally. Don't use words just because they sound "important." Your writing should have your own voice—and sound like you.

On page 45 is the first draft of a paragraph about Mary McLeod Bethune, an African American educator from South Carolina who lived from 1875 to 1955. Notice the writer's questions that appear in brackets. These show that the writer will later return to the prewriting stage to find more information before writing the final draft. Notice, also, that the writing in this draft does not sound as polished as the final draft will. In this first draft there are problems with both content and organization that the writer will fix later.

HERE'S
HOW

Mary McLeod Bethune was the first in her family to go to school. She started when she was eleven. [Twelve? Check this.] The school was a mission school for black children. [Where? Go back for details.] Mary was a fast learner. She had to walk a long way to and from school. Mary's family sacrificed to let her attend school. When she was in school, she couldn't help with all the chores on the family farm. Mary liked to plow. When she started her third year, she helped the teacher. She also began teaching her brothers and sisters at home to read. Mary was good at math. She helped people with their accounts so the big planters couldn't cheat them.

E X E R C I S E 11 ▶ **Writing a First Draft**

Many children and adults in the world today don't know how to read any language. Imagine that you were never taught to read. What would you miss? How would it change your life? Get ready to write a draft of a paragraph telling how you'd feel if you couldn't read. Use one or more of the prewriting techniques on pages 26–36 to explore your thoughts on this topic. Arrange your ideas in a way that makes sense. For this topic, logical order or order of importance might work well. Draft your paragraph and share it with your classmates.

Evaluating and Revising

You can't fix a TV set—or anything else—until you figure out what's wrong with it. In the same way, after you've finished your first draft and are looking over what you've written, you'll need to figure out what parts aren't working so that you can fix them. *Evaluating* and *revising* are really two separate steps in the writing process, but most people do them together.

Evaluating

When you *evaluate* your writing, you judge what's good about it and what needs to be improved. You evaluate writing more often than you realize. Each time you decide whether you like a book or magazine, you're evaluating.

Self-Evaluation. It's often harder to judge your own writing than someone else's. Use these tips to evaluate your own writing.

- Put your draft aside for awhile. Rest your brain.
- Read your paper carefully at least three times. Each time focus on something different. For example, you might ask yourself questions like these:
    Are the ideas clear?
    Are the ideas in the most effective order?
    Are sentences well worded and smoothly connected to each other?
- Read your paper aloud to yourself. Listen for awkward or unclear spots.

Peer Evaluation. You can get some feedback on your writing from a partner or several classmates. (A peer is someone who is your equal—in this case, your classmate.) When you use peer evaluation, get ready to play two roles: (l) a writer whose work is being evaluated, and (2) a reader who is evaluating a classmate's writing.

GUIDELINES FOR PEER EVALUATION

Tips for the Writer

1. Make a list of questions for the reader. Ask what the reader thinks about parts of your paper you're not sure about.
2. Keep an open mind. Take all of the comments that your reader makes seriously, and don't be offended by any criticism. Even professional writers get suggestions for improvement from their editors.

Tips for the Reader

1. Always tell the writer something good about the paper.
2. Focus on content and organization. Don't point out spelling and grammar errors.
3. Put your suggestions into helpful questions: "Can you say this in easier words?" or "Can you add some specific details?"
4. Suggest something specific the writer can do to improve the paper.

CRITICAL THINKING

Evaluating Writing

Whenever you evaluate, you judge something by measuring it against established standards. Here are some basic standards for judging good writing. (See page 51 for a more detailed list of standards.)

1. The writing is interesting. It grabs and holds your attention.
2. The writing has a clear main idea.
3. The main idea is supported with enough details.
4. The ideas are presented in a clear and reasonable order.

CRITICAL THINKING EXERCISE:
Evaluating a Paragraph

If you think octopuses are scary, wait till you meet the giant squid. With one or two classmates, evaluate the following paragraph. Use the standards for good writing given on page 47. Write at least one comment on what's good about the paragraph. Then write at least one comment on what needs to be improved.

A strange sea creature that people rarely see because it lives in deep waters is the giant squid. Giant squids can grow up to sixty feet long. There are old sea stories about giant squids attacking boats. They wrap their tentacles around them. Rows of sucking disks line the arms. The giant squid's eyes are huge, up to 15 inches wide. Boy, I wouldn't want to meet one, would you? Old sailors called giant squids sea monsters.

Revising

When you *revise,* you make changes to improve your writing. You can make your changes by hand or on a typewriter or word processor. Whatever you use as your writing tool, to revise your writing you'll use just four basic revision techniques: *adding, cutting, replacing,* and *reordering.* (To understand the examples, see the chart of symbols on page 56.)

REVISION TECHNIQUES	
TECHNIQUE	EXAMPLE
1. **Add.** Add new information and details. Add words, sentences, or paragraphs.	The book *Lovey: A Very Special Child* is written by a *with severe emotional problems,* woman who teaches children.
2. **Cut.** Take out repeated, unnecessary, or related ideas.	The children have serious problems. One of the children, Hannah, hides in a closet at first.
3. **Replace.** Replace weak or awkward wording with precise words or details.	Hannah doesn't talk to the teacher or other kids, but *cries and screams* she acts up when she's upset.
4. **Reorder.** Move information, sentences, and paragraphs for clear order.	In time, Hannah joins the class and begins to talk and learn. The teacher patiently works with Hannah.

In the following revised paragraph (you read it earlier as a first draft, page 45), the writer has used these four revision techniques. Do you think the changes improve the paragraph? How?

Mary McLeod Bethune was the first in
her family to go to school. She started
when she was eleven. ~~[Twelve? Check~~
~~this.]~~ The Presbyterian school was a mission school for **cut/add**
black children in Mayesville, South Carolina. ~~[Where? Go back for~~ **add/cut**
~~details.]~~ Mary was a fast learner. She had **cut/reorder**
to walk ~~a long way~~ three miles to and from school. **replace**
Mary's family sacrificed to let her attend
school. When she was in school, she
couldn't help with all the chores on the
family farm. ~~Mary liked to plow.~~ When she **cut**
started her third year, she helped the
teacher. She also began teaching her
brothers and sisters at home to read. Mary
was good at math. She helped ~~people~~ both black and white neighbors with **replace**
their accounts so the big planters couldn't
cheat them.

Mary McLeod Bethune at the college she founded in 1904 in Daytona Beach, Florida.

GUIDELINES FOR EVALUATING AND REVISING

EVALUATION GUIDE	REVISION TECHNIQUE
CONTENT	
1 Is the writing interesting?	**Add** specific examples, a brief story, dialogue, or details. **Cut** repeated or boring details.
2 Are there enough details?	**Add** details, facts, statistics, or examples to support the main idea.
3 Is the main idea clear?	**Add** a sentence that clearly states your main idea.
4 Are there unrelated ideas?	**Cut** the ideas that are not related to your topic.
ORGANIZATION	
5 Are ideas and details arranged in a clear order?	**Reorder** ideas and details to make the meaning more easily understood.
6 Are the connections between ideas and sentences clear?	**Add** transitional words and phrases, such as *first, next, finally, similarly, because, for example*, and so on. (See pages 74–75.)
STYLE	
7 Does the language fit the audience and purpose?	**Replace** slang and contractions in formal writing. Use *I* and *me* when you need to create a relaxed feeling.
8 Do sentences read smoothly?	**Reorder** words to vary sentence beginnings. Reword to vary sentence structure.

EXERCISE 12 ▶ Evaluating and Revising a Paragraph

With a partner, evaluate the following first draft. Then, revise the paragraph. Use the Guidelines for Evaluating and Revising on page 51. You may add, cut, reorder, or replace words and details.

Many Arab Americans live in the United States. Syrians began to arrive in the late nineteenth century. They taught their heritage to their American-born children. Arab American children often learn to read and write the Arabic language. In Detroit, there is an Arab World Festival every year. Many Arab Americans share a common faith, Islam. Believers in Islam gather to practice their faith in mosques throughout the United States. Doug Flutie, an Arab American, won the Heisman Trophy in 1984. There are many Arabic-language newspapers and journals in the United States. Many people from Egypt, Lebanon, and Jordan came to the United States after World War II.

Islamic Center of Greater Toledo, Ohio

Proofreading and Publishing

One last step to finish your writing, then you'll need to find a way to share what you've written with an audience.

Proofreading

Remember puzzle pictures that asked, "What's wrong with this picture?" You had to search carefully to find mistakes—a cat wearing one plaid sock, a man writing with a fish, a woman wearing a reversed coat. Think of *proofreading* as solving a puzzle—searching out and fixing all the mistakes in grammar, spelling, capitalization, and punctuation.

Be sure to allow enough time to put your paper aside for awhile. It's easier to find mistakes when you've had a break. Try peer proofreading, too. Exchange papers with a partner and see if you can find errors in each other's papers.

GUIDELINES FOR PROOFREADING

1. Is every sentence a complete sentence, not a fragment or run-on? (See pages 354–360.)
2. Does every sentence begin with a capital letter? Does every sentence end with the correct punctuation mark? Are punctuation marks used correctly within sentences? (See pages 675–676 and pages 701–761.)
3. Do plural subjects have plural verbs? And do singular subjects have singular verbs? (See pages 551–569.)
4. Are verb forms and verb tenses used correctly? (See pages 580–598.)
5. Are adjective and adverb forms used correctly in comparisons? (See pages 629–636.)
6. Are the forms of personal pronouns used correctly? (See pages 606–621.)
7. Does every pronoun agree with its antecedent (the word it refers to) in number and gender? Are pronoun references clear? (See pages 572–574.)
8. Is every word spelled correctly? (See pages 764–793.)

EXERCISE 13▶   Proofreading a Paragraph

Can you find and correct the mistakes in this paragraph? (You should find six.) You can use a dictionary and the **Handbook** on pages 394–823.

> When she heard the words <u>tropical rain forest</u>, Janet always thinked of a jungle. She was surprized to learn that few bushes grow in most parts of a tropical rain forest. The crowns of trees blocks the sunlight from the ground, so you can easy walk through most areas of a rain forest. Only where enough sunlight hits the ground do you find jungles. Thick, tangled masses of plants. Grow by rivers and in places where the land was once cleared.

Publishing

After proofreading your paper, find yourself a reader—or a listener. Remember that the purpose of most writing is to communicate with a reader. You may want to try one of the following ideas.

- Submit your writing to the school newspaper, yearbook, or magazine.
- Read aloud what you've written to your classmates or family or friends.
- Post book and movie reviews. You could use your class or library bulletin board.
- Make a class booklet.

CRITICAL THINKING

Reflecting on Your Writing

Once you've found a way to communicate with an audience, take some time to communicate with yourself. You can round out your writing experience by deciding whether your papers are keepers and by thinking about what you learned while writing them.

A **portfolio** is a collection of your writing designed to show your growth as a writer and thinker. Its purpose is to allow you to analyze and evaluate your writing and your writing process. You analyze by reflecting over the different stages of the writing process. Which ones are easiest? hardest? You evaluate by forming your own judgments. How satisfied are you? What would you do differently next time? This "thinking about thinking" helps you to identify your strengths and to set personal goals.

By the end of the school year, your portfolio will contain both a wide range of your work (stories, poems, reports, and so on) written for a variety of purposes, and a collection of your answers to the reflection questions. These different forms and purposes will call for different thinking skills and writing strategies. As a result, you may sometimes choose to include a paper that doesn't completely satisfy you but does show that you're making progress in certain areas. When you're deciding whether to include a particular piece of writing in your portfolio, don't be too critical of your writing, but do be honest— that's how writers grow.

 CRITICAL THINKING EXERCISE:
Reflecting on Your Writing

Think about the writing you've done in the past few weeks. You have probably written papers for several of your teachers. If you have some of your papers, reread them. Then, reflect on your writing process by answering these questions. Add your responses to your portfolio.

1. Which part of the writing process generally goes most smoothly for you? least smoothly? Why?
2. Which part of each paper are you most pleased with and why? Which part might you handle differently the next time you write that type of paper?
3. What did you discover about yourself by writing these papers? about your writing process?

Follow these guidelines to prepare your final copy.

GUIDELINES FOR THE FORM OF A PAPER

1. Use only one side of a sheet of paper.
2. Write in blue or black ink, type, or use a word processor.
3. Leave margins of about one inch at the top, sides, and bottom of each page.
4. Follow your teacher's instructions for heading your paper.
5. Double-space if you type. Don't skip lines if you write.
6. Indent the first line of each paragraph.
7. Keep your paper neat and clean.

E X E R C I S E **14** ▶ **Identifying Ways to Publish**

Think about all the types of writing that can be shared in different ways. Brainstorm with classmates to list other publishing ideas.

SYMBOLS FOR REVISING AND PROOFREADING

SYMBOL	EXAMPLE	MEANING OF SYMBOL
≡	San juan	Capitalize a lowercase letter.
/	Ruth's Father	Lowercase a capital letter.
∧	the name of ^the^ school	Insert a missing word, letter, or punctuation mark.
℘	Take it it back.	Leave out a word, letter, or punctuation mark.
∩	bel(ei)f	Change the order of letters or words.
¶	¶"Help!" he called.	Begin a new paragraph.
⊙	Dr⊙Chiang Woo	Add a period.
⋏	Oh⋏I don't know.	Add a comma.

MAKING CONNECTIONS

Revising with a Computer

Your pages can start to look pretty cluttered when you revise your writing by hand. You'll need to cross out words and sentences you want to delete, write down things you want to squeeze in, and draw lines or arrows next to parts you want to move. Even if you're careful, you could end up with a jumbled, hard-to-read mess.

If you revise on a computer, though, you can avoid this clutter. Computers let you experiment with deleting or moving words and sentences, without any scratching out or erasing. For example, you can make use of your word-processing program's Cut and Paste commands to find the best place for a sentence in your draft. If you change your mind, you don't need to do any retyping—just move the sentence back.

Find and Replace are two more word-processing commands that can save you a lot of time. If, for example, you discover you've misspelled a name that shows up ten times in your draft, you need only to type the new spelling once, and the computer will automatically change all ten misspellings in your draft at the same time.

Many word-processing programs also contain thesauruses you can use to find synonyms. You just highlight a word in your draft, select the Thesaurus command, go through a list of suggested replacements, and make a selection.

Take an assignment you've started, and retype it using a computer. Then, use a word-processing program to make your changes. If you don't have access to a computer, interview people who do and ask them to explain how computers can make revision easier. Report back to the class with what they tell you.

2 LEARNING ABOUT PARAGRAPHS

Looking at the Parts

Have you ever thought about the **parts** of a bicycle? A bike has handlebars, wheels, and a seat, but not all bikes are alike. Some are bigger than others; some have more parts than others.

You can think of paragraphs that way, too. They all have words, and they all say something. But some are bigger than others and some have more parts than others.

Writing and You. Some paragraphs stand alone, but most of them work together like links in a chain. Have you ever noticed that paragraphs can be very short—even a single word or sentence, and that other paragraphs go on and on?

As You Read. The following paragraphs are from a book about the life of a Native American, Black Elk. What do you notice about the sizes of the paragraphs?

Frank Frazier, *Senegalese Fishing Village* (1989). Visions in Black Gallery.

"They put us in some of those shining wagons and took us to a very beautiful place..."

FROM

► Black Elk ◄
Speaks

as told through

JOHN G. NEIHARDT

(Flaming Rainbow)

Black Elk (at left) and his friend, Elk, participating in Buffalo Bill's Wild West Show, touring England.

One day we were told that Majesty was coming. I did not know what that was at first, but I learned afterward. It was Grandmother England (Queen Victoria), who owned Grandmother's Land [Canada] where we lived awhile after the Wasichus murdered Crazy Horse.

She came to the show in a big shining wagon, and there were soldiers on both sides of her, and many other shining wagons came too. That day other people could not come to the show— just Grandmother England and some people who came with her.

Sometimes we had to shoot in the show, but this time we did not shoot at all. We danced and sang, and I was one of the dancers chosen to do this for the Grandmother, because I was young and limber then and could dance many ways. We stood right in front of Grand-mother England. She was little but fat and we liked her, because she was good to us. After we had danced, she spoke to us. She said some-thing like this: "I am sixty-seven years old. All over the world I have seen all kinds of  people; but today I have seen the best-looking people I know. If you belonged to me, I would not let them take you around in a show like this." She said other good things too, and then she said we must come to see her, because she had come to see us. She shook hands with all of us. Her hand was very little and soft. We gave a big cheer for her, and then the shining wagons came in and she got into one of them and they all went away.

In about a half-moon after that we went to see the Grand-mother. They put us in some of those shining wagons and took us to a very beautiful place where there was a very big house with sharp, pointed towers on it. There were many seats built high in a circle, and these were just full of Wasichus who were all pounding their heels and yelling: "Jubilee! Jubilee! Jubilee!" I never heard what this meant.

They put us together in a certain place at the bottom of the seats. First there appeared a beautiful black wagon with two black horses, and it went all around the show place. I heard that the Grandmother's grandson, a little boy, was in that wagon. Next came a beautiful black wagon with four gray horses. On each of the two right hand horses there was a rider, and a man walked, holding the front left hand horse. I heard that some of Grandmother's relatives were in this wagon. Next came eight buckskin horses, two by two, pulling a shining black wagon. There was a rider on each right hand horse and a man walked, holding the front left hand horse. There were soldiers, with bayonets, facing outward all around this wagon. Now all the people in the seats were roaring and yelling "Jubilee!" and "Victoria!" Then we saw Grandmother England again. She was sitting in the back of the wagon and two women sat in the front, facing her. Her dress was all shining and her hat was all shining and her wagon was all shining and so were the horses. She looked like a fire coming.

Afterward I heard that there was yellow and white metal all over the horses and the wagon.

When she came to where we were, her wagon stopped and she stood up. Then all those people stood up and roared and bowed to her; but she bowed to us. We sent up a great cry and our women made the tremolo. The people in the crowd were so excited that we heard some of them got sick and fell over. Then when it was quiet, we sang a song to the Grandmother.

That was a very happy time.

We liked Grandmother England, because we could see that she was a fine woman, and she was good to us. Maybe if she had been our Grandmother, it would have been better for our people.

READER'S RESPONSE

1. Why did Black Elk like "Grandmother" England?
2. Have you ever met anyone you liked as much as Black Elk liked the Queen of England, someone who was very different from you? Write a brief journal entry about the experience.

WRITER'S CRAFT

3. There are two very long paragraphs in this passage. Each one has at least eighteen lines. What is the first of these long paragraphs about? the second?
4. Neihardt uses two very short paragraphs here. Which of these paragraphs do you think moves the reader from one idea to another? Which makes an idea stand out?

LOOKING AHEAD

In this chapter, you'll study the form and structure of paragraphs. Even though most paragraphs are a part of a longer piece of writing, keep in mind that

- most paragraphs have a central, or main, idea
- sensory details, facts, and examples may be used to support the main idea
- description, narration, comparison and contrast, and evaluation are four ways of developing paragraphs

The Parts of a Paragraph

The Main Idea

Paragraphs that stand alone almost always have a main idea. So do paragraphs that are part of a longer piece of writing. The *main idea* is the big idea in the paragraph. In the following paragraph, you will find the main idea in the first sentence. It tells you that this paragraph is about how Hopis use Kachina dolls.

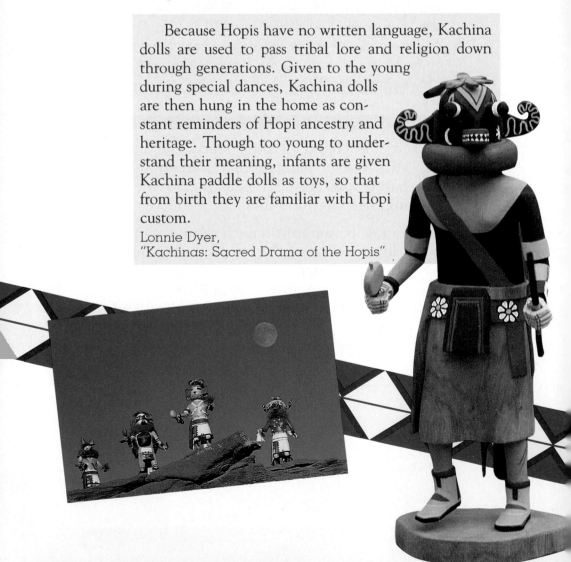

Because Hopis have no written language, Kachina dolls are used to pass tribal lore and religion down through generations. Given to the young during special dances, Kachina dolls are then hung in the home as constant reminders of Hopi ancestry and heritage. Though too young to understand their meaning, infants are given Kachina paddle dolls as toys, so that from birth they are familiar with Hopi custom.

Lonnie Dyer,
"Kachinas: Sacred Drama of the Hopis"

The Topic Sentence

Location of the Topic Sentence.   The *topic sentence* states the main idea of the paragraph. You may find it at the beginning of the paragraph, in the middle, or even at the end. Then it's like a surprise ending. In the paragraph on page 64, the topic sentence is the first sentence of the paragraph: *Because Hopis have no written language, Kachina dolls are used to pass tribal lore and religion down through generations.*

In the paragraph below, the topic sentence is last. This sentence makes clear that the villagers are preparing for a battle. The other sentences lead up to that point.

Quickly, quickly we gathered the sheep into the pens. Children rushed through the village gathering firewood to pile inside the homes. Men and women scooped up pots and pots of water, filling cisterns and containers as rapidly as possible. People pulled the last ears of corn from the fields and turned their backs on the dry stalks. Finally, we all stood together in the plaza in the center of the village for just a moment before the fighters went to stand near the walls and the wide-eyed children were coaxed inside the houses. And so we prepared for the coming battle.

Importance of a Topic Sentence. Paragraphs that relate a series of events or that tell a story often don't have a topic sentence. Read the following paragraph. It doesn't have a topic sentence. But all the sentences are about one main idea—a relationship between two women.

"Oh, Lottie, it's good to see you," Bess said, but saying nothing about Lottie's splendid appearance. Upstairs Bess, putting down her shabby suitcase, said, "I'll sleep like a rock tonight," without a word of praise for her lovely room. At the lavish table, top-heavy with turkey, Bess said, "I'll take light and dark both," with no marveling at the size of the bird, or that there was turkey for two elderly women, one of them too poor to buy her own bread.

Dorothy West, "The Richer, the Poorer"

Although all paragraphs don't have to have topic sentences, it is helpful to use them when you are writing. They may help you focus on your main idea. They also help the reader find the main idea.

COMPUTER NOTE: Use your word-processing program's Cut and Paste commands to find the best placement of a topic sentence within a paragraph. You can always move or replace the sentence if you change your mind.

WRITING NOTE In a longer piece of writing, start a new paragraph when you change ideas. Also, if you are writing dialogue (the actual words of people), start a new paragraph when you change speakers.

E X E R C I S E 1 ▶ **Identifying Main Ideas and Topic Sentences**

Finding a main idea is like detective work. In each of the following paragraphs search out the main idea. If there's a topic sentence, identify it. If there is no topic sentence, look at all the details in the paragraph and tell in your own words the main idea of the paragraph.

1.   He turned and looked back at the stand of raspberries. The bear was gone; the birds were singing; he saw nothing that could hurt him. There was no danger here that he could sense, could feel. In the city, at night, there was sometimes danger. You could not be in the park at night, after dark, because of the danger. But here, the bear had looked at him and had moved on and—this filled his thoughts—the berries were so good.

Gary Paulsen, from *Hatchet*

2.   Like lots of other kids her age, eight-year-old Aura-lea Moore plays baseball, swims and skis. She also has a favorite plaything: a 19-inch doll named Susan, who was handcrafted to look like her. Auralea was born with spina bifida, a birth defect that has left her paralyzed from the waist down. Her look-alike doll, equipped with a pair of blue and silver "designer" braces, helps her remember that although she may be handicapped, she is definitely not out of the action.

"A Doll Made to Order," *Newsweek*

3.   Personally, I thought Maxwell was just about the homeliest dog I'd ever seen in my entire life. He looked like a little old man draped in a piece of brown velvet that was too long, with the leftover cloth hanging in thick folds under his chin. Not only that, his long droopy ears dragged on the ground; he had sad wet eyes and huge thick paws with splayed toes. I mean, who could love a dog like that, except my brother Joji, aged nine, who is a bit on the homely side himself.

Yoshiko Uchida, *A Jar of Dreams*

Supporting Sentences

Supporting sentences give details that explain or prove the main idea. These sentences are called *supporting sentences* because they contain *sensory details, facts,* or *examples* that support the main idea of the paragraph.

Sensory details are words that describe one of the five senses—sight, sound, touch, taste, and smell. *Facts* give information that can be proved true in a concrete way. For instance, it's a fact that sea gulls drop clams on rocks to break them open. It's also a fact that great herds of buffalo once roamed the western plains. *Examples* give typical instances of an idea. A manatee is an example of a mammal that lives in the water. A chameleon is a lizard whose changes in coloring are an example of protective coloration. This chart shows the kinds of details you can use to support the main idea of the paragraph.

SUPPORTING SENTENCES	
Sensory Details	Examples
Sight	The bright sun glared off the front windshield of the car.
Sound	Thunder boomed down the canyon, echoing off the walls.
Touch	My hands felt frozen to the cold, steel handlebars.
Taste	Thirstily, she gulped down the sweet orange juice.
Smell	The sharp, unpleasant odor of fresh asphalt met his nose.
Facts	In 1961, Roger Maris slammed sixty-one home runs to break the old record of sixty held by Babe Ruth.
Examples	Fierce windstorms occur throughout the world. In the central United States, tornadoes have wind speeds over two hundred miles per hour.

EXERCISE 2 ▶   **Collecting Supporting Details**

When you write paragraphs, you have to collect (find or think up) details of support. You can practice with the following topic sentences. For each, one kind of supporting detail is suggested—sensory details, facts, or examples. List at least two details to support each topic sentence.

EXAMPLE   **1.** The appliance that toasts our bread has changed over the years. (facts)
   1. *Details: It originated in the early 1900s. It consisted of bare wires with no thermostat. The first pop-up toaster appeared in 1926.*

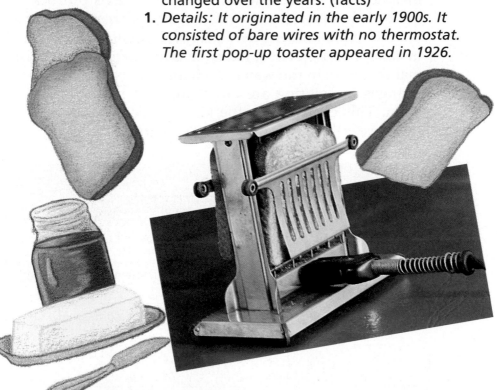

1. The time I spend getting ready for school in the mornings is not my favorite part of the day. (sensory details)
2. My dream is to spend two days in a shopping mall. (examples)
3. One person's actions can make a difference in the lives of others. (facts)
4. When I'm hungry, I can just imagine my favorite meal. (sensory details)

Unity and Coherence

A paragraph is a little like a car. It has to have *unity*—you don't want one blue fender on a red car. And it has to have *coherence*—the back of the car has to be connected to the front.

Unity

A paragraph has **unity** when all the sentences support, or tell something about, one main idea. A paragraph that doesn't have unity may confuse your readers. For example, in a paragraph about Bonnie St. John, you might tell how she became a skiing champion despite losing a leg. But if you mentioned a friend who is also a skier, you would destroy the unity. That information wouldn't be related to your main idea.

People Weekly/Time Inc., © 1986 Richard Howard.

In the paragraph on the following page, the first sentence states the main idea. Notice how all the other sentences tell something more about the heavy snow.

The snow began quietly this time, like an after-thought to the gray Sunday night. The moon almost broke through once, but toward daylight, a little wind came up and started white curls, thin and lonesome, running over the old drifts left from the New Year storm. Gradually the snow thickened, until around eight-thirty the two ruts of the winding trails were covered and undisturbed, except down in the Lone Tree district, where an old, yellow bus crawled heavily along, feeling out the ruts between the choppy sand hills.

Mari Sandoz, *Winter Thunder*

EXERCISE 3 ▶   **Identifying Sentences That Destroy Unity**

Each of the following paragraphs has one sentence that destroys the unity. Try your skill at finding the sentences that don't belong. [Hint: First, decide what the main idea is. Next, decide whether each supporting sentence is closely connected to the main idea.]

1.   It felt like an oven to Tamara as she walked up the street toward the park. It was a hot day for baseball practice. She wondered if the Cardinals game would be on television that evening. Tamara told herself she couldn't let the heat slow her down, though. The coach would be deciding today who would start in the season's first game. And she wanted to be playing third.

2.   Canoes are made for many different purposes. White-water canoes are for use in fast, rock-filled streams. They're made to turn quickly to avoid obstacles. Other canoes are made for lakes and quiet rivers. They don't turn too quickly, so they won't be your first choice for use on a river with lots of rapids. On the other hand, they're easy to paddle in a straight line. The white-water canoe can't be paddled in a perfectly straight line no matter what you do. You can also find canoes that are made to carry either one or two people. Before choosing a canoe, think about what kind of water you'll be using it in.

Coherence

A paragraph has *coherence* when readers can tell how and why ideas are connected.

To create coherence you can do two things. First, you can arrange your details in an *order* that makes sense to the reader. In the section Ways of Developing Paragraphs (page 77), you'll learn more about how to organize details.

The second way of creating coherence in paragraphs is to use *transitional words* or *phrases* to connect ideas. These are words and phrases like *for example, mainly*, and *in addition*. They not only connect ideas, but also tell why and how they're related.

The following chart shows examples of some of the common words and phrases used for transitions that help to create coherence.

TRANSITIONAL WORDS AND PHRASES		
COMPARING AND CONTRASTING IDEAS		
also	another	similarly
although	but	too
and	however	yet
SHOWING CAUSE AND EFFECT / NARRATION		
as a result	for	so that
because	since	therefore
SHOWING TIME / NARRATION		
after	first, second, etc.	then
before	next	until
finally	often	when
SHOWING PLACE / DESCRIPTION		
above	down	next
around	here	over
before	in	there
beside	into	under

The following paragraph tells how Native Americans are recognized everywhere. The writer uses transitional words to show how ideas are connected. Notice, for example, how the writer says that at "first" kids pretend they don't see him. "Then" they turn and look.

When I go someplace, most of the time those little people see me. At first they'll pretend not to see me. They go past me a little ways, and then they will turn back and look at me. Then they'll nudge their mama or daddy or grandma or grandpa, and I'll hear them say, "There's an Indian back there." So the Indians are still here. We never phased away. We didn't just blend into society and vanish. In fact, we're appearing more and more and more. We get around more now, too. Indians are not just confined only to the United States or one state or one county or one city or one house. They know us all over this Earth.

Wallace H. Black Elk and William S. Lyon,
Black Elk: The Sacred Ways of a Lakota

EXERCISE 4▶ **Identifying Transitional Words and Phrases**

Identifying transitional words and phrases can help you see how they work when they are used in paragraphs. Using the chart on page 74 as a guide, make a list of all the transitional words and phrases in the following paragraph.

> When she was elected to be chief of the Cherokee Nation in 1987, Wilma Mankiller took on a huge job. But she was used to challenges. In 1976, she had developed many needed projects for Cherokees in rural Oklahoma. First, she taught people how to build their own homes. Next, she installed new water supply lines. Finally, she started new rural health clinics. Then she had to overcome serious injuries she suffered in an auto accident in late 1979. So while others were impressed with the new chief's dedication, no one who really knew her well found her leadership ability surprising. Once elected as chief, Mankiller continued her work to improve Cherokee communities. She focused on housing and education needs, and she encouraged her people to be proud of their language and culture. Wilma Mankiller served one more term as chief of the Cherokee Nation before a serious illness forced her to retire.

Ways of Developing Paragraphs

What you're writing about, your subject or topic, usually determines the way you develop it. Here are four ways of writing a paragraph.

WAYS OF DEVELOPING PARAGRAPHS	
Description	Looking at parts of a person, place, or thing
Narration	Looking at changes in a person, place, or thing over time
Comparison and Contrast	Finding likenesses and differences between people, places, or things
Evaluation	Judging the person, place, or thing's value or worth

Description

How would you describe your favorite hangout to one of your friends? What does the Ninja Turtle Michelangelo look like?

In answering either of these questions, you're *describing* something. That means you're picking out specific details, or features, to tell about that will help someone else recognize it.

In describing something, you often use *spatial order*. Spatial order organizes details according to their location. In the following paragraph, notice how the writer uses sensory details and spatial order to describe her father's farm.

> The farm my father grew up on, where Grandpa Welty and Grandma lived, was in southern Ohio in the rolling hills of Hocking County, near the small town of Logan. It was one of the neat, narrow-porched, two-story farmhouses, painted white, of the Pennsylvania-German country. Across its front grew feathery cosmos and barrel-sized peony bushes with stripy heavy-scented blooms pushing out of the leaves. There was a springhouse to one side, down a little

walk only one brick in width, and an old apple orchard in front, the barn and the pasture and fields of corn and wheat behind. Periodically there came sounds from the barn, and you could hear the crows, but everything else was still.

Eudora Welty, *One Writer's Beginnings*

EXERCISE 5 ▶   Collecting Descriptive Details

How would you describe an insect, a rock star, or a movie set? Work in a group of two or three classmates. Choose one of the subjects below and list sensory details that describe it. Then, arrange them in spatial order.

1. the creepiest animal you've ever seen
2. your favorite car
3. the best setting for a science fiction movie
4. your classroom, moments before a holiday break
5. your favorite season

Narration

What happened when a character lost in the frigid arctic wilderness couldn't build a fire? How is soccer played? What caused the ocean liner *Titanic* to sink?

When you answer any of these questions, you are ***narrating***. That means you are telling about an event or an action as it changes over time. Because narrating tells about changes in time, you usually use ***chronological***, or time, ***order***.

You can use narration to tell a story (what happened to the character in the Arctic), to explain a process (how to play soccer), or to explain causes and effects (what caused the *Titanic* to sink).

Telling a Story.   Everybody loves a good story. You've probably listened to one or told one today. It may have been made up, or it may have been about something that really happened.

The following is a story slaves told many years ago about some strange escapes from slavery.

Uncle Mingo's forehead wrinkled like a mask in the moonlight. "Don't make light of what old folks tell you, son," he warned. "If the old folks say they seen slaves pick up and fly back to Africa, like birds, just don't you dispute them. If they tell you about a slave preacher what led his whole flock to the beach and sat down on the sand with them, looking across the ocean toward home, don't ask no questions. Next morning nobody could find trace of that preacher or his people. And no boat had been there neither. One day when I was chopping cotton in the field, I looked up and the old fellow working in the row next to mine was gone. He was too feeble to run away, and I couldn't see no place for him to hide. None of the others in the field saw him leave either, but later on an old woman drinking water at a well, told us she noticed something pass in front of the sun about that time, like a hawk or a buzzard maybe, but she didn't pay it much mind."

Arna Bontemps, *Chariot In the Sky: A Story of the Jubilee Singers*

Explaining a Process. When you tell how to do something or how something works, you're *explaining a process.* Often, this means telling how to do something step by step—what is done first, then next, and so on. This is chronological order.

The following paragraph tells how kites may have been developed.

Like a lot of very old activities, no one is quite sure how kite flying started. Perhaps an ancient Chinese first noticed big leaves of certain plants fluttering at the end of long vines. Then, after watching "leaf-kites" for a while, he tied his straw hat to a string just for fun and happily found that the wind kept it flying. Later, he may have stretched a piece of animal skin over a bamboo frame and flown that from the end of a line.

Dan Carlinsky, "Kites"

Explaining Causes and Effects. Narrating is also used to *explain causes and effects.* In other words, narrating can be used to tell how one event is a result of an earlier event.

The following paragraph tells what causes crickets to stop chirping. It also tells one helpful effect of their sudden silence.

Effect

Cause

Cause

Effect

As you walk along the sidewalk, the tree crickets keep up their song until you are quite close; then they stop. They can sense your presence and fall silent. If, as sometimes happens in Blantyre, there is a leopard prowling around among the trash cans a few blocks away, then the tree crickets near to it will stop singing, and you will be warned of its presence in time to turn back. So singing insects are excellent watchdogs.

Carson I. A. Ritchie, *Insects, The Creeping Conquerors and Human History*

EXERCISE 6 ▶ **Using Narration to Develop Paragraphs**

Can you tell a story about the time you were most frightened? Can you explain how to tie your shoes? Can you tell the causes and effects of not cleaning up your room for a month? The following exercises will give you some practice in telling about events in the order in which they happen. Follow the directions for each item.

1. Each of the topics below could be the subject of a story. Select one of these topics and make up three or more events that might be in the story. Arrange all of the events in chronological order. Don't forget to use your imagination.
    a. A mysterious light follows your family's car down a lonesome, country road one night.
    b. A tall, shy, new student enters your school. He doesn't really fit in at first, but soon the situation changes.

2. Pick one of the following activities. Then list three or more steps you'd need to take in order to perform this activity. Arrange the steps in chronological order—that is, the order in which they should happen.
    c. how to boot up (start) a computer
    d. how to clean up your room

3. Choose one of the following. Give at least three possible causes or three possible effects.
    e. missing the school bus (give causes)
    f. a water shortage in your town or region (give effects)

Comparison and Contrast

A car manufacturer may want to know how its car compares to a competitor's car. The manufacturer will want to analyze the similarities and differences. Whenever you *compare,* you tell how things are alike. Whenever you *contrast,* you tell how things are different from one another. Students, as well as professionals, are asked to make such comparisons.

When you compare and contrast, you can use *logical order.* Something that is logical is something that makes sense. When you compare and contrast, it is logical to group related ideas together.

Read the following paragraph. The writer compares and contrasts her two sisters. How are the sisters alike? How are they different?

Comparison

　　My sisters may be twins, but they are very different. Sara and Sally look exactly alike. They both have long, braided black hair and big black eyes with eyelashes out to there. But the resemblance stops with looks. If they just stand still, they can pretend to be each other. If they talk or move, the joke is over. Sara talks all the time and bounces just like Winnie the Pooh's friend Tigger. Sally never says anything except "Pass the peanut butter," and she moves like a sick snail. How can they be twins?

Contrast

EXERCISE 7 ▶ **Speaking and Listening: Comparison and Contrast**

Now it's your turn to think about two subjects that are enough alike to be compared and different enough to be interesting. Write one statement that tells how these subjects are alike and one statement that tells how they are different. Share your statements with a small group. With the help of the group, think of some other similarities and differences.

　　You might compare and contrast the following items:

1. being a child and being a teenager
2. good horror movies and bad horror movies
3. living in a large city and living in a small community

Evaluation

Do you like broccoli? Did you enjoy Robert M. Service's poem "The Cremation of Sam McGee"?

Whenever you answer questions like these, you're *evaluating.* In other words, you're telling whether you think broccoli and the poem are good or bad. You'd want to give reasons for your answer. For example, you might say you gagged on cooked broccoli, but you love raw broccoli with cheese dip. You might say you enjoyed the poem because of its rhyme or because of its humor.

When writing an evaluation, you will probably organize it by *order of importance.* For example, you might place your most important information first. Then you'd put your next most important information, and so on. Or, you might arrange your most important information last, so that you gradually lead up to your biggest point.

The following paragraph was written to persuade people not to build more buildings in Yellowstone National Park. Notice the reasons the writer gives for the evaluation.

Reason

Reason

Evaluation

I don't think that more hotels, campgrounds, and restaurants should be built in Yellowstone National Park. The park is set aside to protect the animals and plants that live there and to allow people to experience the wilderness. When more buildings go up, more people crowd into the park. And the more people there are, the less room there is for wildlife and for wilderness. People don't just take up space. They also scare the animals and keep them from living as they would naturally live in the wild. In Yellowstone National Park, I think the most important thing is to protect the animals and the natural wilderness. If this means putting a stop to more building, then the building should be stopped.

EXERCISE 8 ▶ Developing an Evaluation

What's your evaluation? Why do you think so? Choose one of the following subjects and write your evaluation of it. Give at least two reasons for your opinion. List first the reason you think is more important.

EXAMPLE   **1.** our school's basketball team
   1. *Evaluation:* *It's a very good team.*
       Reasons: *(1) Our center is five foot ten.*
             (2) Our guards are very quick.
             (3) Players who are not even
                 starting are also good shooters.

1. the street you live on
2. a book you've read lately or movie you've seen recently
3. the newest fad in clothes

MAKING CONNECTIONS

Now that you know the form and structure of paragraphs, how do you use your knowledge? Try applying what you've learned as you write paragraphs for different purposes. Remember that the basic purposes of writing are self-expression, information, persuasion, and creativity.

WRITING PARAGRAPHS FOR DIFFERENT PURPOSES

Writing a Paragraph to Express Yourself

Have you ever thought about writing as a way to think problems through? as a way to explore an idea you're puzzling over? or maybe as just a way to decide what you really do think about something? Writing can help you sort out your thoughts.

On a separate sheet of paper—or in your journal or diary if you keep one—write an expressive paragraph. Use one of the following sentences to get started. See where it leads you.

1. My closest friend means so much to me because ____.
2. I'm happiest when I'm ____ because ____.
3. One thing I'd like to change about myself is ____.
4. I get sad when I think about ____.
5. Something I'd really like to do within the next year is ____.

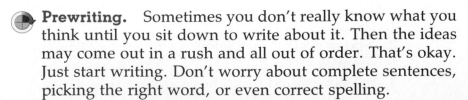 **Prewriting.** Sometimes you don't really know what you think until you sit down to write about it. Then the ideas may come out in a rush and all out of order. That's okay. Just start writing. Don't worry about complete sentences, picking the right word, or even correct spelling.

Writing, Evaluating, and Revising. Expressive writing is often a very personal kind of writing. You may not want to share this writing with others. In that case, just write a draft. You may not need to revise it. If you want to share it with others, though, you should reread it. Check it for unity and coherence. Are the sentences organized so the ideas are clear?

Proofreading and Publishing. If you have decided to share your writing with others, be sure that you proofread it carefully. Check your usage and mechanics. You may want to make a clean copy for others to read.

Writing a Paragraph to Persuade

One of the earliest skills you learned was persuasion. You may have used it to get your mom or dad to buy a certain cereal in the supermarket. Sometimes parents are easy to persuade. Sometimes they aren't. Convincing other people can be just as hard or harder. You need to have reasons that support the point you want to make.

Look at the photographs. One shows an abandoned railroad track. The other shows a bike path that was built along a strip of land that was once a railroad. Imagine that a railroad that runs through your county has been abandoned. The railroad company is willing to give it to the county, but the county doesn't know what to do with it.

Some people want to turn it into a bikeway, like the one in the photograph. But many people, especially people who own land along the railway, oppose the bikeway. They are afraid that they'd lose their privacy and that the county can't afford to build and maintain the bikeway.

Write a paragraph in which you try to persuade county leaders either to support the bikeway or to oppose it. Think about the advantages and disadvantages of your proposal and organize your reasons carefully. You may want to review the section on Evaluation (page 84) before you begin writing.

Prewriting. You may want to begin by listing your reasons for supporting or opposing the bikeway. Choose the best two or three reasons for your paragraph.

Writing, Evaluating, and Revising. You'll want to begin your paragraph with a clear topic sentence that states your opinion. You can use one of these topic sentences or make up your own.

> The county government should support making a bikeway where the railroad used to run.

> The county government should oppose making a bikeway where the railroad used to run.

After completing your draft, review it carefully. Do you have two or three reasons? Do they support your topic sentence? Have you arranged them in the best order? Revise your paragraph to make it more convincing.

Proofreading and Publishing. Proofread your final draft and correct any errors in usage and mechanics. Then share your paragraph with classmates, your parents, or neighbors. Ask them if it persuaded them.

Writing a Paragraph to Inform

In school and out, you'll be asked to write paragraphs that inform. Your teachers want to see what you have learned in class. A friend may want your recipe for making a pizza. A relative in another state may want to know what you did on vacation.

The chart below gives information about the 1989 San Francisco earthquake. Use the information to write an informative paragraph. Here's a topic sentence to get you started.

Topic Sentence: The 1989 San Francisco earthquake caused a great deal of damage.

THE SAN FRANCISCO EARTHQUAKE OF 1989

Occurred October 17, 1989, with many aftershocks
Measured 7.1 on the Richter scale
Collapsed $1\frac{1}{4}$-mile section of double-decker Nimitz Freeway (I-880)
Caused delay of third game of World Series
Hundreds of buildings destroyed; thousands damaged
Damage of approximately six billion dollars
Official death toll of 63
More than 3,000 injured

Prewriting. Use notes from the chart to develop your paragraph. Before you begin, however, you might look for ways to organize them.

Writing, Evaluating, and Revising. Begin with your topic sentence. Then write two or three additional sentences, using information from the chart. You can add more information, if you like, from your own research. Evaluate your paragraph. Does it make sense? Do your facts support the topic sentence? Can the paragraph be reorganized so the information is clearer to readers?

Proofreading and Publishing. Reread your paragraph, looking carefully for errors in usage or mechanics. Make any needed corrections. Then share your paragraph with a friend.

Writing a Paragraph That Is Creative

It's a dark, moonless night. You've been walking along a sandy beach for more than an hour, and you're all alone. There are no lights anywhere to be seen. The wind is getting stronger and stronger. Waves are crashing against the beach. Suddenly, you hear the sound of horse hooves pounding into the sand. Then you hear a dog barking. You turn and look toward the sounds. You can't see anything at first. But then, the sounds draw closer. You can just make out the dark shape of a rider and horse coming toward you. A large dog races alongside.

What happens next? Make it up. Write a paragraph that tells about the next event. Your paragraph doesn't have to tell the rest of the story. Just add some information about what occurs next. Use the following questions to help you write the paragraph.

- Is the rider a stranger or a friend?
- Is the dog chasing the horse or running with it?
- Do you feel threatened or relieved that the rider has come?
- Does the rider stop in front of you or go on past?

Prewriting. Think about possible answers to the questions. You might try freewriting about the situation for a few minutes. Just let your ideas develop as you go.

When you finish, read what you've written. Use the ideas to develop your paragraph.

Writing, Evaluating, and Revising. Using the ideas from freewriting, write three or four sentences that tell what happens next. Your paragraph doesn't have to complete the story. It only needs to tell the next part.

When you've finished your paragraph, review it. Does it leave the reader wanting to know more? Revise your paragraph to improve any weaknesses you've noticed.

Proofreading and Publishing. Read your final draft again, and correct any errors in usage or mechanics. Then, share your paragraph with a group of classmates. Discuss your ideas about how the story ends.

 Reflecting on Your Writing

If you plan to put one or more of these paragraphs in your **portfolio,** date each one. Include with them brief reflections based on these questions.

- How did you decide whether to state your main idea in a topic sentence or just to suggest it?
- Which was harder for you, collecting supporting details or keeping out unrelated ideas? Why?
- Did writing only one paragraph seem just right, or did it make you want to write more? Explain your response.

---

3 LEARNING ABOUT COMPOSITIONS

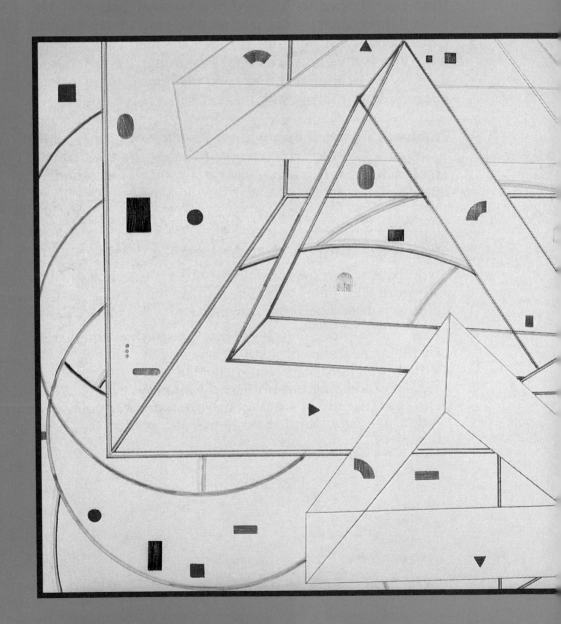

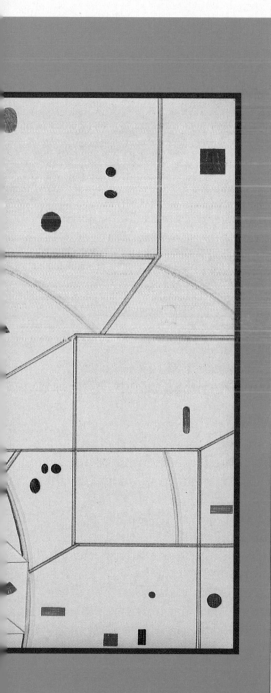

Looking at the Whole

When you think about the volleyball team, do you think about the individual players? *Daniel has a strong serve, but Sarah is more accurate.* Or do you think about the whole team? *Our seventh-grade team is going to win the tournament.* In writing, you can think of words, sentences, or paragraphs as parts. A composition is a **whole** piece of writing.

Writing and You. A magazine article tells about a baseball superstar. A newspaper report tells about a teenager doing volunteer work. A student's history paper explains how the Civil War started. Each of these is a whole piece of writing, a kind of composition. Why do you think the composition form is used so often?

As You Read. On the next pages is a magazine article about manatees. What can you tell about composition form from reading this article?

Al Held, *76 C-7* (1976). Colored pencil, graphite, crayon, and felt-tip pen on paper. Sheet and image 27 × 39 15/16". Frame 34 7/8 × 47 3/4". Collection of Whitney Museum of American Art. Purchase, funds from the Drawing Committee. 86.2. Photograph © 1996 Whitney Museum of American Art. © 1996 Al Held/Licensed by VAGA, New York, N.Y.

the spaceport mermaids

by Greg Walz-Chojnacki

For centuries, sailors have told of the legendary mermaid which appeared to lonely mariners during their long sea voyages. Nowadays, astronauts, too, have the chance to see mermaids— at Kennedy Space Center in Florida.

Mermaids?

Well, manatees, actually. Some people think these large, flippered creatures may have looked like humanoids—mermaids—to bored, superstitious seamen after months at sea.

Thousands of these gentle sea mammals live in the coastal waters of Florida, including the waterways of the Kennedy Space Center.

Unfortunately, these creatures, which have poor eyesight, are an endangered species. They are often injured by the propellers of power boats that cruise under the Florida sunshine. But the playful animals have been finding a safe haven in the waters surrounding the space center.

When NASA purchased 188,000 acres for the Apollo program, it set aside a large part of the land for the Merritt Island Wildlife Refuge. NASA has a policy of protecting many species there, including bald eagles, alligators, and sea turtles.

NASA has been protecting manatees since 1977. Although manatee deaths have been increasing in Florida, only two have died in space center waters since 1984, and those two died of natural causes.

NASA, in cooperation with state and federal wildlife agencies, has attached space-age radio monitors to some manatees to identify and protect their habitats. NASA also gives special training to space center personnel who operate boats, so they can avoid harming the creatures.

Even the boats used to recover the Shuttle's solid rocket boosters have been built with the manatees in mind. When retrieving the boosters in the Atlantic Ocean, the ships use ordinary propellers. But the ships are powered by water jets when they reach the waters inhabited by manatees.

The manatees seem to know a safe place when they find one. Their numbers have been increasing at the space center since 1984.

NASA's manatee protection policy has been a real success. Kennedy Space Center employees have many opportunities to see these fascinating creatures in the waterways of America's spaceport.

Now, if astronauts start seeing mermaids in orbit, that will be a completely different kind of problem!

"Some people think these large, flippered creatures may have looked like humanoids—mermaids—to bored, superstitious seamen after months at sea."

READER'S RESPONSE

1. If you have ever seen a manatee or a dolphin, tell about your experience with the animal. Why do you think people like these animals so much?
2. When you think of NASA and the Kennedy Space Center, what usually comes to your mind? Do you think of manatees?

WRITER'S CRAFT

3. How do you know that the main idea of the article is about NASA protecting the manatee?
4. The first paragraph talks about astronauts seeing mermaids. You know that mermaids don't exist. Why do you think the author begins the article this way?
5. How does the ending relate to the first paragraph?

LOOKING AHEAD

In this chapter, you'll learn about the parts of a composition. You'll find that most compositions are alike in certain ways. Most of them

- have one main idea
- have three main parts—an introduction, a body, and a conclusion
- have several paragraphs that work together to support the main idea

What Makes a Composition

Writing compositions in school may not be your favorite activity. But most people, whether they are writing compositions for school or writing memos or reports for work, find writing to be challenging. As a student, you have probably written several compositions. Even with this practice, it might be hard to think of something to write about, and hard to decide exactly how to begin or end a composition.

In this chapter, you'll learn about composition form—how the different parts work together to create a whole piece of writing. Then you'll be able to use that form in other chapters to explain a process, to persuade, to write about literature, and to write a research report.

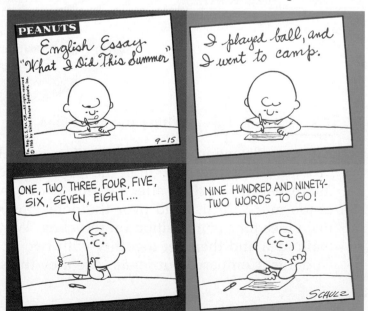

The Composition Plan

What are you doing this weekend? Will you work, play a sport, or take music lessons? You've probably already made some plans for this weekend and maybe for future ones. Compositions, like weekends, usually turn out much better when they are planned.

The Main Idea

When you have a topic for your composition, think what you want to say about it. What is most important and interesting? What you want to say about your topic is your *main idea.*

One writer wanted to write about competing in a skateboarding contest. He thought about the days of practicing, the new tricks, and the excitement. He finally decided to focus on how much fun the contest was. "Skateboard contests are fun" became his main idea.

EXERCISE 1 ▶   **Writing the Main Idea**

Are you throwing away things that could be recycled instead? The writer who took the following notes became interested in recycling after hearing about the problems of too much trash. Read over the notes and decide on a main idea for a composition on recycling. Write down the main idea and then get together with two or three other students. Compare your ideas. Are they the same?

You can set up a recycling center in your home or school.

Try not to buy items in jars or boxes that can't be recycled.

Find out how to get a community recycling program started.

Don't accept food that's in plastic containers at fast-food restaurants.

Separate your trash, and throw away only what can't be recycled.

Don't waste paper—use both sides of your notebook and other writing paper.

Don't wrap your lunch in plastic.

Buy or make canvas or nylon grocery bags and lunch sacks that you can use again.

Don't buy things you don't really want or need.

WRITING NOTE   You can always change your main idea for your composition. As you find ideas and think about your topic, you may decide that you want to say something different.

Early Plans

An *early plan,* sometimes called an *informal outline,* is a way to organize your ideas. First, put your ideas into related groups. Then, arrange the groups in an order that makes sense to readers.

Grouping.   Look at the information you have. Which details belong together? Do you have several notes about one part of your topic? Follow these steps to group ideas.

1. Group notes that have something in common.
2. Write a heading for each group of notes.
3. Put the heading with that group of notes.
4. Set aside for later use notes that don't seem to fit.

Ordering.   The order you use depends partly on your information. What should come first? What last? If your composition tells how to perform skateboarding tricks, you're writing about a step-by-step process. You should use *chronological* (time) *order.* Is your composition about a trip to see the giant redwoods? You might use *spatial order* and describe the trees in the order you see them.

Be sure to arrange your ideas in an order that makes sense to readers. The writer of the composition on pet pigs (page 102) uses *logical order,* in which related ideas are grouped together. The writer tells first about the benefits of having a pet pig and then tells about the drawbacks. The early plan on page 101 also uses logical order.

COMPUTER NOTE: You can create tables within your word-processing program and use them to organize your prewriting notes.

TOPIC: PET PIGS	
BENEFITS	DRAWBACKS
clean easier than some other animals to housebreak don't shed or get fleas can communicate easy to train will play and do tricks easy to feed	can get very large can be lazy can be too playful not a good watch animal

E X E R C I S E 2 ▶   **Making an Early Plan**

Working with a partner, make an early plan for a composition based on the notes on recycling in Exercise 1. What will be the best order for the composition? After you decide, group the notes in that order. Then arrange the notes within the groups in a way that makes sense.

☞ REFERENCE NOTE: For more help in arranging ideas, see pages 77–84.

Formal Outlines

A *formal outline* is more structured than an early plan. It uses letters and numbers to label main headings and ideas that belong below those headings. A formal outline can have either topics (single words or phrases) or complete sentences.

Here's a topic outline for the essay on pet pigs. Compare it to the finished composition, below. Notice that the introduction and conclusion aren't a part of the outline.

Title: The Patter of Little Hooves
Main Idea: Pigs make great pets.

I. Benefits
   A. Characteristics
      1. Cleanliness
      2. Ease of housebreaking
      3. Lack of fur and fleas
      4. Friendliness
   B. Enjoyment of games
      1. Fetching
      2. Swimming
      3. Rolling over
      4. Climbing stairs
II. Drawbacks
   A. Playfulness
   B. Inability to protect

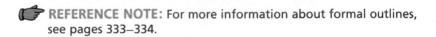 **REFERENCE NOTE:** For more information about formal outlines, see pages 333–334.

A WRITER'S MODEL

Here's the composition on pet pigs. See how the paragraphs are based on the parts of the outline? Does every paragraph support the idea that pigs make great pets?

The Patter of Little Hooves

INTRODUCTION

     What comes to mind when you think about pigs? Many people think of words like <u>dirty, smelly, unfriendly</u>, and even <u>stupid</u>. It may surprise you, but these words don't describe pigs at all. You may be even more surprised that

Main idea

many people think that pigs make great pets.

BODY

Main topic: Characteristics

Main topic: Enjoyment of games

Main topic: Playfulness and inability to protect

CONCLUSION

As a matter of fact, pig lovers will tell you that pigs are very pleasant. Many people say that pigs are much better pets than cats or dogs. They point out that pigs are really very clean and are more easily housebroken than most other pets. Pigs don't shed or get fleas. And they are friendly companions. They are happy to sit quietly and watch TV with you and never complain about your choice of programs.

Pigs learn quickly and enjoy playing games. They will happily fetch sticks that are thrown for them. They can also be taught to swim, roll over, climb stairs, or do just about any other pet trick.

On the other hand, pet pigs have their drawbacks. For one thing, they can be too playful. One pig owner found that nothing could stop her pet pig from taking the phone off the hook. He liked to hear the dial tone! Also, they won't protect you. They're more likely to smile at a burglar than to run the criminal off.

Pigs have been around for a long time. Yet it's only recently that people have begun to use words like cuddly, sweet, and smart to describe them. The day of the pig has finally arrived. Who knows? Maybe someday you'll hear the patter of little hooves around your house.

The Parts of a Composition

A composition may have several paragraphs, but it has three basic parts. The first part is the *introduction*. It's a little bit like the topic sentence in a paragraph. The second part may be much longer. It's called the *body*. The last part is the *conclusion*. It ends the composition.

The Introduction

Does the first paragraph of a book or an article sometimes capture your interest immediately? Do you keep reading to find out more?

Capturing the Reader's Interest. A good *introduction* grabs the reader's attention. It makes the reader want to read the rest of the composition. For example, the writer of the composition about pet pigs asks a question and follows it with a surprising statement. Just when the reader begins thinking about the usual bad words used to describe pigs, the writer says that pigs are not at all like most people think. Most readers will want to keep reading to find out why this is so.

Stating the Main Idea. A good introduction also states the main idea. This tells the reader what the composition will be about.

Ways to Write Introductions

You can use several different ways to make an introduction interesting. The following numbered examples show a few techniques you might try.

1. **Ask a question.** You've seen how a question works in the introduction to the composition on pigs. Here's another example. The writer asks a question and then immediately answers it.

   What's a top-notch sport that's rolling its way from coast to coast? In-line skating!

2. **Tell an anecdote.** An *anecdote* (a short, interesting, or even humorous story or incident) adds drama to your composition. Your reader will be caught by the humor or the human interest. Anecdotes add intriguing details to an introduction. This anecdote is from the introduction to an autobiographical work by Jesse Stuart.

> In Milwaukee I spoke to 14,400 educators. It was hard for me to realize that so many people were listening to me. After my talk, teachers came up and brought my books for me to sign. It was a great meeting for me. I had never dreamed in my youth of addressing an audience of this size.
>
> Jesse Stuart, "What America Means to Me"

3. **State an interesting or startling fact.** Curiosity also makes a reader want to read on. An exciting statement of fact creates curiosity.

> Most people know about the huge Saint Bernards who save travelers lost in the mountains, but a tiny canary once saved its owner's life. As its injured owner lay unconscious on the floor, the bird flew to a niece's house and got attention by tapping again and again on the window. It seems that pets of all kinds have saved human lives.

| EXERCISE 3 ▶ | **Identifying Types of Introductions** |

Can you recognize the three ways of writing introductions? Working with two or three classmates, try to identify the technique used in each of these introductions.

1.   There's a mystery in the sky. Centuries ago, ancient astronomers wrote about it. But when later astronomers looked for it, most of them thought the ancient astronomers were wrong. The mystery in the sky is whether there is a tenth planet, out beyond Neptune and Pluto. Many scientists believe Planet X is lurking out there waiting to be rediscovered!

2.   *Do, re, mi, fa, sol, la, ti, do.* Did you ever wonder where in the world such words came from? An Italian monk named Guido d'Arezzo used the first syllable of each line of a Latin hymn to represent the music scale. Guido taught music in the monasteries, and the musical note system he developed made his work easier. Many people believe he is the inventor of written music.

3.   Susanne woke up early on the morning of her thirteenth birthday. Someone had tied a string to the foot of her bed. On the string was a note that said, "Follow me." She put her hand on the string and started walking. The string led first to her brother's room, where he and their parents were waiting to go with her while she followed the string. It was the beginning of the most exciting birthday Susanne ever had.

The Body

The *body* of a composition usually contains several para-graphs, and every paragraph helps to support the main idea by developing a part of it.

All these paragraphs somehow have to stick together, too. Have you noticed that you lose interest if what you're reading never makes a point or connects ideas? Compositions that bore you probably don't have *unity* and *coherence*.

Unity.   *Unity* means that the paragraphs in the body of your paper all work together to support your main idea. Look at the model composition on pigs (page 102). Notice how each of the paragraphs has its own main idea (topic). Now look at each of the paragraph topics again. Notice how each of these paragraph topics ties in with the main idea of the whole composition—"Pigs make great pets."

In addition, as you read each paragraph, you'll see that the details in it tie directly to the paragraph topic. So every sentence in every paragraph leads back to the main idea of the composition.

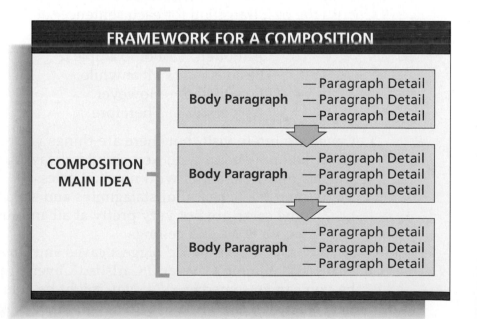

FRAMEWORK FOR A COMPOSITION

COMPOSITION MAIN IDEA

Body Paragraph
— Paragraph Detail
— Paragraph Detail
— Paragraph Detail

Body Paragraph
— Paragraph Detail
— Paragraph Detail
— Paragraph Detail

Body Paragraph
— Paragraph Detail
— Paragraph Detail
— Paragraph Detail

Coherence. Have you ever noticed how some things you read are easier to follow than others? One sentence leads easily into another, and one paragraph to the next. This type of writing has *coherence.*

You can do two things to make sure your composition has coherence. First, arrange your ideas in an order that makes sense. Second, make sure it's obvious to your readers how your ideas are connected. For example, you can let your readers know how your ideas are connected by using *transitional words and phrases* such as *for example, first, then, next,* and *finally.* In the composition on pigs, words and phrases such as *for one thing, on the other hand,* and *as a matter of fact* help the reader see the connections the writer is making.

👉 **REFERENCE NOTE:** See pages 74–75 for more information on transitional words and phrases.

| EXERCISE 4 ▶ | **Using Transitions** |

Some transitional words and phrases are listed below. They are followed by some sentence sets that need them. Choose the best transition for each sentence set, but don't use the same word or phrase more than once.

Although	For example
Besides	Meanwhile
Eventually	However
As a result	Therefore

1. Caves are fun to visit, but there are things you should know before you go. ____, you should always dress warmly and wear shoes with nonskid soles.
2. Many caves have beautiful stalagmites and stalactites. ____, some caves are not very pretty at all and just have smooth walls and ceilings.
3. If you haven't been to the biggest caves and caverns, such as Mammoth Cave and Carlsbad Caverns, maybe you can go someday. ____, you might be able to visit a smaller cave close to where you live.

4. Caves are usually formed by water that flows underground and wears away rock over long periods of time. ____, the water can form enormous rooms underground.
5. When caves are formed in limestone, dripping water dissolves the rock. Over time, the drips harden into crystal formations. ____, limestone caves often have beautiful sparkling shapes in them.

The Conclusion

Your *conclusion* should let your readers feel that your composition is complete. It shouldn't stop suddenly so that they feel let down. Your conclusion needs to tie the ideas together and flow once again into your main idea.

Ways to Write Conclusions

1. **Refer to your introduction.** In the model composition on pigs (pages 102–103), the writer brings readers back to the idea of "words used to describe pigs."

> **Introduction:** Many people think of words like *dirty*, *smelly*, *unfriendly*, and even *stupid*.
> **Conclusion:** Yet it's only recently that people have begun to use words like *cuddly*, *sweet*, and *smart* to describe them.

2. **Close with an interesting comment.** Another way to end your composition is to leave your readers with an interesting statement that clearly signals "the end."

> In-line skating may not replace bicycling as a way to travel, but for some people, it's the only way to roll!

3. **Restate your main idea.** One direct way to wrap up a composition is to restate your main idea *in different words.* This conclusion restates the idea that there is a mysterious planet somewhere out in space.

> Are some modern astronomers right about a tenth planet? Is it orbiting far beyond Pluto and Neptune, waiting for astronomers to find it? Maybe someday soon there will be a tenth planet to learn about: the mysterious Planet X.

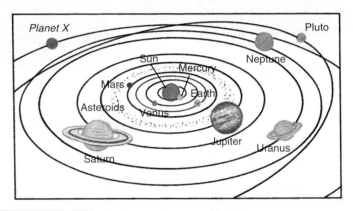

E X E R C I S E 5 ▶ **Writing a Conclusion**

The two models in this chapter—about manatees (page 94) and about pigs (page 102)—both use the same way of ending the composition. They both refer to the introduction. Write a new conclusion for one of these two models, using a different technique (pages 109–110). Then get together with two or three classmates and compare your conclusions.

MAKING CONNECTIONS

A Composition to Inform

You write for different purposes. You write to express your feelings, to tell a story, to persuade, or to inform. You can use the composition form you learned in this chapter for all these purposes.

Here are some notes about Saint Augustine, Florida, one of the oldest cities in the United States. To help you get started, the information has been organized into three groups. Study the notes until you're familiar with the information. Then write a short composition to *inform* your readers about this historic city. You may not want to use all the information.

SAINT AUGUSTINE, FLORIDA
HISTORY
1. Ponce de León landed near the area in 1513, looking for the fountain of youth.
2. He claimed the land for Spain.
3. The settlement of Saint Augustine was established in 1565 by Pedro Menéndez de Avilés.
4. Saint Augustine is the oldest continuously settled site (by Europeans) in the United States.
5. It was nearly destroyed by Sir Francis Drake and his English forces in 1586.
6. Spain transferred Florida to the United States in 1821.

SAINT AUGUSTINE, FLORIDA *(continued)*

LOCATION

1. Saint Augustine is located in northeastern Florida.
2. It is on a narrow peninsula formed by the Matanzas and San Sebastian rivers.
3. It is one-half mile from the Atlantic Ocean.

POINTS OF INTEREST

1. The Spanish fortress of Castillo de San Marcos was built in 1672 of coquina, a local shellrock. This is the oldest masonry fort in the United States.
2. The Cathedral of Saint Augustine was built in 1790. This is the seat of the oldest Catholic parish in the United States.
3. The Spanish Quarter is an area of reconstructed and restored buildings.

Writing a Composition to Inform

Prewriting. Based on the facts you've read, think about your main idea. Write the idea down. Then, use the three groups to create an early plan of your own.

Writing, Evaluating, and Revising. Think about how to grab your reader's attention. Then, write an introduction that will make someone want to read more of your paper.

Next, draft the body paragraphs. Remember that each paragraph must have a topic that ties in to your main idea. Then, write a conclusion that ties your information together and ends your composition in a satisfactory way.

After writing, look over your draft, and see what can be done to improve it. You might trade papers with a classmate and evaluate each other's writing. Ask these questions about your paper:

1. Does the introduction grab the reader's attention?
2. Is the main idea stated clearly?
3. Does each body paragraph connect to the main idea?
4. Do the details in each paragraph connect to the paragraph topic?
5. Does the conclusion tie the composition together?

 Proofreading and Publishing. Set your paper aside for a while. Come back to it later, and read over it again. Look for and correct any mistakes in grammar, usage, and mechanics. Then, write or print out a clean copy.

 Reflecting on Your Writing

If you decide to add your paper to your **portfolio,** answer the following questions and attach them to your composition.

- How long did it take to come up with your main idea? Did it change as you wrote?
- How did you decide which information to include and how to arrange it?
- Did you use your peer reviewer's suggestions when you revised your paper? Why or why not?

---

4 EXPRESSIVE WRITING: NARRATION

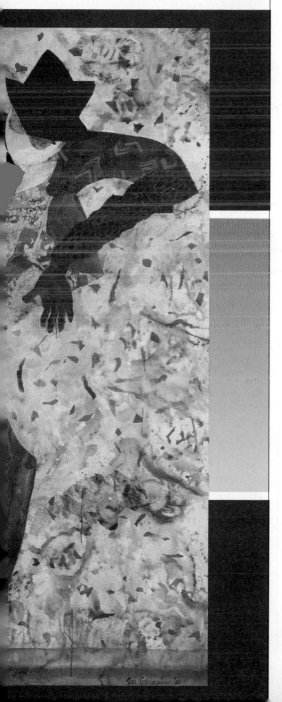

Discovering Yourself

You've already discovered many things about yourself. You hate math, but not English. You like to sit in your room and listen to all kinds of music. But you hate green peas and liver. Yet there is still more you can **discover about yourself,** through expressive writing.

Writing and You. A teenager writes to his cousin about how excited he is to be going away to basketball camp this summer. A famous actress writes a book telling her life story. A young girl tells her diary how much she likes her new bike. When have you expressed your personal feelings in writing?

As You Read. Here's an autobiographical piece in which a man expresses his feelings about a jacket he had to wear as a boy. What are his feelings?

Miriam Schapiro, *Pas de Deux* (1986). Acrylic and fabric on canvas, 90 × 96". Collection of Dr. and Mrs. Acinapura. Courtesy Steinbaum Krauss Gallery, New York City.

115

THE JACKET

by Gary Soto

My clothes have failed me. I remember the green coat that I wore in fifth and sixth grades when you either danced like a champ or pressed yourself against a greasy wall, bitter as a penny toward the happy couples.

When I needed a new jacket and my mother asked what kind I wanted, I described something like bikers wear: black leather and silver studs with enough belts to hold down a small town. We were in the kitchen, steam on the windows from her cooking. She listened so long while stirring dinner that I thought she understood for sure the kind I wanted. The next day when I got home from school, I discovered draped on my bedpost a jacket the color of day-old guacamole. I threw my books on the bed and approached the jacket slowly, as if it were a stranger whose hand I had to shake. I touched the vinyl sleeve, the collar, and peeked at the mustard-colored lining.

From the kitchen mother yelled that my jacket was in the closet. I closed the door

"From my bed, I stared at the jacket. I

wanted to cry because it was so

ugly and so big that I knew I'd have

to wear it a long time."

to her voice and pulled at the rack of clothes in the closet, hoping the jacket on the bedpost wasn't for me but my mean brother. No luck. I gave up. From my bed, I stared at the jacket. I wanted to cry because it was so ugly and so big that I knew I'd have to wear it a long time. I was a small kid, thin as a young tree, and it would be years before I'd have a new one. I stared at the jacket, like an enemy, thinking bad things before I took off my old jacket whose sleeves climbed halfway to my elbow.

I put the big jacket on. I zipped it up and down several times, and rolled the cuffs up so they didn't cover my hands. I put my hands in the pockets and flapped the jacket like a bird's wings. I stood in front of the mirror, full face, then profile, and then looked over my shoulder as if someone had called me. I sat on the bed, stood against the bed, and combed my hair to see what I would look like doing something natural. I looked ugly. I threw it on my brother's bed and looked at it for a long time before I slipped it on and went out to the back-yard, smiling a "thank you" to my mom as I passed her in the kitchen. With my hands in my pockets I kicked a ball against the fence, and then climbed it to sit looking into the alley. I hurled orange peels at the mouth of an open garbage can and when the peels were gone I watched the white puffs of my breath thin to nothing.

I jumped down, hands in my pockets, and in the backyard on my knees I teased my dog, Brownie, by swooping my arms while making bird calls. He jumped at me and missed. He jumped again and again, until a tooth sunk deep, ripping an L-shaped tear on my left sleeve. I pushed Brownie away to study the tear as I would a cut on my arm. There was no blood, only a few loose pieces of fuzz. Damn dog, I thought, and pushed him away hard when he tried to bite again. I got up from my knees and went to my bedroom to sit with my jacket on my lap, with the lights out.

That was the first afternoon with my new jacket. The next day I wore it to sixth grade and got a D on a math quiz. During the morning recess Frankie T., the playground terrorist, pushed me to the ground and told me to stay there until recess was over. My best friend, Steve Negrete, ate an apple while looking at me, and the girls turned away to whisper on the monkey bars. The teachers were no help: they looked my way and talked about how foolish I looked in my new jacket. I saw their heads bob with laughter, their hands half-covering their mouths.

Even though it was cold, I took off the jacket during lunch and played kickball in a thin shirt, my arms feeling like braille from goose bumps. But when I returned to class I slipped the jacket on and shivered until I was warm. I sat on my hands, heating them up, while my teeth chattered like a cup of crooked dice. Finally warm, I slid out of the jacket but a few minutes later put it back on when the fire bell rang. We paraded out into the yard where we, the sixth graders, walked past all the other grades to stand against the back fence. Everybody saw me. Although they didn't say out loud, "Man, that's ugly," I heard the buzz-buzz of gossip and even laughter that I knew was meant for me.

And so I went, in my guacamole jacket. So embarrassed, so

hurt, I couldn't even do my homework. I received Cs on quizzes, and forgot the state capitals and the rivers of South America, our friendly neighbor. Even the girls who had been friendly blew away like loose flowers to follow the boys in neat jackets.

I wore that thing for three years until the sleeves grew short and my forearms stuck out like the necks of turtles. All during that time no love came to me—no little dark girl in a Sunday dress she wore on Monday. At lunchtime I stayed with the ugly boys who leaned against the chain-link fence and looked around with propellers of grass spinning in our mouths. We saw girls walk by alone, saw couples, hand in hand, their heads like bookends pressing air together. We saw them and spun our propellers so fast our faces were blurs.

I blame that jacket for those bad years. I blame my mother for her bad taste and her cheap ways. It was a sad time for the heart. With a friend I spent my sixth-grade year in a tree in the alley waiting for something good to happen to me in that jacket, which had become the ugly brother who tagged along wherever I went. And it was about that time that I began to grow. My chest puffed up with muscle and, strangely, a few more ribs. Even my hands, those fleshy hammers, showed bravely through

the cuffs, the fingers already hardening for the coming fights. But that L-shaped rip on the left sleeve got bigger; bits of stuffing coughed out from its wound after a hard day of play. I finally Scotch-taped it closed, but in rain or cold weather the tape peeled off like a scab and more stuffing fell out until that sleeve shriveled into a palsied arm. That winter the elbows began to crack and whole chunks of green began to fall off. I showed the cracks to my mother, who always seemed to be at the stove with steamed-up glasses, and she said that there were children in Mexico who would love that jacket. I told her that this was America and yelled that Debbie, my sister, didn't have a jacket like mine. I ran outside, ready to cry, and climbed the tree by the alley to think bad thoughts and watch my breath puff white and disappear.

But whole pieces still casually flew off my jacket when I played hard, read quietly, or took vicious spelling tests at school. When it became so spotted that my brother began to call me "camouflage," I flung it over the fence into the alley. Later, however, I swiped the jacket off the ground and went inside to drape it across my lap and mope.

I was called to dinner: steam silvered my mother's glasses as she said grace; my brother and sister with their heads bowed made ugly faces at their glasses of powdered milk. I gagged too, but eagerly ate big rips of buttered tortilla that held scooped-up beans. Finished, I went outside with my jacket across my arm. It was a cold sky. The faces of clouds were piled up, hurting. I climbed the fence, jumping down with a grunt. I started up the alley and soon slipped into my jacket, that green ugly brother who breathed over my shoulder that day and ever since.

READER'S RESPONSE

1. The narrator blames his ugly jacket for the bad things that happen to him for three years while he wears it. Do you agree with this way of looking at things? How could a piece of clothing be responsible?
2. Have you ever had to wear a piece of clothing that you thought was ugly? In a short journal entry, write about how the experience made you feel.

WRITER'S CRAFT

3. In expressive writing, writers use sensory details—details of sight, sound, taste, touch, and smell—to make experiences seem real. What details of sight does the narrator use to make the jacket seem real to readers?
4. Expressive writing tells about experiences that are meaningful, or significant, for the writer. Where does Gary Soto reveal that this experience was significant for him? What do you think he discovered about himself?

Ways to Express Yourself

You'll find expressive writing all around you. You'll read it in magazines and newspapers and write it in journals and letters. Your writing is expressive when the focus is on you—what you experience, think, and feel. Here are some ways to develop expressive writing.

- in your journal, writing about an event that happened to you because you were in a wheelchair
- in an essay for a job application, writing about a significant life experience
- in a story, describing your grandparents' house to show how you feel about it
- in an article for the school's humor magazine, writing a funny description of the broccoli served in the lunchroom
- in a letter to your cousin, comparing your two best friends
- in your journal, exploring which you enjoy more, tennis or basketball
- in an essay, evaluating the water quality in your neighborhood park's drinking fountains
- in a letter to a friend, explaining why the Dallas Cowboys are the best NFL team

LOOKING AHEAD

In the main assignment in this chapter, you'll use narration to write about an incident that happened to you. As you work through the chapter, keep in mind that a good autobiographical narrative

- tells about the events in the order in which they happened
- gives details about the events
- explains the significance of the incident to the writer

Writing on an Autobiographical Incident

Prewriting

Choosing an Incident to Write About

When you write about an autobiographical incident, you tell of a particular event in your life that has significance for you. You often tell good friends about incidents in your life. How do you decide which incidents to write about?

Think about experiences that touched your feelings. Perhaps they were funny, sad, or scary. Or consider "first-time" events. For example, you may remember your first day at a new school, your first stage performance, or the first time you hit a home run. Finally, think about incidents that changed you in some way or that taught you something; during a family move for example, you may have learned how hard it is to say goodbye to friends.

Keep these points in mind when you choose an incident to write about.

- *Write about something you remember well.* You want to *tell* about and *show* your experience to readers. You can't if you don't remember details about it.
- *Write about an incident that was important to you.* It doesn't have to be a big adventure, but it should have meaning for you.

■ *Write about an incident you're willing to share.* You want to be comfortable sharing the experience with others.

EXERCISE 1 ▶ **Speaking and Listening: Exploring Topics for Autobiographical Incidents**

Get together with a partner or a few classmates and read the statements below. Can you remember an incident that fits each description? Tell each other the best stories you remember. Discuss what makes them interesting as stories. Create lists for your favorite two or three stories.

1. You and a friend disagreed.
2. Something happened that was embarrassing (at the time) but funny (later).
3. An event made strangers notice or hear about you.
4. You won a contest or some other honor.
5. You spent a frightening night, perhaps at a camp-out during a bad storm.

WRITING ASSIGNMENT

PART 1:
Choosing a Topic for an Autobiographical Incident

What experiences have you had that you want to explore in your writing? Choose one incident to write about. Try looking through the list you made with your classmates for Exercise 1. Or look through your journals, talk to your friends, or do a little private brainstorming.

Prewriting

Gathering and Organizing Your Ideas

In talking with friends, you often just start a story and hope to remember it as you go along. You write better, however, when you plan what to say and how to say it.

Thinking About Purpose and Audience

The *purpose* for writing about an autobiographical incident is to discover your own thoughts and feelings and to learn a little about yourself. You also write to share the experience, and what it meant to you, with others.

Your *audience* is probably made up of your classmates and teacher and perhaps other adults you trust. Try to make your narrative interesting to them. Remember to give them the background information they will need to understand your incident. Did you lose a pet you loved? Explain the pet's special qualities. Ask yourself what your audience will need to know in order to "be there" with you.

Recalling Details

A narrative of an autobiographical incident is different from most other types of writing. That's because many of the details and events are stored inside your memory. You'll need to recall these details to make your experiences seem real for readers. Did you win or lose a special contest? What sights and sounds will help you *tell* about the incident so that readers can share it? What did people say and do? How did you feel?

As you plan to write about your incident, try to remember the following kinds of details.

1. **Events.** What happened? Make notes about all the little individual events that made up the whole event. You went to your first big dance. *We decorated the gym with crepe paper and balloons; we danced for hours; we went for pizza afterward . . .*

2. **Sensory details.** What did you hear, see, feel, and maybe even smell and taste? *The rhythmic beat of the music; my dance partner's light-blue dress; the warm, humid night air . . .*

3. **Characters and places.** What other people were involved in your experience? What places were important? *My friend Takara came running down the stairs of her apartment building. For one evening the gym changed from a world of basketballs and hoops into a magical place.*

4. **Dialogue and quotations.** Did you and others say anything interesting during the incident? *"Takara, they're organizing a dance contest in front of the stage! Let's go!"*

5. **Thoughts and feelings.** What did you think and feel? Why? *At first, I was embarrassed—I'm not a very good dancer; but then I felt the music wash over me.*

WRITING NOTE   An autobiographical narrative is a first-person story, so the words *I* and *me* play an important part. Even though others shared the experience, remember that you're writing from your point of view. As you jot down details, stress what *you* saw and heard and felt, what *you* did, what *you* thought, and what the event meant to *you*.

CRITICAL THINKING

Showing, Not Telling

When you write your autobiographical narrative, you should *show* your experience to your readers—not just *tell* them about it. One way to do this is to collect sensory details about places, people, and things to use in your writing.

For example, you could collect sensory details about a specific moment during a lightning storm. Note what you observe with all your senses, not just your eyes. What do you see? What sounds do you hear? What do you feel, both with your skin and in your emotions? Does anything have a taste or smell? Either during or soon after the event, jot down notes of your observations. As you write, try to use precise words to describe your impressions.

Don't give up too quickly. Collecting sensory details is like the poem about shaking the ketchup bottle—none'll come and then a lot'll, but you have to keep at it.

CRITICAL THINKING EXERCISE:
Showing, Not Telling

Think of an event or occasion that was special to you. Maybe you spent a perfect day with friends at the beach last summer; maybe you saw a beautiful sunset or attended a track meet. Close your eyes and visualize the experience. Then, list as many *showing* details as you can for each sense. You might want to use a cluster diagram to collect your details.

Arranging Details

The next step in writing about an autobiographical incident is to arrange the details you've recalled. You need to put them in an order that will make sense to your readers. Many writers begin with background information and then use chronological order for the other details. Using *chronological order* (time order) means telling about events in the order they happened. You begin with the event that happened first, then go on to the second, and so on.

REFERENCE NOTE: For more information on chronological order, see pages 39, 79, and 100.

As you arrange your details, list them in a chart. On the next page you can see how one writer organized details for an autobiographical incident.

The Night the Lights Went Out	
BACKGROUND:	Where: Losoyas' home—my first baby-sitting job When: last spring, Saturday night Who: the Losoyas, baby Anna, me

EVENTS	DETAILS
Arrived at Losoyas' house.	Sight: clutter of toys Feeling: proud to be trusted with baby, nervous
Fed Anna and settled her down for night.	Touch: Anna's soft skin Sound: Anna's low gurgling
Thunderstorm began at eight o'clock.	Sound: sharp crack of nearby thunder Sight: vivid streaks of lightning
Lights and telephone went out at nine o'clock.	Sounds: telephone static; howling wind; branches rattling window; Anna's terrified cry Feeling: fright
I got the baby and quieted her.	Sight: lightning flash lights up room Touch: tense baby Quotation: "Everything's okay, sweetie. We'll be fine." Sound: Anna's steady breathing
Losoyas arrived home.	Sight: glow of candlelight Feeling: I handled the emergency like an adult.

WRITING ASSIGNMENT

PART 2:
Gathering and Organizing Ideas

You chose an experience to write about in Writing Assignment, Part 1. Now make a chart like the one above and list each event in the order it happened. Then, jot down details about each event, including sensory details, dialogue, and thoughts or feelings. Save your work.

Writing Your First Draft

The Parts of an Autobiographical Incident

No two autobiographical narratives are just alike, but they all have three basic parts:

- a *beginning* that grabs the reader's interest; sometimes gives background information and a hint about the importance of the incident
- a *middle* that tells about important events, describes people and places, and tells the writer's thoughts and feelings
- an *ending* in which the writer explains the outcome and shows the meaning of the incident

Here's how one professional writer, Ernesto Galarza, uses these parts to write about an autobiographical incident. Galarza's family lived for a time in the Mexican state of Sinaloa before moving to the United States.

A PASSAGE FROM A BOOK

from Barrio Boy
by Ernesto Galarza

BEGINNING
Attention grabber

There was another red-letter event for me that Christmas season. I saw my first motion picture.

Mazatlán was becoming a modern town. We had electricity at the plaza and on the

Background information

streets. For a penny you could buy electric shocks from a man who handed you two copper tubes wired to a small brown box with a handle which he turned faster and faster until you could not let go of the tubes. On the

Sensory details

salt flats where the bicycle races were held, a new game was being played in which a player threw a small white ball at another who hit it with a stick and ran. José, who was up-to-date on all these matters, found out about the cinema.

California Museum of Photography, Keystone-Mast Collection, University of California, Riverside.

MIDDLE
Sensory details

Event 1

Sensory details

The show was in a large hall somewhere near the market. High up on one wall there was a white screen facing a wooden tower from which a brilliant purple light shone through a small square hole. When we entered, the lights were on. Because there were no seats, the audience was standing. We pushed our way to one corner, where I was hoisted to a windowsill so I could look over the heads of the crowd.

The lights dimmed. There was a whir from the top of the tower and pictures began to flicker on the screen. A murmur of surprise and wonder rose from the audience.

Now it was pitch-dark in the hall except for the beam of light from the tower and the moving pictures above us. Words and the pictures took turns on the screen and the story began to unfold. It was a tragedy at sea, the sinking of a great ship and the drowning of many people.

Quotation

Event 2

All went well during the shore scenes. Suddenly the ship was on the ocean in stormy weather. As the waves broke over the prow someone yelled: "The ocean! Watch out! Run!" The audience turned into a panicky mob. Jammed against the door of the hall they burst it open and poured into the street.

Event 3

The lights went on and a man climbed up the tower. He harangued the few spectators who remained near the door until he convinced them that the ocean on the screen was make-believe. He climbed down, found a ladder somewhere, and propped it against the screen. The pictures went on again and he touched the waves, holding his hand out to show that it was absolutely dry. Little by little the crowd came back and the film was finished.

ENDING

Meaning of experience

On the way home José had much to say about the difference between motion-picture water and the real thing. Now that it was all over I could understand how ridiculous it had all been. But I had felt like running myself.

EXERCISE 2 ▶ **Analyzing the Organization of an Autobiographical Incident**

Read and think about the excerpt from *Barrio Boy*. Then, meet with two or three classmates to discuss the following questions.

1. Does the first sentence grab your attention? Explain why or why not.
2. What background information do you get in the introduction? Do you need this information to understand the incident? Why?
3. In what order are the events discussed? Make a time line to show the chronological order of events.
4. What are some sensory details that Galarza uses to describe his experience at the cinema?
5. How does Galarza let his readers know what he felt about the incident? the meaning he thought it had?

A Writer's Model for You

Although Ernesto Galarza was an accomplished writer, his narrative follows a basic framework. The model below follows that basic framework, too. You may want to use it as a model when you write about your own incident.

A WRITER'S MODEL

The Night the Lights Went Out

BEGINNING
Attention grabber

What would you do if you were alone with a baby in a dark house during the worst thunderstorm of the year?

Background information

Everything was calm when I arrived for my first baby-sitting job. The Losoyas' baby, Anna, was playing in the living room, a clutter of toys all around her. Although nervous, I was proud that the Losoyas trusted me with her and I wanted to prove worthy of that trust.

Thoughts and feelings
Hint of importance

MIDDLE
Event 1
Sensory details

Soon after the Losoyas left, I fed Anna and settled her down for the night. As I tucked the blankets around her, I touched her soft skin and listened to her low gurgling.

Event 2
Sensory details

Event 3

Sensory details

Feelings

Shortly after eight o'clock, I heard the sharp crack of nearby thunder. Every few seconds, vivid streaks of lightning lit up the sky. Then at nine o'clock the lights suddenly went out. I picked up the phone to call my parents, but there was only static. By now the wind was howling, and dead branches rattled the windows. Suddenly, Anna's terrified cry rang out. Controlling my fright, I groped through cabinets to find flashlights and candles. Fumbling in the drawers, I found candles and a box of matches.

Event 4
Sensory details

Quotation
Sensory details
ENDING

Outcome—meaning of incident

I felt my way to Anna. When the next lightning flash lit up the room, I put a candle in a saucer and lit it. I held the tense, frightened baby and rocked her. I crooned to her, "Everything's okay, sweetie. We'll be fine." When I heard her steady breathing, I laid her in the bed. And that's how her parents found her, fast asleep, bathed in the glow of candlelight. That night I learned that I could handle an emergency like an adult.

If you decide to model your autobiographical narrative on the one you've just read, you can use the following framework.

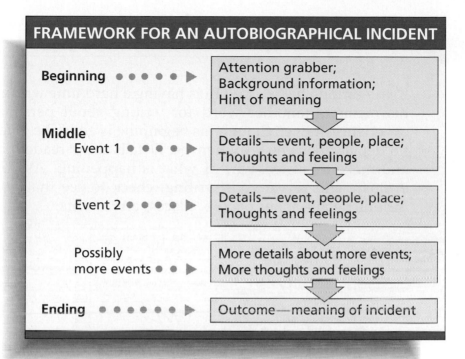

FRAMEWORK FOR AN AUTOBIOGRAPHICAL INCIDENT

Beginning ● ● ● ● ● ▶	Attention grabber; Background information; Hint of meaning
Middle Event 1 ● ● ● ● ▶	Details—event, people, place; Thoughts and feelings
Event 2 ● ● ● ● ▶	Details—event, people, place; Thoughts and feelings
Possibly more events ● ● ▶	More details about more events; More thoughts and feelings
Ending ● ● ● ● ● ● ▶	Outcome—meaning of incident

Reminder

As you write about your autobiographical incident

- arrange details about the events in chronological order
- include sensory details about each event
- include thoughts, feelings, and possibly dialogue, to make the narrative come alive
- help your readers see the meaning of the experience

WRITING ASSIGNMENT

PART 3:

Writing a Draft of Your Autobiographical Incident

Now it's time to write. Use the chart you developed in Writing Assignment, Part 2 (page 129). Then, just write about the incident as if you were telling it to a friend. Don't forget to end your narrative by telling its outcome and showing what the experience meant to you.

Evaluating and Revising

In the cartoon below, Calvin is having a hard time writing his memoirs (another word for writing about personal experiences). Even though his beginning is good, he gives no details about his experiences. Details draw readers in and make them feel part of what is happening. As you evaluate and revise your writing, check to see that you include details about people, places, and events.

 COMPUTER NOTE: Your word-processing program's built-in thesaurus can help you find vivid words to replace flat ones.

Use the chart on the next page to help you evaluate and revise your writing. First, ask yourself a question from the left-hand column. Then, if you find a weakness in the narrative of your incident, use the revision technique suggested in the right-hand column.

EVALUATING AND REVISING AUTOBIOGRAPHICAL INCIDENTS

EVALUATION GUIDE	REVISION TECHNIQUE
1 Does the writer grab the reader's interest in the introduction?	**Add** an interesting statement or question.
2 Has the writer given enough background information?	**Add** important details about where and when the incident happened. Tell who was there.
3 Are the events told in an order that makes sense?	**Reorder** events in the order they happened.
4 Has the writer used details that make events, people, and places seem real?	**Cut** dull or needless details. **Add** sensory details, possibly quotations, and details about your thoughts and feelings.
5 Are the outcome and significance of the incident clear?	**Add** a sentence or two that tells the outcome. **Add** information to show the significance of the incident to you.

EXERCISE 3 ▶ **Analyzing a Writer's Revisions**

Now's your chance to see inside an editor's mind. Working with a partner or in a small group, study these revisions from the last paragraph of the writer's model on pages 133–134, and then answer the questions that follow. Get together with another group to compare your answers.

That night I learned that I could handle an emergency like an adult. I felt   **reorder**

my way to Anna. When the next lightning flash lit up the room, I put ~~one~~ *a candle* in a saucer   **replace**

and lit it. I held the tense ∧*frightened* baby and rocked   **add**

her. I ~~talked~~ *crooned* to her ∧ *"Everything's okay, sweetie.* ~~I told her everything~~   **replace**

We'll ~~would~~ be fine." When I heard her ∧*steady* breathing,   **replace/add**

I laid her in the bed. And that's how her parents found her ∧*fast* asleep, bathed in ∧*the glow of*   **add**

candlelight. ∧

1. Why does the writer move the first sentence? Why is it more effective at the end?
2. How does replacing the word *one* with the words *a candle* improve the third sentence?
3. In the sixth sentence, why does the writer add the quotation? How does it improve the paragraph?
4. In the fourth, seventh, and eighth sentences, how does adding the words *frightened*, *steady*, *fast*, and *the glow of* improve the paragraph?

WRITING NOTE

Dialogue—words people actually say—can bring an autobiographical incident to life. For example, read the following two passages. Both express the same information. Isn't the second one much livelier?

1.   Mario had called the National Weather Service and learned from a man there that it was snowing in the pass. Carmen thought we should go anyway and asked for my opinion. I agreed that we should try.

2.　　"I just called the National Weather Service," Mario announced. "The guy says it's snowing in the pass."
　　　"Oh, let's go anyway," said Carmen. "We can make it. What do you think, Ginny?"
　　　"I'm game," I replied.

PART 4:
Evaluating and Revising Your Autobiographical Incident

You've seen how someone else improved the telling of an autobiographical incident. Now it's time to decide how to evaluate and improve your own narrative. Read your draft with a partner, and evaluate each other's work. Use the evaluating and revising guidelines on page 137. (You might also want to use the peer evaluation guidelines on page 47.) When you get your paper back, think about your partner's suggestions. Then, revise your work.

Proofreading and Publishing

Proofreading.   Even simple mistakes in usage or mechanics can make your paper hard to understand. Proofread your work carefully, and correct any mistakes you find.

MECHANICS HINT

Using Dialogue

You may often use dialogue in your narrative. The correct punctuation of dialogue is important so that readers know who is talking. In the first sentence below, you can't be sure who has called the National Weather Service. In the second sentence, punctuation makes the point clear.

EXAMPLES   Henry said I called the National Weather
              Service.
              Henry said, "I called the National Weather
              Service."

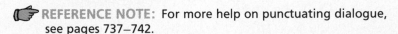 REFERENCE NOTE: For more help on punctuating dialogue, see pages 737–742.

Publishing.   Once you have revised, proofread, and made corrections, make a clean copy. Readers always find a clean, neat paper more inviting than a messy, difficult-to-read one. Here are two ways you can publish your writing.

■ One audience for your work may be your own future self. Start a scrapbook of memories, beginning with this piece. Years from now, you may be surprised at the picture you get of yourself.

■ With your classmates, make an anthology of auto-biographical incidents. Create groupings based on similar topics: outdoor adventures, conflicts with friends or family, school experiences, and so forth.

WRITING ASSIGNMENT

PART 5:
Proofreading and Publishing Your Autobiographical Incident

You've worked hard, so reward yourself now with your best effort. Proofread your work carefully and correct the errors. (See page 53 for more help with proofreading.) Share your work in one of the ways suggested above or in any other way you like.

 Reflecting on Your Writing

If you'd like to add your autobiographical incident paper to your **portfolio,** date it and include with it the answers to these questions.

■ What prewriting technique led you to your topic?
■ How did you try to make your incident interesting for readers? How well do you think you succeeded? Why?
■ Which did you find more difficult, recalling details or organizing your ideas? Why?

A STUDENT MODEL

Jerry Bonner believes that writers who tell about personal experiences should remember that "you are trying to interest the reader about something that was true and happened to you." Jerry is a student at Cumberland Middle School in Cumberland, Rhode Island. Here is part of his narrative about a very special race.

Personal Best
by Jerry Bonner

What was I doing in Reno, Nevada, in the middle of winter? I was at the National Cross-Country Championships competing with my team, the Sentinel Striders.

Just before the race I started to get nervous and began to doubt my own ability, but after a while I calmed down. Before I knew it, we were at the starting line.

The gun went off and so did I. There was nothing but silence in the crowd. I led the pack right from the start. My strategy was to go out as fast as I could for as long as I could. There was a hill half a mile long; it felt as though it was never going to end, and that was the toughest part of the race. There were two kids right behind me, so close I could feel them breathing down my back and their feet pounding against the ground right behind me. Before I knew it, though, I was on the back straightaway, the crowd cheering and screaming as I ran toward the finish line. The race was over and I had won the National Cross-Country Championships. It was the greatest feeling in the world.

Finally, all the hard work and training paid off. I had broken the course record in Reno, Nevada, and my team finished third in the nation. A great thing about the day of the race was that it was my grandfather's birthday and coming in first was a nice gift for him. I realized that this was my best vacation and my greatest experience.

WRITING WORKSHOP

A Journal Entry

Some types of expressive writing, such as a work based on an autobiographical incident, are meant to be shared. But other types of expressive writing are just for the writer. For example, a journal is a tool for exploring what you think and feel. A journal is more than a record of events—it's a place where you can write freely about events, reveal your thoughts, and express your anger and other emotions.

The following excerpt is from *The Diary of a Young Girl*, by Anne Frank. Anne was a Jewish girl who, along with her family and four Jewish family friends, spent much of World War II on the top floor of an Amsterdam house, hiding from Holland's Nazi occupiers. Eventually they were discovered and arrested. Anne died in a concentration camp a few months before Germany surrendered.

from The Diary of a Young Girl
by Anne Frank

Wednesday, February 23, 1944

My dearest Kitty,

The weather's been wonderful since yesterday, and I've perked up quite a bit. My writing, the best thing I have, is coming along well. I go to the attic almost every morning to get the stale air out of my lungs. This morning when I went there, Peter was busy cleaning up. He finished quickly and came over to where I was sitting on my favorite spot on the floor. The two of us looked out at the blue sky, the bare chestnut tree glistening with dew, the seagulls and other birds glinting with silver as they swooped through the air, and we were so moved and entranced that we couldn't speak. He stood with his head against a thick beam, while I sat. We breathed in the air, looked outside and both felt that the spell shouldn't be broken with words. We remained like this for a long while, and by the time he had to go to the loft to chop wood, I knew he was a good, decent boy. He climbed the ladder to the loft, and I followed; during the fifteen minutes he was chopping wood, we didn't say a word either. I watched him from where I was standing, and could see he was obviously doing his best to chop the right way and show off his strength. But I also looked out the open window, letting my eyes roam over a large part of Amsterdam, over the rooftops and on to the horizon, a strip of blue so pale it was almost invisible.

Thinking It Over

1. Anne addresses her diary entries to "Kitty," an imaginary friend. What does Anne tell "Kitty" that she might not share with others?
2. What is your impression of Anne? of her feelings for Peter?

Writing a Journal Entry

Prewriting. In your journal, you can write about any subject. Don't worry about coming up with something that you can show the world. Just write to explore what you think and remember.

Writing. Write your journal entry. Then reread it, and think about whether there's anything else you want to say or explore.

Publishing. You might want to share your journal entry with a friend or family member. Or you can save your entry in your **portfolio.** If you choose to save your entry, date it and include your responses to these questions.
- Did you discover anything new about yourself or your subject?
- How freely do your ideas flow in this type of informal writing? Is writing easier when you prewrite?
- Could you use your entry in a more formal piece of writing, such as an autobiographical incident or a short story?

MAKING CONNECTIONS

WRITING ACROSS THE CURRICULUM

Expressive Writing and History

Historians learn about the past from public documents, such as newspapers and treaties, as well as from private documents, such as letters and journals. In the following journal entry, a trader describes a meeting with a group of American Indians in Texas in 1808. As you read the entry, look for details about the events, people, and places that were part of the trader's experience. Remember that the year is 1808. Some of the spelling and capitalization will seem strange to you.

August 11th

The Messenger we sent to the Village returned early this Morning accompanied by six Indians and we were met by fifty men on Horseback, who Escorted us into the Village   when in sight of the town we hoisted our flag and they immediately hoisted a similar one which they had received of Dr. Sibly of Nacki-tosh. a man met us with an Invitation to the Chief's house. But we preferred encamping near the great spring and were conducted thither where I pitched my tent and hoisted my flag in front of it, about fifty yards from the Chiefs house.—a band of Women came immediately [and] pulled up and cleared away the grass and weeds from about the camp and also cleared a path down to the spring. I then waited on the Great Chief and was received with every token of Friendship I informed him I would wait on him again the next day & inform[ed] him for what purpose we had come to his

Country & returned to my tent   we found our Camp filled with a quantity of green Corn, Beans, Water and Mus Melons.

Anthony Glass, *Journal of an Indian Trader*

An autobiographical incident you write about might one day become an important document about life today. Choose an event you remember—perhaps a severe storm or memorable trip—that might tell people a hundred years from now about life today. Write about how you experienced the incident. Include details that would help explain your experience to someone from a later time.

EXPRESSIVE WRITING AND PERSONAL LETTERS

Personal letters may be informative. For example, you might write to your aunt to tell her when you're arriving to visit. They also may be persuasive. You might write to a friend who moved away, trying to persuade him to come visit you in the summer. But often personal letters are expressive. We sometimes want to share our personal thoughts and feelings with good friends and close relatives, and a letter is one way to do that. In the following personal letter, a girl shares her feelings about her grandparents with a friend who lives some distance away.

December 2, 1998

Dear Joanna,

Thanks for the letter. It seems funny to think about you playing in the sun in Florida when it's already snowing here in Chicago. We got up early this morning to listen to the weather report. We were hoping the snow would be heavy enough that we wouldn't have to go to school. No such luck!

We had a great Thanksgiving. My grandparents cooked the meal, and we had Chinese food instead of turkey and dressing. While we were eating, they told me some stories about their life in China that I'd never heard before. It was kind of strange. I'd never thought much about China before. You know what I mean. The fact that my grandparents came from there didn't mean much to me.

Now I feel different. They made China sound so beautiful and so interesting. My grandfather says that Kweilin, where they lived, has lots of hills and rivers. I'd like to go there to visit when I get older. Want to go along?

Tell everybody I said hello, and tell your parents to let you come stay when school is out. You'll like Chicago, especially in the summer.

Your friend,
Amy

In this letter, Amy shares her thoughts and feelings about her experience with her grandparents. Do you have any thoughts or feelings you'd like to share with someone? Instead of calling, try writing a letter.

5 USING DESCRIPTION

Creating Pictures and Images

Words are a writer's paintbrush. With words, a writer can create a **picture** so funny, so sad, or so frightening, that you feel like laughing, crying, or shuddering in fright at the "sight" of it.

Writing and You. A science fiction writer describes how the sun looks when it becomes a nova. A newspaper reporter describes the terrible damage left by a killer hurricane. With their vivid words, writers make you feel as though you were there—hearing, seeing, feeling, smelling, or tasting what they are writing about. Have you ever described something in writing?

As You Read. Here's an excerpt from a short story that describes a Japanese meal. As you read, look for words that make the meal seem real to you. Can you see or taste it?

Bev Doolittle

Bev Doolittle, *Doubled Back* (1988) © The Greenwich Workshop, Inc., Shelton, CT 06484.

149

FROM 二世 NISEI DAUGHTER

BY MONICA SONE

While the Matsuis and our parents reminisced about the good old days, we thumbed through the worn photograph albums and old Japanese tourist magazines. Finally Mrs. Matsui excused herself and bustled feverishly around the dining room. Then she invited us in. "*Sah*, I have nothing much to offer you, but please eat your fill."

"*Mah, mah*, such a wonderful assortment of *ogochi-soh*," Mother bubbled.

Balding Mr. Matsui snorted deprecatingly. Mrs. Matsui walked around the table with an enormous platter of *osushi*, rice cakes rolled in seaweed. We each took one and nibbled at it daintily, sipping tea. Presently she sailed out of the kitchen bearing a magnificent black and silver lacquered tray loaded with carmine lacquer bowls filled with fragrant *nishime*. In pearly iridescent china bowls, Mrs. Matsui served us hot chocolatey *oshiruko,* a sweetened bean soup dotted with tender white *mochi,* puffed up like oversized marshmallows.

F ather and Mother murmured over the superb flavoring of each dish, while Mr. Matsui guffawed politely, "*Nani,* this woman isn't much of a cook at all."

I was fascinated with the *yakizakana,* barbecued perch, which, its head and tail raised saucily, looked as if it were about to flip out of the oval platter. Surrounding this centerpiece were lacquer boxes of desserts, neatly lined rows of red and green oblong slices of sweet bean cakes, a mound of crushed lima beans, tinted red and green, called *kinton.* There was a vegetable dish called *kimpira* which looked like a mass of brown twigs. It turned out to be burdock, hotly seasoned with red pepper.

READER'S RESPONSE

1. Have you ever eaten a meal cooked by someone from a culture or country different than your own? Describe the meal for your classmates.
2. Imagine a meal in an unusual place. For example, perhaps you have lunch on Mount Everest or breakfast on the ocean floor. Write a short journal entry about the meal.

WRITER'S CRAFT

3. In this description, Monica Sone uses words like *enormous platter* and *magnificent black and silver lacquered tray* to create a picture of a Japanese meal. What are some other words she uses to paint a picture of the meal for you?
4. When they describe, writers often use *sensory details,* words that describe sights, sounds, tastes, textures, and smells. For example, "an enormous platter of *osushi*" helps you see the dish. What are some texture, or touch, words that Monica Sone uses? What are some taste words she uses?

"THE DISCOVERY OF A NEW DISH DOES MORE FOR HUMAN HAPPINESS THAN THE DISCOVERY OF A STAR."

ANTHELME BRILLAT-SAVARIN

Uses of Description

Writers of description always want to create a picture with words. But they don't always use description in the same way or for the same purpose. Here are several ways you might use description in your writing.

- in a journal entry, describing the emptiness in your old room as you pack for a move to a new house
- in a letter to a friend, describing the frightening characters and amazing special effects in a science fiction movie you watched
- in a note to your parents, describing the colorful, prize-filled piñata at a birthday party so that your parents will let you have one at yours
- in a newspaper ad, describing a puppy so that someone will adopt it
- in an e-mail message to a coworker, describing problems you are having with your computer
- in a bulletin board notice, giving an accurate description of your missing bicycle
- in a short story, describing the little alien from Mars who is the main character
- in a poem, describing a spider spinning a web

When you start your first part-time job, you'll need descriptions of the materials you'll use and the duties you'll perform. When you read your newspaper, you'll read descriptions of soccer or football games. Descriptions are also in ads on the veterinarian's bulletin board and in pamphlets about computers

in the computer store. And you can relax and enjoy description in stories, novels, poems, and plays. The purpose of the descriptions may be different, but they're all alike in one way. All the writers want you to form a picture or image of their subjects.

LOOKING AHEAD

In the main assignment in this chapter, you'll write a description. Your basic purpose will be to express yourself or to be creative. As you work through this chapter, keep in mind that an expressive or creative description

- is filled with details that create a picture or image of the subject
- uses sensory details, exact words, and figures of speech
- is clearly organized and easy to follow

Calvin & Hobbes copyright 1986 Watterson. Distributed by Universal Press Syndicate. Reprinted with permission. All rights reserved.

Writing a Description

Prewriting

Planning a Description

A good description doesn't just come out of thin air. It's the result of thinking and planning.

Thinking About Subject, Purpose, and Audience

A Subject. You usually don't have to look around for a *subject* to describe. The subject is already there. For example, you need to describe a new jacket you want for your birthday. Or you need to describe your state capitol building in your history report. If you do have to think of a subject to write about, it helps to choose something you know well. You might think of an object in your own home or a place you know very well. If you don't know the subject well, you may have to use your imagination.

A Purpose. Your *purpose* for writing can take you in two different directions. The first direction is to describe something *exactly as it is*. For example, if you've lost your pet dog, Flash, you need to describe his exact color, size, and markings. Otherwise you might get the wrong dog back.

The second direction is the one you take in expressive or creative descriptions. You describe something in a way that will *create a feeling or mood*. You may want to describe your day at the beach to make your readers feel how exciting it was. You could show that excitement by describing how it felt to surf in on a big wave or to catch and reel in a fifty-pound shark or to watch the volleyball soar across the net.

An Audience.   Your *audience* will also make a difference in your description. Your best friend would remember that Flash was brown and white, but she might not remember the black spot on his ear. Always ask yourself what your audience will need to know to clearly see what you describe.

Calvin & Hobbes copyright 1986 Watterson. Distributed by Universal Press Syndicate. Reprinted with permission. All rights reserved.

WRITING NOTE   When you want to show readers how you feel about a subject, put yourself into the picture. Use words like *I, me, my,* and *mine* when you talk about yourself. However, when you write a description for a formal report—like a science report—it may not be appropriate to use these words or to include your thoughts and feelings. You will have to decide which of these types of description—one that includes your feelings or one that is more focused on facts—better suits your purpose.

WRITING ASSIGNMENT

PART 1:
Beginning Your Description

In this chapter, you'll be writing a description of an object that expresses your feeling about it. First, you'll have to decide what you want to describe. You will be trying to create a feeling or mood, so you might want to choose something you have a specific feeling about. Also, make sure it's something you know well. Remember that your audience will include your teacher and classmates.

After you've finished thinking, write the name of your subject. Then, write three sentences that tell how you feel about it or how you want your readers to feel about it.

Collecting Details

Now that you have an interesting subject, how do you describe it? Where do you get the details to make it clear? You can observe, recall, or imagine it.

Observing.   *Observing* a subject means paying close attention to it. It also means using all your senses. What do you see and hear? What do you feel, taste, and touch?

Recalling.   Sometimes you can't observe a subject, but you can *recall* certain memories of it. You remember a park because you had a good time there. Close your eyes and think about your subject. What animals do you see? What sounds do you hear?

Imagining.   You can *imagine* details about things you've never seen. What's it like inside a race car? What do you imagine you'd see? hear? smell? Or think about an alien from a distant solar system. How does it look? walk? talk?

COMPUTER NOTE: To avoid the urge to correct errors as you're typing details from memory, type with the monitor off or dimmed. When you want to see what you've typed, turn the monitor back up.

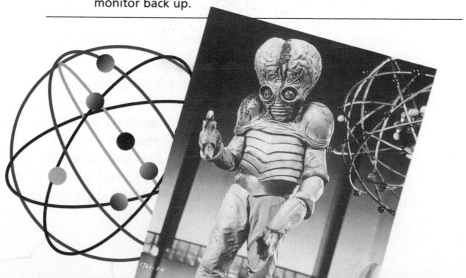

Here are one writer's notes to describe the dark, scary experience she had the time she crawled under a house. Notice that the writer used two of the three ways of collecting details (page 157).

HERE'S HOW

| What I observe: | darkness under house; muffled sounds; rays of light from house; damp smell; rough ground |
| What I recall: | trash; sweating; imagining spiders and snakes; spider webs in my mouth; seeing my brother and his friend running toward house; hands and knees hurting |

EXERCISE 1 ▶ **Speaking and Listening: Collecting Details**

If you're describing a book, you don't have to worry too much about sounds. But you can't describe a herd of elephants or a rock concert without details about sound. That means you need to train your ears to listen for details. Use the following suggestions to practice your listening skills.

1. Take five minutes to listen for all the sounds in your home. Jot down notes as you listen. Can you hear a car motor outside? a creaky sound in the walls? the humming of the refrigerator? the ticking of a clock?
2. Get together with a partner. Take turns reading the list of sounds you heard. Did you and your partner hear similar sounds? What are some differences in your lists?

CRITICAL THINKING

Observing Details

When you are writing a description of something, remember to include vivid details that will help your readers visualize what you describe. Take a minute to look at the picture on the right. Then, think about how you would describe it to someone who hasn't seen it. What details would you focus on? How would you describe the colors?

You don't observe details with just your eyes. You also observe them by hearing, tasting, touching, and smelling. Make yourself aware of even the smallest details. Sit on a park bench. What strikes you first? Is the bench wooden or concrete? Are there names or initials carved or drawn on the bench? Can you smell flowers nearby or the fumes of traffic? What do you hear?

 CRITICAL THINKING EXERCISE:
Observing Details

Practice your observing skills. Choose something you can observe directly, like the subjects listed below. Use all your senses to observe the subject. Make a list of as many details about it as you can. Compare with classmates who chose similar subjects. What details are different?

1. your bedroom closet
2. your back yard late at night or early in the morning
3. an aquarium
4. your favorite food
5. the refrigerator in your house

PART 2:
Collecting Details

Put your observing, recalling, and imagining skills into action! Collect the details for the subject you chose for Writing Assignment, Part 1 (page 156). Write your details in a chart like the one on page 158.

Selecting and Organizing Details

Sometimes, when you're going out, you choose everything you wear just to create a certain effect. You decide between a T-shirt and a shirt with buttons, or between a flashy belt and a plain one. You do the same kind of thing when you try to create a particular feeling or mood in a description. You use some details and leave out others. For example, if you want to show that the park was gloomy and depressing, you probably won't include details about the beautiful rose garden.

After you've chosen your details, you need to think about how to put them together. Here are two of the many ways you can arrange descriptive details.

spatial order: arrange details by location—good for describing places and objects
- from top to bottom or bottom to top
- from near to far or far to near
- from left to right or right to left

order of importance: arrange details by the importance you want to give them—good for describing people and animals
- from least to most important
- from most to least important

You don't have to use one of these organizations. Sometimes a description just won't work that way. However, it is important that you create a clear picture for your readers.

👉 **REFERENCE NOTE:** For more help on arranging information, see pages 39–42 and 77–84.

When you plan a description

- collect details by observing, recalling, or imagining
- select the details that will help you create a special feeling
- decide the best way to organize the details

E X E R C I S E **2**▶ **Selecting and Organizing Details**

Write a description of the house pictured here to create a feeling of mystery and suspense. Make a list of all the details from the picture that would help create that feeling. Think how to arrange the details. Which would be better—spatial order or order of importance? Arrange your details in the order you've chosen. Next, work with two or three classmates to compare details and the order you used. Try to decide which details and which order work the best.

WRITING ASSIGNMENT

PART 3:
Selecting and Organizing Details

Look over the details in the chart you made for Writing Assignment, Part 2 (page 160). Think about the feeling you want to create. Choose details and an order you think are best. Then list your details in that order.

Writing Your First Draft

An artist paints a picture with brushes and paint. These are the artist's tools. When you write a description, you're painting a picture, too. Your tools are words.

The Basic Elements of Description

Sensory details.   Sensory details come from using your senses—sight, touch, hearing, smell, and taste. In this paragraph, many sensory details help create a strong picture of hard work.

> It was hot work, dusty work. Chemicals used for spraying the vines smelled bad and choked him. Spider webs got in his face. Broken vines scratched his arms. Grapes stained his hands. Sweat poured into his eyes, in spite of the handkerchief wrapped around his forehead.
>
> James P. Terzian and Kathryn Cramer,
> *Mighty Hard Road*

Here's the beginning of a *word bank* for sensory details. You might start your own word bank in your journal. That way, you can add new words as you learn them.

A WORD BANK			
Sight	shiny faded broad	copper tall silvery	spotted rosy round
Touch	fuzzy scratchy	slippery cool	bumpy damp
Sound	screech mutter	murmur rumble	whisper roar
Smell	smoky rotten	fresh stale	spicy perfumy
Taste	warm sour	salty fresh	bitter sweet

Exact Words. Exact words make your description sharp. For example, an exact word for the color of your favorite sweater might be *turquoise* or *navy*, not *blue*. A duck doesn't *walk*, it *waddles*. In the following paragraph, a young boy finds a fawn, or young deer, that he has been looking for. As you read, notice how the writer uses exact words such as *startled*, *fawn*, and *stare*.

Movement directly in front of him startled him so that he tumbled backward. The fawn lifted its face to his. It turned its head with a wide, wondering motion and shook him through with the stare of its liquid eyes. It was quivering. It made no effort to rise or run. Jody could not trust himself to move.

Marjorie Kinnan Rawlings, *The Yearling*

Figures of speech. *Figures of speech* compare two things that are very different. When you use a figure of speech, you don't mean exactly what you say. "This room is a pig pen" doesn't *really* mean that pigs live in the room. It just means the room is messy. *Similes* and *metaphors* are two figures of speech that are easy to use.

A *simile* compares two things using the word *like* or *as*.

My mother's voice was like a cool, dark room in summer—peaceful, soothing, quiet.

Eugenia Collier, "Marigolds"

A *metaphor* compares two things directly. It doesn't use *like* or *as*.

> During the storm, the *sky was a cloudy sea.*

MECHANICS HINT

Noun Plurals

The exact words that you use in your descriptions are often nouns. Remember that nouns form their plurals in different ways.

Form the plural of many nouns by adding *s.*

EXAMPLES   Little *rays* of light helped me see.

I imagined hairy *spiders* and coiled *snakes* in the darkness.

Add *es* to nouns ending in *s, x, z, ch,* or *sh.*

EXAMPLE   In the dim light, I saw two small *foxes* hiding in the *bushes.*

Other nouns form their plurals in different ways. Use your dictionary to find the correct noun plurals.

☞ REFERENCE NOTE: For more about noun plurals, see pages 773–776.

Maybe you recall a special place from your childhood. Could you describe that place vividly? Read the following description of a special place that one girl shared with her parents. As you read, look for details that make the place and the people seem real.

A PASSAGE FROM A NOVEL

from Water Girl
by Joyce Carol Thomas

Simile
Metaphor

Exact words

Amber's mother had scrubbed the oak floors until they gleamed like gold, until the seams in the parquet danced with light. A center rug embroidered with blue trumpet vines hooking themselves into a round wreath added warmth and comfort. The mother had rinsed the enormous plate-glass window in vinegar water and shined it with a soft lintless rag until one wondered whether or not there really was any glass in the pane. Amber often looked out this window to capture a panoramic view of the sea. It was a simple room, sparsely furnished but alive with light and warmth.

A rocking chair sat next to a little wicker table. When Amber was much younger, her father would rock her to sleep here. A couch, upholstered in a fabric woven from blue and red threads, sat opposite the rocker. Before her father would rock her to sleep, her mother would tell her stories on this couch. From a distance the blue and red threads

Sensory details

gave off the color of purple. It was only when Amber was closer, sitting on the couch in her mother's lap, sucking on her three middle fingers and listening to the story of the bear who went fishing in a lake, that she could see where the red stopped and the blue began.

E X E R C I S E 3 ▶   **Analyzing a Description**

After reading the description, can you see Amber's living room in your mind? Discuss the following questions with your class or small group.

1. What feeling about Amber's family does the passage give you? What word describes the feeling?
2. How does the first sentence create a vivid image?
3. What are two sensory details the writer uses to describe the living room? What specific information does she give about the couch?
4. The writer uses order of importance and spatial order. Which object in the room seems to be most important to her? How does she use spatial order?

A Writer's Model for You

Joyce Carol Thomas is a skilled professional writer, so her model may be hard for you to match. Before you begin writing your description, read the following model. It's probably more like what you might write yourself.

A WRITER'S MODEL

Simile
Exact words

Last summer I discovered a different world when I crawled under the house to look for a lost baseball. The crawl space was like a secret cave. Mostly it was dark, but little rays of light from the

Sensory details

house above helped me see. The ground smelled musty and damp, and it was rough on my hands and knees. Above me I could just barely hear music from the radio. Sticky cobwebs got in my mouth. It was cool, but I began to sweat. I

Writer's feelings

imagined hairy spiders and coiled snakes in the darkness. I crawled quickly back to the front and poked my head out of the opening. Bright

Simile

sunlight blinded my eyes. I felt like a bear coming out of its cave after a long winter's nap.

PART 4:

Writing a Draft of Your Description

Are you ready to paint a picture with words? Using the details that you've collected, write the first draft of your description. As you write, focus on the feeling you want to create about your subject. Remember to use sensory details, exact words, and figures of speech so that your description will seem real to your readers.

Evaluating and Revising

On page 156 you saw how Calvin's mother helped him evaluate his description. Next, he must revise his work. This same process of evaluating and revising will help you improve your first draft. Use the following chart and ask yourself each question in the left-hand column. If you find a problem, use the ideas in the right-hand column to solve it.

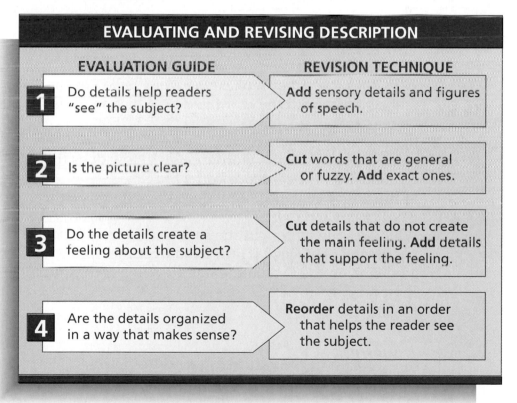

EVALUATING AND REVISING DESCRIPTION

EVALUATION GUIDE	REVISION TECHNIQUE
1 Do details help readers "see" the subject?	**Add** sensory details and figures of speech.
2 Is the picture clear?	**Cut** words that are general or fuzzy. **Add** exact ones.
3 Do the details create a feeling about the subject?	**Cut** details that do not create the main feeling. **Add** details that support the feeling.
4 Are the details organized in a way that makes sense?	**Reorder** details in an order that helps the reader see the subject.

E X E R C I S E 4 ▶ Analyzing a Writer's Revisions

On the following page is part of the description you read on page 168. As you read, think about the changes the writer made during revision. With your class or in a small group, answer the questions that follow.

> Above me I could just barely hear
> ~~sounds~~ *music* from the radio. *Sticky* ₍C₎obwebs got in my   **replace/add**
> mouth. It was cool, but I began to sweat. I
> imagined ₍*hairy*₎ spiders and ₍*coiled*₎ snakes in the   **add**
> darkness. I crawled quickly back to the
> front and poked my head out of the
> opening. ~~The crawl space was about 4 1/2~~   **cut**
> ~~feet long.~~ Bright sunlight blinded my eyes.
> I felt like a bear coming out of its cave
> after a long winter's nap.

1. Why does the writer replace the word *sounds* in the first sentence with the word *music*? Which word is more exact?
2. In the second sentence, why does the writer add the word *Sticky* before the word *cobwebs*? How does this change make the sentence better?
3. In the fourth sentence, why does the writer add the words *hairy* and *coiled*?
4. Why does the writer cut the sentence *The crawl space was about 4 ½ feet long*? [Hint: Read over the third guideline on the Evaluating and Revising Description chart on page 169.]

| **WRITING ASSIGNMENT** | PART 5: **Evaluating and Revising Your Description** |

It's a good idea to take advantage of other people's evaluations of your writing. Exchange papers with a partner or with a small group of classmates, and comment on each other's descriptions. (Don't forget to use the peer-evaluation guidelines on page 47.) Think about your own evaluations and your classmates' or partner's. Then revise your first draft.

Proofreading and Publishing

In proofreading, you catch and correct errors in grammar, usage, and mechanics.

 COMPUTER NOTE: If you use a spell-checking program, remember that it won't catch homonym errors. For example, it won't reveal that you typed *their* when you meant to type *there*.

When your description is ready, share it with others.

- Make a classroom display of the places and objects everyone described. Draw, find, or create pictures, cartoons, or photos to go along with the descriptions.
- Play a guessing game with a small group of classmates. Read your description aloud. Then, ask your classmates to identify the main feeling. Is it the same as or different from the one you wanted to create?

PART 6:

Proofreading and Publishing Your Description

You've created a clear picture with your description. Now get your picture ready for viewing by proofreading and correcting it carefully. Exchange papers with a partner, who may catch errors you missed. Then, share your description.

 Reflecting on Your Writing

To add your description to your **portfolio,** date it and include your responses to the following questions.

- Which was easier—finding sensory details and exact words, or arranging them clearly? Why?
- How well did you create a feeling or mood? What might you do differently next time?

A STUDENT MODEL

In the following paper, Matt Harris—a student at the University Laboratory School in Baton Rouge, Louisiana—writes about his dog, Sherman. Matt says it was hardest to "find the right words to describe Sherman, for he is difficult to describe." Even so, you'll probably notice that Matt finds just the right words to create a clear picture of Sherman.

No-Tail Sherman
by Matt Harris

Every time someone sees him, they ask what he is. We always tell them that Sherman is his name, and he is a Schipperke. He is a black, small, compact dog that is half fur. He has a fox- or wolf-like face, short fox ears, and no tail. Sherman weighs seventeen pounds and is a sweet, affectionate dog, although he is hyper and jumps up on everyone he sees. He doesn't smell bad too often; but when he does smell, he smells like a rotten onion just found on the bottom of an old grocery sack. Unfortunately, his bark can often be heard with a yip-brop-rorp and a bu-ru-ru-ru that is sharper than a razor blade. He prances lightly and with a bouncing motion, like a cat with springs on his feet. When he wants to go out, he whines like a hungry seal. If he gets the chance, he will get into the refrigerator and eat the peanut butter if the jar is left open. Sherman has a different attitude from most dogs. Most dogs lick the garbage can and attack the postman. Sherman licks the postman and attacks the garbage can.

Sherman is the most unusual dog I have ever known. I guess that is why I love him so much.

WRITING WORKSHOP

A Descriptive Poem

In this chapter, you've learned how to create a word-picture with sensory details, exact words, and figures of speech. You can use these same skills to write poetry. A kind of poetry that creates very small word-pictures is *haiku*.

Haiku is a Japanese form of poetry that describes one moment in nature. A haiku has seventeen syllables—five in lines one and three, and seven in line two. As you read the following poems, notice how the writer captures a very simple but vivid scene in just three lines.

The lightning flashes!
And slashing through the darkness,
A night-heron's screech.
Matsuo Bashō, *translated by Earl Minor*

An old silent pond . . .
A frog jumps into the pond,
splash! Silence again.
Matsuo Bashō, *translated by Harry Behn*

Thinking It Over

1. Which haiku do you like more? Why?
2. What details of sight does the poet use in each haiku?
3. What details of sound or touch do the poems include?

Writing a Descriptive Poem

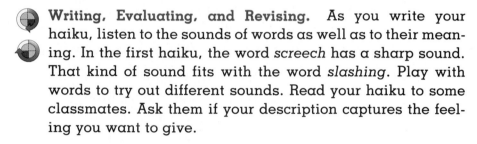

Prewriting.   Choose a scene in nature that you can observe, recall, or imagine clearly. You might choose the sun rising over the ocean, fireworks in a dark sky, a dog shaking off water after a swim. Visualize the subject, and jot down sensory details that describe it. Can you think of comparisons that might help you?

Writing, Evaluating, and Revising.   As you write your haiku, listen to the sounds of words as well as to their meaning. In the first haiku, the word *screech* has a sharp sound. That kind of sound fits with the word *slashing.* Play with words to try out different sounds. Read your haiku to some classmates. Ask them if your description captures the feeling you want to give.

Proofreading and Publishing.   Check spelling, punctuation, and capitalization before you write a final copy. Then, decide how to arrange your poem on a page. Leave white space around it to draw attention to how brief it is. Sign your poem, and if you wish, illustrate it with a drawing or decoration.

   If you decide to include your poem in your **portfolio,** date the poem and attach a note responding to these questions: How did you decide which kind of scene to use? Was it easy for you to find sounds that went with your meaning? Why or why not?

MAKING CONNECTIONS

MASS MEDIA AND DESCRIPTION

A Classified Ad

Classified ads are another form of description. They are called *classified* because they are arranged in categories, such as "Jobs," "Cars," or "Yard Sales."

Classified ads are usually short, because newspapers charge by the word or line. Within a short space, the writer must make the item sound better than other, similar items. As you read this type of ad, look for words that might make you want to buy the item. Ads often use abbreviations such as *w/* for *with* and *inc.* for *includes.*

Men's 10-speed bike. Black w/silver pinstripe. Excellent condition, new tires; inc. pump, water bottle, wrench. $70. Call Ed. 555–1685.

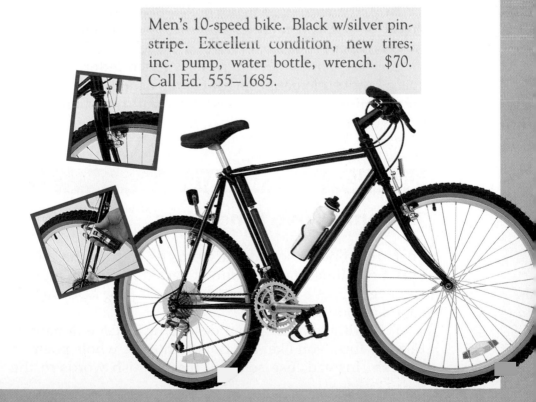

Cute, friendly gerbils. Clean, fun, easy
to keep. No smells, little work. $5 each
with week's food. Call Marin 555–5984.

Now try writing your own classified ad. Think of an
object or pet you might sell someday and the way you
would describe it. Then write a three- or four-line ad,
making each line forty characters. (Each letter, number,
space, and punctuation mark counts as a character.) Use
abbreviations whenever possible. Later, exchange ads
with your classmates.

DESCRIPTION AND LITERATURE

A Poem in Two Languages

Poets rely on the sounds of words as well as the meanings. Sometimes a word sounds very different in another
language. Does a *perro* sound nicer than a *dog*? Does *agudo*
sound as pointed as *sharp*?

Try writing a brief poem describing a scene in nature.
Use any form you like. But don't write the whole poem in
English. Instead, use some of the Spanish words in the

following charts. If possible, have the words read aloud by someone who knows Spanish. Let your ear enjoy the sounds of these words.

The Spanish words that you can choose to use in your poem are shown in the two following charts. A collection of Spanish nouns is shown in the left-hand column of each chart, and a variety of Spanish adjectives is shown in the right-hand columns. You may use any of the nouns or any of the adjectives in your poem, or you can use noun and adjective combinations. However, there are a few important points to keep in mind when you use the words from these charts.

First, note that in Spanish, an adjective usually follows the noun it describes. For example, in English you would say "white flower," but in Spanish you would say *flor blanca*. Second, Spanish has a more complicated system than English for matching adjectives to the nouns they modify. For the purposes of this exercise, if you want to use a Spanish adjective to modify a Spanish noun, be sure to select the noun and adjective from the same numbered chart.

CHART #1	
NOUNS	**ADJECTIVES**
tree—*árbol*	dark—*oscuro*
sun—*sol*	cool—*fresco*
sky—*cielo*	blue—*azul*
day—*día*	red—*rojo*
water—*agua*	quiet—*tranquilo*

CHART #2	
NOUNS	**ADJECTIVES**
grass—*hierba*	cool—*fresca*
leaf—*hoja*	green—*verde*
flower—*flor*	black—*negra*
star—*estrella*	yellow—*amarilla*
night—*noche*	white—*blanca*

6 CREATIVE WRITING: NARRATION

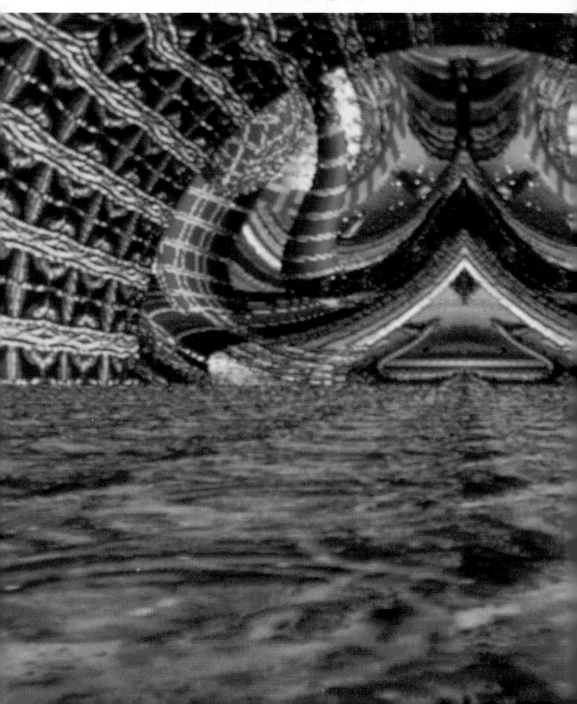

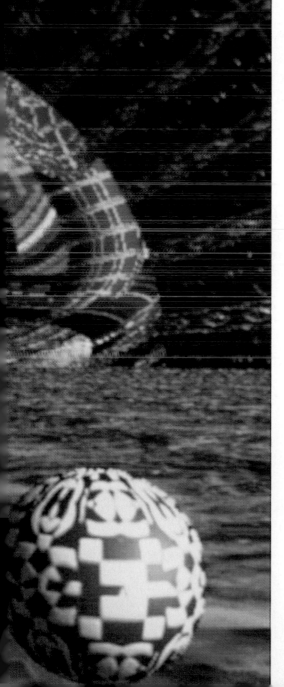

Imagining Other Worlds

You probably like to go to the movies. Most people do. It's a chance to escape—for just a little while—to **other worlds.** Movies allow our **imaginations** to run wild. Anything can happen. And, best of all, things usually come out okay in the end.

Writing and You.   Writers use their imagination to write movie scripts, novels, stories, plays, poems, and even comic strips. They tickle our own imagination by creating, and having us believe in, people and places that never were and never will be. They make us burst with excitement, fear, unreal ex-pectations, and fun. Have you ever used your imagination to make up a story for a little child?

As You Read.   As you read the following myth, you'll see how people can also use imagination to explain the world around them.

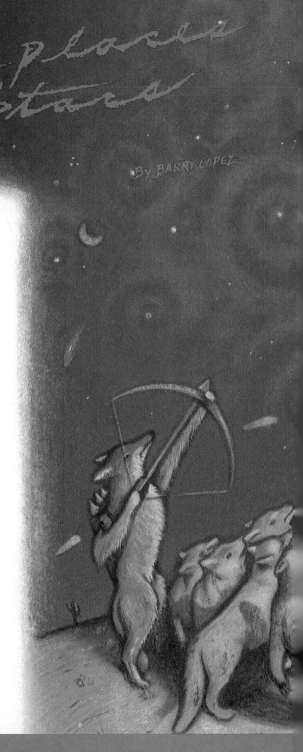

Coyote Places the Stars

BY BARRY LOPEZ

One time there were five wolves, all brothers, who traveled together. Whatever meat they got when they were hunting they would share with Coyote. One evening Coyote saw the wolves looking up at the sky.

"What are you looking at up there, my brothers?" asked Coyote.

"Oh, nothing," said the oldest wolf.

Next evening Coyote saw they were all looking up in the sky at something. He asked the next oldest wolf what they were looking at, but he wouldn't say. It went on like this for three or four nights. No one wanted to tell Coyote what they were looking at because they thought he would want to interfere. One night Coyote asked the youngest wolf brother to tell him and the youngest wolf said to the other wolves, "Let's tell Coyote what we see up there. He won't do anything."

So they told him. "We see two animals up there. Way up there, where we cannot get to them."

"Let's go up and see them," said Coyote.

"Well, how can we do that?"

"Oh, I can do that easy," said Coyote. "I can show you how to get up there without any trouble at all."

Coyote gathered a great number of arrows and then began shooting them into the sky. The first arrow stuck in the sky and the second arrow stuck in the first. Each arrow stuck in the end of the one before it like that until there was a ladder reaching down to the earth.

"We can climb up now," said Coyote. The oldest wolf took his dog with him, and then the other four wolf brothers came, and then Coyote. They climbed all day and into the night. All the next day they climbed. For many days and nights they climbed until finally they reached the sky. They stood in the sky and looked over at the two animals the wolves had seen from down below. They were two grizzly bears.

"Don't go near them," said Coyote. "They will tear you apart." But the two youngest wolves were already headed over. And the next two youngest wolves followed them. Only the oldest wolf held back. When the wolves got near the grizzlies, nothing happened. The wolves sat down and looked at the bears, and the bears sat there looking at the wolves. The oldest wolf, when he saw it was safe, came over with his dog and sat down with them.

Coyote wouldn't come over. He didn't trust the bears. "That makes a nice picture, though," thought Coyote. "They all look pretty good sitting there like that. I think I'll leave it that way for everyone to see. Then when people look at them in the sky they will say, 'There's a story about that picture,' and they will tell a story about me."

So Coyote left it that way. He took out the arrows as he descended so there was no way for anyone to get back. From down on the earth Coyote admired the arrangement he had left up there. Today they still look the same. They call those stars Big Dipper now. If you look up there you'll see three wolves make up the handle and the oldest wolf, the one in the middle, still has his dog with him. The two youngest wolves make up the part of the bowl under the handle and the two grizzlies make up the other side, the one that points toward the North Star.

When Coyote saw how they looked he wanted to put up a lot of stars. He arranged stars all over the sky in pictures and then made the Big Road across the sky with the stars he had left over.

When Coyote was finished he called Meadowlark over. "My brother," he said, "When I am gone, tell everyone that when they look up into the sky and see the stars arranged this way, that I was the one who did that. That is my work."

Now Meadowlark tells that story. About Coyote.

READER'S RESPONSE

1. Would you want Coyote for a friend? In a few words, describe his qualities—good and bad.
2. Were there places in the story where what happened was not what you expected? (What about those grizzlies?) In your journal, rewrite the story. Keep the same characters, but change the events of the story any way you want.

WRITER'S CRAFT

3. Item 1 above asked you to describe Coyote. What details in the story helped you know him?
4. Stories get set in motion because characters have problems and need to solve them. Who has a problem in this story? What is the problem? How is it solved?
5. How did the person who created this story use his imagination to explain a part of the world?

"We are a part of the earth and it is part of us."

Chief Seattle

Ways to Write Creatively

In this chapter you'll write a story and a poem, two types of creative writing. Other types are movie and play scripts, words for songs, children's books, and novels. Creative writing starts in the writer's imagination. Just as an artist uses paint, a writer uses words to create something special. Here are some ways of writing creatively.

- in a television script, telling the story of a child genius and her longing for a normal life
- in a story, telling about a Seminole girl who saves a panther cub in the Florida Everglades
- in a song, describing a girl's long, beautiful hair and sparkling eyes
- in a story about time travel, describing New York City in the year 4000
- in a poem, comparing envy to a wasp's sting
- in a novel, contrasting the life of a big-city girl with the life of a small-town boy
- in a poem, making a statement about the worth of advertising billboards that have been put up along a famous scenic highway
- in a play, showing how too much pride can drive away good friends

LOOKING AHEAD

In this chapter, you'll use narration to write a story. As you write, keep in mind that an effective story

- entertains the reader
- solves a conflict, or problem
- holds the reader's attention with lifelike characters, an interesting plot, and a specific setting

Writing a Story

Prewriting

Finding a Story Idea

Here's the big question: Where do you find a story idea? Here's the answer: Anywhere and everywhere. You might get an idea from a magazine or a photograph, from another story or a cartoon, or from a daydream or a nightmare.

As you look and listen around you, you can also play the "What if?" game: imagining any change or new thing that comes into your head. This is a way writers get some great ideas: *What if* a father shrank his kids? *What if* a man could strap a rocket to his back?

Thinking About Purpose and Audience

In writing a story, the one *purpose* you have is to entertain your readers. You may do it by making them laugh over the mistakes of a silly character. Or you may do it by involving them in a deep mystery. Just give your *audience* something that keeps them turning the pages.

Starting with Characters and Situations

What keeps a reader turning pages? Almost always it's an interesting main *character* faced with a *conflict*—a situation that holds a problem or challenge. How will the brave princess rescue the prince from the tower? How will the class clown ever get the honor roll student to take her seriously?

Character.   You can begin your story idea by thinking of a character. Suppose your little sister has a girlfriend who's very, very, *very* shy but amazingly sharp when you get her to talk. Or pretend that you see a newspaper photo of a ninety-year-old man from Jamaica. These people stick in your mind somehow—perhaps the girl has unusual eyes or the man has an interesting face. Could you put one in a situation with conflict? Of course you don't have to start with a real person. What kind of story could you build around a shy mouse from Jamaica?

Situation.   Or you could begin in the opposite way. Think of an interesting situation or problem. It may be something you've seen on television, heard about from a friend, or actually experienced.

Maybe you know of someone hiding a cat in an apartment where animals are forbidden. Or you've always wondered what it would be like to be lost in a large city where you don't speak the language. From there, you can build a conflict and a story.

Here are just a few examples of how you might start with a character or a situation to build a story idea. A million other ideas are possible. Just feel free to let your imagination run wild!

STORY IDEAS

Character: Ninety-year-old man, born in Jamaica. Has lived almost all his life in New York City.
Situation: *What if* . . . he took his Social Security check, ran away from his niece's apartment, and stowed away on a cruise ship bound for Jamaica.

Situation: Someone who can't speak English or Spanish is lost in Houston, Texas.

Character: *What if* . . . the person is a young boy who speaks Mayan, is visiting with a group of musicians, and has with him a wooden flute that he can play beautifully.

When you're looking for story ideas, remember

- ideas can come from anywhere: your own experience, TV, newspapers, photographs, songs, and more
- your story needs a main character and a conflict
- try starting with a character or situation and asking "What if?" to build a story idea

EXERCISE 1 ▶ **Building Story Ideas**

Now try your hand (and imagination) at using the following characters and situations to come up with story ideas. Work with a small group, and brainstorm as many ideas as you want. [Remember: Your situations must hold a *conflict*, or *problem*.]

1. **Character**: A young girl is extremely clever, but she's also painfully shy, always staying in the background.
   Situation: *What if* _____

2. **Character:** Ahmed Mostafa, with his elderly grandfather, takes care of dozens of homing pigeons on the roof of his building.
   Situation: *What if* _____

3. **Situation:** Someone is hiding a cat in an apartment where animals aren't allowed.
   Character: *What if* _____

4. **Situation:** All of the bicycles, roller skates, and skateboards disappear from a town.
   Character: *What if* _____

John Sloan, American (1871–1951), *Pigeons* (1910). Oil on canvas, 66 × 81.2 cm (26 × 32"). Copyright © 1996, Museum of Fine Arts, Boston, Charles Henry Hayden Fund, 35.52.

PART 1:
Finding a Story Idea

You may have gotten a great idea from the group brainstorming in Exercise 1. But if not, now you know how to go about getting one. Remember that you can use anything around you—from everyday experiences to space monsters on TV—to come up with characters and situations. Decide on your final story idea and write it down.

 *Prewriting*

Planning Your Story

Professional writers plan their stories before they begin. Of course, that doesn't mean they don't make some changes along the way. Writers often surprise themselves!

Imagining Characters. If you want readers to pay attention to your story, your main character (and other important characters) should seem *alive*. The best way to get life into your characters is with specific, sharp *details*.

You can make up details: a lavender kitten with one orange eye and one purple eye. Or you can borrow details from real people: a Civil War general who has your own grandfather's twinkling green eyes. These questions will help you imagine your characters—make them solid.

- *What does the character look like?*
- *What is the character's name?*
- *How would you describe the character's personality?*
- *What does the character love and hate?*
- *What does the character sound like?*

One way to make notes on your characters is to keep the questions in mind and then freewrite a description.

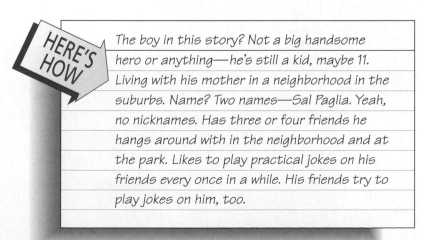

HERE'S HOW

The boy in this story? Not a big handsome hero or anything—he's still a kid, maybe 11. Living with his mother in a neighborhood in the suburbs. Name? Two names—Sal Paglia. Yeah, no nicknames. Has three or four friends he hangs around with in the neighborhood and at the park. Likes to play practical jokes on his friends every once in a while. His friends try to play jokes on him, too.

Describing Setting.   The *setting* is where and when the story takes place. A setting can be the corner of a room at night or a football stadium on Sunday afternoon. It can be the present or the age of dinosaurs.

The setting can give information about characters. A clean room, for example, shows readers that a character likes order and neatness. The setting can also create a mood. An abandoned house and a howling wind will make sure a scary story is scary.

Sometimes setting even creates a conflict. If you set your story in Alaska during a blizzard, your character might be trapped in the snow.

Here are some questions to help you plan your setting.

- *Where and when will my story take place?*
- *What places, weather, things, or times of day could be important in my story?*
- *What sensory details (smells, sights, sounds) can I use to describe these important parts of setting?*

PART 2:
Planning Characters and Setting

To get a clearer picture of your characters and setting, use the questions on pages 189 and 190. You can jot down your responses, freewrite, or even use clustering. Write freely and let your ideas flow.

Planning Your Plot. Suppose you have an interesting character, a girl named Tuyet Nguyen, and a good solid setting for her, an old two-story house in Myer's Cove, where she lives with her parents and grandmother. Now you need a *plot*, or series of events, for the story. While a plot is "what happens," it has these special parts:

- **A conflict:** As you've already learned, the main character must face some problem. *Tuyet wants piano lessons, but her family can't afford to pay for them.*
- **A series of events:** Your story must have action. The events must move forward as the character works on the conflict. *Tuyet may run errands to earn money, count her earnings daily, and dream of the lessons.*
- **A high point:** Your story also needs a moment, the high point, when the problem is going to be *settled* —one way or another. Readers' curiosity or suspense is at a high point. *Perhaps Tuyet's grandmother gets very sick. Will Tuyet have to sacrifice her piano lessons for her grandmother's medicine?*
- **An outcome:** The outcome shows how the problem is solved and what happens when it is. *Tuyet gives her savings to her parents and says she will forget the lessons. Her grandmother sees how much music means to her and promises to help Tuyet earn money when she is better.*

Creating a Story Map. When you plan your plot, you can put it into a story map that outlines your character, setting, and plot all at once. The following example shows how one writer mapped her story about Sal Paglia and his friends.

A STORY MAP	
CHARACTERS:	Sal Paglia, his friends (Chief, Corky, Duane), Mrs. Paglia
SETTING:	Woods, neighborhood, and yard—summertime
PLOT:	Conflict: Sal vs. friends planning to scare him

Events:
(1) Chief tells Corky and Duane about his plan to hide and surprise Sal.
(2) The neighborhood goes to the picnic.

High Point:
(3) The boys sneak back to Sal's house.
(4) They are soaked because Sal has turned the sprinklers around.

Outcome:
(5) Mrs. Paglia thinks the boys watered her roses and gives them flowers.

WRITING ASSIGNMENT

PART 3:
Creating a Story Map

Now it is time for the last stage of your planning. Exactly what will *happen* in your story? Remember that your plot needs certain elements: conflict, events, high point, and outcome. When you decide on the parts, put them into a story map like the one in the Here's How on this page. Don't forget to include characters and settings.

Writing Your First Draft

Combining the Basic Elements of a Story

A map to a place isn't the place. And your story map isn't a story—yet. How do you turn the map into a bursting-with-life tale? Here are some tips.

Making the Plot Move Along. A good *beginning* for a story hooks the reader's attention right away. You might start in the middle of an action—a burglar coming through the window, for example. Or you might describe the dark night and lonely street to set the mood.

In the *middle* of the story, keep your audience guessing. Make every event open up a possibility, create a surprise, or lead to the high point. What happens when Jowela sees the burglar? Don't let her stop to play a video game!

After your strong high point, make sure the *ending* is satisfying. Solve the problem but also tie up any loose ends. If Jowela traps the burglar and the police come, the conflict is over. But don't leave the burglar trapped in the shower stall. Get her out before Jowela and the police say good night.

Making Your Characters Seem Real. You've learned that specific details make lifeless characters into lively ones. Here are three good ways to use details.

- Give clear descriptions of *appearance*. Don't say *She dressed oddly* when you can say *She wore purple felt overalls, green high-heeled sneakers, and a bright red cape.* (For more help with descriptions, see Chapter 5.)

- Make *actions* specific. You could say *He sat down in the chair*. But readers would know this character much better if *He plopped down in the big recliner, dangling his legs over the arm.*
- Use *dialogue.* A summary of speech like *He refused to do it* will move action along. But ***dialogue***—a character's own words—can also reveal emotion and personality. Use fragments, contractions, and slang if they're right for the character. *"No way! Are you nuts? I wouldn't call her if she was Queen of the World."*

EXERCISE 2 ▶	**Speaking and Listening:** **Creating Dialogue**

With a partner, create dialogues for the characters in the following situations. Try to make the dialogue natural—like real speech. Present your dialogues to another partner group. Then ask for feedback about whether you sound real—and why or why not.

1. An elderly woman calls the police to report that her cat is up in a tree. The police officer tries to convince her that the cat will be okay.
2. Two teenage boys try to decide how to spend the afternoon. Should they go to the mall or to the ice skating rink?

Looking at a Short Story

Every story is different. Writers combine plot, characters, and setting in different ways. The writer of the following short story makes sure you're aware of setting at the start. As you read, see if you can guess the surprise ending.

A SHORT STORY

The Dinner Party
by Mona Gardner

BEGINNING
Setting

Situation and
characters

Event 1

Dialogue

The country is India. A colonial official and his wife are giving a large dinner party. They are seated with their guests— army officers and government attachés and their wives, and a visiting American naturalist—in their spacious dining room, which has a bare marble floor, open rafters, and wide glass doors opening onto a veranda.

A spirited discussion springs up between a young girl who insists that women have outgrown the jumping-on-a-chair-at-the-sight-of-a-mouse era and a colonel who says that they haven't.

"A woman's unfailing reaction in any crisis," the colonel says, "is to scream. And while a man may feel like it, he has that ounce more of nerve control than a woman has. And that last ounce is what counts."

The American does not join in the argument but watches the other guests. As he looks, he sees a strange expression come over the face of the hostess. She is staring straight ahead, her muscles contracting slightly. With a slight gesture she summons the native boy standing behind her chair and whispers to him. The boy's eyes widen: He quickly leaves the room.

Of the guests, none except the American notices this or sees the boy place a bowl of milk on the veranda just outside the open doors.

The American comes to with a start. In India, milk in a bowl means only one thing—bait for a snake. He realizes there must be a cobra in the room. He looks up at the rafters—the likeliest place—but they are bare. Three corners of the room are empty, and in the fourth the servants are waiting to serve the next course. There is only one place left—under the table.

His first impulse is to jump back and warn the others, but he knows the commotion would frighten the cobra into striking. He speaks quickly, the tone of his voice so arresting that it sobers everyone.

"I want to know just what control everyone at this table has. I will count to three hundred—that's five minutes—and not one of you is to move a muscle. Those who move will forfeit fifty rupees. Ready!"

The twenty people sit like stone images while he counts. He is saying " . . . two hundred and eighty . . ." when, out of the corner of his eye, he sees the cobra emerge and make for the bowl of milk. Screams ring out as he jumps to slam the veranda doors safely shut.

ENDING

Dialogue

"You were right, Colonel!" the host exclaims. "A man has just shown us an example of perfect control."

Outcome

"Just a minute," the American says, turning to his hostess. "Mrs. Wynnes, how did you know that cobra was in the room?"

Surprise ending

A faint smile lights up the woman's face as she replies: "Because it was crawling across my foot."

EXERCISE 3 ▶ **Analyzing the Elements of a Short Story**

Think about the basic elements of "The Dinner Party." With a partner discuss the following questions.

1. Did you enjoy the story? How do you think you would have reacted if you'd been the American naturalist? or Mrs. Wynnes, the hostess?
2. How important is the story's setting? Could this story happen in your home? in some other setting in India?
3. How did the writer create suspense in the story?
4. Do you think the story has a message—an important idea? What is it?
5. Were you surprised by the story's ending? What clues does the writer give?

Using a Story Framework

"The Dinner Party" has vivid descriptions, great suspense, and a surprise ending. It even has a serious message about mistaken ideas about women. It's polished and professional. But even if your story doesn't have all these elements (plus a high point with a cobra!), it can be just as entertaining.

Notice how the following writer starts with action and gets quickly to characters and conflict. Also, notice how the writer makes the story more interesting by using dialogue and descriptions of specific actions. You might want to follow this model for your story.

A WRITER'S MODEL

Sal's Surprise

BEGINNING	Sal Paglia scrambled over the wall and
Main character/ Setting	dashed to his hide-out under the ivy. From there he eavesdropped on his friends as they discussed
Situation	their secret plans. Chief gave the orders.
Dialogue	"Tomorrow, while Sal's at the cookout, we'll
Event 1	hide in his yard until he comes home," he whispered.
Specific action	Corky gave a chuckle. Duane nodded.
Dialogue	"Corky and I'll hide between Mrs. Paglia's rosebushes and the house, and jump out and scare Sal when he gets there," Chief added.
Background	Sal was the neighborhood trickster. He was always playing jokes on the other boys and getting
Conflict	the best of them. For Chief, this was a chance to get even.
Dialogue	"Duane," Chief went on, "you hide in the dark by the controls for the Paglias' sprinklers—the ones that point toward the street—and turn them on as Sal walks up. When the water starts, we'll rush out screaming and scare Sal."

Specific action

Sal almost had to bite his tongue to keep from laughing. His friends had no idea that he had just overheard Chief's whole plan.

MIDDLE
Event 2

By 6:15 the next day, Sal, his friends, and most of the other people in the neighborhood were eating at the cookout in the park.

Event 3
Specific action
Dialogue
Specific action

At 7:00, Chief, Corky, and Duane sneaked across the green back yards toward the Paglias' house. "Okay, make it fast," said Chief.

Chief and Corky squeezed into the tiny space between the rosebushes and the house. Duane took his position at the sprinkler controls.

Suspense

The street was dark and quiet as Sal walked home a few minutes later. He couldn't see the other boys as he came up to his house, and he wondered for a second if they were there. As he

Event 4

got closer, though, he heard the sound of Duane turning the knob that controlled the sprinklers.

High point

When the sprinklers came on, a yell erupted from behind the rosebushes, but Chief and Corky

Specific action

didn't jump out. Sal laughed because he knew his plan had worked.

Flashback

Before he left for the cookout, Sal had turned the sprinklers around so that they all pointed straight into Chief and Corky's hiding place behind the bushes. Now the boys were trapped. They had no way to escape without running straight into the streams of water and getting even wetter. Chief's plan had backfired!

Specific action

Meanwhile, Duane had rushed right out into the water before he realized what was going on. He quickly returned to shut the water off. As the

Event 5

sprinkler streams slowed to trickles, Chief and Corky finally burst out—straight toward Mrs. Paglia, who had walked home a bit after Sal.

Mrs. Paglia was startled as the two boys sped by her, with Duane following just behind them.

Suspense

Then she noticed that her rosebushes were wet.

"Come back here!" she shouted at the fleeing

**Appearance
detail**

boys. They obeyed. As they slunk back, Sal thought they looked like frightened wet mice.

Dialogue

"Sal, your nice friends watered my rosebushes —as a surprise!" Mrs. Paglia exclaimed. Chief, Corky, and Duane looked at each other, very

ENDING

confused. Sal just smiled.

"Good work," Sal said to himself as Mrs. Paglia

Outcome

handed each soggy boy a yellow rose.

USAGE HINT

Using Verb Tenses

Story events are usually told in chronological order, using the past tense: *The villain* **grasped** *the prune. He* **thrust** *it fiercely toward my mouth.* To explain actions that happened before other past actions, use the past perfect tense.

EXAMPLE   I **had seen** [past perfect] an escape route before the villain grasped [past] the prune.

☞ **REFERENCE NOTE:** For more information on verb tenses, see pages 592–594.

PART 4:
Writing Your First Draft

Now it's time to begin your story. Go over the character and setting descriptions you wrote. Reread your story map, but remember that it's only a guide. You don't have to follow it exactly. Part of the fun of writing stories can be discovering new ideas. Begin writing and see what happens.

Evaluating and Revising

If you're like most writers, you feel a sense of accomplishment after you finish a draft. But part of you knows the story could be better. And you want to make it as good as possible.

Read your story as a critic. Use the guidelines on page 204 to find its strengths and weaknesses. If the answer to any question on the left-hand side of the chart is no, use the techniques on the right-hand side to make revisions.

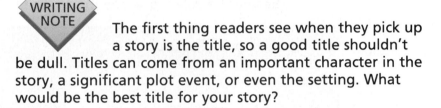

WRITING NOTE The first thing readers see when they pick up a story is the title, so a good title shouldn't be dull. Titles can come from an important character in the story, a significant plot event, or even the setting. What would be the best title for your story?

COMPUTER NOTE: Before you print a copy of a draft you plan to proofread or revise, adjust the line spacing and margins to allow lots of room for handwritten corrections on the hard copy. Use double- or triple-spacing and a wide right margin. When you want to print a final draft, remember to reset the spacing and margins.

CRITICAL THINKING

Analyzing the Elements of a Story

All good writers *analyze* when they evaluate their writing. They look at all the elements and how they fit together. When the writer of "Sal's Surprise" analyzed her first paragraph, she made the following changes.

~~It was a june day in Burnside, before~~   **cut**

~~the neighborhood was going to have a big~~

~~picnic with lots of food. A boy named~~

Sal Paglia ~~went~~ over the wall to his   **replace/add**
(scrambled ... and dashed)

hideout under the ivy. From there he

~~listened in secret to~~ his friends as they   **cut/replace**
(eavesdropped on)

discussed the plans ~~they didn't want him~~   **cut/replace**
(their secret)

~~to hear.~~ Chief told the other boys that   **cut/replace**
(gave the orders ¶ "Tomorrow, while)

~~they would hide in Sal's yard during the~~
(Sal's at the cookout, we'll hide in his yard until he)

~~cookout and wait for Sal to return.~~
(comes home," Chief whispered.)

CRITICAL THINKING EXERCISE:
Analyzing a Writer's Revisions

Work with a partner to analyze the revisions in the paragraph above. Use the following questions to guide your analysis. Also refer to the chart on page 204. It shows you the important elements of a short story.

1. Why did the writer cut so much from the beginning?
2. Why did the writer decide to use *scrambled* and *dashed* in the second sentence?
3. Why were the changes in the third sentence made?
4. Do you think the replacement in the last sentence is a good revision? Why or why not?

WRITING ASSIGNMENT

PART 5:
Evaluating and Revising Your Story

Use the chart on page 204 to help evaluate and revise your first draft. When you finish revising, swap stories with a classmate for feedback and suggestions.

EVALUATING AND REVISING SHORT STORIES

EVALUATION GUIDE	REVISION TECHNIQUE
1 Does the beginning catch readers' interest?	**Add** (or **replace** other) sentences with vivid details of character, action, or setting.
2 Is the conflict clear early in the story?	**Add** or **reorder** sentences in which the main character faces a problem.
3 Do events create suspense or curiosity for readers?	**Cut** events that slow down action. **Add** events that keep readers wondering.
4 Does the plot have a strong high point and a satisfying outcome?	**Add** a tense scene that solves a conflict. **Add** details that explain how everything works out.
5 Are the characters lifelike and believable?	**Add** details about the characters' looks, actions, and thoughts. **Add** dialogue that sounds natural.
6 Is the setting clear? If possible, does it help set a mood?	**Add** specific details of time and place. **Add** vivid sensory details.

"Everyone you meet has a story."

Madeleine L'Engle

Proofreading and Publishing

Proofreading.   Now it's time to polish your story. To make it shine, double-check carefully to find and correct any errors in spelling, usage, and mechanics.

Publishing.   Don't be shy with your story. People *want* to be entertained. Let readers see your special imagination. Here are three possibilities for publishing.

- Ask your principal if you may read some of the stories over the intercom during homeroom.
- Create giant comic-book murals of your stories and use them to decorate your classroom and school hallways.
- Use a paint or draw program to add pictures to your story. Show the illustrated story to your classmates.

PART 6:
Proofreading and Publishing Your Story

Make a neat, final copy of your story. Be sure to give that final copy one last good proofreading—and then share your story with an audience.

 Reflecting on Your Writing

If you would like to add your story to your **portfolio,** date the story and attach your written responses to these questions.

- Did you begin your story idea with a character or with a situation? Would you do the same next time? Explain.
- What techniques helped you develop your characters? your setting? your plot? Did you use a story map? Why or why not?
- Did you make any discoveries as you wrote your draft? Explain your response.

A STUDENT MODEL

Brittany Williams, a student at Heskett Middle School in Bedford Heights, Ohio, says it is important to stick with a story line and not "switch back and forth between ideas."

Excuses, Excuses
by Brittany Williams

"Bring that note up here right now!" yelled Mrs. Hirko.

"Yes, ma'am," I replied. Now what am I going to do? That note is just the secret of the boy I like. If she reads it to the class, I'll be sunk! I have to think of a way to get it back. A plan that is subtle, yet effective.

"Mrs. Hirko, I can't give you the note because I don't want you to read it." Smooth. Now she'll read it for sure.

"Why not, Miss Jackson?"

"Because . . ." I looked at the clock. Wait, that's it. If I can stall for the last five minutes of class, she won't have time to read it! "Because if you do, I will have to turn you in."

"Turn me in?"

"Yes, turn you in," I replied nervously.

"For what, exactly?"

"Well, for not honoring my right to privacy. You know. It's in the Constitution or something."

"Yes, I know what you are saying. Please enlighten me and your classmates on why I should do as you ask."

"Well, if you don't," (two and a half minutes to go!) "you would be breaking a law. A really important one, too. Breaking laws calls for legal action. I would have to call the police. Maybe even the FBI."

"Oh, really," Mrs. Hirko retorted. "Well, after hearing your fascinating rebuttal, I have decided to read it anyway."

"No, wait! What about the Miranda rights? The right to remain silent, and—" Brring! . . .

WRITING WORKSHOP

A Narrative Poem

A poem that tells a story is called a **narrative poem.** A narrative poem is much like the story you just wrote. It has characters, plot, setting, and sometimes even dialogue.

But poetry adds other elements to storytelling—especially sounds and images. To create musical sounds, poets use rhythm, rhyme, and repeated sounds (*"lovely laughing ladies"*). Poets also create word pictures with words that appeal to the senses.

The following poem has rhythm, rhyme, great word pictures, and a hungry weed. Hungry? See for yourself.

My Aunt
by Ted Hughes

You've heard how a green
  thumb
Makes flowers come
Quite without toil
Out of any old soil.

Well, my Aunt's thumbs were
  green.
At a touch, she had blooms
Of prize Chrysanthemums—
The grandest ever seen.

People from miles around
Came to see those flowers
And were truly astounded
By her unusual powers.

One day a little weed
Pushed up to drink and feed
Among the pampered flowers
At her water-can showers.

Day by day it grew
With ragged leaves and bristles
Till it was tall as me or you—
It was a King of Thistles.

"Prizes for flowers are easy,"
My aunt said in her pride.
"But was there ever such a weed
The whole world wide?"

She watered it, she tended it,
It grew alarmingly.
As if I had offended it,
It bristled over me.

"Oh Aunt!" I cried. "Beware
  of that!
I saw it eat a bird."
She went on polishing its points
As if she hadn't heard.

"Oh Aunt!" I cried. "It has a
    flower
Like a lion's beard—"
Too late! It was devouring her
Just as I had feared.

Her feet were waving in the
    air—
But I shall not proceed.
Here ends the story of my Aunt
And her ungrateful weed.

Thinking It Over

1. Who are the characters in this poem? (If you name only two, think again.) What can you tell about them?
2. Gardens are usually peaceful. Is that true of this garden?
3. How many conflicts do you see in the poem? Explain.
4. How would you describe the beat of the poem?
5. What examples of sounds and images do you hear and see?

Writing a Narrative Poem

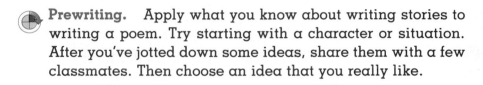

Prewriting. Apply what you know about writing stories to writing a poem. Try starting with a character or situation. After you've jotted down some ideas, share them with a few classmates. Then choose an idea that you really like.

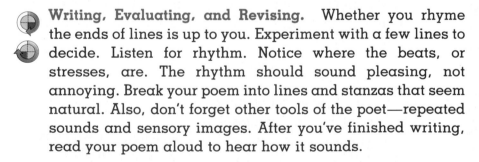

Writing, Evaluating, and Revising. Whether you rhyme the ends of lines is up to you. Experiment with a few lines to decide. Listen for rhythm. Notice where the beats, or stresses, are. The rhythm should sound pleasing, not annoying. Break your poem into lines and stanzas that seem natural. Also, don't forget other tools of the poet—repeated sounds and sensory images. After you've finished writing, read your poem aloud to hear how it sounds.

Proofreading and Publishing. Make a clean copy of your poem, and proofread it carefully. Your class might create a poem clothesline to hang your finished poems on, or you might perform some of your poems in class.

To add your poem to your **portfolio,** date the poem and include a written response to this question: In what ways is writing a poem different from writing a story?

MAKING CONNECTIONS

MYTHS

Writing a Myth

Myths are stories that people have told and passed down to others through the ages. Very often they try to explain something about the natural world. For example, the sun is a god's chariot driven across the sky, or the stars are the result of Coyote's magic handiwork, as in "Coyote Places the Stars" on pages 180–182.

People everywhere tell myths—in the Northern African desert, in the Central American jungle, and on the Canadian Plains. You can, too. Why is the sea salty? Why do people sneeze? Make up a myth to explain anything you like. Or, if you know a myth from your culture, retell it in your own words. That's how myths stay alive.

CREATIVE WRITING AND LITERATURE

Writing a New Ending for a Story

Sometimes when you read a story, it doesn't end quite as you imagine it will. Sometimes you want a different ending, the *right* one—yours. Here's your chance to step into the author's shoes. Pick one of the stories in this chapter—"Coyote Places the Stars," "The Dinner Party," or "Sal's Surprise." Try your hand at writing a new ending for it. Begin at the story's high point.

Working and Playing

Have dinosaur skeletons been found in the U.S.? How do you do an axel in ice skating? Where is the closest national park? Who wants to know? Someone somewhere does. We spend most hours **working or playing,** so the information we want is often about *processes:* how to do something or how something works.

Writing and You.   You'd be surprised how much writing explains a process. A detective story explains how the murder weapon disappeared: it was an icicle. An article in *WaterSki* magazine gives tips for using a kneeboard. What process could you write about?

As You Read.   Writers sometimes explain a special way of doing a familiar process. Do you think you know how to eat? Maybe not. As you read the following "how-to," notice the steps even a child could follow.

Diego Rivera, *The Making of a Fresco Showing the Building of a City* (1931), San Francisco Art Institute. Photo by Don Beatty © 1984.

How to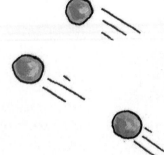
Like a Child

by Delia Ephron

Peas: Mash and flatten into thin sheet on plate. Press the back of the fork into the peas. Hold fork vertically, prongs up, and lick off peas.

Mashed potatoes: Pat mashed potatoes flat on top. Dig several little depressions. Think of them as ponds or pools. Fill the pools with gravy. With your fork, sculpt rivers between pools and watch the gravy flow between them. Decorate with peas. Do not eat.

Alternative method: Make a large hole in center of mashed potatoes. Pour in ketchup. Stir until potatoes turn pink. Eat as you would peas.

Animal crackers: Eat each in this order—legs, head, body.

Sandwich: Leave the crusts. If your mother says you have to eat them because that's the best part, stuff the crusts into your pants pocket or between the cushions of the couch.

Spaghetti: Wind too many strands on the fork and make sure at least two strands dangle down. Open your mouth wide and stuff in spaghetti; suck noisily to inhale the dangling strands. Clean plate, ask for seconds, and eat only half. When carrying your plate to the kitchen, hold it tilted so that the remaining spaghetti slides off and onto the floor.

Ice-cream cone: Ask for a double scoop. Knock the top scoop off while walking out the door of the ice-cream parlor. Cry. Lick the remaining scoop slowly so that ice cream melts down the outside of the cone and over your hand. Stop licking when the ice cream is even with the top of the cone. Be sure it is absolutely even. Eat a hole in the bottom of the cone and suck the rest of the ice cream out the bottom. When only the cone remains with ice cream coating the inside, leave on car dashboard.

Ice cream in bowl: Grip spoon upright in fist. Stir ice cream vigorously to make soup. Take a large helping on a spoon, place spoon in mouth, and slowly pull it out, sucking only the top layer of ice cream off. Wave spoon in air. Lick its back. Put in mouth again and suck off some more. Repeat until all ice cream is off spoon and begin again.

Cooked carrots: On way to mouth, drop in lap. Smuggle to garbage in napkin.

Spinach: Divide into little piles. Rearrange into new piles. After five or six maneuvers, sit back and say you are full.

Chocolate-chip cookies: Half-sit, half-lie on the bed, propped up by a pillow. Read a book. Place cookies next to you on the sheet so that crumbs get in the bed. As you eat the cookies, remove each chocolate chip and place it on your stomach. When all the cookies are consumed, eat the chips one by one, allowing two per page.

Milk shake: Bite off one end of the paper covering the straw. Blow through straw to shoot paper across table. Place straw in shake and suck. When the shake just reaches your mouth, place a finger over the top of the straw—the pressure will keep the shake in the straw. Lift straw out of shake, put bottom end in mouth, release finger, and swallow.

Do this until the straw is squished so that you can't suck through it. Ask for another. Open it the same way, but this time shoot the paper at the waitress when she isn't looking. Sip your shake casually—you are just minding your own business—until there is about an inch of shake remaining. Then blow through the straw until bubbles rise to the top of the glass. When your father says he's had just about enough, get a stomachache.

Chewing gum: Remove from mouth and stretch into spaghetti-like strand. Swing like a lasso. Put back in mouth. Pulling out one end and gripping the other end between teeth, have your gum meet your friend's gum and press them together. Think that you have just done something really disgusting.

Baked apple: With your fingers, peel skin off baked apple. Tell your mother you changed your mind, you don't want it. Later, when she is harassed and not paying attention to what she is doing, pick up the naked baked apple and hand it to her.

French fries: Wave one French fry in air for emphasis while you talk. Pretend to conduct orchestra. Then place four fries in your mouth at once and chew. Turn to your sister, open your mouth, and stick out your tongue coated with potatoes. Close mouth and swallow. Smile.

READER'S RESPONSE

1. You no doubt used a few of Delia Ephron's funny eating techniques when you were younger. Which one in her list was your specialty?
2. Now for the sequel: "How to Eat Like a Child II." Can you give special instructions for eating broccoli, cereal, two foods that no adult would combine, or something else? Share your technique.

WRITER'S CRAFT

3. The information you give in a "how-to" paper, even one about eating, usually includes equipment. Where does Ephron tell about equipment and how to use it?
4. Is Ephron writing for young children or for other readers? Is her article a real "how-to" paper or actually a "how-it-happens" paper? Does she want you to take her seriously? Give reasons for your answers.

Ways to Inform

There are several different ways to share information in writing. You can use some ways for similar purposes. For example, the way you explain a process is similar to the way you tell a story. So, you can think of a "how-to" process paper as a step-by-step "story" about how to do something. Here are more specific examples of how you can share information in different ways.

- in a magazine article, telling how you make tempura
- in an office memo, telling a coworker how to fill out a shipping bill for an overnight package
- in a letter to your grandfather, describing the set you helped paint for a play
- in a report, describing a bird's nest that you found
- in an essay for science class, explaining what the different parts of a plant are for
- in a letter to your parents, pointing out the differences between two bikes that you like
- in a movie review, telling whether the plot was interesting and logical
- in an article for your school newspaper, explaining how well a new "instant" camera works

LOOKING AHEAD

In your main assignment in this chapter, you'll be writing a process paper explaining how to do something. Your purpose will be to give information. As you work through the exercises and the writing assignment, keep in mind that a "how-to" paper

- includes all necessary materials and steps
- presents the steps of the process in the order they're done

Writing a "How-to" Paper

Prewriting

Choosing a Process to Explain

You can do many things that someone else might want to learn. Do you know how to keep your cat from getting fleas? Can you explain how to run a baby sitters' club? Are you good at racing dirt bikes? One way to look for a topic is to brainstorm a list of things you do well. Then, to narrow down the list, ask yourself these questions:

- What do I most like to spend time doing?
- What can I do best?

Thinking About Interest. To pick a topic, focus on interest—in two ways. Think about what interests you *and* what will interest your *audience*. A paper on how to get ready for school will bore an audience of teenagers— unless you make it funny! And most of your classmates already know how to heat up a pizza. But they might want to find out how to make a special food that you have at home, Navajo bread, for instance, or Japanese sushi. Or, you can write your paper for younger children. Just be sure that your topic and your audience match.

Thinking About Skill. The purpose of a "how-to" paper is to share information about a process so that your readers can do it themselves. This means you have to pick something you're good at. Writing about how to dance a hula might be a good idea. However, you have to be able to dance the hula well enough to explain it. Basically, the test of your explanation will be, "Does it work?" If your readers follow your directions on how to make a boomerang, the boomerangs they make should fly back.

To choose a "how-to" topic

- brainstorm a list of things you do well
- pick something that you really like to do
- pick a process that will interest your audience

EXERCISE 1 ▶ **Exploring Possible Topics**

Meet with a few classmates to discuss possible topics for a "how-to" paper. You might brainstorm from broad areas like "the outdoors," "crafts," and "what I do on Saturday." As you come up with ideas, give each other feedback. Would you like to learn the process? Can an idea be covered in a paragraph or two?

PART 1:
Choosing a Process to Explain

You can pick a topic from your work in Exercise 1 or a topic of your own. Are you known for how well you can lip-sync the words to your favorite song? Can you explain how to do it? Will you write about how to twirl a baton? Would you like to tell younger children how to draw monsters? When you've decided on your topic, write one sentence telling what it is and who your audience will be.

Prewriting

Gathering and Organizing Your Information

Planning your paper before you write will save time and make the writing easier. Since you know how to do the process, you probably have all the information you need. But if you have any questions, look for information in books, articles, or videotapes about the topic.

Listing Steps and Materials.   Your readers need two kinds of information: (1) what steps to do and (2) what materials to use.

Here's a good technique for gathering information. Imagine yourself doing the process on a video screen. What steps do you see yourself going through? As you watch each step on your mental TV, think about the tools and materials you're using.

You can use a chart to organize your notes about steps and materials. Here's a chart one writer made for a "how-to" paper.

HERE'S HOW

How to Do a Magic Trick: Ballooney-Baloney	
Steps	Materials
1. Blow up some balloons.	Three or four balloons of ordinary colors (pink, blue, yellow). One balloon of unusual color (purple).
2. Stick two pieces of tape on one side of unusual balloon.	See-through tape, scissors.
3. Ask someone to stick pin into ordinary balloons.	Pins
4. Stick pin through center of tape on taped balloon.	

As you take notes, jot down any terms that your readers might not know. This is especially important if you're writing for an audience younger than yourself. It's also important if you're writing about an unusual process. Your notes on terms like *karate chop, cakewalk,* and *D & D module* will remind you to define them in the paper.

EXERCISE 2 ▶ **Listing Steps and Materials**

Many processes you do every day have become almost as easy for you as breathing. Do you think you can break them into clear and separate steps? Get together with a group of classmates and divide each of the following processes into steps. Also, list materials you would need.

1. washing your hair
2. fixing your breakfast
3. doing the dishes
4. sharpening a pencil

Organizing Your Information.   On the next page are one writer's directions for making a Huichol yarn painting. Can you follow them?

You put a little liquid glue along the outline of your design. Add more glue inside the design and press yarn into it. The Huichols use traditional designs, and they use beeswax, not glue. They live in a part of Mexico where there are mountains. Cut the yarn for the inside of the design in small pieces. Put the pieces of yarn as close together as possible. You put the long yarn on the outline first. The design should be drawn on cardboard.

Suppose you tried to follow these directions the way they were written. Before you got to the end, you'd have to start over. And you would probably like to get your hands on the writer!

To make your process easy for readers to follow, first tell what materials are needed. Then give the steps in *chronological order,* the order that you'd do them.

As you're writing, many details may come into your mind. It's good to include details that relate directly to the process and help explain it. But don't use details that just get in the way (like the mountains in Mexico) or confuse your readers (like the beeswax).

To plan a "how-to" paper

■ list the steps that you want readers to follow
■ note the materials needed for each step
■ be sure the steps are in chronological order
■ use only details that will help readers do the process

CRITICAL THINKING

Arranging Steps in Chronological Order

Has this ever happened to you?

You ask an expert a simple question. The expert gives you a long and complicated answer. By the end you've forgotten what your question was! You're also more confused than you were before you asked the question.

That's one way an explanation can be confusing. Another way is to have an explanation move back and forth in time—jumping from what to do first to what to do last to everything in between! This is especially frustrating in a "how-to" paper. You want to go straight forward in time, or *chronologically:* what comes first, second, and so on.

 CRITICAL THINKING EXERCISE:
Arranging Steps in Chronological Order

On the next page are out-of-order directions for preparing to fly a kite. Working with one or two classmates, put the steps into chronological order—the order in which someone who wanted to fly a kite would need to do them. (You and your classmates might even enjoy actually following these directions after you're done.)

Release the kite while you are running, and let out the
    twine or string as the wind pulls the kite into the air.
Start running.
Find a long spool or ball of strong twine or string. Make
    sure it's at least a hundred feet long.
Take the kite in one hand, and the string or twine in the
    other, and place yourself at one end of the open space,
    with lots of room to run ahead of you.
Go to a big open space, such as a football field or a park.
Tie one end of the twine or string to the middle of
    your kite.

EXERCISE 3 ▶   **Evaluating Details**

All of the details in your "how-to" paper should help
readers do the process. If a detail doesn't help, take it out.
Ask yourself *Could readers make a mistake if I leave this detail
out? Is this detail something my audience already knows?* On
the next page are some notes for a paper about making
fried plantains or bananas. The audience is a class of seventh-graders. Which information would you cross out?

Buy ripe bananas or plantains.
Plantains are not as sweet as bananas.
You can't get plantains in most places in this country.
Peel bananas or plantains.
Cut them in half lengthwise and across.
Be sure you don't cut yourself.
Put butter or margarine in frying pan on medium heat.
Fry the fruit until it's golden brown.
Take bananas or plantains out of pan.
Sprinkle with sugar and cinnamon.
Eat now.
Clean up kitchen.
Save peelings for compost pile.

 **WRITING ASSIGNMENT**

PART 2:
Gathering and Organizing Information

Flying kites and making fried bananas: That's enough practice. Now plan *your* "how-to" paper. Begin with a chart like the one on page 219. Be sure to list your steps in chronological order and jot down all materials. [Remember: You could find some terms to define.]

Writing Your First Draft

Putting Your Ideas on Paper

Thinking and planning are important, but you've probably done enough for now. It's time to get down to the business of writing.

Introduction. The introduction of a "how-to" paper can be just two or three sentences. As usual, you want to begin by catching your readers' interest. One way to do this is by giving the reader a reason for learning the process. Show that it's fun, challenging, or useful.

Body. Begin the body of your paper by listing the materials. Then, give the steps in chronological order. You can explain steps when needed and give helpful tips, but include only information that's directly related to the process. Also use transitional words like *first, now,* and *after this* to make the steps clear and easy to follow.

 REFERENCE NOTE: For more information on transitional words and phrases, see pages 74–75.

Conclusion. Your conclusion should be brief. Probably one or two sentences will do. You might repeat why learning the process is a good idea, give another reason, or end with a final tip.

In the following explanation, the writer tells you how to make beads the way young people in southern Africa do it. As you read, ask yourself if you could follow her directions.

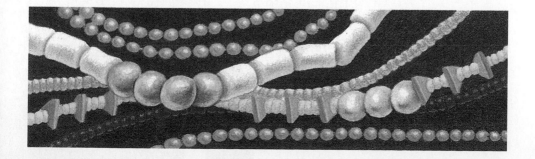

A PASSAGE FROM A BOOK

from Ubuhlali and Umnaka — Beaded Necklaces and Bangles

INTRODUCTION
Attention grabber
Reason for learning process

In the old days men and women as well as children wore beads; they were not simply decorations. In southern Africa, it was traditional to give beaded articles with special messages woven into them to loved ones and friends. . . .

The meanings of certain patterns and colors varied from place to place in southern Africa. Yellow usually symbolized wealth, and pink indicated poverty. Red showed anger and blue meant departure. White usually signified love. . . .

Process to be explained

Young people begin to learn beadwork by making simple necklaces of seeds and homemade beads. You can make your own beads as they were made long ago.

BODY
Step 1

For paste beads: Heat 3/4 cup of fine salt in a dry pan for a few minutes until it pops. Pour the salt into a bowl with 1/2 cup of flour.

Step 2

Step 3
Explanation

Step 4
Step 5

Step 6

Step 7
Helpful
hint

Step 8

Helpful
hint

Add 1/2 cup of water to which you have added a few drops of food coloring if you want tinted beads. Knead this mixture thoroughly.

Roll out a snake of the paste and cut into equal pieces. Roll each of the pieces into a smooth round ball.

To make flat beads, roll the paste out with a jar or rolling pin and cut beads into the desired shape.

Pierce each ball with a round toothpick. Stick toothpicks into a ball of soft clay or grapefruit rind to dry. Turn the beads periodically to prevent them from sticking to the toothpicks and allow them to dry thoroughly.

If you have not already tinted the paste, paint your beads with poster paint and cover with clear nail polish. For silver and gold beads use metallic nail polish.

from *African Crafts*

E X E R C I S E **4**▶   **Analyzing a "How-to" Explanation**

Did you realize you could make beads using just salt, flour, and water? Take a closer look at this process by discussing the following questions with two or three classmates.

1. This passage is part of a chapter about African beadwork. How does the beginning introduce the topic? Do the first sentences grab your attention? Explain why or why not.
2. What are the basic steps in making both round and flat beads? What steps are different for round beads and flat beads?

3. The writer doesn't list all materials before giving the steps. Do you think she should have? Explain.

4. Are the steps in chronological order? Would you change the order of any information to make the process easier to follow? If so, what and why?

5. Because this chapter goes on, the model does not have a conclusion. Make up one or two sentences that give the passage a good ending.

Following a Basic Framework for a "How-to" Paper

The explanation you've just read about making beads is part of a whole book about African crafts, so it isn't exactly like the paper you'll write. Your readers will want to know right away what materials they will need, and they may need more explanation of steps—not just a recipe approach. The following writer's model is an example of the kind of paper you'll write.

A WRITER'S MODEL

INTRODUCTION
Attention grabber
Reasons for learning process

Magic tricks are fun to do. This one will wake up anyone in your audience who's decided to take a little nap. It's sure to surprise your friends. To make sure it doesn't surprise you, practice before you do it for a real audience.

BODY
List of materials

You need to buy three or four balloons that are ordinary in color and one balloon that's an unusual color. Pink, blue, or yellow will do for the

Helpful hints

ordinary balloons. Try to get purple or black for the unusual one—your magic balloon. You also need a roll of tape, two or three long pins, and a pair of scissors. (Be sure that you get see-through tape.)

Step 1

Before you do the trick for your audience, you have to prepare. First, blow up the balloons. Next,

Step 2
Explanation

Helpful hint

Step 3
Explanation

Step 4

Helpful hint
Step 5
Explanation
CONCLUSION
Final hints

cut two one-inch pieces of tape and stick them on the "magic" balloon. It's important that both pieces be on one side of the balloon, so that you can turn that side <u>away from</u> the audience. Also make sure the tape is perfectly smooth.

Now you're ready to show your trick. Ask volunteers from the audience to pop the ordinary balloons. Give each volunteer a pin and cover your ears for the big bang. Then, tell the audience you have a magic balloon. Say some "magic" words like "Fiddle-faddle, Ballooncy-baloney" while you carefully stick a pin through the center of each tape. The tape keeps the "magic" balloon from popping.

After you've amazed your friends, you might want to show them how it's done. Otherwise, keep this trick a secret and add it to other tricks you can do.

WRITING NOTE You may want to add drawings or diagrams to your paper. Pictures often help explain a process. A diagram showing foot patterns, for instance, might help you tell how to do a Native American ceremonial dance. (Remember, in some cases one picture is worth a thousand words.)

It's often helpful to have a pattern to follow when you write. You may want to model your "how-to" paper on the one you've just read about the magic trick. Here is the framework it follows:

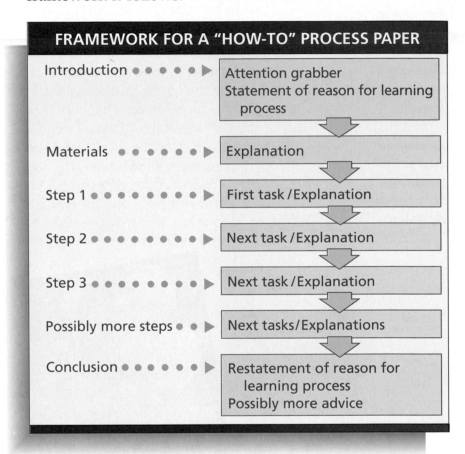

FRAMEWORK FOR A "HOW-TO" PROCESS PAPER

Introduction • • • • • ▶ Attention grabber
Statement of reason for learning
process

Materials • • • • • • ▶ Explanation

Step 1 • • • • • • • • ▶ First task / Explanation

Step 2 • • • • • • • • ▶ Next task / Explanation

Step 3 • • • • • • • • ▶ Next task / Explanation

Possibly more steps • • ▶ Next tasks / Explanations

Conclusion • • • • • • ▶ Restatement of reason for
learning process
Possibly more advice

WRITING
ASSIGNMENT

PART 3:
Writing Your First Draft

Now you're ready to put your process on paper from beginning to end. Be sure to use the chart of steps and materials you created in Writing Assignment, Part 2 (page 224). Whenever you have a question about what to do, look back at the basic framework above.

Evaluating and Revising

Evaluating a "how-to" paper with a partner is a big help. You know your process, but someone who *doesn't* can quickly see what's missing or confused. Use Exercise 5 with a partner as a "test run" of your "how-to" paper.

Then, use the chart on the next page to find problems and to fix them. If you answer "no" to a question on the left, use the revision technique on the right.

COMPUTER NOTE: Use your word-processing program's Cut and Paste commands to reorder steps that seem to be out of sequence. Move them back if you change your mind.

EXERCISE 5 **Speaking and Listening: Explaining and Following a Process**

Now you're going to read your draft out loud while a partner "acts out" the process. You'll need some imagination, but you have plenty—and this is a good test! First, read out your list of materials. Have your partner write each of the materials on a slip of paper. Then, read out the steps. Have your partner "use" the slips while pretending to do each step. Your partner can stop you and ask questions whenever something isn't clear. And *you* can call "Wait!" if there's a big mess. Make notes about problems right on your draft. Then, change roles.

"Oh, wait! Wait, Cory! ... Add the cereal *first* and *then* the milk!"

EVALUATING AND REVISING PROCESS ESSAYS

EVALUATION GUIDE	REVISION TECHNIQUE
1 Does the introduction grab the reader's attention and give reasons for learning the process?	**Add** interesting details to the beginning. **Add** a sentence that gives a reason for learning the process.
2 Does the paper list the materials before explaining the first step?	**Add** a list of all the materials needed before giving the first step.
3 Are the steps in chronological order? Are all the details necessary to explain the process?	**Reorder** the steps to put them in the order they must be done. **Cut** unnecessary details. **Add** any necessary details.
4 Do transitions help the reader follow the steps?	**Add** words like *first, then, before,* and *after*.
5 Does the paper end with a clear conclusion?	**Add** a sentence or two that restates the reason for learning the process or gives another reason. Offer a last hint.

Reminder

As you evaluate and revise your "how-to" paper

- use specific words so your readers won't become confused by vague language
- vary sentence beginnings to keep your readers interested
- ask yourself if any part of your paper sounds complicated

USAGE HINT

Using Specific Adjectives and Nouns

It's especially important to use specific, exact adjectives and nouns in "how-to" papers. Specific adjectives and nouns answer the questions "How many?" or "What kind?" or "How much?" These kinds of words will make your paper more accurate and precise.

EXAMPLES   *Vague Adjectives and Nouns*:
Heat **some** salt in a **container.**

Specific Adjectives and Nouns:
Heat **3/4 cup** of **fine** salt in a **dry pan.**

☞ **REFERENCE NOTE:** For more information on specific adjectives and nouns, see pages 434–437 and 423–426.

EXERCISE 6▶   **Analyzing a Writer's Revisions**

Here's the way the writer revised the third paragraph in the model on pages 228–229. Study the changes. Then answer the questions that follow the paragraph.

Before you do the trick for your

audience, you have to prepare. ~~Your~~   **cut**

~~audience may be made up of friends,~~

~~relatives, or neighbors.~~ (Next,) Cut two (one-inch) pieces of   **add**

tape and stick them on the "magic"

balloon. But first blow up the balloons. It's   **reorder/cut/add**

important that both pieces be on one side

↑ so that you can turn that side away from the audience

of the balloon. Also make sure the tape is   **add**

perfectly smooth.

1. Why did the writer cut the second sentence?
2. What is the reason for moving the sentence about blowing up the balloons?
3. In the third sentence, why are *Next* and *one-inch* good additions?
4. How does the addition in the next-to-last sentence make the directions clearer for the reader?

WRITING ASSIGNMENT

PART 4:
Evaluating and Revising Your Paper

Now it's time to use the chart on page 232 to evaluate and revise your paper. You can use it for a peer evaluation first. Then you can evaluate your own paper. When you're ready to make changes, look at what other students say about your paper. Which suggestions will you take? It's your paper, so the decision is up to you.

Peanuts reprinted by permission of United Feature Syndicate, Inc.

Proofreading and Publishing

Proofreading. Every detail is important in a "how-to" paper. That's why you need to proofread carefully. If you're telling how to make beads and you write "1/4 cup salt" instead of "3/4 cup salt," your readers won't end up with beads. One last check can help you catch this kind of mistake.

Publishing. Now you need to find a way to reach the audience you had in mind when you wrote your paper. Here are two ways:

- If your paper is about a craft, give a copy to a store that sells craft supplies. The store could post your paper for its customers to read.
- Stage a class demonstration day. Some of your classmates can demonstrate the processes they wrote about. Others can pick a topic and follow the "how-to" paper's directions to do the process.

| WRITING ASSIGNMENT | PART 5: **Proofreading and Publishing Your Paper** |

Proofread your "how-to" paper. Then, correct any mistakes you find in it. When your paper is as good as you can make it, choose a way to share it.

 Reflecting on Your Writing

Along with your "how-to" paper, include in your portfolio your answers to these questions:

- How did you go about choosing your topic? Are you pleased with your choice? Explain.
- Which was harder, thinking of all the steps in the process or arranging them clearly? Why?

A STUDENT MODEL

Not every "how-to" paper tells how to make something, as shown in this process paper by Stephanie
Pearl, a student at Randolph Intermediate School
in Randolph, New Jersey. Notice how the body of
her paper gives clear, step-by-step instructions in
chronological order.

How to Choose a Puppy
by Stephanie Pearl

Everyone knows that puppies are cute. What some people
don't know is that a puppy requires planning and responsibility, even before you bring it home. By following the steps
below, you can find the puppy that's right for you and make
a home that's right for your puppy.

Before adopting a puppy, you must prepare for one. Make
sure you have a crate or area set aside in your home for the
puppy to stay in when you are not around. Have all the supplies you'll need before you bring the puppy home. You
should have a collar and leash, some toys, and puppy food.
You may want to consider fencing in a part of your yard.

After you have decided to get a puppy, and you are prepared and have all necessary supplies, you need to decide
where to get one. The best place to go to adopt a puppy is an
animal shelter. Animal shelters usually have a wide variety
of puppies that people have abandoned.

When choosing a puppy, there are a number of qualities
you should look for. The puppy should not be too timid or too
aggressive. It should respond to noises and allow you to pet it.
It should appear healthy and have all necessary vaccinations.

First, you should pick out a puppy you like. Then, take
that puppy into a separate room. Sit down on the floor and
call it. The puppy should come, or at least look at you. If it
doesn't come, walk over and pet the puppy, letting it smell
your hand first. If it cringes or snarls, you may want to think
twice about adopting it. Overly aggressive or submissive puppies require more patience to train.

WRITING WORKSHOP

The Cause-and-Effect Paper

The "how-to" paper you just wrote gives information. It answers the question *How do you do that?* Another kind of paper that informs is a cause-and-effect paper. It answers the question *Why does that happen?* or *What is the result?* When you write a cause-and-effect paper, you start with an event or situation. Then you explain the causes for it (*Why?*) or its effects (*What's the result?*).

Here's an example. Teenagers often have messy rooms. You could explore the causes of this situation: Teenagers are too busy to keep their rooms looking neat. Or, you could write about the effects of teenagers' messy rooms: Homework—and many other things—get lost forever in them.

Causes and effects are sometimes obvious. But usually you do some thinking—exploring—to discover them. In this passage, astronaut Sally Ride writes about the effects of weightlessness that she discovered in space. Would you have guessed that these effects would happen?

Weightless in Space
by Sally Ride with Susan Okie

The best part of being in space is being weightless. It feels wonderful to be able to float without effort; to slither up, down, and around the inside of the shuttle just like a seal; to be upside down as often as I'm right side up and have it make no difference. On Earth being upside down feels different because gravity is pulling the blood toward my head. In space I feel exactly the same whether my head is toward the floor or toward the ceiling.

When I'm weightless, some things don't change. My heart beats at about the same rate as it does on Earth. I can still

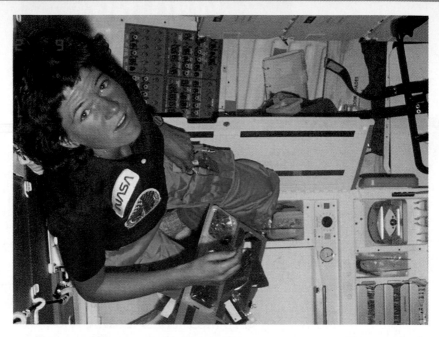

swallow and digest food. My eyes, ears, nose, and taste buds work fine; I see, hear, smell, and taste things just as I do at home.

I *look* a little different, though—all astronauts do. Since the fluid in our bodies is not pulled toward our feet as it is on Earth, more of this fluid stays in our faces and upper bodies. This makes our faces a little fatter and gives us puffy-looking cheeks. We are also about an inch taller while in orbit because in weightlessness our spines are not compressed. Unfortunately (for me, anyway), we shrink back to normal height when we return to Earth. . . .

In weightlessness the slightest touch can start an astronaut's body floating across the room or drifting over in a slow-motion somersault. The only way to stop moving is to take hold of something that's anchored in place. . . .

Some astronauts are uncomfortable while their bodies are adjusting to weightlessness. Almost half of all shuttle crew members are sick for the first day or two. . . .

By the third day of a week-long shuttle flight, though, all the astronauts are feeling fine. Weightlessness is pure fun, once everyone gets the hang of it.

from *To Space & Back*

Thinking It Over

1. What three effects of weightlessness does Sally Ride mention in the first paragraph?
2. Ride doesn't just list effects. She also explains them for readers. Find details that explain these effects: feeling the same whether upside down or right side up, the changed look of astronauts' faces, and being taller.
3. If you were in orbit, which effect would you like best?

Writing a Cause-and-Effect Paper

Prewriting. Like Sally Ride, you will write about effects in this paper. So think about something that makes you want to ask *What's the result of that?* Use one of the following ideas or think of one of your own. Just choose a situation you really want to explore, and then brainstorm all the effects you can.

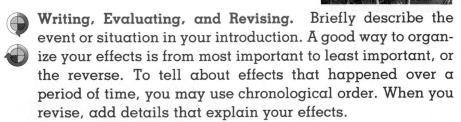

- the effects of being an only child
- the effects of having a disability
- the effects of a hurricane on your town
- the effects of a school volunteer project

Writing, Evaluating, and Revising. Briefly describe the event or situation in your introduction. A good way to organize your effects is from most important to least important, or the reverse. To tell about effects that happened over a period of time, you may use chronological order. When you revise, add details that explain your effects.

Proofreading and Publishing. Before you share your paper, check your capitalization, spelling, and punctuation. Think about who your audience will be: your family, an older friend, or the school newspaper, perhaps.

If you include this paper in your **portfolio,** add the date and a note reflecting on these questions: What did you learn by exploring your topic? Were you surprised by what you learned?

MAKING CONNECTIONS

PROCESS ACROSS THE CURRICULUM

Folk Tales, Riddles, and Brainteasers

Here's a brainteaser in the form of an old folk tale. It's about a crow who has an idea for a process that will let him get a drink of water. Exactly what does the crow do? Can you figure out his process?

A Drink for Crow
told by George Shannon

Once there was a crow who had grown so thirsty he could barely caw. He flew down to a big pitcher where he had gotten a drink of water the day before, but there was only a little bit of water remaining at the bottom. He tried and tried to reach it with his beak, but the pitcher was too deep and his beak was too short. But just as he was about to give up, he knew what to do. He flew back and forth from the garden to the pitcher until he was able to drink easily from the pitcher while sitting on its edge.

What did the crow do?

Answer: The crow dropped pebbles in the pitcher, and the water level rose.

Make up or find other riddles or brainteasers that involve figuring out a process. (Remember *What am I?* riddles? They sometimes describe a process.) Ask your parents or relatives, too. Then, try to stump your classmates.

SPEAKING AND LISTENING

Process in Social Studies: Mapping and Directions

Giving clear directions is important. Here's a way to practice this skill by making a treasure map.

First, you need to decide what you're going to use for your "treasure." The value of the treasure doesn't matter, because the fun comes from looking for it. Your treasure can be anything small that's easily hidden, such as a plastic figure or a key ring. Hide the treasure somewhere in your neighborhood.

Next, draw a map of the neighborhood. You can put real names of things on your map (pine tree, garbage cans, Fourth Street). Or you can pretend that the neighborhood is an imaginary place with imaginary names. The pine tree might become "Giant's Tower"; the garbage cans, "Smelly Swamp"; and Fourth Street, "Dragon's Lair." Use an arrow to mark a starting point. Use an *X* to mark the spot where the treasure is. Then, figure out five or six directions that would lead someone to the treasure, and write them down.

Give your map to a friend who's going to hunt for the treasure. Then, go together to the starting point. Read your first direction—for instance, "Walk straight ahead to Smelly Swamp, turn left, and stop at the blinking light." Then, give the next direction. Read each one *only once*. When your friend finds the treasure (or gets lost), talk about what was good and bad about the map. The directions might be faulty—or your friend's listening powers.

8 WRITING TO PERSUADE

Paul Newman
for America's
Libraries

Taking a Stand

When John Parker's Minutemen stood facing the advancing British troops at Lexington in 1775, Parker said, "Stand your ground." And they did. It's often important to **take a stand**—to have a belief you're willing to argue and defend. Doing so won't usually result in a revolution. But you may be able to persuade others that you're right.

Writing and You. Persuasion comes into every part of your life. You might try to talk your classmates into having a class picnic. You might write a speech persuading others how to vote in a school election. You might convince your big brother to lend you his radical shirt. Have you tried to persuade someone lately? Did it work?

As You Read. Advertisers often try to persuade us. Look at the ad on the next page. What is its purpose? Who is it trying to convince? Why?

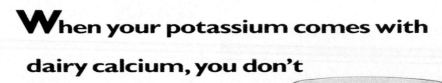

READER'S RESPONSE

1. Does this ad persuade you that milk and other dairy foods are "the perfect way to avoid nutritional slip-ups"? Why or why not?
2. Which part of the ad did you look at first? What part of the ad do you find the most convincing? Why?
3. What's your favorite food? Is it as good as ads for it say it is? In your journal, brainstorm some vivid words to describe it. Create your own ad slogan; for instance, "Scrumptious Smithers' soup—steaming, zesty, robust."

WRITER'S CRAFT

4. Who is the audience for the ad for dairy foods? How can you tell? What kind of magazine do you think it appeared in?
5. What advantages does the ad writer claim for milk and other dairy products?
6. Milk has many nutrients, not just potassium. Why would the Dairy Board compare milk with bananas? [Hint: Have you seen any banana ads?]
7. What does the ad try to get the reader to do?

"Advertising is what you do when you can't go see somebody. That's all it is."

Fairfax Cone

Ways to Persuade

Persuasive writing tries to convince you to *do* something or *believe* something. Advertising comes in many forms— radio, television, newspapers, and billboards. And there are many kinds of persuasion besides advertising—editorials, speeches, sermons, and even songs. Here are some forms that persuasion can take.

- in an article for a school newspaper, telling about a homeless family to persuade students to volunteer at a shelter
- in a letter to your parents, trying to convince them that a trip to the lake will help you to get a better grade on your paper about turtles
- in a speech to the school board, describing your school's gym to persuade them to buy new bleachers
- in a newspaper ad, describing kittens in an animal shelter to urge readers to adopt one
- in a cover letter for a job application, classifying your skills and personal qualities to persuade an employer to hire you
- in a paper for English class, asking your classmates to listen to a new CD by a musical group that you think is great
- in a letter to the editor, stating your opinion about safe biking and suggesting that bike lanes be added to streets

LOOKING AHEAD

In the main assignment in this chapter, you'll be writing a persuasive paper. As you work, keep in mind that an effective persuasive paper

- states the writer's opinion about the issue
- provides information to support the opinion
- may appeal to the reader's emotions

Writing a Persuasive Paper

Prewriting

Choosing a Topic

You may not realize how often you use persuasion. Think about it. Have you ever tried to convince your parents to increase your allowance? Have you ever tried to get a friend to try out for a team? Have you ever tried to persuade someone to go to a movie with you? All these situations involve persuasion. And just think—the more persuasive you are, the better your chances of having things go your way.

In this chapter, you'll get to practice your powers of persuasion. You'll be writing about an *issue*, a topic or idea that people have different opinions about.

Finding an Issue That Matters. It's important to choose an issue that matters to you. It should also be one that people around you think is important. Why try to convince people of something that neither you nor they have any interest in? Look for things that are happening in your school or neighborhood that you feel strongly about. For example, is your school setting up a new dress code? Should your community build a hockey rink? Does air pollution upset you? Is there too much violence in movies? Any one of these topics would be a good issue for persuasive writing. Just be sure it really matters to you.

COMPUTER NOTE: The World Wide Web is a great place to begin prewriting research for a persuasive paper. To locate Web sites that have information on contemporary issues, do a keyword search using an Internet search engine. Use the information you find to choose a topic for your paper.

Identifying Your Opinion.   Your *opinion* is something you believe. It isn't something that can be proven true. For example, it's your opinion that Nolan Ryan is the greatest baseball pitcher of all time. You believe it, but others may disagree. A *fact,* on the other hand, can be proven true. It's a fact that Nolan Ryan pitched seven no-hit games. No one can deny it. As the famous baseball manager Casey Stengel used to say, "You could look it up."

Putting your opinion down in black and white is the first step in writing a persuasive paper. You can do this by writing a *statement of opinion* that tells your topic and what you believe about it. Here are some examples of statements of opinion:

Driving a motorboat should require a license.
The city schools should set up tutoring classes for
    students who don't speak English.
Too many movies today use violence as entertainment.

Reminder

When choosing a topic for persuasive writing

- brainstorm, listen to television and radio, and look through newspapers and magazines to find an issue you care about
- write a sentence identifying your issue and telling your opinion about it

---

EXERCISE 1 ▶ **Distinguishing Fact from Opinion**

With a small group, decide which of the following statements is a *fact* and which is an *opinion*. Keep in mind that a fact can be proven true while an opinion is a belief. Be ready to explain your reasoning about each statement.

1. Our school really should celebrate Harriet Tubman's birthday.
2. Some of the largest cities in the United States have Spanish names.
3. New York City is the largest city in the United States.
4. I. M. Pei, the architect, is the greatest American of Chinese descent.

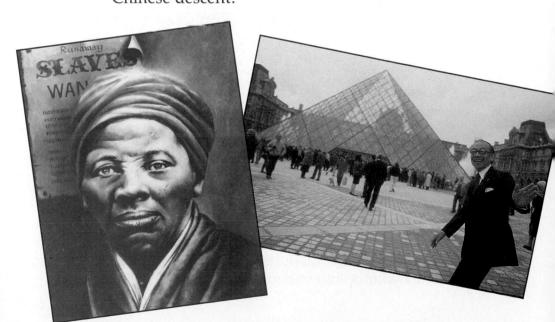

EXERCISE 2 ▶   **Exploring Possible Topics**

With a small group of classmates, brainstorm possible topics for persuasive writing. Talk about what's going on at school. Think about issues you have heard about on television or radio. Look through copies of magazines such as *Sports Illustrated* or *Time* in your library. Make a list of at least five issues.

PART 1:
Choosing an Issue to Write About

Pick an issue for persuasive writing. Perhaps you'll stay with one you came up with in Exercise 2. Or you may want to take a stand on something else. Should we have a new national anthem because "The Star-Spangled Banner" is too hard to sing? Should all experiments on animals be outlawed? When you've decided what you want to write about, write a sentence that names the issue and states your opinion about it.

Prewriting

Planning Your Paper

Have you ever set out to get something you wanted—and succeeded? Then you probably gave your "plan of action" some careful thought. Persuading on paper takes the same planning.

Thinking About Purpose and Audience

Your *purpose* in persuasive writing is to make readers think a certain way or act a certain way. You can't do that without paying pretty close attention to *them*—to your *audience*. On your issue, what will be their interests and concerns? How can you appeal to your readers?

Suppose you want your classmates to support a city hockey rink. They'll be interested in being able to watch good teams play. Suppose you want to convince the city council. They'll worry about building costs. So to have the right appeal and answers, think ahead about audience.

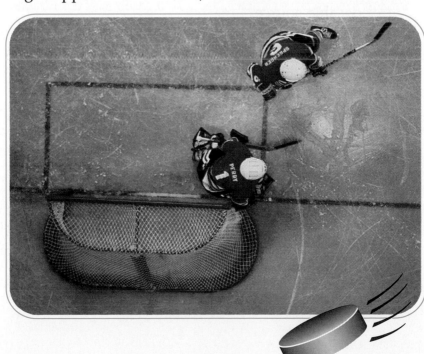

Supporting Your Opinion

Do you always accept what other people say just because they seem to believe their own words? Probably not. You have opinions of your own that may be completely different from theirs. How, then, do you go about changing other people's opinions? It *can* be done. You just have to give convincing *support,* or proof, for what you believe.

Finding Information to Support Your Opinion. There are several ways to find support for your opinions. Here are three.

1. Talk to friends and others interested in the issue.
2. Talk to experts—people who are knowledgeable about the issue.
3. Look in books, magazines, and newspapers.

As you use these methods, look for *reasons, facts,* or *opinions* from knowledgeable sources. The more support you find, the more likely you are to sway your readers. For example, one writer needed to support his opinion that everyone in Fresno, California, should be required to ration water. He found facts and the opinion of a knowledgeable source.

> Support/Opinion of an expert: According to Water Commissioner Carol Main, "Some people are cutting their water use, but not enough are doing it to save the amount of water we need."

> Support/Fact: In Fresno, people were asked to cut their water use voluntarily by 25 percent. They cut their use by 17.7 percent.

WRITING NOTE As you talk to people and read about the issue, you may find your opinion changing. That's okay. It simply means you've become better informed and better able to explain and defend your true point of view.

Using Appeals to the Emotions.   Not all the support in good persuasive writing is factual. Some is emotional. You want to appeal to people's hearts as well as to their minds.

An organization is raising money to save California's redwood trees. You've been asked to write the appeal for donations. Will you just tell them how many trees will be saved? No. You'll describe a family enjoying a hike through a redwood forest. Then you'll say that a forest just like this one is being logged less than a hundred miles away. You'll describe the ugly, treeless landscape after the logging.

As you write, you'll consider how *you* feel about the issue. Do you feel fear? concern? hope? anger? Then you'll try to create the same emotions in your audience. Draw vivid word pictures. Use a powerful quotation. Tell about a sad incident. Make the audience feel the rightness of your cause.

Emotional appeals alone aren't enough, though. The best persuasion has a base of solid information. Then you can add feelings.

When you're gathering support, you can use a chart like the one in the Here's How on page 254.

OPINION:	Athletes shouldn't charge for autographs.
AUDIENCE:	Junior high school students
SUPPORT:	1. The most popular players already earn millions. 2. Fans will think less of their favorite players if they have to pay for autographs. 3. Players in the past didn't ask fans to pay for autographs. Today's players should be more like them.

CRITICAL THINKING
Evaluating Reasoning

Sometimes what seems like support for an opinion isn't support at all. Some reasons aren't really reasonable (logical), and some emotional appeals are tricks, not truth. Unsuspecting readers and listeners can be fooled by these "statements masquerading as reasons."

So be careful. If you use misleading support, some readers will spot it. Those who do won't be convinced.

STATEMENTS MASQUERADING AS REASONS		
TECHNIQUE	**STRATEGY**	**EXAMPLE**
False Cause and Effect	Assumes that one event caused another just because one came before the other	"Not sending the band to out-of-town games put the team on a losing streak."
Attacking the Person	Ignores the issue by attacking the person instead of the person's view on the topic	"Supporters of this leash law are dog haters at heart."
Bandwagon	Asks you to believe or do something because many other people do	"Don't be the only family in your neighborhood without a CD player."

⚡ CRITICAL THINKING EXERCISE:
Evaluating Persuasive Statements

With a small group, study each statement below. Why is each statement misleading? Which technique from page 254 is being used? Be prepared to explain.

1. Everyone is buying Bright-O toothpaste. The stores can hardly keep it on the shelves. Buy yours today!
2. Because the principal shortened the homeroom period, many students got poorer grades.
3. Since he is an active deer hunter, it's no wonder that Bob says hunting helps conserve deer.
4. The kids at Del Rio Middle School who started skateboarding lost their A and B averages. Skateboarding definitely eats up study time.

WRITING ASSIGNMENT	PART 2: **Finding Support for Your Opinion**

You'll need information and perhaps emotional appeals to support the opinion statement you wrote for your paper. Use a chart like the one on page 254, and start backing up your belief. What reasons or facts can you think of? Whose expert opinion can you quote? What feelings can you tap—and how? Line up some strong support.

Writing Your First Draft

Combining the Elements of Persuasion

You've seen that the basic elements of persuasive writing are (1) a clear statement of your opinion and (2) support for that opinion. Now that you have both, you need to put them together in a way that's really convincing—in a way that gets your audience to think or to act as you'd like.

A Good Beginning. You need to try to grab your readers' attention from the start. You could begin with a question that creates strong feelings: "Would you want a nuclear waste dump across the street from your house?" Or you might begin with an interesting *anecdote* (little story): "Yesterday I walked out of a movie and asked for my money back. I got it." Once you have everyone's attention, you can state your opinion. With a good beginning, you've made the first step toward convincing your readers.

Clearly Organized Support. One way to organize support in persuasion is *order of importance.* Go from your most important reason to your least important, or the opposite. In other words, you try to capture your readers' sympathy at the start, or you build up to a powerful punch at the end. Either way can work. Just be sure to decide what's most important to *your readers*, not only to you.

A Good Ending. Leave your audience convinced that you're right. Your best ending might be a strong restatement of your opinion. Or it might be a *call to action*, a specific suggestion about something the audience can do.

The writer of the following chapter from a book wants readers to go without meat one day a month. Notice how she uses both information and emotion to support her opinion. Does she put it all together in a strong, persuasive package?

A CHAPTER FROM A BOOK

Title/Call to action

One Day a Month, Go Without Meat
by Marjorie Lamb

BEGINNING

Statement of opinion
SUPPORT
Expert opinion

Reason

Many North Americans are eating less meat than we used to, partly for our health, and partly out of the knowledge that meat consumption wastes our planet's resources. Frances Moore Lappé, in her wonderful book, *Diet For a Small Planet* (Ballantine Books), documents the hideous waste of protein fed to livestock compared to the minuscule amount of protein we receive from livestock in return. We could easily supply the human population of the Earth with enough protein if we stopped feeding it to our livestock. Cattle consume more than 15 pounds of grains for every pound of beef they give us in return.

Reason

Facts

The demand for beef also means the clearing of vast tracts of tropical rainforest for cattle grazing. The land rapidly deteriorates, the soil erodes and becomes infertile.

Emotional appeal

Then more acreage must be cleared for cattle grazing. Land which once supported farmers in tropical countries now grows soya—not to feed the people, but for export as livestock feed. Some fast-food chains get their beef from tropical lands such as Costa Rica. Ask your fast-food outlet where their beef comes from.

Facts
Reason

Reason

Fact and emotional appeal

As cattle digest, they give off methane, a greenhouse gas. The world's cattle population, along with large areas of rice paddies, accounts for nearly half the global release of methane. More beef means more global warming.

Finally, livestock grazing requires tremendous amounts of water to irrigate pasture land. California alone uses enough water to meet the domestic needs of 22 million people, just to turn the desert into grassland for cattle and sheep grazing.

ENDING

Summary of reasons

> If we all reduced our meat consumption, we'd make a significant impact on the protein available for the rest of the world, save water for more reasonable uses and

Emotional appeal

> help preserve our tropical rainforests, which we desperately need for the health and survival of the planet.
>
> from *2 Minutes a Day for a Greener Planet*

EXERCISE 3 ▶ Analyzing Persuasive Writing

After you read the excerpt from *2 Minutes a Day for a Greener Planet*, discuss it with some classmates. Use these questions to guide your analysis.

1. Many people who read Marjorie Lamb's book already believe we need a "greener planet." If her readers *did not*, do you think her opening sentence would be different? What opening would you write?
2. What words and phrases make the expert opinion of Frances Moore Lappé also an emotional appeal?
3. How many facts does Lamb give in comparison to her emotional appeals? Is there a good balance between facts and opinions?
4. Lamb's title contains her call to action. How does she conclude her chapter?
5. Does Lamb convince you of her opinion? Why or why not? If you were a cattle rancher, what specific objections to Lamb's comments would you make?

Using a Basic Framework

The excerpt from Lamb's book shows you effective persuasion in action, but it's different from the composition you'll write. You'll probably be writing a simpler paper, with less extensive support—and of course you're not writing a whole book! On page 261 is a framework you can use when you're learning to write persuasion.

A WRITER'S MODEL

BEGINNING
Attention grabber—anecdote

Last week at a baseball card show, I asked a well-known baseball player for his autograph. Imagine my surprise when a man standing next to him said I would have to pay fourteen dollars before the player would sign his name!

Opinion
SUPPORT
Fact

Emotional appeals

Athletes shouldn't charge fans for autographs. The fans help many athletes get huge salaries in the first place. The most popular players—the ones fans ask for autographs most often—already earn millions of dollars. They don't really need this extra money. And how can you have respect for a player who won't even take a minute to sign his name for you? Babe Ruth was flattered just to have kids look up to him. He wouldn't have dreamed of asking people to pay for his autograph.

ENDING
Call to action
Restatement of opinion

Don't cave in and pay for an autograph. Players should see that an autograph is a way of saying "thank you" to loyal fans, and they shouldn't charge money.

You can use the following framework as a guide. The paper about athletes' autographs uses this framework.

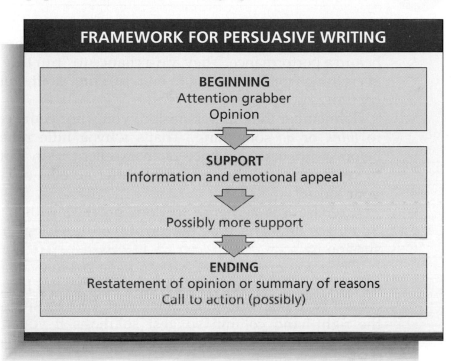

FRAMEWORK FOR PERSUASIVE WRITING

BEGINNING
Attention grabber
Opinion

SUPPORT
Information and emotional appeal

Possibly more support

ENDING
Restatement of opinion or summary of reasons
Call to action (possibly)

WRITING NOTE
As you write the draft of your paper, remember to grab your audience's attention. When you're trying to persuade, you may be able to get their attention just by stating your opinion: "I think seventh-grade students should have a class party." But most of the time you'll need to do something special to make your audience want to read on.

WRITING ASSIGNMENT

PART 3:
Writing Your First Draft

It's time to start writing. Look back at your statement of opinion and your chart of supporting information. Use the framework as a guide, and don't forget your audience.

Evaluating and Revising

By now you know that your drafts are like rehearsals before a performance. They are a chance to "run through" everything from beginning to end. In a first draft, you can try things out to see if they work.

Remember that, in persuasion, you want your readers to *think* or *do* something. That's why a little rehearsal before a preview audience is an excellent idea. You get to see how a real, live audience either accepts or rejects your ideas.

Exercise 4 is a chance to do a preview with a peer. You'll see firsthand how powerful (you hope!) your persuasion is.

Then you can use the chart on page 263 to evaluate all the parts of your paper. The questions in the left-hand column will help you judge each part. The techniques in the right-hand column suggest solutions if you find a problem.

> **EXERCISE 4** ▶ **Speaking and Listening: Responding to an Argument**

Try out your draft—out loud—with a partner. The listener will use the questions below to take notes as you speak. You can read your draft twice so your partner has a chance to catch everything. After you finish, look at your partner's responses to the questions. Jot down anything you want to keep in mind for your revising. Then change roles. You might even want to get another partner and repeat the process.

1. Can I state the speaker's issue and opinion in my own words?
2. Did the speaker grab my attention right from the start?
3. What supporting point really stood out for me?
4. Did my opinion change by the end? Why or why not?
5. What helpful suggestions can I give the speaker?

EVALUATING AND REVISING PERSUASIVE WRITING

EVALUATION GUIDE	REVISION TECHNIQUE
1 Does the beginning grab the reader's attention?	**Add** an interesting question or brief story.
2 Is the writer's opinion clearly stated early in the paper?	**Add** a sentence giving your opinion, or **replace** the statement of opinion with a clearer one.
3 Is there enough support to convince the audience?	**Add** reasons, facts, or opinions from experts. **Add** a sentence that will appeal to your reader's feelings.
4 Does the writer include any incorrect or misleading statements?	**Cut** statements that depend on false cause and effect, attacking the person, or bandwagon.
5 Is the ending strong?	**Add** a sentence that restates your opinion or calls your reader to action.

"Just get it down on paper, and then we'll see what to do with it."

Maxwell Perkins

EXERCISE 5 ▶ **Analyzing a Writer's Revisions**

Study the writer's revisions of the middle paragraph of the composition on page 260. Then answer the questions that follow.

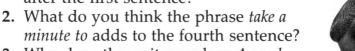

Athletes shouldn't charge fans for

(The fans help many athletes get huge salaries in the first place⊙)

autographs. The most popular players—

add

the ones fans ask for autographs most

often—already earn millions of dollars.

They don't really need this extra money.

And how can you have respect for a

take a minute to

player who won't even sign his name for

add

Babe Ruth

you? ~~A good player in the past~~ was

replace

flattered just to have kids look up to him.

He wouldn't have dreamed of asking

people to pay for his autograph. ~~Anyone~~

cut

~~who pays for an autograph is pretty dumb.~~

1. What's the writer's reason for adding a new sentence after the first sentence?
2. What do you think the phrase *take a minute to* adds to the fourth sentence?
3. Why does the writer replace *A good player in the past* with *Babe Ruth*?
4. Do you see a good reason to cut the last sentence?

GRAMMAR HINT

Using Comparatives

In writing persuasion, you will sometimes want to compare one person or thing to another. You may want to show that your candidate for class president is *more experienced* than the other candidate. You may want to say that one brand of sneaker feels *better* than another. Be sure not to use the word *more* if the modifier is already in the comparative form (*longer*).

INCORRECT	Powermax batteries last more longer than batteries from other manufacturers.
CORRECT	Powermax batteries last **longer** than batteries from other manufacturers.

INCORRECT	Super Crunchies cereal will make your breakfast more better every day!
CORRECT	Super Crunchies cereal will make your breakfast **better** every day!

 REFERENCE NOTE: For more information on using comparatives, see pages 629–635.

WRITING ASSIGNMENT	PART 4: **Evaluating and Revising Your Persuasive Paper**

Do you have your notes from the "peer listening" in Exercise 4? Keep them in mind as you use the chart on page 263 to evaluate your paper. Start by exchanging papers with another student. Using the questions, write an evaluation of each other's work. Then evaluate your essay yourself. Revise it to correct any problems you or your partner has found.

Proofreading and Publishing

Proofreading. Correct spelling, capitalization, punctuation, and usage errors. Otherwise, readers may suspect you've made mistakes in your thinking, too.

Publishing. Here are two ways to publish your writing.

- Join with three of your classmates to make an illustrated bulletin board display from your four papers.
- Present the ideas from your paper as part of a debate with a student who disagrees with your opinion.

 | PART 5:
WRITING | **Proofreading and Publishing**
ASSIGNMENT | **Your Persuasive Paper**

Proofread and then discuss your paper with a partner.

 Reflecting on Your Writing

If you include your essay in your **portfolio,** attach written responses to the following questions.

- Did your opinion change as you wrote? Explain.
- How did you shape your support to fit your audience?

A STUDENT MODEL

A persuasive composition may sometimes be just a single paragraph, such as this one by Kathy Bobek, a student at Henry David Thoreau Intermediate School in Vienna, Virginia. Notice how her paragraph clearly focuses on a single topic. Also, look for the specific reasons she gives to support her topic sentence. Does she convince you of her opinion about school dances?

School Dances
by Kathy Bobek

I feel that our school should let the seventh- and eighth-grade classes have their own dances. Wouldn't you and your friends love to have dances with just your friends and peers of only your grade? I'm sure most people want to socialize with friends who are in the same grade. They would want to do this and not have to worry about being made fun of by people of a higher or lower grade. The dances wouldn't have mixed grades, so more people would come to the dances, which would bring in more money. I also think there would be fewer people at each individual dance, which would also bring more order. Last but not least, I feel that the dances would be decorated more to the liking of the students. Each grade could have different people from their grade decorate each dance. What one grade might think is stupid or baby-ish, another might like. For these reasons, I think that having individual school dances for each grade would be a very good idea.

WRITING WORKSHOP

A Newspaper or Magazine Ad

Advertising is everywhere. Television and radio ads bombard your eyes and ears. Magazine and newspaper ads draw you in with pictures and bold words. All these ads have one aim—to grab your attention and convince you to buy or do something.

How do ads do it? They use certain techniques that have proved successful. Here are four.

1. *"We're the best."* The ad claims its product or service is better than that of its competitors. The ad may give facts to support the claim.
2. *"You'll feel or look better."* The ad promises you health, comfort, or beauty.
3. *"We'll solve your problem."* The ad suggests a problem (maybe one you never thought of) and offers to solve it.
4. *"A star athlete says . . ."* The ad quotes a famous person who uses or recommends the product or service.

"Do you know me? I have to deal with lions, wolves, and saber-toothed tigers . . . That's why I carry one of THESE."

THE GOLD CLUB
John Q Caveman
123 456 7890

These techniques aren't always so obvious in an ad. Advertisers can use them in very clever ways. But if you look closely, you can usually figure out which techniques are being used. What does this cereal ad promise you?

Every round a winner...
and every triangle, too!

Spelling bee champion Pia Sanchez says,
"I start every day with Double Oats. They're simply supercalifragilistic-expialidocious."

Introducing Double Oats

Who says a health-packed cereal can't be a taste sensation? Try this great new treat—toasty oat triangles and hearty oat puffs. With twelve essential vitamins and minerals. Extra low in sugar. Extra high in crunchy goodness.

T O A S T E D

DOUBLE OATS

Crisp, Wholesome, Delicious! New Nifty Shapes!

Ideal Source of Oat Bran

Thinking It Over

1. Which of the four techniques does the ad use to make you want to try Double Oats? (More than one is possible.) Does the ad persuade you?
2. How does the ad's headline connect the spelling bee with Double Oats?
3. Does the ad use any facts to support the claim that Double Oats is "a winner"? If so, identify them.
4. Why do you think the illustration includes the spelling-bee scene? Why wouldn't a picture of the cereal box be enough? Why does the ad use sentence fragments?

Writing an Ad

Prewriting.   You're going to create an ad of your own. What will you sell? A new shampoo? A bicycle? Sneakers? List some possible products for your ad and choose one. Give it a good name. To plan your ad, think about the four advertising techniques. Which will you use? Jot down ideas for words and pictures. Also decide what audience you'll be trying to persuade.

Writing, Evaluating, and Revising.   All three parts of an ad must work together—the headline, the information (a short paragraph), and the illustration. Keeping that in mind, write your headline. Make it short, direct, and catchy. Think about the ad techniques as you write your paragraph. What will appeal to your audience? Why will they want to buy the product? You can sketch your illustration, or clip it from a magazine. Arrange your ad on a sheet of paper. Then look it over carefully with a partner. Would you stop to read it in a magazine? Could you make it stronger?

Proofreading and Publishing.   Since ads are brief and eye-catching, any mistakes in spelling, capitalization, or punctuation jump out at readers. Errors will take away from your message. Proofread carefully. Consider publishing your ad as part of a bulletin board display or class album. Or put together a class magazine. Your persuasion papers from this chapter can be the articles. Ads can then be placed throughout the magazine. You may also want to include other writing—stories and poems, for instance.

   If you choose to include your ad in your **portfolio,** date it and add a note responding to these questions: Which advertising techniques did you use? Why is your ad effective? How does the headline relate to the product?

MAKING CONNECTIONS

SPEAKING AND LISTENING

Comparing Persuasion in Different Forms

Join with two or three classmates in an ad hunt. Find one product that is advertised in two or more forms.

- Some *products* to consider are toothpaste, soap, cereal, shoes, clothing, cameras, and watches.
- Some *forms of advertising* to consider are television, magazines, newspapers, radio, and direct mail (ads that come in the mail).

The Pierce Arrow

LUXURY in a car is as much a matter of engine building as it is of upholstery. Luxury as expressed in a Pierce-Arrow means efficiency first, attractive design second, a perfectly appointed car, built around a thoroughly tried-out machine.

THE PIERCE-ARROW MOTOR CAR COMPANY, BUFFALO, N. Y.
Licensed under Selden Patent

You may want to divide the forms among yourselves. That way, everybody won't be searching in the same places. Try to find your product advertised in as many different forms as possible. (You probably won't find it in all forms.) Cut out or record the ads if possible. Otherwise, take notes.

When the group gets together, ask yourselves:

1. How are the ads alike, and how are they different? Describe the ads. [Hint: What do you notice about words, pictures, color, sound, and motion?]
2. Which ad in which form is the most convincing to you? Why?

Report your findings to the class. Use the ads you've collected in your report.

PERSUASION IN ACTION

Letters to the Editor

Almost all newspapers and magazines have a "Letters to the Editor" section. It gives readers a chance to say what's on their minds. They may respond to a news item or an editorial. Or they may bring up a whole new issue.

The real audience for such letters is all the readers of a newspaper or magazine, not just an editor. The purpose often is to persuade. Here's a letter from a writer who wants readers to be aware that wild plants can be useful.

> CURES FROM THE JUNGLE
>
> I really enjoyed reading "In Search of Jungle Secrets" in the February 1990 issue of *Ranger Rick*. When I was nine years old, I got a very rare type of blood cancer. One of the drugs that was used to cure me came from the *rosy periwinkle*. This flower grows in Madagascar, an island off the African coast.

I am 15 years old now and very happy to be alive. I'm thankful for tropical plants that can be used to make medicines like the one that cured me.

Please tell everyone how important it is to save wild plants and other living things. Not only are they beautiful, but they also might contain some "secret" medicines that can save other people's lives too.

Whitney Hair, Cary, NC
Ranger Rick

Read a few more letters to the editor, and write one of your own. Think of an issue that concerns you, and choose a specific magazine or newspaper to write to.

Use the elements you've learned in this chapter: opinion statement, supporting information, emotional appeal (not overexcited, though), and perhaps a call to action. But be very brief. Editors often shorten long letters.

Then mail your letter. If it's published, bring the clipping to class.

Reading and Responding

Every day you spend time **reading and responding.** You read your favorite comic strips and laugh. You put a book down because it's so boring you can't stay awake. You have feelings and thoughts about almost everything you read.

Writing and You.   People often put their responses in writing. Newspaper and TV critics respond to movies, books, and TV shows. Your friend may write in her journal about a movie she liked. Your teacher may ask you to respond in writing to a poem you read. Or you may be asked to write an in-depth book report. Did you realize that all these were responses?

As You Read.   Following is a response about a book you may have read—*Number the Stars*, by Lois Lowry. As you read, think about the reviewer's opinion. Does she like the book? If so, why does she?

Steven Cortright, *Book Objects* (1986), Santa Barbara Museum of Art.

A Review of Lois Lowry's

NUMBER THE STARS

by Louise L. Sherman

Annemarie's life in occupied Copenhagen in 1943 seemingly is not much changed by the war—until the Nazi persecution of Danish Jews begins. Annemarie's family becomes involved in the Resistance effort, helping a Jewish friend by having her pose as Annemarie's dead sister Lise. When an important packet must be taken to the captain of one of the ships smuggling Jews to neutral Sweden, Annemarie finds the courage needed to deliver it despite grave danger to herself. Later her Uncle Henrik tells her that *brave* means "not thinking about the dangers. Just thinking about what you must do." Lowry's story is not just of Annemarie; it is also of Denmark and the Danish people, whose Resistance was so effective in saving their Jews. Annemarie is not just a symbol, however. She is a very real child who is equally involved in playing with a new kitten and running races at school as in the dangers of the occupation. *Number the Stars* brings the war to a child's level of understanding, suggesting but not detailing its horrors. It is well plotted, and period and place are convincingly recreated. An afterword answers the questions that readers will have and reiterates the inspirational idealism of the young people whose courage helped win the war.

"...brave

means 'not thinking about the dangers.

Just thinking about what you must do.' "

READER'S RESPONSE

1. Does *Number the Stars* seem like a book you'd want to read? Explain why or why not.
2. If you've read this book, tell why you think it is or is not a good story.

WRITER'S CRAFT

3. What is the reviewer's opinion of *Number the Stars*? Does she like or dislike it? What sentences tell you this?
4. The reviewer uses details from the book to support her opinion about it. What does she say about why she likes or dislikes *Number the Stars*?

"She is a very real child who is equally involved in playing with a new kitten and running races at school as in the dangers of the occupation."

Purposes for Writing About Literature

The purpose of a review, like the one about *Number the Stars*, is to tell whether or not others should read a story, poem, or book. You might also write about literature in your journal or in a letter to friends, or make a poster showing your responses to a book. Then your purpose for writing about literature might be different—just to give your own feelings or to persuade someone else to read something. Here are some examples of possible purposes.

- in a journal entry, writing about a short-story character that seems just like you
- in a letter, writing about your favorite TV show
- in a note to your parents or guardians, describing a movie so that they will let you see it
- in a poster for the library, describing a book to persuade other students to read it
- in a report on Italy for social studies class, telling about a movie you saw about the country
- in a message for a bulletin board at work, telling coworkers about a book they might enjoy
- in a poem, writing as though you were a character in a story you read
- in your journal, imagining what happens to a character ten years after the story ends

LOOKING
AHEAD

In the main assignment in this chapter, your purpose for writing about literature will be informative. You'll be analyzing a character in a story and telling about him or her. Keep in mind that a good character analysis

- tells about two or three character traits
- gives story details to support the analysis

Writing a Character Analysis

Prewriting

Reading and Responding to Stories

Before you can write about literature, you have to read it, respond to it, and think about it. You start with the story or poem itself and your reactions to it. Then you try to understand it.

Starting with a Personal Response

A personal response usually happens automatically. You know right away whether you like a movie or not. You walk out of the theater saying, "Those battle scenes were great!" or "What a boring movie!" You respond to literature—a poem, a novel, or a story—in the same way.

There is no right or wrong way to respond to literature. That's why it's called a "personal" response.

The following story is about a young boy who is embarrassed about the way his great-grandfather looks and acts. As you read, think about your personal response. Can you understand how the boy feels?

A SHORT STORY

The Medicine Bag

by Virginia Driving Hawk Sneve

My kid sister Cheryl and I always bragged about our Sioux grandpa, Joe Iron Shell. Our friends, who had always lived in the city and only knew about Indians from movies and TV, were impressed by our stories. Maybe we exaggerated and made

Grandpa and the reservation sound glamorous, but when we'd return home to Iowa after our yearly summer visit to Grandpa we always had some exciting tale to tell.

We always had some authentic Sioux article to show our listeners. One year Cheryl had new moccasins that Grandpa had made. On another visit he gave me a small, round, flat, rawhide drum which was decorated with a painting of a warrior riding a horse. He taught me a real Sioux chant to sing while I beat the drum with a leather-covered stick that had a feather on the end. Man, that really made an impression.

We never showed our friends Grandpa's picture. Not that we were ashamed of him, but because we knew that the glamorous tales we told didn't go with the real thing. Our friends would have laughed at the picture, because Grandpa wasn't tall and stately like TV Indians. His hair wasn't in braids, but hung in stringy, gray strands on his neck and he was old. He was our great-grandfather, and he didn't live in a tepee, but all by himself in a part log, part tar-paper shack on the Rosebud Reservation in South Dakota. So when Grandpa came to visit us, I was so ashamed and embarrassed I could've died.

There are a lot of yippy poodles and other fancy little dogs in our neighborhood, but they usually barked singly at the mailman from the safety of their own yards. Now it sounded as if a whole pack of mutts were barking together in one place.

I got up and walked to the curb to see what the commotion was. About a block away I saw a crowd of little kids yelling, with the dogs yipping and growling around someone who was walking down the middle of the street.

I watched the group as it slowly came closer and saw that in the center of the strange procession was a man wearing a tall black hat. He'd pause now and then to peer at something in his hand and then at the houses on either side of the street. I felt cold and hot at the same time as I recognized the man. "Oh, no!" I whispered. "It's Grandpa!"

I stood on the curb, unable to move even though I wanted to run and hide. Then I got mad when I saw how the yippy dogs were growling and nipping at the old man's baggy pant legs and how wearily he poked them away with his cane. "Stupid mutts," I said as I ran to rescue Grandpa.

When I kicked and hollered at the dogs to get away, they put their tails between their legs and scattered. The kids ran to the curb where they watched me and the old man.

"Grandpa," I said and felt pretty dumb when my voice cracked. I reached for his beat-up old tin suitcase, which was tied shut with a rope. But he set it down right in the street and shook my hand.

"*Hau, Takoza,* Grandchild," he greeted me formally in Sioux.

All I could do was stand there with the whole neighborhood watching and shake the hand of the leather-brown old man. I saw how his gray hair straggled from under his big black hat, which had a drooping feather in its crown. His rumpled black suit hung like a sack over his stooped frame. As he shook my hand, his coat fell open to expose a bright-red, satin shirt with a beaded bolo tie under the collar. His get-up wasn't out of place on the reservation, but it sure was here, and I wanted to sink right through the pavement.

"Hi," I muttered with my head down. I tried to pull my hand away when I felt his bony hand trembling, and looked up to see fatigue in his face. I felt like crying. I couldn't think of anything to say so I picked up Grandpa's suitcase, took his arm, and guided him up the driveway to our house.

Mom was standing on the steps. I don't know how long she'd been watching, but her hand was over her mouth and she looked as if she couldn't believe what she saw. Then she ran to us.

"Grandpa," she gasped. "How in the world did you get here?"

She checked her move to embrace Grandpa and I remembered that such a display of affection is unseemly to the Sioux and would embarrass him.

"*Hau*, Marie," he said as he shook Mom's hand. She smiled and took his other arm.

As we supported him up the steps the door banged open and Cheryl came bursting out of the house. She was all smiles and was so obviously glad to see Grandpa that I was ashamed of how I felt.

"Grandpa!" she yelled happily. "You came to see us!"

Grandpa smiled and Mom and I let go of him as he stretched out his arms to my ten-year-old sister, who was still young enough to be hugged.

"*Wicincala*, little girl," he greeted her and then collapsed.

He had fainted. Mom and I carried him into her sewing room, where we had a spare bed.

After we had Grandpa on the bed Mom stood there helplessly patting his shoulder.

"Shouldn't we call the doctor, Mom?" I suggested, since she didn't seem to know what to do.

"Yes," she agreed with a sigh. "You make Grandpa comfortable, Martin."

I reluctantly moved to the bed. I knew Grandpa wouldn't want to have Mom undress him, but I didn't want to, either. He was so skinny and frail that his coat slipped off easily. When I loosened his tie and opened his shirt collar, I felt a small leather pouch that hung from a thong around his neck. I left it alone and moved to remove his boots. The scuffed old cowboy boots were tight and he moaned as I put pressure on his legs to jerk them off.

I put the boots on the floor and saw why they fit so tight. Each one was stuffed with money. I looked at the bills that lined the boots and started to ask about them, but Grandpa's eyes were closed again.

Mom came back with a basin of water. "The doctor thinks Grandpa is suffering from heat exhaustion," she explained as she bathed Grandpa's face. Mom gave a big sigh, *"Oh hinh,* Martin. How do you suppose he got here?"

We found out after the doctor's visit. Grandpa was angrily sitting up in bed while Mom tried to feed him some soup.

"Tonight you let Marie feed you, Grandpa," spoke my dad, who had gotten home from work just as the doctor was leaving. "You're not really sick," he said as he gently pushed Grandpa back against the pillows. "The doctor said you just got too tired and hot after your long trip."

Grandpa relaxed, and between sips of soup he told us of his journey. Soon after our visit to him Grandpa decided that he would like to see where his only living descendants lived and what our home was like. Besides, he admitted sheepishly, he was lonesome after we left.

I knew everybody felt as guilty as I did—especially Mom. Mom was all Grandpa had left. So even after she married my dad, who's a white man and teaches in the college in our city, and after Cheryl and I were born, Mom made sure that every summer we spent a week with Grandpa.

I never thought that Grandpa would be lonely after our visits, and none of us noticed how old and weak he had become. But Grandpa knew and so he came to us. He had ridden on buses for two and a half days. When he arrived in the city, tired and stiff from sitting for so long, he set out, walking, to find us.

He had stopped to rest on the steps of some building downtown and a policeman found him. The cop, according to Grandpa, was a good man who took him to the bus stop and waited until the bus came and told the driver to let Grandpa out at Bell View Drive. After Grandpa got off the bus, he started walking again. But he couldn't see the house numbers on the other side when he walked on the sidewalk so he walked in the middle of the street. That's when all the little kids and dogs followed him.

I knew everybody felt as bad as I did. Yet I was proud of this eighty-six-year-old man, who had never been away from the reservation, having the courage to travel so far alone.

"You found the money in my boots?" he asked Mom.

"Martin did," she answered, and roused herself to scold. "Grandpa, you shouldn't have carried so much money. What if someone had stolen it from you?"

Grandpa laughed. "I would've known if anyone tried to take the boots off my feet. The money is what I've saved for a long time—a hundred dollars—for my funeral. But you take it now to buy groceries so that I won't be a burden to you while I am here."

"That won't be necessary, Grandpa," Dad said. "We are honored to have you with us and you will never be a burden. I am only sorry that we never thought to bring you home with us this summer and spare you the discomfort of a long trip."

Grandpa was pleased. "Thank you," he answered. "But do not feel bad that you didn't bring me with you, for I would not have come then. It was not time." He said this in such a way that no one could argue with him. To Grandpa and the Sioux, he once told me, a thing would be done when it was the right time to do it and that's the way it was.

"Also," Grandpa went on, looking at me, "I have come because it is soon time for Martin to have the medicine bag."

We all knew what that meant. Grandpa thought he was going to die and he had to follow the tradition of his family to pass the medicine bag, along with its history, to the oldest male child.

"Even though the boy," he said still looking at me, "bears a white man's name, the medicine bag will be his."

I didn't know what to say. I had the same hot and cold feeling that I had when I first saw Grandpa in the street. The medicine bag was the dirty leather pouch I had found around his neck. "I could never wear such a thing," I almost said aloud. I thought of having my friends see it in gym class, at the swimming pool, and could imagine the smart things they would say. But I just swallowed hard and took a step toward the bed. I knew I would have to take it.

But Grandpa was tired. "Not now, Martin," he said, waving his hand in dismissal, "it is not time. Now I will sleep."

So that's how Grandpa came to be with us for two months. My friends kept asking to come see the old man, but I put them off. I told myself that I didn't want them laughing at Grandpa. But even as I made excuses I knew it wasn't Grandpa that I was afraid they'd laugh at.

Nothing bothered Cheryl about bringing her friends to see Grandpa. Every day after school started there'd be a crew of giggling little girls or round-eyed little boys crowded around the old man on the patio, where he'd gotten in the habit of sitting every afternoon.

Grandpa would smile in his gentle way and patiently answer their questions, or he'd tell them stories of brave warriors, ghosts, animals, and the kids listened in awed silence. Those little guys thought Grandpa was great.

Finally, one day after school, my friends came home with me because nothing I said stopped them. "We're going to see the great Indian of Bell View Drive," said Hank, who was supposed to be my best friend. "My brother has seen him three times so he oughta be well enough to see us."

When we got to my house Grandpa was sitting on the patio. He had on his red shirt, but today he also wore a fringed leather vest that was decorated with beads. Instead of his usual cowboy boots he had solidly beaded moccasins on his feet that stuck out of his black trousers. Of course, he had his old black hat on—he was seldom without it. But it had been brushed and the feather in the beaded headband was proudly erect, its tip a brighter white. His hair lay in silver strands over the red shirt collar.

I started just as my friends did and I heard one of them murmur, "Wow!"

Grandpa looked up and when his eyes met mine they twinkled as if he were laughing inside. He nodded to me and my face got all hot. I could tell that he had known all along I was afraid he'd embarrass me in front of my friends.

"*Hau, hoksilas,* boys," he greeted and held out his hand.

My buddies passed in a single file and shook his hand as I introduced them. They were so polite I almost laughed. "How, there, Grandpa," and even a "How-do-you-do, sir."

"You look fine, Grandpa," I said as the guys sat on the lawn chairs or on the patio floor.

"*Hanh,* yes," he agreed. "When I woke up this morning it seemed the right time to dress in the good clothes. I knew that my grandson would be bringing his friends."

"You guys want some lemonade or something?" I offered. No one answered. They were listening to Grandpa as he started telling how he'd killed the deer from which his vest was made.

Grandpa did most of the talking while my friends were there. I was so proud of him and amazed at how respectfully quiet my buddies were. Mom had to chase them home at suppertime. As they left they shook Grandpa's hand again and said to me:

"Martin, he's really great!"

"Yeah, man! Don't blame you for keeping him to yourself."

"Can we come back?"

But after they left, Mom said, "No more visitors for a while, Martin. Grandpa won't admit it, but his strength hasn't returned. He likes having company, but it tires him."

That evening Grandpa called me to his room before he went to sleep. "Tomorrow," he said, "when you come home, it will be time to give you the medicine bag."

I felt a hard squeeze from where my heart is supposed to be and was scared, but I answered, "OK, Grandpa."

All night I had weird dreams about thunder and lightning on a high hill. From a distance I heard the slow beat of a drum. When I woke up in the morning I felt as if I hadn't slept at all. At school it seemed as if the day would never end and, when it finally did, I ran home.

Grandpa was in his room, sitting on the bed. The shades were down and the place was dim and cool. I sat on the floor in front of Grandpa, but he didn't even look at me. After what seemed a long time he spoke.

"I sent your mother and sister away. What you will hear today is only for a man's ears. What you will receive is only for a man's hands." He fell silent and I felt shivers down my back.

"My father in his early manhood," Grandpa began, "made a vision quest to find a spirit guide for his life. You cannot understand how it was in that time, when the great Teton Sioux were first made to stay on the reservation. There was a strong need for guidance from *Wakantanka*, the Great Spirit. But too many of the young men were filled with despair and hatred. They thought it was hopeless to search for a vision when the glorious life was gone and only the hated confines of a reservation lay ahead. But my father held to the old ways.

"He carefully prepared for his quest with a purifying sweat bath and then he went alone to a high butte top to fast and pray. After three days he received his sacred dream—in which he found, after long searching, the white man's iron. He did not understand his vision of finding something belonging to the white people, for in that time they were the enemy. When he came down from the butte to cleanse himself at the stream below, he found the remains of a campfire and the broken shell of an iron kettle. This was a sign which reinforced his dream. He took a piece of the iron for his medicine bag, which he had made of elk skin years before, to prepare for his quest.

"He returned to his village, where he told his dream to the wise old men of the tribe. They gave him the name Iron Shell, but neither did they understand the meaning of the dream. This first Iron Shell kept the piece of iron with him at all times and believed it gave him protection from the evils of those unhappy days.

"Then a terrible thing happened to Iron Shell. He and several other young men were taken from their homes by the soldiers and sent far away to a white man's boarding school. He was angry and lonesome for his parents and the young girl he had wed before he was taken away. At first Iron Shell resisted the teachers' attempts to change him and he did not try to learn. One day it was his turn to work in the school's blacksmith shop. As he walked into the place he knew that his medicine had brought him there to learn and work with the white man's iron.

"Iron Shell became a blacksmith and worked at the trade when he returned to the reservation. All of his life he treasured the medicine bag. When he was old, and I was a man, he gave it to me, for no one made the vision quest anymore."

Grandpa quit talking and I stared in disbelief as he covered his face with his hands. His shoulders were shaking with quiet sobs and I looked away until he began to speak again.

"I kept the bag until my son, your mother's father, was a man and had to leave us to fight in the war across the ocean. I gave him the bag, for I believed it would protect him in battle, but he did not take it with him. He was afraid that he would lose it. He died in a faraway place."

Again Grandpa was still and I felt his grief around me.

"My son," he went on after clearing his throat, "had only a daughter and it is not proper for her to know of these things."

He unbuttoned his shirt, pulled out the leather pouch, and lifted it over his head. He held it in his hand, turning it over and over as if memorizing how it looked.

"In the bag," he said as he opened it and removed two objects, "is the broken shell of the iron kettle, a pebble from the butte, and a piece of the sacred sage." He held the pouch upside down and dust drifted down.

"After the bag is yours you must put a piece of prairie sage within and never open it again until you pass it on to your son." He replaced the pebble and the piece of iron, and tied the bag.

I stood up, somehow knowing I should. Grandpa slowly rose from the bed and stood upright in front of me, holding the bag before my face. I closed my eyes and waited for him to slip it over my head. But he spoke.

"No, you need not wear it." He placed the soft leather bag in my right hand and closed my other hand over it. "It would not be right to wear it in this time and place where no one will understand. Put it safely away until you are again on the reservation. Wear it then, when you replace the sacred sage."

Grandpa turned and sat again on the bed. Wearily he leaned his head against the pillow. "Go," he said, "I will sleep now."

"Thank you, Grandpa," I said softly and left with the bag in my hands.

That night Mom and Dad took Grandpa to the hospital. Two weeks later I stood alone on the lonely prairie of the reservation and put the sacred sage in my medicine bag.

EXERCISE 1 ▶ **Responding to a Story**

What's your personal response to "The Medicine Bag"? How many stars would you give it? (Use four stars as the highest rating and one star as the lowest.) Draw the number of stars in your journal. Then write two or three sentences in your journal about your personal response to the characters and story events. What do you think of Martin? How did you feel about the way he treated his great-grandfather? Did events in the story keep your interest? Would you like to read another story like this one?

Reading for Understanding

After reading some stories, you may stop at your personal response. But sometimes you need to go beyond it. For instance, you may want to explain to a friend why you want him or her to read a story. Or, you may have a school assignment to read a story and analyze it. Then you'll need to have some understanding of the basic parts, or elements, of a story. These are the characters, the plot, the setting, and the meaning.

BASIC ELEMENTS OF STORIES
CHARACTERS. The *characters* of a story are its actors—the people, animals, or creatures who play parts. You get to know characters in a story the same way you get to know people in real life. You observe what they say, what they think, and what they do. You also notice how they look and how other people respond to them.
PLOT. *Plot* is what happens in the story—the events that unfold from the beginning to the end. The plot almost always presents a *conflict,* or problem, that the main character has to overcome.
SETTING. Where and when a story's events occur make up its *setting.* In some stories, the setting causes things to happen. In others, the events might happen anywhere.
THEME. The *theme,* or main idea, of a story is what it tells you about people or life. The theme of a story about a village hit by an earthquake could be "Hard times can bring out the best in people."

EXERCISE 2 ▶ Analyzing the Elements of a Story

How well do you understand the basic parts of a story? Read back over "The Medicine Bag" on pages 280–291. Then, with two or three classmates, answer the following questions.

1. Who are the two main characters? Imagine telling a friend about them. What word or two would you use to describe each one?
2. What conflict, or problem, does Martin face?
3. Briefly describe what happens at the most exciting point (the climax) in the story.
4. What is the setting? Why does this setting cause events in the story to happen?
5. The theme, or main idea, of this story focuses on the way a boy reacts to his great-grandfather. Tell the theme of the story in your own words.

WRITING ASSIGNMENT

PART 1:

Reading and Responding to a Story

Choose a story, either one that you would like to read or one your teacher suggests. First, read it and check your own response. How do you feel about this story? Then, look at it more closely. Use the questions in Exercise 2 to analyze the story's basic elements.

Planning a Character Analysis

In a literature class, you are often asked to analyze a story or some part of it. A *character analysis* is one type of story analysis.

Studying a Character

When you analyze a character in a story, you try to find out what makes that character "tick." In your everyday life, you do this all the time. You pick up clues about the people around you by noticing what they do and say. To pick up clues about a character in a story, you do the same thing. These are the things you should especially watch for.

- Notice how the character **looks.** Does his or her appearance affect what happens?
- Watch how the character **behaves.** Does he or she take action to face the conflict? What do the character's actions show about what the character feels inside? Are the character's actions and feelings related in any way?
- Listen to what the character **says.** Does the character say how he or she feels? What kind of language does the character use?
- Notice the character's **thoughts.** What goes on in the character's mind? What does that tell you about him or her? Do any thoughts keep popping up over and over again?

As you read a story closely, take notes. Write down details that show how a character feels or thinks. Beside each note, write your own reaction or evaluation (for example: "he's embarrassed"; "cares what his friends think"; "shows honesty"; "proud"). On the next page are some notes one writer made about Martin.

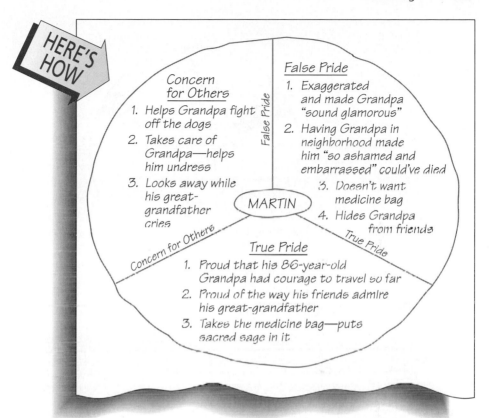

HERE'S HOW

False Pride

Concern
for Others
1. Helps Grandpa fight
   off the dogs
2. Takes care of
   Grandpa—helps
   him undress
3. Looks away while
   his great-
   grandfather
   cries

False Pride
1. Exaggerated
   and made Grandpa
   "sound glamorous"
2. Having Grandpa in
   neighborhood made
   him "so ashamed and
   embarrassed" could've died
3. Doesn't want
   medicine bag
4. Hides Grandpa
   from friends

MARTIN

Concern for Others

True Pride
1. Proud that his 86-year-old
   Grandpa had courage to travel so far
2. Proud of the way his friends admire
   his great-grandfather
3. Takes the medicine bag—puts
   sacred sage in it.

True Pride

CRITICAL THINKING
Analyzing a Character

When you *analyze* something, you look at its parts. This analysis helps you understand something better. When you analyze a character, you think about what the character says, does, thinks, and so on.

One way to analyze a character is to create a character wheel. To make one, first think about the character overall. What are his or her *major traits,* or characteristics? Choose two or three traits that you think are the most important. Then, look back through the story to find details that show those traits.

The Here's How above is an example of an analysis using a character wheel. Here are the parts of the wheel.

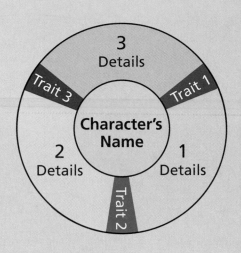

 CRITICAL THINKING EXERCISE:
Analyzing a Character

Work with some classmates to analyze a character—perhaps Grandpa in "The Medicine Bag," a character in another story, or a character from one of your favorite TV shows. Work together to make a character wheel. Identify two or three character traits. Then have one person draw the wheel and write the traits on the spokes. As the group identifies details to go with each trait, one person can write them in the wheel between the spokes. What kind of person is this character? Can you write one or two sentences to summarize what you think?

EXERCISE 3 ▶ **Speaking and Listening: Creating and Analyzing a Character**

Make up your own character. Then tell a small group of classmates about your character. What does your character look like? How does he or she speak? walk? dress? Suppose the character takes your place at school today. How does he or she behave? Do your classmates like the character? Tell why. Now, listen to your classmates speak. What do you learn about their characters?

WRITING ASSIGNMENT

PART 2:
Choosing a Character to Analyze

Choose a character from the story you read for Writing Assignment, Part 1 (page 293). The character should be one you either liked or disliked very much. Next, make a character wheel like the one on page 295. Find two or three traits for your character to put on the wheel. Between the spokes, write details that support those traits.

Developing a Writing Plan

Thinking About Purpose and Audience.   The *purpose* of a character analysis is to find out what kind of person a story character is. You do this so that you and your readers can understand a character better. When you know a story character in this way, you can often understand yourself or others better. The *audience* for the analysis is usually your teacher and classmates. You may also want to share your analysis with a friend or family member.

Stating Your Main Idea.   Think about how you describe someone new in school to friends who have never met him or her. Usually, you describe a few major traits of that person. You may say, for example, that the person seems lonely or cheerful or very shy. In a character analysis, these traits become your *main idea.*

For your character analysis, choose one or two, perhaps three, major traits about your character. (It's better to look at fewer traits and explain them clearly.) Then write a sentence about them. That sentence is your *main idea statement.* If your character changes, you may need two or more sentences to express your main idea. Here's the main idea statement for the character wheel on page 295. The writer uses only two of the traits on his wheel.

EXAMPLE   At first, Martin feels false pride. However, it becomes a true pride after he learns more about his great-grandfather and his heritage.

Organizing Your Information. One way to organize a character analysis is to decide which trait is most important and start or end with it. Another way is to treat the traits chronologically, in the order in which they appear in the story. Just be sure that you don't mix the details that support one trait with the details for another trait.

To develop a plan for your character analysis

- think about your purpose and audience
- identify some traits of the character
- look for details from the story to explain the traits
- decide what traits you will discuss in your paper
- write a main idea statement about those traits

 PART 3:
Developing a Writing Plan

Think about the character you chose for Writing Assignment, Part 2 (page 297). Review the traits on your character wheel and choose one or two that you think are very important. Write a main idea statement about them. Then decide how you will organize your analysis. List the traits and supporting details in the order you will use them.

Writing Your First Draft

The Parts of a Character Analysis

Now it's time to write your character analysis and turn your notes into sentences and paragraphs. Your paper should be four or five paragraphs long. It will be organized like a composition.

- First paragraph: Name the title and author of the story and tell what character you're analyzing. State your main idea in one or two sentences.
- Middle (or body) paragraphs: In each paragraph, write about one trait and the details that explain it. Start a new paragraph for each trait.
- Last paragraph: Sum up the main points of your paper and restate your main idea.

☞ **REFERENCE NOTE:** For more information on the parts of a composition, see pages 104–110.

Here's a model character analysis of Martin, the main character of "The Medicine Bag." It tells about two of Martin's character traits. As you read, notice how each trait has details to support it.

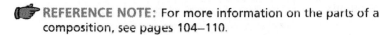

A WRITER'S MODEL

The Discovery of True Pride

INTRODUCTION
Author/Title
Character
Main idea

The main character in Virginia Driving Hawk Sneve's "The Medicine Bag" is a young boy named Martin. One of the strongest traits of this character is his pride. At the beginning of the story it is a false, bragging kind of pride. But at the end of the story it is a true pride—in his heritage.

BODY
First trait

At the beginning of the story, Martin admits that he and his sister always brag about their Sioux "grandpa," who is actually their great-grandfather. For Martin, though, this pride in a way isn't sincere. He exaggerates and makes his great-grandfather sound like Indians in the movies and on TV.

Details—
Martin's actions

When Grandpa actually walks into his neighborhood, Martin is embarrassed. He says that he feels hot and cold all over and is "so ashamed and embarrassed" he could die. When Martin holds his head down and pulls his hand away, he shows how his pride in his great-grandfather is not real. He is proud only of his pretend "grandpa," not the real one.

Details—
Martin's words and actions

How Martin feels about the medicine bag also shows his false pride. His great-grandfather has come to give the medicine bag to Martin. But Martin doesn't want it. He doesn't want his friends to see him wearing it.

Details—
Martin's thoughts

Second trait
Details—
Martin's actions

He doesn't even want them to see his great-grandfather. They ask to, but Martin won't let them. But one day they go right into Martin's house anyway. Grandpa seems to have known they were coming. He has put on his best clothes, and he is impressive in his beaded vest and moccasins. When Martin sees that his friends think Grandpa is great, he begins to feel a true pride.

Details—
Martin's thoughts

Details—
Martin's thoughts
and actions

The next day, Grandpa tells Martin about the medicine bag. He explains how his father had passed it on to him. Then he asks Martin to find a piece of sacred sage to add to the medicine bag and save it for his own son. As Martin listens to the story, he begins to understand his heritage and be proud of it. Soon after that Grandpa dies. At the end of the story, Martin stands alone on the prairie and puts the sacred sage in his medicine bag. He is now proud of the medicine bag and what it means to his family.

CONCLUSION

Main idea in different words

Martin always had pride. But as he comes to know his great-grandfather, that pride changes. It goes from a false pride to a sincere pride and feeling of honor in his heritage.

WRITING NOTE

Use details from the story to support the traits of your character. But don't just tell your readers what happens in the story. Many of your readers may already know the story, and it's boring to read something you already know.

Peanuts reprinted by permission of United Feature Syndicate, Inc.

A Framework for a Character Analysis

On the next page is a framework for a character analysis like the one about Martin. You may want to use this framework when you write your own analysis.

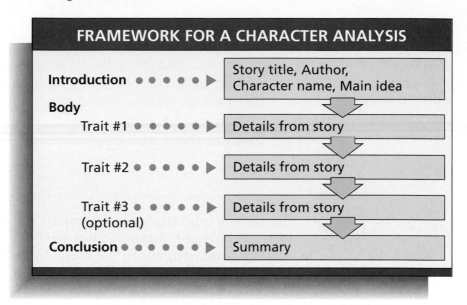

FRAMEWORK FOR A CHARACTER ANALYSIS

Introduction • • • • • ▶ | Story title, Author, Character name, Main idea

Body

   Trait #1 • • • • • ▶ | Details from story

   Trait #2 • • • • • ▶ | Details from story

   Trait #3 • • • • • ▶ | Details from story
   (optional)

Conclusion • • • • • • ▶ | Summary

WRITING ASSIGNMENT

PART 4:
Writing Your First Draft

You've already done most of the work for your analysis. Now, use your main idea statement and the details on your character wheel to write a rough draft of a character analysis. Remember that you'll have a chance to make changes in your analysis later. It doesn't have to be perfect on the first try.

Evaluating and Revising

To evaluate your analysis, use the following guide. Ask yourself each question in the left-hand column. If you find a problem, use the ideas in the right-hand column to fix it.

EVALUATING AND REVISING A CHARACTER ANALYSIS

EVALUATION GUIDE	REVISION TECHNIQUE
1 Does the introduction identify the story's author and title? Does it name the character who is analyzed?	**Add** the missing information.
2 Does the introduction state the main idea?	Review your character wheel and **add** a main idea statement.
3 Does the body have enough details from the story to support each character trait?	**Add** direct quotations and other story details that describe the words, thoughts, actions, and appearance of the character.
4 Does the conclusion sum up the main points and restate the main idea?	**Add** one or two sentences or rewrite sentences in the conclusion.

EXERCISE 4 ▶ **Analyzing a Writer's Revisions**

On the next page is a first draft of the first paragraph of the analysis of Martin. With two or three classmates, figure out why the writer made the changes. Then answer the questions that follow.

The main character in Virginia
Driving Hawk Sneve's ~~story~~ "The Medicine Bag" is a young   **replace**
boy. named Martin. One of the strongest traits of this   **add**

character is his pride. At the beginning of

the story it is a false, bragging kind of

pride. But at the end of the story it is a

true pride—in his heritage. ~~That's because~~   **cut**

~~he'd gotten to know his great-grandfather~~

~~and learned about the medicine bag.~~

1. Why does the writer replace the word *story* with *"The Medicine Bag"*?
2. In the same sentence, what words does the writer add after the word *boy*? What important information do the new words add to the paragraph?
3. Why does the writer cut out the last sentence? [Hint: Where does this information belong?]

| WRITING ASSIGNMENT | PART 5: **Evaluating and Revising Your Character Analysis** |

A first draft is like a caterpillar; a revision is the butterfly. Reread your own first draft, and think of ways to "make it fly." The questions from the evaluating and revising chart on page 303 will help you.

Proofreading and Publishing

Proofreading.   You've "given wings" to your paper. Now it's time to take care of the finishing details. Read over your paper at least twice to check for mistakes.

 COMPUTER NOTE: Your word-processing program may allow you to add character names from the story to a user dictionary so the names will not be flagged as errors during a spelling check.

MECHANICS HINT

Using Quotation Marks

Use quotation marks around the title of the story. And when you quote directly from a story, put quotation marks around the words. Do this even when a character isn't speaking.

EXAMPLES   The main character in Virginia Driving Hawk Sneve's **"The Medicine Bag"** is a young boy named Martin.
He says that he feels hot and cold all over and is **"so ashamed and embarrassed"** he could die.

 REFERENCE NOTE: For more information on quotation marks, see pages 737–744.

Publishing.   With your teacher's help, plan some special ways to share your papers. Here are two ideas:

- Create a "movie poster" for the story. Include quotations from your paper. Place the posters in your classroom.

■ Get together with a classmate and share your papers. Write a short dialogue between one character from your story and one character from your partner's story.

WRITING ASSIGNMENT

PART 6:
Proofreading and Publishing Your Character Analysis

You're at the finish line. Proofread your paper and make sure it has no errors and is clear to your readers. Use one of the ideas on page 305 and above, or another idea of your own, to share your paper with others.

 Reflecting on Your Writing

You may want to add your character analysis to your **portfolio.** If so, date your paper and include it with a brief reflection based on the following questions.

■ How did you choose which character traits to focus on?
■ Which was harder for you, expressing your main idea or finding story details to support it? Explain.
■ Did writing a character analysis help you better understand yourself or others? If so, how?

A STUDENT MODEL

David Street, a student at West Ridge Middle School in Austin, Texas, writes about a well-known short story in his paper. David recommends "asking yourself questions about the story" and "working through many drafts before the final copy." As you read his paper, ask yourself if David makes you want to read O. Henry's story "After Twenty Years."

Evaluation of "After Twenty Years"
by David Street

I enjoyed reading the story "After Twenty Years" by
O. Henry because of the surprising twist at the end. My
attention was quickly absorbed when the policeman, Jimmy
Wells, notices his old friend Bob and starts carrying on a
conversation with him. Bob's quick talking in the beginning
of the conversation caught my attention, and his unusual
and suspicious story kept me listening. O. Henry sets up the
meeting with an appropriate setting, which helped to attract
my attention. He describes the weather as "chilly gusts of
wind with a taste of rain in them," and he makes the streets
nearly vacant. This scenery gives an eerie feeling to help
elaborate on the mystery. The characters are described
enough to set up the reader but not too much. He describes
Bob as having "a pale, square-jawed face with keen eyes, and
a little white scar near his right eyebrow." Then he tells how
his "scarfpin was a large diamond, oddly set." These details
give the reader a subtle clue that Bob might be some sort of
a gangster. The plot is well thought out and fairly easy to
follow. It gives the reader many clues that lead up to the
surprise ending. Overall, I enjoyed "After Twenty Years"
because of the suspense and the ending. I would recommend
it to anyone who enjoys unexpected twists in stories.

WRITING WORKSHOP

A Comparison of Two Characters

Sometimes you write an analysis of one character. But many times you can understand one character better by comparing him or her to another character.

When you compare two characters, you start by looking at their similarities. How are they alike? Sometimes you may also contrast them. How are they different?

When you write a paper or paragraph comparing two characters, you can organize it in one of two ways.

1. Present everything you have to say about one character, and then present everything you have to say about the other character, or
2. Present one detail about both characters, then a second detail about both characters, then a third detail about both characters, and so on.

Here's a writer's model comparing Martin in "The Medicine Bag" with the main character in "The All-American Slurp."

Martin, a young boy whose ancestry is part Native American, is the main character in Virginia Driving Hawk Sneve's "The Medicine Bag." At the beginning of the story, he is embarrassed by his family background. Because his great-grandfather, called "Grandpa," doesn't look like the Indians in the movies, Martin is afraid his friends will laugh at him. The Chinese American girl in Lensey Namioka's "The All-American Slurp" is also embarrassed by her family background. At the beginning of the story she and her family are invited out to their first dinner in America. She feels her family has "disgraced" themselves because they don't know how to eat American food.

Both Martin and the Chinese American girl learn to be proud of their own families and heritage. Martin discovers that his friends really think Grandpa is great. He also listens to Grandpa tell about the medicine bag and begins to understand his heritage. The Chinese American girl learns that their American friends have as much trouble with chopsticks as her family had with the celery. She even discovers that the embarrassing sounds her family make when they eat soup, "Shloop, shloop," aren't so unusual. Her friend Meg makes the same sound when she drinks a milkshake. The Chinese American girl, like Martin, is no longer embarrassed by her heritage.

Thinking It Over

1. In what ways are Martin and the Chinese American girl alike?
2. When you compare two things, you sometimes contrast (show differences) as well. Does this paper show any differences between the two characters? Can you think of any obvious differences?
3. How is this comparison paper organized? Did the writer use the first method or the second one (page 308)?

Writing a Comparison of Two Characters

 Prewriting.   Choose a character from another story to compare with the character in your analysis. The two characters
should have something in common. They may face a similar
conflict or be the same age. In the writer's model, both characters learn to be proud of their heritage.

Develop a chart like the one below. List the main traits
the characters have in common. If there are important differences between them, list those too.

Martin	Chinese American girl
1. embarrassed by great-grandfather (false pride)	1. embarrassed by family
2. accepts his heritage (sincere pride)	2. accepts her heritage

Writing, Evaluating, and Revising.   Follow the model on
pages 308–309 to write your paper. First, compare one quality of each character. Then, compare the next quality. You
can also discuss differences between the characters.
Include details from each story to support your main points.

Ask a classmate to read your draft and to tell you in his
or her own words how your two characters are alike. Take
notes on anything your reader seems confused about. Then,
make changes in your paper to clarify those points.

Proofreading and Publishing.   Correct any mistakes in
your paper, and then share it with your classmates. Did
anyone else write about either of your characters?

If you include this paper in your **portfolio,** date it and
add answers to these questions: Did comparing characters
help you understand the stories better? In what ways?

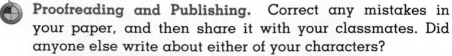

MAKING CONNECTIONS

INFORMING THROUGH EVALUATION

Writing a Review

You have learned to analyze a story character by looking closely at his or her actions and words. People who write reviews of movies, books, or restaurants use similar methods. For example, a restaurant reviewer analyzes the quality of the food and service and makes an evaluation.

McHenry's Steak House

Subject

Detail 1

Main idea

When you enter McHenry's Steak House, you're greeted warmly. The hosts make you feel as though you're a friend who has come to eat in their home. It's obvious from the start: This restaurant delivers more than just excellent food.

Detail 2

The food at McHenry's *is* excellent. Especially good are the fresh swordfish and thick, juicy burgers. They are seasoned well and served with a big tossed salad and fresh vegetable. And if you aren't in the mood for these, try McHenry's special pizza for one. It's delicious!

Detail 3

Summing up

Prices at McHenry's are low. My meal came to only $8.95. This is a restaurant that you'll return to again and again. The people at McHenry's serve great food in a friendly way, without taking a big bite out of your budget.

Now, try your hand at writing a restaurant review. Pick a restaurant that you know well. It doesn't have to be a fancy one. You might write about a fast-food restaurant or even the school cafeteria!

Think of details to support your opinions. Be specific about the food, the service, the prices, and the appearance of the restaurant itself. Your audience will be your classmates. Give them a good "picture" of the restaurant. Through your writing, persuade them either to go to this restaurant or to avoid it!

WRITING ACROSS THE CURRICULUM

Analyzing Great Characters in History

You can use what you have learned about analyzing characters in literature to learn more about real people in history. You usually don't have any way of finding out what historical figures were thinking because you can't read their minds. But you can find out some of the things they said and did, as well as what other people said or wrote about them.

Pick some historical figure you have always been interested in—Abraham Lincoln, Pocahontas, Cleopatra, Martin Luther King, Jr. It's your decision. Then use your history book, encyclopedia articles, and biographies to catch up on the figure's personality. Was honesty really one of Lincoln's important character traits? Was Cleopatra a strong leader? Was Eleanor Roosevelt (pictured below) really one of the most active first ladies of all time? Decide which character trait seems to stand out or be most interesting in the figure you've chosen. Then choose one of the following ways to illustrate that trait:

1. Draw a picture showing the historical figure doing something that shows the trait.
2. Pretend you are the historical figure and write an entry in your diary. Use the figure's thoughts to show his or her character trait.
3. Write a dialogue between the historical figure you've chosen and someone else. Have your figure say something that shows the character trait.
4. Write a paragraph identifying the trait and telling about something the historical figure did that illustrates the trait

10 WRITING A REPORT: EXPOSITION

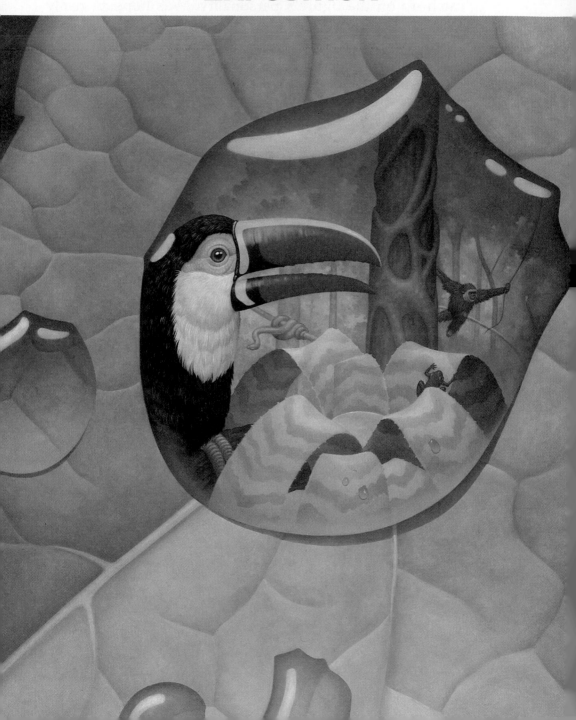

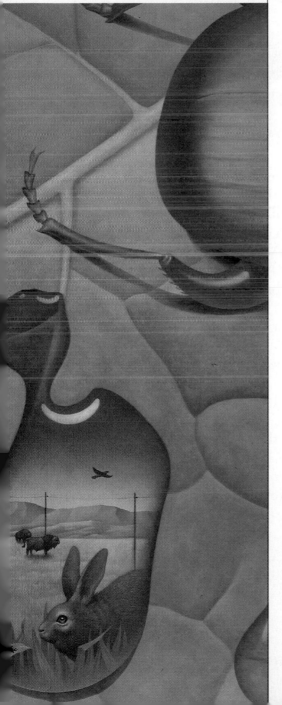

Exploring Your World

The **world** around you is full of things to **explore** and learn about. Many of these wonders you'll be able to explore for yourself. Others you'll explore through the eyes of someone who wrote about them.

Writing and You. Reports are summaries of knowledge. Scientists write reports to tell what they know about the environment. Employees share their knowledge of the workplace world in business reports. And we learn about the most distant planets from what is written about them. Reports are everywhere—in e-mail messages, books, magazines, newspapers, and on the Internet. What is the last thing you read a report about?

As You Read. Reports are based on fact. As you read the following report about the cheetah, look for the facts that help you learn more about this great animal.

Detail of poster for the National Forum on BioDiversity, Robert Goldstrom (1986).

from MEET-A-

Cheetah

BY FRED JOHNSON

All members of the cat family can move fast when they really want to. But there is one who can easily leave all the others far behind. In fact, he can leave any animal far behind. Nothing can outrun a cheetah (CHEE-tuh).

Cheetahs are found in Africa, in India, Afghanistan, and Arabia. Some scientists think that the cheetah is between the cat and dog families. They have the body build of dogs rather than cats.

Their claws, like dogs', are dull. And they cannot be pulled back into the paw. Their claws are of little use in fighting or killing. But like all cats, cheetahs have one claw that is very sharp and dangerous. This is a claw on the inside of the foreleg, something like your thumb. It can be pulled into the paw.

The cheetah's sense of smell is poor, but its eyesight is keen. Its fur is brownish-yellow with black or brown "polka dots." A clear black line runs from the inside corner of each eye down the side of the nose. A full-grown cheetah may measure as much as 7 feet long with his tail outstretched. How tall is the door to your room? A cheetah may be as long as your door is tall.

One surprising fact about the cheetah is that it can be tamed easily. Once it has become used to people, it seems to enjoy being a member of a human family.

The cheetah is also one of the few big cats which purr when happy, just as a pet cat does. However, its purr is far louder and sounds more like an engine.

But the most amazing thing about cheetahs is their speed. They have been timed at speeds up to 80 miles an hour! Daniel P. Mannix is an animal owner and trainer. He tells of a cheetah which saw a man going down the road on a motorcycle. The cheetah went out to look at this strange, noisy animal. The man speeded up to 60 miles an hour—and the cheetah ran along beside him!

READER'S RESPONSE

1. What facts about the cheetah seem unusual or surprising to you? Would you like to read more about the animal? Why?
2. A *fact* can be something you observe directly—for example, that your cat has gray fur and likes milk. In your journal jot down some facts you know about a cat, dog, or some other pet.
3. Would you like to have a cheetah for a pet? Why?

WRITER'S CRAFT

4. What facts did you learn about the cheetah's length? about its speed?
5. One source for this report is an animal expert named Daniel P. Mannix. What information does he give about the cheetah?

"Nothing can outrun a cheetah..."

Ways to Develop a Report

Reports come in many forms—in magazines and newspapers, or on television news shows or science programs like *NOVA*. You can even get them by telephone if you call for a weather report. All these kinds of reports give you information, developed in different ways. Here are some ways to develop information in writing.

- in a history report, telling about how the Spanish settled St. Augustine
- in an essay for English class, telling about the life of a civil rights leader
- in a travel brochure, describing the Anasazi cliff dwellings
- in a gardening article for a newspaper, describing a ruby-throated hummingbird
- in a report for science class, comparing cheetahs with house cats
- in a report for a nature club, explaining how to tell the difference between two similar-looking lizards
- in a builder's report, estimating how long it will take to frame a house
- in an article for a consumer magazine, reporting on durability tests of several brands of mountain bikes

In this chapter, you'll learn how to gather information about a subject—information stored away in sources like books and computer databases. To write your report, you'll unlock and use these storehouses of information.

LOOKING AHEAD

In the main assignment in this chapter, you will write a short, informative report. You'll need to choose a subject and find information about it. Then, you'll need to write a report that

- gives the information you found
- uses a variety of sources
- lists the sources where you found the information

Writing a Report

 *Prewriting*

Choosing and Narrowing a Subject

What causes earthquakes? Do vampire bats really exist? When did dogs first become pets? Who invented tab-top cans for carbonated soda? Writing a report is your chance to learn about an interesting subject.

Choosing Your Subject

To choose a subject, think about your interests. What kinds of books or magazines do you like to read? What kinds of subjects do you like hearing about on television programs like *NOVA* or *National Geographic World*? Do you have special collections of things like stamps or insects? What subjects do you enjoy talking, thinking, and wondering about?

Here are some ideas for general subjects. Try to think of three or four other subjects you'd like to learn more about.

dinosaurs	ancient kingdoms
pyramids	bats
early explorers of the United States	Native Americans the Old West
the Civil War	exploring space

Narrowing Your Subject

You probably realize that there's a great deal of information about a broad subject like dinosaurs—hundreds of books, articles, and TV programs. That's way too much information to try to sift through and include in a short report. You need to narrow broad subjects by focusing on just one part. The subjects you've just read include many smaller *topics*. On the next page you'll find some of them.

why dinosaurs
   disappeared
the pyramids
   of Egypt
the Spanish explorer
   Ponce de León
photography in
   the Civil War

the ancient kingdom
   of Kush
vampire bats
the Cherokee
   "Trail of Tears"
African American cow-
   boys in the Old West
the first moon landing

As you narrow your subject, remember that any broad subject includes many smaller topics. For example, the subject "dinosaurs" also includes these topics: renaming the brontosaurus, famous dinosaur discoveries, and forms of protection against enemies.

Not all topics work equally well for a report. Here are some questions that will help you figure out if your topic will work for a report.

- Can you find facts about your topic? (*Facts* are information that experts have checked and believe is true.)
- Can you find enough information about your topic? (If your topic is *too* narrow, you may not find enough information.)
- Will you have enough time to find the information you need? (If you write a letter to get information, how long will it take to get an answer?)
- Is your topic interesting enough to hold your attention? (You'll put a great deal of time and effort into your report. If you like your topic, you'll be more willing to put the time and effort into it.)

EXERCISE 1 ▶ **Choosing Topics for a Report**

What's a good topic? Here are some topics for a report. Get together with one or two classmates and discuss each topic. Try to decide which topics are suitable for a short report. Can you find facts about the topic from sources like books or videotapes? Is it narrow enough? Is it appropriate for a report?

1. robots for surgery
2. why I like soccer
3. space—the final frontier
4. Egyptian mummies
5. Sarah Winnemucca, a Native American hero
6. the history of horses
7. Mexican birthday customs
8. my most exciting birthday
9. the killer fish—the piranha
10. schools in Japan

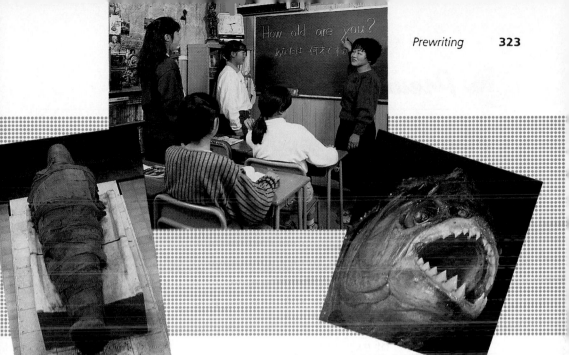

WRITING ASSIGNMENT	PART 1:

WRITING
ASSIGNMENT ➤ **Choosing a Topic for Your Report**

What would you like to know more about? Think of a subject you're interested in. Then, narrow it to a topic for your report. Check your library or the World Wide Web to be sure it's a topic you can find facts about.

WRITING NOTE   Writing a report takes more time than one or two days. Don't try to do most of your report in one weekend. To do a good job in the time you have, make a schedule now. Then, stick to it. In your schedule, allow time to do five things:

1. Find information about your topic.
2. Take notes about the information.
3. Write your first draft.
4. Evaluate and revise your draft.
5. Proofread and publish your report.

Prewriting

Planning Your Report

When is the last time you planned a surprise for someone? You probably planned it carefully ahead of time so that it would work out just right. If you plan your report ahead, it should work out right, too.

Thinking About Audience and Purpose

The purpose for writing a report is to discover information and share it with other people. Most of the information in a report is made up of facts. Some information may be the opinions of experts on the topic.

Your teacher and classmates will probably be the first readers of your report. (On page 346, you'll find ideas you can use to share your report with other readers.) As you write your report, think about three things.

1. What information will interest your readers?
2. What do your readers already know?
3. What information do your readers need?

Reports are boring to readers if they already know all the facts you give, so look for new or unusual information about your topic. Try to give your readers all the information they need to understand the topic. If you think they may not know a word, tell them what it means. If they may not understand how something works, explain it to them.

   **Deciding About Audience and Purpose**

On the next page is some information you might put in a report on giant snakes. You are writing this report to give both your teacher and classmates facts about the snakes. Which information would you put in your report? Why wouldn't you include the other information?

1. *Giant* means "big."
2. One giant snake, the anaconda, can be as long as thirty feet.
3. I hate snakes.
4. Boa constrictor babies are born live; python babies are hatched from eggs.
5. There are many kinds of snakes.

▲ **boa constrictor** babies are born live.

python babies are hatched from eggs ▼

Asking Questions

What would you like to know about your topic? What would your readers like to know? Make a list of questions that will help you find this information. First try the *5W-How?* questions—*Who? What? When? Where? Why? How?* Which questions you ask will depend on your topic. For a report on Africanized honeybees, also called "killer" bees, you might ask these questions.

What are Africanized honeybees?
When will they come here?
Where do they come from?
Why are they called "killer" bees?
How are they different from native bees?
How can they be stopped?

Reminder

If you don't know much about your topic, get some general information about it first. Read one or two encyclopedia articles about your topic, or do a search on the World Wide Web. You might also talk to other people who know about the topic. Then make your list of questions.

WRITING
ASSIGNMENT

PART 2:
**Asking Questions About
Your Topic**

What do you want to know about your topic? What do you think your readers will want to know? Make a list of *5W-How?* questions that you'll answer in your report.

Finding Sources

Reading and Viewing.   It's a good idea to have at least three sources for your report. When you use more sources, you can combine facts and opinions in new ways.

The library is a good place to start your hunt for information. It's full of *print sources* like encyclopedias, books, magazines and newspapers, and pamphlets. And don't forget about *nonprint sources* like videotapes, audiotapes, slides, and CD-ROMs. (For help in finding and using library sources, see pages 848–854.)

Other places to look for information depend on your topic. You might check radio and TV guides for programs that will give you some information. You can also find up-to-date information on the World Wide Web. Here are some ideas for other places to look for sources.

museums	hospitals	bookstores
government offices	planetariums	zoos

 REFERENCE NOTE: For help with finding information using online catalogs, databases, and the Internet, see pages 849 and 853.

Interviewing. Here's an idea for a nonprint source. Interview someone who's an expert on your topic, perhaps a teacher, someone at a zoo or museum, or even a parent or high school student. It's only important that this person know a great deal about your topic. Suppose your topic is "mountain bikes." Your expert might be a bike store owner or a high school student who has taken trips on a mountain bike.

Before the interview, do some reading about your topic. Make a list of questions to ask. Write each question at the top of a sheet of paper. To avoid *yes* or *no* answers, ask questions that begin with *Who, What, When, Where, Why,* and *How.* (For more information about interviewing, see page 841.)

EXERCISE 3▶ **Speaking and Listening: Interviewing**

Practice your interviewing skills with a classmate. Ask a classmate to name a special interest. Make out a list of *5W-How?* questions about it. Then, interview your classmate about that interest. When you finish, change places and let your classmate interview you.

WRITING NOTE
Not all sources will be helpful to you. To judge how useful a source is, ask yourself these questions about it.

■ *Is the information up-to-date?* Some topics simply need more up-to-date information than others. If your topic is "Ponce de León, early sixteenth-century Spanish explorer," you may not need many recent books and articles. If your topic is "robots for people who have disabilities," you will need new information.

■ *Can you trust the information?* Some sources give a truer picture of the facts than others. You can usually trust reference books more than the magazines you buy at the grocery store checkout stand. Can you tell why?

Listing Sources

The next step is to list each of your sources. Then, give each source a number. You'll use these *source numbers* later when you take notes. There are several different ways to list sources. The chart on the next page shows the way the Modern Language Association recommends.

MLA GUIDE FOR LISTING SOURCES

Books. Give this information: author, title, city of publication, publisher, and copyright year.

> Pringle, Laurence. Here Come the Killer Bees.
> New York: William Morrow, 1986.

Magazines and Newspapers. Give this information: author, title of article, name of magazine or newspaper, date, and page numbers.

> Alper, Joseph. "The Big Sting." Health Apr. 1989:
> 53–54.
> Sidener, Jonathan. " 'Killer Bees' May Reach
> Arizona Within a Year." The Arizona Republic
> 25 Oct. 1990: A1.

Encyclopedia Articles. Give this information: author, title of article, name of encyclopedia, year and edition (ed.).

> Heinrich, Bernd. "Bee." The World Book Encyclopedia.
> 1995 ed.

Interviews. Give this information: expert's name, the words *Personal interview* or *Telephone interview,* and date.

> Hardy, Ann. Telephone interview. 12 Dec. 1997.

Television or Radio Programs. Give this information: title of program, producer or director if available, network, local station call letters and city, and date of broadcast.

> Living with Killer Bees. Prod. Tony Burden. PBS.
> KUHT, Houston. 24 Nov. 1991.

Electronic Materials. Give this information: author (if any), title, electronic posting date (online), type of source (*CD-ROM* or *Online*), location of source (*Internet,* online service, or city, if given, for CD-ROMs), distributor (CD-ROMs), publication date (CD-ROMs) or access date, and Internet address (if any).

> Africanized Honey Bees Home Page. 1995. Online.
> Internet. 29 Dec. 1997. Available HTTP:
> 128.194.30.1/agcom/news/hc/ahb/ahbhome.htm

PART 3:
Finding and Listing Sources for Your Report

Where can you find information? What books and articles does your library have? Can you find World Wide Web sites related to your topic? Do you know someone you can interview? Find three or four different sources of information about your topic. Then, use the guide on page 329 to list them.

Taking Notes

Now you're ready to start gathering information from your sources. Be sure to keep your list of questions in mind as you work. Your questions will help keep you focused on gathering the information you need to write about your topic. Here are some other tips for taking good notes.

- Write your notes on 4″ × 6″ cards, on sheets of paper, or in computer files.
- Use abbreviations and short phrases. You can also make lists of details and ideas. You don't have to write complete sentences.
- Use your own words unless the exact words in the source are especially interesting.
- Put quotation marks around an author's or interviewee's exact words. (Not using quotation marks around someone else's words is called *plagiarism.* Plagiarizing is not identifying the source of ideas and words that are not your own.)
- Write the source number you're using at the top of the note card, piece of paper, or file. You'll use that number later when you need to identify where you got your information.
- Give each note a short label telling what the note is about. Write each label at the top of each card, piece of paper, or file.
- At the bottom, write the page number(s) where you found the information.

These two examples show you how to take notes.

How Different	2
	label/source number

Africanized bees chase 1/2 mi.
Native bees lose interest
after a few yds.

note written in your own words

p. 54 — *page number(s)*

This note is from the second source (see page 329), a magazine article titled "The Big Sting," by Joseph Alper. Notice how the card includes a label, a source number, and a page number. This information will come in handy later when the writer is planning and writing the report.

Where They'll Go	1

label/source number

Where there are mild winters:
Fla., Ga., Miss., La., Tex., Ariz.,
Calif., Va., N.C., S.C.

note written in your own words

p. 35 — *page number(s)*

This note is from the first source (see page 329), a book titled *Here Come the Killer Bees,* by Laurence Pringle. Notice how the writer uses abbreviations. This usage simplifies note taking. (Just be sure you understand the abbreviations you use!)

To keep from getting confused

- don't put notes from different sources on the same card, sheet of paper, or computer file
- don't place notes in your own words and quotations on the same card, sheet of paper, or computer file
- do use a new card, sheet of paper, or computer file whenever you write a new label

---

 REFERENCE NOTE: For more help with taking notes, see pages 886–887.

 PART 4:
Taking Notes for Your Report

What interesting information can you gather about your topic? Take notes from the sources you listed for Writing Assignment, Part 3 (page 330). Use half-sheets of paper if you don't have note cards or a computer. Save your notes to use in writing your report.

 *Prewriting*

Organizing and Outlining Your Information

By now you've found most of the information you will use in your report. The next step is to organize your notes into groups, like an *early plan* (see pages 100–101), and to make an *outline*. First, sort through your note cards, sheets of paper, or computer files. (You want to figure out which of them deal with the same or similar information.) Make several sets. In each set, put notes with the same or similar labels. Then, choose a heading for each set.

The headings of your sets are the main ideas for your report. Decide how you will arrange these ideas in your report. Which ones will come first? last? What order of ideas will help your readers understand your topic? The writer of the killer bee report arranged headings this way, making an *early plan* for the report.

> Nature of the bees
> History of the bees
> Africanized bees in the United States
> Attempts to stop the bees
> Ways to protect people

Next, make an *outline* for your report. You already have the main headings. These directions can help you with the rest of the outline.

1. Go through each set of notes. Take out notes that aren't about the heading.
2. Put the rest of the notes in the order you'll discuss them in your report.
3. Use these notes to make subheadings for your outline.

The example on the next page shows how you might write your outline.

The Invasion of the Killer Bees

I. Nature of the bees
  A. Behavior of United States bees and killer bees
    1. Gentleness of United States bees
    2. Fierceness of Africanized bees
  B. Danger of United States bees and killer bees
    1. Little danger of United States bees
    2. Great danger of Africanized bees

II. History of Africanized bees
  A. Import of African bees to Brazil in 1956
  B. Escape of queen bees
  C. Spread of bees

III. Africanized bees in the United States
  A. Movement to western and southern states
  B. Effects on honey industry
  C. Effects on agriculture

IV. Attempts to stop Africanized bees
  A. Attempts to crossbreed bees
  B. Attempts to kill bees

V. Ways to protect people
  A. Knowledge about bees
  B. Advice from beekeeper

 REFERENCE NOTE: For more help with making an early plan and outlining, see pages 100–102.

WRITING ASSIGNMENT

PART 5:
Writing an Outline for Your Report

You probably have many pieces of information for your report. Now you need to organize these pieces into groups and put them in order by writing an outline. You don't need to include everything in your outline. Just use headings and subheadings that will guide you when you write.

Writing Your First Draft

In one way, a report is not very different from other compositions you write. Like them, it has an introduction, a body, and a conclusion. The difference is that you use information from outside sources in your report. At the end of the report, you write a list of your sources to show readers where you found the information. That way, interested readers can look up your sources if they want to.

Understanding the Parts of a Report

Title Page. A report printed in a newspaper or magazine doesn't need a title page; it just needs a title. But reports that stand alone, like a school report or a business report, often need a cover page. On the cover page you put your name, the title of your report, the date, and any other information your teacher recommends.

Introduction. The *introduction* of the report isn't in your outline. It's a short opening paragraph where you do two things:

- catch your reader's attention
- tell what the report is about

Notice the introduction in the sample report on page 338. The writer first catches the reader's attention with a vivid example of attacking bees. At the same time, she introduces the topic of her report—Africanized honeybees, also known as "killer" bees.

Body. The *body* of the report contains paragraphs that discuss the information on your note cards and outline. The body of the sample report on pages 338–341 has nine paragraphs. Your own report may be shorter. Each paragraph should have enough information to inform readers about the main idea of each paragraph.

Conclusion.   The *conclusion* is the final paragraph of your report, where you sum up your ideas. You may want to state the main idea of your report in a new way. Without writing the words *The End,* make sure your readers know your report is finished.

 REFERENCE NOTE: For more information on how to write the introduction, body, and conclusion, look at Chapter 3, "Learning About Compositions," pages 104–110.

List of Sources.   What if your readers want to know more about your topic? They can turn to your *list of sources,* the place where you list the information about the sources you've used. After your conclusion, begin a new page. At the top of the page, write the words *Works Cited.* (Some people use the word *Bibliography,* but it refers only to print sources like books.) List your sources in alphabetical order by the author's last name. If there is no author, alphabetize by the first word in the title.

List your sources in the way described on page 329. The Works Cited page of the sample report on page 341 shows you how to do this.

 COMPUTER NOTE: Most word-processing programs have features to help automatically format and alphabetize a Works Cited list.

 CRITICAL THINKING

Synthesizing Information

To *synthesize* means "to combine different things in a new way." A green plant synthesizes light, water, carbon dioxide, and certain minerals to make food. A music video synthesizes music, dance, and special effects to make a "mini-movie." When you write a report, you synthesize the information in your notes. You use other people's ideas, but you put them together in a new way.

Here are some notes for the report on killer bees.

Bees in the United States	1
Where they'll go depends on mild winters.	
Could live year-round in parts of the U.S.: as	
far north as San Francisco and S. Maryland,	
all Ala., Miss., La., Tex., Ariz., Va., N.C. & S.C.	
	pp. 34-35

This paragraph from the sample report on page 340 shows how this information is put into the writer's own words. This is a synthesis of the information.

> Killer bees can live where the winters are mild. They will be year-round residents as far north as San Francisco and southern Maryland. They will also live all year in southern Texas and in Arizona, Alabama, Mississippi, Louisiana, Virginia, North Carolina, and South Carolina. In the summer, killer bees will live even in the northern states. They will die off there when it gets cold.

CRITICAL THINKING EXERCISE:
Synthesizing Your Notes

Go over your notes under one heading of your outline. Try out different ways of putting the notes into your own words. Make up a paragraph that includes the information you found. Next, find a partner and read your paragraph aloud as he or she listens and suggests changes. Then, change places with your partner, and do the same with your partner's paragraph.

Writing Your Report

Use your outline as a guide while you write. You may want to turn each of the main headings in your outline into a topic sentence for a paragraph. (Be sure that each sentence has a subject and a verb.) The subheadings can become the details for each paragraph.

You can use the following sample report as a model for your own. Remember that your report doesn't have to be this long. Writing a good, short report can teach you just as much as writing a longer one.

A WRITER'S MODEL

The Invasion of the Killer Bees

INTRODUCTION
Main idea

> Very soon, much of the United States may be invaded by fierce Africanized honeybees from Brazil called "killer" bees. The invasion seems like a horror movie. In such a movie, millions of
>
Attention grabber
> bees are attacking the people. They try to run, but there are so many bees that they can't see. They are stung over and over and over!

BODY
Nature of the bees

The Africanized bees are very different from native bees that live in the United States. These bees, which first came from Europe, live mostly in hives and hollow trees. They have few enemies and are usually gentle. In Africa, honeybees build their nests in the open because the weather is so warm. To protect their nests, they have become very fierce.

Killer bees are extremely nervous, and they are also fighters. Native bees chase people for a yard or so when they are bothered. Africanized bees, however, will chase for more than half a mile. Their poison is not different from the poison of ordinary bees, but they come after people in a big swarm. No one can survive a hundred or more stings. Dr. Kenneth Schuberth of the Johns Hopkins Medical Institutions says, "When you get that much venom in your system at once, it's like receiving a giant snake bite."

History of killer bees

The invasion of the killer bees began in 1956. In that year a scientist in Brazil imported seventy-five fierce queen bees from Africa. He wanted to crossbreed them with peaceful European bees. Twenty-six of these African bees accidentally escaped in 1957. They began attacking and killing animals and people.

The descendants of the African bees are the killer bees. They spread all over South America, flying more than five thousand miles in thirty years. Some of them have already crossed the United States' border. Many more of them will be here by the mid-1990s.

Killer bees in the United States

Killer bees can live where the winters are mild. They will be year-round residents as far north as San Francisco and southern Maryland. They will also live all year in southern Texas and in Arizona, Alabama, Mississippi, Louisiana, Virginia, North Carolina, and South Carolina. In the summer killer bees will live even in the northern states. They will die off there when it gets cold.

The invasion of the killer bees is serious. They kill people and animals, and they could ruin the honey industry. This industry is worth 150 million dollars a year. Wherever killer bees have gone, many beekeepers have changed jobs. Also, many crops cannot be grown without the pollinating that native bees do. After killer bees get here, fruits and vegetables may become much more expensive.

Attempts to stop the bees

Scientists have tried to tame the killer bees. The United States Department of Agriculture has tried to mate them with the European bees, which are much more peaceful. The results have not been too good because the resulting bees are still very fierce. There has also been an attempt to kill the bees. So far, the USDA has trapped and destroyed 13,700 swarms of killer bees in Mexico.

Ways to protect people

There is some hope. Most deaths from killer bees happen in the first four years after they come to a new place. Then people learn how to avoid them. Also, killer bees may become more peaceful in cool weather.

In an interview, a beekeeper had some advice about preparing for killer bees. She pointed out

that people who live in South America have
learned how to deal with African bees. Only
strangers to these bees and their ways get killed.

According to the beekeeper, here's what to
do once the killer bees get here. She said, "When
you see a bee, run as far and as fast as you can.
Run behind things that block the bee's vision.
Run to a house. Then call the fire department."

CONCLUSION
Restatement of
main idea

The fierce killer bees are on their way
through the United States. If people are not
ready for them, they can cause great harm to
the honey industry and to agriculture. Killer
bees can seriously hurt or even kill people.
Will this country be ready for them?

Works Cited

Africanized Honey Bees Home Page. 1995. Online.
    Internet. 29 Dec. 1997. Available HTTP:
    128.194.30.1/agcom/news/hc/ahb/ahbhome.htm
Alper, Joseph. "The Big Sting." Health Apr. 1989: 53–54.
Hardy, Ann. Telephone interview. 12 Dec. 1997.
Kerby, Mona. Friendly Bees, Ferocious Bees New York:
    Franklin Watts, 1987.
Patoski, Joe Nick. "Killer Buzz." Texas Monthly Dec. 1990:
    104.
Pringle, Laurence. Here Come the Killer Bees. New York:
    William Morrow, 1986.

MECHANICS HINT

Punctuating Titles

In a printed book or magazine, italics are used to identify titles of books and magazines. In a handwritten or typewritten report, underlining does the same thing. In your report or list of sources, underline the title of each book, magazine, or encyclopedia. Notice this, however: don't underline the title of your own report or the titles of articles. Put quotation marks around the titles of articles in magazines or encyclopedias.

EXAMPLES   **Book:**

Pringle, Laurence. <u>Here Come the Killer Bees</u>. New York: William Morrow, 1986.

Magazine:

Alper, Joseph. "The Big Sting." <u>Health</u> Apr. 1989: 53–54.

Encyclopedia:

Heinrich, Bernd. "Bee." <u>The World Book Encyclopedia</u>. 1995 ed.

 REFERENCE NOTE: For more help with punctuating titles, see pages 735–736 and 743–744.

PART 6:
Writing Your First Draft

Using your notes and outline as a guide, write your first draft. Remember that it doesn't have to be as long as the sample report. At the end of your report, list your sources on a Works Cited page.

Evaluating and Revising

After you've written your first draft, put it away for a day. Then use the chart below to evaluate and improve it. Ask yourself each question at the left. Whenever you answer a question no, use the technique in the right-hand column to revise your report.

EVALUATING AND REVISING REPORTS

EVALUATION GUIDE	REVISION TECHNIQUE
1 Does the report use at least three different sources?	**Add** sources. Try to use at least one nonprint source.
2 Does the report have enough information?	**Add** facts or the ideas of an expert.
3 Does the report give credit to an author's words?	**Add** quotation marks where you use someone's words.
4 Is information in the report clearly organized?	**Reorder** paragraphs so that the order of ideas is clear.
5 Does an interesting introduction give the report's topic?	**Add** (or rewrite) a sentence that tells your main idea.
6 Does a conclusion let readers know the report is over?	**Add** eye-catching details. **Add** a paragraph that summarizes or restates the main idea.
7 Does a list of sources in the correct form end the report?	**Add** a list of your sources. Use the form on page 341.

E X E R C I S E   4 ▶   **Analyzing a Writer's Revisions**

Before you revise your own draft, look at the changes another writer made. Working with a partner, study the writer's changes to one paragraph in the report on killer bees. Then answer the questions that follow. You and your partner might compare your answers to another pair's answers. Do your answers agree?

> No one can survive a hundred or more   **reorder**
>
> stings. Killer bees are extremely nervous,
>
> and they are also fighters. Native bees
> (for a yard or so)
> chase people when they are bothered.   **add**
>
> Africanized bees, however, will chase for
>
> more than half a mile. Their poison is not
>
> different from the poison of ordinary bees,
>
> but they come after people in a big swarm.
>
> ~~I wouldn't want them chasing after me!~~   **cut**
>
> Dr. Kenneth Schuberth of the Johns
>
> Hopkins Medical Institutions says, When   **add**
>
> you get that much venom in your system at
>
> once, it's like receiving a giant snake bite.   **add**

1. Why did the writer move the first sentence to a new place in the paragraph? Where does it make more sense?
2. Why did the writer add the words *for a yard or so* to the third sentence? [Hint: Does the reader need this information?]
3. Why did the writer cut the sentence *I wouldn't want them chasing after me!*? [Hint: Does this sentence give a fact or an expert's ideas? How does this sentence change the way the paragraph sounds?]
4. Why did the writer add quotation marks to the last sentence?

| EXERCISE 5 ▶ | **Evaluating a Report** |

Have you ever heard the song "Swing Low, Sweet Chariot"? It's a spiritual, a song first sung by slaves. Here's a paragraph from a report on spirituals. Get together with one or two classmates, and evaluate the paragraph. What are its weaknesses? What changes should be made? Use the evaluating and revising chart on page 343 to decide.

> Spirituals were sung by slaves on southern plantations. Frederick Douglass, a former slave, said, Slaves are generally expected to sing as well as to work. Most of the songs were very sorrowful. Many of these spirituals are still sung today. They were often about a better life to come. Some of the spirituals had codes in them.

| WRITING ASSIGNMENT | PART 7: **Evaluating and Revising Your Report** |

What changes will you make in your first draft to improve it? Read your report to a small group of classmates. Listen carefully to their suggestions. You might even want to take notes on what they like and dislike about your report. Then use the chart on page 343 to evaluate and revise the draft by yourself.

Proofreading and Publishing

Read your report carefully to make sure it has no mistakes. Think of a way to share your report. Here are two ideas.

■ Bind all the reports in your class on similar subjects into a book. Number the pages, make up a table of contents page, and give the book a title. Place a copy of the book in your school library.
■ If your topic is about science or history, give an oral report in your science or history class based on the information in your report.

WRITING ASSIGNMENT

PART 8:
Proofreading and Publishing Your Report

Make a clean copy of your report and proofread it carefully. Then, use one of the ideas above or one of your own to share your report. Give a copy of your report to anyone you interviewed for information.

 Reflecting on Your Writing

Before adding your report to your **portfolio,** date it and include your answers to the following questions.

■ How did you feel about your topic when you began your report? Did your feelings change? Explain.
■ What would you do differently if you were just beginning a report on the same topic?

A STUDENT MODEL

Allison Hamilton, a student in Hillsboro, Ohio, says that index cards and outlines are important to report writers because "they help to keep you on track."

Nature's Recyclers
by Allison Hamilton

If there was an oil spill off the coast of Alaska, how would you clean it up? You may think this is a machine's job, but scientists have proven that a tiny bug, usually invisible to the naked eye, could take on the work of a one-hundred-ton piece of steel! This bug, known as the microbe, has been the key to unlocking many doors to science.

Microbe is the name for any of millions of microscopic organisms. Microbes are tiny cells. They are so small you can't see them without a microscope. Some of the most common are the ones called bacteria. Bacteria are some of the oldest life forms, and some of the simplest, not having the cell nucleus found in most other microbes.

Most bacteria are harmless to plants and animals. Only a small fraction cause disease. Some attack living things after they're dead. If it wasn't for bacteria, animal wastes and dead organisms would build up. Bacteria also make the soil rich. They take nitrogen gas from the air and convert it to a form that green plants use for growth. Bacteria create fertilizer, too. They break down compost made of soil and dead plants.

Scientists have discovered how to use microbes to clean up oil spills. The scientists found a type of bacteria that feeds on oil and breaks it down into hydrogen, carbon, and oxygen.

The microbe is very important to us. I guess you could look at it as nature's recycler. Life as we know it today would never exist without these powerful bugs. Scientists have explored only a fraction of these amazing creatures' potential. Microbes could be another step into the future.

WRITING WORKSHOP

A Book Report

How do you evaluate (or judge) a book? You can start by saying whether or not you liked it. But most readers want a little more information. Here are some questions you can ask yourself to evaluate a novel.

1. *Do the characters seem like real people?*
2. *Do they change or grow in some way?*
3. *Do the events occur for a reason, or just by accident?*
4. *Does the novel's theme apply to real life?*
5. *Is the novel suspenseful? Did it hold my interest?*

If you answer most of these questions yes, the book is probably very good. It's worth reading. If you answer most of them no, you probably shouldn't recommend the book to others.

Now back to your book report. How do you put it together? First, you have to get your readers' attention. Then, you have to tell them the title and the author's name. After that you can begin to say a little about the plot and characters. Finally, give your recommendation.

A sample book report appears below. As you read it, look for the writer's recommendation.

Carlota, a Woman of Courage

Have you ever dived for sunken treasure? Ridden in a horse race? Faced a hostile army? The main character of Carlota, by Scott O'Dell, does all these things and more. Carlota is a good, exciting novel that readers will enjoy.

Carlota is about a young woman named Carlota de Zubarán, who lives with her grandmother and her father in California. The novel takes place in the last part of the 1848

war between the United States and Mexico. At that time, California was still a part of Mexico. Carlota's family, whose Spanish ancestors settled Mexico, is on the side of Mexico.

In many ways Carlota is like my friends and me. Sometimes she does not get along with the adults around her. For example, Carlota enjoys riding her horse out on the ranch with her father. This fact bothers her grandmother, who wants her to dress and behave like a young woman. Later, in a serious incident, Carlota stands up to her father. Not knowing the war is over, some American soldiers are making their way to California. Carlota's father and some other ranchers track the soldiers and attack them. Carlota wounds one of the soldiers with her lance and then insists on taking care of him. This action makes her father very angry.

The main idea of this novel is that sometimes courage means standing up for what you believe, something that is harder to do when other people do not feel the same way you do. At first, Carlota hates the Americans because her father does. Then she realizes that the wounded American is also a human being, and she takes care of him. To do this, she must show courage and stand up against her father. As Carlota says, "I was ashamed, now, of what I had tried to do. The shame gave me courage" (125). In real life, there are many times when you must show this kind of courage.

Carlota is very suspenseful; it holds the reader's interest. Carlota has many adventures and many close calls. One of these adventures is the horse race at her sister's wedding. She has a dangerous fall from her horse, but she goes on to win a close and exciting victory. To share in these adventures and to enjoy a good book, read Carlota.

Thinking It Over

1. In the first two paragraphs, what information do you learn about the novel *Carlota*?
2. Does the writer think *Carlota* is a good or bad novel?
3. Why does the writer feel this way? Give two reasons.

Writing a Book Report

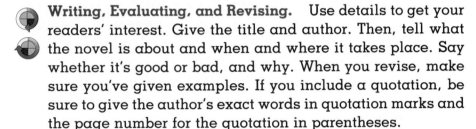

Prewriting. For your report, choose a novel that you feel strongly about. After you've read it, take notes on it. To evaluate the book, answer the questions on page 348.

Writing, Evaluating, and Revising. Use details to get your readers' interest. Give the title and author. Then, tell what the novel is about and when and where it takes place. Say whether it's good or bad, and why. When you revise, make sure you've given examples. If you include a quotation, be sure to give the author's exact words in quotation marks and the page number for the quotation in parentheses.

Proofreading and Publishing. Proofread your book report and correct any errors. Be sure that you've underlined the name of the book whenever it appears. Don't underline your own title for the report. Put a copy of your report into a file for other students to use when they select books.

If you decide to include your book report in your **portfolio,** date it and attach a note responding to these questions: What did you do to get your readers' attention? How was this paper different from others you've written?

MAKING CONNECTIONS

RESEARCH ACROSS THE CURRICULUM

History

Do you ever wonder what your city (or a nearby city) looked like many years ago? What the place looked like even before a city was there? You can find out by doing some research, perhaps about the following things.

1. What's the history of the city? How old is it? Who first settled it? Why was a city started here? Who were some of the first families? What's the oldest building?
2. What was here two hundred years ago? Did Native Americans live here? Who were they, and how did they live? What happened to them?
3. Who is the oldest living resident of the city? Could you interview this person? In what ways has the town changed since this person was a child?

4. What natural resources made the area a good place to live? What are the native plants and animals? How might this place have looked before people arrived?

5. What ethnic groups from other countries settled in the city? When did they arrive? What part of the city did they settle in?

6. How do people earn their living in your city? Have the jobs changed since the city was started?

Get together with several of your classmates and find out about the history of the place where you live. Divide the questions, and decide on a research job for each classmate. The library is a good place to start your research. Other sources might be your local newspaper or a historical society or museum.

Take careful notes from your sources. Then, prepare a group report on the history of your city. Include drawings of important events, or of buildings, plants, and animals that have made your city an interesting place to live.

SPEAKING AND LISTENING

Reporting on the Weather

You've probably seen weather forecasters on TV. Some read reports put out by the National Weather Service. But others are *meteorologists*, highly trained scientists who study weather and report on it. They base their reports on facts collected from a vast network of weather stations. They also check records of weather patterns from earlier years. Then they make a forecast, a prediction of future weather.

Here's your chance to gather weather information and present a weather report to your class. You may want to do this activity with a partner.

First, listen to the TV or radio meteorologist on at least two stations. Notice the kind of information they report. Also pay attention to how they present the information they've gathered.

Next, take notes on the weather information that has been in your local paper for the past week. At the library, find last year's newspapers for that week. Read what the weather was like at this time last year. What, if anything, do you find is unusual about this year's rainfall, wind, or temperature?

Now gather information on this year's weather. Keep a record of your town's weather for at least three days. To collect your own data, record the temperature three times each day. Note the amount of precipitation (rain or snow). Describe the type and quantity of clouds. If you prefer, you can get this information from the National Weather Service. The closest airport will also have it.

Finally, make some weather charts:

- one chart comparing the weather last week to the weather at the same time last year
- one chart showing what the weather has been like for the past three days
- one chart showing what the weather will be like tomorrow

Then, make notes on the information you want to present along with your charts. Practice your weather report out loud until you can present your report in an interesting way.

11 WRITING EFFECTIVE SENTENCES

LOOKING AHEAD

In this chapter, you will learn how to make your sentences clearer and more interesting by

- writing complete sentences
- combining sentences
- improving your sentence style

Writing Clear Sentences

One of the best ways to make your writing clear is to use *complete sentences.* A complete sentence

- has a subject
- has a verb
- expresses a complete thought

EXAMPLES   Some birds can imitate human speech.
              Parrots and myna birds are great mimics.
              Listen to that bird talk!

Each of the example word groups expresses a complete thought. Each has a verb. The last example may not appear to have a subject in it, but it actually has the unstated subject *you:* (You) Listen to that bird talk!

There are two common errors that get in the way of writing complete sentences: *sentence fragments* and *run on sentences.* Once you learn how to recognize fragments and run-ons in your writing, you can revise them to form clear, complete sentences.

Sentence Fragments

A *sentence fragment* is a part of a sentence that has been punctuated as if it were a complete sentence. Because it is incomplete, a sentence fragment sends a confusing message.

FRAGMENT   Was the first African American man to win the Wimbledon tennis championship. [The subject is missing. *Who* was the first African American man to win Wimbledon?]

SENTENCE   Arthur Ashe was the first African American man to win the Wimbledon tennis championship.

FRAGMENT   Ashe the Wimbledon singles title in 1975. [The verb is missing. What's the connection between Ashe and the singles title?]

SENTENCE   Ashe won the Wimbledon singles title in 1975.

FRAGMENT   While he was a student at the University of California. [This has a subject and a verb, but it doesn't express a complete thought. *What happened* while Ashe was a student?]

SENTENCE   Ashe also won several championships in college tennis while he was a student at the University of California.

As you can see from the first two examples, you can correct some sentence fragments by adding a subject or verb. Other times a sentence fragment just needs to be attached to the sentence next to it. You may have accidentally separated it from the sentence it belongs with by putting in a period and a capital letter too soon.

FRAGMENT   The crowd cheered wildly. **When Leon scored the winning touchdown.**

SENTENCE   The crowd cheered wildly when Leon scored the winning touchdown.

GRAMMAR HINT

Identifying Fragments

Some words look like verbs but really aren't. These "fake" verbs can fool you into thinking a group of words is a sentence when it is really a fragment. A word that ends in *–ing* can't stand as a verb unless it has a helping verb (such as *is, are, were*) with it.

FRAGMENT   The children playing on the swings. [Without the helping verb, this isn't a complete thought.]

SENTENCE   The children **were playing** on the swings.

EXERCISE 1 ▶ Identifying Sentence Fragments

Decide which of the following groups of words are sentence fragments and which are complete sentences. This simple three-part test will help you.

1. Does the group of words have a subject?
2. Does it have a verb?
3. Does it express a complete thought?

If you answer *no* to any of the questions, write *F* to show that the group of words is a fragment. If the group of words is a complete sentence, write *S*. (Remember, the subject "you" isn't always stated directly in a sentence.)

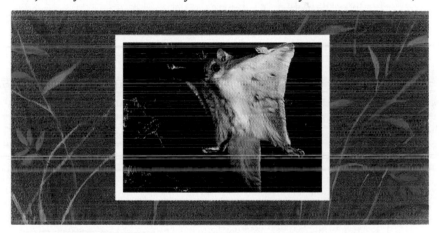

1. A flying squirrel a squirrel that can glide through the air.
2. Some Asian flying squirrels three feet long.
3. Leaps from one tree to another.
4. The squirrel glides downward, then straight, and finally upward.
5. Some flying squirrels more than fifty feet.
6. If they use a higher starting point.
7. Flying squirrels live in the forests of Asia, Europe, and North America.
8. Eat berries, birds' eggs, insects, and nuts.
9. Nest in the hollows of trees.
10. Notice how this squirrel stretches out its legs to help it glide.

EXERCISE 2 ▶ **Finding and Revising Fragments**

Some of the following groups of words are sentence fragments. Revise each fragment by (1) adding a subject, (2) adding a verb, or (3) attaching the fragment to a complete sentence. You may need to change the punctuation and capitalization, too. If the word group is already a complete sentence, write *S*.

EXAMPLE   **1.** As soon as we finished eating breakfast.
            1. *We left for our camping trip as soon as we finished eating breakfast.*

  1. The whole family into the car.
  2. We traveled for hours.
  3. When we arrived at the campground.
  4. My sister and I down to the river.
  5. Took our fishing gear with us.
  6. We cast our lines the way our aunt had taught us.
  7. Because we didn't have the best bait.
  8. We headed back to the campsite at sunset.
  9. Dad cooking bean soup over the fire.
10. Mom and my sister the tent.

Run-on Sentences

A *run-on sentence* is actually two complete sentences punctuated like one sentence. In a run-on, the thoughts just run into each other. The reader can't tell where one idea ends and another one begins.

RUN-ON   Edna Ferber was a novelist and playwright she wrote about American life in the 1800s.

CORRECT   Edna Ferber was a novelist and playwright. She wrote about American life in the 1800s.

RUN-ON   Ferber's novel *Show Boat* was made into a musical play, some of her other novels were made into movies.

CORRECT   Ferber's novel *Show Boat* was made into a musical play. Some of her other novels were made into movies.

To spot run-ons, try reading your writing aloud. As you read, you will usually pause where one thought ends and another begins. If you pause at a place where you don't have any end punctuation, you may have a run-on sentence.

MECHANICS HINT

Using Commas Correctly

A comma does mark a brief pause in a sentence, but it doesn't show the end of a sentence. If you use just a comma between two sentences, you create a run-on sentence.

RUN-ON   Clogging is a lively kind of dancing, the dancers wear special shoes to tap out the rhythm.

CORRECT   Clogging is a lively kind of dancing. The dancers wear special shoes to tap out the rhythm.

Revising Run-on Sentences

There are several ways you can revise run-on sentences. Here are two of them.

1. You can make two sentences.

> RUN-ON   Asteroids are tiny planets they are sometimes called planetoids.
>
> CORRECT   Asteroids are tiny planets. They are sometimes called planetoids.

2. You can use a comma and the coordinating conjunction *and, but,* or *or.*

> RUN-ON   Some asteroids shine with a steady light, others keep changing in brightness.
>
> CORRECT   Some asteroids shine with a steady light, **but** others keep changing in brightness.

E X E R C I S E   3 ▶   **Identifying and Revising Run-ons**

Decide which of the following groups of words are run-ons. Then revise each run-on by (1) making it into two separate sentences or (2) using a comma and a coordinating conjunction. If the group of words is already correct, write *C.*

1. Saturn is a huge planet it is more than nine times larger than Earth.
2. Saturn is covered by clouds, it is circled by bands of color.
3. Some of the clouds are yellow, others are off-white.
4. Saturn has about twenty moons Titan is the largest.
5. Many of Saturn's moons have large craters the crater on Mimas covers one third of its diameter.
6. Saturn's most striking feature is a group of rings that circles the planet.
7. The rings of Saturn are less than two miles thick, they spread out from the planet for a great distance.
8. The rings are made up of billions of tiny particles.

9. Some of the rings are dark, but others are brighter.
10. Saturn is a beautiful planet you need a telescope to see its rings.

REVIEW A ▶

The following paragraph is confusing because it contains some fragments and run-ons. First, identify the fragments and run-ons. Then, revise each fragment and run-on to make the paragraph clearer.

Many deserts have no plant life, some desert regions have a variety of plants. Many plants can survive. Where the climate is hot and dry. Cacti, Joshua trees, palm trees, and wildflowers grow in deserts. These plants. Do not grow close together. Are spread out, each plant gets water and minerals from a large area.

Combining Sentences

Short sentences can sometimes express your ideas well. But if you use only short sentences, your writing will sound choppy and dull. For example, read the following paragraph, which has only short sentences.

Thomas Edison invented the phonograph. He also experimented with robots. A lot of people don't know this. Edison created a talking doll. He created the talking doll in 1894. The doll would recite a nursery rhyme or poem. It said the words when a crank in its back was turned. The talking doll was very popular. Edison opened a factory. The factory made five hundred of the dolls every day.

Now read the revised paragraph. Notice how the writer has combined some of the short sentences to make longer, smoother sentences.

Thomas Edison invented the phonograph. A lot of people don't know that he also experimented with robots. Edison created a talking doll in 1894. When a crank in its back was turned, the doll would recite a nursery rhyme or poem. The talking doll was very popular, and Edison opened a factory that made five hundred of the dolls every day.

As you can see from the revision, sentence combining has also helped to reduce the number of repeated words and ideas. The revised paragraph is clearer, shorter, and more interesting to read.

Combining Sentences by Inserting Words

One way to combine short sentences is to take a key word from one sentence and insert it into the other sentence.

ORIGINAL   The Easter lily is a flower. It is a white flower.
COMBINED   The Easter lily is a **white** flower.

Sometimes you'll need to change the form of the key word before you can insert it. You can change the forms of some words by adding an ending such as *–ed*, *–ing*, *–ful*, or *–ly*. In its new form, the key word can be used to describe another word in the sentence.

ORIGINAL   Easter lily plants have leaves. The leaves have points.

COMBINED   Easter lily plants have **pointed** leaves.

| EXERCISE 4 ▶ | **Combining Sentences by Inserting Words** |

Each of the following items contains two sentences. To combine the two sentences, take the italicized key word from the second sentence and insert it into the first sentence. The directions in parentheses will tell you how to change the form of the key word if you need to do so.

EXAMPLE   **1.** Peanuts are the tiny fruit of the peanut plant. They have a good *taste.* (Change *taste* to *tasty.*)

           1. *Peanuts are the tiny, tasty fruit of the peanut plant.*

1. This picture shows peanuts underground. They *grow* underground. (Add *–ing.*)
2. Peanuts are a crop of many warm regions. They are a *major* crop.
3. Peanuts are a food for snacking. Peanuts are good for your *health.* (Add *–ful.*)
4. The oil from peanuts is used in many dressings. The dressings are for *salad.*
5. Grades of peanut oil are used to make soap and shampoo. The *low* grades are used for these products.

Combining Sentences by Inserting Phrases

A *phrase* is a group of words that doesn't have a subject and a verb. You can combine sentences by taking a phrase from one sentence and inserting it into the other sentence.

ORIGINAL   Arachne is a famous figure. She is a figure in Greek mythology.

COMBINED   Arachne is a famous figure **in Greek mythology.**

Using Commas with Phrases

Some phrases need to be set off by commas. Before you insert a phrase into a sentence, ask yourself whether the phrase renames or explains a noun or pronoun. If it does, set it off with a comma (or two commas if the phrase is in the middle of the sentence).

ORIGINAL   Arachne challenged Athena to a weaving contest. Athena was the goddess of wisdom.

COMBINED   Arachne challenged Athena**, the goddess of wisdom,** to a weaving contest.

☞ REFERENCE NOTE: For more information about phrases that need to be set off by commas, see pages 712–719.

Sometimes you can change the verb in a sentence to make a phrase. Just add *–ing* or *–ed* to the verb or put the word *to* in front of it. You can then use the phrase to describe a noun or pronoun in a related sentence. Be sure to place the phrase near the word(s) it modifies.

ORIGINAL   The name *Inuit* refers to several groups of people. These people live in and near the Arctic.

COMBINED   The name *Inuit* refers to several groups of people **living in and near the Arctic.**

ORIGINAL   Early Inuit, or Eskimos, followed a special way
            of life. They did this so they could survive in a
            harsh environment.
COMBINED   **To survive in a harsh environment,** early Inuit,
            or Eskimos, had to follow a special way of life.

☞ REFERENCE NOTE: For more information about verb forms using
    –ing, –ed, or *to,* see pages 502–508.

| EXERCISE 5 | **Combining Sentences by Inserting Phrases** |

Each of the following items contains two sentences. Combine the two sentences by taking the italicized word group from the second sentence and inserting it into the first sentence. The hints in parentheses tell you how to change the forms of words. Remember to insert commas where they are needed.

EXAMPLE   **1.** The Inuit followed their traditional way of life.
            They followed this way of life *for thousands
            of years.*

            1. *The Inuit followed their traditional way of life
            for thousands of years.*

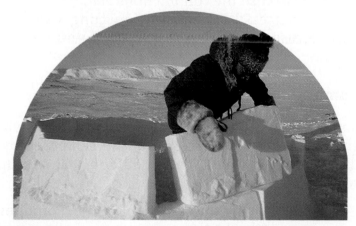

1. The Inuit could build winter shelters in a few
   hours. They *stacked blocks of snow.* (Change *stacked*
   to *stacking.*)
2. They used harpoons. This is how they *hunted seals.*
   (Change *hunted* to *to hunt.*)

3. The Inuit also hunted and ate caribou. Caribou are *a type of deer*.
4. Whalers and fur traders came to the region and affected the Inuit way of life. They arrived in the region *in the 1800s*.
5. Most Inuit today follow a modern way of life. They are *like these Canadian Inuit*.

Combining Sentences by Using *And, But,* or *Or*

You can also use the conjunctions *and, but,* and *or* to combine sentences. With these connecting words, you can make a *compound subject*, a *compound verb*, or a *compound sentence*.

Compound Subjects and Verbs

Sometimes two sentences have the same verb with different subjects. You can combine the sentences by linking the two subjects with *and* or *or*. You will end up with a **compound subject.**

ORIGINAL   Dolphins look a little like fish. Porpoises look a little like fish.
COMBINED   **Dolphins and porpoises** look a little like fish.

Two sentences can also have the same subject with different verbs. You can use *and, but,* or *or* to connect the two verbs. The result is a **compound verb.**

ORIGINAL   Dolphins swim like fish. They breathe like other
           mammals.
COMBINED   Dolphins **swim** like fish **but breathe** like other
           mammals.

GRAMMAR HINT

Checking for Subject–Verb Agreement

When you use the conjunction *and* to link two subjects, your new compound subject will be a plural
subject. Don't forget to make the verb agree with the
subject in number.

ORIGINAL   Harry likes visiting the sea mammals at the
           aquarium. Dorothy likes visiting the sea
           mammals at the aquarium.
REVISED   **Harry and Dorothy like** visiting the sea
           mammals at the aquarium. [The plural
           subject *Harry and Dorothy* takes the
           verb *like.*]

👉 REFERENCE NOTE: For more information about agreement
   of subjects and verbs, see pages 551–569.

EXERCISE 6 ▶ **Combining Sentences by Creating
              Compound Subjects and Verbs**

Combine each of the following pairs of short, choppy sentences by using *and*, *but*, or *or*. If the two sentences have
the same verb, make a compound subject. If they have
the same subject, make a compound verb. Remember
to check your combined sentences for subject–verb
agreement.

1. Dolphins can't smell things as people do. They can't
   taste things as people do.
2. Dolphins hunt fish. Dolphins eat fish.

3. Baby dolphins catch waves near the beach. Baby dolphins ride waves near the beach.

4. Sharks sometimes attack porpoises. Sharks sometimes kill porpoises.

5. A porpoise could outswim most sharks. A tuna could outswim most sharks.

Compound Sentences

Sometimes you will want to combine two sentences that express equally important ideas. You can connect two closely related, equally important sentences by using a comma plus the coordinating conjunction *and, but,* or *or.* This creates a *compound sentence.*

ORIGINAL   My brother entered the Annual Chili Cook-off. His chili won a prize.

COMBINED   My brother entered the Annual Chili Cook-off**, and** his chili won a prize.

ORIGINAL   I didn't help him cook the chili. I helped him clean up the kitchen.

COMBINED   I didn't help him cook the chili**, but** I helped him clean up the kitchen.

ORIGINAL   We can help cook the meal. We can help wash the dishes.

COMBINED   We can help cook the meal**, or** we can help wash the dishes.

WRITING NOTE   A compound sentence tells the reader that the two ideas are closely related. If you combine two short sentences that are not closely related, you will confuse your reader.

UNRELATED   Fernando mowed the grass, and I brought a broom.

RELATED   Fernando mowed the grass, and I swept the sidewalk.

| EXERCISE 7 ▶ | **Combining Sentences by Forming a Compound Sentence** |

Each of the following pairs of sentences is closely related. Make each pair into a compound sentence by adding a comma and a coordinating conjunction (*and, but,* or *or*).

EXAMPLE **1.** The Pueblos have lived in the same location for a long time. They have strong ties to their homeland.

1. *The Pueblos have lived in the same location for a long time, and they have strong ties to their homeland.*

1. Some Pueblos built villages in the valleys. Others settled in desert and mountain areas.
2. Desert surrounded many of the valleys. The people could grow crops with the help of irrigation systems.
3. Women gathered berries and other foods. Men hunted game.
4. Their adobe homes had several stories. The people used ladders to reach the upper levels.
5. Today, each Pueblo village has its own government. The Pueblo people still share many customs.

Combining Sentences by Using a Subordinate Clause

A *clause* is a group of words that contains a subject and verb. Some clauses can stand alone as a sentence. We call them *independent.* Other clauses can't stand alone as a sentence because they don't express a complete thought. We call them *subordinate.*

INDEPENDENT CLAUSE   Gertrude Ederle swam the English Channel. [can stand alone]
SUBORDINATE CLAUSE   when she was nineteen years old [can't stand alone]

If two sentences are closely related, you can combine them by using a subordinate clause. Just turn one of the sentences into a subordinate clause and attach it to the other sentence (the independent clause). The subordinate clause will give information about a word or idea in the independent clause.

TWO SENTENCES   Gertrude Ederle swam the English Channel. She was nineteen years old at the time.
ONE SENTENCE   Gertrude Ederle swam the English Channel **when she was nineteen years old.**

Clauses Beginning with *Who, Which,* or *That*

You can make a short sentence into a subordinate clause by inserting *who, which,* or *that* in place of the subject.

ORIGINAL   The Everglades is an area of swamps. It covers the southern part of Florida.
COMBINED   The Everglades is an area of swamps **that covers the southern part of Florida.**

Clauses Beginning with Words of Time or Place

Another way to turn a sentence into a subordinate clause is to add a word that tells time or place at the beginning. Some words that can begin this type of clause are *after, before, where, wherever, when, whenever,* and *while.* You may also need to delete some words before you can insert the clause into another sentence.

ORIGINAL   No humans lived in the Everglades until 1842. In 1842, Seminoles fled to the area.
COMBINED   No humans lived in the Everglades until 1842, **when Seminoles fled to the area.**

MECHANICS HINT

Using Commas with Introductory Clauses

If you put your time or place clause at the beginning of the sentence, use a comma after the clause.

ORIGINAL   People began draining the swamps to make farmland. The Everglades was in danger.

COMBINED   **When people began draining the swamps to make farmland,** the Everglades was in danger.

 REFERENCE NOTE: For more about the use of commas with subordinate clauses, see pages 713 and 720.

EXERCISE 8 ▶ **Combining Sentences by Using a Subordinate Clause**

Combine each sentence pair by making the second sentence into a subordinate clause and attaching it to the first sentence. The hints in parentheses tell you how to begin the subordinate clause. You may need to delete a word or two from the second sentence.

1. The pearl is a gem. It is made by certain kinds of oysters and clams. (Use *that.*)
2. Beautiful pearls are found in tropical seas. The best pearl oysters live there. (Use a comma and *where.*)
3. A valuable pearl has a shine. The shine comes from below its surface. (Use *that.*)
4. A pearl becomes round. It is formed in the soft part of the oyster. (Use *when.*)
5. Pearls should be wiped clean with a soft cloth. They are worn as jewelry. (Use *after.*)

REVIEW B ▶ **Revising a Paragraph by Combining Sentences**

These paragraphs sound choppy because they have too many short sentences. Use the methods you've learned in this section to combine sentences in the paragraphs.

Pegasus is a winged horse. He is a beautiful horse. He is a horse from Greek mythology. Pegasus was created by Poseidon. Poseidon was the god of the sea. He was a Greek god. Athena caught Pegasus. Athena tamed Pegasus. Athena was the goddess of wisdom.

A hero could ride Pegasus. A true poet could ride Pegasus. These were the only kinds of people who could ride him. The first person to ride the winged horse was a Greek youth. The youth was sent by a king to kill a monster. The youth destroyed the monster. He became a hero.

Improving Sentence Style

When you combine short, choppy sentences, your writing is easier and more interesting to read. You can also make your writing more effective by revising *stringy* and *wordy sentences* to make them shorter and clearer.

COMPUTER NOTE: When you're working on your first draft, use bold, italic, or underline formatting to mark sentences you plan to revise.

Revising Stringy Sentences

A *stringy sentence* is made up of several independent clauses strung together with words like *and* or *but*. Stringy sentences just ramble on and on. They don't give the reader a chance to pause before each new idea.

To fix a stringy sentence, you can

- break the sentence into two or more sentences
- turn some of the independent clauses into phrases or subordinate clauses

STRINGY   Martina climbed the stairs of the haunted house and she knocked on the door several times but no one answered and she braced herself and then she opened the door.

REVISED   Martina climbed the stairs of the haunted house. She knocked on the door several times, but no one answered. Bracing herself, she opened the door.

MECHANICS HINT

Punctuating Compound Sentences

When you revise a stringy sentence, you may decide to keep *and* or *but* between two closely related independent clauses. If you do this, remember to add a comma before the *and* or *but*.

ORIGINAL   She knocked on the door several times but no one answered.

REVISED   She knocked on the door several times, but no one answered.

☞ **REFERENCE NOTE:** For more about compound sentences, see pages 536–538.

EXERCISE 9 ▶ **Revising Stringy Sentences**

Some of the following sentences are stringy and need to be improved. First, identify the stringy sentences. Then, revise them by (1) breaking each sentence into two or more sentences or (2) turning some of the independent clauses into phrases or subordinate clauses. If the sentence is effective and doesn't need to be improved, write *C*.

1. Mercedes O. Cubría was born in Cuba, but her mother died, and she moved to the United States, and she moved with her two sisters.

2. She worked as a nurse, and then she joined the Women's Army Corps, and she soon became an officer in the army.
3. Cubría was the first Cuban-born woman to become an officer in the U.S. Army.
4. Her job during World War II was to put important government papers into a secret code.
5. The war ended, and she was promoted to captain, and later her official rank rose to major.
6. Then there was the Korean War, and she worked as an intelligence officer, and she studied information about the enemy.
7. Cubría retired from the army in 1953 but was called to duty again in 1962.
8. After the Castro revolution, thousands of Cubans fled to the United States, and Cubría interviewed many of these refugees, and she also prepared reports on Cuba.
9. In her spare time, she helped people from Cuba find jobs and housing.
10. She retired again in 1973, and she settled in Miami, Florida, and she was surrounded by friends and family there.

Revising Wordy Sentences

Sometimes you use more words in a sentence than you really need. Extra words don't make writing sound better. They just get in the reader's way. Short, well-written sentences help the reader understand your message, whether you are writing in school or in the workplace. You can revise *wordy sentences* in three different ways.

1. Replace a phrase with one word.

    WORDY   In the event that we win this game, our team will go to the playoffs.

    REVISED   **If** we win this game, our team will go to the playoffs.

    WORDY   In a state of exhaustion, Tony slumped across the bus seat and fell asleep.

    REVISED   **Exhausted,** Tony slumped across the bus seat and fell asleep.

2. Take out *who is* or *which is.*

    LENGTHY   Yesterday I went for a hike with Sonya, who is my best friend.

    REVISED   Yesterday I went for a hike with Sonya, **my best friend.**

    LENGTHY   Afterward, we drank some apple juice, which is a good thirst quencher.

    REVISED   Afterward, we drank some apple juice, **a good thirst quencher.**

3. Take out a whole group of unnecessary words.

    WORDY   What I mean to say is that I am going to work on my report tonight.

    REVISED   I am going to work on my report tonight.

    WORDY   I spent a lot of time writing my report because I really want people to learn about manatees so they can know all about them.

    REVISED   I spent a lot of time writing my report because I want people to learn about manatees.

Here is a list of some common wordy phrases and their shorter, simpler replacements. Be on the lookout for these wordy phrases as you revise your writing.

WORDY	SIMPLER
at the point at which	when
by means of	by
due to the fact that	because, since
in spite of the fact that	although
in the event that	if
the fact is that	actually

EXERCISE 10 ▶ **Revising Wordy Sentences**

Some of the following sentences are wordy and need improving. Decide which of the sentences are wordy; then, revise them. You can (1) replace a phrase with one word, (2) take out *who is* or *which is*, or (3) take out a whole group of unnecessary words. If a sentence is effective as it is, write *C*.

1. Our science class has been learning about the starfish, which is a strange and beautiful fish.
2. What I want to say is that starfish are fascinating creatures.
3. A starfish has little feet tipped with suction cups that have suction power.
4. At the end of each arm is a sensitive "eyespot."
5. In spite of the fact that the eyespot cannot really see things, it can tell light from dark.
6. The starfish's mouth is in the middle of its body.
7. When it uses its arms, it can pull at the shells of clams.
8. At the point at which the clam's shell opens, the starfish can feed on the clam.
9. Starfish come in a variety of colors, shapes, and sizes, and some are bigger than others.

10. This photograph shows a candy cane starfish holding onto a soft coral by holding it with its suction cups.

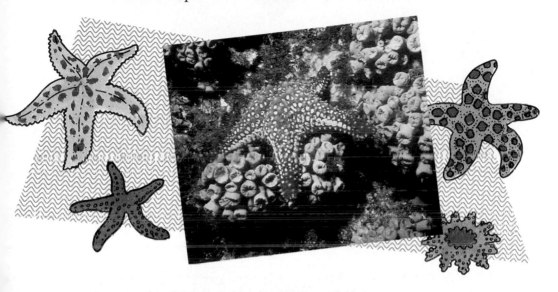

REVIEW C ▶

The following paragraph is hard to read because it contains stringy and wordy sentences. First, identify the stringy and wordy sentences. Then, revise them by using the methods you've learned. Notice how your revisions improve the style of the paragraph.

The movie *The Dark Crystal* features a lot of strange characters, and the characters are actually puppets, and they were designed by Jim Henson, and he was the man who created the Muppets. The puppets used in *The Dark Crystal* were different from the original Muppets, having things about them that were different. One thing is that they weren't as brightly colored as the TV Muppets. They also had legs and could move through a scene with their whole bodies showing. Some of the *Dark Crystal* characters were radio-controlled, and others were operated by puppeteers, and the puppeteers were hidden under the movie set.

MAKING CONNECTIONS

Fill in the Missing Pieces

You are fishing in a bay when you suddenly spot a corked bottle bobbing in the water near the pier. You guess that the bottle has floated over from the summer camp across the bay. You pull the bottle out of the water and take out the cork. Inside is a piece of paper with a mysterious message. But some water has leaked into the bottle, and parts of the sentences have been washed away. Try to reconstruct the message by adding the missing words.

To whoever finds this message: my _____ is Claudia. I was walking _____ at the northern end of the bay when I saw a mysterious shadow near the cave opening. _____ could be some kind of dangerous monster or even a ghost. I _____ ly the cave almost every day. _____ can't get anyone to help me explore the cave. If you want to help me _____

12 ENGLISH: ORIGINS AND USES

LOOKING AHEAD

In this chapter, you will take a close look at the English language—where it comes from, how it has grown, and how it is used today. You will also examine your own use of language with an eye for style, learning

- what kinds of language are appropriate for particular situations
- how to improve your writing by choosing clearer, more effective words

A Changing Language

Languages have ancestors just as people do. English and dozens of other languages come from a single early language that was spoken thousands of years ago on the other side of the globe.

Although each language is unique, you can still see the family resemblance among words with the same meaning in related languages.

ENGLISH	GERMAN	FRENCH	SPANISH
new	neu	nouveau	nuevo
nose	Nase	nez	nariz
salt	Salz	sel	sal
young	jung	jeune	joven

No one knows exactly when English branched off as a separate language. However, we do know that a form of English was being spoken by tribes of people in the fifth century. These tribes migrated to the island of Britain and conquered the area that is now England. Their language is the ancestor of modern-day English.

The earliest known English writings date back about 1,300 years. This early form of English is so different from our English that it looks like a foreign language to us.

> He þæt ful geþeáh
> wæl-reow wíga, æt Wealhþeówe,
> and þá gyddode, gúðe gefýsed.
> Beowulf maðelode, bearn Ecgþeówes:
>
> from *Beowulf*

The Growth of English

English didn't grow up all at once. If you had a time machine, you could stop off in England every few hundred years and witness gradual changes taking place in people's language. You would hear and see new pronunciations, forms, and meanings of words. You would also notice many new words being added to the language. By about 1500, you would probably be able to understand the English of the time. However, it would still sound strange to you.

How Do You Spell It?

Some English words have traveled through the centuries with only small changes in spelling. Others have undergone greater change. Here are some examples of present-day English words and their original forms.

PRESENT-DAY	red	three	summer	sheep	fish
ORIGINAL	read	threo	sumor	sceap	fisc

Even today, the spellings of words vary. Different spellings of a word can be standard in different places. For example, compare standard American and standard British spellings of some everyday words.

AMERICAN	color	flavor	theater	tire
BRITISH	colour	flavour	theatre	tyre

How Do You Say It?

By the 1300s, written English looked similar to the English we use. But English-speaking people of that time still pronounced words differently from the way we do. For example, they pronounced *meek* like *make*, *boot* like *boat*, and *mouse* like *moose*.

The Granger Collection, New York.

Changes in pronunciations help account for many of the English words that aren't spelled as they sound. For example, the word *knight* used to be pronounced with a strong *k* sound at the beginning. The letter remained part of the spelling even though the *k* sound was eventually dropped.

EXERCISE 1 ▶   **Giving Present-Day Forms of Words**

Here are five sets of English words written with their original spellings. See if you can figure out what the words are in present-day English.

1. bryht, deorc   **4.** docga, hors
2. sealt, mete   **5.** plante, saed
3. muth, lippa

What Does It Mean?

Read the following sentence:

> Without reply, the typewriter rose and withdrew, thrusting her pencil into the coil of her hair. . . .
>
> Frank Norris, *The Octopus*

When people read Frank Norris's sentence in the early 1900s, they didn't see anything strange about it. In those days, it wasn't unusual for a typewriter to get up and walk out of a room. The word *typewriter* could mean "typist" as well as "typewriting machine."

The meaning of *typewriter* has changed only slightly. But some words have ended up with meanings entirely different from their original ones. Nine hundred years ago, *awful* meant "awe-inspiring, very impressive." Today, it usually means "terrifying" or "very bad." Another good example is the word *nice*. In the 1300s, *nice* didn't mean "pleasant"; it meant "lazy" or "foolish."

The meanings of words are still changing today. For example, the word *bad* can now mean "good" in informal English. And *bonnet* means only "a hat" in the United States but also "the hood of a car" in Great Britain.

EXERCISE 2 ▶   Answering Word-Origin Riddles

See if you can answer each of the following riddles. First, look up the italicized word in a dictionary that gives word origins. (*Webster's New World Dictionary* is one.) The earliest meaning listed for the word will be your clue to the riddle. Give this meaning along with your answer.

EXAMPLE   **1. Where should a *villain* work?**
          1. *on a farm* (villain *meant "farm tenant"*)

1. Why do *silly* people smile all the time?
2. What should you do with a *brat*?
3. Why do *comets* need shampoo?
4. Why is cheese a good food for your *muscles*?
5. What should you buy with your *salary*?

Where Does It Come From?

Have you ever *munched* a *burrito* or *feasted* on *chop suey*? If so, then you haven't just eaten foods from different cultures. You've also used words from different languages.

About 15 percent of the words we use are native to English. The rest have been borrowed or adapted from other languages. Many nonnative words were borrowed as English people came into contact with people from other cultures and lands. Here are a few examples of words that have been borrowed in the past one thousand years.

NORSE	leg, fellow, get
LATIN	area, candle, decorate, joke
FRENCH	beauty, dance, study
SPANISH	chili, hurricane, mustang
NATIVE AMERICAN LANGUAGES	bayou, chipmunk, squash
AFRICAN LANGUAGES	jazz, okra, gumbo

LOOKING AT

Name Your Phobia

Can you catch *brontophobia* from a brontosaurus? Has someone with *anthophobia* been bitten by ants? Neither of these words means what it sounds like. For each, the key to the meaning is the ending –*phobia*, which comes from the Greek word *phobos*, "fear."

The ending –*phobia* is added to Greek and Latin root words to describe all kinds of fears. *Brontophobia*, from *bronte*, "thunder," means "fear of thunder." *Anthophobia*, from *anthos*, "flower," means "fear of flowers." Some better-known phobias include *claustrophobia*, "fear of closed-in spaces," and *arachnophobia*, "fear of spiders."

See how Gary Larson came up with the –*phobia* word that he used in the following cartoon. Why would his made-up word look familiar to an *ornithologist*, someone who studies birds?

Anatidaephobia: The fear that somewhere, somehow, a duck is watching you.

In coming up with the name for the phobia, I played around with words like "quackaphobia" and "duckalookaphobia" and so on. But then I got the bright idea to look up the scientific name for ducks, and discovered their family name is *Anatidae*. And so, I ended up coining a word that twelve ornithologists understood and everyone else probably went, "Say what?"

Gary Larson,
The PreHistory of the Far Side

EXERCISE 3 ▶   Researching Word Origins

Each of the following words came into English from another language. Using a dictionary that gives word origins, find out what language each word was borrowed from. Give a date for the word's entry into English if your dictionary lists one.

1. tea
2. sketch
3. shawl
4. parade
5. census

6. same
7. school
8. command
9. salsa
10. skunk

Dialects of American English

You probably know people whose English is different from yours. Maybe they pronounce words strangely, or maybe they use words in unfamiliar ways. Your English probably sounds as "funny" to them as theirs sounds to you.

Because ways of speaking vary so widely, the English of one group of people is bound to sound "funny" to another group. There are many different forms of English, and no form is better or worse than another. The variety of English used by a particular group of people is called a *dialect.* In this section, you'll learn about two types of American English dialects, *regional dialects* and *ethnic dialects*.

Regional Dialects

Do you carry a *pail* or a *bucket*? Do you *wash* (or *warsh*) the *car* (or *cah*)? Do you stand *on* line or *in* line? Where you come from can help determine what words you use, how you pronounce words, and how you put words together. A dialect shared by people from the same area of the United States is called a *regional dialect.*

Not everyone who lives in a region uses that region's dialect. Someone from Alabama or Georgia won't necessarily say *y'all*, and someone from Boston may not pronounce *farm* like *fahm*. When people move from place to place, they often lose some of their old dialect and learn a new one.

Ethnic Dialects

People who share the same cultural heritage may share a dialect of English, too. The English used by a particular cultural group is called an *ethnic dialect.* Widely used American ethnic dialects include the Black English of many African Americans and the Spanish-influenced English of many people whose families come from Mexico, Central America, Cuba, and Puerto Rico.

Many words that are now part of general English usage originally came from ethnic dialects. For example, the words *afro, jazz,* and *jukebox* were originally Black English dialect words, and *arroyo, mesa,* and *taco* were originally from Hispanic English.

EXERCISE 4 ▶ **Reading a Dialect**

In the following excerpt, the speaker, Stanley Hicks, is describing some happy memories from his childhood. He is from Sugar Grove, North Carolina, and speaks Appalachian dialect. Read the passage aloud to hear the sounds of Hicks's dialect. Try to pronounce the words as the writer has spelled them. Is Stanley Hicks's dialect different from yours? If it is, tell how you would say the same things in your own words.

> And we used to play fox and goose. You've got two red foxes—you know, red grains of corn—and the rest of them is white. Play on a board like a checkerboard. And then the geese tries to hem these foxes up. Dad'd get 'em hemmed up and he'd say, "Que-e-e-e-e-e-e! Listen to her wheeze!" He'd say, "Watch her wiggle her tail, boys! She's a-dying!" It'd made us so cussed mad, you know. He was good on it. And then every time he'd jump one of our geese, he'd go "Quack!" Make like a goose a-hollering, you know.
>
> Eliot Wigginton,
> *I Wish I Could Give My Son a Wild Raccoon*

Standard American English

Every variety of English has its own set of rules and guidelines. No variety is the best or the most correct. However, one kind of English is more widely used and accepted than others in the United States. This variety is called *standard American English.*

Standard American English is the one variety that belongs to all of us. Because it's commonly understood, it allows people from many different regions and cultures to communicate with one another clearly. It is the variety of English used most often in books and magazines, on radio and television. It is the variety people are expected to use in most school and business situations.

The **Handbook** in this textbook gives you some of the rules and guidelines for using standard American English. To identify the differences between standard American English and other varieties of English, the **Handbook** uses the labels *standard* and *nonstandard. Nonstandard* doesn't mean wrong language. It means language that is inappropriate in situations where standard English is expected.

☞ REFERENCE NOTE: For more about standard English, see page 653

Choosing Your Words

Because English offers you many different ways to say the same thing, you have to make decisions every time you speak and write. Sometimes you make these choices naturally. For example, you probably don't think much about word choice when you're talking with a friend. But at other times, especially when you write, you need to give some thought to the words you use. You need to make sure your words are clear, effective, and appropriate.

Formal and Informal English

Read the following sentences:

> I really enjoyed that story about the men who climbed Mount Everest.
> I really got into that story about the guys who climbed Mount Everest.

Just a few words have been changed from the first sentence to the second, but the effect of each sentence is different. One is written in *formal English* and the other in *informal English.*

Different levels of formality in language are appropriate for different situations. You might use the more formal language of the first example sentence if you were telling a teacher how you liked a story. But if you were talking about the story to a classmate, you might use informal expressions like *got into* and *guys.*

Uses of Informal English

There are two kinds of informal English that you should be familiar with: *colloquialisms* and *slang.*

Colloquialisms are the casual, colorful expressions that we use in everyday conversation. Many colloquialisms aren't meant to be taken literally. They have understood meanings that are different from the basic meanings of the words.

EXAMPLES The band **brought down the house** with the last number.
The plot of that movie was **hard to swallow.**
We'll order some sandwiches **to go.**

Slang consists of made-up words or old words used in new ways. Slang words are usually the special language of a particular group of people, such as teenagers or musicians. You and your friends probably use slang that's unique to your generation.

Although slang words seem up-to-date when they're first used, they tend to fall out of style very quickly. Some of the slang words in the following sentences probably seem dated to you.

EXAMPLES That's a **groovy** set of **wheels, man.**
That last scene really **broke me up.**
Where did you get those **neat** shoes?
Tim just got a **rad** new haircut.

> **STYLE NOTE** Don't use slang in essays, test answers, or reports. If you use slang in a formal speaking or writing situation, your audience may think you are not serious about your subject. However, you may want to use slang in short stories. For example, if one of your characters is a teenager, slang will help make the character's dialogue seem realistic.

EXERCISE 5 ▶ **Writing Letters in Formal or Informal English**

You've just returned from visiting a friend in another state. You want to write letters to your friend and your friend's parents telling them what a good time you had.

Write the thank-you note you would send to your friend's parents and the letter you would send to your friend. In each letter, mention some parts of your visit that you especially enjoyed—for example, a sightseeing trip, a day at an amusement park, or a family barbecue. Use the formal or informal English that you think is appropriate for each letter.

Denotation and Connotation

Suppose you heard someone say, "Cara is beautiful and scrawny." You'd probably wonder whether the person meant to compliment or insult Cara. *Scrawny* is another way of saying "thin." That is the word's basic meaning, or **denotation.** But *scrawny* and *thin* create very different pictures of a person. *Scrawny* suggests that Cara is bony and looks underfed. This is the emotional association, or **connotation,** of the word.

It's important to think about the connotations of the words you use. If you use a word without knowing its connotations, you may send the wrong message to your audience.

EXERCISE 6 ▶ **Responding to Connotations**

Which of the words in each pair would you prefer if someone were describing you? Why?

1. stubborn, determined
2. serious, grim
3. eccentric, weird
4. wishy-washy, undecided
5. sensitive, touchy

Tired Words and Expressions

A tired word is a dull, worn-out word. It has been used so often and so carelessly that it has become almost meaningless. Tired words like *nice, fine, great,* and *wonderful* are common in everyday conversation, but they are too dull and vague to be effective in writing.

Tired expressions are often called *clichés.* Many clichés were striking and vivid the first time they were used. But after a while, they lost their originality and their expressiveness. Here are some examples of clichés; you can probably think of many more.

break the ice	easier said than done
busy as a bee	eat like a horse
the crack of dawn	on top of the world
clear as a bell	sadder but wiser

STYLE NOTE Most writers have a few favorite words that they tend to overuse. If a word appears too often in your writing, find *synonyms* for it— words that have a similar meaning. You can look up synonyms in a *thesaurus,* a dictionary of synonyms. Keep in mind, though, that no two words have exactly the same meaning. Before you use a synonym, look up the word in a dictionary to make sure it has the meaning you intend.

COMPUTER NOTE: Use your word-processing program's thesaurus to help you find vivid words to replace overused ones as you draft or revise.

EXERCISE 7 ▶ **Identifying Tired Words and Clichés**

Make a list of all the tired words and expressions you can think of. You may want to spend a few days watching and listening for them, jotting down words and expressions as you hear them. Then compare your list with those of your classmates. By combining lists, you'll have a handy collection of words and expressions to avoid when you write.

Jargon

Jargon is special language that is used by a particular group of people, such as people who share the same profession, occupation, sport, or hobby. For example, the word *set* is used as theater jargon for "the props and scenery arranged on a stage" or "the act of arranging scenery on a stage." Like *set*, many jargon words are ordinary words that have been given special meanings.

Jargon can be practical and effective because it reduces many words to just one or two. However, don't use jargon when you are writing for or speaking to a general audience who may not be familiar with the terms. Even people working in the same company may not understand each other's jargon if they work in different areas.

☞ REFERENCE NOTE: For an example of how dictionaries label special uses of words, see page 858.

EXERCISE 8 ▶ **Translating Jargon**

Look up each of the following words in a dictionary to find out what the word means for the group indicated. For help with looking up special uses of words, see page 858.

1. *taw*—marble players
2. *strike*—baseball players
3. *pan*—filmmakers
4. *lock*—wrestlers
5. *proof*—photographers

MAKING CONNECTIONS

Identify Dated Language

When you watch reruns of old television shows, you probably notice that the people's clothes and cars seem out of style. But have you ever noticed that their way of talking seems dated, too? By watching a television show from twenty years ago, you can get a good sense of how people's everyday language has changed over time.

Watch at least one rerun of a situation comedy from the 1970s. Listen to the characters' language—especially that of teenage characters. Jot down any words and expressions that seem dated or unfamiliar to you.

Which of the words and expressions on your list are colloquialisms or slang? What words and expressions do you and your friends use today to mean the same things?

HANDBOOK

GRAMMAR

USAGE

MECHANICS

13 THE SENTENCE

Subject and Predicate, Kinds of Sentences

Diagnostic Test

A. Identifying Sentences

Some of the following groups of words are sentences; others are not. If a group of words is a sentence, add a capital letter at the beginning and an appropriate punctuation mark at the end. If a group of words is not a sentence, write *sentence fragment*.

EXAMPLES **1.** revised the paper and then proofread it
1. *sentence fragment*

2. we can meet you at the bus stop after school
2. *We can meet you at the bus stop after school.*

1. one day this week or maybe next week
2. will you lend me that book
3. on her vacation she met her pen pal for the first time
4. his favorite meal, cheese enchiladas with refried beans
5. lock the door on your way out

B. Identifying Simple Subjects and Simple Predicates

Identify each *simple subject* and *simple predicate* in the following sentences. [Hint: Be on the alert for compound subjects, compound verbs, and verb phrases.]

EXAMPLE **1.** Foods and beverages with large amounts of sugar can contribute to tooth decay.
          1. *Foods, beverages—simple subject; can contribute—simple predicate*

  6. The lava from a volcano can be very dangerous.
  7. The earthquake survivors camped on blankets in the streets.
  8. In Beijing, cyclists pedal on the sidewalks and weave expertly through the busy streets.
  9. Between 1896 and 1899, gold prospectors rushed to Alaska.
10. The weather during an Alaskan summer can be very hot.
11. Have you read this collection of Claude McKay's poems?
12. In the center of the table was a huge bowl of fruit.
13. Linked forever in legend are Paul Bunyan and Babe the Blue Ox.
14. Many famous racehorses have been raised or trained in Kentucky.
15. The bright lights and the tall buildings amaze and delight most visitors to New York City.

C. Classifying and Punctuating Sentences

For each of the following sentences, add the correct end mark of punctuation. Then label each sentence *declarative, interrogative, imperative,* or *exclamatory.*

EXAMPLE **1.** Has anyone guessed the right number
          1. *Has anyone guessed the right number?— interrogative*

GRAMMAR

16. We celebrate our parents' anniversary every year
17. Don't tell them about our surprise
18. Our cousins are coming all the way from Hawaii
19. Who is in charge of decorations
20. What a beautiful Navajo blanket that is

Sentence Sense

13a. A *sentence* is a group of words that expresses a complete thought.

A sentence begins with a capital letter and ends with a period, a question mark, or an exclamation point.

EXAMPLES **Alice Walker won a prize for her book.**
Please fasten your seat belt.
Why did you stop running?
Watch out for the car!

When a group of words looks like a sentence but does not express a complete thought, it is a *sentence fragment.*

SENTENCE FRAGMENT **After they pitched the tent.** [This is not a complete thought. What happened after they pitched the tent?]

SENTENCE **After they pitched the tent, they built a campfire.**

SENTENCE FRAGMENT **Sailing around the world.** [The thought is not complete. Who is sailing around the world?]

SENTENCE **Some marine biologists are sailing around the world.**

SENTENCE FRAGMENT **Her hike through the Grand Canyon.** [The thought is not complete. What about her hike?]

SENTENCE **Sheila enjoyed her hike through the Grand Canyon.**

▶ EXERCISE 1   **Identifying Sentences**

Tell whether each of the following groups of words is a *sentence* or a *sentence fragment*. If a group of words is a sentence, use a capital letter at the beginning and add a mark of punctuation at the end.

EXAMPLES   [1] during her vacation last summer
1. *sentence fragment*

[2] my friend Michelle visited Colorado
2. *sentence—My friend Michelle visited Colorado.*

[1] she took an exciting boat trip on the Colorado River [2] running the rapids [3] at first her boat drifted calmly through the Grand Canyon [4] then the river dropped suddenly [5] and became foaming rapids full of dangerous boulders [6] which can break a boat [7] Michelle's boat was small, like the one in this picture [8] with one guide and four passengers [9] some people prefer large inflatable boats with outboard motors [10] that can carry eighteen passengers

The Subject and the Predicate

Every sentence has two parts: a *subject* and a *predicate*.

The Subject

13b. The *subject* tells whom or what the sentence is about.

EXAMPLES   **Nicholasa Mohr** is a writer and an artist.
The girls on the team were all good students.

To find the subject, ask *who* or *what* is doing something, or *whom* or *what* is being talked about. The subject may come at the beginning, middle, or end of a sentence.

EXAMPLES   **The pitcher** struck Felicia out. [*Who* struck Felicia out? *The pitcher* did.]
After practicing for hours, **Timmy** bowled two strikes. [*Who* bowled two strikes? *Timmy* did.]
Hiding in the tall grass was **a baby rabbit**. [*What* was hiding? *A baby rabbit* was.]

EXERCISE 2   **Identifying Subjects**

Identify the subject of each of the following sentences.

EXAMPLE   **1.** Have you read a book by N. Scott Momaday?
1. *you*

1. Born in 1934 in Oklahoma, Momaday lived on Navajo and Apache reservations in the Southwest.
2. Momaday's father was a Kiowa.
3. As a young man, Momaday attended the University of New Mexico and Stanford University.
4. In *The Way to Rainy Mountain*, Momaday tells about the myths and history of the Kiowa people.
5. The book includes poems, an essay, and stories about the Kiowa people.
6. *The Way to Rainy Mountain* was published in 1969.

7. After Momaday's book came other works by Native American writers.
8. William Least Heat-Moon traveled in a van across the United States and wrote about his journey.
9. Was he inspired to write by his travels?
10. Readers of this Osage writer enjoy his beautiful descriptions of nature.

 EXERCISE 3   **Writing Subjects and Punctuating Sentences**

Add subjects to fill in the blanks in the following sentences. Begin each sentence with a capital letter, and end it with a mark of punctuation.

EXAMPLE   **1.** ＿＿ is very heavy
            1. *This bag of cement is very heavy.*

1. ＿＿ is a difficult game to play
2. ＿＿ works in the post office
3. Luckily for me, ＿＿ was easy to read
4. Tied to the end of the rope was ＿＿
5. Did ＿＿ help you

Complete Subject and Simple Subject

The *complete subject* consists of all the words needed to tell *whom* or *what* a sentence is about.

13c.   The *simple subject* is the main word or words in the complete subject.

EXAMPLES   **The four new students** arrived early.
            Complete subject   The four new students
              Simple subject   students

            A round walnut table with five legs stood in the middle of the dining room.
            Complete subject   A round walnut table with five legs
              Simple subject   table

If you leave out the simple subject, a sentence does not make sense.

EXAMPLES   The four new . . . arrived early.
A round walnut . . . with five legs stood in the middle of the dining room.

A simple subject may consist of one word or several words.

EXAMPLES   **Jets** break the sound barrier. [one word]
Does **Aunt Carmen** own a grocery store? [two words]
On the library shelf was ***The Island of the Blue Dolphins.*** [six words]

NOTE: In this book, the term *subject* refers to the simple subject unless otherwise indicated.

EXERCISE 4 — Identifying Complete Subjects and Simple Subjects

Identify the complete subject in each of the following sentences. Then, underline the simple subject.

EXAMPLES   1. Stories about time travel make exciting reading.
1. *Stories* about time travel
2. Samuel Delany writes great science fiction.
2. *Samuel Delany*

1. Ray Bradbury is also a writer of science fiction.
2. *The Golden Apples of the Sun* is a collection of his short stories.
3. My favorite story in that book is "A Sound of Thunder."
4. The main character in the story is called Mr. Eckels.
5. For ten thousand dollars, Mr. Eckels joins Time Safari, Inc.
6. He is looking for the dinosaur *Tyrannosaurus rex.*
7. With four other men, Bradbury's hero travels over sixty million years back in time.
8. On the safari, trouble develops.

9. Because of one mistake, the past is changed.
10. The results of that mistake affect the future.

The Predicate

13d. The *predicate* of a sentence is the part that says something about the subject.

EXAMPLES   Old Faithful **is a giant geyser in Yellowstone National Park.**
Jade Snow Wong **wrote about growing up in San Francisco's Chinatown.**

Like the subject, the predicate may be found anywhere in a sentence.

EXAMPLES   **Outside the tent was** a baby bear.
Late in the night we **heard a noise.**

EXERCISE 5   **Identifying Predicates**

Identify the predicate in each of the sentences in the following paragraph.

EXAMPLE   [1] My favorite sports poster is this one of Roberto Clemente.
1. *is this one of Roberto Clemente*

[1] Also among my treasures is a book about Clemente. [2] Clemente played right field for the Pittsburgh Pirates. [3] During his career, he won four National League batting titles. [4] In 1966, he was named the league's Most Valuable Player. [5] Twice Clemente helped lead the Pirates to World Series victories. [6] In fourteen World Series games, Clemente

Roberto Clemente
Pittsburgh Pirates

never went without a hit. [7] Roberto Clemente died in a plane crash off the coast of his homeland, Puerto Rico. [8] The crash occurred on a flight to Nicaragua to aid earthquake victims. [9] After his death, Clemente was elected to the National Baseball Hall of Fame. [10] In New York, a park has been named for this beloved ballplayer.

▶ EXERCISE 6 **Writing Predicates**

Make a sentence out of each of the following groups of words by adding a predicate to fill the blank or blanks.

EXAMPLES **1.** A flock of geese ____.
1. *A flock of geese flew high overhead.*

2. ____ a poster of Nelson Mandela.
2. *Over Kim's desk hung a poster of Nelson Mandela.*

1. My favorite food ____.
2. A course in first aid ____.
3. ____ our car ____.
4. Rock climbing ____.
5. Spanish explorers in the Americas ____.
6. Several computers ____.
7. ____ a new pair of roller skates.
8. The skyscrapers of New York City ____.
9. Some dogs ____.
10. ____ my family ____.

Complete Predicate and Simple Predicate

The *complete predicate* consists of all the words that say something about the subject.

13e. The *simple predicate,* or *verb,* is the main word or group of words in the complete predicate.

EXAMPLES The pilot broke the sound barrier.
Complete predicate broke the sound barrier.
Simple predicate (verb) broke

We should have visited the diamond field in Arkansas.

> *Complete predicate*   should have visited the diamond field in Arkansas.
>
> *Simple predicate (verb)*   should have visited

NOTE: In this book, the simple predicate is usually referred to as the *verb*.

▶ EXERCISE 7   **Identifying Complete Predicates and Verbs**

Identify the complete predicate of each of the following sentences. Then, underline the verb.

EXAMPLE   **1.** Nobody knows the creator of the U.S. flag.
   1. <u>knows</u> *the creator of the U.S. flag*

1. Scholars are unsure about the history of the Stars and Stripes.
2. The Continental Congress approved a design for the flag.
3. The design included thirteen red stripes and thirteen white stripes.
4. The top inner quarter of the flag was a blue field with thirteen white stars.
5. The name of the designer remains a mystery.
6. During the American Revolution, the colonists needed a symbol of their independence.
7. George Washington wanted flags for the army.
8. Unfortunately, Washington's flags arrived after the end of the Revolutionary War.
9. According to legend, Betsy Ross made the first flag.
10. Historians doubt the Betsy Ross story.

The Verb Phrase

Some verbs consist of more than one word. Such a verb is called a *verb phrase.*

EXAMPLES   Kathy **is riding** the Ferris wheel.
The carnival **has been** in town for two weeks.
Bernice **should have been** here sooner.

NOTE: The words *not* and *never* are not verbs. They are never part of a verb or verb phrase.

        EXAMPLES   She **has** not **written** to me recently.
                   I **will** never **forget** her.

EXERCISE 8   **Identifying Verbs and Verb Phrases**

Identify the verb or verb phrase in each of the following sentences.

EXAMPLES   **1.** Look at these beautiful pictures of Hawaii.
              1. *Look*

             2. They were taken by our science teacher.
             2. *were taken*

1. Hawaii is called the Aloha State.
2. It was settled by Polynesians around the year 750.
3. The musical heritage and rich culture of the original Hawaiians have contributed much to the islands' popularity.
4. Hawaii has the largest, most active volcanoes in the world.
5. These volcanoes may be viewed by tourists in Hawaii Volcanoes National Park.

Finding the Subject

Sometimes it's difficult to locate the subject of a sentence. In such cases, it can help to find the verb first and then to ask yourself *whom* or *what* the verb is referring to.

EXAMPLES   In high school we will have more homework. [The verb is *will have*. *Who* will have? *We* will have. *We* is the subject of the sentence.]

Can you untie this knot? [*Can untie* is the verb. *Who* can untie? *You* can untie. *You* is the subject of the sentence.]

The peak of Mount Everest was first reached by Sir Edmund Hillary and Tenzing Norgay. [The verb is *was reached*. *What* was reached? The answer is *peak*. *Peak* is the subject of the sentence.]

Ahead of the explorers lay a vast wilderness. [The verb is *lay*. What *lay*? The answer is *wilderness*. *Wilderness* is the subject of the sentence.]

NOTE: The subject of a sentence is never part of a prepositional phrase.

EXAMPLE   The papayas on the table look tasty. [*What* look tasty? *Papayas.* To say *table look tasty* doesn't make sense.]

WRITING APPLICATION

Using Complete Sentences in a Letter

Sometimes a thought or an impression is so clear in your mind that you forget that others do not see it as clearly. Where you express such thoughts and expressions, you may be tempted to use a single word or phrase rather than a complete statement.

GRAMMAR

SENTENCE FRAGMENTS	What a great birthday party! All my friends. Good eats—popcorn, roasted peanuts, lots of goodies. Playing games. Music. Dancing.
COMPLETE SENTENCES	I had a great birthday party. All my friends were there. My mom and I made popcorn, roasted peanuts, and made lots of other goodies. Everybody had fun playing games, listening to music, and dancing.

To make sure that others can clearly understand you, use complete sentences.

▶ WRITING ACTIVITY

Yesterday, you went to a birthday party. Write a letter to a friend or relative who lives far away. In your letter, describe where the party was held, how long it lasted, and what refreshments were served. Also include details about the activities you enjoyed and about the other people who were there. Use complete sentences to make sure your thoughts are clear.

Prewriting   Make a list of the details that you'd like to include in your letter. At this stage, you don't have to use complete sentences—just jot down your thoughts as they come to you.

Writing   Use your prewriting list of details as you write your rough draft. Choose details that would be interesting to your friend or relative. You might organize your letter chronologically (telling about events in the order they occurred). Or you might want to tell about one or two important events.

Evaluating and Revising   Read your letter aloud. As you read, mark any parts of the letter that seem unclear. Add, cut, or rearrange details to make your letter clear and interesting to your reader. (See pages 361–371 for information on combining sentences.) Check your work once again to make sure you have used only complete sentences.

Proofreading   Read over your letter for errors in spelling and punctuation. Be sure that you have capitalized the first word of each sentence and have ended each sentence with correct punctuation.

Compound Subjects and Compound Verbs

Compound Subjects

13f.   A *compound subject* consists of two or more connected subjects that have the same verb. The usual connecting word is *and* or *or*.

EXAMPLES   **Paris** and **London** remain favorite tourist attractions. [The two parts of the compound subject have the same verb, *remain.*]
Nelson Mandela or **Archbishop Desmond Tutu** will speak at tomorrow's conference. [The two parts of the compound subject have the same verb phrase, *will speak.*]
Among my hobbies are **reading, snorkeling,** and **painting.** [The three parts of the compound subject have the same verb, *are.*]

▶ EXERCISE 9   **Identifying Compound Subjects**

Identify the compound subject in each of the following sentences.

EXAMPLE   **1.** The shapes and sizes of sand dunes are determined by the wind.
      1. *shapes, sizes*

1. The national parks and monuments of the United States include many of the world's most spectacular landforms.

2. The Grand Canyon and the waterfalls of Yosemite are examples of landforms shaped by erosion.
3. Water and other natural forces are continuing the age-old erosion of landforms.
4. On the Colorado Plateau, for example, natural bridges and arches like the ones shown below have been produced by erosion.
5. Likewise, Skyline Arch and Landscape Arch in Utah are two natural arches formed by erosion.
6. Underground, caves and immense caverns are created by rushing streams and waterfalls.
7. Stalagmites and stalactites such as the ones in the photo on the right are formed by lime deposits from drops of water seeping into these caverns.
8. In river systems throughout the world, canyons and gorges are cut into the earth by erosion.
9. Many rapids and waterfalls have also originated through erosion.
10. Do steep areas with heavy rainfall or dry regions with few trees suffer more from erosion?

EXERCISE 10 Writing Compound Subjects

Add a compound subject to each of the following predicates. Use *and* or *or* to join the parts of your compound
subjects.

EXAMPLE **1.** ____ were at the bottom of my locker.
1. *My bus pass and a pair of gym socks were at
the bottom of my locker.*

1. Yesterday ____ arrived in the mail.
2. ____ make loyal pets.
3. On the beach ____ spotted a dolphin.
4. ____ will present their report on Álvar Núñez Cabeza
de Vaca.
5. In the attic were piled ____.

Compound Verbs

13g. A *compound verb* consists of two or more
connected verbs that have the same subject. A
connecting word—usually *and, or,* or *but*—is
used to join the verbs.

EXAMPLES The basketball team **played** well but **lost** the
game anyway.
The rain **has fallen** for days and **is** still **falling** in
some areas.

A sentence may have both a *compound subject* and a
compound verb. Notice in the following example that both
subjects carry out the action of both verbs.

EXAMPLE A few **vegetables** and many **flowers sprouted**
and **grew** in the rich soil. [The vegetables
sprouted and grew, and the flowers sprouted
and grew.]

EXERCISE 11 Identifying Compound Verbs

Identify each compound verb or verb phrase in the following sentences.

EXAMPLE   **1.** Just like children today, children in ancient
              Egypt played games and enjoyed toys.
            1. *played, enjoyed*

1. Have you heard of the game Serpent or learned the game Senet?
2. For the Egyptian board game Serpent, players found or carved a serpent-shaped stone.
3. Players placed the serpent in the center of the board and then began the game.
4. They used place markers and threw bones or sticks as dice.
5. The players took turns and competed with one another in a race to the center.
6. Senet was another ancient Egyptian board game and was played by children and adults alike.
7. Senet looked like an easy game but was actually quite difficult.
8. Players moved their playing pieces toward the ends of three rows of squares but sometimes were stopped by their opponents.
9. Senet boards were complex and had certain squares for good luck and bad luck.
10. These squares could help players or could block their playing pieces.

▶ EXERCISE 12   **Writing Appropriate Compound Verbs**

Where in the solar system are you? That's what you—the captain of this spaceship—want to find out. To do so, you've called up on your viewing screen the map shown on the next page. Look at the map and find your spaceship among the planets. Then use the map and the accompanying notes you've made in your log to write your official report for the last three days of June. (Be as imaginative as you want.) Use at least five sentences that have compound verbs.

EXAMPLE   *We then landed on Jobel's Dark Spot and captured Shelzan, king of the Noidles.*

LOG NOTES

FRIDAY
JUNE
28

rough trip through Banzoi Asteroid Belt
contacted Intergalactic Command for
instructions   Dark Spot on Jobel   captured
Shelzan—king of the Noidles

SATURDAY
JUNE
29

surveyed Prog   strange light   spotted
ancient satellite Voyager I   lost gravity field
crater creature

SUNDAY
JUNE
30

ship's fuel low   sighted Bittzer's Comet
landing on Grepinak   took on supplies
frozen fog   plan next course

MONDAY
JULY

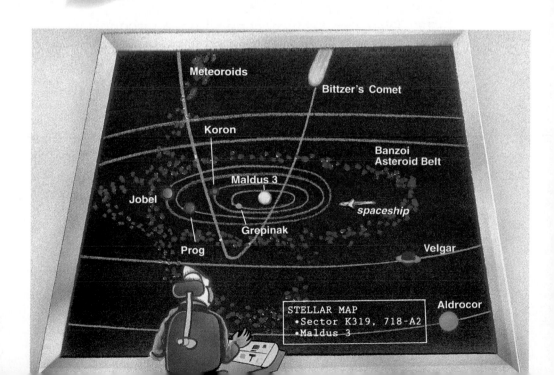

▶ EXERCISE 13   **Identifying Subjects and Verbs**

Identify the subject and verb in each of the following sentences. Some of the subjects and verbs are compound.

EXAMPLE   **1.** American pioneers left their homes and traveled to the West.
　　　　 1. *pioneers—subject; left, traveled—verbs*

1. Settlers faced and overcame many dangers.
2. Mount McKinley and Mount Whitney are two very high mountains.
3. Sacagawea of the Shoshones helped open the West.
4. Every winter many skiers rush to the Grand Tetons.
5. Few Hollywood stars have been both born and raised in California.
6. Broad valleys and dense forests cool and refresh travelers through the Appalachian Mountains.
7. On Beartooth Highway in Montana, excellent campgrounds and scenic overlooks provide many views of distant glaciers.
8. Mount Evans is west of Denver and can be reached by the highest paved road in America.
9. The view from the top slopes of Mount Evans is breathtaking.
10. The name *Kentucky* comes from an Iroquois word and means "meadowland."

▶ REVIEW A   **Identifying Subjects and Predicates**

Write the following sentences. Underline the complete subjects once and the complete predicates twice. Then, circle each simple subject and each verb or verb phrase.

EXAMPLE   **1.** The seven continents are divisions of the earth's land.
　　　　 1. The seven (continents) (are) divisions of the earth's land.

1. The entire continent of Australia is occupied by a single nation.
2. Can you name the capital of Australia?

3. Australia is a federation of six states and two territories.
4. The continent was claimed for Britain by Captain James Cook.
5. The native people of Australia live mainly in the desert regions and have a very close bond to their environment.
6. British colonists settled in cities on the coast.
7. Many ranchers raise sheep and export wool.
8. In addition, large quantities of gold and uranium are mined in Australia.
9. The country is also highly industrialized and produces a variety of goods, ranging from shoes to airplanes.
10. Among Australia's unusual animals are the platypus and the anteater.

Kinds of Sentences

13h. A *declarative sentence* makes a statement. It is always followed by a period.

EXAMPLES   Amy Tan was born in Oakland, California.
I couldn't hear what Jason said.

13i. An *imperative sentence* gives a command or makes a request. It is usually followed by a period. A strong command is followed by an exclamation point.

EXAMPLES   Be quiet during the play.
Please give me another piece of melon.
Stop!

The subject of a command or a request is always *you*, although *you* doesn't appear in the sentence. In such cases, *you* is called the **understood subject.**

EXAMPLES (You) Be quiet during the play.
(You) Please give me another piece of melon.
(You) Stop!

The word *you* is the understood subject even when the person spoken to is addressed by name.

EXAMPLE Miguel, (you) please answer the door.

13j. An *interrogative sentence* asks a question. It is followed by a question mark.

EXAMPLES When did Thurgood Marshall retire from the Supreme Court?
Did the surfboard cost much?

13k. An *exclamatory sentence* shows excitement or expresses strong feeling. It is followed by an exclamation point.

EXAMPLES Gabriella won the match!
How terrifying that movie was!

PICTURE THIS

The time is the 1960s. The young men on stage are the Beatles. You are a reporter for *Rock Roots,* a music databank that is popular in the twenty-third century. You've been transported back in time to write a short review of this Beatles concert. You find the Beatles' hair styles and clothes most unusual, and you're amazed at the number of police on the scene to protect the group from the crowd. As you watch the concert, you compare it with rock concerts of the twenty-third century. Because space is limited on the databank, your review must be no longer than ten sentences. In your review, use at least one example of each of the four kinds of sentences (declarative, imperative, interrogative, and exclamatory).

Subject: Beatles concert
Audience: users of music history databank *Rock Roots*
Purpose: to inform

▶ EXERCISE 14 **Classifying Sentences by Purpose**

Label each of the following sentences as *declarative, imperative, interrogative,* or *exclamatory.*

EXAMPLE **1.** Ask Yoshiko for the address.
               1. *imperative*

1. Will your grandfather compete in the Kansas Senior Olympics again this year?
2. Our school's clean-up project was so successful that the local newspaper ran a story about us.
3. What enthusiasm those dancers showed!
4. Is the Rig-Veda the oldest of the Hindu scriptures?
5. Read this poem by Naomi Shihab Nye.
6. How huge this library is!
7. Origami is a fascinating Japanese folk art.
8. How did you make that paper crane?
9. Please line up alphabetically in front of the bleachers on the left side of the gymnasium.
10. After we eat supper, we're going to my aunt's house.

GRAMMAR

▶ REVIEW B   **Classifying and Punctuating Sentences**

Add the correct end mark of punctuation to each of the following sentences. Then, label each sentence as *declarative*, *imperative*, *interrogative*, or *exclamatory*.

EXAMPLE   **1.** Are prairie dogs social creatures

         1. *Are prairie dogs social creatures?—interrogative*

1. Many of these small mammals live together in underground "towns" like the one shown below
2. As you can see, American prairie dogs dig family burrows
3. These burrows sometimes cover several acres
4. Have you ever seen a prairie dog
5. These creatures can usually be seen at night or in the early morning
6. What alert animals prairie dogs are
7. At least one prairie dog always keeps a constant lookout for threats to the community
8. Look at how it sits up to see better
9. It will make a shrill whistle of alarm at the first sign of danger
10. It then dives headfirst into the burrow and alerts the entire colony

Review: Posttest 1

A. Identifying Sentences

Label each of the following groups of words as a *sentence* or a *sentence fragment*. Write each sentence, using a capital letter at the beginning and an end mark of punctuation.

EXAMPLES   **1.** having forgotten their homework
               1. *sentence fragment*

               2. how strong the wind is
               2. *sentence—How strong the wind is!*

1. after we visit the library and gather information for the report
2. are you ready for the big game next week
3. listen closely to our guest speaker
4. have read the first draft of my paper
5. an excellent short story, "The Medicine Bag," is in that book

B. Identifying Simple Subjects and Verbs

Identify the simple subject and the verb in each of the following sentences.

EXAMPLE   **1.** A computer can be a wonderful tool for people with disabilities.
               1. *computer—simple subject; can be—verb*

6. Specially designed machines have been developed in recent years.
7. Have you ever seen a talking computer?
8. It is used by both visually impaired people and sighted people.
9. Its electronic voice speaks the words typed into the machine.
10. Most computers show their writing on a screen.

11. However, these special models can give information by voice.
12. Closed-captioned television is another interesting invention.
13. Subtitles appear on the television screens of hearing-impaired viewers.
14. These viewers can read the subtitles and enjoy their favorite shows.
15. Many new inventions make life easier and more enjoyable nowadays.

C. Classifying and Punctuating Sentences

Add the correct end mark of punctuation after the last word in each of the following sentences. Then, label each sentence *declarative, interrogative, imperative,* or *exclamatory.*

EXAMPLE   **1.** Flowers and insects depend on one another for life
    1. *life.—declarative*

16. Have you ever watched a bee in a garden
17. The bee flies busily from one flower to another
18. Notice the pollen on the legs and body of the bee
19. The bee is carrying pollen from flower to flower
20. What a remarkable insect the bee is

Review: Posttest 2

Writing Sentences

Identify each of the following sentence parts as a *complete subject* or a *complete predicate.* Then, use each sentence part in a sentence. Begin each sentence with a capital letter and end it with the correct mark of punctuation.

EXAMPLE   **1.** the tides of the oceans

         1. *complete subject*
         Are the tides of the oceans influenced by the moon?

1. the path through the woods
2. the city of San Juan
3. found a four-leaf clover
4. my favorite television show
5. can call a meeting and take a vote on the matter
6. splashed happily in the shallow water
7. one of the nurses
8. our broken VCR
9. will represent us at the meeting
10. mentioned rain and high winds

14 THE PARTS OF SPEECH

Noun, Pronoun, Adjective

Diagnostic Test

Identifying Nouns, Pronouns, and Adjectives

Identify each italicized word in the following paragraph as a *noun*, a *pronoun*, or an *adjective*.

EXAMPLE The mangrove [1] *tree* grows in [2] *coastal* areas, and [3] *it* sends down roots from its branches.
  1. *noun*
  2. *adjective*
  3. *pronoun*

In [1] *this* country [2] *mangroves* grow along the coasts of [3] *Florida*. [4] *They* form a [5] *wonderland* where land, water, and [6] *sky* blend. [7] *The* lush, green [8] *mangrove* islands and [9] *shoreline* are both beautiful and valuable. Mangroves are [10] *important* to [11] *our* [12] *environment*. They produce [13] *tons* of valuable [14] *vegetable* matter and are an essential part of [15] *tropical* biology. So far as [16] *we* know, the

[17] *first* reference to mangroves dates back to [18] *Egyptian* times. A [19] *South African* expert has also discovered evidence of mangrove islands along the [20] *Red Sea*.

The Eight Parts of Speech			
noun	adjective	adverb	conjunction
pronoun	verb	preposition	interjection

The Noun

14a. A *noun* is a word that names a person, place, thing, or idea.

PERSONS	Jessye Norman, teacher, Dr. Ling, first baseman
PLACES	Grand Canyon, city, Nigeria, kitchen
THINGS	lamp, canary, Nobel Prize, Empire State Building
IDEAS	happiness, self-control, democracy, bravery

Notice that some nouns are made up of more than one word. Such nouns are called *compound nouns.* They may be written as one word, as a hyphenated word, or as two or more words.

ONE WORD	grandmother
HYPHENATED WORD	great-grandmother
TWO WORDS	grand piano

▶ EXERCISE 1   **Identifying Nouns**

Identify the twenty-five nouns in the following paragraph. Some nouns will be used more than once.

EXAMPLE   [1] We have been reading about patriots in our
textbook.
1. *patriots, textbook*

[1] Rebecca Motte was a great patriot. [2] During the Revolutionary War, British soldiers seized her mansion in South Carolina. [3] General Harry Lee told Motte that the Americans would have to burn her home to smoke out the enemy. [4] Motte supported the plan and was glad to help her country. [5] She even supplied the bow and set the arrows on fire for the attack. [6] But the enemy raised the white flag of surrender, and the house was saved. [7] Afterward, Motte invited soldiers from both sides to dinner.

Proper Nouns and Common Nouns

A *proper noun* names a particular person, place, thing, or idea. It always begins with a capital letter. A *common noun* names any one of a group of persons, places, things, or ideas. It is generally not capitalized.

COMMON NOUNS	PROPER NOUNS
girl	Kay O'Neill
writer	Octavio Paz
country	Panama
monument	Eiffel Tower
team	Atlanta Braves
book	*Tiger Eyes*
religion	Buddhism

▶ EXERCISE 2   **Identifying Common and Proper Nouns**

Identify the nouns in the following paragraph as *common* or *proper*. [Note: Some nouns are used more than once.]

EXAMPLE   [1] Mark visited an interesting museum in
Colorado last month.
1. *Mark—proper; museum—common;*
Colorado—proper; month—common

[1] Mark and his parents went to the Black American West Museum and Heritage Center in Denver. [2] The

museum displays many items that cowboys used. [3] These items are from the collection of Paul Stewart, the man who founded the museum. [4] Mark saw saddles, knives, hats, and lariats. [5] He also saw many pictures of African American cowboys. [6] The museum is located in an old house that is listed in the National Register of Historic Places. [7] The house once belonged to Dr. Justina L. Ford. [8] She was the first black woman to become a physician in Colorado. [9] Mark was amazed by all of the old medical instruments in one display. [10] He said he was glad doctors don't use equipment like that anymore.

▶ EXERCISE 3   **Revising Sentences by Using Proper Nouns**

Revise the following sentences by replacing each common noun with a proper noun. You may need to change other words in each sentence. You may also make up proper names to use. Be sure you capitalize all proper nouns.

EXAMPLE   **1.** An ambassador visited a local school and spoke about his country.
             1. *Ambassador Rios visited Jackson High School and spoke about Brazil.*

1. That painting is in a famous museum.
2. The police officer directed us to the building on that street.
3. My relatives, who are from a small town, now live in a large city.
4. The librarian asked my classmate to return the book.
5. That newspaper is published daily; this magazine is published weekly.
6. The girl read a poem for the teacher.
7. That state borders on the ocean.
8. The owner of that store visited two countries during a spring month.
9. A man flew to a northern city one day.
10. The mayor visited our school and talked about our city.

Concrete Nouns and Abstract Nouns

A *concrete noun* names a person, place, or thing that can be perceived by one or more of the senses (sight, sound, taste, touch, smell). An *abstract noun* names an idea, a feeling, a quality, or a characteristic.

CONCRETE NOUNS	poster, music, beans, heat, Florida
ABSTRACT NOUNS	love, fun, freedom, pride, beauty

▶ EXERCISE 4 **Writing Sentences with Concrete and Abstract Nouns**

Identify each noun in the following list as *concrete* or *abstract*. Then, use each noun in an original sentence.

EXAMPLE **1.** truth
       1. *abstract—My mother said I should always tell the truth.*

1. soy sauce   **3.** laughter   **5.** excitement
2. brotherhood   **4.** ice

▶ REVIEW A **Identifying and Classifying Nouns**

Identify the twenty nouns in the following paragraph. Then tell whether each noun is a *common noun* or a *proper noun*. Be sure to capitalize all proper nouns.

EXAMPLE [1] Lillian evanti sang operas in europe, latin america, and africa.
      1. *Lillian Evanti—proper noun; operas—common noun; Europe—proper noun; Latin America—proper noun; Africa—proper noun*

[1] Evanti was the first African American woman to sing opera anywhere in the world. [2] Her talent was recognized early, when at the age of four, she gave a solo concert in washington, d.c. [3] As an adult, she performed in a special concert at the white house for president franklin roosevelt and his wife. [4] Evanti also composed a

musical piece titled *"Himno Panamericano,"* which was a great success. [5] Her career inspired many other African American singers.

▶ REVIEW B   **Using the Different Kinds of Nouns**

Complete the following poem, which is based on this painting titled *Strong Man.* Insert common, proper, concrete, or abstract nouns as directed. Choose nouns that you think will best help to describe or explain the picture. For proper nouns, you will need to make up names of people and places. Be sure you capitalize all proper nouns.

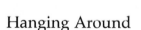

Jacob Lawrence, *Strong Man*, Gouache on paper, 22 × 17". Photo by Chris Eden, Francine Seders Gallery.

Hanging Around

Meet my [1] *(common)* , the really amazing,
Truly tremendous [2] *(proper)* , that's who.
You can see what [3] *(abstract)* he gives
His fans who hang on him like glue.

The walls of his [4] *(concrete)* on [5] *(proper)*
Are covered with [6] *(concrete)* that show
The muscled, tussled [7] *(common)* aplenty,
Who work out there, come rain or come snow.

Eduardo, [8] *(proper)* , and I really enjoy
The [9] *(abstract)* of hanging on tight
Way above the [10] *(concrete)* and swinging,
Held up by the muscle man's might.

The Pronoun

| **14b.** | A *pronoun* is a word used in place of one or more nouns or pronouns. |

EXAMPLES   Ask Dan if Dan has done Dan's homework.
Ask Dan if **he** has done **his** homework.

Both of Lois's friends said both would help Lois find Lois's books.
Both of Lois's friends said **they** would help Lois find **her** books.

The word that a pronoun stands for (or refers to) is called its *antecedent.*

              antecedent   pronoun   pronoun
EXAMPLE   **Frederick,** have **you** turned in **your** report?

Sometimes the antecedent is not stated.

              pronoun
EXAMPLE   **It** was hot outside today.

Personal Pronouns

A *personal pronoun* refers to the one speaking (*first person*), the one spoken to (*second person*), or the one spoken about (*third person*).

PERSONAL PRONOUNS		
	SINGULAR	PLURAL
First person	I, me, my, mine	we, us, our, ours
Second person	you, your, yours	you, your, yours
Third person	he, him, his, she, her, hers, it, its	they, them, their, theirs

NOTE: Some teachers prefer to call possessive pronouns (such as *my, your,* and *their*) possessive adjectives. Follow your teacher's directions in labeling these words.

Reflexive and Intensive Pronouns

A *reflexive pronoun* refers to the subject and directs the action of the verb back to the subject. An *intensive pronoun* emphasizes a noun or another pronoun.

REFLEXIVE AND INTENSIVE PRONOUNS	
FIRST PERSON	myself, ourselves
SECOND PERSON	yourself, yourselves
THIRD PERSON	himself, herself, itself, themselves

REFLEXIVE   Tara enjoyed **herself** at the party.
The band members prided **themselves** on their performance.

INTENSIVE   I **myself** cooked that delicious dinner.
Did you redecorate the room **yourself**?

NOTE: If you are not sure whether a pronoun is reflexive or intensive, use this test. Read the sentence aloud, omitting the pronoun. If the meaning of the sentence stays the same, the pronoun is intensive. If the meaning changes, the pronoun is reflexive.

EXAMPLES   The children enjoyed **themselves** all morning. [Without *themselves,* the sentence doesn't make sense. The pronoun is reflexive.]
Mark repaired the car **himself.** [Without *himself,* the meaning stays the same. The pronoun is intensive.]

Demonstrative Pronouns

A *demonstrative pronoun* points out a person, a place, a thing, or an idea.

Demonstrative Pronouns			
this	that	these	those

GRAMMAR

EXAMPLES **This** is the book I told you about.
Are **these** the kinds of plants that bloom at night?

NOTE: Demonstrative pronouns can also be used as adjectives. When they are used in this way, they are called *demonstrative adjectives.*

DEMONSTRATIVE PRONOUN **Those** are very sturdy shoes.
DEMONSTRATIVE ADJECTIVE **Those** shoes are very sturdy.

Interrogative Pronouns

An *interrogative pronoun* introduces a question.

Interrogative Pronouns				
what	which	who	whom	whose

EXAMPLES **What** is the best brand of frozen yogurt?
Who wrote *Barrio Boy*?

Indefinite Pronouns

An *indefinite pronoun* does not refer to a definite person, place, thing, or idea.

Common Indefinite Pronouns				
all	both	few	nobody	other
any	either	more	none	several
anyone	everything	much	no one	some

EXAMPLES **Both** of the girls forgot their lines.
I would like **some** of that chow mein.

NOTE: Indefinite pronouns can also be used as adjectives.

PRONOUN **Some** are bored by this movie.
ADJECTIVE **Some** people are bored by this movie.

GRAMMAR

Relative Pronouns

A *relative pronoun* introduces a subordinate clause.

Relative Pronouns				
that	which	who	whom	whose

EXAMPLES   Thomas Jefferson, **who** wrote the Declaration of Independence, was our country's third president.

Exercise is one of several methods **that** people use to control their weight.

☞ REFERENCE NOTE: For more information about subordinate clauses, see pages 516–525.

▶ EXERCISE 5   **Identifying Pronouns**

Identify each pronoun and its antecedent in the following sentences. [Note: A sentence may have more than one pronoun.]

EXAMPLE   **1.** The drama coach said he would postpone the rehearsal.

1. *he—coach*

1. "I want you to study," Ms. Gaines said to the class.
2. The firefighter carefully adjusted her oxygen mask.
3. The children made lunch themselves.
4. Jenny and Rosa decided they would get popcorn, but Amy didn't want any.
5. Dad said to let him know when Tamisha came home.

▶ EXERCISE 6   **Writing Appropriate Pronouns**

Rewrite each sentence, replacing the repeated nouns with pronouns.

1. Put the flowers in water before the flowers' petals droop.
2. The canoe capsized as the canoe neared the shore.

3. The players convinced the players that the players would win the game.
4. Lorraine oiled the bicycle before Lorraine put the bicycle in the garage.
5. Tim said, "Tim answered all six questions on the quiz."

▶ EXERCISE 7   **Writing Sentences with Pronouns and Antecedents**

Your pen pal in another country has written you to ask about the American pastimes of roller-skating and in-line skating. In your next letter, you send this photograph along with a written description of these types of skating. In your letter, use at least five pronouns. Underline each pronoun and draw an arrow to its antecedent.

EXAMPLE   *The skater slowly increases his speed.*

asked about skating. They're wearing
in-line skates in the picture. Some people
harder to balance on these
single

WRITING APPLICATION

Using Pronouns Clearly

When you write about people, you nearly always use pronouns for variety. Sometimes, though, pronouns can be confusing.

CONFUSING Joel wrote to Mark while he was on vacation.
[Who was on vacation, Joel or Mark?]
CLEAR While Joel was on vacation, **he** wrote to Mark.
or
CLEAR While Mark was on vacation, Joel wrote to **him**.

When you use a pronoun, make sure that it refers clearly to its antecedent. If the pronoun reference is not clear, change the order of the sentence or reword parts of the sentence.

▶ WRITING ACTIVITY

Your class is creating a bulletin board display for the school's Special People Day. For the display, write a brief report about someone you think is special. Tell why you think so. Be sure that the pronouns you use refer clearly to their antecedents.

Prewriting First, you'll need to select your subject. Someone special—perhaps a friend, a neighbor, or a relative—may come to mind immediately. If not, make a list of the different people you know. Which of these people really stands out? After you choose a subject, freewrite about that person. What makes this person special? Tell what that person has done to earn your respect and admiration.

Writing As you write your first draft, refer to your freewriting notes. In your first paragraph, catch the reader's attention and identify your subject. Your thesis statement should briefly state what is special about your subject. In the rest of your paragraphs, give specific examples that illustrate why the person is special.

Evaluating and Revising Now, read through your report and imagine that you don't know the subject. What do you think about him or her? Does the person sound special? If not, you may want to add or cut details or rearrange your report. Read your report aloud to hear whether it sounds choppy. Combine short, related sentences by inserting prepositional phrases or appositive phrases. For more about combining sentences, see pages 361–371. Look closely at your use of pronouns. Be sure that each pronoun has a clear antecedent. You may need to revise some sentences to make the antecedents clear.

 Proofreading and Publishing Check to see that you have spelled and capitalized all proper names correctly. You and your classmates may want to use your reports to make a classroom bulletin board display. If possible, include pictures or drawings of your subjects. You may also wish to send a copy of your report to the person you wrote about.

The Adjective

14c. An *adjective* is a word that modifies a noun or a pronoun.

To *modify* a word means to describe the word or to make its meaning more definite. An adjective modifies a noun or a pronoun by telling *what kind, which one, how much,* or *how many.*

WHAT KIND?	WHICH ONE OR ONES?	HOW MANY OR HOW MUCH?
happy children	seventh grade	full tank
busy dentist	these countries	five dollars
sunny day	any book	no marbles

Sometimes an adjective may come after the word that it modifies.

EXAMPLES **The box is empty.** [The adjective *empty* modifies *box.*]

A woman, kind and helpful, gave us directions. [The adjectives *kind* and *helpful* modify *woman*.]

Articles

The most commonly used adjectives are *a, an,* and *the.* These adjectives are called *articles. A* and *an* are called *indefinite articles* because they refer to someone or something in general. *The* is called a *definite article* because it refers to someone or something in particular.

Nouns Used as Adjectives

When a noun modifies another noun or a pronoun, it is considered an adjective.

NOUNS	NOUNS USED AS ADJECTIVES
bean	**bean** soup
spring	**spring** weather
gold	**gold** coin
football	**football** game

Demonstrative Adjectives

This, that, these, and *those* can be used both as adjectives and as pronouns. When they modify a noun, they are called *demonstrative adjectives.* When they are used alone, they are called *demonstrative pronouns.*

DEMONSTRATIVE   Did Jennifer draw **this** picture or **that**
ADJECTIVES   one?
              Let's take **these** sandwiches and **those**
              apples on our picnic.

DEMONSTRATIVE   **This** is mine and **that** is his.
PRONOUNS   **These** are much more expensive than
              those are.

👉 **REFERENCE NOTE:** For more information about demonstrative pronouns, see pages 429–430.

▶ EXERCISE 8   **Identifying Adjectives**

Identify the twenty adjectives in the following paragraph and give the noun or pronoun each modifies. Do not include the articles *a, an,* and *the.*

EXAMPLE   **[1] Why don't you take the local bus on cold**
           days?
        1. *local—bus; cold—days*

[1] On winter afternoons, I sometimes walk home after basketball practice rather than ride on a crowded, noisy bus. [2] I hardly notice the heavy traffic that streams past me. [3] The wet sidewalk glistens in the bright lights from the windows of stores. [4] The stoplights throw green, yellow, and red splashes on the pavement. [5] After I turn the corner away from the busy avenue, I am on a quiet street, where a jolly snowman often stands next to one of the neighborhood houses. [6] At last, I reach my peaceful home. [7] There I am often greeted by my brother and sister. [8] I know they are glad to see me. [9] Delicious smells come from the kitchen. [10] This walk home always makes me feel tired but happy.

► EXERCISE 9   **Writing Appropriate Adjectives**

Complete the following story by writing an appropriate adjective to fill each blank.

EXAMPLE   [1] ____ parks have [2] ____ trails for hikers.
      1. *National*
      2. *many*

    The hikers went exploring in the [1] ____ woods. Sometimes they had difficulty getting through the [2] ____ undergrowth. On [3] ____ occasions they almost turned back. Yet they kept going and were rewarded for their [4] ____ effort. During the [5] ____ hike through the woods, they discovered [6] ____ kinds of [7] ____ animals. In the afternoon the [8] ____ hikers pitched camp in a [9] ____ clearing. They were [10] ____ for supper and rest.

Proper Adjectives

A *proper adjective* is formed from a proper noun.

PROPER NOUNS	PROPER ADJECTIVES
Thanksgiving	**Thanksgiving** dinner
Catholicism	**Catholic** priest
Middle East	**Middle Eastern** country
Africa	**African** continent

Notice that a proper adjective, like a proper noun, always begins with a capital letter.

► EXERCISE 10   **Identifying Common and Proper Adjectives**

Identify the ten adjectives in the following paragraph. Then tell whether each is a *common* or a *proper* adjective. Do not include the articles *a, an,* and *the.*

EXAMPLE   [1] **We have been studying how various animals protect themselves.**
1. *various—common*

[1] Many small animals defend themselves in clever ways. [2] For example, South American armadillos wear suits of armor that consist of small, bony scales. [3] As you can see from the photograph, armadillos seem delicate, with their narrow faces. [4] However, their tough armor protects them well. [5] Likewise, the Asian anteater has scales that overlap like the shingles on a roof.

armadillos

▶ EXERCISE 11   **Using Proper Adjectives in Sentences**

Change the following proper nouns into proper adjectives. Then use each proper adjective in a sentence. Use a dictionary to help you spell the adjectives.

EXAMPLE   **1.** Spain
1. *Spanish—Those Peace Corps volunteers take Spanish lessons every Tuesday.*

1. Mexico   **3.** Memorial Day   **5.** Congress
2. Hawaii   **4.** Korea

PICTURE THIS

You're a mobile reporter for a radio station, and you travel around looking for interesting stories. You just received a call about something strange happening at the beach. When you arrive, this is the amazing scene you see! Of course, you immediately call the station and start a live broadcast from the beach. Write at least five sentences that you would use in your broadcast. In your sentences, use a variety of adjectives that appeal to the senses. Remember, your radio listeners have only your words to help them visualize this scene.

Subject: unusual beach scene
Audience: radio listeners
Purpose: to inform

Kenny Scharf, *Feliz a Praia* (1983–1984). Acrylic and spraypaint on canvas, 6'10 1/2" × 12'2". Collection Mr. Tony Shafrazi, N.Y. Photo, Ivan Dalla Tana. © 1996 Kenny Scharf/Artists Rights Society (ARS), N.Y.

Changing Parts of Speech

The way that a word is used in a sentence determines what part of speech it is. Some words may be used as nouns or as adjectives.

NOUN The helmet is made of **steel.**
ADJECTIVE It is a **steel** helmet.

Some words may be used as pronouns or as adjectives.

PRONOUN **That** is a surprise.
ADJECTIVE **That** problem is difficult.

▶ REVIEW C **Identifying Nouns, Pronouns, and Adjectives**

Identify all of the nouns, pronouns, and adjectives in the following paragraph. Do not include the articles *a, an,* and *the.*

EXAMPLE **1.** We walked along the empty beach at sundown.
1. *We—pronoun; empty—adjective; beach—noun; sundown—noun*

[1] When the tide comes in, it brings a variety of interesting items from the sea. [2] When it ebbs, it leaves behind wonderful treasures for the watchful beachcombers. [3] Few creatures live here, but you almost certainly will find several animals if you try. [4] Some live in shallow burrows under the wet sand and emerge in the cool evening to dine on bits of plants and other matter. [5] A number of different species of beetle like this part of the beach. [6] Around them you can find bristly flies and tiny worms. [7] You might also come across old pieces of wood with round holes and tunnels in them. [8] These holes are produced by shipworms. [9] If you watch the shoreline carefully, you will see many signs of life that casual strollers miss. [10] Low tide is a marvelous time to search along the shore.

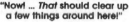

"Now! ... *That* should clear up
a few things around here!"

Review: Posttest 1

Identifying Nouns, Pronouns, and Adjectives

Identify each italicized word in the following paragraphs as a *noun*, a *pronoun*, or an *adjective*.

EXAMPLE   The [1] *achievements* of the [2] *native* peoples of
North America have sometimes been overlooked.
1. *noun*
2. *adjective*

Recent [1] *studies* show that the Winnebago people
developed a [2] *calendar* based on careful observation of the
[3] *heavens*.

An [4] *archaeologist* has found that the markings on
an old [5] *calendar* stick are the precise records of a [6] *lunar*
year and a solar year. These records are remarkably accurate, considering that at the time the [7] *Winnebagos* had
neither a [8] *written* language nor a [9] *mathematical* system.

[10] *The* calendar stick is a carved [11] *hickory* branch with [12] *four* sides. [13] *It* is worn along the [14] *edges* and shows other signs of frequent use. A [15] *similar* stick appears in a portrait of an early chief of the Winnebagos. In it, the chief holds a calendar stick in [16] *his* right hand. [17] *Our* current theory is that the chief went out at [18] *sunrise* and sunset to observe the sun and the moon. [19] *He* then marked on the stick what he saw. According to one researcher, this is the [20] *first* indication that native North American peoples recorded the year day by day.

Review: Posttest 2

Using Words as Different Parts of Speech

Write ten sentences using each of the following words first as a noun or pronoun and then as an adjective. Underline the word and give its part of speech after the sentence.

EXAMPLES   **1.** silk
     1. *Leonie's scarf is made of <u>silk</u>.—noun*
        May I borrow your <u>silk</u> scarf?—adjective

     2. that
     2. *<u>That</u> is a silly idea!—pronoun*
        <u>That</u> idea is very silly!—adjective

1. this   **2.** radio   **3.** few   **4.** light   **5.** April

15 THE PARTS OF SPEECH

Verb, Adverb, Preposition, Conjunction, Interjection

Diagnostic Test

Identifying Verbs, Adverbs, Prepositions, Conjunctions, and Interjections

Identify each numbered, italicized word or word group in the following paragraphs as a *verb,* an *adverb,* a *preposition,* a *conjunction,* or an *interjection.*

EXAMPLES [1] *Tomorrow,* we [2] *will order* equipment [3] *for* our summer camping trip.

1. *adverb*
2. *verb*
3. *preposition*

Have you ever [1] *hiked* into the wilderness [2] *with* a pack on your back and [3] *camped* under the stars? Backpacking [4] *was* once popular mainly with hardy mountaineers, [5] *but* now almost anyone who loves the outdoors [6] *can become* a backpacker.

First, however, you [7]*must be* able to carry a heavy pack long distances [8]*over* mountain trails. To get in shape, start with short walks and [9]*gradually* increase them to several miles. Doing leg exercises [10]*and* going on organized hikes can [11]*further* help build your strength. [12]*After* a few hikes, you [13]*should be* ready.

[14]*Oh,* you [15]*may be thinking,* what equipment and food should I take? Write [16]*to* the International Backpackers Association [17]*for* a checklist. The first item on the list will [18]*usually* be shoes with rubber [19]*or* synthetic soles. The second will [20]*certainly* be a sturdy backpack.

The Verb

15a. A *verb* is a word that expresses an action or a state of being.

EXAMPLES We **celebrated** the Chinese New Year yesterday.
The holiday **is** usually in February.

Action Verbs

(1) An *action verb* is a verb that expresses physical or mental action.

EXAMPLES The owls **hooted** all night.
Gloria **plays** with the children.
She **thought** about the problem.
I **believe** you.
Finish your work by three o'clock, please.

EXERCISE 1 **Identifying Action Verbs**

Identify the action verb in each of the following sentences.

EXAMPLE **1.** I saw that movie last week.
1. *saw*

1. For a science project, Elena built a sundial.
2. Mr. Santos carefully explained the problem again.
3. I enjoy soccer more than any other sport.
4. This waterfall drops two hundred feet.
5. Mike's bicycle skidded on the pavement.
6. Mrs. Karras showed us the recipe for stuffed grape leaves with tomato sauce.
7. Mix the ingredients slowly.
8. The heavy traffic delayed us.
9. For the Jewish holiday of Purim, Rachel gave a costume party.
10. The early Aztecs worshiped the sun.

▶ EXERCISE 2 **Writing Action Verbs**

Your pen pal in another country wants to know what students at your school do at school dances. To explain, you send this photograph to your pen pal. In addition, you write a letter describing the things that people do at school dances. In your letter, use at least ten action verbs. Include at least three verbs that do not express physical actions. Then, underline the action verbs in your letter.

EXAMPLES   **1.** *Everyone <u>dances</u> to the fast songs.*
            2. *Darnell and I sometimes <u>invite</u> the chaperone to dance.*

Transitive and Intransitive Verbs

(2) A ***transitive verb*** is an action verb that expresses an action directed toward a person or thing.

EXAMPLES   Derrick **greeted** the visitors. [The action of *greeted* is directed toward *visitors.*]
Felicia **painted** her room. [The action of *painted* is directed toward *room.*]

With transitive verbs, the action passes from the doer—the subject—to the receiver of the action. Words that receive the action of a transitive verb are called *objects.*

☞ REFERENCE NOTE: For more information about objects and their uses in sentences, see pages 474–477.

An ***intransitive verb*** expresses action (or tells something about the subject) without passing the action to a receiver.

EXAMPLES   The train **stopped.**
Last night we **ate** on the patio.

A verb may be transitive in one sentence and intransitive in another.

EXAMPLES   The children **play** checkers. [transitive]
The children **play** quietly. [intransitive]

Mr. Lopez **is baking** bread. [transitive]
Mr. Lopez **is baking** this afternoon. [intransitive]

▶ EXERCISE 3   **Identifying Transitive and Intransitive Verbs**

In each of the following sentences, identify the italicized action verb as *transitive* or *intransitive.*

EXAMPLE   **1.** She *runs* early in the morning.
1. *intransitive*

1. If you do different kinds of exercises, you *are exercising* in the correct way.

2. When you exercise to improve endurance, flexibility, and strength, your body *develops*.
3. Aerobic exercise *builds* endurance.
4. When you *walk* quickly, you do aerobic exercise.
5. Many people *attend* classes in aerobic dancing.
6. They *enjoy* the fun of exercising to music.
7. Exercises that *improve* flexibility require you to bend and stretch.
8. *Perform* these exercises slowly for maximum benefit.
9. Through isometric and isotonic exercises, your muscle strength *increases*.
10. These exercises *contract* your muscles.

▶ EXERCISE 4 **Writing Sentences with Transitive and Intransitive Verbs**

For each verb given below, write two sentences. In one sentence, use the verb as a *transitive* verb and underline its object. In the other, use the verb as an *intransitive* verb. You may use different tenses of the verb.

EXAMPLE **1.** write
1. *Alex is writing a research <u>report</u>. (transitive)*
Alex writes in his journal every day.
(intransitive)

1. fly   **2.** leave   **3.** return   **4.** draw   **5.** drive

Linking Verbs

(3) A *linking verb* is a verb that expresses a state of being. A linking verb connects the subject of a sentence with a word in the predicate that identifies or describes the subject.

EXAMPLES Howard Rollins **is** an actor. [The verb *is* connects *actor* with the subject *Howard Rollins.*]
The children **remained** quiet during the puppet show. [The verb *remained* links *quiet* with the subject *children.*]

Linking Verbs Formed from the Verb *Be*

am	has been	may be
is	have been	might be
are	had been	can be
was	will be	should be
were	shall be	would have been

Other Linking Verbs

appear	grow	seem	stay
become	look	smell	taste
feel	remain	sound	turn

Some words may be either action verbs or linking verbs, depending on how they are used.

ACTION   Amy **looked** through the telescope.
LINKING   Amy **looked** pale. [The verb links *pale* with the subject *Amy.*]

ACTION   **Remain** in your seats until the bell rings.
LINKING   **Remain** quiet. [The verb links *quiet* with the understood subject *you.*]

☞ REFERENCE NOTE: For more about understood subjects in imperative sentences, see pages 415–416.

▶ EXERCISE 5   **Identifying Linking Verbs**

Identify the linking verb in each sentence in the following paragraphs.

EXAMPLE   [1] A radio station can be the voice of a community.
      1. *can be*

[1] "Good morning, listeners! This is Roberto Martínez, your weather forecaster. [2] Unfortunately, the forecast looks bad today. [3] Outside the window here at Station

WOLF, the skies appear cloudy. [4] It certainly felt rainy earlier this morning. [5] And, according to the latest information, it should be a damp, drizzly day with an 85 percent chance of rainfall. [6] Now, for the latest scores, our sportscaster this morning is Marta Segal."

[7] "Well, Roberto, things have been quiet here around Arlington for the past few days. [8] But stay alert for sports action tonight. [9] It should be a great game between our own Arlington Angels and the visiting Jackson City Dodgers. [10] The team looked great at practice today, and I predict a hometown victory."

▶ EXERCISE 6   **Identifying Action Verbs and Linking Verbs**

Identify the verb in each of the following sentences. Then label each verb as either an *action verb* or a *linking verb*. If the verb is a linking verb, give the two words that it connects.

EXAMPLES   **1.** We sent our dog to obedience school.
1. *sent—action verb*

2. Some breeds are extremely nervous.
2. *are—linking verb; breeds, nervous*

1. Everyone felt sorry about the misunderstanding.
2. In daylight, this sweater looks blue.
3. The temperature plunged to almost ten degrees below zero.
4. The museum exhibited Inuit sculptures of whales and seals.
5. Loretta felt her way carefully through the dark, quiet room.
6. The city almost always smells musty after a heavy summer storm.
7. Dakar is the capital of Senegal.
8. The firefighter cautiously smelled the burned rags.
9. Antonia Novello was the Surgeon General of the United States.
10. They looked handsome in their party clothes.

▶ EXERCISE 7 **Identifying Action Verbs and Linking Verbs**

Identify the twenty verbs in the following paragraphs. Then label each verb as either an *action verb* or a *linking verb*.

EXAMPLE [1] I always enjoy field trips.
 1. *enjoy—action verb*

[1] Last spring, our class visited the Hayden Planetarium. [2] It is a wonderful place, full of amazing sights. [3] We wandered through the various displays and saw a collection of fascinating exhibits. [4] One showed a space vehicle. [5] Another displayed a thirty-four-ton meteorite. [6] When this meteorite fell to earth many years ago, it made a huge crater.

[7] After lunch, we went to the show in the observatory. [8] As the room became darker, the picture of a galaxy appeared on the dome above us. [9] The lecturer said that the galaxy is so far away from here that its light reaches us centuries after its first appearance. [10] When we look at such stars, we actually see the ancient past! [11] I still feel a little strange when I think about the galaxy and its history. [12] We really live in a universe that is full of wonders.

▶ EXERCISE 8 **Writing Sentences with Action Verbs and Linking Verbs**

The circus is in town! Unfortunately, your best friend is sick and can't go. So that your friend won't miss out entirely, you take some photographs. Using the pictures on the next page and your imagination, write ten sentences describing the circus to your friend. In five of the sentences, use action verbs. In the other five, use linking verbs. Underline each verb that you use.

EXAMPLES **1.** *The trapeze artist* <u>*leaps*</u> *from the trapeze into the air.*
 2. *He probably* <u>*feels*</u> *nervous, but he certainly* <u>*looks*</u> *brave!*

Helping Verbs

A *verb phrase* contains one main verb and one or more helping verbs.

EXAMPLES   Many people in Africa **can speak** more than one language.
Kansas **has been named** the Sunflower State.
The ball **should have been caught** by the nearest player.

(4) A *helping verb* helps the main verb to express action or a state of being.

EXAMPLES   **can** speak
has been named
should have been caught

Helping Verbs				
am	be	do	might	shall
is	been	does	must	should
are	has	did	can	will
was	have	may	could	would
were	had			

Sometimes a verb phrase is interrupted by another part of speech, such as an adverb or a pronoun.

EXAMPLES   Ken **does** not **have** a new desk.
Our school **has** always **held** a victory celebration.
Did you **hear** Carmen Zapata's speech?

▶ EXERCISE 9 **Identifying Verb Phrases and Helping Verbs**

Identify the verb phrases in the following paragraphs. Underline the helping verbs.

EXAMPLE   [1] You can recognize redwoods and sequoias by their bark.
    1. *can recognize*

[1] Have you ever visited Redwood National Park? [2] The giant trees there can be an awesome sight. [3] For centuries, these trees have been an important part of the environment of the northwest United States. [4] Surely, these rare trees must be saved for future generations.

[5] More than 85 percent of the original redwood forest has been destroyed. [6] Because of this destruction, the survival of the forest is being threatened. [7] With proper planning years ago, more of the forest might already have been saved. [8] Unfortunately, redwood forests are still shrinking rapidly. [9] According to some scientists, redwood forests outside the park will have disappeared before the year 2000. [10] However, according to other experts, the redwood forests can still be saved!

▶ EXERCISE 10 **Writing Sentences with Verb Phrases**

You are a member of the city planning board. Your job is to figure out what kind of traffic control is needed at the busy street corner shown on the next page. Does the intersection require stoplights, stop signs, or a traffic police officer? After you investigate the street corner, you will make your recommendation to the rest of the planning board. Using this photograph, make some notes about what is happening at the intersection. Write at least five sentences containing verb phrases. Then, underline each verb phrase and circle the helping verb.

EXAMPLE   **1.** *The number of crosswalks* (can) *confuse people.*

 REVIEW A   **Identifying Action Verbs and Linking Verbs**

Identify the verbs in the following paragraphs. Then, label each verb as an *action verb* or a *linking verb.* [Note: A sentence may contain more than one verb.]

EXAMPLE   **[1] Have you ever seen a play in Spanish?**
          1. *Have seen—action verb*

[1] The Puerto Rican Traveling Theatre presents plays about Hispanic life in the United States. [2] Over the past twenty years, this group has become a leader in Hispanic theater. [3] Sometimes, a production has two casts—one that performs in English and one that speaks in Spanish. [4] In this way, speakers of both languages can enjoy the play.

[5] In recent years many young Hispanic playwrights, directors, and actors have begun their careers at the Traveling Theatre. [6] Some became well-known at the Puerto Rican Traveling Theatre and then moved on to

Broadway or Hollywood. [7] Others remain happy at the Traveling Theatre, where they enjoy the warm, supportive atmosphere.

[8] Each production by the Traveling Theatre has its own style. [9] Some shows are musicals, full of song and dance, while other plays seem more serious. [10] Light or serious, Puerto Rican Traveling Theatre productions present a lively picture of Hispanic life today.

The Adverb

15b. An *adverb* is a word that modifies a verb, an adjective, or another adverb.

An adverb answers the following questions:

Where?	How often?	To what extent?
When?	*or*	*or*
How?	How long?	How much?

EXAMPLES **The sprinter ran swiftly.** [The adverb *swiftly* modifies the verb *ran* and tells *how.*]
Jolene was comforting a very small child. [The adverb *very* modifies the adjective *small* and tells *to what extent.*]
The fire blazed too wildly for anyone to enter. [The adverb *too* modifies the adverb *wildly* and tells *to what extent.* The adverb *wildly* modifies the verb *blazed* and tells *how.*]
Dad often quotes from Archbishop Desmond Tutu's speech. [The adverb *often* modifies the verb *quotes* and tells *how often.*]
Put the apples there, and we'll eat them later. [The adverb *there* modifies the verb *put* and tells *where.* The adverb *later* modifies the verb *eat* and tells *when.*]

WORDS OFTEN USED AS ADVERBS	
Where?	away, here, inside, there, up
When?	ago, later, now, soon, then
How?	clearly, easily, quietly, slowly
How often? or *How long?*	always, usually, continuously, never, forever, briefly
To what extent? or *How much?*	almost, so, too, more, least, extremely, quite

NOTE: The word *not* is nearly always used as an adverb to modify a verb. When *not* is part of a contraction, as in *hadn't, aren't,* and *didn't,* the *–n't* is still an adverb and is not part of the verb.

Adverbs and Adjectives

Many adverbs end in *–ly.* These adverbs are formed by adding *–ly* to adjectives.

> **Adjective + *–ly* = Adverb**
> clear + –ly = clearly
> quiet + –ly = quietly

However, some words ending in *–ly* are used as adjectives.

> **Adjectives Ending in *–ly***
> daily   friendly   lonely
> early   kindly   timely

If you aren't sure whether a word is an adjective or an adverb, ask yourself what it modifies. If a word modifies a noun or a pronoun, it is an adjective.

EXAMPLES   She gave us a **friendly** hello. [*Friendly* modifies the noun *hello* and is used as an adjective.]
Were you **lonely** yesterday? [*Lonely* modifies the pronoun *you* and is used as an adjective.]

☞ **REFERENCE NOTE:** For more about adjectives, see pages 434–437.

If a word modifies a verb, an adjective, or an adverb, then it's an adverb.

EXAMPLES   People from many nations have come to the United States **recently.** [The adverb *recently* modifies the verb *have come.*]
English can be a **fairly** difficult language to learn. [The adverb *fairly* modifies the adjective *difficult.*]
Newcomers study **incredibly** hard to learn the language. [The adverb *incredibly* modifies the adverb *hard.*]

NOTE: The adverb *very* is overused. In your writing, try to use adverbs other than *very* to modify adjectives.

EXAMPLE   Arnold Schwarzenegger is very strong.
Arnold Schwarzenegger is **amazingly** strong.

▶ EXERCISE 11   **Identifying Adverbs**

Identify the adverb and the word or words it modifies in each sentence in the following sentences.

EXAMPLE   **1.** Today, many Cherokee people make their homes in Oklahoma.
1. *Today—make*

1. Oklahoma is not the Cherokees' original home.
2. The Cherokees once lived in Georgia, North Carolina, Alabama, and Tennessee.
3. A number of Cherokees still live in the mountains of North Carolina.
4. In 1829, people hurried excitedly to northern Georgia for the first gold rush in the United States.
5. Many white settlers of the region fought greedily for the gold.

6. These settlers totally ignored the Cherokees' right to the land.
7. Feeling threatened, some Cherokees finally signed a treaty with the U.S. government.
8. Later, the Cherokees were forced to leave their land.
9. The people were hardly given a chance to collect their belongings.
10. Many Cherokees will never forget the "Trail of Tears" that led their ancestors to Oklahoma.

The Position of Adverbs

One of the characteristics of adverbs is that they may appear at various places in a sentence. Adverbs may come before, after, or between the words they modify.

EXAMPLES We **often** study together.
We study together **often**.
Often we study together.

When an adverb modifies a verb phrase, it frequently comes in the middle of the phrase.

EXAMPLE We have **often** studied together.

An adverb that introduces a question, however, must be placed at the beginning of a sentence.

EXAMPLES **When** does your school start? [The adverb *when* modifies the verb phrase *does start.*]
How did you spend your vacation? [The adverb *how* modifies the verb phrase *did spend.*]

▶ EXERCISE 12 **Identifying Adverbs**

Identify the twenty adverbs and the words they modify in the following paragraphs.

EXAMPLE [1] "To Build a Fire" is a dramatically suspenseful short story.
1. *dramatically—suspenseful*

[1] "To Build a Fire" is probably one of Jack London's best stories. [2] In this story, a nameless character goes outdoors on a terribly cold day in the Yukon. [3] Except for a dog, he is traveling completely alone to a mining camp. [4] Foolishly confident of his ability to survive the unusually harsh cold, he does not understand the dangers of the northern wilderness.

[5] The dog knows instinctively that they are certainly in a bad situation. [6] It slinks fearfully along at the man's heels and seems to question his every movement. [7] Soon both the dog's muzzle and the man's beard are frosted with ice.

[8] Along the way, the man accidentally falls into a hidden stream. [9] Desperately, he builds a fire under a tree to avoid frostbite. [10] The flames slowly grow stronger. [11] Unfortunately, he has built his fire in the wrong place. [12] A pile of snow suddenly falls from a tree limb and kills the fire. [13] Unable to relight the fire, the man again finds himself in serious trouble. [14] Based on what you now know about the story, what kind of ending would you write for "To Build a Fire"?

▶ EXERCISE 13 **Writing Adverbs**

Supply ten different adverbs to fill the blanks in the following paragraph.

EXAMPLE [1] I have ____ been a real music lover.
     1. *always*

Every Friday I [1]____ go to the record store. I can [2] ____ wait to see what new cassettes and CDs have arrived. As soon as school is out, I bicycle [3] ____ to the store and join other [4] ____ enthusiastic customers. [5] ____ I stroll through the aisles and [6] ____ study the selections. I listen [7] ____ as the loudspeaker announces the day's specials. When I have decided what I want, I [8] ____ figure out which items I can afford. Then I walk [9] ____ to the cash register. I grin [10] ____ as I think of how much I will enjoy the music.

GRAMMAR

PICTURE THIS

You are part of an important deep-sea expedition. Your job is to record what you see down in the ocean. The other members of your team lower your diving bell into the water. The diving bell is a heavy steel cabin with thick windows. When you reach the right depth, you switch on the outside light. Through the window in front of you, you see this scene. Write a brief report describing your observations. In your report, use at least five adverbs. Underline each adverb that you use.

Subject: underwater observations
Audience: scientists and others interested in undersea
             exploration
Purpose: to inform

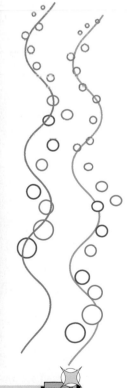

The Preposition

15c. A *preposition* is a word that shows the relationship between a noun or pronoun and another word in the sentence.

Notice how changing the preposition in these sentences changes the relationship of *cat* to *door* and *kite* to *tree*.

The cat walked **through** the door.
The cat walked **toward** the door.
The cat walked **past** the door.

The kite **in** the tree is mine.
The kite **beside** the tree is mine.
The kite **next to** the tree is mine. [Notice that a preposition may be made up of more than one word.]

Commonly Used Prepositions				
aboard	before	for	off	toward
about	behind	from	on	under
above	below	in	out	underneath
across	beneath	in front of	out of	unlike
after	beside	inside	over	until
against	between	instead of	past	up
along	beyond	into	since	up to
among	by	like	through	upon
around	down	near	throughout	with
as	during	next to	till	within
at	except	of	to	without

▶ EXERCISE 14 **Writing Prepositions**

In each of the following sentences, a preposition is missing. Choose two prepositions that would make sense in each sentence.

EXAMPLE **1.** The car raced ____ the highway.
          1. *along, across*

1. We watched television _____ dinner.
2. She ran _____ the park.
3. A boat sailed _____ the river.
4. The dog crawled _____ the fence.
5. The runner jogged _____ the gym.

The Prepositional Phrase

A *prepositional phrase* includes a preposition, a noun or pronoun called the *object of the preposition,* and any modifiers of that object.

EXAMPLES You can press those leaves **under glass.** [The preposition *under* relates its object, *glass,* to *can press.*]
The books **in my pack** are heavy. [The preposition *in* relates its object, *pack,* to *books.*]
Fred stood **in front of us.** [The preposition *in front of* relates its object, *us,* to the verb *stood.*]

A preposition may have more than one object.

EXAMPLE Thelma's telegram **to Nina and Ralph** contained good news. [The preposition *to* relates its objects, *Nina* and *Ralph,* to *telegram.*]

The objects of prepositions may have modifiers.

EXAMPLE It happened **during the last examination.** [*The* and *last* are adjectives modifying *examination,* which is the object of the preposition *during.*]

NOTE: Be careful not to confuse a prepositional phrase beginning with *to* (*to the park, to him*) with a verb form beginning with *to* (*to sing, to be heard*). Remember that a prepositional phrase always ends with a noun or a pronoun.

▶ EXERCISE 15 **Identifying Prepositional Phrases**

Identify the prepositional phrases in the following paragraphs. Underline the preposition once and its object twice. [Note: A sentence may contain more than one prepositional phrase.]

GRAMMAR

EXAMPLE [1] Lieutenant Robert Peary and Matthew Henson reached the North Pole in 1909.

1. *in 1909*

[1] Lieutenant Peary looked for the North Pole for many years. [2] Matthew Henson traveled with him on every expedition except the first one. [3] However, for a long time, Henson received no credit for his role.

[4] Peary had hired Henson as his servant on a trip to Nicaragua. [5] There, Peary discovered that Henson had sailing experience and could also chart a path through the jungle. [6] As a result, Peary asked Henson to join his Arctic expedition. [7] The two explorers became friends during their travels in the North. [8] On the final push to the North Pole, Henson was the only other American who went with Peary.

[9] Yet because Peary was leader of the expedition, he received all the credit for the discovery. [10] Finally, after many years, Henson was honored by Congress, Maryland's state government, and two U.S. presidents.

WRITING APPLICATION

Using Prepositional Phrases to Write Directions

You have probably given directions many times. They may have been directions telling how to get somewhere or how to do something. Using prepositional phrases can help you give directions that are clear and complete.

INCOMPLETE Walk straight ahead a little bit. Then turn and keep going. You will see the house.

COMPLETE Walk straight ahead *for four blocks, to the first stoplight.* Turn *to the right at that corner* and go *for two more blocks.* The house is *at the end of the driveway with the mailbox with flowers on it.*

▶ WRITING ACTIVITY

Your class has decided to provide a "how-to" manual for seventh-graders. The manual will have chapters on crafts and hobbies, personal skills, school skills, and other topics. Write an entry for the manual, telling someone how to do a particular activity. You may use one of the following ideas or one of your own. In your entry, be sure to use prepositional phrases to make your directions clear and complete. Underline the prepositional phrases that you use.

1. how to keep a bicycle in good condition
2. how to care for houseplants
3. how to study for an essay test
4. how to bathe a cat or a dog
5. how to make friends at a new school
6. how to amuse a younger child

Prewriting   First, picture yourself doing the activity you are describing. As you imagine doing the activity, jot down each thing that you do. Then put each step in the order that you do it. If necessary, change the order or add steps to make your directions clear and complete.

Writing   Refer to your prewriting notes as you write your first draft. You may find it necessary to add or rearrange steps to make your directions clear and complete.

Evaluating and Revising   Ask a friend or a classmate to read your paragraph. Then have your reader repeat the directions in his or her own words. If any part of the directions is unclear, revise your work.

Proofreading and Publishing   Read over your entry again to check your spelling, grammar, and punctuation. Make sure you have used prepositional phrases correctly. (See pages 640–643 for more about the correct placement of phrase modifiers.) You and your classmates may wish to photocopy your manual entries or input them on a computer. You could then share your how-to hints with other students.

Prepositions and Adverbs

Some words may be used as prepositions or as adverbs. Remember that a preposition always has an object. An adverb never does. If you can't tell whether a word is used as an adverb or a preposition, look for an object.

ADVERB	I haven't seen him **since.**
PREPOSITION	I haven't seen him **since** Thursday. [*Thursday* is the object of the preposition *since.*]
ADVERBS	The bear walked **around** and then went **inside.**
PREPOSITIONS	The bear walked **around** the yard and then went **inside** the cabin. [*Yard* is the object of the preposition *around. Cabin* is the object of *inside.*]

▶ EXERCISE 16   **Identifying Adverbs and Prepositions**

Identify the italicized word in each sentence in the following paragraphs as either an *adverb* or a *preposition.*

EXAMPLE   [1] He watches uneasily as the hunter brings the pistol *up.*

    1. *up—adverb*

[1] "The Most Dangerous Game" is the story of Rainsford, a famous hunter who falls *off* a boat and swims to a strange island. [2] Rainsford knows that this island is feared by every sailor who passes *by.* [3] In fact, *among* sailors, the place is known as "Ship-Trap Island."

[4] After looking *around* for several hours, Rainsford can't understand why the island is considered so dangerous. [5] Finally, he discovers a big house *on* a high bluff. [6] A man with a pistol *in* his hand answers the door. [7] Putting his pistol *down,* the man introduces Rainsford to the famous hunter General Zaroff. [8] Zaroff invites Rainsford *inside.* [9] Soon, however, Rainsford wishes he could get *out* and never see Zaroff again. [10] Rainsford has finally discovered the secret *about* the island—Zaroff likes to hunt human beings!

The Conjunction

15d. A *conjunction* is a word that joins words or groups of words.

Coordinating conjunctions connect words or groups of words used in the same way.

GRAMMAR

Coordinating Conjunctions						
and	but	for	nor	or	so	yet

EXAMPLES   Jill **or** Anna [two nouns]
strict **but** fair [two adjectives]
over the river **and** through the woods [two prepositional phrases]
Alice Walker wrote the book, **yet** she did not write the movie script. [two complete ideas]

The word *for* may be used either as a conjunction or as a preposition. When *for* joins groups of words that are independent clauses or sentences, it is used as a conjunction. Otherwise, it is used as a preposition.

CONJUNCTION   He waited patiently, **for** he knew his ride would be along soon.
PREPOSITION   He waited patiently **for** his ride.

NOTE: When *for* is used as a conjunction, there should always be a comma in front of it.

EXAMPLE   I'll be home late**,** for I have basketball practice today.

Correlative conjunctions are pairs of conjunctions that connect words or groups of words used in the same way.

Correlative Conjunctions	
both . . . . . . and	not only . . . . but also
either . . . . or	whether . . . . or
neither . . . . . nor	

EXAMPLES **Both** Bill Russell **and** Larry Bird have played for the Celtics. [two nouns]
She looked **neither** to the left **nor** to the right. [two prepositional phrases]
Not only did Wilma Rudolph overcome her illness, **but** she **also** became an Olympic athlete. [two complete ideas]

▶ EXERCISE 17 **Identifying Conjunctions**

Identify the conjunction in each of the following sentences. Be prepared to tell what words or groups of words each conjunction joins.

EXAMPLE **1.** Both she and her mother enjoy sailing.
1. *Both . . . and*

1. I wanted to see Los Lobos in concert, but I didn't have the money.
2. Our class is recycling not only newspapers but also aluminum cans.
3. He set the table with chopsticks and rice bowls.
4. Have you seen either Whitney Houston or Janet Jackson in person?
5. We learned to use neither too many adjectives nor too few.
6. That diet is dangerous, for it does not meet the body's needs.
7. Both the Mohawk and the Oneida are part of the Iroquois Confederacy.
8. It rained all day, yet we enjoyed the trip.
9. Shall we walk home or take the bus?
10. Revise your paper and proofread it carefully.

GRAMMAR

▶ EXERCISE 18 **Writing Conjunctions**

For each blank in the following sentences, choose an appropriate conjunction.

EXAMPLE **1.** ___ solve the problem yourself ___ ask your teacher for help.
      1. *Either—or* ·

1. We will visit ___ the Johnson Space Center ___ AstroWorld.
2. Alaska ___ Hawaii were the last two states admitted to the Union.
3. Those two students are twins, ___ they do not dress alike.
4. They were ___ hungry ___ thirsty.
5. ___ turn that radio down ___ take it into your room.

▶ EXERCISE 19 **Writing Sentences with Conjunctions**

Follow the directions given below to write sentences using conjunctions.

EXAMPLE **1.** Use *and* to join two verbs.
      1. *Jessye Norman smiled at the audience and bowed.*

1. Use *and* to join two adverbs.
2. Use *or* to join two prepositional phrases.
3. Use *for* to join groups of words that are sentences.
4. Use *but* to join two linking verbs.
5. Use *either . . . or* in an imperative sentence.

The Interjection

15e. An *interjection* is a word that expresses strong emotion.

An interjection has no grammatical relationship to the rest of the sentence. Usually an interjection is followed by an exclamation point.

EXAMPLES **Ouch!** That hurts!
Goodness! What a haircut!
Aha! I know the answer.

Sometimes an interjection is set off by a comma or commas.

EXAMPLES I'll be back in, **oh,** an hour or so.
Well, what have you been doing?

EXERCISE 20 **Writing Interjections**

The people at this video arcade need your help. To express their excitement, they want to use some interjections—but they don't know any. Write five sentences that might be spoken by these people. In each sentence, use a different interjection from the list below. Underline the interjections you use. (Remember that an interjection may be followed by either an exclamation point or a comma.)

yikes	yay	oh	wow	hey
right	no	oops	yes	whew

EXAMPLE *Wow! That's the highest score ever!*

REVIEW B **Identifying Parts of Speech**

For the following sentences, identify the part of speech of each italicized word as a *verb*, an *adverb*, a *preposition*, a *conjunction*, or an *interjection*.

GRAMMAR

EXAMPLE **1.** *Both* otters *and* owls hunt *from* dusk to dawn.
1. both . . . and—*conjunction; from—preposition*

1. *Oh!* I *just* spilled soup on the new white tablecloth!
2. Luis Alvarez *closely* studied atomic particles *for* many years.
3. *Did* Toni Morrison *or* Toni Cade Bambara *write* that book?
4. The Inuit hunters *ate* their meal *inside* the igloo.
5. They were tired, *yet* they did *not* quit working.

Determining Parts of Speech

Remember that you can't tell what part of speech a word is until you know how it is used in a particular sentence. A word may be used in different ways.

NOUN The **play** had a happy ending.
VERB The actors **play** their roles.

NOUN The **outside** of the house needs paint.
ADVERB Let's go **outside** for a while.
PREPOSITION I saw the birds' nest **outside** my window.

▶ REVIEW C **Writing Sentences**

Write ten sentences that meet the requirements in the following directions. Underline the given word in each sentence, and identify how it is used.

EXAMPLE **1.** Use *yet* as an adverb and as a conjunction.
1. *Are we there yet?—adverb*
The sky grew brighter, yet the rain continued falling.—conjunction

1. Use *walk* as a verb and a noun.
2. Use *like* as a preposition and a verb.
3. Use *well* as an interjection and an adverb.
4. Use *inside* as an adverb and a preposition.
5. Use *fast* as an adjective and an adverb.

Review: Posttest

A. Identifying Verbs, Adverbs, Prepositions, Conjunctions, and Interjections

Identify the part of speech of each italicized word in the following paragraphs.

EXAMPLES   Some [1] *very* unusual words [2] *are used* [3] *in* crossword puzzles.
    1. *adverb*
    2. *verb*
    3. *preposition*

The first crossword puzzle was published [1] *in* 1913. It [2] *appeared* on the Fun Page [3] *of* a New York City newspaper, [4] *and* readers [5] *immediately* [6] *asked* the editors [7] *for* more. [8] *Almost* every newspaper in the United States [9] *now* publishes a daily crossword puzzle.

Every day millions of Americans [10] *faithfully* work crossword puzzles. Many people take their puzzles [11] *quite* seriously. For many, solving puzzles [12] *is* a competitive game.

I [13] *do* puzzles [14] *strictly* for fun. Best of all, I can work on them [15] *by* myself. That way, no one knows whether I succeed [16] *or* fail. I [17] *occasionally* [18] *brag* about my successes. [19] *"Aha!"* I exclaim. "That was a tough one, [20] *but* I filled in every space."

B. Writing Sentences Using Words as Different Parts of Speech

Write ten sentences, using each of the following words first as an adverb and then as a preposition. Underline the word, and give its part of speech after the sentence.

EXAMPLE   **1.** around
    1. We walked around.—*adverb*
       We walked around the mall.—*preposition*

1. up   **2.** near   **3.** over   **4.** through   **5.** by

SUMMARY OF PARTS OF SPEECH

Rule	Part of Speech	Use	Examples
14a	noun	names	**Marie** had a good **idea**.
14b	pronoun	takes the place of a noun	Bill had an idea, but **he** would't tell **it** to **anyone**.
14c	adjective	modifies a noun or pronoun	I have **two Mexican** bowls, and both are **large** and **heavy**.
15a	verb	shows action or a state of being	Ada **has met** you, but she **is** not sure where.
15b	adverb	modifies a verb, an adjective, or another adverb	We left **early** when the sky was **almost completely** dark.
15c	preposition	relates a noun or a pronoun to another word	We looked **for** you **next to** the gate **at** the game.
15d	conjunction	joins words or groups of words	Bill **or** she will call us later **and** give us directions.
15e	interjection	shows strong feeling	**Ouch!** My arm is caught.

GRAMMAR

16 COMPLEMENTS

Direct and Indirect Objects, Subject Complements

Diagnostic Test

Identifying Complements

Identify the complement or complements in each of the following sentences. Then, label each complement as a *direct object*, an *indirect object*, a *predicate nominative*, or a *predicate adjective*.

EXAMPLE **1.** My mother bought us some tamales.
   1. *us—indirect object; tamales—direct object*

1. Native American peoples taught the English colonists many useful skills for survival.
2. Rhode Island is the smallest state in the United States.
3. A hurricane of immense power lashed the Florida coast.

4. They became very anxious during the final minutes of the game.
5. This winter was colder and drier than normal.
6. My aunt showed us pictures of her new puppy.
7. The new homeowners found some rare photographs in the attic.
8. Although many eggshells are white, others are brown, and still others are bluish green.
9. Some consumers prefer eggs with brown shells.
10. During this entire month, Mars is so close to the sun that it cannot be seen easily from Earth.
11. Congress gave the president its support on the bill.
12. The movers carried the heavy sofa up the stairs.
13. I found a dollar in the pocket of my jeans.
14. That gigantic reflector is the world's most powerful telescope.
15. Did our representative lead the state delegation at the convention last month?
16. *A Raisin in the Sun* was Lorraine Hansberry's most successful play.
17. Why do animals seem nervous during a storm?
18. The manager will pay all of the ushers an extra five dollars this week.
19. Susumu Tonegawa won a Nobel Prize for his research into the body's defenses against certain diseases.
20. Our neighbor has offered my mother a good price for her car.

Recognizing Complements

16a. A *complement* is a word or a group of words that completes the meaning of a verb.

Every sentence has a subject and a verb. In addition, the verb often needs a complement to complete its meaning.

S   V
INCOMPLETE Dr. Charles Drew researched [*what?*]

S   V   C
COMPLETE Dr. Charles Drew researched blood **plasma.**

S   V
INCOMPLETE Medical societies honored [*whom?*]

S   V C
COMPLETE Medical societies honored **him.**

S V
INCOMPLETE Dr. Drew's research was [*what?*]

S V C
COMPLETE Dr. Drew's research was **important.**

Direct Objects

The *direct object* is one type of complement. It completes the meaning of a transitive verb.

☞ **REFERENCE NOTE:** Transitive verbs are discussed on page 446.

16b. A *direct object* is a noun or a pronoun that receives the action of the verb or shows the result of that action. A direct object answers the question *Whom?* or *What?* after a transitive verb.

EXAMPLES Today, I met **Dr. Mason.** [*Dr. Mason* receives the action of the verb *met* and tells *whom* I met.]
My uncle repairs small **engines,** and then he sells **them.** [*Engines* tells *what* receives the action of the verb *repairs. Them* tells *what* receives the action of the verb *sells.*]

A direct object can never follow a linking verb because a linking verb does not express action. Also, a direct object is never in a prepositional phrase.

LINKING VERB Augusta Savage **was** a sculptor during the Harlem Renaissance. [The verb *was* does not express action and therefore has no direct object.]

PREPOSITIONAL   **She worked with clay.** [*Clay* is not the
PHRASE   direct object of the verb *worked; clay* is
the object of the preposition *with.*]

☞ **REFERENCE NOTE:** For more about linking verbs, see pages 447–448.
For more about prepositional phrases, see pages 491–497.

A direct object may be a compound of two or more objects.

EXAMPLE   **We bought ribbon, wrapping paper, and tape.**
[The compound direct object of the verb *bought*
is *ribbon, wrapping paper,* and *tape.*]

▶ EXERCISE 1   **Identifying Direct Objects**

Identify the direct object in each of the following sentences. [Remember: A direct object may be compound.]

EXAMPLE   **1. Many sports test an athlete's speed and agility.**
1. *speed, agility*

1. However, long-distance, or marathon, swimming requires strength and endurance from an athlete.
2. A swimmer in training may swim five or six miles every day.
3. Marathon swimmers smear grease on their legs and arms for protection against the cold water.
4. During a marathon, some swimmers may lose seventeen pounds.
5. Fatigue, pain, and huge waves challenge marathon swimmers.
6. As they swim, they endure extreme isolation from the rest of the world.
7. Toward the end of the marathon, swimmers hear the loud applause and shouts of encouragement from their fans.
8. Spectators can watch only the finish of a marathon.
9. Nevertheless, they know the long distance that the athletes have traveled.
10. Emerging from the water, exhausted swimmers have successfully completed another marathon.

GRAMMAR

 EXERCISE 2   **Identifying Direct Objects**

Identify the ten direct objects in the following paragraph. If a sentence does not contain a direct object, write *no direct object*. [Remember: Objects follow action verbs only.]

EXAMPLES   [1] Have you ever flown a hang glider?
1. *hang glider*

[2] Hang gliding has become a popular sport.
2. *no direct object*

[1] Many adventurous people enjoy the thrill of gliding through the air. [2] As you can see, a hang glider can carry a full-grown person in its harness. [3] The hang glider has a lightweight sail with a triangular control bar underneath. [4] At takeoff, the pilot lifts the glider shoulder-high and runs hard down a slope into the wind. [5] The wind lifts the glider and carries the pilot off the ground. [6] Because of the wind currents, takeoffs from a hilltop or a cliff are the easiest. [7] Once airborne, the pilot directs the path of flight. [8] He or she also controls the glider's speed by pushing or pulling on the control bar. [9] For example, a gentle pull increases speed. [10] To land, the pilot stalls the glider near the ground and drops lightly to his or her feet.

Indirect Objects

The *indirect object* is another type of complement. Like a direct object, an indirect object helps to complete the meaning of a transitive verb. If a sentence has an indirect object, it always has a direct object also.

16c. An *indirect object* is a noun or pronoun that comes between the verb and the direct object. It tells *to whom* or *to what,* or *for whom* or *for what,* the action of the verb is done.

EXAMPLES   The waiter gave **her** a smile. [The pronoun *her* is the indirect object of the verb *gave.* It answers the question *"To whom* did the waiter give a smile?"]

Pam left the **waiter** a tip. [The noun *waiter* is the indirect object of the verb *left.* It answers the question *"For whom* did she leave a tip?"]

NOTE: Linking verbs do not have indirect objects, because they do not show action. Also, an indirect object is never in a prepositional phrase.

INDIRECT OBJECT	Vinnie made **us** some lasagna.
PREPOSITIONAL PHRASE	Vinnie made some lasagna **for us.**

Like a direct object, an indirect object can be a compound of two or more objects.

EXAMPLE   Felicia threw **Jane** and **Paula** slow curveballs until they had warmed up. [*Jane* and *Paula* are the indirect objects of the verb *threw.* They answer the question *"To whom* did Felicia throw curveballs?"]

▶ EXERCISE 3   **Identifying Direct Objects and Indirect Objects**

Identify the direct object and the indirect object in each of the following sentences.

EXAMPLE   **1.** Did you buy Mom a calculator for her birthday?
           1. *Mom—indirect object; calculator—direct object*

1. The usher found us seats near the stage.
2. I'll gladly lend you my typewriter.
3. The Nobel Committee gave Octavio Paz the Nobel Prize for literature.
4. Please show me your beaded moccasins.
5. Mai told the children stories about her family's escape from Vietnam.
6. Our teacher taught us some English words of Native American origin.
7. I fed the horse some hay.
8. My secret pal sent me a birthday card.
9. They owe you an apology.
10. Will you please save Ricardo a seat?

▶ EXERCISE 4   **Identifying Objects of Verbs**

All of the following sentences contain direct objects. Some sentences contain indirect objects, too. Identify the object or objects in each sentence.

EXAMPLE   **1.** My parents gave me a choice of places to go on our camping vacation.
           1. *me—indirect object; choice—direct object*

1. I told them my answer quickly.
2. I had recently read a magazine article about the Flathead Reservation in Montana.
3. We spent five days of our vacation there.
4. We liked the friendly people and the rugged land.
5. A Salishan tribe known as the Flatheads govern the huge reservation.
6. I especially liked the beautiful mountains and twenty-eight-mile-long Flathead Lake.
7. My parents assigned me the job of putting up our tent beside the lake.

8. Someone gave my father directions to the National Bison Range, and we went there one day.
9. We also attended the Standing Arrow Pow-Wow, which was the highlight of our stay.
10. The performers showed visitors traditional Flathead dances and games.

PICTURE THIS

The year is 1924, and you're a customer in this toy store. You are looking for gifts for your friends, but your attention soon turns to the conversations at the counter. The two sales clerks seem to be having some trouble with their customers. The customers have seen nearly every toy in the shop, yet they have not decided which ones to buy. As you watch and listen, you decide to write a story about this amusing incident. In your writing, use at least three direct objects and two indirect objects.

Subject: customers in a toy store
Audience: friends
Purpose: to entertain

Wyndam Payne, illustration from *The Mysterious Toyshop: A Fairy Tale*, by Cyril W. Beaumont. Published in London, 1924. Commercial color relief process, 6 × 9". Copyright 1984 By The Metropolitan Museum of Art, Rogers Fund, 1970. (1970.544.1).

Subject Complements

16d. A *subject complement* completes the meaning of a linking verb and identifies or describes the subject.

EXAMPLES   Julio has been **president** of his class since October. [*President* identifies the subject *Julio.*]
Was it **you**? [*You* identifies the subject *it.*]
Barbara looks **sleepy** this morning. [*Sleepy* describes the subject *Barbara.*]

☞ REFERENCE NOTE: For more information about linking verbs, see pages 447–448.

There are two kinds of subject complements—the *predicate nominative* and the *predicate adjective*.

Predicate Nominatives

16e. A *predicate nominative* is a noun or pronoun that follows a linking verb and explains or identifies the subject of the sentence.

EXAMPLES   A good dictionary is a valuable **tool.** [*Tool* is a predicate nominative that follows the linking verb *is* and explains the subject *dictionary.*]
This piece of flint may be an old **arrowhead.** [*Arrowhead* is a predicate nominative that follows the linking verb *may be* and identifies the subject *piece.*]
The winner of the race was **she.** [*She* is a predicate nominative that follows the linking verb *was* and identifies the subject *winner.*]

NOTE: Expressions such as *It is I* and *That was he* sound awkward even though they are correct. In conversation, you would probably say *It's me* and *That was him.* Such nonstandard expressions may one day become acceptable in writing as well as in speech. For now, however, it is best to follow the rules of standard English in your writing.

Like other sentence complements, a predicate nominative may be compound.

EXAMPLE   The discoverers of radium were **Pierre Curie** and **Marie Sklodowska Curie.**

Be careful not to confuse a predicate nominative with a direct object. A predicate nominative always follows a linking verb. A direct object always follows an action verb.

PREDICATE NOMINATIVE   We are the **delegates** from our school.

DIRECT OBJECT   We elected the **delegates** from our school.

The predicate nominative is never part of a prepositional phrase.

PREDICATE NOMINATIVE   Bill Russell became a famous basketball **coach.**

PREPOSITIONAL PHRASE   Bill Russell became famous **as coach** of the Boston Celtics.

▶ EXERCISE 5   **Identifying Predicate Nominatives**

Identify the linking verb and the predicate nominative in each of the following sentences.

EXAMPLE   **1.** Are whales mammals?
              1. *Are—mammals*

1. Mount Kilimanjaro is the tallest mountain in Africa.
2. The kingdom of Siam became modern-day Thailand.
3. Dandelions can be a problem.
4. Sue Mishima is a lawyer.
5. When will a woman be President of the United States?
6. Reuben has become a fine pianist.
7. Variety is the spice of life.
8. At the moment, she remains our choice for mayor.
9. Alaska is the largest state in the United States.
10. *Philately* is another name for stamp collecting.

GRAMMAR

Predicate Adjectives

16f. A *predicate adjective* is an adjective that follows a linking verb and describes the subject of the sentence.

EXAMPLES   Cold milk tastes **good** on a hot day. [*Good* is a predicate adjective that describes the subject *milk.*]
The pita bread was **light** and **delicious.** [*Light* and *delicious* form a compound predicate adjective that describes the subject *bread.*]

▶ EXERCISE 6   **Identifying Predicate Adjectives**

Identify the linking verb and the predicate adjective in each of the following sentences.

EXAMPLE   **1.** The crowd became restless.
                1. *became—restless*

1. Everyone felt good about the decision.
2. That container of milk smells sour.
3. Don't the Cuban black beans with rice and onions taste delicious?
4. The situation appears complicated.
5. Everyone remained calm during the emergency.
6. Why does the water in that pond look green?
7. During Barbara Jordan's speech, the audience grew thoughtful and then enthusiastic.
8. Jan stays cheerful most of the time.
9. She must be happy with the results.
10. From here, the drums sound too loud.

▶ EXERCISE 7   **Using Predicate Adjectives and Predicate Nominatives**

You want to write an adventure story, but you aren't sure how to begin. You remember reading about a professional writer who gets ideas from watching people and making up interesting identities for them. You decide to try this method of writing while you are sitting in this waiting room. Write a brief description of the other patients in the waiting room. Imagine the patients' jobs, families, backgrounds, and personalities. In your description, use five predicate adjectives and five predicate nominatives. Underline each predicate adjective once. Underline each predicate nominative twice. You may want to use your description to write the whole adventure story.

EXAMPLES   *The woman next to the coats is <u>Julia Johnson</u>.*

She looks <u>friendly</u>, but she is really an international <u>spy</u>.

▶ REVIEW A   **Identifying Complements**

Identify the complement or complements in each of the following sentences. Then, label each complement as a *direct object*, an *indirect object*, a *predicate nominative*, or a *predicate adjective*.

EXAMPLES   **1.** Our teacher read us stories from the Leatherstocking Tales.
          1. *us—indirect object; stories—direct object*
          2. James Fenimore Cooper is the author of these tales.
          2. *author—predicate nominative*

1. Leatherstocking was a fictional scout in Cooper's Leatherstocking Tales.
2. He was also a woodcrafter and a trapper.
3. He could not read, but he understood the lore of the woods.
4. To generations of readers, this character has become a hero.
5. He could face any emergency.
6. He always remained faithful and fearless.
7. Leatherstocking loved the forest and the open country.
8. In later years he grew miserable.
9. The destruction of the wilderness by settlers and others greatly disturbed him.
10. He told no one his views and retreated from civilization.

WRITING APPLICATION

Using Subject Complements to Write Riddles

Popcorn pops, flashlights light, and linking verbs link. Like popcorn and flashlights, linking verbs do just what their name suggests. They link subjects with subject complements, which identify or describe the subject. Notice how the subject complements in the following riddle give clues to the identity of the subject *I*.

RIDDLE   I feel **smooth** to the touch.
I can be **white** or **brown**.
I am a **box** without a lid.
Inside me, you'll find gold.
What am I?

ANSWER   an egg

GRAMMAR

▶ WRITING ACTIVITY

A magazine for young people is sponsoring a riddle-writing contest. Whoever writes the best riddle will win the most advanced video game system on the market. You are determined to write the best riddle and win. Write two riddles to enter in the contest. In each one, use at least two subject complements.

Prewriting The best way to make up a riddle is to begin with the answer. List some animals, places, and things that suggest funny or hidden meanings. For instance, the example riddle plays on the idea that an egg is like a box of treasure. For each animal, place, or thing, jot down a description based on a funny or hidden meaning. Then choose the four animals, places, or things that you think will make the best riddles.

Writing Use your prewriting notes as you write your first draft. In each riddle, make sure that your clues will help your audience guess the answer. Be sure that you use a subject complement (a predicate nominative or a predicate adjective) in the riddle.

Evaluating and Revising Ask a friend to read your riddles. If the riddles are too difficult or too simple, revise them. You may want to add details that appeal to the senses. Linking verbs such as *appear*, *feel*, *smell*, *sound*, and *taste* can help you add such details. (For a longer list of linking verbs, see page 448.)

Proofreading and Publishing Read through your riddles again to check for errors in spelling, punctuation, and capitalization. Pay special attention to the capitalization of proper nouns. You and your classmates may want to publish a book of riddles. Collect your riddles and draw or cut out pictures as illustrations. Make photocopies for all the members of the class.

▶ REVIEW B   **Identifying Complements**

Identify the complement or complements in each sentence in the following paragraphs. Then label each complement as a *direct object,* an *indirect object,* a *predicate nominative,* or a *predicate adjective.* [Remember: A complement may be compound.]

EXAMPLE   [1] Sean, my brother, won three medals at the
                    Special Olympic games.
           1. *medals—direct object*

[1] Sean was one of more than one hundred special-education students who competed in the regional Special Olympics last month. [2] The games brought students from many schools to our city. [3] The highlights of the games included track events such as sprints and relay races. [4] These were the closest contests. [5] Sean's excellent performance in the relays gave him confidence. [6] The softball throw and high jump were especially challenging events. [7] Sean looked relaxed but determined as he prepared for the high jump. [8] He certainly felt great after he made the best jump.

[9] The Special Olympics are exciting and inspiring. [10] Many of the contestants have physical impairments; some cannot walk or see. [11] Teachers and volunteers train contestants in the different events. [12] However, the young athletes themselves are the force behind the program. [13] The pictures on the next page give you a glimpse of the excitement at the Special Olympics. [14] The two smiling girls on the left are winners of a sprint. [15] On the right, this determined boy gains the lead in the wheelchair race.

[16] Mrs. Duffy, one of the coaches, told us the history of the Special Olympics. [17] Eunice Kennedy Shriver founded the program in 1961. [18] To begin with, the program was a five-week camp. [19] Several years later, however, the camp became an international sports event with contestants from twenty-six states and Canada. [20] Today, the organizers of the Special Olympics sponsor regional and international games.

FINISH LINE

GRAMMAR

Review: Posttest 1

Identifying Complements

Identify the complement or complements in each of the following sentences. Label each complement as a *direct object*, an *indirect object*, a *predicate nominative*, or a *predicate adjective*.

EXAMPLE **1.** A respirator pumps oxygen into the lungs.
1. *oxygen—direct object*

1. Our cat avoids skunks and raccoons.
2. Jim Thorpe was a famous American Indian athlete.
3. The teacher showed us a film about drug abuse.
4. The television commercials for that new product sound silly.
5. Who put the roses in that vase?
6. I sent my grandparents a card for their anniversary.
7. During her interview on television, Zina Garrison-Jackson appeared relaxed and confident.
8. At first the colt seemed frightened.
9. Mrs. Karras offered us olives and stuffed grape leaves.

10. The DJ played songs by Freddie Jackson, Gloria Estefan, and Paula Abdul.
11. The newspaper story prompted an investigation by the mayor's office.
12. My sister has become a computer repair technician.
13. Write your name and address on the envelope.
14. The weather forecasters haven't issued a tornado warning.
15. Before long, the mistake became obvious to nearly everyone.
16. The sky looked gray and stormy.
17. The Egyptian writer Naguib Mahfouz won the Nobel Prize for literature in 1988.
18. The consumer group wrote the senator a letter.
19. *Barrio Boy* is the autobiography of Ernesto Galarza.
20. The candidate seems ambitious but sincere.

Review: Posttest 2

Writing Sentences with Complements

Write two sentences for each of the following kinds of complements. Underline each complement.

EXAMPLE **1.** a direct object
1. *We heard the president's <u>speech</u>.*
Both of my parents enjoy <u>novels</u> set in ancient Rome.

1. a compound direct object
2. an indirect object followed by a direct object
3. a predicate nominative after a form of *be*
4. a predicate adjective after a form of *become* or *seem*
5. a compound predicate adjective after a linking verb other than *be, become,* or *seem*

17 THE PHRASE

Prepositional and Verbal Phrases

Diagnostic Test

A. Identifying Phrases

Identify the phrase in each of the following sentences.

EXAMPLES
1. Payat drew a picture of his adobe house.
   1. *of his adobe house*

2. Returning her library books, Janelle chose two more.
   2. *Returning her library books*

1. Organized in 1884, the first African American professional baseball team was the Cuban Giants.
2. The jacket with a blue collar is mine.
3. My goal is to become a forest ranger.
4. On the sidelines, the coach paced nervously.
5. The student, frowning slightly, erased the title.
6. Guillermo hopes to visit us soon.
7. The charity received donations for the hungry.
8. Immediately after school, we left.

9. I practice my Japanese calligraphy on Mondays, Wednesdays, and Saturdays.
10. Several of my friends are absent today.

B. Identifying and Classifying Prepositional Phrases

Identify the prepositional phrase in each sentence, and classify the phrase as an *adjective phrase* or an *adverb phrase*. Then, give the word or words that the phrase modifies.

EXAMPLE **1.** Harvest festivals are celebrated throughout the world.

1. *throughout the world—adverb phrase; are celebrated*

11. The view from Mount Fuji is spectacular.
12. Has the search party returned to the campsite yet?
13. After the game, we got something to eat.
14. We heard stories about our Cherokee ancestors.
15. An umbrella tent has supports on the outside.
16. The second-longest river in Africa is the Congo.
17. Jody was late for the party.
18. Boulder Dam was the original name of Hoover Dam.
19. The Hudson River was once the chief trading route for the western frontier.
20. Hearing a loud noise, Mr. Cárdenas stopped his car, got out, and looked underneath it.

17a. A *phrase* is a group of related words that is used as a single part of speech and does not contain both a subject and a verb.

EXAMPLES **in the kitchen** [phrase; no subject or verb]
playing the guitar [phrase; no subject]

☞ **REFERENCE NOTE:** If a group of words has both a subject and a verb, it is called a *clause*. See Chapter 18 for more about clauses.

▶ EXERCISE 1   **Identifying Phrases**

Identify each of the following groups of words as a *phrase* or *not a phrase*.

EXAMPLES   **1.** on the paper
            1. *phrase*

            2. after we eat
            2. *not a phrase*

1. when you know
2. as they walked in
3. in the garden
4. is sleeping
5. until Mom gets home

6. smiling brightly
7. to the supermarket
8. with a warm smile
9. around the table
10. if he says so

Prepositional Phrases

17b.   A *prepositional phrase* includes a preposition, a noun or a pronoun called the *object of the preposition,* and any modifiers of that object.

EXAMPLES   under the umbrella
            among good friends
            for ourselves

Notice that an article or another modifier may appear in a prepositional phrase. The first example contains the article *the.* In the second example, *good* modifies *friends.*

☞ REFERENCE NOTE: See page 460 for a list of commonly used prepositions.

The noun or pronoun that ends a prepositional phrase is called the *object of the preposition.*

EXAMPLES   Linh Phan has the lead in the school **play.** [The noun *play* is the object of the preposition *in.*]
            They divided the prize between **them.** [The pronoun *them* is the object of the preposition *between.*]

EXERCISE 2   **Identifying Prepositional Phrases**

Identify each prepositional phrase in the following sentences. [Note: A sentence may contain more than one prepositional phrase.]

EXAMPLE   [1] Many soldiers fought bravely during the Vietnam War.

1. *during the Vietnam War*

[1] One of these soldiers was Jan C. Scruggs. [2] When the war was over, he and other veterans wondered why there was no national memorial honoring those who had served in Vietnam. [3] Scruggs decided he would raise funds for a Vietnam Veterans Memorial. [4] The memorial would include the names of all American soldiers who had died or were missing in action. [5] Organizing the project took years of great effort. [6] Many different people contributed their talents to the project. [7] Maya Ying Lin, a college student, designed the memorial that now stands in Washington, D.C. [8] This picture shows the V-shaped, black granite wall that was built from Lin's design. [9] A glass company from Memphis, Tennessee, stenciled each name on the shiny granite. [10] Now, the men and women who fought and died in Vietnam will never be forgotten by the American people.

GRAMMAR

Adjective Phrases

A prepositional phrase used as an adjective is called an *adjective phrase.*

ADJECTIVE   Rosa chose the **blue** one.
ADJECTIVE PHRASE   Rosa chose the one **with blue stripes.**

17c. An *adjective phrase* modifies a noun or a pronoun.

Adjective phrases answer the same questions that single-word adjectives answer.

> *What kind?   Which one?*
> *How many?   How much?*

EXAMPLES   The music store is the one **with the neon sign.** [The prepositional phrase *with the neon sign* is used as an adjective modifying the pronoun *one.* The phrase answers the question *Which one?*]

We bought a tape **by Janet Jackson.** [*By Janet Jackson* is used as an adjective modifying the noun *tape.* The phrase answers the question *What kind?*]

▶ EXERCISE 3   **Identifying Adjective Phrases**

Identify the adjective phrase in each of the following sentences, and give the word that each phrase modifies.

EXAMPLE   1. Marie Sklodowska Curie, a scientist from Poland, was awarded the Nobel Prize.
1. *from Poland—scientist*

1. While still a student, Marie became friends with Pierre Curie.
2. Pierre had already gained fame as a scientist.
3. Paris, France, was where the two of them met.

4. Their enthusiasm for science brought them together.
5. The marriage between the two scientists was a true partnership.
6. The year after their marriage another scientist discovered natural radioactivity.
7. The Curies began researching the radiation in certain substances.
8. Their theories about a new element were proved to be true.
9. Their research on the mineral pitchblende uncovered a new radioactive element, radium.
10. The Curies won a Nobel Prize for their discovery.

More than one adjective phrase may modify the same noun or pronoun.

EXAMPLE   The sign **with neon letters near my house** flashes on and off all night long. [The two phrases, *with neon letters* and *near my house*, both modify the noun *sign.*]

An adjective phrase may also modify the object in another adjective phrase.

EXAMPLE   A majority **of the mammals in the world** sleep during the day. [The adjective phrase *of the mammals* modifies the noun *majority.* The adjective phrase *in the world* modifies the noun *mammals,* which is the object of the preposition in the first phrase.]

▶ EXERCISE 4   **Identifying Adjective Phrases**

Each numbered sentence in the following paragraph contains at least one adjective phrase. Identify each phrase and give the word that it modifies.

EXAMPLE   [1] R.I.C.E. is the recommended treatment for minor sports injuries.
1. *for minor sports injuries—treatment*

[1] The first letters of the words *Rest, Ice, Compression,* and *Elevation* form the abbreviation *R.I.C.E.* [2] Total rest is

not necessary, just rest for the injured part of the body. [3] Ice helps because it deadens pain and slows the loss of blood. [4] Ice also reduces swelling in the injured area. [5] Compression with a tight bandage of elastic cloth prevents further strain on the injury. [6] This photograph shows a compression bandage treating the pulled hamstring of Carl Lewis. [7] The last step in the treatment is elevation of the injury. [8] The effect of gravity helps fluid drain away. [9] If pain continues, someone with medical training should be called. [10] Even injuries of a minor nature need proper attention.

EXERCISE 5 **Using Adjective Phrases**

In the following sentences, insert an adjective phrase for each blank. Then, give the word that the phrase modifies. Remember that an adjective phrase must modify a noun or a pronoun.

EXAMPLE **1.** A flock _____ flew overhead.
　　　　 1. *A flock of small gray birds flew*
　　　　　　overhead.—flock

1. The sound _____ suddenly filled the air.
2. The theater _____ often shows kung-fu movies.
3. May I have some more _____?
4. Our vacation _____ was relaxing.
5. Her photograph _____ looks like a prizewinner.
6. Baki found the answer _____.
7. He put the flowers in a vase _____.
8. A boy _____ hung a piñata in the tree.
9. The nest is in the top branch _____.
10. Someone _____ shouted for quiet.

Adverb Phrases

A prepositional phrase used as an adverb is called an *adverb phrase.*

ADVERB   The cavalry **soon** reached the fort.

ADVERB PHRASE   **By noon** the cavalry reached the fort.

17d. An *adverb phrase* modifies a verb, an adjective, or another adverb.

Adverb phrases answer the same questions that single-word adverbs answer.

When?	*Why?*
Where?	*How often?*
How?	*To what extent?*

EXAMPLES   We got our new puppy **at the animal shelter.**
[The adverb phrase *at the animal shelter* modifies the verb *got,* telling *where.*]
A puppy is always ready **for a game.** [The adverb phrase *for a game* modifies the adjective *ready,* telling *how.*]
He barks loudly **for a puppy.** [The adverb phrase *for a puppy* modifies the adverb *loudly,* telling *to what extent.*]

Unlike adjective phrases, which usually follow the word or words they modify, adverb phrases may appear at various places in sentences.

EXAMPLES   We planted elm seedlings **along the driveway.**
Along the driveway we planted elm seedlings.

At our house we have dinner early.
We have dinner early **at our house.**

▶ EXERCISE 6   **Identifying Adverb Phrases**

Identify the adverb phrase in each of the following sentences, and give the word that each phrase modifies. [Note: Do not list adjective phrases.]

EXAMPLE   **1. Pecos Bill will live forever in the many legends about him.**
　　　　　　　1. *in the many legends—will live*

1. When he was only a baby, Pecos Bill fell into the Pecos River.
2. His parents searched for him but couldn't find him.
3. He was saved by coyotes, who raised him.
4. He thought for many years that he was a coyote.
5. After a long argument a cowboy convinced him that he was not a coyote.
6. During a drought he dug the bed of the Rio Grande.
7. On one occasion Bill rode a cyclone.
8. A mountain lion once leaped from a ledge above Bill's head.
9. Bill was ready for trouble and soon had the mountain lion tamed.
10. Stories like these about Pecos Bill are common in the West.

Like adjective phrases, more than one adverb phrase may modify the same word.

EXAMPLES   She drove **for hours through the storm.** [Both adverb phrases, *for hours* and *through the storm,* modify the verb *drove.*]
　　　　　　　The library is open **during the day on weekends.** [Both adverb phrases, *during the day* and *on weekends,* modify the adjective *open.*]

NOTE: An adverb phrase may be followed by an adjective phrase that modifies the object in the adverb phrase.

EXAMPLE   The boat landed **on an island near the coast.** [The adverb phrase *on an island* modifies the verb *landed.* The adjective phrase *near the coast* modifies the noun *island.*]

▶ EXERCISE 7   **Identifying Adverb Phrases**

Identify the ten adverb phrases in the following paragraphs. Then, give the word or words that each phrase
modifies. [Note: Do not list adjective phrases.]

EXAMPLE [1] Never before had a blizzard struck the coastal
area with such force.
1. *with such force—had struck*

[1] The raging wind blew eleven-year-old Andrea over
a sea wall near her home and trapped her in a deep snow-
drift. [2] No one could hear her shouts over the howling
wind.

[3] Suddenly, Andrea's dog charged through the snow
toward the beach. [4] He plunged into the snow around
Andrea and licked her face, warming the skin. [5] Then
the huge dog walked around Andrea until the snow was
packed down. [6] The dog pulled her to an open area on
the beach. [7] With great effort, Andrea and her dog made
their way home. [8] Grateful to their dog, Andrea's family
served him a special steak dinner.

▶ EXERCISE 8   **Writing a Paragraph Using Adjective
and Adverb Phrases**

You are working with a
park ranger for the summer.
Together you are writing
a safety pamphlet for
campers. One part of the
pamphlet will explain how
to avoid coming into contact
with poison ivy and poison
oak. Using these drawings
the ranger has given you
and the notes on the next
page, write a paragraph
informing campers about these
plants. Use at least two adjective phrases
and three adverb phrases in your paragraph.

GRAMMAR

Notes

poison ivy and poison oak—plants can cause an
allergic reaction when touched

some people react worse than others—some not at all

reaction includes itching and blistering of the skin

best method to deal with these plants—learn to
recognize and avoid them

poison ivy—leaf made up of three leaflets that are
glossy green, oval-shaped, and smoothly textured

poison oak—similar to poison ivy, but leaflets are
thicker and smaller, and the ends are rounded
rather than pointed

first aid—wash the area thoroughly with soap and
water; visit a doctor if itching, swelling, and
redness develop

▶ REVIEW A **Identifying and Classifying Prepositional Phrases**

In the following sentences, identify each prepositional phrase and classify it as an *adjective phrase* or an *adverb phrase*. Then, give the word or words the phrase modifies.

EXAMPLE **1. Here is some information about sharks.**
1. *about sharks—adjective phrase; information*

1. Did you know that there are hundreds of types?
2. Scientists group these different types into twenty-eight large families.
3. Sharks within the same family share many traits.
4. The body shape, tail shape, and teeth determine the differences among families.

5. Sharks are found throughout the world's oceans.
6. As the chart shows, some sharks prefer cold waters, and others live mostly in warm tropical oceans.
7. Only thirty kinds of sharks are dangerous.
8. The huge whale shark, however, falls under the "not dangerous" category.
9. Divers can even hitch a ride on its fins.
10. Beautiful yet frightening to most people, sharks are perhaps the world's most awesome creatures.

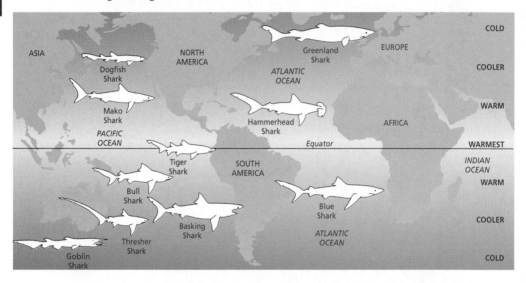

▶ REVIEW B

Writing Sentences with Prepositional Phrases

Write five sentences of your own. In each sentence, use a different prepositional phrase from the following list. After each sentence, label the phrase as an *adjective phrase* or an *adverb phrase*.

EXAMPLE   **1.** through the toll booth
           1. *A car passed through the toll booth.—adverb phrase*

1. in the movie theater
2. for the Cinco de Mayo party
3. along the water's edge
4. about General Colin Powell
5. into the crowded department store

GRAMMAR

WRITING APPLICATION

Using Prepositional Phrases to Add Detail to Your Writing

Prepositional phrases add information to a sentence. Adjective phrases give details about *what kind, which one,* and *how many.* Adverb phrases tell details about *when, where, how, why, how much,* and *to what extent.*

WITHOUT PHRASES	We fed the cat.
WITH PHRASES	In the morning we fed the cat from the blue box of dry Kitty Bits.

▶ WRITING ACTIVITY

You are writing a note to a friend explaining how to care for your pet while you are away on vacation. In your note, use a combined total of at least ten adjective phrases and adverb phrases to give detailed instructions to your friend.

Prewriting Begin by thinking about a pet you have or would like to have. Then, make a chart or list of the pet's needs. If you need more information about a particular pet, ask a friend or someone else who owns such a pet.

Writing As you write your first draft, focus on giving information about each of your pet's needs. Tell your friend everything he or she needs to know to care for your pet properly.

Evaluating and Revising Ask a family member or friend to read your note. Add any missing information and take out any unnecessary instructions. Be sure that you have used both adjective phrases and adverb phrases and that you have used a total of at least ten phrases.

Proofreading Read over your note again to check the grammar, punctuation, and spelling. Be sure that your prepositional phrases are properly placed. Remember that an adjective phrase follows the noun or pronoun it modifies. An adverb phrase may occur at various places in a sentence. (See page 720 for information on when to use commas with introductory prepositional phrases.)

Verbals and Verbal Phrases

A *verbal* is a word that is formed from a verb but is used as a noun, an adjective, or an adverb.

The Participle

17e. A *participle* is a verb form that can be used as an adjective.

There are two kinds of participles: *present participles* and *past participles*.

(1) *Present participles* end in *–ing*.

EXAMPLES   Mr. Sanchez rescued three people from the **burning** building. [*Burning* is the present participle of the verb *burn*. The participle modifies the noun *building*.]
We skated on the **frozen** pond. [The irregular past participle *frozen* modifies the noun *pond*.]
Chasing the cat, the dog ran down the street. [*Chasing* is the present participle of the verb *chase*. The participle acts as an adjective modifying the noun *dog*.]

(2) *Past participles* usually end in *–d* or *–ed*. Some past participles are irregularly formed.

EXAMPLES   Well **trained** in gunnery, the soldier successfully carried out her mission. [The past participle *trained* modifies the noun *soldier*.]
We skated on the **frozen** pond. [The irregular past participle *frozen* modifies the noun *pond*.]

GRAMMAR

☞ **REFERENCE NOTE:** For a list of irregular past participles, see pages 583–586.

NOTE: Be careful not to confuse participles used as adjectives with participles used in verb phrases. Remember that the participle in a verb phrase is part of the verb.

PARTICIPLE	**Discouraged,** the fans went home.
VERB PHRASE	The fans **were discouraged** and went home.
PARTICIPLE	**Singing** cheerfully, the birds perched in the trees.
VERB PHRASE	The birds **were singing** cheerfully in the trees.

▶ EXERCISE 9 ## Identifying Participles and the Nouns They Modify

Identify the participles used as adjectives in the following sentences. After each participle, give the noun that the participle modifies.

EXAMPLE **1.** The deserted cities of the Anasazi are found in the Four Corners area of the United States.
1. *deserted—cities*

1. Utah, Colorado, New Mexico, and Arizona are the bordering states that make up the Four Corners.
2. Because of its natural beauty, Chaco Canyon is one of the most visited sights in this region of the Southwest.
3. Among the remaining ruins in Chaco Canyon are the houses, public buildings, and plazas of the Anasazi.
4. What alarming event may have caused these people to leave their valley?
5. Historians are studying the scattered remains of the Anasazi culture to learn more about these mysterious people.

▶ EXERCISE 10 ## Identifying Participles and the Nouns or Pronouns They Modify

Identify the participles used as adjectives in the following sentences. Then, give the noun or pronoun the participle modifies.

EXAMPLE **1.** Buzzing mosquitoes swarmed around me.
1. *Buzzing—mosquitoes*

1. Annoyed, I went inside to watch TV.
2. I woke my sleeping father to ask about mosquitoes.
3. Irritated, he directed me to the encyclopedia.
4. I learned that some flying insects carry diseases.
5. Biting mosquitoes put liquid chemicals into the skin.
6. The swollen skin itches.
7. Sucking blood for food, mosquitoes survive in many different climates.
8. Sometimes you can hear mosquitoes humming.
9. Their vibrating wings make the sound.
10. Mosquitoes, living only a few weeks, may go through as many as twelve generations in a year.

The Participial Phrase

17f. A *participial phrase* consists of a participle together with its modifiers and complements. The entire phrase is used as an adjective.

EXAMPLE **Stretching slowly,** the cat jumped down from the windowsill. [The participle *stretching* is modified by the adverb *slowly.*]

The tornado **predicted by the weather forecaster** did not hit our area. [The participle *predicted* is modified by the prepositional phrase *by the weather forecaster.*]

Reading the assignment, she took notes carefully. [The participle *reading* has the direct object *assignment.*]

A participial phrase should be placed close to the word it modifies. Otherwise the phrase may appear to modify another word, and the sentence may not make sense.

☞ REFERENCE NOTE: For information on how to place participial phrases correctly, see page 643.

▸ EXERCISE 11   **Identifying Participial Phrases and the Nouns or Pronouns They Modify**

Identify the participial phrases in the following sentences. Then, give the word or words each phrase modifies.

EXAMPLE   **1.** Living over four hundred years ago, Leonardo da Vinci kept journals of his many ideas and inventions.

1. *Living over four hundred years ago—Leonardo da Vinci*

1. The journals, written in "mirror writing," are more than five thousand pages long.
2. Leonardo drew many pictures showing birds in flight.
3. He hoped that his machines based on his sketches of birds would enable humans to fly.
4. Shown here, his design for a helicopter was the first one in history.

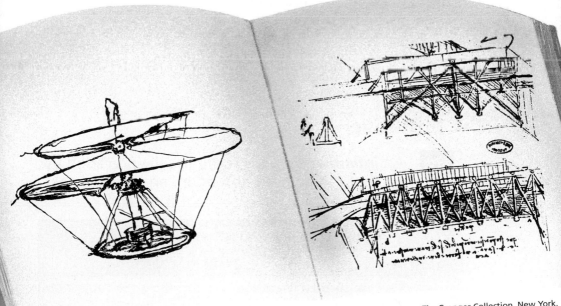

The Granger Collection, New York.

5. Studying the eye, Leonardo understood the sense of sight.
6. He worked hard, filling his journals with sketches like the ones above for a movable bridge.

7. The solutions reached in his journals often helped Leonardo when he created his artworks.
8. He used the hands sketched in his journals as models when he painted the hands in the *Mona Lisa*.
9. Painting on a large wall, Leonardo created *The Last Supper*.
10. Leonardo, experimenting continually, had little time to paint in his later years.

▶ EXERCISE 12   **Writing Sentences with Participial Phrases**

Write five sentences, using in each sentence a different participial phrase from the following list. [Note: Place a comma after a participial phrase that begins a sentence.]

EXAMPLE   **1.** cheering for the team
            1. *Cheering for the team, we celebrated the victory.*

1. confused by the directions
2. gathering information on the Hopi
3. practicing my part in the play
4. followed closely by my younger brother
5. searching through the crowd

The Infinitive

17g. An *infinitive* is a verb form, usually preceded by *to,* that can be used as a noun, an adjective, or an adverb.

INFINITIVES	
USED AS	EXAMPLES
Nouns	**To succeed** is my goal. [*To succeed* is the subject of the sentence.] My ambition is **to teach** Spanish. [*To teach* is a predicate nominative.] She tried **to win.** [*To win* is the direct object of the verb *tried.*]

(continued)

INFINITIVES *(continued)*	
USED AS	**EXAMPLES**
Adjectives	The place **to meet** tomorrow is the library. [*To meet* modifies the noun *place.*] She is the one **to call.** [*To call* modifies the pronoun *one.*]
Adverbs	Tamara claims she was born **to surf.** [*To surf* modifies the verb *was born.*] This math problem will be hard **to solve** without a calculator. [*To solve* modifies the adjective *hard.*]

NOTE: *To* plus a noun or a pronoun (*to Washington, to her*) is a prepositional phrase, not an infinitive.

PREPOSITIONAL PHRASE   I am going **to the mall** today.
INFINITIVE   I am going **to shop** for new shoes.

EXERCISE 13   **Identifying Infinitives**

Identify the infinitives in the following sentences. If a sentence does not contain an infinitive, write *none*

EXAMPLE   **1.** I would like to go to New York City someday.
1. *to go*

1. My first stop would be to visit the Statue of Liberty.
2. Thousands of people go to see the statue every day.
3. They take a boat to Liberty Island.
4. The statue holds a torch to symbolize freedom.
5. The idea of a statue to represent freedom came from a French historian.
6. France gave the statue to the United States in 1884.
7. It was a gift to express the friendship between the two nations.
8. The statue was shipped to this country in 214 cases.
9. In the 1980s, many people helped to raise money for repairs to the statue.
10. The repairs were completed in time to celebrate the statue's 100th anniversary on October 28, 1986.

The Infinitive Phrase

17h. An *infinitive phrase* consists of an infinitive together with its modifiers and complements. It may be used as a noun, an adjective, or an adverb.

EXAMPLES **To be a good gymnast** takes hard work. [The infinitive phrase is used as a noun. The infinitive *to be* has a complement, *a good gymnast.*]

The first person **to fly over both the North Pole and the South Pole** was Richard Byrd. [The infinitive phrase is used as an adjective modifying the noun *person.* The infinitive *to fly* is modified by the prepositional phrase *over both the North Pole and the South Pole.*]

Are you ready **to go to the gym now?** [The infinitive phrase is used as an adverb modifying the adjective *ready.* The infinitive *to go* is modified by the prepositional phrase *to the gym* and by the adverb *now.*]

▶ EXERCISE 14 **Identifying Infinitive Phrases**

Identify the infinitive phrase in each of the following sentences.

EXAMPLE **1.** We went to the park to watch birds.
1. *to watch birds*

1. A bird is able to control each of its feathers.
2. Birds use their feathers to push their bodies through the air.
3. Human beings learned to build aircraft by studying birds.
4. A bird sings to claim its territory.
5. To recognize the songs of different birds takes practice.
6. By molting (or gradual shedding), birds are able to replace their feathers.

7. Eagles use their feet to catch small animals.
8. Since they have no teeth, many birds have to swallow their food whole.
9. In many cases both parents help to build a nest.
10. Most birds feed their young until the young are ready to fly from the nest.

PICTURE THIS

Wow! Whoever drew this sketch is a good artist. You found this sketch on the bus this morning, and you wish you knew who lost it. What is the artist like? Who are the people in the sketch? You find yourself thinking about these things and making up stories. You decide to write a short story about the artist or about the people in the sketch. Use at least three participial phrases and two infinitive phrases in your story. Underline the phrases you use.

Subject: sketch by an unidentified artist
Audience: classmates
Purpose: to entertain

GRAMMAR

▶ EXERCISE 15   **Writing Sentences with Infinitive Phrases**

Write five sentences, using in each sentence a different infinitive phrase from the following list. Try to vary your sentences as much as possible.

EXAMPLE   **1.** to see the carved masks of the Haida people
            1. *Terry wants to see the carved masks of the Haida people.*

1. to sing with the Boys Choir of Harlem
2. to ask a question about the test
3. to write a poem to his girlfriend
4. to understand the assignment
5. to give a report on the Spanish exploration of California

▶ REVIEW C   **Identifying and Classifying Participial Phrases and Infinitive Phrases**

Identify the participial phrase or the infinitive phrase in each sentence of the following paragraph. Label each phrase as a *participial phrase* or an *infinitive phrase*.

EXAMPLES   [1] My family is proud to celebrate our Jewish holidays.
            1. *to celebrate our Jewish holidays—infinitive phrase*

            [2] Observing Jewish traditions, we celebrate each holiday in a special way.
            2. *Observing Jewish traditions—participial phrase*

[1] During Rosh Hashanah we hear the Torah read in our synagogue. [2] Celebrated in September or October, Rosh Hashanah is the Jewish New Year. [3] On this holiday, the rabbi at our synagogue chooses to wear white robes instead of the usual black robes. [4] Representing newness and purity, the white robes symbolize the new year. [5] My favorite food of Rosh Hashanah is the honey cake baked by my grandmother. [6] During this holiday we plan to eat a lot. [7] We know that in only ten days

we will be fasting for Yom Kippur, considered the holiest day of the Jewish year. [8] To attend services like the one you see below is part of my family's Yom Kippur tradition. [9] I am always pleased to see many of my friends and neighbors there. [10] Sunset, marking the end of the day, brings Yom Kippur to a peaceful close.

Review: Posttest 1

A. Identifying and Classifying Prepositional Phrases

Identify each prepositional phrase in the following sentences and classify it as an *adjective phrase* or an *adverb phrase*. Then, give the word that the phrase modifies.

EXAMPLE   **1.** The chairs in the kitchen need new cushions.
            1. *in the kitchen—adjective phrase; chairs*

1. Cathy Guisewite is the creator of the cartoon strip "Cathy."
2. The Rio Grande is the boundary between Texas and Mexico.

3. Those totem poles come from Washington State.
4. The most popular name for the United States flag is the Stars and Stripes.
5. Heu Feng was a finalist at the international violin competition.
6. Through the window crashed the baseball.
7. I wish I were better at tennis.
8. During the Persian Gulf Conflict, we watched the news often.
9. The first United States space shuttle was launched in 1981.
10. Outside the door the hungry cat waited patiently.

B. Identifying and Classifying Verbal Phrases

Identify the verbal phrase in each of the following sentences. Then, tell whether it is a *participial phrase* or an *infinitive phrase*.

EXAMPLE **1.** The snow, falling steadily, formed huge drifts.
1. *falling steadily—participial phrase*

11. We expect to do well on the test.
12. The bus, slowed by heavy traffic, arrived later than it usually does.
13. Breaking the eggs into the wok, he made egg foo yong.
14. To remain calm is not always easy.
15. She wants to study Spanish in high school.
16. The magazine featuring that article is in the school library.
17. Chilled to the bone, the children finally went inside.
18. Who are the candidates that they plan to support in the election?
19. Bethune-Cookman College, founded by Mary McLeod Bethune, is in Daytona Beach, Florida.
20. Teresa called to ask about tonight's homework assignment.

Review: Posttest 2

Writing Phrases for Sentences

For each of the following sentences, write the kind of phrase that is called for in parentheses.

EXAMPLE **1.** _____ , the audience cheered Yo-Yo Ma's performance. (*participial phrase*)

1. *Clapping loudly, the audience cheered Yo-Yo Ma's performance.*

1. We walked slowly _____. (*adverb phrase*)
2. The people _____ applauded Barbara Jordan's speech. (*adjective phrase*)
3. My little brother is afraid _____. (*adverb phrase*)
4. The water _____ dripped steadily. (*adjective phrase*)
5. _____ we saw many beautiful Navajo rugs. (*adverb phrase*)
6. _____, the principal entered the classroom. (*participial phrase*)
7. Suddenly, _____, the lion pounced. (*participial phrase*)
8. My friends and I like _____. (*infinitive phrase*)
9. _____ is my one ambition. (*infinitive phrase*)
10. She wrote a poem _____. (*participial phrase*)

18 THE CLAUSE

Independent and Subordinate Clauses

Diagnostic Test

A. Identifying Clauses

Label each of the following groups of words as a *clause* or *not a clause*.

EXAMPLES **1.** last winter we ice-skated
1. *clause*

2. on the frozen pond
2. *not a clause*

1. until tomorrow
2. for lunch they had tacos
3. their pictures in the newspaper
4. waiting at the corner for the bus

5. because they are twins
6. neither answer is right
7. after the concert last Saturday
8. that honors Rosa Parks
9. which happened before I was born
10. playing first base

B. Classifying Subordinate Clauses

Label each italicized clause in the following sentences as an *adjective clause* or an *adverb clause*. Then give the word or words each clause modifies.

EXAMPLES   **1.** Manuel's paper route has doubled *since he took it over.*

      1. *adverb clause—has doubled*

      2. The present *that I bought for Mother's Day* is in my closet.

      2. *adjective clause—present*

11. Everyone *who signed up for the marathon* should meet at 8:00 A.M. tomorrow in the parking lot.
12. Tuesday we went to the Mardi Gras Parade, *which is held every year in New Orleans.*
13. Can you go to the park *when school is over today?*
14. The CD *that I wanted to buy* was out of stock.
15. Loretta stayed home today *because she has a bad case of the flu.*
16. I play soccer *so that I will get more exercise.*
17. We met the García family *as we were leaving the grocery store.*
18. My older sister, *who is on the varsity basketball team,* practices after school every day.
19. *Since it was such a beautiful evening,* we decided to take a long walk.
20. The students *whose families observe the Jewish Sabbath* will be excused early on Friday.

18a. A *clause* is a group of words that contains a verb and its subject and is used as a part of a sentence.

Every clause contains a subject and a verb. However, not all clauses express complete thoughts. Clauses that do express a complete thought are called *independent clauses.* Clauses that do not make complete sense by themselves are called *subordinate clauses.*

The Independent Clause

18b. An *independent* (or *main*) *clause* expresses a complete thought and can stand by itself as a sentence.

EXAMPLES   I woke up late this morning.
The alarm clock never rang.

When an independent clause stands alone, it is called a sentence. Usually, the term *independent clause* is used only when such a clause is joined with another clause.

SENTENCE   **My mother drove me to school.**
INDEPENDENT CLAUSE   Since I missed the bus, **my mother drove me to school.**

The Subordinate Clause

18c. A *subordinate* (or *dependent*) *clause* does not express a complete thought and cannot stand alone.

A subordinate clause must be joined with at least one independent clause to make a sentence and express a complete thought.

GRAMMAR

SUBORDINATE CLAUSES | since we first met
that the veterinarian recommended
if the dress is too long
SENTENCES | You and I have been good friends **since we first met.**
We give our hamster the food **that the veterinarian recommended.**
If the dress is too long, we will hem it.

Notice that words such as *since, that,* and *if* signal the beginning of a subordinate clause.

▶ EXERCISE 1   **Identifying Independent and Subordinate Clauses**

For each of the following sentences, label the italicized clause as *independent* or *subordinate.*

EXAMPLE   **1.** *If you know any modern music history,* you are probably familiar with the Motown sound.
     1. *subordinate*

1. Do you recognize any of the entertainers *who are shown in the photographs on the next page?*
2. These performers all had hit records in the 1950s and 1960s *when the music business in Detroit (the Motor City, or "Motown") was booming.*
3. Berry Gordy, *who founded the Motown record label,* began his business in a small office in Detroit.
4. He was a songwriter and producer, and *he was able to spot talent.*
5. Gordy went to clubs to hear local groups *whose sound he liked.*
6. The Miracles, *which was the first group he discovered,* had a lead singer named Smokey Robinson.
7. *Robinson was also a songwriter,* and Gordy included him in the Motown team of writers and musicians.
8. Gordy carefully managed all aspects of the Motown sound, *which is a special combination of rhythm and blues and soul.*

9. Diana Ross and the Supremes, Stevie Wonder, Marvin Gaye, Gladys Knight and the Pips, the Four Tops, and the Temptations are just some of the performers *that Gordy discovered.*
10. *As you look at the photographs again,* can you recognize more of these Motown music legends?

▶ EXERCISE 2   **Identifying Subordinate Clauses**

Identify the subordinate clause in each of the following sentences.

EXAMPLE   1. When you get up in the morning, do you look at your sleepy face in a mirror?
            1. *When you get up in the morning*

1. A mirror is a piece of polished metal or glass that is coated with a substance such as silver.

2. The most common type of mirror is the plane mirror, which is flat.
3. The image that is reflected in a plane mirror is reversed.
4. As you look into a mirror, your left hand seems to be the image's right hand.
5. When an image is reversed, it is called a mirror image.
6. A sailor who looks through the periscope of a submarine is using a system of lenses and mirrors to see above the water's surface.
7. Right-hand rear-view mirrors on cars, which show a wide area of the road behind, are usually convex, or curved outward.
8. Drivers must be careful because convex mirrors make reflected objects appear far away.
9. Because the mirror in a flashlight is concave, or curved inward, it strengthens the light from a small light bulb.
10. When you look in a concave mirror, you see a magnified reflection.

▶ EXERCISE 3 **Writing Sentences with Subordinate Clauses**

Write five sentences by adding an independent clause to each of the following subordinate clauses. Underline the independent clause in each of your sentences. Make your sentences interesting by adding a variety of independent clauses.

EXAMPLE **1.** who lives next door to us
      1. *The woman* who lives next door to us *is a computer programmer.*

1. when I bought the CD
2. who won the contest
3. if my parents agree
4. as Jessye Norman began to sing
5. because we are going to a fiesta

The Adjective Clause

18d. An *adjective clause* is a subordinate clause that modifies a noun or a pronoun.

Like an adjective or an adjective phrase, an adjective clause may modify a noun or a pronoun. Unlike an adjective phrase, an adjective clause contains a verb and its subject.

ADJECTIVE	a **blue** flower
ADJECTIVE PHRASE	a flower **with blue petals** [does not have a verb and its subject]
ADJECTIVE CLAUSE	a flower **that has blue petals** [does have a verb and its subject]

An adjective clause usually follows the noun or pronoun it modifies and tells *which one* or *what kind.*

EXAMPLES   Emma Willard was the one **who founded the first women's college in the United States.** [The adjective clause modifies the pronoun *one,* telling *which one.*]
I want a bicycle **that I can ride over rough ground.** [The adjective clause modifies the noun *bicycle,* telling *what kind.*]

The Relative Pronoun

An adjective clause is almost always introduced by a *relative pronoun.*

Relative Pronouns				
that	which	who	whom	whose

These words are called *relative pronouns* because they *relate* an adjective clause to the noun or pronoun that the clause modifies.

EXAMPLES   A snorkel is a hollow tube **that lets a diver breathe underwater.** [The relative pronoun *that* begins the adjective clause and relates it to the noun *tube.*]

The team's mascot, **which is a horse,** is called Renegade. [The relative pronoun *which* begins the adjective clause and relates it to the noun *mascot.*]

Gwendolyn Brooks is the writer **who is the poet laureate of Illinois.** [The relative pronoun *who* begins the adjective clause and relates it to the noun *writer.*]

Those **whose library books are overdue** must pay fines. [The relative pronoun *whose* begins the adjective clause and relates it to the pronoun *Those.*]

▶ EXERCISE 4   **Identifying Adjective Clauses**

Identify the adjective clause in each of the following sentences. Underline the relative pronoun that begins the clause.

EXAMPLE   **1.** The person who wrote the Declaration of Independence was Thomas Jefferson.
   1. *who wrote the Declaration of Independence*

 1. In his later years, Jefferson lived at Monticello, which he had designed.
 2. Jefferson planned a daily schedule that kept him busy all day.
 3. He began each day by making a note that recorded the morning temperature.
 4. Then he did his writing, which included letters to friends and businesspeople.
 5. Afterward, he ate breakfast, which was served around 9:00 A.M.
 6. Jefferson, whose property included stables as well as farm fields, went horseback riding at noon.

7. Dinner was a big meal, which began about 4:00 P.M.
8. From dinner until dark, he talked to friends and neighbors who came to visit.
9. He also spent time with his family, which included twelve grandchildren.
10. Jefferson, whose interests ranged from art and architecture to biology and mathematics, read each night.

▶ EXERCISE 5   **Writing Appropriate Adjective Clauses**

Complete each of the following sentences by adding an adjective clause that will make sense in the blank. Then, underline the relative pronoun. Remember that a clause must contain a verb and its subject.

EXAMPLE   **1.** We read the Greek legend ____.
          1. *We read the Greek legend <u>that</u> tells the story of the Trojan horse.*

1. You should proofread every composition ____.
2. My friend ____ is a good student.
3. Mrs. Echohawk ____ was my fifth-grade teacher.
4. We heard a sound ____.
5. Our neighbors ____ are from Fez, Morocco.

PICTURE THIS

You are visiting a small company that creates greeting cards. The artist shown on the next page is a family friend, and she designs cards that will be marketed to young people. She has asked you to help her write messages for the cards that she illustrates. For example, she might design a card with a rabbit on the cover, and you might write *This is a bunny who has something to say: Have a Hoppy Birthday!* Write messages for at least five greeting cards. Use an adjective clause in each message, and circle each relative pronoun. Following each message, write a brief description of a photo or illustration to go with your message.

Subject: greeting card messages
Audience: people your age
Purpose: to entertain

The Adverb Clause

18e.   An *adverb clause* is a subordinate clause that is used as an adverb.

Like an adverb or an adverb phrase, an adverb clause may modify a verb, an adjective, or an adverb. Unlike an adverb phrase, an adverb clause contains a verb and its subject.

ADVERB	**Bravely,** Jason battled a fierce dragon.
ADVERB PHRASE	**With great bravery,** Jason battled a fierce dragon. [does not have a verb and its subject]
ADVERB CLAUSE	**Because Jason was brave,** he battled a fierce dragon. [does have a verb and its subject]

GRAMMAR

An adverb clause answers the following questions: *How? When? Where? Why? To what extent? How much? How long?* or *Under what conditions?*

EXAMPLES I feel **as though I will never catch up.** [The adverb clause tells *how* I feel.]

After I finish painting my bookcases, I will call you. [The adverb clause tells *when* I will call you.]

I paint **where there is plenty of fresh air.** [The adverb clause tells *where* I paint.]

I have more work to do today **because I didn't paint yesterday.** [The adverb clause tells *why* I have more work to do.]

I will paint **until Mom comes home;** then I will clean my brushes and set the table for supper. [The adverb clause tells *how long* I will paint.]

If I paint for two more hours, I should be able to finish. [The adverb clause tells *under what conditions* I should be able to finish.]

Notice in these examples that adverb clauses may be placed in various positions in sentences. When an adverb clause comes at the beginning, it is usually followed by a comma.

 REFERENCE NOTE: For more about punctuating introductory adverb clauses, see page 720.

Subordinating Conjunctions

Adverb clauses begin with *subordinating conjunctions.*

Common Subordinating Conjunctions			
after	as soon as	in order that	until
although	as though	since	when
as	because	so that	whenever
as if	before	than	where
as long as	how	though	wherever
as much as	if	unless	while

Some subordinating conjunctions, such as *after, as, before, since,* and *until,* may also be used as prepositions.

PREPOSITION	**Before** sunrise, we left for the cabin.
SUBORDINATING CONJUNCTION	**Before** the sun had risen, we left for the cabin.
PREPOSITION	In the nineteenth century, buffalo skins were used **as** blankets and clothing.
SUBORDINATING CONJUNCTION	Around 1900, **as** the buffalo became nearly extinct, conservationists fought for its protection.

▶ EXERCISE 6 **Identifying Adverb Clauses**

Identify the adverb clause in each sentence in the following paragraph. Then write whether the clause tells *when, where, how, why, how much,* or *under what condition.*

EXAMPLE [1] More than two thousand years ago, the Chinese were making kites.
　　　　 1. *More than two thousand years ago—when*

[1] Although this story is only a legend, many people believe that a kite like the one pictured on the next page may have saved the people of China's Han Dynasty. [2] The Chinese were about to be attacked by an enemy army when an adviser to the emperor came up with a plan. [3] As the adviser stood beside an open window, his hat was lifted off by a strong wind. [4] He immediately called for a number of kites to be made so that they might be used to frighten the enemy. [5] The kite makers had no trouble finding lightweight bamboo for their kite frames because bamboo is native to China. [6] As soon as each frame was completed, silk was stretched over it. [7] The emperor's adviser attached noisemakers to the kites so that they would produce an eerie sound. [8] He ordered his men to fly the kites in the darkest hour of night because then the enemy would hear the kites but not see them. [9] Unless the adviser had misjudged the enemy,

they would be fooled into thinking that the kites were gods warning them to retreat. [10] According to the legend, the enemy retreated as if they were being chased by a fire-breathing dragon.

David F. Jue, *Chinese Kites, How to Make and Fly Them*, Charles E. Tuttle Co., Inc., of Tokyo, Japan.

▶ REVIEW

Identifying and Classifying Subordinate Clauses

Identify the subordinate clause in each of the following sentences. Then, label each clause as an *adjective clause* or an *adverb clause.*

EXAMPLES **1.** American history is filled with stories of people who performed heroic deeds.
1. *who performed heroic deeds—adjective clause*

2. As the American colonists struggled for independence, women played important roles.
2. *As the American colonists struggled for independence—adverb clause*

1. When you study the American Revolution, you may learn about the adventures of a woman known as Molly Pitcher.

2. Molly, whose real name was believed to be Mary Ludwig, was the daughter of farmers.
3. Although she was born in New Jersey, she moved to Pennsylvania.
4. There she married John Hays, who was a barber.
5. Hays joined the colonial army when the Revolution began.
6. Mary Ludwig Hays went to be with her husband in Monmouth, New Jersey, which was the site of a battle on a hot June day in 1778.
7. At first, she carried water to the soldiers so that they would not be overcome by the intense heat.
8. The soldiers nicknamed her "Molly Pitcher" because she carried the water in pitchers.
9. Later, when her husband collapsed from the heat, she took over his cannon.
10. George Washington, who was the commander of the Continental Army, made Molly an honorary sergeant.

WRITING APPLICATION

Using Subordinating Conjunctions to Explain a Process

Subordinating conjunctions don't just connect ideas. They show the relationships between ideas. Notice how the subordinating conjunctions in the following examples show the different time relationships between the two clauses.

1. Squeeze the trigger of the fire extinguisher **before** you aim the nozzle.
2. Squeeze the trigger of the fire extinguisher **as** you aim the nozzle.
3. Squeeze the trigger of the fire extinguisher **after** you aim the nozzle.

Which of the instructions on the previous page would help you put out a fire efficiently?

Clearly showing relationships between clauses in your writing is always important. However, it is particularly necessary when you are giving instructions or explaining a process.

▶ WRITING ACTIVITY

Your class project for National Safety Week is to write a safety manual. Each class member will write one page of instructions telling what to do in a particular emergency. You may write about a major emergency, such as a fire, an earthquake, or a tornado. Or you may write about a minor emergency, such as a brief power outage, a sprained ankle, or a case of poison ivy. Use subordinating conjunctions to show the relationships between your ideas.

Prewriting   Think of a specific emergency that you know how to handle. List the steps that someone should follow in this emergency. Number the steps in order. If you aren't sure of the order or don't know a particular step, stop writing and get the information you need. A health teacher, the school nurse, or an organization such as the Red Cross should be able to provide information. [Remember: Readers will rely on your manual in an emergency. *The information you present must be accurate.*]

Writing   Use your prewriting list to begin your first draft. As you write, make your instructions as clear as possible. Define or explain terms that might be unfamiliar to your readers. Be sure that your instructions are in the right order.

Evaluating and Revising   Read over your instructions to be sure that you've included all necessary information. Add, cut, or rearrange steps to make the instructions easy to follow. Be sure to use appropriate subordinating conjunctions to make the order of the steps clear. You may want to present your instructions in a numbered list rather than in a paragraph.

Proofreading and Publishing Check your work carefully for any errors in grammar, punctuation, or spelling. For information on punctuating introductory adverb clauses, see page 720. To publish your class safety manual, gather all the pages and input them on a computer or make photocopies. Organize your topics alphabetically, or group them by kinds of emergencies.

Review: Posttest 1

A. Identifying and Classifying Independent and Subordinate Clauses

Label each of the following clauses as either *independent* or *subordinate*.

EXAMPLES **1.** when I was eleven years old
     1. *subordinate*

     2. he was eleven years old
     2. *independent*

1. because I have lived in Chile and Ecuador
2. his writing has improved
3. although Gullah is still spoken on South Carolina's Sea Islands
4. when the Philadelphia Phillies won the National League pennant
5. she served as Secretary of Labor
6. that we brought to the Juneteenth picnic
7. everyone laughed
8. who heard the Navajo story about Coyote
9. during the storm the power failed
10. which seemed to be the reason for the delay

B. Identifying and Classifying Subordinate Clauses

Identify the subordinate clause in each of the following sentences. Then, label each clause as either an *adjective clause* or an *adverb clause*.

EXAMPLES
  1. Today is the day that you are having dinner at my house.
     1. *that you are having dinner at my house—adjective clause*

  2. I will give you a map so that you can find my house easily.
     2. *so that you can find my house easily—adverb clause*

11. If you have never eaten Caribbean food, you are in for a big treat.
12. My mother, who was born and raised in Jamaica, really knows how to cook.
13. Whenever I have a chance, I help her in the kitchen to learn her secrets.
14. My grandmother, whose cooking is even better than my mother's, is making her special sweet potato pone for dessert.
15. Some of the fruits and vegetables that grow in Jamaica are hard to find in the markets around here.
16. Today we are shopping for yams, cantaloupes, and okra, which were introduced to the Caribbean by Africans.
17. We must also remember to buy fresh hot peppers, onions, and spices that are needed for seasoning the meat.
18. Although my mother never uses measuring spoons, she seems to know just how much of each spice to add.
19. As soon as we pay for these items, let's take them to my house.
20. Part of your treat will be to sniff the delicious smells from the kitchen before you even begin eating.

Review: Posttest 2

Writing Sentences with Subordinate Clauses

Write ten different sentences of your own. In each sentence, include a subordinate clause that begins with one of the following words. Underline the subordinate clause. After the sentence, label the subordinate clause as an *adjective clause* or an *adverb clause*.

EXAMPLES   **1.** so that
           1. *We hurried <u>so that we wouldn't miss the bus.</u>—adverb clause*

           2. whom
           2. *Jim Nakamura, <u>whom I met at summer camp,</u> is now my pen pal.—adjective clause*

1. which   **4.** who   **7.** as though   **9.** that
2. before   **5.** than   **8.** although   **10.** if
3. since   **6.** whose

19 KINDS OF SENTENCE STRUCTURE

Simple, Compound, and Complex Sentences

Diagnostic Test

A. Identifying Independent and Subordinate Clauses

Identify each clause in the following sentences as either an *independent clause* or a *subordinate clause*.

EXAMPLES
1. I waved to them, but they didn't see me.
1. *I waved to them—independent clause; they didn't see me—independent clause*

2. All tennis players who are renting rackets should pay their rental fees today.
2. *All tennis players should pay their rental fees today—independent clause; who are renting rackets—subordinate clause*

1. She raked the leaves, and I mowed the lawn.
2. Lupe and Ben rode their bicycles to the park so that they could watch the fireworks.

3. We chose tacos instead of sandwiches from the cafeteria's menu.
4. The new camp that offers instruction in computer programming will be in session from August 17 through August 28.
5. The rain changed to snow mixed with sleet.
6. At the beach, Mei-Ling and her parents practiced their tai chi exercises.
7. My grandparents, who enjoy exciting vacations, are planning to visit Nepal this year.
8. Since last year I have grown three inches, but I still can't reach the top shelf in the kitchen.
9. Uncle Martin gave me this book by Jamaica Kincaid because he enjoyed it.
10. She wants to be a veterinarian, for she likes to be around animals.

B. Classifying Sentences by Structure

Classify each of the following sentences as a *simple sentence*, a *compound sentence*, or a *complex sentence*.

EXAMPLE   **1.** The religion of the Muslims is called Islam, and it is based on a belief in one God.
          1. *compound sentence*

11. Muslims live in various parts of the world, though mostly in Africa, the Middle East, and Malaysia.
12. In recent years many Muslims have come to the United States, and they have brought their religion with them.
13. In May 1991, a mosque opened in New York.
14. When the mosque was opened, religious leaders and other Muslims went there to pray.
15. Some worshipers wore the traditional clothing of their homelands, and others were dressed in typical American clothes.
16. Muslims were particularly pleased that the new mosque opened in the spring.

17. The month of fasting called Ramadan had just ended, so the holiday after Ramadan could be celebrated in the new house of worship.
18. Although Muslims share a common religion, their languages differ.
19. Many Muslims speak Arabic, but those in Iran, Turkey, and neighboring countries, for example, speak other languages, too.
20. Of course, Muslims in the United States speak English, or they are learning it as a new language.

The Simple Sentence

19a. A *simple sentence* has one independent clause and no subordinate clauses.

                          S   V

EXAMPLES   A good **rain helps** the farmers.

                              V   S

                 Up for the rebound **leaped Kareem.**

A simple sentence may have a compound subject, a compound verb, or both.

                        S   S   V

EXAMPLES   **Burritos** and **fajitas are** two popular Mexican dishes. [compound subject]

               S   V

              Susan read *The Planet of Junior Brown* and
              V
              reported on it last week. [compound verb]

               S   S   V

              The huge **dog** and the tiny **kitten lay** down in
                      V
              the sunshine and **napped.** [compound subject and compound verb]

▶ EXERCISE 1   **Identifying Subjects and Verbs in Simple Sentences**

Identify the subject(s) and the verb(s) in each sentence of the following paragraph. [Note: Some sentences have a compound subject, a compound verb, or both.]

EXAMPLE   **[1] I enjoy urban life but need to escape from the city once in a while.**
        1. *I—subject; enjoy, need—verbs*

[1] My favorite escape from city life is the green world of Central Park in New York City. [2] Its beautiful woods and relaxing outdoor activities are just a few minutes from our apartment. [3] The enormous size of the park, however, can sometimes be a problem. [4] Often, I take this map along with me for guidance. [5] Using the map, I can easily find the zoo, the bandshell, and the Lost Waterfall. [6] In the summertime my brothers and I row boats on the lake, climb huge rock slabs, and have picnics in the Sheep Meadow. [7] I also watch birds and often wander around the park in search of my favorite species. [8] Last month a pair of purple finches followed me along the pond. [9] Near Heckscher Playground, the birds got tired of the game and flew off. [10] In Central Park my family and I can enjoy a little bit of nature in the middle of a bustling city.

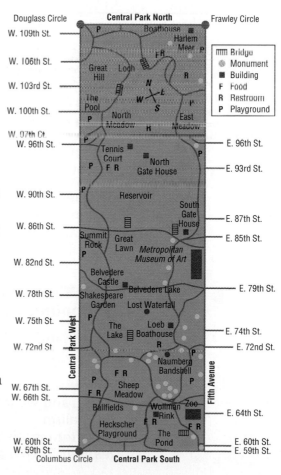

GRAMMAR

The Compound Sentence

19b.	A *compound sentence* has two or more independent clauses and no subordinate clauses.

INDEPENDENT CLAUSE	Melvina wrote about her mother's aunt
INDEPENDENT CLAUSE	Leroy wrote about his cousin from Jamaica
COMPOUND SENTENCE	Melvina wrote about her mother's aunt, and Leroy wrote about his cousin from Jamaica.

The independent clauses of a compound sentence are usually joined by a comma and a coordinating conjunction (*and, but, or, nor, for, so,* or *yet*).

EXAMPLES	A variety of fruits and vegetables should be a part of everyone's diet, **for** they supply many important vitamins.
	No one was injured in the fire, **but** several homes were destroyed, **and** many trees burned down.

The independent clauses of a compound sentence may be joined by a semicolon.

EXAMPLE	Pedro Menéndez de Avilés founded Saint Augustine, the first permanent settlement in the United States; he also established six other colonies in the Southeast.

▶ EXERCISE 2   **Identifying Subjects and Verbs in Compound Sentences**

Identify the subject and verb in each independent clause. Then, give the coordinating conjunction.

EXAMPLE	**1.** A newspaper reporter spoke to our class last week, and we learned about careers in journalism.
	1. *reporter—subject; spoke—verb; we—subject; learned—verb; and*

1. Ruth Benedict was a respected anthropologist, and Margaret Mead was one of her students.
2. An area's weather may change rapidly, but its climate changes very slowly.
3. Linh Phan lived in Vietnam for many years, so he was able to tell us about Vietnamese foods such as *nuoc mam*.
4. Students may type their reports, or they may write them neatly.
5. Our landlord is kind, yet she will not allow pets in the building.
6. Daniel Boone had no formal education, but he could read and write.
7. Sofia's favorite dance is the samba, and Elena enjoys the merengue.
8. Benjamin Franklin was known for his inventions, yet he should also be remembered for his work during the Constitutional Convention.
9. Sheena did not play soccer this week, for she had sprained her ankle.
10. They did not watch the shuttle take off, nor did they watch it land

Distinguishing Compound Sentences from Compound Subjects and Compound Verbs

A simple sentence has only one independent clause. It may have a compound subject or a compound verb or both. A compound sentence has two or more independent clauses. Each independent clause has its own subject and verb. Any of the independent clauses in a compound sentence may have a compound subject, a compound verb, or both.

                         S   S   V

SIMPLE SENTENCE   **Kim** and **Maureen read** each other's

                                  V

                        stories and **made** suggestions for improvements. [compound subject and compound verb]

$$\overset{\text{S}}{} \qquad \overset{\text{S}}{} \overset{\text{V}}{}$$

COMPOUND SENTENCE   **Kim** and **Maureen read** each other's

$$\overset{\text{S}}{} \overset{\text{V}}{}$$

stories, and **they gave** each other suggestions for improvements. [The first independent clause has a compound subject and a single verb. The second independent clause has a single subject and a single verb.]

NOTE: When a subject is repeated after a coordinating conjunction, the sentence is compound.

$$\overset{\text{S}}{} \overset{\text{V}}{}$$

SIMPLE SENTENCE   **We studied** about the artist

$$\overset{\text{V}}{}$$

Romare Bearden and **went** to an exhibit of his paintings.

$$\overset{\text{S}}{} \overset{\text{V}}{}$$

COMPOUND SENTENCE   **We studied** about the artist

$$\overset{\text{S}}{} \overset{\text{V}}{}$$

Romare Bearden, and **we went** to an exhibit of his paintings.

▶ EXERCISE 3   ### Distinguishing Compound Sentences from Compound Subjects or Compound Verbs

Identify each of the following sentences as either *simple* or *compound*. Then identify the subject(s) and verb(s) in each sentence.

EXAMPLES   1. A rain forest is a tropical evergreen forest and has heavy rains throughout the year.
1. *simple; rain forest—subject; is, has—verbs*

2. The trees and other plants in a rain forest grow close together, and they rise to different heights.
2. *compound; trees, plants—subjects; grow—verb; they—subject; rise—verb*

1. The Amazon River is located in South America and is one of the longest rivers in the world.

2. The Amazon begins in Peru, and it flows across Brazil to the Atlantic Ocean.
3. Of all the rivers in the world, this river carries the most water and drains about one fifth of the earth's fresh water.
4. The Amazon is actually a network of several rivers, but most people think of these combined rivers as only one river.
5. These rivers drain the largest rainy area in the world, and during the flood season, the main river often overflows its banks.
6. Unlike many other rivers, the Amazon does not twist and curve.
7. Instead, it follows a fairly straight course and flows at an average rate of about one and one-half miles an hour.
8. The Amazonian rain forest is only two hundred miles wide along the Atlantic, but it stretches to twelve hundred miles wide at the foot of the Andes Mountains in Peru.
9. The variety of plant life in the Amazonian rain forest is remarkable; in fact, of all rain forests in the world, this area may contain the greatest number of species of plants.
10. Raw materials are shipped directly from ports deep in the rain forest, for oceangoing ships can sail more than two thousand miles up the Amazon.

PICTURE THIS

Your community has been given the abandoned theater shown on the next page. Now the local citizens' council must decide what to do with the building. They could sell the theater, they could restore it, or they might find some other use for it. Write a letter to the council, giving your opinion on what should happen to the theater. To make your letter more interesting, vary your sentence structure. Use at least three simple sentences and two compound sentences.

Subject: an abandoned theater
Audience: community leaders
Purpose: to persuade

The Complex Sentence

19c. A *complex sentence* has one independent clause and at least one subordinate clause.

Two kinds of subordinate clauses are adjective clauses and adverb clauses. Adjective clauses usually begin with relative pronouns such as *who, whose, which,* and *that.* Adverb clauses begin with subordinating conjunctions such as *after, as, because, if, since,* and *when.*

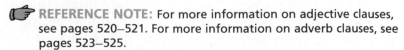

REFERENCE NOTE: For more information on adjective clauses, see pages 520–521. For more information on adverb clauses, see pages 523–525.

EXAMPLES   Patricia Roberts Harris, **who served as President Carter's Secretary of Housing and Urban Development,** was the first African American woman Cabinet member. [complex sentence with adjective clause]

When I hear ukulele music, I think of my cousin Alani. [complex sentence with adverb clause]

One interesting annual event **that is held in the Southwest** is the Inter-Tribal Ceremonial, **which involves many different Native American peoples.** [complex sentence with two adjective clauses]

👉 REFERENCE NOTE: For help in deciding when to use commas with subordinate clauses, see pages 713 and 720.

▶ EXERCISE 4   **Identifying Subordinate Clauses**

Identify the subordinate clause in each of the following sentences. Then, circle the subordinating conjunction or the relative pronoun that begins the subordinate clause.

EXAMPLES   **1.** Helen Keller, who overcame severe handicaps, showed courage and determination.

1. (who) *overcame severe handicaps*

2. Keller was fortunate because she had such a skillful and loving teacher.

2. (because) *she had such a skillful and loving teacher*

1. Helen Keller, who is shown in the photographs on the next page, became very ill as a small child.
2. After she recovered from the illness, she could no longer see or hear.
3. Because she could not hear, she also lost her ability to speak.
4. Helen's parents asked Alexander Graham Bell, who trained teachers of people with hearing impairments, for his advice about the child's education.
5. Upon Bell's suggestion, a special teacher, whose name was Annie Sullivan, stayed at the Kellers' home to teach Helen.

6. Sullivan spelled words into Helen's hand as the child touched the object represented by the word.
7. From this basic understanding of language, Helen went on to learn Braille, which is the alphabet used by people with visual impairments.
8. Sullivan, who had been partly cured of blindness herself, remained with Helen for many years.
9. Because she had triumphed over her handicaps, Helen Keller was awarded the Presidential Medal of Freedom.
10. Her autobiography, which is titled *The Story of My Life*, tells about her remarkable achievements.

WRITING APPLICATION

Using a Variety of Sentence Structures in Your Writing

"I'm bored!" That's how a reader responds to writing that uses the same kind of sentence structure over and over again. Using a variety of sentence structures can make your writing more interesting to read.

SIMPLE SENTENCES	Josh and I went to the supermarket. Josh watched the lobsters in the fish tank. I picked out some flowers to surprise Mom. We got everything on our shopping list. We paid for our groceries. We walked home.
SENTENCE VARIETY	Josh and I went to the supermarket. [simple] While Josh watched the lobsters in the fish tank, I picked out some flowers to surprise Mom. [complex] We got everything on our shopping list. [simple] Then we paid for our groceries, and we walked home. [compound]

▶ WRITING ACTIVITY

Anyone can enter the "Win Your Dream Home" Contest. All you have to do is describe your ideal house. Write a letter to the contest judges, describing where your dream house would be and what it would look like. Use a variety of sentence structures to make your letter interesting for the judges to read.

Prewriting   Make a list of the special features of the house you want to describe. To help you think of ideas, you may want to look through magazines or books to find pictures of interesting homes. You may also find it helpful to draw a rough diagram of the rooms, yard, and other features you would want. Take notes for details you want to include.

Writing   As you write your first draft, use your notes to include vivid details that will give the contest judges a clear picture of your dream house.

Evaluating and Revising   Read over your letter to make sure it is interesting and clear. Also, check to see whether you can combine similar ideas by using either compound or complex sentences. Ask an adult to read your letter. Does he or she think your description would impress the contest judges?

Proofreading   Check over the grammar and spelling in your letter. Also, make sure that you have used commas correctly in compound sentences and complex sentences. (For information on using commas, see pages 706–720.)

 REVIEW A   ## Classifying Simple, Compound, and Complex Sentences

Classify each of the following sentences as *simple, compound,* or *complex.*

EXAMPLE   **1.** The Mississippi River, which is the second longest river in the United States, begins in the town of Lake Itasca, Minnesota.
      1. *complex*

1. I drew an illustration for a poem that was written by Robert Hayden.
2. The Olympic skaters felt anxious, but they still performed their routine perfectly.
3. Kamehameha Day is an American holiday that honors the king who united the islands of Hawaii.
4. For the first time in his life, José saw the ocean.
5. If you had a choice, would you rather visit China or Japan?
6. The bull was donated to the children's zoo by the people who bought it at the auction.
7. Lookout Mountain, which is in Tennessee, was the site of a battle during the Civil War.
8. The guide led us through Mammoth Cave, and she explained the difference between stalactites and stalagmites.
9. Wilhelm Steinitz of Austria became famous after he was officially recognized as the first world champion of chess.
10. Amy Tan is the author of the book *The Joy Luck Club.*

▶ REVIEW B   **Classifying Simple, Compound, and Complex Sentences**

Classify each sentence in the following paragraphs as *simple, compound,* or *complex.*

EXAMPLE   **[1] The Iroquois people traditionally held a Green Corn Festival in August when their crops were ready for harvesting.**

   1. *complex*

[1] For the early Iroquois, the Green Corn Festival was a celebration that lasted several days. [2] During the celebration, all children who had been born since midwinter received their names. [3] Tribal leaders made speeches, and adults and children listened to them carefully. [4] In one traditional speech, the leader would give thanks for the harvest. [5] After they had heard the speeches, the people sang and danced.

[6] On the second day of the festival, the people performed the special dance pictured here, and during the dance they gave thanks for the sun, the moon, and the stars. [7] On the third day, the Iroquois gave thanks for the helpfulness of their neighbors and for good luck. [8] The festival ended on the fourth day when teams of young people would play a bowling game. [9] During the festival the people renewed their friendships and rejoiced in their harmony with nature. [10] This Iroquois festival resembles the U.S. Thanksgiving holiday, which has its roots in similar Native American celebrations.

THE CORN DANCE.

Review: Posttest 1

A. Identifying and Classifying Clauses

Label each clause in the following sentences as an *independent clause* or a *subordinate clause*.

EXAMPLE   **1.** We did warm-up exercises before we practiced the difficult routine.
          1. *We did warm-up exercises—independent clause; before we practiced the difficult routine—subordinate clause*

1. Students who are interested in attending the science fair at the community college should sign up now.
2. The musical *West Side Story* is a modern version of the story of Romeo and Juliet.
3. The first poem in the book is about spring, and the second one is about autumn.
4. Molasses, which is made from sugar cane, is a thick brown liquid used in human food and animal feed.
5. Before the test we studied the chapter and did the review exercises.
6. We took notes while our teacher discussed the formation of the African nation of Liberia.
7. It rained Saturday morning, but the sun came out in time for the opening of the Special Olympics.
8. The player whose performance is judged as the best receives the Most Valuable Player Award.
9. The tourists went to the Japanese exhibit after they had reached the museum.
10. Not all stringed instruments sound alike, for their shapes and the number of their strings vary.

B. Identifying Simple, Compound, and Complex Sentences

Identify each of the following sentences as *simple, compound,* or *complex*.

EXAMPLE   **1.** The Museum of Science and Industry, which is in Chicago, features a German submarine captured during World War II.
      1. *complex*

11. Either Ana or Lee will sing the opening song for the international fair.

12. We always visit the Liberty Bell whenever we go to Philadelphia.

13. Have you chosen a topic for your report yet, or are you still making your decision?

14. George Washington Carver's work on soil improvement and plant diseases helped the South in its recovery from the effects of the Civil War.

15. *A Tree Grows in Brooklyn*, which was written by Betty Smith, is one of my favorite books.

16. The call of a peacock sounds very much like that of a person in distress, so its cries can often be quite startling to people.

17. My younger sister and brother enjoy Beatrix Potter's Peter Rabbit stories and usually ask for them at bedtime.

18. The student whose photographs of Native American cliff dwellings won the contest was interviewed on the local news.

19. The house looked completely deserted when I first saw it.

20. The game was tied at the top of the ninth inning, but then Earlene hit a home run.

Review: Posttest 2

Writing Simple, Compound, and Complex Sentences

Write five sentences of your own, following the guidelines given on the next page.

EXAMPLE **1.** a simple sentence with a compound subject
1. *Jorge and Pilar gave me their recipe for guacamole.*

1. a simple sentence with a compound verb
2. a compound sentence with two independent clauses joined by the coordinating conjunction *and*
3. a compound sentence with two independent clauses joined by the coordinating conjunction *but*
4. a complex sentence with an adjective clause
5. a complex sentence with an adverb clause

20 AGREEMENT

Subject and Verb, Pronoun and Antecedent

Diagnostic Test

A. Identifying and Correcting Errors in Subject-Verb Agreement

If the underlined verb in each sentence does not agree with its subject, write the correct form of the verb. If the verb does agree with its subject, write C.

EXAMPLE **1.** A car with five forward gears <u>cost</u> extra.
         1. *costs*

1. <u>Don't</u> anybody know how to make egg rolls?
2. "Those Winter Sundays" <u>was</u> written by Robert Hayden.
3. Mathematics <u>are</u> taught every day at 9:00 A.M.

4. Seventy dollars <u>seem</u> like a high price for a pair of skates.
5. Here <u>is</u> your tickets for tomorrow's basketball game, Jennifer.
6. Dolores and Frank <u>wear</u> glasses only for reading.
7. One of the batteries <u>do not</u> work.
8. Everyone except us <u>know</u> some Spanish.
9. My family <u>are</u> originally from Thailand.
10. Neither of these cassette recorders <u>have</u> automatic reverse.

B. Identifying and Correcting Errors in Pronoun-Antecedent Agreement

If the underlined pronoun in each of the following sentences does not agree with its antecedent, write the correct form of the pronoun. If the pronoun does agree with its antecedent, write *C*.

EXAMPLE   **1.** Someone left <u>their</u> skis here.
           1. *his or her*

11. Neither of these plants should have <u>their</u> roots disturbed.
12. Did anyone forget <u>their</u> CDs?
13. Either Maria or Louise will receive <u>their</u> award today.
14. Everybody should know <u>their</u> ZIP Code.
15. Each student has given <u>their</u> report on an African American folk tale.
16. Every one of the dogs obeyed <u>its</u> owner.
17. Each of the components has <u>its</u> own on-off switch.
18. Will either Hector or Tony read <u>his</u> paper aloud?
19. Not one of the students had finished <u>their</u> science project on time.
20. She borrowed my Navajo silver jewelry and forgot to return <u>them</u>.

Number

Number is the form of a word that indicates whether the word is singular or plural.

20a. When a word refers to one person, place, thing, or idea, it is *singular* in number. When a word refers to more than one, it is *plural* in number.

SINGULAR	igloo	she	one	child	joy
PLURAL	igloos	they	some	children	joys

☞ REFERENCE NOTE: For more information about forming plurals, see pages 754 and 773–776.

▶ EXERCISE 1   **Classifying Nouns and Pronouns by Number**

Classify each of the following words as *singular* or *plural*.

EXAMPLES   **1.** girl
            1. *singular*
           2. rivers
            2. *plural*

1. evening   **4.** leaf   **7.** tacos   **9.** thief
2. wolves   **5.** they   **8.** we   **10.** armies
3. women   **6.** teeth

Agreement of Subject and Verb

20b. A verb agrees with its subject in number.

Two words *agree* when they have the same number. The number of a verb must always agree with the number of its subject.

USAGE

(1) Singular subjects take singular verbs.

EXAMPLES   The **lightning fills** the sky. [The singular verb
fills agrees with the singular subject *lightning.*]
Jan begins her vacation today. [The singular verb
begins agrees with the singular subject *Jan.*]

(2) Plural subjects take plural verbs.

EXAMPLES   **Cheetahs run** fast. [The plural verb *run* agrees
with the plural subject *cheetahs.*]
New **families move** into our neighborhood
frequently. [The plural verb *move* agrees with
the plural subject *families.*]

When a sentence contains a verb phrase, the first helping verb in the verb phrase agrees with the subject.

EXAMPLES   The **motor is** running.
The **motors are** running.

The **girl has** been delayed.
The **girls have** been delayed.

Is anyone filling the piñata?
Are any **students** filling the piñata?

☞ REFERENCE NOTE: Most nouns ending in *–s* are plural (*cheetahs,
families*). Most verbs that end in *–s* are singular (*fills, begins*). For
more about spelling the plural forms of nouns, see pages 773–776.

▶ EXERCISE 2   **Identifying Verbs That Agree in
Number with Their Subjects**

Choose the form of the verb in parentheses that agrees
with the given subject.

EXAMPLE   **1.** wind (*howls, howl*)
1. *howls*

1. people (*talks, talk*)
2. rain (*splashes, splash*)
3. birds (*flies, fly*)
4. we (*helps, help*)
5. it (*appears, appear*)

6. geese (*hisses, hiss*)
7. night (*falls, fall*)
8. roofs (*leaks, leak*)
9. baby (*smiles, smile*)
10. tooth (*aches, ache*)

▶ EXERCISE 3 ### Identifying Verbs That Agree in Number with Their Subjects

For each of the following sentences, choose the form of the verb in parentheses that agrees with the subject.

EXAMPLE **1.** Special tours (*is, are*) offered at the National Air and Space Museum, Washington, D.C.
1. *are*

1. This museum (*has, have*) been called the best of all the Smithsonian museums.
2. The huge building (*covers, cover*) three blocks.
3. Twenty-three galleries (*offers, offer*) visitors information and entertainment.
4. The different showrooms (*deals, deal*) with various aspects of air and space travel.
5. As you can see, the exhibits (*features, feature*) antique aircraft as well as modern spacecraft.
6. In another area, a theater (*shows, show*) films on a five-story-high screen.
7. A planetarium (*is, are*) located on the second floor.
8. Projectors (*casts, cast*) realistic images of stars on the ceiling.
9. Some tours (*is, are*) conducted by pilots.
10. In addition, the museum (*houses, house*) a large research library.

USAGE

EXERCISE 4

Proofreading for Errors in Subject-Verb Agreement

Most of the following sentences contain errors in subject-verb agreement. If a verb does not agree with the subject, write the correct form of the verb. If a sentence is correct, write C.

EXAMPLE **1.** More than fifteen million people lives in and around Mexico's capital.
    1. *live*

1. Located in an ancient lake bed, Mexico City have been built on Aztec ruins.
2. Visitors admire the paintings of Diego Rivera at the National Palace.
3. In one of the city's subway stations, an Aztec pyramid still stand.
4. Sculptures grace the Alameda, which is Mexico City's main park.
5. Atop the Latin American Tower, an observatory offer a great view on a clear day.
6. At the National Autonomous University of Mexico, the library's outer walls is famous as works of art.
7. Juan O'Gorman's huge mosaics shows the cultural history of Mexico.
8. Usually, tourists is fascinated by the Great Temple of the Aztecs.
9. Many fiestas fills Mexico City's social calendar.
10. In addition, the city has one of the largest soccer stadiums in the world.

Problems in Agreement

Prepositional Phrases Between Subject and Verb

20c. The number of a subject is not changed by a phrase following the subject.

EXAMPLES   The **hero** of those folk tales **is** Coyote. [The verb
is agrees with the subject *hero.*]

The successful **candidate,** along with two of her
aides, **has entered** the auditorium. [The helping
verb *has* agrees with the subject *candidate.*]

Scientists from all over the world **have gathered**
in Geneva. [The helping verb *have* agrees with
the subject *Scientists.*]

☞ **REFERENCE NOTE:** If the subject is an indefinite pronoun, its
number may be determined by a prepositional phrase that follows
it. See page 430 for a discussion of indefinite pronouns.

▶ EXERCISE 5   **Identifying Verbs That Agree in
Number with Their Subjects**

In the following sentences, choose the form of the verb in
parentheses that agrees with the subject.

EXAMPLE   **1.** The water in the earth's oceans (*cover, covers*)
much of the planet's surface.
1. *covers*

1. A tidal wave, despite its name, (*is, are*) not caused by
the tides.
2. An eruption beneath the sea (*causes, cause*) a tidal
wave.
3. A network of warning signals (*alert, alerts*) people in
coastal areas of an approaching tidal wave.
4. The tremendous force of tidal waves (*causes, cause*)
great destruction.
5. Walls of earth and stone along the shore (*is, are*) often
too weak to protect coastal villages.

▶ EXERCISE 6   **Using Correct Subject-Verb Agreement**

What do you notice first about the painting shown on the
next page? Is it the floating people? the upside down
train? the multicolored cat? Look at the painting closely,
and identify at least five features you notice. Then, write
five sentences about the unusual features you find. Be sure

that each of your sentences has correct subject-verb agreement. You may want to compare your findings with those of other students.

EXAMPLE   **1.** *The man in the painting has two faces.*

Marc Chagall, *Paris Through the Window* (1913). Oil on canvas, 53 1/2 × 55 3/4". Solomon R. Guggenheim Museum, New York. Gift, Solomon R. Guggenheim, 1937. Photo David Heald, copyright Solomon R. Guggenheim Foundation, New York, FN 37.438. © 1996 Artists Rights Society (ARS), N.Y.

Indefinite Pronouns

You may recall that personal pronouns refer to specific people, places, things, or ideas. A pronoun that does not refer to a definite person, place, thing, or idea is called an *indefinite pronoun.*

PERSONAL PRONOUNS	we	you	she	them
INDEFINITE PRONOUNS	anybody	both	either	everyone

20d.   The following indefinite pronouns are singular: *each, either, neither, one, everyone, everybody, no one, nobody, anyone, anybody, someone, somebody.*

EXAMPLES **Each** of the newcomers **was welcomed** to the city.
Neither of these papayas **is** ripe.
Does anybody on the bus **speak** Arabic?

 EXERCISE 7 **Choosing Verbs That Agree in Number with Their Subjects**

In the following sentences, choose the form of the verb in parentheses that agrees with the subject. Remember that the subject is never part of a prepositional phrase.

EXAMPLE **1.** One of these books (*is, are*) yours.
1. *is*

1. Neither of the movies (*was, were*) especially funny.
2. Everybody in those classes (*gets, get*) to see the Balinese dancers.
3. Someone among the store owners (*donates, donate*) the trophy each year.
4. Each of the Washington brothers (*studies, study*) with a Zulu dance instructor.
5. No one on either team (*was, were*) ever in a playoff before.
6. Everyone with an interest in sports (*is, are*) at the tryouts.
7. Anybody with binoculars (*is, are*) popular at a large stadium.
8. Each of our neighbors (*has, have*) helped us plant the community garden.
9. One of the Spanish teachers (*supervises, supervise*) the language lab.
10. Nobody in our family (*is, are*) able to speak Greek well, but we all can speak a little bit.

20e. The following indefinite pronouns are plural: *both, few, many, several.*

EXAMPLES **Few** of our neighbors **have** parakeets.
Many of them **keep** dogs as pets.

USAGE

20f. The indefinite pronouns *all, any, most, none,* and *some* may be either singular or plural.

The number of the pronouns *all, any, most, none,* and *some* is determined by the number of the object in the prepositional phrase following the subject. If the subject refers to a singular object, the pronoun is singular. If the subject refers to a plural object, the pronoun is plural.

EXAMPLES **All** of the fruit **looks** fresh. [*All* is singular because it refers to one thing—*fruit.* The verb *looks* is singular to agree with the subject *All.*]
All of the pears **are** ripe. [*All* is plural because it refers to more than one thing—*pears.* The verb *are* is plural to agree with the subject *All.*]

    Some of the crowd **has** left. [*Some* is singular because it means "a part" of the crowd. The helping verb *has* is singular to agree with the subject *Some.*]
Some of the fans **are getting** autographs. [*Some* is plural because it refers to more than one fan. The helping verb *are* is plural to agree with the subject *Some.*]

EXERCISE 8 **Choosing Verbs That Agree in Number with Their Subjects**

For each of the following sentences, choose the form of the verb in parentheses that agrees with the subject.

EXAMPLE **1.** All of the new research on dreams (*is, are*) fascinating.
    1. *is*

1. Most of our dreams (*occur, occurs*) toward morning.
2. Few of us really (*understand, understands*) the four cycles of sleep.
3. Most of the research (*focus, focuses*) on the cycle known as rapid eye movement (REM).
4. None of last night's dream (*is, are*) clear to me.
5. Many of our dreams (*is, are*) about that day's events.

REVIEW A

Identifying Verbs That Agree in Number with Their Subjects

For each sentence in the following paragraph, choose the verb form in parentheses that agrees with the subject.

EXAMPLE   [1] These flying objects probably (*look, looks*) familiar to you.

  1. *look*

USAGE

[1] Many people throughout the world (*claims, claim*) to have seen objects like these. [2] However, no one (*know, knows*) for sure what they are. [3] They (*resembles, resemble*) huge plates or saucers. [4] Not surprisingly, everyone (*call, calls*) them "flying saucers." [5] Since 1947, they (*has, have*) been officially called unidentified flying objects, or UFOs. [6] The U.S. government (*has, have*) investigated many UFO sightings. [7] The Air Force (*was, were*) responsible for conducting these investigations. [8] Government records (*shows, show*) that more than twelve thousand sightings were reported between 1948 and 1969. [9] Most reported sightings (*has, have*) turned out to be fakes, but others remain unexplained. [10] None of the official reports positively (*proves, prove*) that UFOs are real.

Compound Subjects

20g. Subjects joined by *and* usually take a plural verb.

EXAMPLES Our **dog and cat get** baths in the summer.
Mr. Duffy and his **daughter have gone** fishing.

A compound subject that names only one person or thing takes a singular verb.

EXAMPLES **A famous singer and dancer is going** to speak at our drama club meeting. [One person is meant.]
Macaroni and cheese is my favorite supper. [One combination is meant.]

USAGE

▶ EXERCISE 9 **Identifying Verbs That Agree in Number with Their Subjects**

For each of the following sentences, choose the correct form of the verb in parentheses. If you choose a singular verb with any of these compound subjects, be prepared to explain why.

EXAMPLE **1.** Chris and her sister (*is, are*) in the school band.
1. *are*

1. (*Is, Are*) the brown bear and the polar bear related?
2. Fruit and cheese (*tastes, taste*) good together.
3. My guide and companion in Bolivia (*was, were*) Pilar, a high school student.
4. New words and new meanings for old words (*is, are*) included in a good dictionary.
5. Mrs. Chang and her daughter (*rents, rent*) an apartment in San Francisco's Chinatown.
6. Both iron and calcium (*needs, need*) to be included in a balanced diet.
7. Mr. Marley and his class (*has, have*) painted a wall-size map of the Caribbean islands.
8. A horse and buggy (*was, were*) once a fashionable way to travel.

9. Tornadoes and hurricanes (*is, are*) dangerous storms.
10. Wind and water (*erodes, erode*) valuable farmland throughout the United States.

20h. Singular subjects joined by *or* or *nor* take a singular verb.

EXAMPLES   The chief **geologist or** her **assistant is** due to arrive tonight. [Either one is due, not both.]
Neither a **rabbit nor** a **mole does** that kind of damage in a garden. [Neither one does the damage.]

Plural subjects joined by *or* or *nor* take a plural verb.

EXAMPLES   **Either mice or squirrels are** living in our attic.
Neither the **senators nor** the **representatives want** the bill to be vetoed by the president.

20i. When a singular subject and a plural subject are joined by *or* or *nor*, the verb agrees with the subject nearer the verb.

EXAMPLE   A **book or flowers** usually **make** an appropriate **gift**. [The verb agrees with the nearer subject, *flowers.*]
Flowers or a **book** usually **makes** an appropriate **gift**. [The verb agrees with the nearer subject, *book.*]

Compound subjects that have both singular and plural parts can sound awkward even though they are correct. Whenever possible, revise a sentence to avoid such constructions.

AWKWARD   Two small boards or one large one is what we need to patch that hole.
REVISED   We need two small boards or one large one to patch that hole.

AWKWARD   Neither the lights nor the microwave is working.
REVISED   The lights aren't working, and neither is the microwave.

USAGE

Identifying Verbs That Agree in Number with Their Subjects

Choose the correct form of the verb in parentheses in each of the following sentences. Be able to explain the reason for your choice.

EXAMPLE   **1.** The club president or the officers (*meets, meet*) regularly with the sponsors.
         1. *meet*

1. Neither pens nor pencils (*is, are*) needed to mark the ballots.
2. Either my aunt or my uncle (*is, are*) going to drive us to the lake.
3. That table or this chair (*was, were*) made by hand in Portugal.
4. (*Has, Have*) the sandwiches or other refreshments been served?
5. Index cards or a small tablet (*is, are*) handy for taking notes.
6. Neither that clock nor my watch (*shows, show*) the correct time.
7. One boy or girl (*takes, take*) the part of the narrator.
8. During our visit to Jamaica, a map or a guidebook (*was, were*) my constant companion.
9. The dentist or her assistant (*checks, check*) my braces.
10. Either Japanese poetry or Eskimo myths (*is, are*) going to be the focus of my report.

▶ REVIEW B   **Proofreading Sentences for Subject-Verb Agreement**

Identify each verb that does not agree with its subject in the following sentences. Then supply the correct form of each incorrect verb.

EXAMPLE   **1.** The players in the photograph on the next page is competing in the most popular sport in the world—soccer.
         1. *is—are*

1. One expert in the field of sports have described soccer as the world's favorite type of football.
2. Some sports writers has estimated that there are over thirty million registered soccer players around the globe.
3. Youth leagues and coaching clinics has helped make amateur soccer the fastest-growing team sport in the United States.
4. In Dallas, Texas, neither baseball nor American football attract as many young players as soccer does.
5. Also, more colleges now has varsity soccer teams than football teams.
6. This increase in soccer fans are a trend that started in 1967, when professional teams began playing in the United States.
7. Additional interest were generated when the U.S. Youth Soccer Association was formed.
8. Both males and females enjoys playing this sport.
9. In fact, by the 1980s, many of the soccer teams in the country was women's teams.
10. In the past, professional soccer were mostly a foreign game, but the United States was selected to host the World Cup in 1994.

USAGE

Other Problems in Subject-Verb Agreement

20j. Collective nouns may be either singular or plural.

A *collective noun* is singular in form but names a group of persons, animals, or things.

Common Collective Nouns			
audience	committee	group	swarm
class	family	herd	team
club	flock	jury	troop

A collective noun takes a singular verb when the noun refers to the group as a unit. A collective noun takes a plural verb when the noun refers to the individual parts or members of the group.

EXAMPLES The **class were divided** in their opinions of the play. [The members of the class were divided in their opinions.]
The **class has decided** to have a science fair in November. [The class as a unit has decided.]

My **family are coming** from all over the state for the reunion. [The members of the family are coming.]
My **family plans** to attend Beth's graduation. [The family as a unit plans to attend.]

20k. When the subject follows the verb, find the subject and make sure that the verb agrees with it. The subject usually follows the verb in sentences beginning with *here* or *there* and in questions.

EXAMPLES Here **is** my **umbrella.**
Here **are** our **umbrellas.**

There **is** a scary **movie** on TV.
There **are** scary **movies** on TV.

Where **was** the **cat**?
Where **were** the **cats**?

Does Jim know the Chens?
Do the **Chens** know Jim?

NOTE: When the subject of a sentence follows the verb, the word order is said to be *inverted.* To find the subject of a sentence with inverted order, restate the sentence in normal word order.

INVERTED	Here **are** your **gloves.**
NORMAL	Your **gloves are** here.

INVERTED	**Were you** late, too?
NORMAL	**You were** late, too?

INVERTED	In the pond **swim** large **goldfish.**
NORMAL	Large **goldfish swim** in the pond.

The contractions *here's, there's,* and *where's* contain the verb *is* and should be used only with singular subjects.

EXAMPLES   There's our new **neighbor.**
Where's my lunch **money**?

☞ REFERENCE NOTE: For more information about contractions, see pages 749–750.

▶ EXERCISE 11   **Identifying Verbs That Agree in Number with Their Subjects**

Identify the subject in each of the following sentences. Then, choose the correct form of the verb in parentheses.

EXAMPLE   **1.** That flock of geese (*migrates, migrate*) each year.
1. *flock—migrates*

1. There (*is, are*) at least two solutions to this Chinese puzzle.
2. The Austrian Olympic team (*was, were*) all getting on different buses.

3. (*Is, Are*) both of your parents from Korea?
4. Here (*comes, come*) the six members of the dance committee.
5. Here (*is, are*) some apples and bananas for the picnic basket.
6. There (*is, are*) neither time nor money for that project.
7. (*Here's, Here are*) the social studies notes I wrote about Mohandas Gandhi.
8. At the press conference, there (*was, were*) several candidates for mayor and two for governor.
9. The family (*has, have*) announced its plans to celebrate Grandma's promotion.
10. Here (*is, are*) some masks carved by the Haida people in Alaska.

20l. Words stating amounts are usually singular.

A word or phrase stating a weight, measurement, or an amount of money or time is usually considered one item. Such a word or phrase takes a singular verb.

EXAMPLES   Sixteen **ounces equals** one pound.
Ten **feet is** the height of a regulation basketball hoop.
Seventy-five **cents is** enough money for my lunch today.
Two **weeks** never **seems** long enough for vacation.

20m. The title of a book, or the name of an organization or a country, even when plural in form, usually takes a singular verb.

EXAMPLES   ***World Tales* is** a collection of folk tales retold by Idries Shah. [one book]
The **United Nations has** its headquarters in New York City. [one organization]
The **Philippines is** an island country that is located in the southwest Pacific Ocean. [one country]

▶ EXERCISE 12   **Identifying Verbs That Agree in Number with Their Subjects**

Choose the correct form of the verb in parentheses in each of the following sentences.

EXAMPLE   **1.** Three inches (*is, are*) a great deal to grow in one year.
   1. *is*

   1. *The Friends* (*is, are*) a book about a girl from the West Indies and a girl from Harlem.
   2. Two cups of broth (*seems, seem*) as if it is too little for that recipe.
   3. Fifteen feet (*was, were*) the length of the winning long jump.
   4. Navarro and Company (*is, are*) selling those jackets.
   5. The National Council of Teachers of English (*is, are*) holding its convention in our city this year.
   6. The United States (*is, are*) home to many different peoples.
   7. Three hours of practice (*is, are*) not unusual for the band.
   8. *Arctic Dreams* (*was, were*) written by Barry Lopez.
   9. Two weeks of preparation (*has, have*) been enough.
   10. Seventy-five cents (*is, are*) the cost of a subway ride.

20n.   *Don't* and *doesn't* must agree with their subjects.

The words *don't* and *doesn't* are contractions of *do not* and *does not*. Use *don't* with all plural subjects and with the pronouns *I* and *you*.

EXAMPLES   The children **don't** seem nervous.
   I **don't** understand.
   You **don't** remember.

   Use *doesn't* with all singular subjects except *I* and *you*.

EXAMPLES   Kim **doesn't** ride the bus.
   He **doesn't** play tennis.
   It **doesn't** snow here.

USAGE

USAGE

Using *Don't* and *Doesn't*

Read the following sentences aloud, stressing the italicized words.

1. My friend *doesn't* understand the problem.
2. *Doesn't* she want to play soccer?
3. The tomatoes *don't* look ripe.
4. Our school *doesn't* have a gymnasium.
5. Italy *doesn't* border Germany.
6. The geese *don't* hiss at Mr. Waverly.
7. Our Muslim neighbors, the Nassers, *don't* eat pork.
8. He *doesn't* play chess.

EXERCISE 13

Writing Original Sentences with *Don't* and *Doesn't*

You're cleaning out your closet and deciding what to do with the things you don't want any more. You plan to give reusable items to a thrift store, but some things just can't be saved. Here are some of the items you've found:

a flat football
a picture made with glue and beans
a T-shirt with a cartoon on the front
a stuffed toy dinosaur
one red and one green tennis shoe
a bug collection
several *Cricket* magazines
pieces of jigsaw puzzles
a brown sock
dried-up paint brushes

Write five sentences telling why you're getting rid of some of these items. Use *don't* or *doesn't* to agree with a different subject in each sentence.

EXAMPLE 1. *This stuffed toy dinosaur doesn't have all its stuffing any more.*

20o. A few nouns, though plural in form, take a singular verb.

EXAMPLES   **Mathematics seems** easier this year.
                   Civics is being taught by Ms. Gutierrez.
                   Mumps is the most uncomfortable disease I've
                     ever had.
                   The **news was** not **encouraging.**

▶ REVIEW C   **Identifying Verbs That Agree in Number with Their Subjects**

For each of the following sentences, choose the verb form in parentheses that agrees with the subject.

EXAMPLE   **1. New wheelchairs with lifts (*help, helps*) many people reach objects up high.**
                1. *help*

1. Twenty-five cents (*is, are*) not enough money to buy that newspaper.
2. Everyone in her company (*prefers, prefer*) to take winter vacations.
3. Allen and his parents (*enjoy, enjoys*) the Puerto Rican Day Parade in New York City.
4. Jan (*don't, doesn't*) know the rules for volleyball.
5. Neither the cassette player nor the speakers (*work, works*) on my stereo.
6. There (*is, are*) 132 islands in the state of Hawaii.
7. Many of the place names in California (*comes, come*) from Spanish words.
8. The principal or her assistant (*is, are*) the one who can help you.
9. Home economics (*is, are*) a required course in many schools.
10. A flock of sheep (*was, were*) grazing on the hill.

▶ REVIEW D   **Proofreading Sentences for Subject-Verb Agreement**

Most of the sentences in the following paragraph contain errors in subject-verb agreement. If a verb does not agree with its subject, give the correct form of the verb. If a sentence is correct, write C.

EXAMPLE   [1] Here is two pictures of Wang Yani and her artwork.

   1. *are*

[1] There surely is few teenage artists as successful as Yani. [2] In fact, the People's Republic of China regard her as a national treasure. [3] She has shown her paintings throughout the world. [4] A painter since the age of two, Yani don't paint in just one style. [5] Her ideas and her art naturally changes over the years. [6] The painting at the bottom of this page shows one of Yani's favorite childhood subjects. [7] Many of her early paintings features monkeys. [8] In fact, one of her large works picture 112 monkeys. [9] However, most of her later paintings is of landscapes, other animals, and people. [10] As her smile suggests, Yani fill her paintings with energy and life.

Wang Yani, Little Monkeys and Mummy

WRITING APPLICATION

Using Subject-Verb Agreement in Formal Writing

You would probably write a thank-you note more neatly than you would write a grocery list. Like penmanship, English usage depends upon the situation. A formal piece of writing calls for special care with language. In formal writing, standard usage, like good penmanship, helps you make a good impression on your audience. Subject-verb agreement is one of the basic rules of standard usage.

NONSTANDARD   The last two governors of the state has **been** highly respected.

STANDARD   The last two **governors** of the state **have** been highly respected.

▶ WRITING ACTIVITY

If you could be any person in history, who would you be? Why? Your social studies teacher has asked you to answer these questions in a short composition. Be sure to use correct subject-verb agreement in explaining your choice.

Prewriting   First, decide what historical person you would like to be. You can be someone out of ancient history or someone who is alive today. List some types of people such as heads of government, inventors, military leaders, explorers, writers, and artists. Then write the names of people you admire under each type. Select the person you would most like to be and freewrite about that person. As you write, think about why the person is noteworthy and why you would want to be him or her.

Writing   Use your freewriting ideas to write your first draft. Begin with a sentence that states the purpose of your composition and identifies your historical figure. Then, give your main reasons for wanting to be that person. If you have several main reasons, you may want to write about each reason in a separate paragraph. Summarize your main points in a conclusion.

 Evaluating and Revising Read through your composition and then answer these questions:

- Is it clear what person from history I want to be? If not, revise your main idea statement. For more about writing main ideas, see pages 64–67 and 98.
- Is it clear why I want to be that person? If not, explain your reasons in more detail. See page 69 for more about using supporting details.

Make sure that all subjects and verbs agree in number. Pay special attention to the subject-verb agreement in subordinate clauses. For more about subordinate clauses, see pages 516–525.

 Proofreading and Publishing Check your composition for errors in spelling, capitalization, and punctuation. Your class may want to create a display using the compositions and pictures of the people written about. One type of display is a time line. Arrange the compositions and pictures to show where each subject fits in time—from ancient to recent. Another type of display requires a large world map. Use straight pins and yarn to connect each composition to the place on the map where that person lived.

Agreement of Pronoun and Antecedent

A pronoun usually refers to a noun or another pronoun called its *antecedent.* Whenever you use a pronoun, make sure that it agrees with its antecedent.

 REFERENCE NOTE: For more information about antecedents, see page 428.

20p. A pronoun agrees with its antecedent in number and gender.

Some singular personal pronouns have forms that indicate gender. Feminine pronouns refer to females. Masculine pronouns refer to males. Neuter pronouns refer to things (neither male nor female) and sometimes to animals.

FEMININE	she	her	hers
MASCULINE	he	him	his
NEUTER	it	it	its

EXAMPLES **Carlotta** said that **she** found **her** book.
Aaron brought **his** skates with **him**.
The **plant** with mold on **it** is losing **its** leaves.

The antecedent of a personal pronoun can be another kind of pronoun. In such cases, you may need to look in a phrase that follows the antecedent to determine which personal pronoun to use.

EXAMPLES **Each** of the **girls** has offered **her** ideas.
One of the **men** lost **his** key.

Some antecedents may be either masculine or feminine. In such cases, use both the masculine and the feminine forms.

EXAMPLES Every **one** of the parents praised **his or her** child's efforts.
No one in the play forgot **his or her** lines.

NOTE: In conversation, people often use a plural personal pronoun to refer to a singular antecedent that may be either masculine or feminine. This form is becoming more common in writing, too, and it may someday be considered standard written English.

EXAMPLES **Everybody** brought **their** swimsuits.
Each **member** of the club sold **their** tickets.

USAGE

☞ **REFERENCE NOTE:** For lists of the different kinds of pronouns, see pages 428–431.

(1) Use a singular pronoun to refer to *each, either, neither, one, everyone, everybody, no one, nobody, anyone, anybody, someone,* **or** *somebody.*

EXAMPLES   **Someone** in the class left behind **his or her** pencil.
Each of the snakes escaped from **its** cage.

(2) Use a singular pronoun to refer to two or more singular antecedents joined by *or.*

EXAMPLES   Either **Ralph or Carlos** will display **his** baseball card collection.
Nina or Mary will bring **her** CD player.

Sentences with singular antecedents joined by *or* can sound awkward if the antecedents are of different genders. If a sentence sounds awkward, revise it to avoid the problem.

AWKWARD   Odessa or Raymond will bring her or his road map.
REVISED   Either **Odessa** will bring **her** road map, or **Raymond** will bring **his.**

NOTE: Rules (1) and (2) are often ignored in conversation; however, they should be followed in writing.

(3) Use a plural pronoun to refer to two or more antecedents joined by *and.*

EXAMPLES   **Isaac and Jerome** went to the playground so that **they** could practice shooting baskets.
Elena and Roberto sent letters to **their** cousin in Costa Rica.

NOTE: Be sure that any pronoun referring to a collective noun has the same number as the noun.

EXAMPLES   The **cast** is giving **its** final performance tonight.
The **cast** are trying on **their** costumes.

EXERCISE 14 **Identifying Antecedents and Writing Pronouns That Agree with Them**

For each blank in the following sentences, give a pronoun that will complete the meaning of the sentence. Then identify the antecedent or antecedents for that pronoun.

EXAMPLE **1.** Dominic or Martin will show ____ slides.
1. *his—Dominic, Martin*

1. A writer should proofread ____ work carefully.
2. The store sent Paula and Eric the posters that ____ had ordered.
3. Mark or Hector will arrive early so that ____ can help us prepare the dim sum.
4. One of the students raised ____ hand.
5. Each of the dogs ate the scraps that we gave ____.
6. The principal and the Spanish teacher announced ____ plans for the Cinco de Mayo fiesta.
7. Everyone in my class has ____ own writer's journal.
8. Neither recalled the name of ____ first-grade teacher.
9. Anyone may join if ____ collects stamps.
10. Either Vanessa or Marilyn was awarded the blue ribbon for ____ design.

REVIEW C **Proofreading a Paragraph for Correct Pronoun-Antecedent Agreement**

Most of the following sentences contain errors in pronoun-antecedent agreement. Identify each error and give the correct pronoun. If a sentence is correct, write *C*.

EXAMPLE **[1]** At the meeting, each member of the Small Business Council spoke about their concerns.
1. *their—his or her*

[1] Everybody had a chance to express their opinion about the new shopping mall. [2] Mrs. Gomez and Mr. Franklin are happy about his or her new business locations at the mall. [3] Both said that his profits have increased significantly. [4] Neither Mr. Chen nor Mr. Cooper, however, feels that their customers find parking

convenient enough. [5] Anyone shopping at the mall has to park their car too far from the main shopping area. [6] Several members of the council said that the mall has taken away many of their customers. [7] One of the new women on the council then presented their own idea about creating a farmers' market on weekends. [8] Many members said he or she favored the plan, and a proposal was discussed. [9] Each farmer could have their own spot near the town hall. [10] The Small Business Council then agreed to take their proposal to the mayor.

PICTURE THIS

You are a sportswriter for the school newspaper and are covering this bicycle race. As the cyclists zoom by, you quickly take notes. Write several sentences that describe this exciting moment in the race. In your sentences, use five of the following pronouns: *her, nobody, his, each, its, one, their, anyone, they.* Remember that a pronoun should agree with its antecedent in number and gender.

Subject: bicycle race
Audience: school newspaper readers
Purpose: to inform

Review: Posttest

A. Identifying Correct Subject-Verb and Pronoun-Antecedent Agreement

Choose the correct word in parentheses in each of the following sentences.

EXAMPLE   **1.** Some of the paintings (*is, are*) dry now.
          1. *are*

1. Three hours of work (*is, are*) needed for a charcoal drawing.
2. Everybody has offered (*his or her, their*) advice.
3. *Harlem Shadows* (*is, are*) a collection of poems by Claude McKay.
4. Either Stu or Ryan can volunteer (*his, their*) skill in the kitchen.
5. Black beans, rice, and onions (*tastes, taste*) good together.
6. Not one of them has offered (*his or her, their*) help.
7. Sometimes my family (*disagrees, disagree*) with one another, but usually we all get along fairly well.
8. There (*is, are*) a beaded belt and a pair of moccasins in that box.
9. (*Doesn't, Don't*) too many cooks spoil the broth?
10. One of my aunts gave me (*her, their*) silk kimono.

B. Proofreading Sentences for Subject-Verb and Pronoun-Antecedent Agreement

Most of the following sentences contain an agreement error. For each error, identify the incorrect verb or pronoun, and supply the correct form. If the sentence is correct, write *C*.

EXAMPLE   **1.** Most stargazers has seen points of light shooting across the night sky.
          1. *has—have*

11. These points of light is commonly called shooting stars.
12. Scientists who study outer space calls these points of light meteors.
13. A meteor is a piece of an asteroid that exploded long ago.
14. Each of these pieces are still flying through space on the path of the original asteroid.
15. Most nights, a person is lucky if they can see a single meteor now and then.
16. Throughout the year, however, there is meteor "showers."
17. None of these showers are as big as the ones in August and November.
18. These large showers come at the same time each year.
19. In November 1833, one of the largest meteor showers in history were recorded.
20. Two hundred forty thousand meteors observed in just a few hours are a record that has never been matched!

21 USING VERBS CORRECTLY

Principal Parts, Regular and Irregular Verbs, Tense

Diagnostic Test

Using the Past and Past Participle Forms of Verbs

For each of the following sentences, give the correct form (past or past participle) of the verb in parentheses.

EXAMPLE **1.** The mayor has (*speak*) at our school's assemblies several times.
      1. *spoken*

1. The sun (*rise*) over the pyramids of Giza in Egypt.
2. We have (*swim*) only three laps.
3. Vera was (*choose*) captain of the volleyball team.
4. I have (*go*) to visit the Grand Canyon twice with my family.
5. The tiny tree frog (*sit*) motionless.
6. Joan has (*write*) a story about aliens from Venus.
7. During lunch hour, Jorge (*do*) his impersonation of Rubén Blades.
8. Someone (*lay*) a mysterious package on my desk.

9. This summer's heat wave has (*break*) all records.
10. Have you (*drink*) all of the tomato juice?
11. The log slowly (*sink*) into the quicksand.
12. The old postcards have (*lie*) in the box for years.
13. Have you ever (*drive*) across the state of Texas?
14. Our local PBS station (*begin*) its fund-raising drive yesterday.
15. Have you (*set*) the paper plates and napkins on the picnic table?
16. Who (*throw*) the ball to first base?
17. I have (*know*) some of my classmates for six years.
18. Kadeem Niles (*take*) the part of Frederick Douglass in the play.
19. The supermarket has (*raise*) the price of eggs.
20. We (*come*) close to winning the tournament.

Principal Parts

The four basic forms of a verb are called the *principal parts* of the verb.

21a. The principal parts of a verb are the **base form,** the **present participle,** the **past,** and the **past participle.**

Notice that the present participle and the past participle require helping verbs (forms of *be* and *have*).

BASE FORM	PRESENT PARTICIPLE	PAST	PAST PARTICIPLE
talk	(is) talking	talked	(have) talked
draw	(is) drawing	drew	(have) drawn

NOTE: Some teachers refer to the base form as the infinitive. Follow your teacher's directions in labeling these words.

The principal parts of a verb are used to express time.

PRESENT TIME   He **draws** excellent pictures.
Susan **is drawing** one now.
PAST TIME   Last week they **drew** two maps.
She **has** often **drawn** cartoons.
FUTURE TIME   Perhaps she **will draw** one for you.
By next Thursday, we **will have
drawn** two landscapes.

© 1992 by Sidney Harris

Because *talk* forms its past and past participle by adding –*ed,* it is called a *regular verb. Draw* forms its past and past participle differently, so it is called an *irregular verb.*

USAGE

Regular Verbs

21b.   A *regular verb* forms its past and past participle by adding –*d* or –*ed* to the base form.

BASE FORM	PRESENT PARTICIPLE	PAST	PAST PARTICIPLE
clean	(is) cleaning	cleaned	(have) cleaned
hope	(is) hoping	hoped	(have) hoped
inspect	(is) inspecting	inspected	(have) inspected
slip	(is) slipping	slipped	(have) slipped

👉 REFERENCE NOTE: Most regular verbs that end in –*e* drop the –*e* before adding –*ing.* Some regular verbs double the final consonant before adding –*ing* or –*ed.* For a discussion of these spelling rules, see pages 770–771.

One common error in forming the past or the past participle of a regular verb is to leave off the –*d* or –*ed* ending.

NONSTANDARD   Our street use to be more quiet.
STANDARD   Our street **used** to be more quiet.

👉 REFERENCE NOTE: For a discussion of standard and nonstandard English, see page 387.

USAGE

▶ ORAL
PRACTICE 1   **Using Regular Verbs**

Read each of the following sentences aloud, stressing the italicized verbs.

1. We are *supposed* to meet at the track after school.
2. The twins *happened* to buy the same shirt.
3. They have already *called* me about the party.
4. Do you know who *used* to live in this house?
5. I *hoped* they could go to the concert with us.
6. The chairs have been *moved* for the dance.
7. That salesclerk has *helped* my mother before.
8. Eli may not have *looked* under the table for the cat.

▶ EXERCISE 1   **Writing the Forms of Regular Verbs**

For each of the following sentences, fill in the blank with the correct present participle, past, or past participle form of the verb given.

EXAMPLE   **1.** *learn* Many people today are ____ folk dances from a variety of countries.
          1. *learning*

1. *practice*   These Spanish folk dancers must have ____ for a long time.
2. *perform*   Notice that they are ____ in colorful, native costumes.
3. *wish*   Have you ever ____ that you knew how to do any folk dances?

4. *use* Virginia reels ____ to be popular dances in the United States.

5. *promise* Mrs. Stamos, who is from Greece, ____ to teach her daughter the Greek chain dance.

6. *lean* The Jamaican dancer ____ backward before he went under the pole during the limbo competition.

7. *start* The group from Estonia is ____ a dance about a spinning wheel.

8. *request* Someone in the audience has ____ an Irish square dance called "Sweets of May."

9. *dance* During the Mexican hat dance, the girl ____ on the rim of the sombrero.

10. *fill* The Jewish wedding dance ____ the room with music and movement.

Irregular Verbs

21c. An *irregular verb* forms its past and past participle in some other way than by adding –*d* or –*ed* to the infinitive form.

An irregular verb forms its past and past participle in three ways:

- by changing vowels *or* consonants

BASE FORM	PAST	PAST PARTICIPLE
ring	rang	(have) rung
make	made	(have) made

- by changing vowels *and* consonants

BASE FORM	PAST	PAST PARTICIPLE
do	did	(have) done
go	went	(have) gone

■ by making no changes.

BASE FORM	PAST	PAST PARTICIPLE
hurt	hurt	(have) hurt
put	put	(have) put

NOTE: If you are not sure about the principal parts of a verb, look in a dictionary. Entries for irregular verbs list the principal parts of the verb. If the principal parts are not given, the verb is a regular verb.

COMMON IRREGULAR VERBS			
BASE FORM	**PRESENT PARTICIPLE**	**PAST**	**PAST PARTICIPLE**
begin	(is) beginning	began	(have) begun
bite	(is) biting	bit	(have) bitten
blow	(is) blowing	blew	(have) blown
break	(is) breaking	broke	(have) broken
bring	(is) bringing	brought	(have) brought
build	(is) building	built	(have) built
burst	(is) bursting	burst	(have) burst
catch	(is) catching	caught	(have) caught
choose	(is) choosing	chose	(have) chosen
come	(is) coming	came	(have) come
cost	(is) costing	cost	(have) cost
do	(is) doing	did	(have) done
draw	(is) drawing	drew	(have) drawn
drink	(is) drinking	drank	(have) drunk
drive	(is) driving	drove	(have) driven
eat	(is) eating	ate	(have) eaten
fall	(is) falling	fell	(have) fallen
feel	(is) feeling	felt	(have) felt
freeze	(is) freezing	froze	(have) frozen
get	(is) getting	got	(have) got *or* gotten

(continued)

USAGE

COMMON IRREGULAR VERBS *(continued)*			
BASE FORM	PRESENT PARTICIPLE	PAST	PAST PARTICIPLE
give	(is) giving	gave	(have) given
go	(is) going	went	(have) gone
grow	(is) growing	grew	(have) grown
know	(is) knowing	knew	(have) known
lead	(is) leading	led	(have) led

ORAL PRACTICE 2 **Using Irregular Verbs**

Read each of the following sentences aloud, stressing the italicized verbs.

1. Ellen's sister *drove* her to the mall this afternoon.
2. My parents *came* to the spelling bee last year.
3. I should have *known* the test would be difficult.
4. He's *going* to Cape Canaveral this summer.
5. Maya has been *chosen* to play Emily in *Our Town*.
6. The water pipe *burst* during the ice storm.
7. *Did* you see the northern lights last night?
8. Wyatt *brought* his new computer game to the party.

EXERCISE 2 **Writing the Past and Past Participle Forms of Irregular Verbs**

For each of the following sentences, give the past or past participle form of the verb that will fit correctly in the blank.

EXAMPLE **1.** *choose* Sara has _____ her song for the recital.
    1. *chosen*

1. *drive* Last summer we _____ to Denver, where we visited the U.S. Mint.
2. *begin* The concert _____ an hour ago.
3. *break* Mike Powell _____ the world long jump record by jumping 29 feet, $4\frac{1}{2}$ inches.
4. *blow* The wind has _____ the tent down.

5. *get*   We've ＿＿ tickets to ride *The Silverton.*
6. *fall*   People have ＿＿ over that log several times.
7. *do*   Mother ＿＿ her best, and she got a promotion.
8. *drink*   According to legend, the Aztec emperor Montezuma ＿＿ chocolate.
9. *build*   People in Africa ＿＿ large cities hundreds, even thousands, of years ago.
10. *go*   You've never ＿＿ to Puerto Rico, have you?

MORE COMMON IRREGULAR VERBS			
BASE FORM	**PRESENT PARTICIPLE**	**PAST**	**PAST PARTICIPLE**
lend	(is) lending	lent	(have) lent
lose	(is) losing	lost	(have) lost
make	(is) making	made	(have) made
meet	(is) meeting	met	(have) met
ride	(is) riding	rode	(have) ridden
ring	(is) ringing	rang	(have) rung
run	(is) running	ran	(have) run
say	(is) saying	said	(have) said
see	(is) seeing	saw	(have) seen
sell	(is) selling	sold	(have) sold
send	(is) sending	sent	(have) sent
shrink	(is) shrinking	shrank	(have) shrunk
sing	(is) singing	sang	(have) sung
sink	(is) sinking	sank	(have) sunk
speak	(is) speaking	spoke	(have) spoken
stand	(is) standing	stood	(have) stood
steal	(is) stealing	stole	(have) stolen
swim	(is) swimming	swam	(have) swum
swing	(is) swinging	swung	(have) swung
take	(is) taking	took	(have) taken
tell	(is) telling	told	(have) told
throw	(is) throwing	threw	(have) thrown
wear	(is) wearing	wore	(have) worn
win	(is) winning	won	(have) won
write	(is) writing	wrote	(have) written

USAGE

▶ ORAL PRACTICE 3   **Using Irregular Verbs**

Read each of the following sentences aloud, stressing the italicized verbs.

1. When the bell *rang*, we hurried out of the building.
2. The audience was quiet as the acrobats *swung* from the trapeze.
3. That dress *shrank* because it was washed in hot water.
4. Otherwise, Lily would have *worn* it to the dance.
5. Have you *met* the foreign exchange student this year?
6. We were late to the picnic because I *lost* the map.
7. My father *lent* me the money to buy a new watch.
8. Would you believe that Raymond *took* singing lessons?

▶ EXERCISE 3   **Writing the Past and Past Participle Forms of Irregular Verbs**

For each of the following sentences, give the past or past participle form of the verb that will fit correctly in the blank.

EXAMPLE   **1.** *see*   I have ____ that movie twice already.
          1. *seen*

1. *run*   Carl Lewis ____ the 100-meter dash in record-breaking time.
2. *sell*   My aunt has ____ more houses than any other real estate agent in the city.
3. *speak* The director of the state health department ____ to our class today.
4. *win*   Mexican poet Octavio Paz ____ the Nobel Prize for literature.
5. *write* I have ____ some poems, but I am shy about showing them to anyone.
6. *ride*   Tamisha's whole family ____ on mules to the bottom of the Grand Canyon.
7. *sing*   At the concert, the group ____ my favorite song.

 8. *throw*   This trash must have been ____ from a car.
 9. *swim*   Two swans ____ across the lake.
10. *sink*   King Arthur's sword Excalibur ____ slowly to the bottom of the lake.

▶ REVIEW A

Writing the Past and Past Participle Forms of Irregular Verbs

For each of the following sentences, give the past or past participle form of the verb that will fit correctly in the blank.

EXAMPLE   **1.** *tell*   Has Alameda ____ you about the book *The Indian Tipi: Its History, Construction, and Use?*
          1. *told*

 1. *write*   Reginald and Gladys Laubin ____ that book and several others about Native American culture.
 2. *come*   The word *tepee*, or *tipi*, has ____ into English from the Sioux language.
 3. *stand*   Tepees of various sizes once ____ all across the plains.
 4. *see*   I have ____ pictures of camps full of decorated tepees.
 5. *make*   For many years, Native Americans have ____ tepees out of cloth rather than buffalo hides.
 6. *build*   The Laubins ____ their own tepee and lived in it.
 7. *draw*   On the outside of their tepees, the Sioux and Cheyenne peoples ____ designs like the ones shown on the next page.
 8. *take*   Because the Plains peoples followed the animal herds, they needed housing that could be ____ from place to place.
 9. *know*   Even before reading the book, I ____ that tepee covers were rarely painted inside.
10. *do*   Women ____ all the work of making tepees and putting them up.

USAGE

 REVIEW B

Writing the Past and Past Participle Forms of Irregular Verbs

For each of the following sentences, give the past or past participle form of the verb that will fit correctly in the blank.

EXAMPLE **1.** *write*   I _____ a report on Jim Thorpe.
           1. *wrote*

1. *blow*   Yesterday the wind _____ the leaves into our yard.
2. *break* My pen pal from Australia has never _____ his promise to write once a week.
3. *bring* I _____ the wrong book to class.
4. *burst* The children almost _____ with excitement.
5. *choose* The director _____ James Earl Jones to star in the new series.
6. *come* My aunt and her friend _____ to dinner last night.

7. *do*   I have always ___ my homework right after supper.

8. *drink*   The guests ___ four quarts of fruit punch.

9. *fall*   One of my Russian nesting dolls has ___ off the shelf.

10. *freeze*   Has the pond ___ yet?

11. *go*   We have never ___ to see the Parthenon in Nashville, Tennessee.

12. *know*   Had I ___, I would have called you sooner.

13. *ring*   Suddenly the fire alarm ___.

14. *run*   Joan Samuelson certainly ___ a good race.

15. *see*   I ___ you in line at the movies.

16. *shrink*   We dried apples in the sun, and they ___.

17. *speak*   After we had ___ to George Takei, who plays Mr. Sulu, we went to the *Star Trek* convention banquet.

18. *throw*   You shouldn't have ___ the ball to second base.

19. *write*   She has ___ me several long letters.

20. *swim*   We ___ out to the float and back.

▶ REVIEW C   **Using Past and Past Participle Forms of Irregular Verbs**

You've won a radio contest called "Ask a Star." Now you get to interview the celebrity of your choice. You name the star, and the radio station will arrange the interview. Pick a celebrity to interview, and write ten questions to ask him or her. In your questions, use the past or past participle forms of ten of the following verbs. Underline each verb you use.

begin	cost	know	sing
break	do	meet	tell
build	drive	ride	throw
catch	feel	say	wear
choose	get	sell	write

EXAMPLE   **1.** *Have you really <u>ridden</u> a camel down Hollywood Boulevard?*

PICTURE THIS

The year is 2030. Just ten years ago scientists made great advances in time travel. Now, time-travel booths like this one are common in malls and shopping centers. For a small fee, you can travel to any place at any time in history. You sit down in the booth, fasten your seat belt, and set the dials for the time and place of your choice. When the machine stops, you get out and begin to explore your surroundings. You take notes about what you see so that you won't forget anything when you tell your family and friends about your trip. In your notes, describe how life in this time and place is similar to or different from life as you know it. Use at least ten irregular verbs, underlining each one you use.

Subject: a journey to a different place and time
Audience: your family and friends
Purpose: to inform and entertain

USAGE

Tense

21d. The *tense* of a verb indicates the time of the action or of the state of being expressed by the verb.

Every verb has six tenses.

Present	Past	Future
Present Perfect	Past Perfect	Future Perfect

The following time line shows the relationship between the six tenses.

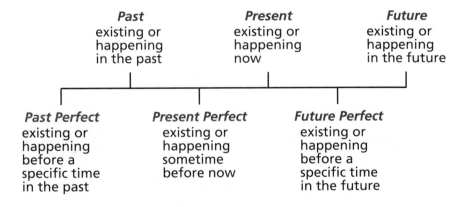

Past	*Present*	*Future*
existing or happening in the past	existing or happening now	existing or happening in the future

Past Perfect	*Present Perfect*	*Future Perfect*
existing or happening before a specific time in the past	existing or happening sometime before now	existing or happening before a specific time in the future

Listing all the forms of a verb is called *conjugating* the verb.

CONJUGATION OF THE VERB *SEE*	
PRESENT TENSE	
SINGULAR	**PLURAL**
I see	we see
you see	you see
he, she, or it sees	they see

(continued)

CONJUGATION OF THE VERB *SEE* (continued)	
PAST TENSE	
SINGULAR	**PLURAL**
I saw	we saw
you saw	you saw
he, she, or it saw	they saw
FUTURE TENSE	
SINGULAR	**PLURAL**
I will (shall) see	we will (shall) see
you will see	you will see
he, she, or it will see	they will see
PRESENT PERFECT TENSE	
SINGULAR	**PLURAL**
I have seen	we have seen
you have seen	you have seen
he, she, or it has seen	they have seen
PAST PERFECT TENSE	
SINGULAR	**PLURAL**
I had seen	we had seen
you had seen	you had seen
he, she, or it had seen	they had seen
FUTURE PERFECT TENSE	
SINGULAR	**PLURAL**
I will (shall) have seen	we will (shall) have seen
you will have seen	you will have seen
he, she, or it will have seen	they will have seen

USAGE

Consistency of Tense

21e. Do not change needlessly from one tense to another.

When writing about events that take place in the present, use verbs that are in the present tense. When writing about events that occurred in the past, use verbs that are in the past tense.

INCONSISTENT   When we **go** to the movies, we **bought** some popcorn. [*Go* is in the present tense, and *bought* is in the past tense.]

CONSISTENT   When we **go** to the movies, we **buy** some popcorn. [Both *go* and *buy* are in the present tense.]

CONSISTENT   When we **went** to the movies, we **bought** some popcorn. [Both *went* and *bought* are in the past tense.]

USAGE

▶ EXERCISE 4   **Revising a Paragraph to Make the Tenses of the Verbs Consistent**

Read the following paragraph and decide whether it should be rewritten in the present or past tense. Then rewrite the paragraph, changing the verb forms to make the verb tense consistent.

EXAMPLE   [1] I picked up the telephone receiver, but the line is still dead.

1. *I picked up the telephone receiver, but the line was still dead.*

or

I pick up the telephone receiver, but the line is still dead.

[1] Lightning struck our house, and I run straight for cover. [2] "Oh, no!" I exclaim. [3] The electricity had gone out! [4] My parents light candles, and we played a game by candlelight. [5] We know that lightning had hit our telephone answering machine, because it keeps playing the same message over and over. [6] My younger brother asks me what lightning is. [7] "Lightning is a big spark of electricity from a thundercloud," I tell him. [8] He nods. [9] I started to tell him about positive and negative charges creating lightning, but he doesn't understand what I'm talking about and walks away. [10] In the morning, we were all glad when the sun shone and our phone works again.

Six Troublesome Verbs

Sit and *Set*

The verb *sit* means "to be seated" or "to rest." *Sit* seldom takes an object.

The verb *set* means "to place" or "to put (something)." *Set* usually takes an object. Notice that *set* has the same form for the base form, past, and past participle.

BASE FORM	PRESENT PARTICIPLE	PAST	PAST PARTICIPLE
sit	(is) sitting	sat	(have) sat
set	(is) setting	set	(have) set

EXAMPLES   Three girls **sat** on the platform. [no object]
Set those geraniums in a sunny place. [Set what? *Geraniums* is the object.]

I **will sit** here for a while. [no object]
I **will set** your dinner on the table. [I will set what? *Dinner* is the object.]

ORAL PRACTICE 4   **Using the Forms of *Sit* and *Set* Correctly**

Read each of the following sentences aloud, stressing the italicized verbs.

1. Darnell and I *sat* down to play a game of chess.
2. After he had been *sitting* for a while, Darnell decided to make banana bread.
3. I *set* the pan on the table.
4. Darnell *set* out the ingredients; then he mixed them.
5. We returned to our game but could not *sit* still for long.
6. We had not *set* the pan in the oven.
7. Then we almost *sat* too long.
8. The pan had been *set* on the wrong rack, and the bread was beginning to burn.

▶ EXERCISE 5 **Writing the Forms of *Sit* and *Set***

For each blank in the following sentences, supply the correct form of *sit* or *set*.

EXAMPLE **1.** I ____ my suitcase on the rack.
            1. *set*

1. On the train to Boston, I ____ next to a middle-aged woman wearing a shawl.
2. She ____ a large basket on the floor by her feet.
3. When the conductor asked her if she would like to ____ it in the baggage rack, she refused.
4. She insisted that the basket must ____ by her feet.
5. As I ____ beside her, I wondered what was in the basket.
6. I ____ my book down and tried to see inside the tightly woven basket.
7. Perhaps I was ____ next to a woman with a picnic lunch to share.
8. Maybe she had ____ next to me because I looked hungry.
9. As the woman ____ her packages down, I watched the basket.
10. A sudden movement of the train caused the basket to open, and inside it ____ a small white rabbit.

Rise and *Raise*

The verb *rise* means "to move upward" or "to go up." *Rise* never takes an object.

    The verb *raise* means "to lift (something) up." *Raise* usually takes an object.

BASE FORM	PRESENT PARTICIPLE	PAST	PAST PARTICIPLE
rise	(is) rising	rose	(have) risen
raise	(is) raising	raised	(have) raised

EXAMPLES   Coretta **has** already **risen** from the bench. [no object]
My brother **has raised** the curtain. [My brother has raised what? *Curtain* is the object.]

The fans **were rising** to sing the national anthem. [no object]
Passing cars **were raising** clouds of dust. [Cars were raising what? *Clouds* is the object.]

▶ ORAL PRACTICE 5   **Using Forms of *Rise* and *Raise***

Read each of the following sentences aloud, stressing the italicized verbs.

1. Mount Everest *rises* over 29,000 feet.
2. The flag was *raised* at sunrise.
3. The TV reporter *raised* her voice to be heard.
4. She *rose* from her seat and looked out the window.
5. The constellation Orion had not yet *risen* in the southern sky.
6. They had *raised* the piñata high in the tree.
7. I hope the bread is *rising*.
8. He will be *raising* the bucket from the well.

▶ EXERCISE 6   **Identifying the Correct Forms of *Rise* and *Raise***

For each of the following sentences, choose the correct verb of the two in parentheses.

EXAMPLE   **1.** After the storm, Diana (*rose, raised*) the window.
1. *raised*

1. The audience (*rose, raised*) for the "Hallelujah Chorus."
2. They used a jack to (*rise, raise*) the car so that they could change the tire.
3. The fire juggler is (*rising, raising*) two flaming batons over his head to signal the start of the show.
4. Some people have trouble remembering that the sun (*rises, raises*) in the east.

USAGE

5. He gently (*rose, raised*) the injured duckling from the lake.
6. Only half of Mauna Kea, a volcano on this island of Hawaii, (*rises, raises*) above the ocean.
7. The proud winner has (*risen, raised*) her trophy so that everyone can see it.
8. The guests have (*risen, raised*) from their seats to see the bride enter.
9. Yeast makes the pizza dough (*rise, raise*).
10. They will (*rise, raise*) the couch while I look under it for the hamster.

Lie and *Lay*

The verb *lie* means "to recline," "to be in a place," or "to remain lying down." *Lie* never takes an object.

The verb *lay* means "to put (something) down," "to place (something)." *Lay* usually takes an object.

BASE FORM	PRESENT PARTICIPLE	PAST	PAST PARTICIPLE
lie	(is) lying	lay	(have) lain
lay	(is) laying	laid	(have) laid

EXAMPLES   **Rocky Ridge lies** twenty miles east of here. [no object]
Aunt Martha lays her apple dolls in the sun to dry. [Aunt Martha lays what? *Dolls* is the object.]

That bicycle has lain in the driveway for a week. [no object]
Dad has laid your clean shirts on the bed. [Dad has laid what? *Shirts* is the object.]

 ORAL PRACTICE 6   **Using Forms of *Lie* and *Lay* Correctly**

Read each of the following sentences aloud, stressing the italicized verbs.

1. If you are tired, *lie* down for a while.
2. *Lay* your pencils down, please.
3. Two huge dogs *lay* by the fire.
4. The cat has been *lying* on the new bedspread.
5. Mr. Cortez *laid* the map of Puerto Rico on the table.
6. In our state, snow usually *lies* on the ground until early spring.
7. *Lay* your coats on the bed in my room.
8. After the baby had *lain* down for a nap, she wanted to play.

▶ EXERCISE 7   **Identifying the Correct Forms of *Lie* and *Lay***

For each of the following sentences, choose the correct verb of the two in parentheses.

EXAMPLE   **1.** Marc (*lay*, *laid*) his new tennis shoes on the floor.
   1. *laid*

1. The islands of American Samoa (*lie*, *lay*) about 4,800 miles southwest of San Francisco.
2. We quickly (*lay*, *laid*) the crab down when it began to pinch.
3. I don't know where I have (*lain*, *laid*) my copy of *Chinese Proverbs* by Ruthanne Lum McCunn.
4. Cattle often (*lie*, *lay*) under trees during sunny days.
5. Many visitors (*lie*, *lay*) flowers and wreaths at the Vietnam Veterans Memorial in Washington, D.C.
6. My brother, who is sick, has been (*lying*, *laying*) in bed all day.
7. The postal employee (*lay*, *laid*) the small package on the scales.
8. (*Lie*, *Lay*) your backpack down and come see my new comic books.
9. Those clothes will (*lie*, *lay*) on the floor until you pick them up.
10. You're sore because you've been (*lying*, *laying*) in one position too long.

▶ REVIEW D   **Identifying the Correct Forms of *Sit* and *Set*, *Rise* and *Raise*, *Lie* and *Lay***

For each of the following sentences, choose the correct verb of the two in parentheses.

EXAMPLE   **1.** The bricklayer (*rose, raised*) from the patio floor and dusted himself off.
    1. *rose*

1. These rocks have (*lain, laid*) here for centuries.
2. (*Sit, Set*) there until your name is called.
3. The nurse (*lay, laid*) her cool hand on the sick child's brow.
4. The cows are (*lying, laying*) in the pasture.
5. The senator and her advisers (*sat, set*) around the huge conference table.
6. After the picnic, everyone (*lay, laid*) on blankets to rest.
7. Smoke (*rose, raised*) from the chimney.
8. The farmhands (*sat, set*) their lunch pails under a tree.
9. Have you been (*sitting, setting*) there all afternoon?
10. The sun has already (*risen, raised*).

▶ REVIEW E   **Proofreading a Paragraph for Correct Verb Forms**

Most sentences in the following paragraph contain incorrect verb forms. If a sentence contains the wrong form of a verb, write the correct form. If a sentence is correct, write *C*.

EXAMPLE   [1] During the 1800s, many German settlers choosed to live in the Hill Country of central Texas.
    1. *chose*

[1] These hardy, determined pioneers builded towns and cleared land for farming. [2] I have went to this town, Fredericksburg, several times. [3] This interesting town lays about eighty miles west of Austin. [4] Fredericksburg

use to be in Comanche territory. [5] Early on, German settlers made peace with the Comanche chiefs. [6] The town then growed rapidly. [7] German-style houses, churches, and public buildings like these raised along the town's central street. [8] On one of our visits, my family set and talked about the town with a woman who was born there. [9] She said that she had spoken German all her life. [10] When we left, she raised a hand and said, *"Auf Wiedersehen"* (until we meet again).

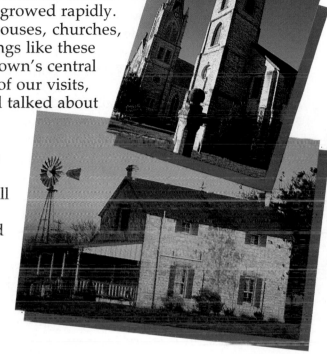

WRITING APPLICATION

Using Different Verb Forms and Tenses in a Story

When you write a story, you use verbs to express the action. The use of correct verb forms and consistent tense helps show your readers the order of events.

INCORRECT FORM AND INCONSISTENT TENSE	The gale wind blowed the tiny boat off course. Huge waves batter the craft. The weary crew will bail out the water.
CORRECT FORM AND CONSISTENT TENSE	The gale wind **blew** the tiny boat off course. Huge waves **battered** the craft. The weary crew **bailed** out the water.

USAGE

▶ WRITING ACTIVITY

A local writers' club is sponsoring a contest for the best "cliffhanger" opening of an adventure story. Write an exciting paragraph to enter in the contest. Your paragraph should leave readers wondering, "What happens next?" In your paragraph, use at least five verbs from the lists of **Common Irregular Verbs** on pages 584–586.

Prewriting First, you'll need to imagine a suspenseful situation to describe. Maybe your characters will actually be hanging on the edge of a cliff, or maybe they'll be in another type of life-or-death situation. Jot down several ideas for your story opening. Then, choose the one you like best. With that situation in mind, scan the lists of irregular verbs. List at least ten verbs that you might be able to use. (You can weed out some of them later.) Include some lively action verbs like *burst, swing, throw*.

Writing As you write your rough draft, think of your readers. Choose words that create a suspenseful, believable scene. Remember that you have only one paragraph to catch your readers' interest.

Evaluating and Revising Ask a friend to read your paragraph. Does your friend find it interesting? Can he or she picture the scene clearly? If not, you may want to add, delete, or revise some details. Check to see if you've used any tired words like *great* or *bad* that you can replace with more specific ones. For more about replacing tired words, see page 391.

Proofreading Check over your spelling, usage, punctuation, and grammar. Be sure that you've used at least five irregular verbs from the lists on pages 584–586. Use your textbook or a dictionary to check the spellings of these verbs. Also, check to make sure the forms are correct and the tenses are consistent.

Review: Posttest

Proofreading Sentences for Correct Verb Forms

If a sentence contains an incorrect past or past participle form of the verb, write the correct form. If a sentence is correct, write *C*.

EXAMPLE **1.** Melissa drunk the medicine in one gulp.
1. *drank*

1. We swum in the lake last weekend.
2. Carlos come from the Dominican Republic.
3. The crow just set there on the barbed wire fence and wouldn't move.
4. I seen that magician on television.
5. The balloon burst with a loud pop.
6. The gypsy raised his tambourine to begin the dance.
7. You should have went with me to the Native American celebration in Gallup, New Mexico.
8. The block of ice shrunk to half its original size.
9. Meanwhile, the water level has rose.
10. I would have wrote to you much sooner, but I lost your address.
11. Sandra throwed the ball to the shortstop.
12. Ms. Lopez has spoke before many civic groups.
13. All of these photographs were taken in Florida's Everglades National Park.
14. The bell has rang for fourth period.
15. While visiting Los Angeles, I run into an old friend in the city's Little Tokyo district.
16. I laid down under a tree to rest.
17. I done everything asked of me.
18. It begun to rain shortly after dusk.
19. Sue lay her pen down and studied the question again.
20. Some of the saucers were broken.

USAGE

22 USING PRONOUNS CORRECTLY

Nominative and Objective Case Forms

Diagnostic Test

A. Identifying the Correct Forms of Pronouns

For each of the following sentences, choose the correct form of the pronoun in parentheses.

EXAMPLE   **1.** Mrs. Boyd gave Jeff and (*I, me*) a ride to school.
          1. *me*

1. The closing procession of the powwow will be led by (*he, him*) and the other Dakota dancers.
2. May (*we, us*) choir members leave science class a few minutes early today?
3. (*Who, Whom*) do you think will win today?
4. Please hand out these copies of Consuelo's report to (*she, her*) and the committee members.
5. (*He, Him*) and his cat relaxed in the easy chair and listened to the rain.

6. Darnell certainly was enjoying (*himself, hisself*) at the African Heritage Festival last night.
7. The last tennis player to beat Martina Navratilova in straight sets was (*her, she*).
8. (*Who, Whom*) have you asked for help with your math homework?
9. Mom, will you take (*we, us*) tired yard workers out for dinner tonight?
10. Collect about a dozen colorful leaves, and then brush (*they, them*) with a thin coat of shellac.

B. Identifying the Correct Forms of Pronouns

For each of the following sentences, choose the correct form of the pronoun in parentheses.

EXAMPLE **1.** The most loyal sports fans at our school are Glenn and (*I, me*).
   1. *I*

11. (*We, Us*) baseball fans are going to the playoff game on Saturday.
12. (*Who, Whom*) will we see at the game?
13. Mario's mother will be driving (*we, us*) and Elena to the stadium.
14. Elena and (*he, him*) volunteered to design a banner.
15. "Tell Jennifer and (*I, me*) your slogan," Glenn said to Mario.
16. "Neither Elena nor (*I, me*) can decide which one we like best," Mario answered.
17. "Well, (*who, whom*) are the two best slogan inventors in the whole school?" I boasted, pointing at Glenn and myself.
18. Last year, the biggest banner was designed by the twins and (*she, her*).
19. They really outdid (*theirselves, themselves*)!
20. You should see the banner designed by (*we, us*) four fans this year, though!

Case

Case is the form of a noun or pronoun that shows its use in a sentence. There are three cases:

- nominative
- objective
- possessive

The form of a noun is the same for both the nominative and the objective cases. For example, a noun used as a subject (nominative case) will have the same form when used as a direct object (objective case).

NOMINATIVE CASE   That Ming **vase** is very old. [subject]
    OBJECTIVE CASE   Who bought the **vase?** [direct object]

A noun changes its form only in the possessive case, usually by adding an apostrophe and an *s*.

POSSESSIVE CASE   The Ming **vase's** new owner is pleased.

☞ **REFERENCE NOTE:** For more information about forming the possessive case of nouns, see pages 746–748.

Unlike nouns, most personal pronouns have different forms for all three cases.

PERSONAL PRONOUNS		
SINGULAR		
NOMINATIVE CASE	OBJECTIVE CASE	POSSESSIVE CASE
I	me	my, mine
you	you	your, yours
he, she, it	him, her, it	his, her, hers, its
PLURAL		
NOMINATIVE CASE	OBJECTIVE CASE	POSSESSIVE CASE
we	us	our, ours
you	you	your, yours
they	them	their, theirs

NOTE: Some teachers prefer to call possessive forms of pronouns (such as *our, your,* and *their*) adjectives. Follow your teacher's instructions regarding possessive forms.

Drawing by Ziegler; © 1988 The New Yorker Magazine, Inc.

USAGE

The Nominative Case

22a. The subject of a verb is in the nominative case.

EXAMPLES   **They** made candles from antique molds. [*They* is the subject of *made.*]
We admired the Navajo rugs. [*We* is the subject of *admired.*]
He and **I** mowed lawns. [*He* and *I* are used together as the compound subject of *mowed.*]

To help you choose the correct pronoun in a compound subject, try each form of the pronoun separately.

EXAMPLE: The guide and (*I, me*) looked for tracks.
I looked for tracks.
Me looked for tracks.
ANSWER: The guide and **I** looked for tracks.

EXAMPLE: (*She, Her*) and (*I, me*) found them.
She found them.
Her found them.
I found them.
Me found them.
ANSWER: **She** and **I** found them.

▶ ORAL PRACTICE 1   **Using Pronouns in Compound Subjects**

Read each of the following sentences aloud, stressing the italicized pronouns.

1. Dr. Chen and *they* discussed the usefulness of herbal medicines.
2. *He* and *I* live next door to each other.
3. *They* and *we* should try to get along better.
4. Yesterday *she* and *they* gave their reports on African American poets.
5. You and *she* left the party early.
6. Since the third grade, you and *I* have been friends.
7. *He* and his family are moving to Puerto Rico.
8. *She* and *I* will miss them.

▶ EXERCISE 1   **Identifying Correct Pronoun Forms**

For each sentence in the following paragraph, choose the correct form of the pronoun in parentheses.

EXAMPLE   **1.** My friends and (*I, me*) like to spend time outdoors.
            1. *I*

[1] Lou and (*I, me*) asked my mother to drive us to a nearby state park. [2] There (*he and I, him and me*) set out on a marked trail through a wooded area. [3] Before long, (*he and I, him and me*) were exploring a snowy area off the beaten track. [4] At dusk Lou and (*I, me*) reluctantly followed our tracks back to the path. [5] (*We, Us*) had had the best time of our lives.

22b. A predicate nominative is in the nominative case.

A *predicate nominative* follows a linking verb and identifies or explains the subject of the verb. A pronoun used as a predicate nominative usually follows a form of the verb *be* (such as *am, are, is, was, were, be, been,* or *being*) and identifies the subject.

EXAMPLES The candidates should have been **he** and **she.**
[*He* and *she* follow the linking verb *should have been* and identify the subject *candidates.*]
The members of the debating team are **they.**
[*They* follows the linking verb *are* and identifies the subject *members.*]

NOTE: Expressions such as *It's me* and *That's her* are acceptable in everyday speaking. However, such expressions should be avoided in writing.

☞ REFERENCE NOTE: For more information about predicate nominatives, see pages 480–481.

▶ ORAL PRACTICE 2 **Using Pronouns as Predicate Nominatives**

Read each of the following sentences aloud, stressing the italicized pronouns.

1. Were the only Spanish-speaking people you and *they*?
2. The caller could have been *she.*
3. The leaders will be my mother and *he.*
4. The three candidates for class president are you and *we.*
5. That must be the pilot and *he.*
6. The three winners were Frank, May, and *I.*
7. The first ones on the scene were our neighbors and *they.*
8. The speakers at the rally were *she* and Jesse Jackson.

▶ EXERCISE 2 **Identifying Correct Pronoun Forms**

For each of the following sentences, choose the correct form of the pronoun in parentheses.

EXAMPLE 1. Could it be (*they, them*)?
1. *they*

1. It must be (*them, they*).
2. Two witnesses claimed that the burglar was (*him, he*).

3. Is the last performer (*her, she*)?
4. The next speaker will be (*him, he*).
5. Among the invited guests are Luther and (*us, we*).
6. I knew it was (*her, she*), of course.
7. The hardest workers are Susan, Tranh, and (*me, I*).
8. Can that be (*her, she*) in that sombrero?
9. The next batter should be (*her, she*).
10. Our newest neighbors are the Blumenthals and (*them, they*).

REVIEW A **Writing Sentences That Contain Pronouns in the Nominative Case**

The busy scene you see on the next page was painted by the Mexican American artist Carmen Lomas Garza. It shows one of her childhood birthday parties. The fish-shaped object hanging from the tree is a piñata, full of gifts and treats for the children. Carmen is getting ready to take a swing at the piñata. Answer each of the following questions by writing a sentence. Follow the directions after each question.

EXAMPLE 1. What are the kneeling boys in the lower left-hand corner doing? (*Use a plural personal pronoun as the subject.*)
1. *They are getting ready to play marbles.*

1. What is Carmen using to hit the piñata? (*Use a singular personal pronoun as the subject.*)
2. Whom are the presents on the table for? (*Use a plural personal pronoun as the subject.*)
3. Who will get the gifts and treats inside the piñata? (*Use a person's name and a plural personal pronoun as the compound subject.*)
4. Have you and your classmates ever played a game that requires a blindfold? (*Use a plural and a singular personal pronoun as the compound subject.*)
5. Why does the boy at the far right have presents in his hand? (*Use a singular personal pronoun as the subject.*)

6. What would Carmen say if you asked her, "Who's the birthday girl?" (*Use a singular personal pronoun as a predicate nominative.*)
7. Did Carmen's parents and her grandmother plan the party? (*Use a plural and a singular personal pronoun as a compound predicate nominative.*)
8. Are the baby and his mother standing near the table having a good time? (*Use the baby and a singular personal pronoun as the compound subject.*)
9. Is Carmen's father the man holding the piñata rope? (*Use a singular personal pronoun as a predicate nominative.*)
10. Who are the ones now looking at the picture of this long-ago birthday party? (*Use a plural personal pronoun as a predicate nominative.*)

Reprinted by permission of GRM Associates, Inc., Agents for Children's Book Press, from the book *Family Pictures* by Carmen Lomas Garza, copyright 1990 by Carmen Lomas Garza

The Objective Case

22c. *Direct objects* and *indirect objects* of verbs are in the objective case.

A *direct object* follows an action verb and tells *who* or *what* receives the action of the verb.

EXAMPLES   Mom called **me** to the phone. [*Me* tells *whom* Mom called.]
Julia bought sweet potatoes and used **them** to fill the empanadas. [*Them* tells *what* she used.]

An *indirect object* comes between an action verb and a direct object and tells *to whom* or *to what* or *for whom* or *for what*.

EXAMPLES   The hostess handed **her** a name tag. [*Her* tells *to whom* the hostess handed the name tag.]
Mr. Tanaka raises large goldfish; he often feeds **them** rice. [*Them* tells *to what* Mr. Tanaka feeds rice.]

To help you choose the correct pronoun in a compound object, try each form of the pronoun separately in the sentence.

EXAMPLE: The teacher chose Luisa and (*I, me*).
The teacher chose *I.*
The teacher chose *me.*
ANSWER: The teacher chose Luisa and **me.**

☞ **REFERENCE NOTE:** For more information about direct and indirect objects, see pages 474–477.

▶ ORAL   **Using Pronouns as Direct Objects and**
PRACTICE 3   **Indirect Objects**

Read each of the following sentences aloud, stressing the italicized pronouns.

1. I took Joe and *her* to a performance by French mimes.
2. The bus driver let Melba, Joe, and *me* off at the next corner.
3. An usher gave *us* programs.
4. Another usher guided *them* and *me* to our seats.
5. The performers fascinated Melba and *me.*
6. Their costumes delighted the crowd and *her.*
7. No one else impressed Joe and *me* as much as the youngest mime.
8. We watched *her* explore the walls of an invisible room.

▶ EXERCISE 3　**Writing Pronouns Used as Direct Objects and Indirect Objects**

For each blank in the following sentences, give an appropriate pronoun. Use a variety of pronouns, but do not use *you* or *it*.

EXAMPLE　**1.** Have you seen Kim and ____?
　　　　　　1. *her*

1. The manager hired Susana and ____.
2. Lana sent ____ and ____ invitations.
3. We gave Grandpa López and ____ round-trip tickets to Mexico City.
4. The firefighters rescued ____ and ____.
5. Aunt Coretta showed my cousins and ____ a carved mask from Nigeria.
6. The show entertained the children and ____.
7. The waiter served ____ and ____ a variety of dim sum dumplings.
8. Our team chose ____ and ____ as representatives.
9. The election committee nominated Gerry and ____.
10. The clerk gave Misako and ____ the receipt for the paper lanterns.

▶ REVIEW B　**Identifying Correct Pronoun Forms**

For each sentence in the following paragraph, choose the correct form of the pronoun in parentheses.

EXAMPLE　**1.** Paul told Ms. Ésteban that (*he, him*) and
　　　　　　(*I, me*) need a topic for our report.
　　　　　　1. *he, I*

[1] Some of the other students and (*he, him*) thought that there should be more reports on women in American history. [2] (*They, Them*) and their achievements are sometimes overlooked. [3] The picture on the next page, showing Amelia Earhart looking cheerful and confident, interested Paul and (*I, me*). [4] Both (*he, him*) and (*I, me*) were eager to find out more about her contribution to aviation. [5] We learned that it was (*she, her*) who made the

USAGE

first solo flight by a woman across the Atlantic. [6] The fact that Amelia Earhart was the first pilot to fly from Hawaii to California surprised the rest of the class and (*we, us*), too. [7] In 1937, her navigator and (*she, her*) took off in a twin-engine plane for a trip around the world. [8] After (*they, them*) had completed two thirds of the trip, Earhart and her navigator lost contact with radio operators. [9] Neither the plane nor (*they, them*) were ever sighted again. [10] Ms. Ésteban and (*we, us*) are among the many people still puzzling over this mystery.

22d. The *object of a preposition* is in the objective case.

The *object of a preposition* is a noun or a pronoun that follows a preposition. Together, the preposition, its object, and any modifiers of the object make a *prepositional phrase*.

EXAMPLES   **We waited for them.** [*Them* is the object of the preposition *for.*]

The secret is between him and me. [*Him* and *me* are the compound object of the preposition *between.*]

☞ REFERENCE NOTE: For a list of prepositions, see page 460.

▶ ORAL
PRACTICE 4   **Using Pronouns as Objects of Prepositions**

Read each of the following sentences aloud, stressing the italicized prepositions and pronouns.

1. Mr. Torres divided the burritos *among them* and *us.*
2. At the game Maria sat *near him* and *her.*
3. Rose walked *toward* Nell and *me.*
4. Sam stood *between him* and *me.*
5. Mom ordered sandwiches *for* Hannah and *her.*
6. "*Without* Squanto and *me,* the Pilgrims won't last through another winter," thought Samoset.
7. I have read biographies *about him* and Martin Luther King, Jr.
8. David's parents gave a bar mitzvah party *for him.*

▶ EXERCISE 4   **Choosing Correct Pronouns Used as Objects of Prepositions**

For each of the following sentences, choose the correct form of the pronoun in parentheses.

EXAMPLE   **1. Of all the people who traveled with Lewis and Clark, Sacagawea was particularly helpful to (*them, they*).**
   1. *them*

1. Sacagawea's husband, a guide named Toussaint Charbonneau, joined the expedition with (*her, she*) and their newborn baby.
2. The Shoshone were Sacagawea's people, and she longed to return to (*them, they*).
3. Captain Clark soon realized how important she would be to Lewis and (*he, him*).
4. The land they were traveling through was familiar to (*she, her*).
5. Luckily for (*she, her*) and the expedition, they met a group of friendly Shoshone.
6. From (*they, them*), Sacagawea obtained the ponies that Lewis and Clark needed.

7. Sacagawea's baby boy delighted the expedition's leaders, and they took good care of (*he, him*).

8. In fact, Captain Clark made a promise to (*she, her*) and Charbonneau that he would give the boy a good education.

9. At the age of eighteen, the boy befriended a prince and traveled with (*him, he*) in Europe.

10. Although sources disagree about when Sacagawea died, a gravestone for (*she, her*) in Wyoming bears the date April 9, 1884.

▶ EXERCISE 5   **Writing Sentences That Include Pronouns as Objects of Prepositions**

A day in the life of a guide dog is full of responsibilities. A guide dog leads its owner safely *around* obstacles, *through* traffic, *among* crowds, *up* and *down* stairs, *onto* buses, *into* stores, *under* low-hanging awnings, and *along* busy sidewalks. Write five sentences describing the actions of Duchess as she guides Michael through this busy downtown area. In each sentence, use at least one pronoun as the object of a preposition. In two of your sentences, use a pronoun as part of a compound object.

EXAMPLE   **1.** *Duchess noticed a group of teenagers in front of a store and guided Michael around them and their bicycles.*

USAGE

> ▶ REVIEW C   **Identifying Correct Pronoun Forms**

For each of the following sentences, choose the correct form of the pronoun in parentheses. Then tell what part of the sentence each pronoun is: *subject, predicate nominative, direct object, indirect object,* or *object of a preposition.*

EXAMPLE   **1.** My brother Pete and (*I, me*) wanted to know more about Elizabeth Blackwell.
　　　　　　1. *I—subject*

1. Mom told Pete and (*I, me*) that Elizabeth Blackwell was the first woman ever to graduate from medical school in the United States.
2. Geneva College granted (*she, her*) a degree in 1849.
3. At first, no male doctor would let her work for (*he, him*) because she was a woman.
4. Pete and (*I, me*) admire Elizabeth Blackwell for not giving up.
5. She wanted to help the poor and opened her own clinic for (*they, them*).
6. Wealthy citizens were soon supporting (*she, her*) and the clinic with donations.
7. Before long, one of the most talked about topics in medical circles was (*she, her*) and the excellent work she was doing for the poor.
8. Mom and (*we, us*) read more about Dr. Blackwell, and we learned that she opened a medical school just for women.
9. Dr. Blackwell set high standards for students and gave (*they, them*) hard courses of study to complete.
10. Her teaching prepared (*they, them*) so well that many went on to become successful physicians.

USAGE

You and your family are spending the weekend in a large, unfamiliar city. Too excited to sleep, you watch the traffic and the city lights from the hotel window. As you're watching, you notice this person climbing into a taxi on the street below. You wonder why he is out in the rain on such a dark, chilly night. Is he rushing to meet someone? Is he a doctor called to an emergency? Perhaps he is a spy who must get to the airport in a hurry. You decide to write a brief story based on this scene. Imagine who the man is, where he is coming from, and where he is going. In your story, use pronouns in each of the following ways: as a subject, as a predicate nominative, as a direct object, as an indirect object, or as an object of a preposition.

Subject:	a man climbing into a taxi
Audience:	yourself
Purpose:	to write a story about the man

Yvonne Jacquette, Three Taxis (1983). Oil on canvas. Courtesy Brooke Alexander, New York.

Special Pronoun Problems

Who and *Whom*

The pronoun *who* has different forms in the nominative and objective cases. *Who* is the nominative form; *whom* is the objective form.

NOTE: In spoken English, the use of *whom* is becoming less common. In fact, when you are speaking, you may correctly begin any question with *who* regardless of the grammar of the sentence. In written English, however, you should distinguish between *who* and *whom*.

When you need to decide whether to use *who* or *whom* in a question, follow these steps:

STEP 1: Rephrase the question as a statement.
STEP 2: Decide how the pronoun is used in the statement—as subject, predicate nominative, object of the verb, or object of a preposition.
STEP 3: Determine the case of the pronoun according to the rules of standard English.
STEP 4: Select the correct form of the pronoun.

EXAMPLE: (*Who, Whom*) is she?
STEP 1: The statement is *She is* (*who, whom*).
STEP 2: The subject is *she,* the verb is *is,* and the pronoun is the predicate nominative: *She is* (*who, whom*).
STEP 3: A pronoun used as a predicate nominative should be in the nominative case.
STEP 4: The nominative form is *who.*
ANSWER: **Who** is she?

EXAMPLE: (*Who, Whom*) will you invite to the dance?
STEP 1: The statement is *You will invite* (*who, whom*) *to the dance.*
STEP 2: The subject is *you,* and the verb is *will invite.* The pronoun is the direct object of the verb: *You will invite* (*who, whom*).
STEP 3: A pronoun used as a direct object should be in the objective case.
STEP 4: The objective form is *whom.*
ANSWER: **Whom** will you invite to the dance?

USAGE

Choosing *Who* or *Whom*

Read each of the following sentences aloud, stressing the italicized pronouns.

1. *Who* is captain of the football team this year?
2. To *whom* did you give your old skateboard?
3. *Whom* will you call to come and pick us up after band practice?
4. *Who* were the first Americans?
5. In the last play of the game, *who* passed the ball to *whom?*
6. *Who*'s that woman in the green kimono?
7. For *whom* did you buy those flowers?
8. *Who* painted that beautiful still life?

Pronouns with Appositives

Sometimes a pronoun is followed directly by a noun that identifies the pronoun. Such a noun is called an *appositive.* To help you choose which pronoun to use before an appositive, omit the appositive and try each form of the pronoun separately.

EXAMPLE: On Saturdays, (*we, us*) cyclists ride to Mount McCabe and back. [*Cyclists* is the appositive identifying the pronoun.]
We ride to Mount McCabe.
Us ride to Mount McCabe.

ANSWER: On Saturdays, **we** cyclists ride to Mount McCabe and back.

EXAMPLE: The speaker praised (*we, us*) volunteers. [*Volunteers* is the appositive identifying the pronoun.]
The speaker praised *we.*
The speaker praised *us.*

ANSWER: The speaker praised **us** volunteers.

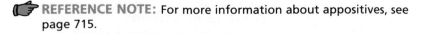 **REFERENCE NOTE:** For more information about appositives, see page 715.

▶ EXERCISE 6   **Choosing Correct Pronouns**

For each of the following sentences, choose the correct form of the pronoun in parentheses.

EXAMPLE   **1.** Hanukkah is always an exciting holiday for (*we, us*) Feldmans.

      1. *us*

1. The famous golfer Lee Trevino is a symbol of pride to (*we, us*) Mexican Americans.
2. (*Who, Whom*) will your brother invite to his birthday party?
3. (*Who, Whom*) will be our substitute teacher while Mr. Chen is away?
4. Miss Jefferson, (*we, us*) students want to thank you for all your help.
5. (*Who, Whom*) has Ms. Spears chosen to serve on the Kite Festival committee?
6. Of the three candidates, (*who, whom*) do you have the most confidence in?
7. (*We, Us*) contestants shook hands warmly.
8. To (*who, whom*) do you wish these flowers sent?
9. (*Who, Whom*) do you admire?
10. (*Who, Whom*) is the leftover macaroni and cheese for?

Reflexive Pronouns

The reflexive pronouns *himself* and *themselves* can be used as objects. Do not use the nonstandard forms *hisself* and *theirselfs* or *theirselves* in place of *himself* and *themselves*.

NONSTANDARD   The secretary voted for hisself in the last election.

    STANDARD   The secretary voted for **himself** in the last election.

NONSTANDARD   The cooks served theirselves some of the won-ton soup.

    STANDARD   The cooks served **themselves** some of the won-ton soup.

▶ EXERCISE 7   **Identifying Correct Pronoun Forms**

For each of the following sentences, choose the correct form of the pronoun in parentheses.

1. Before he started to read, Zack asked (*hisself, himself*) three questions to set his purpose.
2. My little brother often falls down, but he never seems to hurt (*hisself, himself*).
3. The guests helped (*theirselves, themselves*) to the nuts and raisins.
4. John Yellowtail enjoys (*himself, hisself*) making fine silver jewelry.
5. If the early settlers wanted cloth, they had to spin it (*theirselves, themselves*).

▶ REVIEW D   **Identifying Correct Pronoun Forms**

For each of the following sentences, choose the correct form of the pronoun in parentheses.

EXAMPLE   **1. To me, the two most interesting explorers are (*he, him*) and Vasco da Gama.**
          1. he

1. The team captains will be Jack and (*he, him*).
2. Was the joke played on you and (*he, him*)?
3. We were warned by our parents and (*they, them*).
4. The Washington twins and (*I, me*) belong to the same club.
5. Who are (*they, them*)?
6. Pelé and (*he, him*) both played soccer for the New York Cosmos.
7. "What do you think of (*he and I, him and me*)?" I asked.
8. "You and (*he, him*) are improving," they replied.
9. When Miriam Makeba and the troupe of African musicians arrived, we gave (*she and they, her and them*) a party.
10. Do you remember my sister and (*I, me*)?
11. The coach spoke to (*we, us*) players before the game.

12. The finalists in the talent contest are Alfredo, Sylvia, and (*I, me*).
13. Are you and (*she, her*) going to celebrate Kwanzaa this year?
14. Père Toussaint taught my brother and (*I, me*) to play a Cajun fiddle tune.
15. Mom, Andy gave (*himself, hisself*) the biggest piece of banana bread.
16. Both (*he and she, her and him*) have promised to write us this summer.
17. They congratulated (*themselves, theirselves*) on a job well done.
18. Don't leave without (*he and I, him and me*).
19. (*We, Us*) skiers had a beautiful view from the lift.
20. (*Who, Whom*) were you expecting?

WRITING APPLICATION

Using Nouns to Make the Meaning of Pronouns Clear

Using pronouns to take the place of nouns helps you avoid repeating the same nouns over and over. However, it's important not to use so many pronouns that your reader gets confused.

CONFUSING Steve brought two dog biscuits for Duke. As he walked up the steps, he threw them to him. He lay down happily on some towels and ate them. (*Who walked up the steps? What was thrown? To whom was it thrown? Who lay down? What did he eat?*)

CLEAR Steve brought two dog biscuits for Duke. As Steve walked up the steps, he threw both biscuits to the dog. Duke lay down happily on some towels and ate the biscuits.

Be sure that the pronouns you *do* use refer clearly to their antecedents.

USAGE

▶ WRITING ACTIVITY

Your favorite radio station is having a "Create a Radio Show" contest. The show will be produced by and for young people. The station has set aside a half-hour of prime time each week for the winning program. Write a letter to the manager of the station explaining what you would like to include in a radio show. The show can have any format you like. It can be like an existing radio show, or it can be something completely new. In your letter, use a variety of pronouns in the nominative case and the objective case. Be sure to include enough nouns so that the meaning of all your pronouns is clear.

Prewriting Discuss your ideas for a radio program with a group of your classmates. List the kinds of entertainment and information you could present. Above all, think about what *you* would like to hear on the radio. Consider how long each part of your show will be. Remember that you have only thirty minutes each week and that part of that time must be devoted to commercials.

Writing As you write your first draft, follow the format for a business letter. (You will find information about business letters on pages 870–874.) Give specific examples of what you want to do on the show, and give reasons for your choices. Remember that even though your ideas may be very creative, your writing must be formal.

Evaluating and Revising Ask the other group members to read your letter to see if your ideas sound interesting and are clearly stated. Ask them if the relationship between each pronoun and its antecedent is clear. If your meaning is not clear, revise your letter. You may need to include more nouns.

Proofreading and Publishing Reread your letter, and correct any remaining errors in usage, spelling, punctuation, or capitalization. Be sure that you have followed the correct format for a business letter. Also, make sure that you have used all pronouns according to the rules for standard written

English. Your class might want to create a bulletin-board display of the letters, titled "WISH—Imagination Radio." With your teacher's permission, the class might vote on the best idea for a show and then produce and tape the pilot episode.

Review: Posttest

USAGE

Correcting Errors In Pronoun Forms

Most of the following sentences contain errors in the use of pronoun forms. For each sentence, identify the error and give the correct pronoun form. If a sentence is correct, write C.

EXAMPLE 1. The Garcia children and them grew up together In Texas.
   1. *them—they*

1. Omar and him offered us some *pita,* a Middle Eastern bread.
2. Us basketball players know the value of good sneakers.
3. The computer experts in our class are Rosalinda and her.
4. There's more than a three-year age difference between Edward and I.
5. Pablo and me are planning to visit the Andes Mountains someday.
6. At Passover, my grandparents make gefilte fish and other traditional foods for my cousins and I.
7. Give Suki and him this invitation to the Japanese tea ceremony.
8. Josh made hisself a bookcase in industrial arts class.

USAGE

9. Two angry hornets chased Earline and she all the way home.
10. The first actors on stage were Jesse and him.
11. Mr. Mendez and us organized a debate about the rights of students.
12. Will you attend the rally with Dominick and me?
13. I helped Kimberly and they with their play about Hiawatha.
14. Jeannette and her know a great deal about Greek myths.
15. The hickory smoke smelled good to we campers.
16. The only seventh-graders in the marching band are Bianca and me.
17. Liang was telling them and me about his birthplace in Hong Kong.
18. Julia and them learned how to use hot wax to make batik patterns on cloth.
19. During most of the marathon, Lionel ran just behind Jim and she.
20. Thomas asked Marvella and he if they wanted to join a gospel chorus.

23 USING MODIFIERS CORRECTLY

Comparison and Placement

Diagnostic Test

A. Correcting Errors in the Use of Modifiers

The following sentences contain errors in the use of modifiers. Rewrite each sentence, correcting the misuse of the modifier in that sentence.

EXAMPLE **1.** Linen feels more rougher than silk.
1. *Linen feels rougher than silk.*

1. These Hawaiian shirts don't have no pockets.
2. This ring is the most expensive of the two.
3. That striped tie would go good with a white shirt.
4. Is a ticket to Mexico more cheaper than a ticket to Canada?
5. Orange juice tastes more sweetly than grapefruit juice.

6. What is the most funniest thing that ever happened to you?
7. I can't hardly take another step.
8. My uncle thinks that Stevie Wonder sings more well than Ray Charles does.
9. No one is courteouser than Rosa.
10. Ted felt calmly during the test on Greek mythology.

B. Correcting Misplaced and Dangling Modifiers

Each of the following sentences contains a misplaced or dangling modifier. Revise each sentence so that it is clear and correct.

EXAMPLE   1. Hidden in his back pocket, Delbert found the missing ticket.
   1. *Delbert found the missing ticket hidden in his back pocket.*

11. The famous explorer described being attacked by a baboon in today's assembly.
12. Pam examined a plant cell looking through the microscope.
13. Juan read the poem to the class that he had found.
14. My sister promised on Sunday she would take me fishing.
15. Black Hawk was a chief of the Sauk people born in Illinois.
16. Confused, the streets in the neighborhood all looked the same.
17. My favorite character in this African folk tale that outwits all its enemies is a rabbit.
18. A bird landed on the windowsill with a bright red beak.
19. Skateboarding down the street, a large dog chased my brother.
20. The books are now used by many young readers that we donated to the library.

Comparison of Adjectives and Adverbs

A *modifier* is a word, a phrase, or a clause that describes another word or limits the meaning of the word. The two kinds of modifiers–adjectives and adverbs—may be used to compare things. In making comparisons, adjectives and adverbs take different forms. The specific form that is used depends upon how many things are being compared. The different forms of comparison are called *degrees of comparison.*

23a. The three degrees of comparison of modifiers are the *positive*, the *comparative*, and the *superlative.*

(1) The *positive degree* is used when only one thing is being described.

EXAMPLES This suitcase is **heavy**.
Luís **cheerfully** began the job.

(2) The *comparative degree* is used when two things are being compared.

EXAMPLES My suitcase is **heavier** than yours.
He began to talk **more cheerfully** about his plans.

(3) The *superlative degree* is used when three or more things are being compared.

EXAMPLES Sylvia's suitcase is the **heaviest** of all.
Of all the boys, Luís worked at the task **most cheerfully**.

NOTE: In conversation, you may hear and use expressions such as *Put your best foot forward* and *May the best team win*. This use of the superlative is acceptable in spoken English. However, in your writing for school and other formal occasions, you should generally follow the rules above.

Regular Comparison

Most one-syllable modifiers form their comparative and superlative degrees by adding *–er* and *–est*.

POSITIVE	COMPARATIVE	SUPERLATIVE
close	closer	closest
slow	slower	slowest
straight	straighter	straightest
sly	slier	sliest

Notice that both adjectives and adverbs form their degrees of comparison in the same way.

Some two-syllable modifiers form their comparative and superlative degrees by adding *–er* and *–est*. Other two-syllable modifiers form their comparative and superlative degrees by using *more* and *most*.

POSITIVE	COMPARATIVE	SUPERLATIVE
simple	simpler	simplest
easy	easier	easiest
jealous	more jealous	most jealous
swiftly	more swiftly	most swiftly

When you are unsure about which way a two-syllable modifier forms its degrees of comparison, look up the word in a dictionary.

 REFERENCE NOTE: For guidelines on how to spell words when adding *–er* or *–est*, see page 771. For a discussion of the information included in dictionary entries, see pages 856–858.

Modifiers that have three or more syllables form the comparative degree by using *more* and the superlative degree by using *most*.

POSITIVE	COMPARATIVE	SUPERLATIVE
powerful	more powerful	most powerful
illegible	more illegible	most illegible
joyfully	more joyfully	most joyfully
attractively	more attractively	most attractively

USAGE

EXERCISE 1 **Forming the Degrees of Comparison of Modifiers**

Give the forms for the comparative and superlative degrees of the following modifiers. Use a dictionary if necessary.

EXAMPLE **1.** light
1. *lighter; lightest*

1. near
2. proud
3. carefully
4. honestly
5. small
6. tiny
7. timidly
8. enthusiastically
9. safe
10. shady

To show decreasing comparisons, all modifiers form the comparative degree by using *less* and the superlative degree by using *least*.

POSITIVE	COMPARATIVE	SUPERLATIVE
sharp	less sharp	least sharp
costly	less costly	least costly
often	less often	least often
frequently	less frequently	least frequently

Irregular Comparison

The comparative and superlative degrees of some modifiers are not formed by using the regular methods.

POSITIVE	COMPARATIVE	SUPERLATIVE
bad	worse	worst
far	farther	farthest
good	better	best
well	better	best
many	more	most
much	more	most

▶ REVIEW A

Writing Comparative and Superlative Forms of Modifiers

Write the form of the italicized adjective or adverb that will correctly fill the blank in each of the following sentences. You may use a dictionary.

EXAMPLE **1.** *unusual* The Corn Palace in Mitchell, South Dakota, is one of the ____ buildings in the United States.
1. *most unusual*

1. *big* The Corn Palace is ____ than I thought it would be.

2. *pretty* People in Mitchell try to make each year's Corn Palace ____ than the one before.

3. *fresh* The building looks the ____ in September after new corn and grasses are put on it.

4. *easy* Some workers find it ____ to saw and nail the corn to panels while others prefer to hang the panels on the building.

5. *good* I couldn't decide which of the huge corn murals on the Corn Palace I liked ____.

6. *mysterious* The mural of the dancing figure was the ____ one to me.

7. *famous* Until his death in 1983, Mitchell's ____ artist, Oscar Howe, helped to design and paint these murals.

8. *interesting* The life of this Sioux artist is the ____ story I've ever heard.

9. *slowly*   My parents walked ___ around the Corn Palace than I did and studied every design.

10. *far*   The family from Mexico traveled ___ than we did to see the Corn Palace.

Special Problems in Using Modifiers

23b.   Use *good* to modify a noun or a pronoun. Use *well* to modify a verb.

EXAMPLES   The weather was **good** on the day of the match. [*Good* modifies the noun *weather.*]
If you like pears, here is a **good** one. [*Good* modifies the pronoun *one.*]
The trees are producing **well** this fall. [*Well* modifies the verb phrase *are producing.*]

Good should not be used to modify a verb.

NONSTANDARD   Both teams played good.
STANDARD   Both teams played **well.**

👉 **REFERENCE NOTE:** For a discussion of standard and nonstandard English, see page 387.

Although *well* is usually used as an adverb, *well* may also be used as an adjective meaning "in good health" or "healthy."

EXAMPLES Mom feels quite **well** today. [Meaning "in good health," *well* modifies *Mom.*]

👉 REFERENCE NOTE: For more about *good* and *well,* see page 658.

23c. Use adjectives, not adverbs, after linking verbs.

Linking verbs are often followed by predicate adjectives modifying the subject.

EXAMPLES Ingrid looked **sleepy** [not *sleepily*] this morning. [The predicate adjective *sleepy* modifies the subject *Ingrid.*]
Kadeem felt **uncertain** [not *uncertainly*] about the race. [The predicate adjective *uncertain* modifies the subject *Kadeem.*]

NOTE: Some linking verbs can also be used as action verbs. As action verbs they may be modified by adverbs.

EXAMPLES Ingrid looked **sleepily** at the clock. [*Sleepily* modifies the action verb *looked.*]
Kadeem felt his way **uncertainly** along the hall. [*Uncertainly* modifies the action verb *felt.*]

👉 REFERENCE NOTE: For a list of linking verbs, see page 448.

▶ EXERCISE 2 **Using Adjectives and Adverbs Correctly**

Choose the adjective or adverb in parentheses that will make the sentence correct.

EXAMPLE **1.** John seems (*nervous, nervously*) about his speech.
1. *nervous*

1. When we came into the house after ice-skating, the fire felt (*good, well*).
2. The wind blew (*fierce, fiercely*) all night.

3. Tino looked (*good, well*) after his trip to Mexico.
4. We moved (*slow, slowly*) along the trail.
5. Venus looks (*beautiful, beautifully*) tonight.
6. Liang cooked a (*good, well*) meal of vegetables, shrimp, and noodles.
7. We (*sure, surely*) enjoyed seeing you again.
8. We checked the boat (*close, closely*) for leaks.
9. A cup of soup tastes (*good, well*) on a cold day.
10. The ball was caught (*easy, easily*) by the shortstop.

23d. Avoid double comparisons.

A ***double comparison*** is the use of both *–er* and *more* (less) or *–est* and *most* (least) to form a comparison. When you make a comparison, use only one form, not both.

NONSTANDARD   This is Kathleen Battle's most finest performance.
STANDARD   This is Kathleen Battle's **finest** performance.

NONSTANDARD   His hair is more curlier than his sister's.
STANDARD   His hair is **curlier** than his sister's.

 EXERCISE 3   **Revising Sentences to Eliminate Double Comparisons**

For each of the following sentences, identify the incorrect modifier. Then give the correct form of the modifier.

EXAMPLES   **1.** I have been studying more harder lately.
1. *more harder—harder*

2. Frederick Douglass was one of the most brilliantest speakers against slavery.
2. *most brilliantest—most brilliant*

1. Sunday was more rainier than Saturday.
2. That is the most saddest story I have ever heard.
3. Are you exercising more longer than you used to?
4. Native arctic peoples have learned to survive in the most coldest weather.
5. He has a more stronger backhand than his brother.

USAGE

Double Negatives

23e. Avoid the use of double negatives.

A *double negative* is the use of two negative words to express one negative idea.

Common Negative Words			
barely	never	none	nothing
hardly	no	no one	nowhere
neither	nobody	not (–n't)	scarcely

NONSTANDARD	We couldn't hardly move in the subway car.
STANDARD	We **could** hardly move in the subway car.
NONSTANDARD	Yolanda didn't eat no breakfast this morning.
STANDARD	Yolanda didn't eat **any** breakfast this morning.
STANDARD	Yolanda ate **no** breakfast this morning.

▶ EXERCISE 4   **Revising Sentences by Eliminating Double Negatives**

Revise each of the following sentences to eliminate the double negative.

EXAMPLE   **1.** I couldn't find no one to go camping with.
    1. *I couldn't find anyone to go camping with.*
            or
    I could find no one to go camping with.

1. I didn't see no one I knew at the game.
2. Early Spanish explorers searched that area of Florida for gold, but they didn't find none.
3. We couldn't hardly hear the guest speaker.
4. The cafeteria didn't serve nothing I like today.
5. Double negatives don't have no place in standard English.

USAGE

WRITING APPLICATION

Using Clear Comparisons in a Letter

You use comparisons every day to describe changes in the world and in yourself. For instance, your hairstyle may be *shorter* (or *longer*) this year than it was last year. An intersection near your school may be *more dangerous* in the morning than in the afternoon. Complete comparisons help you express your thoughts and observations clearly.

INCOMPLETE   The library seems noisier today. [noisier than what?]

COMPLETE   The library seems noisier today than it was yesterday.

 **WRITING ACTIVITY**

An anonymous donor has given a large sum of money for improvements to your school. The school's administrators have invited students to suggest practical uses for the money. Write a letter to the administrators describing the improvements you'd like to see. Use at least three comparative and two superlative forms of adjectives and adverbs in your writing.

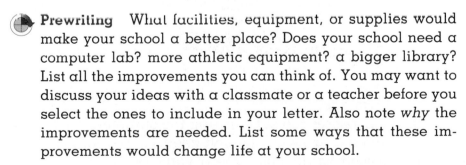

Prewriting   What facilities, equipment, or supplies would make your school a better place? Does your school need a computer lab? more athletic equipment? a bigger library? List all the improvements you can think of. You may want to discuss your ideas with a classmate or a teacher before you select the ones to include in your letter. Also note *why* the improvements are needed. List some ways that these improvements would change life at your school.

Writing   As you write your first draft, use your list to help you make clear and accurate comparisons. Keep your audience in mind. The administrators need practical suggestions for how to spend the money. Let them know exactly what improvements your school needs and why. For more about writing persuasion, see Chapter 8.

Evaluating and Revising Read your letter to a parent or other adult to see if your arguments are convincing. Add, delete, or rearrange details to make your letter more interesting and effective. Finally, be sure you've used the correct comparative and superlative forms of adjectives and adverbs.

 Proofreading Check the form of your letter to make sure it follows the guidelines for business letters (see pages 870–874). Be sure you've used at least three comparative and two superlative forms of adjectives and adverbs. Read through your letter a final time to catch any errors in spelling, grammar, usage, or punctuation.

▶ REVIEW B   **Using Modifiers Correctly**

Most of the following sentences contain errors in the use of modifiers. Revise each incorrect sentence to eliminate the error. If a sentence is correct, write *C*.

EXAMPLE   **1.** My cold is worst today than it was yesterday.
          1. *My cold is worse today than it was yesterday.*

1. She is the funnier of the two comedians.
2. Kendo, a Japanese martial art, is more gracefuller than many other sports.
3. No one in our class can play chess as good as Sylvia Yee.
4. Time passes too slow during the summer.
5. After a long swim, she felt good.
6. I wasn't hardly able to hear you.
7. Which of the twins is strongest?
8. Some people don't seem to have no control over their tempers.
9. He hardly ever visits us.
10. Of all the folk dances my grandfather taught me, the polka is the most funnest.

REVIEW C

Writing Sentences with Correct Forms of Modifiers

When you watch television, you probably don't think about how a show is created. This diagram of a TV studio shows some of the jobs and equipment involved in producing a show. Which of these jobs might you be interested in doing? Would you rather be in front of the camera or behind the scenes? Imagine that you are working in this studio. Write five sentences describing what you do or telling about the show or your coworkers. Use five of the following items correctly in your sentences. Underline each one you use.

- the superlative of *new*
- the comparative of *good*
- a linking verb and a predicate adjective
- *barely* to express a negative idea
- the positive of *well*
- the superlative of *loud*
- the comparative of *popular*
- a decreasing comparison of *costly*

EXAMPLE   **1.** *The new spotlight is <u>better</u> than the old one.*

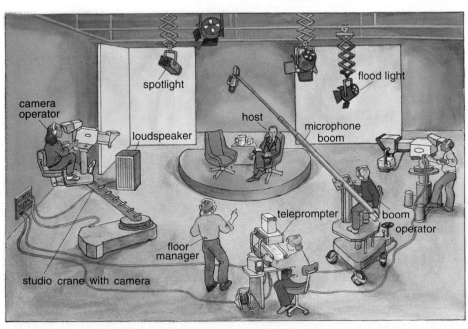

Placement of Modifiers

23f. Place modifying words, phrases, and clauses as close as possible to the words they modify.

Notice how the meaning of this sentence changes when the position of the phrase *from Akron* changes.

EXAMPLES   One ballplayer **from Akron** gave a TV interview for his fans. [The phrase modifies *ballplayer.*]
One ballplayer gave a TV interview for his fans **from Akron**. [The phrase modifies *fans.*]
From Akron, one ballplayer gave a TV interview for his fans. [The phrase modifies *gave.*]

A modifier that seems to modify the wrong word in a sentence is called a ***misplaced modifier.*** A modifier that does not clearly modify another word in a sentence is called a ***dangling modifier.***

MISPLACED   Amazed, the dinosaur exhibit thrilled my brother and his friends.
CORRECT   **Amazed,** my brother and his friends were thrilled with the dinosaur exhibit.

DANGLING   Before moving to Philadelphia, Mexico City had been their home.
CORRECT   **Before moving to Philadelphia,** they had lived in Mexico City.

Prepositional Phrases

A *prepositional phrase* begins with a preposition and ends with a noun or a pronoun.

☞ REFERENCE NOTE: For more information about prepositional phrases, see pages 491–497.

A prepositional phrase used as an adjective should be placed directly after the word it modifies.

MISPLACED   The hat belongs to that girl with blue feathers.
CORRECT   The hat **with blue feathers** belongs to that girl.

A prepositional phrase used as an adverb should be placed near the word it modifies.

MISPLACED   She read that a new restaurant had opened in today's newspaper.

CORRECT   **In today's newspaper** she read that a new restaurant had opened.

Avoid placing a prepositional phrase so that it seems to modify either of two words. Place the phrase so that it clearly modifies the word you intend it to modify.

MISPLACED   Manuel said in the afternoon he would call Janet. [Does the phrase modify *said* or *would call*?]

CORRECT   Manuel said he would call Janet **in the afternoon.** [The phrase modifies *would call*.]

CORRECT   **In the afternoon** Manuel said he would call Janet. [The phrase modifies *said*.]

USAGE

▶ EXERCISE 5   **Revising Sentences with Misplaced and Dangling Modifiers**

The meaning of each of the following sentences is not clear and sensible because the modifier is misplaced or dangling. Decide where the modifier belongs; then revise the sentence. [Hint: You may need to add, delete, or rearrange words.]

EXAMPLE   **1.** In the United States, Zora Neale Hurston grew up in the first self-governed black township.

1. *Zora Neale Hurston grew up in the first self-governed black township in the United States.*

1. That woman was out walking her dog in high heels and a tweed suit this morning.
2. The poster caught my eye on the wall.
3. Hoy taught us with chopsticks how to scoop up rice.
4. Our teacher said on Monday the class would put on a play.
5. Don't forget to take the box to the store with the empty bottles.
6. We saw José Clemente Orozco's beautiful murals on vacation in Guadalajara.

7. Exhausted, an acceptable campsite was finally found.
8. A beautiful Bolivian weaving hangs on our living room wall from the town of Potolo.
9. Did you find the kimonos worn by your grandmother in that old trunk?
10. Surprised, it was hard for little Timmy to decide which birthday gift to open first.

▶ EXERCISE 6   **Placing Prepositional Phrases Correctly**

Rewrite each of the following sentences, adding the prepositional phrase given in parentheses. Be careful to place each prepositional phrase near the word or words it modifies.

EXAMPLE   1. Many paintings show strange, fantastical scenes. (by Marc Chagall)
1. *Many paintings by Marc Chagall show strange, fantastical scenes.*

1. Chagall's *The Green Violinist* contains many delightful mysteries and surprises. (for the eye and mind)
2. As you can see in the painting, a gigantic violinist sits among the buildings of a small village. (with a green face and hand)
3. Dark squares look just like the windows of the houses. (on the musician's pants)
4. A man waves to the violinist, and a dog taller than a house seems to smile at the music it hears. (above the clouds)
5. As you look at the painting's bright colors, perhaps you can almost hear the enchanting music. (of the green violinist)

USAGE

Participial Phrases

A *participial phrase* consists of a verb form—either a present participle or a past participle—and its related words. A participial phrase modifies a noun or a pronoun.

☞ **REFERENCE NOTE:** For more information about participial phrases, see page 504.

Like a prepositional phrase, a participial phrase should be placed as close as possible to the word it modifies.

EXAMPLES **Walking to school,** Celia and James found a wallet. [The participial phrase modifies *Celia and James.*]
I. M. Pei, **born in China,** is a gifted architect. [The participial phrase modifies *I. M. Pei.*]

☞ **REFERENCE NOTE:** For more about using commas with participial phrases, see pages 713 and 720.

A participial phrase that is not placed next to the noun or pronoun that it modifies is a *misplaced modifier.*

MISPLACED **Stolen from the media center,** the deputies found the video recorder. [Were the deputies stolen from the media center?]
CORRECT The deputies found the video recorder **stolen from the media center.**

MISPLACED **Sleeping on the roof,** I saw the neighbor's cat. [Was I sleeping on the roof?]
CORRECT I saw the neighbor's cat **sleeping on the roof.**

MISPLACED We're used to the noise **living by the airport.** [Was the noise living by the airport?]
CORRECT **Living by the airport,** we're used to the noise.

A participial phrase that does not clearly and sensibly modify a word in the sentence is a *dangling modifier.*

DANGLING **Cleaning the attic,** an old trunk was found.
CORRECT **Cleaning the attic, we** found an old trunk.

USAGE

USAGE

▶ EXERCISE 7   **Placing Participles and Participial Phrases Correctly**

Rewrite each of the following sentences, adding the participles or participial phrases given in parentheses. Be sure to use commas to set off participial phrases that begin or interrupt your sentences.

1. I will be working at the garden center near my house. (*beginning next week*)
2. Our new kitten crawled under the sofa. (*exploring*)
3. By mistake, we sat on the swings. (*freshly painted*)
4. Lucy helped her brother find the books. (*lost*)
5. Josie and Fred passed the playground. (*walking through the park*)

▶ EXERCISE 8   **Revising Sentences with Misplaced and Dangling Participial Phrases**

Revise all sentences that contain misplaced or dangling participial phrases. [Hint: You will need to add, delete, or rearrange some words.] Participial phrases that begin or interrupt sentences should be set off by commas. If a sentence is correct, write C.

EXAMPLE   **1.** Made from matzo meal, Rachel shapes tasty dumplings.
           1. *Rachel shapes tasty dumplings made from matzo meal.*

1. Pacing in its cage, I watched the lion.
2. Talking on the telephone, Lori did not hear the doorbell.
3. Exploring the cave, a new tunnel was discovered.
4. Wearing a bright orange suit and floppy yellow shoes, the circus featured a clown.
5. Filled with daisies, the girls walked through the field.
6. Reading his part, the actor felt nervous.
7. The turkey was large enough for three families stuffed with sage and bread crumbs.

8. Tired from the long walk through the snow, food and rest were welcomed.
9. Checking the shelves, Judy found the books she needed.
10. Perched in their nest, we saw the young birds.

Adjective Clauses

An *adjective clause* modifies a noun or a pronoun. Most adjective clauses begin with a relative pronoun—*that, which, who, whom,* or *whose.*

☞ REFERENCE NOTE: For more information about adjective clauses, see pages 520–521.

Like adjective phrases, adjective clauses should be placed directly after the words they modify.

MISPLACED   The Labor Day picnic in the park **that we had** was fun. [Did we have the park?]

   CORRECT   The Labor Day picnic **that we had** in the park was fun.

MISPLACED   The girls thanked their coach **who had won the relay race.** [Did the coach win the relay race?]

   CORRECT   The girls **who had won the relay race** thanked their coach.

▸ EXERCISE 9   **Revising Sentences with Misplaced Clause Modifiers**

Revise each of the following sentences by placing the adjective clause near the word it should modify.

EXAMPLE   1. I showed the fabric to my sister that was made in Kenya.
           1. *I showed the fabric that was made in Kenya to my sister.*

1. The students received an A who made the first presentation.
2. The kitten belongs to my neighbor that is on the branch.

USAGE

3. My friend Beverly visited me who lives in Sarasota, Florida.
4. The doctor said that the triplets were healthy who examined them.
5. The cleanup program was supported by all of the students that the president of the seventh-grade class suggested.

USAGE

PICTURE THIS

You have just witnessed this accident. No one has been hurt, but both drivers are very upset. Each driver insists that the other is to blame. Because you are a witness, the police would like you to describe what happened. Write a brief description of what you saw up to the time of the accident and when the accident occurred. In your description, use at least five adjective clauses.

Subject: traffic accident
Audience: police officers
Purpose: to give an accurate description

▶ REVIEW D　　**Correcting Errors in the Use of Modifiers**

Each of the following sentences contains an error in the form or placement of a modifier. Revise each sentence by changing the form of a modifier or by adding, deleting, or rearranging words.

EXAMPLE　**1.** I have never been more happier in my life.
　　　　　1. *I have never been happier in my life.*

1. My stepsister plays both soccer and softball, but she likes soccer best.
2. The waiter brought plates to Terrell and me piled high with spaghetti and meat sauce.
3. Frustrated, her locker just would not open!
4. Barking and growling, the stranger was frightened by the dogs.
5. The German cuckoo clock still runs good after all these years.
6. I didn't do too bad on the geography quiz this morning.
7. Our puppy is much more playfuller than our older dog is.
8. We drove slow past the duck pond to see if any new ducklings had hatched.
9. They never did find no sponsor for their team.
10. The record was the soundtrack of the movie that we heard.

▶ REVIEW E　　**Proofreading Sentences for Correct Use of Modifiers**

Each of the following sentences contains an error in the form or placement of a modifier. Revise each sentence by changing the form of a modifier or by adding, deleting, or rearranging words.

EXAMPLE　**1.** Of all the women featured in this book, Dolores S. Atencio is the one I admire more.
　　　　　1. *Of all the women featured in this book, Dolores S. Atencio is the one I admire most.*

1. Her mother thought that a law career would offer her daughter the most brightest future.
2. Ms. Atencio always knew she would become a lawyer, but she didn't never expect to be so successful.
3. Looking ahead to college and law school, her grades in high school were excellent.
4. She helped to launch Denver's first bilingual radio station along with two other Hispanic American women in 1985.
5. Ms. Atencio felt proudly about helping to organize Colorado's first minority women lawyers' conference.
6. She decided to run for president of the Hispanic National Bar Association (HNBA), receiving encouragement from a friend.
7. Serving as president of HNBA, the legal rights of Hispanic Americans were her main focus.
8. In 1991 she was named one of the most outstanding Hispanic women by *Hispanic Business Magazine.*
9. She also was given the Outstanding Young Woman Award from the City of Denver which she received for all the time she had devoted to community service.
10. Although she is proud of her accomplishments, Ms. Atencio feels really well when she is spending time with her family.

Review: Posttest

A. Revising Sentences by Correcting Errors in the Use of Modifiers

Most of the following sentences contain errors in the form or placement of modifiers. If a sentence has an error, revise the sentence by adding, deleting, or rearranging words. If a sentence is correct, write *C.*

EXAMPLE **1.** There wasn't nothing missing.
1. *There wasn't anything missing.*
or
There was nothing missing.

1. Please weigh both packages to see which of them is heaviest.
2. Alarmed, the wildfire started to spread quickly toward our camp.
3. Did you read that Eduardo Mata received an award in the newspaper?
4. We pass my aunt and uncle's restaurant walking to school.
5. The bean soup tasted good.
6. I think the play *Fiddler on the Roof* is better than the movie.
7. Reading a magazine, my cat jumped up in my lap.
8. Jason tried to push the huge desk but couldn't hardly move it.
9. The balloons startled the younger children when they burst.
10. A jet taking off can sound more noisier than a jackhammer.

B. Revising Sentences by Correcting Errors in the Use of Modifiers

Most of the following sentences contain errors in the form or placement of modifiers. If a sentence has an error, revise the sentence by adding, deleting, or rearranging words. If a sentence is correct, write C.

EXAMPLE **1.** This gold and silver French franc is the most prettiest coin I've seen.
1. *This gold and silver French franc is the prettiest coin I've seen.*

11. Surprised, my coin collection interested a local coin dealer.
12. He examined two old Greek coins but couldn't see no date on them.

13. The shinier coin looked newer.
14. That coin turned out to be the oldest of the two.
15. I showed one coin to the dealer valued at nearly twenty dollars.
16. He said he couldn't hardly pay more than fifteen dollars for it.
17. If I could have bargained good, I might have gotten more for it.
18. Those two coins come from Ireland that have harp designs on them.
19. Collecting coins, my knowledge about other countries and peoples increases.
20. I polished my Saudi Arabian fifty-halala piece good so that I could see the Arabic writing on it.

24 A GLOSSARY OF USAGE

Common Usage Problems

Diagnostic Test

Revising Sentences by Correcting Errors in Usage

In each of the following sets of sentences, one sentence contains an error in usage. Choose the letter of the sentence that contains an error. Revise the sentence, using standard English.

EXAMPLE **1. a.** Bring the books here.
b. I was somewhat embarrassed.
c. Please return these here books.
1. *c. Please return these books.*

1. **a.** Who's book is it?
   b. There is your hat.
   c. He is the man who owns the shop.
2. **a.** I would of gone with you.
   b. You're my friend.
   c. They're here.

3. **a.** These kinds of games are challenging.
   b. They bought themselves new shoes.
   c. Can you fix this here shelf?

4. **a.** I use to know the title of this song.
   b. That headdress looks as if it is genuine.
   c. Set the bucket down on the porch.

5. **a.** We sat on straw mats called *tatami*.
   b. That fruit salad is real tasty.
   c. You ought to try it.

6. **a.** If we had liked it, we would have bought it.
   b. The cat jumped off of the chair.
   c. Please wait outside the office.

7. **a.** She looks like her sister.
   b. They went somewhere together.
   c. He acts like he is tired.

8. **a.** I made less mistakes this time.
   b. My brother is learning how to dive.
   c. Jack is somewhat nervous.

9. **a.** I like this type of pen.
   b. I know how come he won.
   c. Marco served himself some meatloaf.

10. **a.** The monkey scratched its head.
    b. It's not here.
    c. We had ought to check the weather report.

11. **a.** Our chorus sang good.
    b. Clog dancing gives you a good workout.
    c. Sofía plays the castanets well.

12. **a.** I looked everywhere.
    b. The balloon burst.
    c. Bring the box over there.

13. **a.** You should have been there.
    b. Tom and Sabrena they are in my English class.
    c. It's been a cold winter.

14. **a.** We shared the popcorn among the three of us.
    b. From here she looks like Karen.
    c. Where is the lake at?

15. **a.** Bill looks as if he is upset.
    b. The milk smells badly.
    c. We had scarcely enough books for everyone.

16. **a.** They sang a lot of ballads.
    b. The meal was alright.
    c. Alan had already left.
17. **a.** Everyone can go accept Ramón.
    b. She worked for half an hour.
    c. I rode an elephant.
18. **a.** Marco grew up in Honduras.
    b. The musicians were already to begin playing.
    c. They divided the task among the six workers.
19. **a.** Use less water in the mixture.
    b. Music makes me feel good.
    c. We looked everywheres for red suede shoes.
20. **a.** That kimono looks good on you.
    b. Where did you get them shoes?
    c. They raised the price of stamps.

This chapter contains an alphabetical list, or glossary, of many common problems in English usage. You will notice throughout the chapter that some examples are labeled *standard* or *nonstandard*. **Standard English** is the most widely accepted form of English. It is used in *formal* situations, such as speeches and compositions for school, and in *informal* situations, such as conversations and everyday writing. **Nonstandard English** is language that does not follow the rules and guidelines of standard English.

☞ REFERENCE NOTE: For more discussion of standard and nonstandard English, see page 387.

a, an Use *a* before words beginning with a consonant sound. Use *an* before words beginning with a vowel sound. Keep in mind that the *sound*, not the actual letter, that a word begins with determines whether *a* or *an* should be used.

EXAMPLES They are building **a** hospital near our house.
I bought **a** one-way ticket.
I would like **an** orange.
We worked for **an** hour.

USAGE

accept, except *Accept* is a verb; it means "to receive." *Except* may be either a verb or a preposition. As a verb, it means "to leave out." As a preposition, *except* means "excluding."

EXAMPLES   Ann **accepted** the gift.
No one will be **excepted** from writing a research paper.
All my friends will be there **except** Jorge.

ain't Avoid this word in speaking and writing; it is nonstandard English.

all right Used as an adjective, *all right* means "satisfactory" or "unhurt." Used as an adverb, *all right* means "well enough." *All right* should always be written as two words.

EXAMPLES   Your science project looks **all right** to me. [adjective]
Judy cut her toe, but she is **all right** now. [adjective]
I did **all right** in the drama club tryouts. [adverb]

a lot *A lot* should always be written as two words.

EXAMPLE   I have read **a lot** of Native American folk tales.

already, all ready *Already* means "previously." *All ready* means "completely prepared."

EXAMPLES   By the time my mother came home, I had **already** cooked dinner.
The students were **all ready** for the trip.

among See **between, among.**

anywheres, everywheres, nowheres, somewheres Use these words without the final –*s*.

EXAMPLE   Did you go **anywhere** [not *anywheres*] today?

as See **like, as.**

as if See **like, as if, as though.**

at Do not use *at* after *where.*

> NONSTANDARD   Where are the Persian miniatures at?
> STANDARD   Where are the Persian miniatures?

bad, badly *Bad* is an adjective. It modifies nouns and pronouns. *Badly* is an adverb. It modifies verbs, adjectives, and adverbs.

> EXAMPLES   **The fruit tastes bad.** [The predicate adjective *bad* modifies *fruit.*]
> **Don't treat him badly.** [The adverb *badly* modifies the verb *do treat.*]

NOTE: The expression *feel badly* has become acceptable, though ungrammatical, informal English.

> INFORMAL   Carl felt badly about losing the race.
> FORMAL   Carl felt **bad** about losing the race.

USAGE

▶ EXERCISE 1   **Identifying Correct Usage**

Choose the correct word or words in parentheses in each of the following sentences.

> EXAMPLE   **1.** Navajo people came to the Southwest from (*somewhere, somewheres*) in the North.
> **1.** *somewhere*

1. One group of Navajos settled in the region where the Pueblo people (*lived, lived at*).
2. The Pueblo people were (*already, all ready*) farming and living in permanent dwellings by the time the Navajos arrived.
3. The Navajos may have (*excepted, accepted*) the practice of sand painting from the Pueblos and adapted it to fit their own customs.
4. When the Navajo artists are (*all ready, already*) to begin a sand painting, they gather in a circle, as shown in the picture on the next page.
5. In creating a sand painting, (*a, an*) artist receives directions from the singer who leads the ceremony.

USAGE

6. For example, the painter might make a certain design when things are not (*all right, alright*) in the community.
7. The Navajo sand painter may also use this art to help someone who is injured or feeling (*badly, bad*).
8. Because sand paintings used in healing ceremonies are swept away at the end of each ceremony, the designs are recorded nowhere (*accept, except*) in the artist's imagination.
9. However, the patterns used in sand painting (*ain't, aren't*) limited to this art form.
10. Variations of the sacred designs can be found almost (*anywheres, anywhere*) on items that the Navajos make.

between, among Use *between* when referring to two things at a time, even though they may be part of a group consisting of more than two.

EXAMPLES   Who sits **between** you and Sue?

Between the last three track meets, I trained very hard. [Although there were more than two meets, the training occurred between any two of them.]

There isn't much difference **between** these three brands of juice. [Although there are more than two brands, each one is being compared with the others separately.]

Use *among* when referring to a group rather than to separate individuals.

EXAMPLES   We divided the tacos and burritos **among** the five of us.
There was much disagreement **among** the governors about the new tax plan. [The governors are thought of as a group.]

bring, take   *Bring* means "to come carrying something." *Take* means "to go carrying something." Think of *bring* as related to *come, take* as related to *go.*

EXAMPLES   **Bring** that chair here.
Now **take** this one over there.

bust, busted   Avoid using these words as verbs. Use a form of either *burst* or *break.*

EXAMPLES   The pipe **burst** [not *busted*] after the storm.
The Japanese raku ware vase **broke** [not *busted*] when it fell.

can't hardly, can't scarcely   The words *hardly* and *scarcely* are negative words. They should never be used with another negative word.

EXAMPLES   I **can** [not *can't*] **hardly** wait to hear your new CD.
We **had** [not *hadn't*] **scarcely** enough food for everyone at the Juneteenth picnic.

☞ REFERENCE NOTE: For more on double negatives, see page 636.

could of   Do not write *of* with the helping verb *could.* Write *could have.* Also avoid *ought to of, should of, would of, might of,* and *must of.*

EXAMPLES   Abdul could **have** [not *of*] helped us.
You should **have** [not *of*] hung the piñata higher.

don't, doesn't   See page 567.

except   See **accept, except.**

everywheres See **anywheres,** etc.

fewer, less *Fewer* is used with plural words. *Less* is used with singular words. *Fewer* tells "how many"; *less* tells "how much."

EXAMPLES We had expected **fewer** guests.
Please use **less** salt.

good, well *Good* is always an adjective. Never use *good* to modify a verb; use *well,* which is an adverb.

NONSTANDARD The steel-drum band played good.
STANDARD The steel-drum band played **well.**

Although it is usually an adverb, *well* may be used as an adjective to mean "healthy."

EXAMPLE I did not feel **well** yesterday.

NOTE: *Feel good* and *feel well* mean different things. *Feel good* means "to feel happy or pleased." *Feel well* simply means "to feel healthy."

EXAMPLES Helping others makes me feel **good.**
I went home because I didn't feel **well.**

had of See **of.**

had ought, hadn't ought The verb *ought* should never be used with *had.*

NONSTANDARD You had ought to learn to dance the polka.
You hadn't ought to be late for class.
STANDARD You **ought** to learn to dance the polka.
You **oughtn't** to be late for class.
or
You **should** learn to dance the polka.
You **shouldn't** be late for class.

► EXERCISE 2 **Identifying Correct Usage**

Choose the correct word or words in parentheses in each of the following sentences.

EXAMPLE   **1.** Bike riders (*had ought, ought*) to know some simple rules of safety.
   1. *ought*

1. Just about (*everywheres, everywhere*) you go these days you see people riding bikes.
2. Riders who wear helmets have (*fewer, less*) major injuries than riders who don't.
3. When my aunt came for a visit, she (*brought, took*) her bicycle with her.
4. In choosing clothes, cyclists (*can hardly, can't hardly*) go wrong by wearing bright, easy-to-see colors.
5. On busy streets, groups of cyclists should ride in single file and leave space (*among, between*) their bikes in case of sudden stops.
6. Members of cycling clubs may decide (*between, among*) themselves on special communication signals.
7. A cyclist who is involved in an accident should not try to ride home, even if he or she seems to feel (*well, good*).
8. If possible, call a family member or friend who can (*bring, take*) both the rider and the bike home.
9. A tire that is punctured can usually be patched, but you may not be able to fix one that has (*burst, busted*).
10. Many of the cycling accidents that happened last year (*could of, could have*) been avoided if cyclists and motorists had been more careful.

▶ REVIEW A   **Proofreading a Paragraph for Correct Usage**

Each sentence in the following paragraph contains an error in English usage. Identify each error. Then write the correct usage.

EXAMPLE   **[1]** I should of known that the painting on the next page was done by Grandma Moses.
   1. *should of—should have*

[1] My art teacher gave me a assignment to write a report about any artist I chose. [2] Of all the artists that I could of chosen, Grandma Moses appealed to me the most. [3] I went to the library and looked for a quiet place where I could do my research at. [4] I learned that Anna Mary Robertson Moses didn't start painting until she was all ready in her seventies. [5] By then, her children were grown, and she had less responsibilities. [6] Grandma Moses had no art teacher accept herself. [7] As you can see in the self-portrait *Rockabye,* Grandma Moses felt well about her role as a grandmother. [8] She holds one baby in her lap while the other one rocks in a cradle among the artist and the dog. [9] You can't hardly help feeling that she really loves these children. [10] My report is already for class now, and I can't wait to tell my classmates about this remarkable artist.

Grandma Moses, *Rockabye.* Copyright 1987, Grandma Moses Properties Co., New York.

he, she, they Do not use an unnecessary pronoun after a noun. This error is called the ***double subject.***

| NONSTANDARD | Isiah Thomas he was named Most Valuable Player. |
| STANDARD | Isiah Thomas was named Most Valuable Player. |

hisself, theirself, theirselves These words are nonstandard English. Use *himself* and *themselves*.

EXAMPLES Bob hurt **himself** [not *hisself*] during the game.
They served **themselves** [not *theirselves*] last.

how come In informal English, *how come* is often used instead of *why*. In formal English, *why* is always preferred.

INFORMAL I know how come he's upset.
FORMAL I know **why** he is upset.

its, it's *Its* is a personal pronoun in the possessive case. *It's* is a contraction of *it is* or *it has*.

EXAMPLES The kitten likes **its** new home. [possessive pronoun]
We have Monday off because **it's** the Rosh Hashanah holiday. [contraction of *it is*]
It's been a long day. [contraction of *it has*]

kind, sort, type The words *this, that, these,* and *those* should agree in number with the words *kind, sort,* and *type. This* and *that* are singular. *These* and *those* are plural.

EXAMPLES **That kind** of watch is expensive. [singular]
Those kinds of jokes are silly. [plural]

kind of, sort of In informal English, *kind of* and *sort of* are often used to mean "somewhat" or "rather." In formal English, *somewhat* or *rather* is preferred.

INFORMAL I feel kind of tired.
FORMAL I feel **somewhat** tired.

learn, teach *Learn* means "to acquire knowledge." *Teach* means "to instruct" or "to show how."

EXAMPLES My brother is **learning** how to drive.
The driving instructor is **teaching** him.

less See **fewer, less.**

lie, lay See page 598.

USAGE

like, as *Like* is a preposition and therefore introduces a prepositional phrase. In informal English, *like* is often used as a conjunction meaning "as." In formal English, *as* is always preferred.

EXAMPLES **Your uncle's hat looked like a sombrero.** [*Like introduces the phrase like a sombrero.*]
Marcia trained every day as the coach had suggested. [*As the coach had suggested is a clause and needs the conjunction as (not the preposition like) to introduce it.*]

👉 **REFERENCE NOTE:** For more information about prepositional phrases, see pages 491–497. For more information about clauses, see Chapter 18.

like, as if, as though In formal written English, *like* should not be used for the subordinating conjunction *as if* or *as though*.

EXAMPLES **The Swedish limpa bread looks as if** [not *like*] **it is ready.**
The car looks as though [not *like*] **it needs to be washed.**

might of, must of See **could of.**

nowheres See **anywheres,** etc.

▶ EXERCISE 3 **Identifying Correct Usage**

Choose the correct word or words in parentheses in each of the following sentences.

EXAMPLE **1.** Young rattlesnakes (*learn, teach*) themselves to use their rattles by imitating their parents.
1. *teach*

1. (*Its, It's*) a sound that most people have learned to dread.
2. As you can see on the next page, the snake's rattle consists of "buttons" of flesh at the end of (*its, it's*) tail, which are shaken against rings of loose skin.

3. The rings of skin (*themselves, theirselves*) are fragile and can break.
4. (*As, Like*) zookeepers have discovered, snakes that rattle at visitors all day may damage their rattles.
5. (*This kind, This kinds*) of snake is highly poisonous, but it does not attack unless threatened.
6. Not all scientists agree about (*how come, why*) certain snakes have rattles.
7. According to many scientists, rattlesnakes (*they use, use*) the rattling sound to frighten enemies.
8. Some scientists believe that snakes use the rattles (*like, as*) other animals use different sounds—to communicate with each other.
9. As the photograph below shows, snakes don't have ears; however, they are (*sort of, rather*) sensitive to sound vibrations.
10. When people hear a rattlesnake, they often react (*like, as if*) the situation is an emergency—and it is!

of Do not use *of* with prepositions such as *inside, off,* and *outside.*

EXAMPLES We waited **outside** [not *outside of*] the theater for the ticket window to open.
The glass fell **off** [not *off of*] the table.
Only Muslims are allowed **inside** [not *inside of*] the city of Mecca in Saudi Arabia.

Of is also unnecessary with *had*.

EXAMPLE If we **had** [not *had of*] tried harder, we
would have won.

ought to of See **could of.**

real In informal English, the adjective *real* is often used
as an adverb meaning "very" or "extremely." In
formal English, *very* or *extremely* is preferred.

INFORMAL Basenji puppies are real quiet because they
don't bark.
FORMAL Basenji puppies are **very** quiet because they
don't bark.

rise, raise See pages 596–597.

she, he, they See **he,** etc.

should of See **could of.**

sit, set See page 595.

some, somewhat Do not use *some* for *somewhat* as an
adverb.

NONSTANDARD I like classical music some.
STANDARD I like classical music **somewhat.**

PICTURE THIS

The year is 2045. You are a new crew member on a space
station. The amazing view shown on the next page is your
first glimpse of Earth from your new quarters. Write a letter to a friend back home describing what you see and
explaining how the view makes you feel. In your letter,
correctly use five of the following words or expressions.

already	hardly	ought	real
as if	good	its	except
like	less	it's	well

Subject: the view of Earth from space
Audience: a friend
Purpose: to describe the view and your reaction to it

somewheres See **anywheres**, etc.

sort See **kind**, etc.

sort of See **kind of**, etc.

take See **bring, take.**

teach See **learn, teach.**

than, then *Than* is a conjunction. *Then* is an adverb.

> EXAMPLES   I sing better **than** I act.
> We'll eat first, and **then** we'll ride our bikes.

that See **who**, etc.

that there See **this here, that there.**

their, there, they're *Their* is the possessive form of *they.*
There is used to mean "at that place" or to begin a
sentence. *They're* is a contraction of *they are.*

> EXAMPLES   Do you have **their** CDs?
> The lake is over **there.**
> **There** are five movie theaters in town.
> **They're** writing a report on the poet
> Américo Paredes.

theirself, theirselves See **hisself,** etc.

them *Them* should not be used as an adjective. Use *these* or *those.*

EXAMPLE   Where did you put **those** [not *them*] papers?

they See **he,** etc.

this here, that there The words *here* and *there* are not needed after *this* and *that.*

EXAMPLE   I like **this** [not *this here*] Chinese dragon kite, but I like **that** [not *that there*] one better.

this kind, sort, type See **kind,** etc.

try and In informal English, *try and* is often used for *try to.* In formal English, *try to* is preferred.

INFORMAL   I will try and be there early.
FORMAL   I will **try to** be there early.

type See **kind,** etc.

▶ EXERCISE 4   **Identifying Correct Usage**

Choose the correct word or words in parentheses in each of the following sentences.

EXAMPLE   **1.** The Amish people (*try and, try to*) maintain a simple, traditional way of life.
1. *try to*

1. In the early 1700s, the Amish were not allowed to practice (*their, they're, there*) religion in Germany and Switzerland.
2. Hearing that there was more freedom in North America (*than, then*) in Europe, the Amish came to the New World.
3. Since that time, they have remained (*outside of, outside*) the mainstream of American life.
4. The Amish work (*real, very*) hard at producing organically grown crops.

5. In Amish communities such as (*this, this here*) one, modern conveniences such as telephones, cars, and televisions are not used.
6. The closeness of Amish family life is evident in the way (*these, them*) people build their homes.
7. (*They're, There, Their*) are often three generations— grandparents, parents, and children—living in a large compound made up of several houses.
8. Pictures and photographs are not allowed (*inside of, inside*) Amish homes, but the Amish brighten their plain houses with colorful pillows, quilts, and rugs.
9. If an Amish person gets sick, he or she is almost always cared for by family members rather (*than, then*) by a doctor.
10. The Amish way of life might surprise you (*somewhat, some*), yet Amish communities have thrived in North America for nearly three hundred years.

use to, used to Be sure to add the *–d* to *use. Used to* is in the past form.

> EXAMPLE Gail **used to** [not *use to*] be on the softball team.

way, ways Use *way*, not *ways*, in referring to a distance.

> EXAMPLE Do we have a long **way** [not *ways*] to go?

well   See **good, well.**

when, where   Do not use *when* or *where* incorrectly in writing a definition.

> NONSTANDARD   A *homophone* is when a word sounds like another word but has a different meaning and spelling.
>
> STANDARD   A *homophone* is a word that sounds like another word but has a different meaning and spelling.

where   Do not use *where* for *that.*

> EXAMPLE   Did you read in the newsletter **that** [not *where*] the teen center is closing?

who, which, that   The relative pronoun *who* refers to people only. *Which* refers to things only. *That* refers to either people or things.

> EXAMPLES   Jolene is the one **who** called. [person]
> Here is the salad, **which** is my favorite part of the meal. [thing]
> The book **that** you want is here. [thing]
> He is the salesperson **that** helped me choose the gift. [person]

who, whom   See page 619.

whose, who's   *Whose* is the possessive form of *who. Who's* is a contraction of *who is* or *who has.*

> EXAMPLES   **Whose** book is this? [possessive pronoun]
> **Who's** the new student? [contraction of *who is*]
> **Who's** read "A Walk to the Jetty"? [contraction of *who has*]

without, unless   Do not use the preposition *without* in place of the conjunction *unless.*

> EXAMPLE   I can't go **unless** [not *without*] I ask Dad.

would of   See **could of.**

your, you're *Your* is the possessive form of *you*. *You're* is the contraction of *you are*.

EXAMPLES **Your** Saint Patrick's Day party was great!
You're a good friend.

EXERCISE 5 **Identifying Correct Usage**

Choose the correct word or words in parentheses in the following sentences.

EXAMPLE **1.** Last week I received a letter from Sandra,
(*who's, whose*) a good friend of mine.
1. *who's*

1. When I opened the envelope, I saw (*where, that*) she had sent me these chopsticks and these instructions.

2. "I thought you'd like (*you're, your*) own pair of chopsticks, with instructions for how to use them," Sandra wrote.
3. Instructions like the ones Sandra sent me are helpful because chopsticks can be hard to use (*unless, without*) you are shown how.

USAGE

4. In the letter, Sandra told me (*that, where*) she and her family had taken a trip to visit her grandparents in New York City.

5. Because Sandra lives in a small town, she wasn't (*use, used*) to the crowds.

6. She especially enjoyed visiting Chinatown, (*which, who*) is located on Manhattan Island.

7. While her family was eating in a Chinese restaurant, one of the servers, (*which, who*) was very helpful, showed her how to use chopsticks.

8. "(*Your, You're*) not going to believe this," she wrote, "but by the end of the meal, I was using chopsticks quite well."

9. *Etiquette* is (*when you use good manners, the use of good manners*), and Sandra claimed, "It was only proper etiquette to use chopsticks to eat Chinese food."

10. I'll write Sandra that I have a long (*ways, way*) to go before I'm an expert in using chopsticks.

▶ REVIEW B **Writing Original Sayings with Correct Usage**

People throughout the world pass knowledge along from one generation to another. In many cases, such knowledge is stated in a sentence or two called a *folk saying*. While these sayings express bits of wisdom, they are also often humorous. You've probably heard some of the following folk sayings:

> I have yet to meet a man who, on observing his own faults, blamed himself!
> Learn to behave from those who cannot.
> If I rest, I rust.
> You can't spoil a rotten egg.
> Fish and visitors smell in three days.
> When the wolf shows his teeth, he is not smiling.

Write five sayings of your own. Base each saying on your own experiences or on things you've been told. In your sayings, include the correct use of one of the words in five of the following items. Underline each of these words that you use.

good, well	like, as	who, which, that
its, it's	rise, raise	whose, who's
kind, sort, type	than, then	without, unless
learn, teach	way, ways	your, you're

EXAMPLE   **1.** *A horse that keeps walking can go a long* <u>*way*</u>, *as long as it doesn't walk in circles.*

WRITING APPLICATION

Using Formal English in a Speech

At formal occasions, you probably wear your best clothes and use your best manners. That's expected. In formal writing and speaking situations, people expect you to "dress up" your language. Of course, you can't put a report or a speech in a tuxedo, but you can express your ideas in formal standard English.

INFORMAL /
NONSTANDARD   I'm real upset that the mayor's Clean Air Commission ain't come up with a plan for shutting down that there incinerator.

FORMAL /
STANDARD   I am extremely upset that the mayor's Clean Air Commission has not thought of a plan for shutting down that incinerator.

▶ WRITING ACTIVITY

A local television station has started a new program called *Sound-Off*. Each speaker on the program gets five minutes on the air to express an opinion about a community issue. Some of the issues that have been addressed are crime prevention, pet leash laws, and the addition of more leagues for youth sports. Choose a topic that you think is important, and write a speech to submit to the TV station. Use only formal standard English in your speech.

Prewriting   First, choose a specific topic that interests you. You might ask friends, classmates, or relatives to help you brainstorm some ideas. After you've selected your topic, jot down some notes about it. List important facts and information about the issue. Do you have all the information you need? If not, do some research at your school or local library. Also be sure to include your own feelings and opinions about your topic. Finally, make a rough outline of what you want to say.

Writing   Use your notes and outline to help you write a draft of your speech. Try to write a lively introduction that will grab your listeners' attention. In your introduction, give a clear statement of opinion. (For more about statements of opinion, see page 248.) Then discuss each supporting point in a paragraph or two. Conclude your speech by restating your main point.

Evaluating and Revising   Ask a friend to time you as you read your speech aloud. Then, ask your friend the following questions:

- Is the main idea clear?
- Does the speech give useful information?
- Is the speech convincing?
- Did you hear any informal expressions?

Use the **Glossary of Usage** in this chapter to help you revise any informal or nonstandard usages. If your speech runs longer than five minutes, you'll need to cut or revise some information.

Proofreading   Read your speech slowly to check for any errors in grammar, spelling, or punctuation. Be sure that you have correctly spelled the names of people and organizations. (For more about capitalizing proper names, see pages 676–678.)

Review: Posttest

Revising Sentences by Correcting Errors in Usage

Each of the following sentences contains an error in usage. Write each sentence correctly, using standard formal English.

EXAMPLE   **1.** They did they're best to help.
          1. *They did their best to help.*

1. We are already for our trip to Washington, D.C.
2. Can you tell the difference among these three baseball mitts?
3. Please take those packages to me.
4. Elena had a cold, but she is feeling good now.
5. Mr. Chang he is my t'ai chi ch'uan instructor.
6. Will you learn me how to throw a baseball?
7. May I borrow that there collection of Cheyenne folk tales?
8. Tara might of come with us, but she had to baby-sit.
9. We use to live in Karachi, Pakistan.
10. She is the woman which owns the Great Dane.
11. I dropped the pictures, but I think they're alright.
12. I read in the newspaper where Mayor Alvarez will visit our school.
13. Their the best players on the team.
14. The pipes busted last winter.
15. We cannot go sailing without we wear life jackets.
16. Her new apartment is bigger then her last one.
17. The group went everywheres together.
18. Lydia acted like she was bored.
19. *Antonyms* are when words are opposite in meaning.
20. I hope that you will except my apology.
21. Have you played you're new Natalie Cole CD?
22. Do you know how come the library is closed today?
23. They can't hardly wait for their vacation.
24. I feel well when I am with my friends.
25. Those kind of movies make me laugh.

USAGE

25 CAPITAL LETTERS

Rules for Capitalization

Diagnostic Test

Proofreading Sentences for Correct Capitalization

For each of the following sentences, find the words that should be capitalized but are not. Write the words correctly.

EXAMPLE   **1.** The Mississippi river lies west of illinois.
        1. *River, Illinois*

1. At the crossbay supermarket, i bought a can of jensen's soup, a loaf of garfield bread, and a box of zoom soapflakes.
2. Aunt janice, who lives in holbrook, arizona, took me to visit petrified forest national park.
3. The rosenbach museum and library in philadelphia is open to the public tuesday through Sunday.
4. The bijou theater is next to my junior high school.
5. In world history class, we learned about queen elizabeth I, the defeat of the spanish armada, and the age of exploration.

6. Ares, hera, and zeus are greek gods whose roman names are mars, juno, and jupiter.
7. *The wind in the willows* is a famous children's book.
8. Dave's housewares store has moved from sixteenth avenue to front street.
9. The lozi people in africa live near the Zambezi river.
10. "Stopping by woods on a snowy evening" is by robert frost, an american poet from new england.
11. Do you know when david souter was appointed to the supreme court?
12. Next monday is memorial day.
13. When we traveled through the south, we visited the antietam national battlefield at sharpsburg, maryland.
14. Shirley ling came from hong kong last year, and she is teaching us about chinese culture.
15. Cayuga lake stretches north from ithaca, new york.
16. The main religion in indonesia is islam, but there are many indonesian buddhists and hindus.
17. My older sister, who goes to lincoln high school, is taking spanish, history, mathematics II, and art.
18. Carlos and i had sandwiches made of polish ham with german mustard on french bread.
19. We turned west onto route 95 and stayed on it for five miles.
20. George copway, who was born in canada, wrote about his people, the ojibwa.

MECHANICS

25a. Capitalize the first word in every sentence.

EXAMPLES **That dog knows several tricks. It will shake hands or roll over when I tell it to.**

The first word of a direct quotation should begin with a capital letter, whether or not the quotation starts the sentence.

EXAMPLE **Mrs. Hernandez said, "Don't forget to bring your contributions for the bake sale."**

Traditionally, the first word of every line of poetry begins with a capital letter.

EXAMPLE   **In the night**
The rain comes down.
Yonder at the edge of the earth
There is a sound like cracking,
There is a sound like falling.
Down yonder it goes on slowly rumbling.
It goes on shaking.

A Papago poem, "In the Night"

NOTE: Some modern poets do not follow this style. If you are quoting from a poem, be sure to follow the capitalization that the poet uses.

☞ **REFERENCE NOTE:** For information about using capital letters in quotations, see pages 737–738.

25b.   Capitalize the pronoun *I.*

EXAMPLE   **This week I have to write two papers.**

25c.   Capitalize proper nouns.

A *proper noun* names a particular person, place, thing, or idea. Such a word is always capitalized. A *common noun* names a kind or type of person, place, thing, or idea. A common noun is not capitalized unless it begins a sentence or is part of a title.

PROPER NOUNS	COMMON NOUNS
Central High School	high school
Saturday	day
Barbara Jordan	woman
Cambodia	country
Lassie	dog
USS *Nautilus*	submarine

REFERENCE NOTE: For information about using capital letters in abbreviations, see pages 703–704.

Some proper nouns consist of more than one word. In these names, short prepositions (those of fewer than five letters) and articles (*a, an, the*) are not capitalized.

EXAMPLES House **of** Representatives
Ivan **the** Terrible

 REFERENCE NOTE: For more discussion of proper nouns, see page 424.

(1) Capitalize the names of persons.

EXAMPLES **Monica Sone, Aaron Neville, Mrs. Abrams, Charlayne Hunter-Gault**

(2) Capitalize geographical names.

TYPE OF NAME	EXAMPLES	
Continents	Europe Antarctica	South America Asia
Countries	Australia El Salvador	Egypt Finland
Cities, Towns	Miami Los Angeles	Indianapolis Manila
States	Tennessee Rhode Island	Delaware Wyoming
Islands	Aleutian Islands Crete	Long Island Isle of Pines
Bodies of Water	Amazon River Chesapeake Bay Suez Canal	Lake Ontario Jackson's Pond Indian Ocean
Streets, Highways	Main Street Eighth Avenue	Canary Lane Ventura Highway

NOTE: In a hyphenated street number, the second part of the number is not capitalized.

EXAMPLE West Thirty-fourth Street

MECHANICS

TYPE OF NAME	EXAMPLES	
Parks and Forests	Yosemite Park Sherwood Forest	Everglades National Park
Mountains	Catskills Mount Fuji	Mount Everest Alps
Sections of the Country	New England the West	Corn Belt the Southeast

NOTE: Words such as *east, west, north,* or *south* are not capitalized when the words merely indicate *direction.*

EXAMPLES   A car was going west on Oak Street. [direction]
The South has produced some of America's
great writers. [section of the country]

▶ EXERCISE 1   **Correcting Errors in Capitalization**

Each of the following sentences contains errors in capitalization. Correct these errors either by changing capital letters to small letters or by changing small letters to capital letters.

EXAMPLE   **1.** The original Settlers of hawaii came from the
marquesas islands and tahiti.
1. *settlers, Hawaii, Marquesas Islands, Tahiti*

1. our Class is studying about hawaii.
2. The Hawaiian islands are located in the pacific ocean, nearly twenty-four hundred miles West of san francisco, california.
3. Hawaii became the fiftieth State in the united states in 1959.
4. Our teacher, ms. Jackson, explained that the Capital City is honolulu, and it is located on the southeast Coast of oahu island.
5. The largest of the Islands is hawaii.
6. On the southeast shore of hawaii island is hawaii volcanoes national park.
7. Ms. Jackson asked, "can anyone name one of the Volcanoes there?"

MECHANICS

8. Since i have been reading about National Parks, i raised my hand.
9. "The Park has two active volcanoes, mauna Loa and kilauea," I answered.
10. "This picture shows how lava from kilauea's eruption threatened everything in its path in 1989 " I added.

(3) Capitalize names of organizations, teams, businesses, institutions, and government bodies.

TYPE OF NAME	EXAMPLES	
Organizations	Drama Club Girl Scouts	Modern Language Association
Teams	Boston Celtics Dallas Cowboys	Los Angeles Dodgers
Businesses	Sears, Roebuck and Co.	Fields Department Store
Institutions	Westside Regional Hospital	Roosevelt Junior High School
Government Bodies	United Nations Peace Corps York City Council	Office of Management and Budget

MECHANICS

NOTE: Do not capitalize such words as *hotel, theater,* or *high school* unless they are part of the name of a particular building or institution.

EXAMPLES | **Capital Theater** | a theater
| **Lane Hotel** | the hotel
| **Taft High School** | this high school

EXERCISE 2 **Using Capitalization Correctly**

Mark Twain and his famous character Huckleberry Finn had many adventures on the Mississippi River. It's a big, long river with room for many adventures! Write your own short story about traveling on the Mississippi. Use the map below to tell about the journey. In your story, use at least five words from the map. Remember to capitalize all names of persons and geographical names.

EXAMPLE   *Early on the fourth day, Jason and she knew they were in Kentucky.*

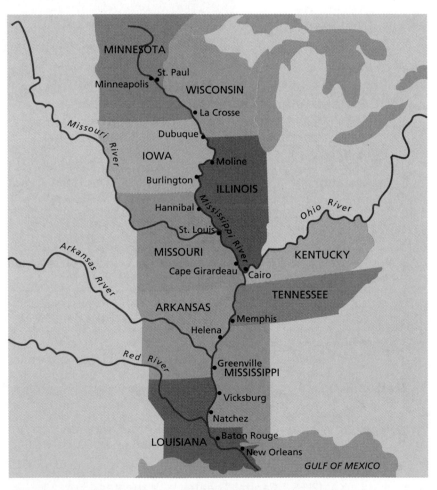

(4) Capitalize the names of historical events and periods, special events, and calendar items.

MECHANICS

TYPE OF NAME	EXAMPLES	
Historical Events and Periods	Revolutionary War Middle Ages Renaissance	United States Bicentennial Age of Reason
Special Events	Texas State Fair Special Olympics	Super Bowl Festival of States
Calendar Items	Monday February	Memorial Day Thanksgiving Day

NOTE: Do *not* capitalize the name of a season unless it is part of a proper name.

EXAMPLES   the **fall** semester
the Quebec **Winter** Carnival

(5) Capitalize the names of nationalities, races, and peoples.

EXAMPLES   **Mexican, Nigerian, Caucasian, Iroquois**

NOTE: The words *black* and *white* may or may not be capitalized when they refer to races.

EXAMPLE   In the **1960s**, both **Blacks** and **Whites** [or **blacks** and **whites**] worked to end segregation.

(6) Capitalize the brand names of business products.

EXAMPLES   **Lux** soap, **General Electric** stove, **Pepsi Cola** bottle [Notice that the names of the types of products are not capitalized.]

(7) Capitalize the names of ships, trains, airplanes, and spacecraft.

TYPE OF NAME	EXAMPLES	
Ships	*Queen Elizabeth 2*	*Kon Tiki*
Trains	*City of New Orleans*	*Orient Express*
Airplanes	*Air Force One*	*Spruce Goose*
Spacecraft	*Voyager II*	*Sputnik*

(8) Capitalize the names of buildings and other structures.

EXAMPLES **Sydney Opera House, World Trade Center, Aswan Dam, Eiffel Tower, Brooklyn Bridge**

(9) Capitalize the names of monuments and awards.

TYPE OF NAME	EXAMPLES	
Monuments	Statue of Liberty Lincoln Memorial	Tomb of the Unknown Soldier
Awards	Emmy Award Nobel Prize	Distinguished Service Medal

(10) Capitalize the names of religions and their followers, holy days, sacred writings, and specific deities.

TYPE OF NAME	EXAMPLES	
Religions and Followers	Judaism Hinduism	Christian Muslim
Holy Days	Easter Ramadan	Yom Kippur Christmas Eve
Sacred Writings	Koran Bible	Talmud Upanishads
Specific Deities	God Allah	Jehovah Krishna

NOTE: The word *god* is not capitalized when it refers to a god of ancient mythology. The names of specific gods *are* capitalized.

EXAMPLE The king of the Norse **gods** was **Odin**.

(11) Capitalize the names of planets, stars, and other heavenly bodies.

EXAMPLES **Mercury, Venus, Sirius, Andromeda, Ursa Major**

NOTE: The words *earth, moon,* and *sun* are not capitalized unless they are used along with the names of other heavenly bodies that are capitalized.

EXAMPLES   Oceans cover three fourths of the **earth's** surface.
Which is larger—Saturn or **Earth?**

▶ EXERCISE 3   **Proofreading Sentences for Correct Capitalization**

For each of the following sentences, supply capital letters where they belong.

EXAMPLE   **1.** Each arbor day the students at franklin junior high school plant a tree.
1. *Arbor Day, Franklin Junior High School*

1. The golden gate bridge spans the entrance of san francisco bay.
2. Yosemite national park in california has the nation's highest waterfall.
3. The peace corps became an agency of the federal government by an act of congress.
4. On august 4, 1984, upper volta, a nation in africa, changed its name to burkina faso.
5. Thousands of cherokee people live in the smoky mountains in and around cherokee, north carolina.
6. To stop flooding in the south, the tennessee valley authority, a government agency, built thirty-nine dams on the tennessee river and the streams that flow into it.
7. The first two states to be admitted to the united states were delaware and pennsylvania.
8. On new year's day, many fans crowd into football stadiums for the annual bowl games.
9. The rose bowl is the oldest of these annual football bowl games.
10. A noted scholar, thomas jefferson, founded the university of virginia.

MECHANICS

▶ EXERCISE 4   **Proofreading Paragraphs for Correct Capitalization**

In the following paragraphs all capital letters have been omitted. Rewrite the paragraphs, using capitals wherever they are needed.

1   the branford mall is the largest in melville county. it
2   is on jefferson parkway, two miles north of duck lake
3   state park and the big bridge that crosses duck lake.
4   across the parkway from the mall is our new local
5   high school with its parking lots, playing fields, and
6   stadium, home of the branford panthers. near the mall
7   are the american legion hall, bowlerama, and king
8   skating rink.
9   the mall includes two jewelry stores, nicholson's
10   department store, the palace cinema, and thirty-five
11   other businesses. they range from small stationery stores
12   to the finest restaurant in the midwest. the restauranté
13   larue is run by marie and jean larue, who are from
14   france. also in the mall is the american box company,
15   which sells boxes for every packaging need. an outlet
16   store for northwestern leather goods of chicago sells
17   uffizi purses and wallets.

▶ REVIEW A   **Correcting Errors in Capitalization**

Each of the following sentences contains errors in capitalization. Correct these errors by either changing capital letters to small letters or changing small letters to capital letters.

EXAMPLE   **1.** African americans in massachusetts have played an important part in american history.
1. *Americans, Massachusetts, American*

1. In Boston, the Crispus attucks monument is a memorial to attucks and the other men who died in the boston Massacre.
2. According to many Historians, attucks was a former slave who fought against the british in the american Revolution.

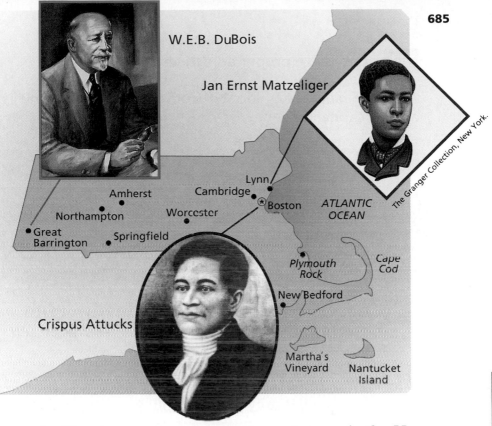

W.E.B. DuBois

Jan Ernst Matzeliger

The Granger Collection, New York.

Amherst
Northampton
Great Barrington
Springfield
Worcester
Cambridge
Lynn
Boston
ATLANTIC OCEAN
Plymouth Rock
Cape Cod
New Bedford
Crispus Attucks
Martha's Vineyard
Nantucket Island

MECHANICS

3. The department of the Interior has made the Home of maria baldwin a historic building in cambridge.
4. Baldwin was a Leader in the league for Community Service, an Organization to help the Needy.
5. One of the founders of the National association for the Advancement of colored people, w.e.b. DuBois, was born in great Barrington, Massachusetts.
6. A marker stands on the Spot where DuBois lived.
7. Jan ernst matzeliger, who lived in lynn, invented a machine that made Shoes easier and cheaper to manufacture.
8. The nantucket historical Association has information about Peter green, a Sailor and Second Mate on the whaling ship *john Adams*.
9. During a storm at sea, Green saved the Ship and crew after the Captain and First Mate had drowned.
10. Use the Map of Massachusetts shown above to locate the Towns and Cities in which these notable african Americans lived.

MECHANICS

25d. Capitalize proper adjectives.

A *proper adjective* is formed from a proper noun and is always capitalized.

PROPER NOUN	PROPER ADJECTIVE
Greece	Greek theater
Mars	Martian moons
Darwin	Darwinian theory
Japan	Japanese tea ceremony

25e. Do *not* capitalize the names of school subjects, except course names followed by a number and languages.

EXAMPLES   history, typing, mathematics, English, Spanish, Latin, History 101, Music III, Art Appreciation I

 EXERCISE 5   **Proofreading Sentences for Correct Capitalization**

In each of the following sentences, find the word or words that should be capitalized but are not. Write the words correctly.

EXAMPLE   **1.** Rosa said we were eating real mexican tamales.
1. *Mexican*

1. The program featured russian ballet dancers.
2. The european Common Market helps improve international trade.
3. The scandinavian countries include both Norway and Sweden.
4. In geography, we learned about the platypus and the koala, two australian animals.
5. Many great english plays were written during the elizabethan age.

6. I am planning to take computer I next year.
7. On the floor was a large persian rug.
8. England, France, Scotland, Russia, and the United States played important roles in canadian history.
9. The back yard was decorated with chinese lanterns.
10. Have you ever tasted indian rice pudding?

PICTURE THIS

The year is 1845. You and your family are pioneers traveling west in one of these covered wagons. You are using this map to find your way from Independence to Los Angeles. Write a letter describing your journey to a friend back in Independence. You may want to tell about your fellow pioneers, the towns you've passed through, or the rivers and land you've crossed. You may also want to mention some of the people, places, and things you miss back home. In your letter, use at least three proper nouns and two proper adjectives.

Subject: heading west in a covered wagon
Audience: a friend
Purpose: to describe your journey

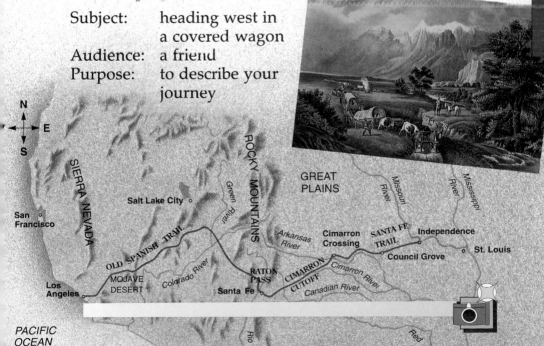

MECHANICS

25f.   Capitalize titles.

(1) Capitalize the title of a person when the title comes before a name.

EXAMPLES   **President Lincoln**   **Mrs.** Wendell
Mayor Bradley   **C**ommissioner Rodriguez

☞ REFERENCE NOTE: For more information about abbreviations, see pages 703–704.

(2) Capitalize a title used alone or following a person's name only when you want to emphasize the title of someone holding a high office.

EXAMPLE   The **S**ecretary of Defense held a news conference.
Lien Fong, class **s**ecretary, read the minutes.

A title used by itself in direct address is usually capitalized.

EXAMPLES   Is it very serious, **D**octor?
How do you do, **S**ir [*or* sir]?

(3) Capitalize a word showing a family relationship when the word is used before or in place of a person's name.

EXAMPLES   We expect **U**ncle **F**red and **A**unt **H**elen soon.
We always go to **G**randma **L**owery's house for Thanksgiving dinner.
Both **M**om and **D**ad work at the hospital.

Do not capitalize a word showing a family relationship when a possessive comes before the word.

EXAMPLE   We asked Pedro's **m**other and his **a**unt Celia to be chaperons.

(4) Capitalize the first and last words and all important words in titles and subtitles of books, magazines, newspapers, poems, short stories, movies, television programs, works of art, and musical compositions.

MECHANICS

Unimportant words in titles include

- articles (*a, an, the*)
- coordinating conjunctions (*and, but, for, nor, or, so, yet*)
- prepositions of fewer than five letters (such as *by, for, on, with*)

TYPE OF NAME	EXAMPLES	
Books	*The Mask of Apollo* *Mules and Men* *The Foxfire Book*	*Chicano Authors:* *Inquiry by* *Interview*
Magazines	*Popular Mechanics* *Ebony*	*Seventeen* *Sports Illustrated*
Newspapers	*The Miami Herald* the *Houston Post*	*The Wall Street* *Journal*
Poems	"Season at the Shore"	"In Time of Silver Rain"
Short Stories	"The Night the Bed Fell"	"Zlateh the Goat"
Movies	*Dances with Wolves*	*It's a Wonderful* *Life*
Television Programs	*Life Goes On* *In Living Color*	*Star Trek: The* *Next Generation*
Works of Art	*Mona Lisa* *David*	*The Old Guitarist* *Mankind's Struggle*
Musical Compositions	"America the Beautiful"	*The Marriage* *of Figaro*

MECHANICS

NOTE: An article (*a, an,* or *the*) before a title is not capitalized unless it is the first word of the title.

EXAMPLES   My father reads *The Wall Street Journal.*
Does she work for the *Texas Review*?

☞ REFERENCE NOTE: For guidelines on what titles are italicized, see pages 735–736. For guidelines on what titles are enclosed in quotation marks, see pages 743–744.

▶ EXERCISE 6   **Proofreading Sentences for Correct Capitalization**

Write the following sentences, using capitals wherever they are needed.

EXAMPLE   **1.** The series *all creatures great and small* is being rerun on public television.
1. *The series* All Creatures Great and Small *is being rerun on public television.*

1. While waiting to interview mayor ward, I read an article in *newsweek*.
2. Have you read leslie marmon silko's poem "story from bear country"?
3. You have probably seen a picture of *the thinker*, one of rodin's best-known sculptures.
4. On television last night we saw a movie called *the three faces of eve*.
5. This year voters will elect a president and several united states senators.
6. Uncle nick read aloud from francisco jiménez's short story "the circuit."
7. The reporter asked, "Can you tell us, senator inouye, when you plan to announce the committee's final decision?"
8. The main speaker was dr. andrew holt, a former president of the university of tennessee.
9. Besides uncle don, our visitors included aunt pat, aunt jean, both of my grandmothers, and my great-grandfather.
10. The president met with his advisers before he spoke to the nation.

▶ REVIEW B   **Proofreading Sentences for Correct Capitalization**

Each of the following sentences contains at least one error in capitalization. Write correctly the words that require capital letters.

EXAMPLE **1.** The waters of the caribbean are pleasantly warm.

       1. *Caribbean*

1. The greeks believed that zeus, the king of the gods, lived on mount olympus.
2. The *titanic* sank after hitting an iceberg off the coast of newfoundland.
3. My cousin collects scandinavian pottery.
4. Stephanie is taking english, math II, biology, and world history.
5. On friday we were cheered by the thought that monday, memorial day, would be a holiday.
6. that chair is made of teakwood.
7. I wanted to name my persian cat after the chief justice of the supreme court.
8. In *roots*, alex haley, a famous journalist, traces the history of his family.
9. She usually travels to boston on american airlines.
10. The quaker oats company has introduced a new corn cereal.

▶ REVIEW C   **Proofreading a Paragraph for Correct Capitalization**

Each sentence in the following paragraph contains at least one error in capitalization. Write correctly the words that require capital letters.

EXAMPLE **[1]** Before the thanksgiving holidays, i learned some interesting facts about africa in my history II class.

      1. *Thanksgiving, I, Africa, History II*

[1] My teacher, mr. davidson, told us about the mighty kingdoms and empires that existed for hundreds of years in africa. [2] some of these kingdoms dated back to the time of the roman empire. [3] Others rose to power during the period known as the middle ages in europe. [4] For many years, the people in the kingdom of cush did iron-work and traded along the nile river. [5] Later, the cush

MECHANICS

were defeated by the people of axum, led by king ezana. [6] As you can see in the map below, kingdoms in west africa developed between lake chad and the atlantic ocean. [7] Three of these kingdoms were ghana, mali, and songhai. [8] These kingdoms established important trade routes across the sahara desert. [9] Tombouctou's famous university attracted egyptian and other arab students. [10] I read more about these african kingdoms and empires in our textbook, *world history: people and nations*.

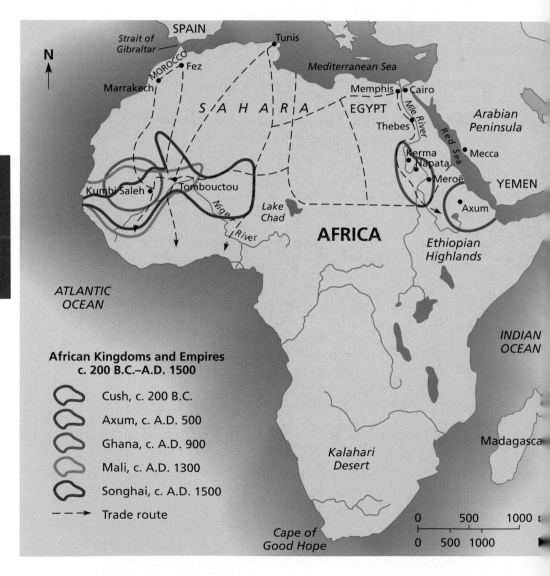

African Kingdoms and Empires
c. 200 B.C.–A.D. 1500

Cush, c. 200 B.C.

Axum, c. A.D. 500

Ghana, c. A.D. 900

Mali, c. A.D. 1300

Songhai, c. A.D. 1500

‑ ‑ → Trade route

WRITING APPLICATION

Using Capital Letters to Make Your Writing Clear

Used correctly, capital letters help your readers understand your writing. Capital letters signal that you mean a particular person, place, thing, or idea. Compare the following sentences:

> I'd like to see the **white house.**
> I'd like to see the **White House.**

The capital letters in the second sentence completely change the meaning of the sentence. The second sentence refers to the home of the President of the United States, not to just any "white house."

▶ WRITING ACTIVITY

Students in your class have become pen pals with students in another country. You have been given the name of someone to write to. Write a letter to your pen pal introducing yourself and telling about your school and your community. In your letter, be sure to use capitalization correctly.

Prewriting Write down the information you want to give in your letter. You may wish to include some of the following information:

- your age
- a description of yourself
- your favorite books, movies, actors, or musicians
- the name of your school
- the courses you are taking in school this year
- some clubs, organizations, or special activities you participate in
- a description of your community
- some special places, events, or attractions in your community or state

Writing As you write your draft, keep in mind that your pen pal may not recognize names of some people, places, and things in the United States. For example, he or she may not recognize the names of your favorite movies or musical groups. Be sure to use correct capitalization and even brief explanations to make your meaning clear.

Evaluating and Revising Read through your letter carefully. Have you left out any important information? Are any parts of your letter confusing? If so, you may want to add, cut, or revise some details. Is the tone of your letter friendly? Have you followed the correct form for a personal letter? (For more about personal letters, see pages 867–869.)

Proofreading Read over your letter carefully to check for any errors in grammar, spelling, or punctuation. Use the rules in this chapter to help you double-check your capitalization.

MECHANICS

▶ REVIEW D   **Correcting Errors in Capitalization**

Each of the following sentences contains errors in capitalization. Correct these errors by either changing capital letters to small letters or changing small letters to capital letters.

EXAMPLE   **1.** On june 25, 1876, the Sioux and cheyenne warriors defeated general george a. Custer and his Troops.
1. *June, Cheyenne, General George A., troops*

1. The Defeat of gen. custer occurred at the battle of the little bighorn.
2. In december of 1890, many Sioux were killed by the Soldiers in a battle at wounded Knee creek in south Dakota.

3. Both Battles have become part of american History, remembered by artists, writers, and filmmakers.
4. In the late nineteenth century, the sioux Artist Kicking bear painted the *Battle Of The little Bighorn.*
5. The painting, done on muslin Cloth, is shown below.

Kicking Bear (Sioux), Battle of the Little Bighorn. Courtesy of the Southwest Museum, Los Angeles. Photo #1026.G.1

6. Kicking bear, who himself fought in the Battle, painted at the pine Ridge agency in south Dakota, where he lived.
7. soldiers who fought against kicking Bear described him as courageous.
8. The well-known American Poet Stephen vincent benét wrote about the battle of wounded knee in a Poem called "american names."
9. More recently, the author Dee brown wrote about the native americans of the west in his book *bury my Heart at Wounded knee.*
10. In 1970, the movie *Little big Man* told the story of a 121-year-old man who survived the Battle against general Custer.

Review: Posttest

Proofreading Sentences for Correct Capitalization

For each of the following sentences, write the words in the sentence that require capitalization. If a sentence is correct, write C.

EXAMPLE   **1.** Next saturday rachel and i will get to watch the filming of our favorite TV show.
      1. *Saturday, Rachel, I*

1. The curtiss soap corporation sponsors the television show called *three is two too many.*
2. The show's theme song is "you and i might get by."
3. My favorite actor on the show is joe fontana, jr., who plays the lovable dr. mullins.
4. The female lead, janelle bledsoe, used to go to our junior high school right here in houston, texas.
5. The action takes place out west, just after the civil war ended.
6. The program is on monday nights, except during the summer.
7. One episode took place at a fourth of july picnic, where dr. mullins challenged the local sheriff to a pie-eating contest.
8. Ms. Bledsoe plays a teacher who is married to Mr. reginald wilson foster II, president of the flintsville National bank.
9. Mrs. foster teaches latin, home economics, and arithmetic I at flintsville's one-room school.
10. One local character, uncle ramón, once played a practical joke on judge grimsby right outside the mayor's office.
11. Some people, including my mother, think that the program is silly, but my father enjoys watching it occasionally.
12. Even i don't think it will receive an emmy from the academy of television arts and sciences.

13. When grandma murray and aunt edna from mobile, alabama, visited us, they watched the program.

14. In that monday night's show, an alien named romax from the planet zarko came to town and stayed at the sidewinder hotel.

15. The alien, who looked like United States president zachary taylor, spoke english perfectly and could read people's minds.

16. He settled a dispute between the union pacific railroad and the flintsville ranchers' association.

17. In another show a united states senator and romax discussed their views of justice.

18. In the silliest show, the people in the next town, longview, thought that a sea monster was living a few miles north in lake cranberry and reported it to the national bureau of endangered species.

19. A week later, mayor murdstone lost his only copy of his secret recipe for irish stew and saw the recipe in the next issue of the *flintsville weekly gazette*.

20. One time a mysterious stranger appeared, claiming he had sailed to the far east around cape horn on the ship *the gem of the ocean*.

21. Another time, wealthy landowner mabel platt hired the law firm of crum, lockwood, and tarr to sue mayor murdstone and threatened to take the case all the way to the united states supreme court.

22. In the next episode, a buddhist priest, who just happened to be traveling through the west on his way back to china, stopped off in flintsville and gave some of the townsfolk a few lessons in manners.

23. Once, when someone mistakenly thought he had found gold down at cutter's creek, thousands of prospectors flocked to flintsville, including three bank-robbing members of the feared gumley gang.

24. The programs are taped before an audience in the universal theater in los angeles, california.

25. You can get tickets to be in the audience by writing to curtiss soap corporation, 151 holly avenue, deerfield, michigan 49238.

MECHANICS

MECHANICS

SUMMARY STYLE SHEET

Names of Persons

Emilio Estevez	an actor
Marie Curie	a scientist
Crazy Horse	a leader

Geographical Names

Fifty-first Street	a dead-end street
Little Rock	the capital of Arkansas
Hidalgo	a county in New Mexico
in the South	traveling south
Kenya	a country in Africa
Galápagos Islands	a group of islands
Indian Ocean	the ocean between Africa and Australia
Everglades National Park	a park in Florida
Appalachian Mountains	hiking in the mountains

Names of Heavenly Bodies

Jupiter, Venus, Earth	the surface of the earth
Ursa Minor	a constellation
Milky Way	a spiral galaxy

Names of Teams, Organizations, Businesses, Institutions, Government Bodies

Overton Owls	a softball team
Westboro Writers' Club	the members of the club
American Printing Company	the company she works for
East Side High School	the local high school
Department of Energy	a department of the government

Names of Historical Events and Periods, Special Events, Calendar Items

Battle of the Little Bighorn	a fierce battle
Ice Age	at an early age
Travis County Fair	a large fair
Veterans Day	a national holiday
June	summer

(continued)

SUMMARY STYLE SHEET *(continued)*

Names of Nationalities, Races, Religions

Turkish	a **n**ationality
Caucasian	a **r**ace
Judaism	a **r**eligion
God	a **g**od of **G**reek mythology

Names of Buildings, Monuments, Awards

Copley **H**otel	a fancy **h**otel
the **G**eneral **A**ssembly **B**uilding	a **U**nited **N**ations building
Washington **M**onument	a national **m**onument

Names of Trains, Ships, Airplanes, Spacecraft

Super Chief	a **t**rain
Titanic	a **s**hip
Air Force One	an **a**irplane
Challenger	a **s**pace shuttle

Brand Names

Nike shoes	**r**ed shoes
Fab detergent	laundry **d**etergent

Names of Languages, School Subjects

English, **D**utch, **C**ree, **S**panish	a **f**oreign language
Algebra I, **B**iology II, **M**usic 104	**a**lgebra, **b**iology, **m**usic

Titles

Senator **S**uarez	a **s**enator from my state
President of the **U**nited **S**tates	the **p**resident of the club
Aunt **M**artha	my **a**unt
How are you, **A**unt?	
Up from Slavery	a book
Teen	a magazine
The New York Times	a newspaper
"Hector the Collector"	a poem
"The House on Mango Street"	a short story
Teenage Mutant Ninja Turtles	a movie, a play
A Different World	a television program
The Pumpkin Patch	a painting
"The Star-Spangled Banner"	a national anthem

MECHANICS

26 PUNCTUATION

End Marks, Commas, Semicolons, Colons

Diagnostic Test

Using End Marks, Commas, Semicolons, and Colons to Punctuate Sentences Correctly

The following sentences lack necessary punctuation. Write each sentence, inserting the correct punctuation.

EXAMPLE
1. After I read my history assignment I did my other homework but I did not finish it
1. *After I read my history assignment, I did my other homework, but I did not finish it.*

1. The following students gave their reports yesterday Carlos Sue and Alan
2. Tanay's grandfather carved this beautiful soapstone cooking pot
3. Have you met Ellen who has recently transferred to our school
4. Calling Simon's name I ran to the door

5. Her new address is 151 Mesa Drive El Paso TX 79912
6. Have you listened to that Bill Cosby tape Felix
7. You will let me know of course if you can't attend
8. Mia will conduct the meeting Gary recently elected secretary will take the minutes
9. Looking out at the harsh bright glare Angela closed the curtains
10. Carlos Montoya picked up the guitar positioned his fingers on the fingerboard just before the frets and strummed a few chords of a flamenco song.
11. If you hurry you can get home before 9 00 PM
12. Help This is an emergency
13. By the way Rosalinda have you seen any of the re-releases of Alfred Hitchcock's old movies
14. Dave hit a long fly ball toward the fence but Phil was there to make the catch
15. *El Norte* which is one of my favorite movies is about a brother and sister fleeing Central America
16. Performed in Spanish the movie that we saw had English subtitles
17. Nicaragua Panama and Honduras are in Central America Peru and Chile are in South America
18. One of our cats Gypsy scooted through the door across the room and out the window
19. The Lock Museum of America a fascinating place in Terryville Conn has over twenty thousand locks on display.
20. Could the surprise gift be in-line skates or a new football or tickets to a concert

MECHANICS

End Marks

An *end mark* is a mark of punctuation placed at the end of a sentence. *Periods, question marks,* and *exclamation points* are end marks.

26a. Use a period at the end of a statement.

EXAMPLES The chess player considered his next move**.**
Tea is grown in Sri Lanka**.**

26b. Use a question mark at the end of a question.

EXAMPLES Did you see the exhibit of Benin bronzes**?**
What time is it**?**

26c. Use an exclamation point at the end of an exclamation.

EXAMPLES What a high bridge**!**
Look at how bright the moon is**!**

26d. Use either a period or an exclamation point at the end of a request or a command.

EXAMPLES Please call the dog**.** [a request]
Call the dog**!** [a command]

▶ EXERCISE 1   **Adding End Marks to Sentences**

Rewrite each of the following sentences, adding the necessary end marks.

EXAMPLE   **1.** Did you know that a choreographer is a person who creates dance steps
            1. *Did you know that a choreographer is a person who creates dance steps?*

1. Why is Katherine Dunham called the mother of African American dance
2. She studied anthropology in college and won a scholarship to visit the Caribbean
3. In Haiti, she was inspired by the dances she saw
4. When Dunham returned to the United States, she toured the country with her own professional dance company

5. How I admire such a talented person
6. Look at the beautiful costume and jewelry worn by Dunham in the photograph below
7. How many honors has Dunham's creativity won her
8. She was named to the Hall of Fame of the National Museum of Dance in Saratoga, New York
9. She was also given the National Medal of Arts Award for exploring Caribbean and African dance
10. The editors of *Essence* magazine praised Dunham for helping to break down racial barriers

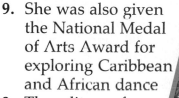

26e. Use a period after most abbreviations.

TYPES OF ABBREVIATIONS	EXAMPLES
Personal Names	F. Scott Fitzgerald Livie I. Durán W.E.B. DuBois
Titles Used with Names	Mr. Mrs. Ms. Jr. Sr. Dr.
Organizations and Companies	Co. Inc. Corp. Assn.

NOTE: Abbreviations for government agencies and some widely used abbreviations are written without periods. Each letter of the abbreviation is capitalized.

EXAMPLES UN, FBI, PTA, NAACP, PBS, CNN, YMCA, VHF

TYPES OF ABBREVIATIONS	EXAMPLES
Times	A.M. P.M. B.C. A.D.
Addresses	Ave. St. Rd. Blvd. P.O. Box
States	Tex. Penn. Ariz. Wash.

NOTE: A two-letter state abbreviation without periods is used only when it is followed by a ZIP Code. Both letters of the abbreviation are then capitalized.

EXAMPLE   Orlando, **FL** 32819

Abbreviations for units of measure are usually written without periods and are not capitalized.

EXAMPLES   mm, kg, dl, oz, lb, ft, yd, mi

However, a period is always used with the abbreviation for *inch* (*in.*) to avoid confusion with the word *in*.

If you're not sure whether to use periods with abbreviations, look in a dictionary.

NOTE: When an abbreviation with a period ends a sentence, another period is not needed. However, a question mark or an exclamation point is used as needed.

EXAMPLES   We will arrive by 3:00 P.M.
Can you meet us at 3:00 P.M.?
Oh, no! It's already 3:00 P.M.!

▶ EXERCISE 2   **Creating and Writing Abbreviations**

Abbreviations provide a quick way to express information. Think of how inconvenient it would be to have to write 10 ante meridiem instead of 10 A.M. Create five abbreviations that you think would be handy timesavers. Use each of your abbreviations in a sentence that tells what it stands for. Be sure to use a period after each letter in your abbreviations.

EXAMPLE   *I.A.F. means "I'm almost finished," an abbreviation students use when they've nearly completed their homework.*

PICTURE THIS

Suddenly last night, monster tomatoes began attacking your town! They're so huge that they have crushed cars, knocked down buildings, and caused general panic. When the attack started, you grabbed your camera and got this amazing shot of one of the giant tomatoes chasing two friends of yours. But now your camera won't work because it is drenched with tomato juice. You remember that you have a small notebook in your pocket. Jot down a description of the attack so that the rest of the world will know what happened. Use all three types of end marks in your description.

Subject: monster tomatoes attacking your town
Audience: people who haven't seen the attack
Purpose: to inform by giving a clear description

MECHANICS

Commas

End marks are used to separate complete thoughts. *Commas*, however, are used to separate words or groups of words within a complete thought.

Items in a Series

> **26f.** Use commas to separate items in a series.

A series is a group of three or more items written one after another. The items in a series may be words, phrases, or clauses.

WORDS IN A SERIES
January, February, and March are all summer months in the Southern Hemisphere. [*nouns*]
The engine rattled, coughed, and stalled. [*verbs*]
The baby was happy, alert, and active after her nap. [*adjectives*]
PHRASES IN A SERIES
There were fingerprints at the top, on the sides, and on the bottom. [*prepositional phrases*]
Cut into pieces, aged for a year, and well dried, the wood was ready to burn. [*participial phrases*]
To pitch in a World Series game, to practice medicine, and to run for mayor are all things I hope to do some day. [*infinitive phrases*]
CLAUSES IN A SERIES
We sang, we danced, and we played trivia games. [*short independent clauses*]

NOTE: Only *short* independent clauses in a series may be separated by commas. Independent clauses in a series are usually separated by semicolons.

Always be sure that there are at least three items in the series; two items do not need a comma between them.

INCORRECT   You will need a pencil, and plenty of paper.
  CORRECT   You will need a pencil and plenty of paper.

NOTE: In your reading, you will find that some writers omit the comma before the *and* joining the last two items of a series. Nevertheless, you should form the habit of always including this comma. Sometimes a comma is necessary to make your meaning clear. Notice how the comma affects the meaning in the following examples.

EXAMPLES   Mom, Jody and I want to go to the movies.
[Mom is being asked for her permission.]
Mom, Jody, and I want to go to the movies.
[Three people want to go to the movies.]

Including a comma before the last item in a series is never incorrect; therefore, it is usually best to do so.

When all the items in the series are joined by *and* or *or*, do not use commas to separate them.

EXAMPLES   Take water **and** food **and** matches with you.
I will take a class in karate **or** judo **or** aikido next year.

▶ EXERCISE 3   **Proofreading Sentences for the Correct Use of Commas**

Some of the following sentences need commas; others do not. If a sentence needs commas, write the word before each missing comma and add the comma. If a sentence is correct, write *C*.

EXAMPLE   **1.** Seal the envelope stamp it and mail the letter.
1. *envelope, it,*

1. The mountains and valleys of southern Appalachia were once home to the Cherokee people.
2. Cleveland Toledo and Dayton are three large cities in Ohio.

3. The captain entered the cockpit checked the instruments and prepared for takeoff.
4. Luisa bought mangos and papayas and oranges.
5. The speaker took a deep breath and read the report.
6. My dog Rover can roll over walk on his hind feet and catch a tennis ball.
7. The neighbors searched behind the garages in the bushes and along the highway.
8. Rubén Blades is an attorney an actor and a singer.
9. Eleanor Roosevelt's courage her humanity and her service to the nation will always be remembered.
10. Rivers overflowed in Virginia and North Carolina.

26g. Use a comma to separate two or more adjectives that come before a noun.

EXAMPLES   Jupiter is a large, strange planet.
Maria Pepe played a powerful, brilliant game.

Do not place a comma between an adjective and the noun immediately following it.

INCORRECT   My spaniel is a fat, sassy, puppy.
CORRECT   My spaniel is a fat, sassy puppy.

Sometimes the final adjective in a series is closely connected to the noun. When the adjective and the noun are linked in such a way, do not use a comma before the final adjective.

EXAMPLES   A huge **horned owl** lives in those woods. [not *huge, horned owl*]
An unshaded **electric light** hung from the ceiling. [not *unshaded, electric light*]

To see whether a comma is needed, insert *and* between the adjectives (*unshaded and electric,* for example). If *and* sounds awkward there, don't use a comma.

☞ REFERENCE NOTE: When an adjective and a noun are closely linked, they may be considered one word. Such a word is called a *compound noun.* For more about compound nouns, see page 423.

MECHANICS

 EXERCISE 4 | **Proofreading Sentences for the Correct Use of Commas**

Most of the following sentences need commas. If a sentence needs any commas, write the word before each missing comma and add the comma. If a sentence is correct, write *C*.

EXAMPLE **1.** Juanita Chen and I are making enchiladas.
1. *Juanita, Chen, and I are making enchiladas.*
or
Juanita, Chen and I are making enchiladas.

1. In judo class I learned that skill balance and timing are more important than strength.
2. Among Robert Fulton's interests were a steam warship and the submarine.
3. Smoking is a costly dangerous habit.
4. In the human ear, the hammer anvil and stirrup carry sound waves to the brain.
5. Buffalo Bill was a Pony Express rider a scout and a touring stunt performer.
6. "The Masque of the Red Death" is a famous horror story by Edgar Allan Poe.
7. According to Greek mythology, the three Fates spin the thread of life measure it and cut it.
8. LeVar Burton plays the intelligent likable character Geordi on *Star Trek: The Next Generation*.
9. Burton also starred in the popular award-winning miniseries *Roots*.
10. Falstaff fought only briefly in a battle ran away and later bragged about his bravery.

MECHANICS

Peanuts reprinted by permission of United Feature Syndicate, Inc.

▶ EXERCISE 5 **Creating Menu Descriptions**

Your parents have opened a restaurant, and they are eager to attract customers. Your job is to list today's specials on a sign outside the restaurant. List at least five food items and give a short description of each one. Try to make the foods sound appealing. Be sure to use commas between a series of adjectives. [Remember: Do not use a comma between an adjective and the noun it modifies.]

EXAMPLE *Delicious homemade chicken soup served with a fresh garden salad and refreshing iced tea—$2.75*

Compound Sentences

26h. Use a comma before *and, but, for, or, nor, so,* and *yet* when they join independent clauses in a compound sentence.

EXAMPLES Tamisha offered to get tickets, and I accepted.
They had been working very hard, but they didn't seem especially tired.
The twins were excited, for they were going to day care for the first time.

NOTE: *So* is often overused. If possible, try to reword a sentence to avoid using *so.*

EXAMPLE It was late, so we went home.
REVISED Because it was late, we went home.

When the independent clauses are very short, the comma before *and, but,* or *or* may be omitted.

EXAMPLES It rained and it rained.
She's going but I'm not.
Come with us or meet us there.

NOTE: Always use a comma before *nor, for, so,* or *yet* joining independent clauses.

EXAMPLE I don't know much about modern art, yet I enjoy the work of Mark Rothko.

Don't be confused by a simple sentence with a compound verb. A simple sentence has only one independent clause.

SIMPLE SENTENCE WITH COMPOUND VERB   Usually we **study** in the morning and **play** tennis in the afternoon.

COMPOUND SENTENCE   Usually we study in the morning**,** and we play tennis in the afternoon. [two independent clauses]

☞ **REFERENCE NOTE:** For more about compound sentences, see pages 536–538. For more about simple sentences with compound verbs, see page 534.

▶ EXERCISE 6   **Correcting Compound Sentences by Adding Commas**

Some of the following sentences are compound and need additional commas. If a sentence needs a comma, write the word before the missing comma and add the comma. If the sentence is correct, write C.

EXAMPLE   **1.** Native American artists have a heritage dating back thousands of years and many of them use this heritage to create modern works.
1. *years,*

1. Today's artists may work with many nontraditional materials but they use traditional techniques.
2. In the photograph on the next page, you can see the work of the Tohono O'odham artist Mary Thomas and begin to appreciate this basket-weaver's skill.
3. The baskets in the photograph are woven in the "friendship design" and show a circle of human figures in a prayer ceremony.
4. Yucca, banana yucca root, and devil's claw are used to make these baskets and each plant's leaves are a different color.
5. The Navajo artist Danny Randeau Tsosie learned about his heritage from his grandmother.
6. She taught him songs and explained the meaning of the different ceremonies.

7. Christine Nofchissey McHorse learned the skill of pottery making from her grandmother and she can make beautiful bowls.
8. McHorse has an unusual style for her designs combine traditional Navajo and Pueblo images.
9. Native American jewelry makers often use pieces of turquoise and coral found in North America but they also use other stones from around the world.
10. Native American art may look very modern yet some of its symbols and patterns are quite old.

Interrupters

26i. Use commas to set off an expression that interrupts a sentence.

Two commas are needed if the expression to be set off comes in the middle of the sentence. One comma is needed if the expression comes first or last.

EXAMPLES   Our neighbor, Ann Myers, is a fine golfer.
Naturally, we expect to win.
My answer is correct, I think.

(1) Use commas to set off nonessential participial phrases or nonessential subordinate clauses.

A *nonessential* (or *nonrestrictive*) phrase or clause adds information that isn't needed to understand the meaning of the sentence. Such a phrase or clause can be omitted without changing the main idea of the sentence.

NONESSENTIAL PHRASES	My sister, **listening to her radio,** did not hear me. Paul, **thrilled by the applause,** took a bow.
NONESSENTIAL CLAUSES	*Out of Africa,* **which I saw again last week,** is my favorite movie. I reported on *Secret of the Andes,* **which was written by Ann Nolan Clark.**

Do not set off an *essential* (or *restrictive*) phrase or clause. Since such a phrase or clause tells *which one(s),* it cannot be omitted without changing the meaning of the sentence.

ESSENTIAL PHRASES	The people **waiting to see Arsenio Hall** whistled and cheered. [Which people?] A bowl **made by Maria Martínez** is a collector's item. [Which bowl?]
ESSENTIAL CLAUSES	The dress **that I liked** has been sold. [Which dress?] The man **who tells Navajo folk tales** is Mr. Platero. [Which man?]

NOTE: A clause beginning with *that* is usually essential.

☞ **REFERENCE NOTE:** For more about phrases, see Chapter 17. For more about subordinate clauses, see pages 516–525.

▶ EXERCISE 7   **Adding Commas with Nonessential Phrases and Clauses**

Some of the following sentences need commas to set off nonessential phrases and clauses. Other sentences are correct without commas. If a sentence needs commas,

MECHANICS

write the word that comes before each missing comma and add the comma. If the sentence is correct, write *C*.

EXAMPLE **1.** This photograph which was taken near Ellis Island shows a family of emigrants from Eastern Europe.
1. *photograph, Ellis Island,*

1. Millions of immigrants who came to the United States between about 1892 and 1954 stopped at Ellis Island which is in Upper New York Bay.
2. Families arriving from Europe were examined and interviewed there.

Photograph by Lewis W. Hine. Courtesy George Eastman House.

3. The island and its buildings which were closed to the public for many years are now part of the Statue of Liberty National Monument.
4. In 1990, Ellis Island rebuilt as a museum was officially opened to the public.
5. Visitors who wish to see the museum can take a ferry ride from Manhattan Island.
6. The museum's lobby crowded with steamer trunks and other old baggage is the visitors' first sight.
7. One special attraction in the museum consists of audiotapes and videotapes that describe the immigrants' experiences.

8. The Registry Room which is on the second floor sometimes held as many as five thousand people.
9. The immigrants who came from many countries hoped to find freedom and a happier life in America.
10. Immigrants who came to the United States brought with them the value of hard work and a variety of skills that helped to make our country great.

(2) Use commas to set off appositives and appositive phrases that are nonessential.

An *appositive* is a noun or a pronoun used to explain or identify another noun or pronoun.

EXAMPLES   Vernon, **my cousin,** was born in Jamaica.
Jamaica, **a popular island for tourists,** is in the Caribbean Sea.

Do not use commas to set off an appositive that is essential to the meaning of a sentence.

EXAMPLES   My sister **Alicia** is at basketball practice. [The speaker has more than one sister and must give a name to identify which sister.]
My sister, **Alicia,** is at basketball practice. [The speaker has only one sister and is giving her name as added information.]

▶ EXERCISE 8   **Proofreading Sentences for the Correct Use of Commas with Appositives**

For each of the following sentences, identify the appositive or appositive phrase. Supply commas where needed. [Hint: Not all of the appositives require commas.]

EXAMPLE   **1.** Mars one of the closest planets can be seen without a telescope.
1. *Mars, one of the closest planets,*

1. The whole class has read the novel *Old Yeller*.
2. Shana Alexander a former editor of *McCall's* was the main speaker.

3. Do you own a thesaurus a dictionary of synonyms and antonyms?
4. The Galápagos Islands a group of volcanic islands in the Pacific Ocean were named for the Spanish word meaning "tortoise."
5. Rubber an elastic substance quickly restores itself to its original size and shape.
6. This bowl is made of clay found on Kilimanjaro the highest mountain in Africa.
7. The North Sea an arm of the Atlantic Ocean is rich in fish, natural gas, and oil.
8. Jamake Highwater a Blackfoot/Eastern Band Cherokee writes about the history of his people.
9. At Gettysburg a town in Pennsylvania an important battle of the Civil War was fought.
10. My friend Juanita is teaching me to make tortillas.

▶ EXERCISE 9   **Writing Sentences with Appositives**

In this painting by Frederic Remington, cowboys break for a midday meal at the chuck wagon. If you'd worked hard on the ranch all morning, you'd gladly join them! Write

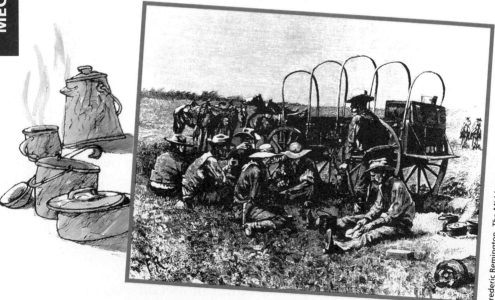

Frederic Remington, *The Midday Meal*, Remington Art Memorial Museum, Ogdensburg, New York.

five sentences about these cowboys and their meal. In your sentences, use five of the following groups of words as appositives or appositive phrases. Be sure that you insert commas wherever they are needed.

EXAMPLE **1.** *The new cook, Jake Thompson, makes great chili.*

the last day on the trail
a terrible cook
our two visitors
the newest ranch hand
the wildest horse in the territory
Jake Thompson
an unusual feast
a good place to eat chow
beans and cornbread again
my partner

(3) Use commas to set off words that are used in direct address.

EXAMPLES **Ben,** please answer the doorbell.
Mom needs you, **Francine.**
Would you show me, **Kadeem,** where the craft store is?

▶ EXERCISE 10 **Correcting Sentences by Adding Commas with Words Used in Direct Address**

Identify the words in direct address from the following sentences. Insert commas before, after, or both before and after the words, as needed.

EXAMPLE **1.** Listen folks to this amazing announcement!
1. *, folks,*

1. Andrea when are you leaving for Detroit?
2. Pay attention now class.
3. Let us my sisters and brothers give thanks.
4. Please Dad may I use your computer?
5. Senator please summarize your tax proposal.

(4) Use commas to set off parenthetical expressions.

A *parenthetical expression* is a side remark that adds information or relates ideas.

EXAMPLES Carl, **on the contrary,** prefers soccer to baseball.
To tell the truth, Jan is one of my best friends.

Common Parenthetical Expressions		
by the way	in fact	of course
for example	in my opinion	on the contrary
however	I suppose	on the other hand
I believe	nevertheless	to tell the truth

Some of these expressions are not always used as parenthetical expressions.

EXAMPLES **Of course** it is true. [not parenthetical]
That is, **of course,** an Indian teakwood screen. [parenthetical]

I **suppose** we ought to go home now. [not parenthetical]
He'll want a ride, **I suppose.** [parenthetical]

▶ EXERCISE 11 **Correcting Sentences by Adding Commas with Expressions That Interrupt**

The following sentences contain parenthetical expressions that require commas. Write the parenthetical expressions, inserting commas as needed.

EXAMPLE **1.** As a matter of fact even a small refracting telescope gives a good view of Saturn's rings.
1. *As a matter of fact,*

1. You don't need a telescope however to see all the beautiful sights in the night sky.
2. For instance on a summer night you can view the Scorpion, the Serpent, and the Serpent Bearer.

3. By the way you should not overlook the Milky Way.
4. The Milky Way in fact is more impressive in the summer than at any other time of year.
5. Hercules of course is an interesting constellation.
6. Studying the constellations is in my opinion a most interesting hobby.
7. It takes an active imagination however to spot some constellations.
8. The Archer for example is hard to see unless you're familiar with a constellation map like this one.
9. The Scorpion on the other hand is quite clearly outlined.
10. Astronomy is a fascinating science I think.

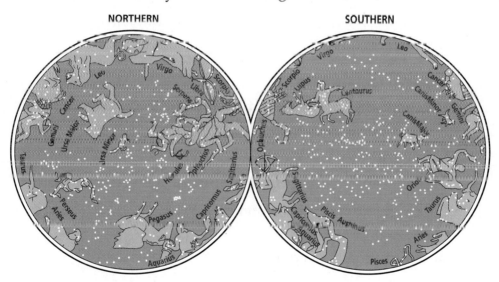

Introductory Words, Phrases, and Clauses

26j. Use a comma after certain introductory elements.

(1) Use a comma after *yes, no,* **or any mild exclamation such as** *well* **or** *why* **at the beginning of a sentence.**

EXAMPLES   **Yes,** you may borrow my bicycle.
Why, it's Lena!
Well, I think you are wrong.

(2) Use a comma after an introductory participial phrase.

EXAMPLES   **Beginning a new school year,** Zelda felt somewhat nervous.

Greeted with applause from the fans, Rashid ran out onto the field.

(3) Use a comma after two or more introductory prepositional phrases.

EXAMPLE   **At the bottom of the hill,** you will see the baseball field.

Use a comma after a single introductory prepositional phrase only when the comma is necessary to make the meaning of the sentence clear.

EXAMPLES   **In the morning they left.** [clear without a comma]

In the morning, sunlight streamed through the window. [The comma is needed so that the reader does not read "morning sunlight."]

(4) Use a comma after an introductory adverb clause.

EXAMPLE   **After I finish my homework,** I will go to the park.

An adverb clause that comes at the end of a sentence does not usually need a comma.

EXAMPLE   I will go to the park **after I finish my homework.**

▶ EXERCISE 12   **Adding Commas with Introductory Elements**

If a comma is needed in a sentence, write the word before the missing comma and add the comma. If a sentence is punctuated correctly, write C.

EXAMPLE   **1.** Walking among the lions the trainer seemed unafraid.

1. *lions,*

1. At our school students eat lunch in the cafeteria.
2. Although the Rev. Jesse Jackson did not win the 1984 or 1988 Democratic presidential nomination he raised many important issues.
3. On the desk in the den you will find your book.
4. Yes I enjoyed the fajitas that Ruben made.
5. Walking home from school Rosa saw her brother.
6. When I go to bed late I have trouble waking up in the morning.
7. Well we can watch *True Colors* or play checkers.
8. Seeing the calculators in the store window George decided to go in and buy one.
9. At the stoplight on the corner of the next block they made a right turn.
10. Because pemmican remained good to eat for several years it was a practical food for many Native American peoples.

Conventional Situations

26k. Use commas in certain conventional situations.

(1) Use commas to separate items in dates and addresses.

EXAMPLES She was born on January 26, 1981, in Cheshire, Connecticut.
A letter dated November 26, 1888, was found in the old house at 980 West Street, Davenport, Iowa.

Notice that a comma separates the last item in a date or in an address from the words that follow it. However, a comma does *not* separate a month and a day (*January 26*) or a house number and a street name (*980 West Street*).

NOTE: Use the correct ZIP Code on every envelope you address. The ZIP Code follows the two-letter state abbreviation without any punctuation between it and the state.

EXAMPLE Fargo, ND 58102

MECHANICS

EXERCISE 13   **Using Commas Correctly**

Rewrite each of the following sentences, inserting commas wherever they are needed.

EXAMPLE   **1.** I received a package from my friend who lives in Irving Texas.
   1. *I received a package from my friend who lives in Irving, Texas.*

1. On May 25 1935 Jesse Owens tied or broke six world track records.
2. The American Saddle Horse Museum is located at 4093 Iron Works Pike Lexington KY 40511.
3. Marian Anderson was born on February 27 1902 in Philadelphia Pennsylvania.
4. Our ZIP Code address is Ames IA 50010.
5. Ocean City New Jersey is a popular seaside resort.

(2) Use a comma after the salutation of a friendly letter and after the closing of any letter.

EXAMPLES   Dear Dad,   Dear Sharon,
   With love,   Yours truly,

 REVIEW A   **Proofreading Sentences for the Correct Use of Commas**

Write each word in the following sentences that should be followed by a comma and add the comma after the word.

EXAMPLE   **1.** The substitute's name is Mr. Fowler I think.
   1. *Fowler,*

1. What time is your appointment Kevin?
2. My aunt said to forward her mail to 302 Lancelot Drive Simpsonville SC 29681.
3. George Washington Carver a famous scientist had to work hard to afford to go to school.
4. Quick violent flashes of lightning caused an average of 14,300 forest fires a year in the United States.

5. My cousin Lono sent me a note on a postcard from Pahala Hawaii.
6. A single branch stuck out of the water and the beaver grasped it in its paws.
7. The beaver by the way is a rodent.
8. This hard-working mammal builds dams lodges and canals.
9. The lodges of American beavers built with their entrances underwater are marvels of engineering.
10. The beaver uses its large tail which is flattened as a rudder.

▶ REVIEW B   **Proofreading Sentences for the Correct Use of Commas**

For the following sentences, write each word that should be followed by a comma and add the comma.

EXAMPLE   1. Kyoto's palaces shrines and temples remind visitors of this city's importance in Japanese history.
   1. *palaces, shrines,*

1. The Procession of the Eras celebrated every autumn takes place in Kyoto.
2. Kyoto a beautiful city was Japan's capital for more than one thousand years.
3. The Procession of the Eras festival which celebrates Kyoto's history begins on October 22.
4. The beautiful solemn procession is a remarkable sight.
5. At the beginning of the festival priests offer special prayers.
6. Portable shrines are carried through the streets and thousands of marchers follow.
7. The photograph on the next page for example shows marchers dressed as ancient warriors.
8. Because the marchers near the front represent recent history they wear costumes from the nineteenth-century Royal Army Era.

MECHANICS

9. Marching at the end of the procession archers wear costumes from the eighth-century Warrior Era.
10. The procession is in fact a rich memorial to Kyoto's long and varied history.

Semicolons

A *semicolon* looks like a combination of a period and a comma, and that is just what it is. A semicolon separates complete thoughts as a period does. A semicolon also separates items within a sentence as a comma does.

26l. Use a semicolon between independent clauses if they are not joined by *and, but, or, nor, for, so,* or *yet.*

EXAMPLES   Jimmy took my suitcase upstairs; he left his own in the car.
            After school, I went to band practice; then I studied in the library for an hour.

26m. Use a semicolon rather than a comma before a coordinating conjunction to join independent clauses that contain commas.

CONFUSING   I wrote to Ann, Ramona, and Mai, and Jean notified Latoya and Sue.

CLEAR   I wrote to Ann, Ramona, and Mai; and Jean notified Latoya and Sue.

NOTE: Semicolons are most effective when they are not over-used. Sometimes it is better to separate a compound sentence or a heavily punctuated sentence into two sentences rather than to use a semicolon.

ACCEPTABLE   In the tropical jungles of South America, it rains every day, sometimes all day; the vegetation there, some of which is found nowhere else in the world, is lush, dense, and fast-growing.

BETTER   In the tropical jungles of South America, it rains every day, sometimes all day. The vegetation there, some of which is found nowhere else in the world, is lush, dense, and fast-growing.

MECHANICS

▶ EXERCISE 14   **Using Semicolons Correctly**

Most of the following sentences have a comma where there should be a semicolon. If the sentence needs a semicolon, write the words before and after the missing semicolon and insert the punctuation mark. If the sentence does not need a semicolon, write C.

EXAMPLE   **1.** Human beings have walked on the moon, they have not yet walked on any of the planets.
1. *moon; they*

1. Miyoko finished her homework, then she decided to go outside.
2. Each January some people predict the major events of the upcoming year, but they are seldom accurate.
3. Tie these newspapers together with string, put the aluminum cans in a bag.

4. I called Tom, Paul, and Francine, and Fred called Amy, Carlos, and Brad.
5. Reading is my favorite pastime, I love to begin a new book.
6. In 1991, Wellington Webb was elected mayor of Denver, he became the first African American to hold that office.
7. The two companies merged, and they became the largest consumer goods firm in the nation.
8. Your grades have improved, you definitely will pass the course.
9. I want to work with animals someday, I might even become a veterinarian.
10. We haven't seen the movie, for it hasn't come to our town yet.

Colons

26n. Use a colon before a list of items, especially after expressions such as *the following* or *as follows.*

EXAMPLES   You will need these items for map work: a ruler, colored pencils, and tracing paper.
Jack's pocket contained the following items: a key, half an apple, a piece of gum, and two rusty nails.
The primary colors are as follows: red, blue, and yellow.

Never use a colon directly after a verb or a preposition. Omit the colon or reword the sentence.

INCORRECT   This marinara sauce is made of: tomatoes, bay leaves, onions, oregano, and garlic.
CORRECT   This marinara sauce is made of the following ingredients: tomatoes, bay leaves, onions, oregano, and garlic.

INCORRECT   My stepsister's favorite sports are: basketball, tennis, swimming, and bowling.

CORRECT   My stepsister's favorite sports are basketball, tennis, swimming, and bowling.

26o. Use a colon between the hour and the minute.

EXAMPLES   8:30 A.M.   10:00 P.M.

26p. Use a colon after the salutation of a business letter.

EXAMPLES   Dear Sir or Madam: Dear Mrs. Foster:
To Whom It May Concern: Dear Dr. Christiano:

26q. Use a colon between chapter and verse in biblical references and between all titles and subtitles.

EXAMPLES   I Chronicles 22:6–19
Harriet Tubman: Conductor on the Underground Railroad

▶ EXERCISE 15   **Using Colons and Commas Correctly**

Make each of the following word groups into a complete sentence by supplying an appropriate list or time. Insert colons and commas where they are needed.

EXAMPLE   **1.** The test will begin at *[time]*
1. *The test will begin at 9:30 A.M.*

1. So far we have studied the following punctuation marks *[list]*
2. You will need these supplies for your project *[list]*
3. If I were writing a book about my friends and me, I would call it *[title with subtitle]*
4. Meet me at the mall at *[time]*
5. My classes this year are the following *[list]*

▶ REVIEW C **Using End Marks, Commas, Semicolons, and Colons Correctly**

The sentences in the following paragraph lack necessary end marks, commas, semicolons, and colons. Write each sentence, inserting the correct punctuation.

EXAMPLE [1] What an unusual clever caring way to help animals
1. *What an unusual, clever, caring way to help animals!*

[1] Animal lovers have you heard about the Sanctuary for Animals [2] Founded by Leonard and Bunny Brook the sanctuary is a safe home for all kinds of animals [3] Through the years hundreds of stray unwanted and abused animals have found a home at the sanctuary [4] It is located on the Brooks' land in Westtown New York [5] On their two hundred acres the Brooks take care of the following animals camels lions elephants and even this Australian kangaroo [6] Of course Mr. and Mrs Brook have cats and dogs and also raise chickens keep horses and look after their other farm animals [7] The Brooks their family and their friends care for animals like this baby cougar they also let

the animals work for themselves [8] How do the animals work [9] The Brooks formed the Dawn Animal Agency and their animals became actors and models [10] You may have seen this camel or some of the other animals in magazines movies television shows and commercials

WRITING APPLICATION

Using Punctuation to Make Your Meaning Clear

When you talk, you have many different ways to make your meaning clear. You pause between ideas, raise and lower your voice, and gesture with your hands. When you write, your words and punctuation have to do all the work. Punctuation helps separate your ideas and show the relationships between them. Notice how changing punctuation changes the meaning in the following sentences.

EXAMPLES   We'll hold the carwash on Saturday, and on Monday we'll be able to buy the new baseball uniforms.
We'll hold the carwash on Saturday and on Monday. We'll be able to buy the new baseball uniforms.

I'll help wash cars with Jeff and Carla, and Susan will put up flyers around town.
I'll help wash cars with Jeff, and Carla and Susan will put up flyers around town.

▶ WRITING ACTIVITY

Your class is sponsoring a carwash to raise money for a special project or trip. You've been chosen to write an announcement about the carwash for publication in a community newsletter. Write a brief announcement telling when and where the carwash will be, how much it will cost, what the money will be used for, and any other important details. In your announcement be sure to use end marks, commas, semicolons, and colons correctly.

Prewriting   List the information that you'll include in your announcement. Clearly state the purpose of the carwash—what your class will spend the money on. You may also want to tell how much money the class needs to raise. Make sure you've included all the facts people will need to know about the time, location, and cost of the carwash.

Writing   As you write your draft, remember that the purpose of your announcement is to attract customers. Write an attention-grabbing first sentence that explains the purpose of the carwash. Be sure to present all your information in clear, complete sentences. Add any important details that you didn't list earlier.

Evaluating and Revising   Ask a friend to read your announcement. Is it clear and straightforward? Does it convince your friend that the carwash is for a good cause? If not, revise, rearrange, or add details.

Proofreading   As you proofread your announcement, pay special attention to your use of punctuation. Remember to check the placement of colons in expressions of time.

Review: Posttest

Using End Marks, Commas, Semicolons, and Colons Correctly

The following sentences lack necessary end marks, commas, semicolons, and colons. Write each sentence, inserting the correct punctuation.

EXAMPLE   **1.** Turtles lizards and crocodiles are reptiles
          1. *Turtles, lizards, and crocodiles are reptiles.*

1. Toads and frogs on the other hand are amphibians
2. Some turtles live on land others live in lakes streams or oceans
3. Although turtles have no teeth they can bite with their strong hard beaks
4. The terms *turtle* and *tortoise* are interchangeable but *tortoise* usually refers to a land dweller.
5. The African pancake tortoise which has a flat flexible shell has a unique means of defense.
6. Faced with a threat it takes the following precautions it crawls into a narrow crack in a rock takes a deep breath and wedges itself in tightly
7. Because some species of tortoises are endangered they cannot be sold as pets
8. Three species of tortoises that live in the United States are the desert tortoise the gopher tortoise and the Texan tortoise.
9. The gopher tortoise lives in the Southeast but the desert tortoise comes from the Southwest
10. The Indian star tortoise now an endangered species is very rare
11. As this kind of tortoise grows older its shell grows larger the number of stars increases and their pattern becomes more complex
12. The Indian star tortoise requires warmth sunlight and a diet of green vegetables
13. Living in fresh water soft-shelled turtles have long flexible noses and fleshy lips
14. Their shells are not really soft however but are covered by smooth skin
15. Wanda may I introduce you to my pet turtle Pokey
16. Pokey who has been part of our family for years is a red-eared slider.
17. The book *Turtles A Complete Pet Owners Manual* has helped me learn how to take care of Pokey

MECHANICS

18. Pokey has been in my family for fifteen years and he could easily live to be fifty
19. If you look at the design on Pokey's shell you can get a good idea of his age
20. Don't you agree with me Wanda that a turtle makes a good pet

SUMMARY OF USES OF THE COMMA

26f	Use commas to separate items in a series—words, phrases, and clauses.
26g	Use a comma to separate two or more adjectives that come before a noun.
26h	Use a comma before *and, but, for, or, nor, so,* and *yet* when they join independent clauses.
26i	Use commas to set off an expression that interrupts a sentence. (1) Use commas to set off nonessential participial phrases and nonessential subordinate clauses. (2) Use commas to set off appositives and appositive phrases that are nonessential. (3) Use commas to set off words used in direct address. (4) Use commas to set off parenthetical expressions.
26j	Use a comma after certain introductory elements. (1) Use a comma after *yes, no,* or any mild exclamation such as *well* or *why* at the beginning of a sentence. (2) Use a comma after an introductory participial phrase. (3) Use a comma after two or more introductory prepositional phrases. (4) Use a comma after an introductory adverb clause.
26k	Use a comma in certain conventional situations. (1) Use commas to separate items in dates and addresses. (2) Use a comma after the salutation of a friendly letter and after the closing of any letter.

27 PUNCTUATION

Underlining (Italics), Quotation Marks, Apostrophes, Hyphens, Parentheses, Dashes

Diagnostic Test

Using Underlining (Italics), Quotation Marks, Apostrophes, Hyphens, Parentheses, and Dashes

The following sentences contain errors in the use of underlining (italics), quotation marks, apostrophes, hyphens, parentheses, or dashes. Write each sentence correctly.

EXAMPLE **1.** My mother's note said, "Please buy celery, rye bread, and milk.

       1. *My mother's note said, "Please buy celery, rye bread, and milk."*

1. Sharon she's my youngest cousin asked me to tell her a bedtime story.
2. "Did you know," asked Kathy, "that the novel *Don Quixote* has seventy four chapters"?

MECHANICS

3. "Have you ever read Robert Hayden's poem 'Those Winter Sundays?" asked Jorge.
4. "Whos your favorite professional baseball player?" asked Don.
5. Randall Jarrell wrote both fiction and nonfiction, but hes best known for his poetry.
6. Many people misspell the word *accommodate* by leaving out one c.
7. "Meet me at 2:30 sharp; don't be late, my mother's note read.
8. The reading list included the novel Island of the Blue Dolphins.
9. My complaint was that the sandwiches we ate at the beach were three fourths sand.
10. In English class today, we read the poem Sisters, which was written by Lucille Clifton.
11. "Can you volunteer just two hours worth of your time a week?" asked Mrs. Jackson.
12. The bearded man you probably guessed is really the jewel thief in disguise.
13. "A group of twenty one students is not a two thirds majority of our class," Stan stated.
14. This coupon is for a free enchilada at Pedros Lunch Palace on Oak Street.
15. The librarian told me that the only copy of the book *Childrens Songs* had been checked out for more than two weeks.
16. Ms. Liu said, Turn to Chapter 7, 'Multiplying Fractions.'"
17. "What is the origin of the word inoculate?" Derrick asked Dr. Jackson.
18. "The state of Massachusetts was named after a Native American people that lived in that area" Jessica said.
19. She added, "The word *Massachusett* also refers to that peoples language."
20. Aunt Rosie and Uncle Fred went to the Bahamas on the cruise ship Princess.

Underlining (Italics)

Italics are printed letters that lean to the right—*like this.* When you write or type, you show that a word should be *italicized* by underlining it. If your composition were to be printed, the typesetter would set the underlined words in italics. For example, if you type

Madeleine L'Engle wrote A Wrinkle in Time.

the sentence would be printed like this:

Madeleine L'Engle wrote *A Wrinkle in Time.*

NOTE: If you use a personal computer, you can probably set words in italics yourself. Most word-processing software and many printers can produce italic type.

27a. Use underlining (italics) for titles of books, plays, periodicals, films, television programs, works of art, long musical compositions, ships, aircraft, and spacecraft.

MECHANICS

TYPE OF NAME	EXAMPLES	
Books	*A Wind in the Door*	*Watership Down* *Mules and Men*
Plays	*Our Town* *Hamlet*	*I Never Sang for My Father*
Periodicals	the *Daily News* *Essence*	*National Geographic*
Films	*The Maltese Falcon*	*Cry Freedom*
Television Programs	*Home Improvement*	*Paleoworld*
Works of Art	*Starry Night* *The Dream*	*Watson and the Shark*
Long Musical Compositions	*Carmen* *An American in Paris*	*Music for the Royal Fireworks*
Ships	the *Titanic* the *Pequod*	the USS *Eisenhower*
Aircraft	the *Silver Dart* the *Hindenburg*	the *Deperdussin Racer*
Spacecraft	*Soyuz XI*	*Atlantis*

NOTE: The article *the* before the title of a newspaper is often neither italicized nor capitalized when it is written within a sentence.

EXAMPLE   Would you like to subscribe to **the** *Chicago Tribune*?

☞ REFERENCE NOTE: For examples of titles that are not italicized but are enclosed in quotation marks, see page 744.

27b. Use underlining (italics) for words, letters, and figures referred to as such.

EXAMPLES   I often confuse the words *accept* and *except*.
Don't forget to double the final *n* before you add *–ing* in words like *running*.
Can you tell whether he wrote a *4* or a *9*?

▶ EXERCISE 1   **Using Underlining (Italics) Correctly**

For each of the following sentences, write each word or item that should be italicized and underline it.

EXAMPLE   **1.** Mike Royko writes a column for the Chicago Tribune.
1. *Chicago Tribune*

1. The British spell the word humor with a u after the o.
2. In Denmark, you might see the spelling *triatlon* for the word triathlon.
3. The current Newsweek has an informative article on the famine in Africa.
4. Our school paper, the Norwalk Valley News, is published weekly.
5. Luis Valdez wrote and directed La Bamba, a movie about the life of Richie Valens.
6. The Oceanic is one of the ocean liners that sail to the Caribbean.
7. The movie Dances with Wolves has some of the most beautiful photography that I have ever seen.
8. Our local theater group is presenting The Time of Your Life, a comedy by William Saroyan.

9. Lindbergh's Spirit of St. Louis is on display at the museum, along with the Wright brothers' Flyer and Gemini IV.
10. The best novel that I read during vacation was The Summer of the Swans.

Quotation Marks

27c. Use quotation marks to enclose a *direct quotation*—a person's exact words.

Be sure to place quotation marks both before and after a person's exact words.

EXAMPLES Emma Lazarus wrote the famous quotation on the Statue of Liberty, which begins with the words "Give me your tired, your poor. . . ."
"When the bell rings," said the teacher, "leave the room quietly."

Do not use quotation marks for an *indirect quotation*—a rewording of a direct quotation.

DIRECT QUOTATION Tom predicted, "It will be a close game." [Tom's exact words]
INDIRECT QUOTATION Tom predicted that it would be a close game. [not Tom's exact words]

27d. A direct quotation begins with a capital letter.

EXAMPLES Maria said, "The *carne asada* isn't ready yet, but please help yourself to the guacamole."
While he was in prison, Richard Lovelace wrote a poem containing the well-known quotation "Stone walls do not a prison make."

27e. When the expression identifying the speaker interrupts a quoted sentence, the second part of the quotation begins with a small letter.

MECHANICS

EXAMPLES   "Lightning has always awed people," explained
Mrs. Worthington, "and many of us are still
frightened by it."
"The time has come," insisted the speaker, "to
improve our educational program."

A quoted sentence that is divided in this way is called a
broken quotation. Notice that each part of a broken quotation is enclosed in a set of quotation marks.

When the second part of a divided quotation is a sentence, it begins with a capital letter.

EXAMPLE   "I can't go today," I said. "Ask me tomorrow."

27f. A direct quotation is set off from the rest of the
sentence by a comma, a question mark, or an
exclamation point, but not by a period.

Set off means "to separate." If a quotation comes at the
beginning of a sentence, a comma follows it. If a quotation
comes at the end of a sentence, a comma comes before it.
If a quoted sentence is interrupted, a comma follows the
first part and comes before the second part.

EXAMPLES   Bernie said**,** "Science is more interesting than
history."
"I especially like to do experiments**,**" Velma
commented.
"Yes**,**" Juan added**,** "Bernie loves to do
experiments, too."

When a quotation ends with a question mark or an
exclamation point, no comma is needed.

EXAMPLES   "Is that a good video game**?**" Jane wanted to
know.
"I'll say it is**!**" Debbie exclaimed.

▶ EXERCISE 2   **Punctuating Quotations**

For each of the following sentences, insert commas, quotation marks, and capital letters where they are needed. If
a sentence is correct, write *C*.

MECHANICS

EXAMPLE   **1.** Let's go to a horror movie this afternoon, said
Bob.

1. *"Let's go to a horror movie this afternoon,"*
said Bob.

1. When I shrieked in fear, the usher warned me to
be quiet.
2. At the same time, Bob whispered it's only a movie—
calm down!
3. He pointed out that the people around us were getting annoyed.
4. I quietly replied I'm sorry.
5. You shouldn't have screamed, he complained.
6. From now on I said to him I promise I'll try to be
quiet.
7. When the lights came on, Bob said it's time to go.
8. Outside the theater he muttered something about
people who shouldn't go to horror movies.
9. But I can't help it I explained.
10. You were even afraid Bob protested during the
credits!

27g.   A period or a comma should always be placed
inside the closing quotation marks.

EXAMPLES   "The Ramses exhibit begins over there," said
the museum guide.
Darnell replied, "I'm ready to see some ancient
Egyptian jewelry and artwork."

27h.   A question mark or an exclamation point should
be placed inside the closing quotation marks
when the quotation itself is a question or an
exclamation. Otherwise, it should be placed
outside.

EXAMPLES   "How far have we come?" asked the exhausted
man. [The quotation is a question.]
Who said, "Give me liberty or give me death"?
[The sentence, not the quotation, is a question.]

MECHANICS

"Jump!" ordered the firefighter. [The quotation is an exclamation.]

I couldn't believe it when he said, "No, thank you"! [The sentence, not the quotation, is an exclamation.]

When both the sentence and the quotation at the end of the sentence are questions (or exclamations), only one question mark (or exclamation point) is used. It is placed inside the closing quotation marks.

EXAMPLE   Did Josh really say, "What's Cinco de Mayo?"

▶ EXERCISE 3   **Punctuating and Capitalizing Quotations**

For each of the following sentences, insert capital letters, quotation marks, and other marks of punctuation where needed.

EXAMPLE   **1.** Ashley Bryan wore traditional African clothes when he came to our school Elton said

1. *"Ashley Bryan wore traditional African clothes when he came to our school," Elton said.*

1. Oh, like the clothes Mr. Johnson showed us in class Janell exclaimed
2. Elton asked have you read any of Ashley Bryan's books about African culture
3. I've read Janell quickly replied the one titled *Beat the Story-Drum, Pum-Pum*
4. I'd like to read that again Elton said those African folk tales are wonderful
5. Mrs. Ray thinks *Walk Together Children* is excellent Janell said
6. Isn't that Elton asked about Negro spirituals
7. You're right Janell answered and Bryan wrote that spirituals are America's greatest contribution to world music
8. She added he grew up in New York City and began writing stories and drawing when he was still in kindergarten

9. Did you know Elton asked that he illustrated his own books

10. This is one of the woodcuts Bryan made to illustrate *Walk Together Children* he added.

Reprinted with the permission of Atheneum Books for Young Readers, an imprint of Simon & Schuster Children's Publishing Division from *Walk Together Children* selected and illustrated by Ashley Bryan. Copyright ©1974 Ashley Bryan.

EXERCISE 4   **Revising Indirect Quotations to Create Direct Quotations**

Revise each of the following sentences by changing the indirect quotation to a direct quotation. Be sure to use capital letters and punctuation wherever necessary.

EXAMPLE   **1.** I asked my grandmother if she would like to help us paint our float.

       1. *"Grandma," I asked, "would you like to help us paint our float?"*

1. Mayor Alaniz announced that he would lead the parade this year.
2. Ms. Feldman asked me what my plans for the big parade were.
3. I answered that my brother and I were building a float.
4. She exclaimed that she thought that was terrific.
5. Ron remarked that our float probably had something to do with sports.

MECHANICS

27i. When you write dialogue (conversation), begin a new paragraph every time the speaker changes.

EXAMPLE   The young man smiled, and said, "My old master, now let me tell you the truth. My home is not so far away. It is quite near your temple. We have been old neighbors for many years."
        The old monk was very surprised. "I don't believe it. You, young man, will have your joke. Where is there another house round here?"
        "My master, would I lie to you? I live right beside your temple. The Green Pond is my home."
        "You live in the pond?" The old monk was even more astonished.
        "That's right. In fact," said Li Aiqi, in a perfectly serious tone, "I'm not a man at all. I am a dragon."

from "Green Dragon Pond," a Bai folk tale

☞ **REFERENCE NOTE:** For more information on writing dialogue, see pages 140 and 194.

27j. When a quotation consists of several sentences, put quotation marks only at the beginning and the end of the whole quotation.

EXAMPLE   "Mary Elizabeth and I will wait for you at Robertson's Drug Store. Please try to get there as soon as you can. We don't want to be late for the concert," Jerome said before he rushed off down the hall.

27k. Use single quotation marks to enclose a quotation within a quotation.

EXAMPLES   Brandon added, "My mom always says, 'Look before you leap.'"
        "Did Ms. Neuman really say, 'It's all right to use your books and your notes during the test'?" asked Sakura.

MECHANICS

PICTURE THIS

Watch out! You and a friend are making sure that no one gets hurt at your little sister's birthday party. If this child hits the piñata hard enough, it will break open. Then all the small toys and treats inside will fall out, and the children will rush for them. Breaking open piñatas, which are papier-mâché figures like this one, is a Latin American party custom. It's also popular in the United States. As you watch the children, you and your friend talk about the scene. Write a short conversation about what you see and hear. Be sure to use quotation marks and punctuation correctly.

Subject: a pinata contest
Audience: a friend
Purpose: to talk about what's happening

MECHANICS

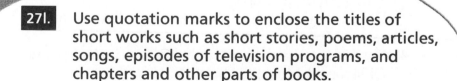

27l. Use quotation marks to enclose the titles of short works such as short stories, poems, articles, songs, episodes of television programs, and chapters and other parts of books.

TYPE OF NAME	EXAMPLES
Short Stories	"A Day's Wait" "The Medicine Bag" "The Circuit"
Poems	"In Time of Silver Rain" "Birdfoot's Grampa" "Annabel Lee"
Articles	"Rooting for the Home Team" "Annie Leibovitz: Behind the Images" "The Storytelling Renaissance"
Songs	"La Cucaracha" "The Star-Spangled Banner" "Swing Low, Sweet Chariot"
Episodes of Television Programs	"Cheap Is Cheap" "This Side of Paradise" "Growing Up Hispanic"
Chapters and Other Parts of Books	"The Natural World" "The Myths of Greece and Rome" "The Double Task of Language"

☞ **REFERENCE NOTE:** For examples of titles that are italicized, see page 735.

▶ EXERCISE 5   **Punctuating Quotations**

Insert quotation marks where they are needed in each of the following items. If a sentence is correct, write C.

EXAMPLE   **1.** Let's sing 'The Ballad of Gregorio Cortez,' suggested Jim.
   1. *"Let's sing 'The Ballad of Gregorio Cortez,'" suggested Jim.*

1. Lani, have you seen my clarinet? asked Rob. It was on this table. I need it for my lesson this afternoon.
2. The most interesting chapter in *The Sea Around Us* is The Birth of an Island.
3. Didn't Benjamin Franklin once say, Time is money? asked Myra.
4. My favorite Langston Hughes poem is As I Grew Older, said Mom.

MECHANICS

5. Lea Evans said, One of the greatest changes in architecture has been in the design of churches. They no longer follow traditional forms. Churches have been built that are shaped like stars, fish, and ships.
6. The latest issue of *Discover* has a fascinating picture of a shark that swallowed an anchor.
7. Do you know which character asked, What's in a name? in *Romeo and Juliet*? I asked.
8. Yes, answered Li. My mother used to say that to me when I was a little girl. That's how I first heard of Shakespeare.
9. A human hand has more than twenty-seven bones and thirty-five muscles! exclaimed Marcus. No wonder it can do so much.
10. There is an article called The Customers Always Write in today's newspaper.

▶ REVIEW A **Punctuating Paragraphs**

Revise the following paragraphs, using quotation marks and other marks of punctuation wherever necessary. Remember to begin a new paragraph each time the speaker changes. If a sentence is correct, write C. [Note: The punctuation marks that are already included in the exercise are correct.]

EXAMPLE [1] **Mr. Brown asked Can you baby-sit tonight?**
1. *Mr. Brown asked, "Can you baby-sit tonight?"*

[1] Last night I baby-sat for the Browns, a new family on our block. [2] Come in Mrs. Brown greeted me. [3] You must be Lisa. [4] Hello, Mrs. Brown I replied. [5] I'm looking forward to meeting the children. [6] First Mrs. Brown explained I want you to meet Ludwig. [7] Is he a member of the family I asked. [8] In a way replied Mrs. Brown as she led me to the kitchen and pointed to an aging dachshund. [9] That is Ludwig. [10] He rules this house and everyone in it.

[11] Mr. Brown entered the kitchen and introduced himself. [12] I see that you've met Ludwig he said. [13] Yes

Mrs. Brown answered for me. [14] Why don't you give Lisa her instructions while I go find the children?

[15] If Ludwig whines said Mr. Brown give him a dog biscuit. [16] Should I take him for a walk I asked. [17] No replied Mr. Brown. [18] Just let him out into the yard.

[19] Mrs. Brown came back into the kitchen with the children. [20] Did my husband remind you to cover Ludwig when he falls asleep she asked. [21] I'll remember I promised [22] But what should I do for the children? [23] Don't worry said Mr. Brown. [24] They'll behave themselves and go to bed when they're supposed to. [25] As I told you laughed Mrs. Brown Ludwig rules this house and everyone in it, even the sitter!

Apostrophes

Possessive Case

The *possessive case* of a noun or a pronoun shows ownership or relationship.

OWNERSHIP	RELATIONSHIP
Kathleen's desk **his** bat **their** car	**anybody's** guess an **hour's** time **horse's** mane

27m. To form the possessive case of a singular noun, add an apostrophe and an *s*.

EXAMPLES   a boy's cap   Cleon's pen
                the baby's toy   Charles's opinion

NOTE: A proper noun ending in *s* may take only an apostrophe to form the possessive case if the addition of *'s* would make the name awkward to say.

EXAMPLES   Philippines' government
              Ms. Rodgers' cat

MECHANICS

▶ EXERCISE 6   ### Using Apostrophes for Singular Possessives

For each sentence in the following paragraph, identify the word that needs an apostrophe. Then, write the word correctly punctuated.

EXAMPLE   [1] **The Prado in Madrid, Spain, is one of the worlds greatest museums.**
   1. *worlds—world's*

[1] Shown here is one of the Prados paintings by Diego Velázquez, *Las Meninas.* [2] Velázquezs painting is known in English as *The Maids of Honor.* [3] In the center of the canvas is Princess Margarita, the royal couples daughter. [4] To the princesss right, a kneeling maid of honor offers her something to drink. [5] To the royal childs left, another maid of honor curtsies. [6] On the far left of the canvas, you can see the artists own image, for he has painted himself! [7] The palaces other important people, such as the chamberlain and a court jester, also appear. [8] The faces of Margaritas parents are reflected in the mirror on the back wall. [9] In the foreground, the royal dog ignores a young guests invitation to play. [10] This paintings fame has grown since it was painted in 1656, and each year millions of people see it while visiting the Prado.

Diego Velázquez, *Las Meninas.* Prado, Madrid, Scala/Art Resource, N.Y.

MECHANICS

27n. To form the possessive case of a plural noun that does not end in *s*, add an apostrophe and an *s.*

EXAMPLES mice's tracks   men's hats
          children's games teeth's enamel

27o. To form the possessive case of a plural noun ending in *s*, add only the apostrophe.

EXAMPLES cats' basket   four days' delay
          brushes' bristles the Carsons' bungalow

NOTE: Do not use an apostrophe to form the *plural* of a noun. Remember that the apostrophe shows ownership or relationship.

INCORRECT Three girls' lost their tickets.
CORRECT Three **girls** lost their tickets. [plural]
CORRECT Three **girls'** tickets were lost. [plural possessive]

▶ EXERCISE 7 **Writing Possessives**

Rewrite each of the following expressions by using the possessive case. Be sure to insert an apostrophe in the right place.

EXAMPLE **1.** food for the dog
         1. *the dog's food*

1. the nominee of the party
2. the clothes of the babies
3. the grades of my sister
4. the name tags of the guests
5. the dish for the cat

▶ EXERCISE 8 **Writing Sentences with Plural Possessives**

Write the plural form of each of the following words. After each plural form, write a sentence using the possessive form of that plural.

1. dog
2. plumber
3. goose
4. friend
5. woman

27p. Do not use an apostrophe with possessive personal pronouns.

EXAMPLES Is that sticker **yours** or **mine**?
Our cat is friendlier than **theirs**.
His report on Cherokee folk tales was as good as **hers**.

☞ REFERENCE NOTE: For more about possessive personal pronouns, see pages 606–607.

27q. To form the possessive case of some indefinite pronouns, add an apostrophe and an *s*.

EXAMPLES neither's homework
everyone's choice
somebody's jacket

☞ REFERENCE NOTE: For more about indefinite pronouns, see page 430.

▶ EXERCISE 9   **Writing Possessives of Indefinite Pronouns**

Rewrite each of the following expressions by using the possessive case of each indefinite pronoun. Be sure to insert an apostrophe in the right place.

EXAMPLE   **1.** the park for everyone
1. *everyone's park*

1. the stereo that belongs to somebody
2. the footprints of anyone
3. the fault of nobody
4. the turn of either
5. the opinion of another

Contractions

27r. Use an apostrophe to show where letters have been omitted (left out) in a contraction.

A *contraction* is a shortened form of a word, a number, or a group of words. The apostrophe in a contraction shows where letters or numerals have been left out.

Common Contractions			
I am	I'm	they have	they've
1993	'93	where is	where's
let us	let's	we are	we're
of the clock	o'clock	he had	he'd
she would	she'd	you will	you'll
book is	book's	Pat has	Pat's

The word *not* can be shortened to *n't* and added to a verb, usually without changing the spelling of the verb.

EXAMPLE
is not	isn't	has not	hasn't
are not	aren't	have not	haven't
does not	doesn't	had not	hadn't
do not	don't	should not	shouldn't
was not	wasn't	would not	wouldn't
were not	weren't	could not	couldn't

EXCEPTIONS   will not . . . . **won't**   cannot . . . . **can't**

Be careful not to confuse contractions with possessive pronouns.

CONTRACTIONS	POSSESSIVE PRONOUNS
It's Friday. [*It is*] **It's** been a pleasure. [*It has*]	**Its** nest is over there.
Who's your server? [*Who is*] **Who's** been practicing the piano? [*Who has*]	**Whose** backpack is this?
You're late. [*You are*]	**Your** mom called
They're arriving soon. [*They are*] **There's** the path. [*There is*]	**Their** parakeet is friendly. That rose bush is **theirs**.

► EXERCISE 10 **Using Apostrophes in Contractions Correctly**

For each of the following sentences, write the word or words requiring an apostrophe and insert the apostrophe. Be sure to spell the word correctly. If a sentence is correct, write *C*.

EXAMPLE **1.** Arent you going with us at one oclock?
   1. *Aren't; o'clock*

1. Wed better chain our bicycles to the rack.
2. That old cars seen better days, hasnt it?
3. She wasnt too happy to see us.
4. Whose ringing the doorbell?
5. We wont forget how helpful youve been.
6. Im certain youll be invited.
7. Whose turn is it to take attendance?
8. Anns an excellent swimmer, but she cant dive.
9. Its almost time to leave, isnt it?
10. Im sure theyll show up before its over.

► EXERCISE 11 **Punctuating Contractions**

For each sentence in the following paragraph, identify the word that needs an apostrophe to indicate a contraction. Then, write the word correctly.

EXAMPLE [1] Whats the best route from Lawrenceville, New Jersey, to Newtown, Pennsylvania?
   1. *What's*

[1] Theres one especially pretty route you can take to get there. [2] I think youll enjoy the drive. [3] You shouldnt go directly west. [4] Youve got to go northwest or south first. [5] Its easier to go south on Route 206 to Route U.S. 1, cross the Delaware River, and then go north on Route 32 to Yardley. [6] From Yardley, turn left on Route 332, and in a little while Im sure you will find yourself in Newtown. [7] If youd prefer a different route, go south on Route 206 to Route 546 and make a right turn to go west. [8] After you cross the Delaware River and the road becomes 532, dont

MECHANICS

turn until Linton Hill Road. [9] When you turn left onto Linton Hill Road, it wont be long before you arrive in Newtown. [10] Heres a map you can use to help you find your way.

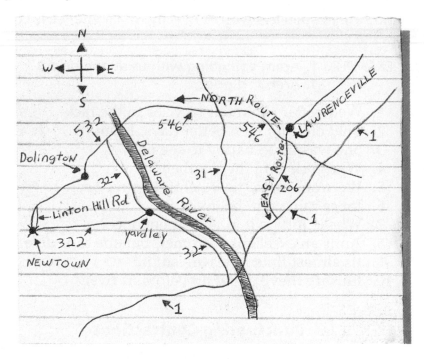

▶ EXERCISE 12   **Writing Contractions**

For each sentence in the following paragraph, write the contraction of the underlined word or words.

EXAMPLE   [1] If you think it <u>should have</u> been easy to visit the building shown on the next page, guess again!
    1. *should've*

[1] <u>It is</u> the Potala Palace in Lhasa, Tibet, which my parents and I visited last year. [2] The city of Lhasa is two miles high in the Himalaya Mountains, and we <u>could not</u> move around much because the lack of oxygen made us tired. [3] The Potala Palace is the former residence of the Tibetan spiritual leader, <u>who has</u> been living in exile in

India. [4] Because this palace is a holy shrine, pilgrims <u>do not</u> mind traveling on foot from all over the country to worship there. [5] After <u>they have</u> bought yak butter in the city square, they take it to the palace as an offering. [6] From the photograph, you <u>cannot</u> imagine how steep those stairs on the right are! [7] Because it <u>would have</u> taken a long time to climb them, our bus driver took us directly to the rear entrance on the left. [8] Once inside, we spent hours exploring the palace, but we <u>were not</u> able to visit most of its more than one thousand rooms! [9] <u>I am</u> sure we would never have found our way out without our guide, who led us to an exit on the right. [10] Walking down the stairs <u>was not</u> too hard, and soon we were in the beautiful central square in the Himalayan sunshine!

▶ EXERCISE 13 **Writing Contractions**

Write a suitable contraction for the blank in each of the following sentences.

1. ___ my sweater?
2. ___ lying on the beach.
3. We ___ help you now.
4. ___ dinner ready?
5. They ___ played that game before.

Plurals

27s. Use an apostrophe and an *s* to form the plurals of letters, numerals, and symbols, and of words referred to as words.

EXAMPLES Your *o*'s look like *a*'s, and your *u*'s look like *n*'s.
There are three *5*'s in his telephone number.
One sign of immature writing is too many *and*'s.
Place *$*'s before monetary amounts and *¢*'s after.

NOTE: Nowadays, many writers leave out the apostrophe if a plural meaning is clear. However, to make your writing clear, you should always use an apostrophe.

▶ REVIEW B **Using Underlining (Italics) and Apostrophes Correctly**

For each of the following sentences, add underlining or apostrophes as necessary. The punctuation already supplied is correct.

EXAMPLE **1.** One of my brothers college textbooks is History of Art by H. W. Janson.
1. *brother's; History of Art*

1. Whos the painter who inspired the musical play Sunday in the Park with George?
2. Hes Georges Seurat, one of Frances greatest painters.
3. "The young childrens reactions to Jacob Lawrences paintings were surprising," Angie said.
4. Didnt you read the review in Rolling Stone of the movie Vincent & Theo?

5. Its about Vincent van Gogh and his brother, who often supported him.
6. "I like Jasper Johns," Rick said, "but I cant tell if that is one of Johnss paintings."
7. Have you ever tried counting all the 2s or 4s in his Numbers in Color painting?
8. On a class trip to Chicago, we saw a bronze statue named Horse by Raymond Duchamp-Villon.
9. In our group, everybodys favorite painting is Cow's Skull: Red, White, and Blue by Georgia O'Keeffe.
10. "On PBS, Ive seen an American Playhouse program about O'Keeffes life," Joyce said.

Hyphens

27t. Use a hyphen to divide a word at the end of a line.

EXAMPLES   In my opinion, what this salad needs is some cu-
cumber slices.
Will you and Marguerite help me put the silver-
ware on the table?

When dividing a word at the end of a line, remember the following rules:

(1) Divide a word only between syllables.

INCORRECT   Mr. Morrison looked around with a bewild-
ered expression.
CORRECT   Mr. Morrison looked around with a bewil-
dered expression.

(2) Do not divide a one-syllable word.

INCORRECT   Exercises like push-ups help to develop strength of the arm muscles.
CORRECT   Exercises like push-ups help to develop
strength of the arm muscles.

(3) Do not divide a word so that one letter stands alone.

INCORRECT	The seating capacity of the new stadium is e-normous.
CORRECT	The seating capacity of the new stadium is enormous.

27u. Use a hyphen with compound numbers from *twenty-one* to *ninety-nine* and with fractions used as modifiers.

EXAMPLES   During a leap year, there are twenty-nine days in February.

Congress may override a president's veto by a two-thirds majority. [*Two-thirds* is an adjective that modifies *majority.*]

The pumpkin pie was so good that only one sixth of it is left. [*One sixth* is not used as a modifier. Instead, *sixth* is a noun modified by the adjective *one.*]

▶ EXERCISE 14   **Using Hyphens Correctly**

Write a number—using words, not numerals—to fit the blank in each sentence. Use hyphens where they are needed.

EXAMPLE   **1.** The sum of ten and fifteen is _____.
            1. *twenty-five*

1. January, March, May, July, August, October, and December are the months that have _____ days.
2. _____ of the moon is visible from the earth, but the other half can be seen only from outer space.
3. In twenty years I will be _____ years old.
4. I used _____ cup, which is 25 percent of the original one cup.
5. Our seventh-grade class has _____ students, fifteen boys and twelve girls.

REVIEW C   **Punctuating Sentences Correctly**

Rewrite the following sentences, inserting underlining, quotation marks, commas, apostrophes, and hyphens as necessary.

EXAMPLE   **1.** For the talent show, Leila recited Poes poem The Raven.

            1. *For the talent show, Leila recited Poe's poem "The Raven."*

1. Queen Hatshepsut seized the throne of Egypt in 1503 B.C. and ruled for twenty one years.
2. Whos borrowed my scissors? demanded Jean.
3. Its hard to decide which authors story I should read first.
4. A weeks vacation never seems long enough.
5. After wed eaten supper, we decided to watch an old episode of Star Trek.
6. The driver shouted Move to the rear of the bus!
7. We didnt eat any salmon during our visit to Oregon.
8. I wasnt sorry admitted the clerk to see those picky customers leave.
9. Very Short on Law and Order is my favorite chapter in Andrew Garcia's autobiographical book Tough Trip Through Paradise.
10. Our new phone number starts with two 6s and ends with two 4s.

Parentheses

27v. Use parentheses to enclose material that is added to a sentence but is not considered of major importance.

EXAMPLES   Emilio Aguinaldo **(**1869–1964**)** was a Filipino patriot and statesman.

           Mom and Dad bought a kilim **(**ki lēm'**)** rug from our Turkish friend Ali.

MECHANICS

Material enclosed in parentheses may be as short as a single word or as long as a short sentence. A short sentence in parentheses may stand alone or be contained within another sentence. Notice that a sentence within a sentence is not capitalized and has no end mark.

EXAMPLES   Please be quiet during the performance.
(Take crying babies to the lobby.)
Jack Echohawk **(he's Ben's cousin)** told us about growing up on a reservation.

▶ EXERCISE 15   **Correcting Sentences by Adding Parentheses**

Insert parentheses where they are needed in the following sentences.

EXAMPLE   **1.** My bicycle I've had it for three years is a ten-speed.
     1. *My bicycle (I've had it for three years) is a ten-speed.*

1. At the age of thirteen, Jennifer Capriati began playing tennis my favorite sport professionally.
2. Elijah McCoy 1843–1929 invented a way to oil moving machinery.
3. I had to buy a new pocket calculator. My old one stopped working.
4. Charlemagne shär'lə mān' was one of Europe's most famous rulers.
5. Lian Young she's a friend of mine told our class about her school in China.

Dashes

A *parenthetical expression* is a word or phrase that breaks into the main thought of a sentence. Parenthetical expressions are usually set off by commas or parentheses.

EXAMPLES   Grandma Moses**, for example,** started painting
in her seventies.
The butler **(Theo Karras)** was the detective's
first suspect.

👉 **REFERENCE NOTE:** For more about using commas with
parenthetical expressions, see page 718. For more about using
parentheses, see pages 757–758.

Some parenthetical elements need stronger emphasis.
In such cases, a dash is used.

27w.   **Use a dash to indicate an abrupt break in
thought or speech.**

EXAMPLES   The right thing to do—I know it'll be hard—is
to apologize.
"Do you think Ann will mind—I really hope she
won't—if I borrow her sunglasses?" asked
Melody.

▶ EXERCISE 16   **Correcting Sentences by Adding
Dashes**

Insert dashes where they are needed in the following
sentences.

EXAMPLE   **1.** The school lunchroom it was a dull green has
been painted a cheery yellow.
1. *The school lunchroom—it was a dull green—
has been painted a cheery yellow.*

1. Fireflies I can't remember where I read this make
what is called cold light.
2. Roberto has always wanted to be can't you guess?
an astronaut.
3. Randy Travis I really want to see his concert has a
new song out.
4. Do you mind I don't if Jill and Mandy go to the mall
with us?
5. The best way to learn how to swim that is, after
you've learned the basic strokes is to practice.

MECHANICS

WRITING APPLICATION

Using Quotations in Reports

In persuasive and informative essays, a direct quotation can sometimes be more effective than a secondhand paraphrase. However, a quotation can be confusing and misleading if it isn't correctly capitalized and punctuated.

CONFUSING   Inés Torro, manager of the Waste Disposal Department, said by the end of December, weekly recycling pickup will be available in all areas of the city.

CLEAR   Inés Torro, manager of the Waste Disposal Department, said, "By the end of December, weekly recycling pickup will be available in all areas of the city."

▶ WRITING ACTIVITY

Your social studies class is taking a survey of people's attitudes toward recycling. Interview at least three people from different households in your community. Ask them specific questions to find out

- whether they think recycling is important
- what items, if any, they recycle
- whether they find it easy or difficult to recycle
- how they think recycling could be made easier for people in the community

Based on the information you gather, write a brief report about recycling in your community. In your report, quote several people's exact words.

Prewriting   First, think of several questions to ask. Word your questions so that they can't be answered with a simple *yes* or *no*. Next, decide whom you want to interview. You might interview friends, family members, or neighbors. Begin each interview by recording the person's name, age, and occupation. During the interview, write down or tape-record what the person says. (If you want to tape the interview, make sure you have the person's permission first.) If you write down the interview, be sure to write the person's answers word for word. (You may need to ask the person to speak slowly.) When all your interviews are completed, compare your interviewees' responses. How are they similar? How are they different? What conclusions can you draw about attitudes toward recycling in your community? Jot down some notes to help you organize your information.

Writing   In the first paragraph of your draft, give a statement that sums up the main idea of your report. Then, use your interviewees' answers to support your main idea. Since you can't quote every word, you'll need to choose your quotations carefully. Quote words and sentences that accurately represent each person's answers and attitudes. Clearly identify each person that you quote. Conclude your report by restating your main idea.

Evaluating and Revising   After you've completed your first draft, reread your main idea. Does the body of your report support that idea? If not, rethink and revise your main idea. Make sure the body of your report follows a logical order. As you organize your report, you may need to add, cut, or rearrange details. Be sure that all direct quotations are correctly quoted. Also, be sure that you have not used a person's words or ideas without giving him or her credit.

Proofreading and Publishing   As you proofread your report, check your quotations against your notes. Be sure you've spelled people's names correctly. Finally, make sure that you've put quotation marks around direct quotations and that you've capitalized and punctuated all quotations correctly. You and your classmates can share your findings and suggestions with the person or agency in charge of recycling in your community. As a class, write a letter that summarizes your findings.

Review: Posttest

A. Proofreading Sentences for the Correct Use of Apostrophes, Quotation Marks, Underlining (Italics), Hyphens, Parentheses, and Dashes

Revise each of the following sentences so that apostrophes, quotation marks, underlining, hyphens, parentheses, or dashes are used correctly. [Note: A sentence may contain more than one error.]

EXAMPLE 1. "May I borrow your copy of 'Life' magazine? Phil asked Alan.

1. *"May I borrow your copy of <u>Life</u> magazine?" Phil asked Alan.*

1. Boris Karloff (his real name was William Henry Pratt played the monster in the original movie version of Frankenstein.
2. "Ive never known—do you? what the word 'kith' means," Phil said.
3. Its just a simple word," Anna said, "that refers to family and friends."
4. I've heard that the programs announcer and inter viewer will be Connie Chung, a favorite of mine.
5. Alan said that "Norma couldn't understand why twenty two people had voted against having the dance on a Friday night.
6. "A two thirds majority of the mens team hadnt played before", Shawn said.
7. Fred said, This magazine article titled *Luxury Liners of the Past* is interesting".
8. "Does the public library have some copies of 'The Seminole Tribune' or any other American Indian newspapers"? Tanya asked.
9. My sisters' like to read folktales in books such as the stories in Two Ways to Count to Ten by Ruby Dee.
10. The Lopezes's cat I dont think they know is living in our garage." Mary said.

B. Punctuating Quotations Correctly

For each of the following sentences, add quotation marks where they are needed.

EXAMPLE **1.** I wonder why so many people enjoy collecting things, said J. D.
1. *"I wonder why so many people enjoy collecting things," said J. D.*

11. I know I do! Julia exclaimed.
12. Tomás said, My grandmother once said, It's the thrill of the hunt.
13. Do you collect anything as a hobby? Josh asked Marsha, who had just entered the room.
14. No, Marsha answered, but I know a person who collects old cameras and antique costume jewelry.
15. My aunt collects John McCormack's records, Kevin said. Do you know who he is?
16. I'm not sure, Julia said, but I think that he was an Irish singer.
17. Yes, he sang in the opera; he also sang popular Irish songs such as The Rose of Tralee, Kevin said.
18. My stepbrother has a collection of arrowheads. He hasn't been collecting them very long, Sydney said.
19. You should see Mrs. Webb's collection of Chinese jade carvings, J. D. said. It's great!
20. Some people—I'm sure you know—have unusual collections, Josh said. For instance, my aunt collects old shoelaces.

28 SPELLING

Improving Your Spelling

Good Spelling Habits

Practicing the following techniques can help you spell words correctly.

1. **To learn the spelling of a word, pronounce it, study it, and write it.** Pronounce words carefully. Mispronunciation can cause misspelling. For instance, if you say *ath • a • lete* instead of *ath • lete,* you will probably spell the word wrong.

   - First, make sure that you know how to pronounce the word correctly, and then practice saying it.
   - Second, study the word. Notice any parts that might be hard to remember.
   - Third, write the word from memory. Check your spelling.
   - If you misspelled the word, repeat the three steps of this process.

2. **Use a dictionary.** When you find that you have misspelled a word, look it up in a dictionary. Don't guess about the correct spelling.

MECHANICS

3. **Spell by syllables.** A *syllable* is a word part that can be pronounced by itself.

   EXAMPLE   thor • ough [two syllables]
              sep • a • rate [three syllables]

   Instead of trying to learn how to pronounce and spell a whole word, break it up into its syllables whenever possible. It's easier to learn a few letters at a time than to learn all of them at once.

   ☞ REFERENCE NOTE: For information on using the dictionary to determine the syllables in a word, see page 857.

▶ EXERCISE 1   **Spelling by Syllables**

Look up the following words in a dictionary, and divide each one into syllables. Pronounce each syllable correctly, and learn to spell the word by syllables.

1. legislature
2. perspire
3. modern
4. temperature
5. probably

6. similar
7. library
8. definition
9. recognize
10. awkward

4. **Proofread for careless spelling errors.** Reread your writing carefully, and correct any mistakes and unclear letters. For example, make sure that your *i*'s are dotted, your *t*'s are crossed, and your *g*'s don't look like *q*'s.

5. **Keep a spelling notebook.** Divide each page into four columns:

   COLUMN 1   Correctly spell the word you missed. (Never enter a misspelled word.)
   COLUMN 2   Write the word again, dividing it into syllables and marking its accents.
   COLUMN 3   Write the word once more, circling the spot that gives you trouble.
   COLUMN 4   Jot down any comments that might help you remember the correct spelling.

MECHANICS

Here is an example of how you might make entries for two words that are often misspelled.

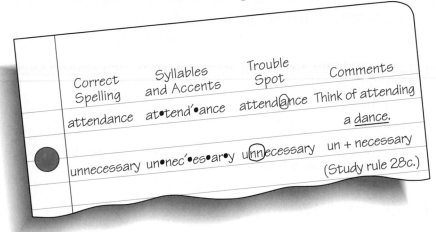

Correct Spelling	Syllables and Accents	Trouble Spot	Comments
attendance	at•tend´•ance	attend@nce	Think of attending a *dance*.
unnecessary	un•nec´•es•ar•y	u(nn)ecessary	un + necessary (Study rule 28c.)

Spelling Rules

ie and *ei*

28a. Write *ie* when the sound is long *e*, except after *c*.

EXAMPLES   chief, brief, believe, yield, receive, deceive
EXCEPTIONS   seize, leisure, either, neither, weird

Write *ei* when the sound is not long *e*, especially when the sound is long *a*.

EXAMPLES   sleigh, veil, freight, weight, height, foreign
EXCEPTIONS   friend, mischief, ancient, pie

You may find this time-tested verse a help.

I before *e*
Except after *c*,
Or when sounded like *a*,
As in *neighbor* and *weigh*.

If you use this rhyme, remember that "*i* before *e*" refers only to words in which these two letters stand for the sound of long *e*, as in the examples under rule 28a.

▶ EXERCISE 2   **Writing Words with *ie* and *ei***

Add the letters *ie* or *ei* to correctly spell each of the following words.

EXAMPLE   **1.** conc . . . t
          1. *conceit*

1. dec . . . ve	**8.** w . . . ght	**15.** rec . . . pt
2. n . . . ther	**9.** . . . ght	**16.** p . . . ce
3. rec . . . ve	**10.** sl . . . gh	**17.** r . . . gn
4. h . . . ght	**11.** fr . . . ght	**18.** th . . . r
5. fr . . . nd	**12.** n . . . ghbor	**19.** s . . . ze
6. l . . . sure	**13.** c . . . ling	**20.** br . . . f
7. misch . . . f	**14.** shr . . . k	

▶ EXERCISE 3   **Proofreading a Paragraph to Correct Spelling Errors**

The following paragraph contains ten spelling errors involving the use of *ie* and *ei*. For each sentence, write the misspelled word or words correctly. If a sentence has no spelling error, write *C*.

EXAMPLE   [1] Last summer I recieved an airline ticket as a
          birthday gift.
          1. *received*

   [1] I used the ticket to fly to Puerto Rico with my freind Alicia to see my grandmother and other relatives. [2] We flew to San Juan, where my grandmother's nieghbor, Mr. Sanchez, met us and drove us to my grandmother's house. [3] When we got there, all of my relatives—aunts, uncles, cousins, neices, nephews—came to welcome us. [4] They couldn't beleive that niether of us had ever been to Puerto Rico before, so the next day, they took us sightseeing. [5] First we went to Humacao, which, as you can see on the map on the next page, is located on the Caribbean. [6] Then we drove along the coast to Ponce, the island's cheif city after San Juan. [7] Continuing north from Ponce, we thought that we'd take a liesurely drive on this mountain road, *Ruta Panoramica*, which means "Panoramic

Road." [8] However, the road turned and twisted so much that I was releived to get back on the main road. [9] After we had a breif rest, we explored the western part of the island. [10] Within two days, Puerto Rico no longer seemed foriegn to us.

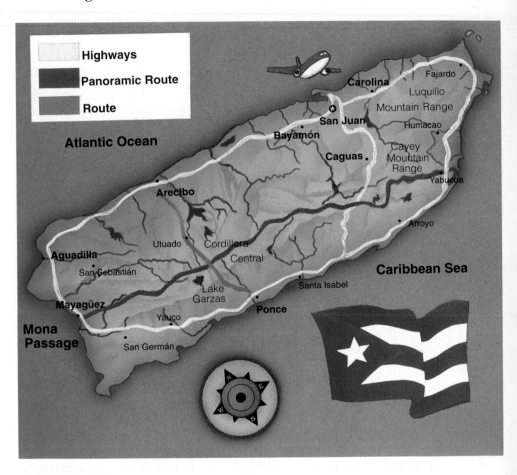

–cede, –ceed, and –sede

28b. The only word ending in *–sede* is *supersede*. The only words ending in *–ceed* are *exceed, proceed,* and *succeed.* Most other words with this sound end in *–cede.*

EXAMPLES   con**cede**, re**cede**, pre**cede**

Prefixes and Suffixes

A *prefix* is a letter or a group of letters added to the begin-ning of a word to change its meaning. A *suffix* is a letter or a group of letters added to the end of a word to change its meaning.

28c. When adding a prefix to a word, do not change the spelling of the word itself.

EXAMPLES   il + legal = **il**legal
un + natural = **un**natural
dis + appear = **dis**appear
mis + spent = **mis**spent

▶ EXERCISE 4   **Spelling Words with Prefixes**

Spell each of the following words, adding the prefix given.

EXAMPLE   **1.** semi + circle
       1. *semicircle*

1. il + legible
2. un + necessary
3. im + partial
4. in + offensive
5. im + mortal

6. mis + spell
7. dis + satisfy
8. dis + approve
9. mis + understand
10. over + rule

28d. When adding the suffix *–ness* or *–ly* to a word, do not change the spelling of the word itself.

EXAMPLES   sudden + ness = sudden**ness**
truthful + ly = truthful**ly**
still + ness = still**ness**
final + ly = final**ly**

EXCEPTION   For most words that end in *y*, change the *y* to *i* before *–ly* or *–ness*.

EXAMPLES   kindly + ness = kindli**ness**
day + ly = daily

MECHANICS

28e. Drop the final silent e before a suffix beginning with a vowel.

Vowels are the letters *a, e, i, o, u,* and sometimes *y.* All other letters of the alphabet are *consonants.*

EXAMPLES   nice + est = nic**est**
                love + able = lov**able**

EXCEPTION   Keep the silent e in words ending in *ce* and *ge* before a suffix beginning with *a* or *o.*

        EXAMPLES   notice + able = notic**eable**
                    courage + ous = courag**eous**

28f. Keep the final e before a suffix beginning with a consonant.

EXAMPLES   care + less = car**eless**
                plate + ful = plat**eful**
                false + hood = fals**ehood**

EXCEPTIONS   argue + ment = argu**ment**
                  true + ly = tru**ly**

MECHANICS

EXERCISE 5   **Spelling Words with Suffixes**

Spell each of the following words, adding the suffix given.

EXAMPLE   **1.** joy + ful
            1. *joyful*

1. hopeful + ly   **5.** desire + able   **9.** true + ly
2. happy + ness   **6.** change + able   **10.** easy + ly
3. sincere + ly   **7.** cross + ing
4. write + ing   **8.** advance + ment

28g. For words ending in *y* preceded by a consonant, change the *y* to *i* before any suffix that does not begin with *i*.

EXAMPLES   friendly + er = friendl**ier**
           beauty + ful = beaut**iful**
           carry + ing = carry**ing**

Words ending in *y* preceded by a vowel do not change their spelling before a suffix.

EXAMPLES   key + ed = key**ed**
           pay + ment = pay**ment**

EXCEPTIONS   lay—la**id**   say—sa**id**   day—da**ily**

28h. Double the final consonant before adding *–ing, –ed, –er,* or *–est* to a one-syllable word that ends in a single consonant preceded by a single vowel.

EXAMPLES   sit + ing = si**tting**
           hop + ed = ho**pped**
           dim + er = di**mmer**

With a one-syllable word ending in a single consonant that is *not* preceded by a single vowel, do not double the consonant before adding *–ing, –ed, –er,* or *–est*.

EXAMPLES   reap + ed = reap**ed**   neat + est = neat**est**
           cold + er = cold**er**   hold + ing = hold**ing**

▶ EXERCISE 6   **Spelling Words with Suffixes**

Spell each of the following words, adding the suffix given.

EXAMPLE   **1.** beauty + ful
          1. *beautiful*

1. bay + ing
2. silly + ness
3. drop + ed
4. deny + ing
5. pity + less
6. swim + er
7. sly + est
8. hurry + ed
9. tap + ing
10. clean + er

> **▶** REVIEW A **Proofreading a Paragraph for Correct Spelling**

Most of the following sentences contain words that have been misspelled. Write each misspelled word correctly. If a sentence is correct, write *C*.

EXAMPLE   [1] Remember the beautyful bonsai trees in the *Karate Kid* movies?
   1. *beautiful*

[1] Bonsai trees can live to be hundreds of years old, yet you can quickly create one of your own in an afternoon. [2] Simpley use these pictures as you proceed through the following steps.

MECHANICS

[3] First, you'll need an inxpensive plant (such as a juniper), some soil, some moss, and a shallow bowl. [4] When you are chooseing a plant, try to get one with a trunk that has some of its roots showing so that your tree will look old. [5] Make a carful study of your plant, and decide how you want the bonsai to look in the bowl. [6] Then, cut or pinch away undesireable branches and leaves until the plant looks like a tree. [7] After triming your plant, remove most of the large roots so that the plant can stand in the bowl. [8] Cover the remaining roots with soil, and if the weather is mild, put your bonsai in a shaded place outside. [9] You don't have to water your plant dayly, but you should keep the soil moist. [10] After your plant has healled, you will have many years of enjoyment from your bonsai.

Forming the Plural of Nouns

28i. Observe the following rules for spelling the plural of nouns:

(1) To form the plural of most nouns, add –s.

SINGULAR	girl	cheese	task	monkey	banana
PLURAL	girls	cheeses	tasks	monkeys	bananas

☞ **REFERENCE NOTE:** Make sure that you do not confuse the plural form of a noun with its possessive form. For a discussion of possessive forms of nouns, see pages 746–748.

(2) Form the plural of nouns ending in *s, x, z, ch,* or *sh* by adding –*es.*

SINGULAR	moss	wax	waltz	birch	dish
PLURAL	mosses	waxes	waltzes	birches	dishes

NOTE: Proper nouns usually follow this rule, too.

EXAMPLES   the Nuñez**es**
the Williams**es**

▶ EXERCISE 7　**Spelling the Plural of Nouns**

Spell the plural form of each of the following nouns.

EXAMPLE　**1.** match
　　　　　　1. *matches*

1. box　　**3.** wrench　**5.** church　**7.** Gómez　**9.** miss
2. crash　**4.** address　**6.** index　　**8.** ditch　**10.** tax

(3) Form the plural of nouns ending in *y* preceded by a consonant by changing the *y* to *i* and adding –*es*.

SINGULAR　lady　　hobby　　county　　strawberry
　PLURAL　lad**ies**　hobb**ies**　count**ies**　strawberr**ies**

EXCEPTION　With proper nouns, simply add –*s*.
EXAMPLES　the Appleby**s**　　the Trilby**s**

(4) Form the plural of nouns ending in *y* preceded by a vowel by adding –*s*.

SINGULAR　toy　　journey　　highway　　Wednesday
　PLURAL　toy**s**　journey**s**　highway**s**　Wednesday**s**

(5) Form the plural of most nouns ending in *f* by adding –*s*. The plural of some nouns ending in *f* or *fe* is formed by changing the *f* to *v* and adding either –*s* or –*es*.

SINGULAR　gulf　　belief　　knife　　loaf　　wolf
　PLURAL　gulf**s**　belief**s**　kni**ves**　loa**ves**　wol**ves**

NOTE:　When you are not sure about how to spell the plural of a noun ending in *f* or *fe*, look in a dictionary.

(6) Form the plural of nouns ending in *o* preceded by a vowel by adding –*s*. The plural of many nouns ending in *o* preceded by a consonant is formed by adding –*es*.

SINGULAR　patio　　ratio　　veto　　hero
　PLURAL　patio**s**　ratio**s**　veto**es**　her**oes**

EXCEPTIONS　Eskimo—Eskimo**s**　silo—silo**s**

Form the plural of most musical terms ending in *o* by adding –*s*.

SINGULAR   piano   alto   solo   trio
PLURAL   pianos   altos   solos   trios

NOTE: To form the plural of some nouns ending in *o* preceded by a consonant, you may add either –*s* or –*es*.

SINGULAR   banjo   mosquito   flamingo
PLURAL   banjos   mosquitos   flamingos
     or   *or*   *or*
     banjoes   mosquitoes flamingoes

(7) The plural of a few nouns is formed in irregular ways.

SINGULAR   man   mouse   foot   ox   child
PLURAL   men   mice   feet   oxen children

▶ EXERCISE 8   **Spelling the Plural of Nouns**

Spell the plural form of each of the following nouns.

EXAMPLE   **1.** industry
           1. *industries*

1. turkey   6. self
2. studio   7. chimney
3. chief   8. baby
4. soprano   9. tomato
5. puppy   10. echo

(8) Form the plural of compound nouns consisting of a noun plus a modifier by making the modified noun plural.

SINGULAR   sister-in-law   coat-of-arms
PLURAL   sisters-in-law   coats-of-arms
SINGULAR   Chief of State   editor in chief
PLURAL   Chiefs of State   editors in chief

☞ REFERENCE NOTE: For more on compound nouns, see page 423.

MECHANICS

(9) The plural of a few compound nouns is formed in irregular ways.

SINGULAR   eight-year-old   tie-up   drive-in
　PLURAL   eight-year-old**s**   tie-up**s**   drive-in**s**

(10) Some nouns are the same in the singular and the plural.

SINGULAR AND PLURAL   deer   sheep   salmon   Sioux

(11) Form the plural of numerals, letters, symbols, and words referred to as words by adding an apostrophe and –s.

SINGULAR   **100**   *B*   **&**   *the*
　PLURAL   **100's**   *B'***s**   **&'s**   *the'***s**

NOTE: In your reading you may notice that some writers do not use apostrophes to form the plurals of numerals, letters, symbols, and words referred to as words. However, using an apostrophe is never wrong. Therefore, it is best always to use the apostrophe.

EXERCISE 9   **Spelling the Plural of Nouns**

Spell the plural form of each of the following nouns.

EXAMPLE   **1.** push-up
　　　　　1. *push-ups*

1. side-wheeler
2. moose
3. mother-in-law
4. 1930
5. *m*
6. thirteen-year-old
7. trout
8. governor-elect
9. Chinese
10. commander in chief

Shoe reprinted by permission: Tribune Media Services.

MECHANICS

Words Often Confused

People often confuse the words in each of the following groups. Some of these words are *homonyms,* which means that their pronunciations are the same. However, these words have different meanings and spellings. Other words in the following groups have the same or similar spellings yet have different meanings.

accept	[verb] *to receive; to agree to* The Lanfords would not *accept* our gift.
except	[preposition] *with the exclusion of; but* Everyone *except* Lauren agreed.
advice	[noun] *a recommendation for action* What is your mother's *advice?*
advise	[verb] *to recommend a course of action* She *advises* me to take the camp job.
affect	[verb] *to act upon; to change* Does bad weather *affect* your health?
effect	[noun] *result; consequence* What *effect* does the weather have on your health?
already	*previously* We have *already* studied the customs of the Navajo people.
all ready	*all prepared* or *in readiness* The crew is *all ready* to set sail.

MECHANICS

 EXERCISE 10   **Choosing Between Words Often Confused**

From each pair in parentheses, choose the word or words that will make the sentence correct.

EXAMPLE   **1.** All of us (*accept, except*) Josh forgot our tickets.
         1. *except*

1. By the time Melba arrived, Roscoe had (*already, all ready*) baked the sweet potatoes.
2. One of the purposes of the Cabinet is to (*advice, advise*) the president.
3. The soft music had a soothing (*affect, effect*) on the tired child.
4. The girls were (*already, all ready*) for the sleigh ride.
5. The arrival of Buddhism in Japan had an enormous (*affect, effect*) on Japanese culture.
6. The snow has melted everywhere (*accept, except*) in the mountains.
7. The doctor's (*advice, advise*) was to drink plenty of fluids and to rest.
8. Sarita was happy to (*accept, except*) the invitation to the party.
9. Reading the newspaper usually (*affects, effects*) my ideas about current events.
10. What do you (*advice, advise*) me to do?

altar	[noun] *a table or stand at which religious rites are performed* There was a bowl of flowers on the *altar*.
alter	[verb] *to change* Another hurricane may *alter* the shoreline near our town.
altogether	*entirely* It is *altogether* too cold for swimming.
all together	*everyone in the same place* Will our class be *all together* at the Ramses exhibit?

brake [noun] *a device to stop a machine*
        I used the emergency *brake* to prevent
            the car from rolling downhill.
break [verb] *to fracture; to shatter*
        Don't *break* that mirror!

capital *a city, the location of a government*
        What is the *capital* of this state?
capitol *building; statehouse*
        The *capitol* is on Congress Avenue.

cloths *pieces of cloth*
        I need some more cleaning *cloths.*
clothes *wearing apparel*
        I decided to put on warm *clothes.*

EXERCISE 11   **Choosing Between Words Often Confused**

From each pair in parentheses, choose the word or words that will make the sentence correct.

EXAMPLE   **1.** If it rains, we will (*altar, alter*) our plans.
           1. *alter*

1. My summer (*cloths, clothes*) are loose and light.
2. In England, you can still see remains of (*altars, alters*) built by early tribes.
3. Going down a steep mountain, a bicyclist can wear out a set of (*brakes, breaks*).
4. You should use soft (*cloths, clothes*) to clean silver.
5. The cold weather did not (*altar, alter*) Ling's plans for the Chinese New Year celebration.
6. Accra is the (*capital, capitol*) of Ghana.
7. Put the pieces of the vase (*altogether, all together*), and I will try to repair it.

8. Did he (*brake, break*) his promise?
9. On the dome of the (*capital, capitol*) stands a large bronze statue.
10. The audience was (*altogether, all together*) charmed by the mime's performance.

coarse	[adjective] *rough, crude, not fine* The *coarse* sand acts as a filter.
course	[noun] *path of action; series of studies* [also used in the expression *of course*] What is the best *course* for me to take? You may change your mind, *of course*.
complement	[noun] *something that completes* Red shoes are a good *complement* to that outfit.
compliment	[verb] *to praise someone;* [noun] *praise from someone* Mrs. Katz *complimented* Jean on her speech. Thank you for the *compliment*.
council	*a group called together to accomplish a job* The mayor's *council* has seven members.
councilor	*a member of a council* The mayor appointed seven *councilors*.
counsel	[noun] *advice;* [verb] *to give advice* He needs legal *counsel* on this matter. His attorney will *counsel* him before the hearing.
counselor	*one who advises* Mr. Jackson is the guidance *counselor* for the seventh grade.

> **des′ert** [noun] *a dry, barren, sandy region; a wilderness*
> This cactus grows only in the *desert.*
>
> **desert′** [verb] *to abandon; to leave*
> Good sports do not *desert* their teammates.
>
> **dessert′** [noun] *the final course of a meal*
> Let's have fresh peaches for *dessert.*

▶ EXERCISE 12   **Choosing Between Words Often Confused**

From each pair in parentheses, choose the word that will make the sentence correct.

EXAMPLE   **1.** At the end of dinner, we ate (*desert, dessert*).
            1. *dessert*

1. The city (*council, counsel*) will not meet unless seven of the ten (*councilors, counselors*) are present.
2. The patient received (*council, counsel*) from the doctor on the best (*coarse, course*) to a speedy recovery.
3. Chutney and yogurt are often the (*complements, compliments*) of Indian food.
4. When we visited Cairo, we saw the Nile River, of (*coarse, course*).
5. Juan is preparing the enchiladas, and I'm making empanadas for (*desert, dessert*) tonight.
6. Marilyn made a hand puppet out of (*coarse, course*) burlap.
7. The major would not (*desert, dessert*) her regiment.
8. I want your (*council, counsel*), not your (*complements, compliments*).
9. My mother and father both took part in Operation (*Dessert, Desert*) Storm.
10. Our camp (*councilor, counselor*) suggested that we eat fruit for (*desert, dessert*).

MECHANICS

formally	*with dignity; following strict rules or procedures* We must behave *formally* at the reception.
formerly	*previously; at an earlier date* *Formerly,* people thought travel to the moon was impossible.
hear	[verb] *to receive sounds through the ears* You can *hear* a whisper through these walls.
here	[adverb] *in this place* How long have you lived *here?*
its	[possessive form of *it*] That book has lost *its* cover.
it's	[contraction of *it is* or *it has*] *It's* the coldest winter anyone can remember. *It's* not rained for two months.
lead	[verb, present tense, rhymes with *feed*] *to go first, to be a leader* Can she *lead* us out of this tunnel?
led	[verb, past tense of *lead*] *went first* Elizabeth Blackwell *led* the movement for hospital reform.
lead	[noun, rhymes with *red*] *a heavy metal; graphite used in a pencil* There is no *lead* in a *lead* pencil.
loose	[adjective, rhymes with *moose*] *not tight* This belt is too *loose.*
lose	[verb] *to suffer loss* Fran will *lose* the argument if she doesn't check her facts.

> **passed** [verb, past tense of *pass*] *went by*
> He *passed* us five minutes ago.
> **past** [noun] *that which has gone by;* [preposition]
> *beyond;* [adjective] *ended*
> Good historians make the *past* come alive.
> We rode *past* your house.
> That era is *past*.

▶ EXERCISE 13 **Choosing Between Words Often Confused**

From each pair in parentheses, choose the word that will make the sentence correct.

EXAMPLE **1.** Kaya (*lead, led*) us to the ceremonial lodge.
1. *led*

1. The woman who (*formally, formerly*) (*lead, led*) the band moved to Alaska.
2. We do not expect to (*loose, lose*) any of our backfield players this year.
3. We (*passed, past*) three stalled cars this morning on our way to school.
4. "Why did you (*lead, led*) us (*hear, here*)?" the angry group demanded.
5. Can you (*hear, here*) the difference between the CD and the album?
6. The workers removed the (*lead, led*) pipes from the old house.
7. How did the ship break (*loose, lose*) from both of its anchors?
8. The guests are to dress (*formally, formerly*) for the inauguration ball.
9. "I think (*it's, its*) time for a pop quiz," announced Mrs. Ferrari.
10. Has the school bus already gone (*passed, past*) our street, Tiffany?

MECHANICS

peace	*quiet order and security* World *peace* is the goal of the United Nations.
piece	*a part of something* Lian bought that *piece* of silk in Hong Kong.
plain	[adjective] *unadorned, simple, common;* [noun] *a flat area of land* Jeans were part of his *plain* appearance. A broad, treeless *plain* stretched before them.
plane	[noun] *a flat surface; a tool; an airplane* Use an inclined *plane* to move that couch. I have just learned how to use a carpenter's *plane*. Have you ever flown in a *plane*?
principal	[noun] *the head of a school;* [adjective] *chief, main* The *principal* spoke of the *principal* duties of students.
principle	[noun] *a rule of conduct; a fundamental truth* Action should be guided by *principles*.
quiet	[adjective] *still and peaceful; without noise* The forest was very *quiet*.
quite	[adverb] *wholly or entirely; to a great extent* Some students are already *quite* sure of their career plans.
shone	[verb, past tense of *shine*] *gleamed; glowed* The moon *shone* softly over the grass.
shown	[verb, past participle of *show*] *revealed* Tamisha has *shown* me how to crochet.

> EXERCISE 14
Choosing Between Words Often Confused

From each pair in parentheses, choose the word that will make the sentence correct.

EXAMPLE   **1.** Mr. Ramírez used a (*plain, plane*) to smooth the board.
1. *plane*

1. Each drop of water (*shone, shown*) like crystal.
2. Motor vehicles are one of the (*principal, principle*) sources of air pollution in our cities.
3. If you don't hurry, you'll miss your (*plain, plane*).
4. The (*principal, principle*) of trust can lead to world (*peace, piece*).
5. Jan has (*shone, shown*) me how to change a tire.
6. It is clear that Luisa is acting on (*principal, principle*), not from a personal motive.
7. On Christmas Eve we always sing carols and have a (*peace, piece*) of fruitcake.
8. "What a (*quiet, quite*) Fourth of July," said Gloria.
9. "For once," the (*principal, principle*) announced with a smile, "you don't have to be (*quiet, quite*)."
10. (*Plain, Plane*) fruits and vegetables can provide a delicious and nutritious meal.

> EXERCISE 15
Proofreading for Words Often Confused

In the following paragraph, identify the ten misspelled words. Then give the correct spelling of each word.

EXAMPLE   [1] Some portraits are quiet striking.
1. *quiet—quite*

[1] The painting on the next page is by Rembrandt, one of the principle painters of the seventeenth century. [2] The portrait, probably of a rabbi in Amsterdam, is quiet lovely even though it is relatively plane. [3] The painting illustrates one of Rembrandt's main artistic principals, the strong contrast between light and dark. [4] Light is shown

MECHANICS

only on the rabbi's face, hands, and a peace of his clothing. [5] The rest of the painting is quiet dark, creating a
somber plain that highlights these lighted features. [6] The
rabbi is shone in a state of piece, and the lack of detail in the
painting gives an impression of quite elegance.

Rembrandt van Rijn, *Portrait of an Old Man.* Florence, Uffizi, Scala/Art Resource, N.Y.

stationary	[adjective] *in a fixed position* Is that chalkboard *stationary?*
stationery	[noun] *writing paper* Do you have any white *stationery?*
than	[a conjunction used in comparisons] Alaska is bigger *than* Texas.
then	[adverb] *at that time* If she will see me after class, we can talk about it *then.*

> **their**   [possessive form of *they*]
>   Can you understand *their* message?
> **there**   [adverb] *a place*; [also used to begin a
>   sentence]
>   Let's meet *there*.
>   *There* are toys hidden inside the piñata.
> **they're**   [contraction of *they are*]
>   *They're* all from Guam.

> **threw**   [verb, past tense of *throw*] *tossed; cast*
>   Ted *threw* me the mitt.
> **through**   [preposition]
>   I can't see *through* the lens.

▶ EXERCISE 16   **Choosing Between Words Often Confused**

From each pair or group in parentheses, choose the word that will make the sentence correct.

EXAMPLE   **1.** When will we arrive (*their, they're, there*)?
              1. *there*

1. That noise is from a jet plane going (*threw, through*) the sound barrier.
2. The stars appear to be (*stationary, stationery*), but we know that (*their, there, they're*) moving at very high speeds.
3. Thailand is much larger (*than, then*) South Korea.
4. The pitcher (*threw, through*) a curveball.
5. A (*stationary, stationery*) store usually sells paper, pencils, and other supplies.
6. We started our trip in Barcelona and (*than, then*) traveled west to Madrid.
7. The girls brought (*their, there, they're*) displays for the science fair.
8. A moving target is much harder to hit (*than, then*) a (*stationary, stationery*) one.

MECHANICS

9. Each time Chris got a free throw, he lobbed the ball neatly (*threw, through*) the net to score one point.
10. (*Their, They're, There*) first rehearsal will be after school today.

to	[preposition] We are going *to* Mexico.
too	[adverb] *also; more than enough* Audrey is going, *too*. Kazuo used *too* much miso; consequently, the soup was very salty.
two	*one plus one* We bought *two* sets of chopsticks.
weak	[adjective] *feeble; not strong* Melinda's illness has left her very *weak*.
week	[noun] *seven days* Let's practice again next *week*.
weather	[noun] *the condition of the atmosphere* The *weather* seems to be changing.
whether	[conjunction] *if* We don't know *whether* to expect rain or snow.
who's	[contraction of *who is* or *who has*] *Who's* going to the museum? "*Who's* been eating my porridge?" asked Papa Bear.
whose	[possessive form of *who*] *Whose* report was the most original?
your	[possessive form of *you*] What is *your* middle name?
you're	[contraction of *you are*] *You're* my best friend.

▶ EXERCISE 17   **Choosing Between Words Often Confused**

From each pair or group in parentheses, choose the word that will make the sentence correct.

EXAMPLE   **1.** What are (*your, you're*) plans for celebrating Juneteenth?
      1. *your*

1. (*Who's, Whose*) the present Secretary of State of the United States?
2. My stepsister and I built (*to, too, two*) snow forts on our front lawn.
3. "(*Your, You're*) late," my friend complained.
4. Would you be able to stand the (*weather, whether*) in Alaska?
5. That sounds like a (*weak, week*) excuse to me.
6. (*Your, You're*) dog is (*to, too, two*) sleepy to learn any new tricks.
7. "(*Who's, Whose*) boots and mittens are these?" Mrs. Allen asked.
8. The pilot must quickly decide (*weather, whether*) to parachute to safety or try to land the crippled plane.
9. Spring break starts next (*weak, week*).
10. My family is going (*too, to, two*) New Orleans for the holidays.

▶ EXERCISE 18   **Writing Sentences with Words Often Confused**

You are the new meteorologist for a local television station. Tonight is your first broadcast, and you still haven't written your script. Using the weather map on the next page, write five sentences for your script. In each sentence, use one of the words from the following list. Underline each one you use.

to	weak	whose
two	weather	your
too	whether	you're
week	who's	

MECHANICS

EXAMPLE   **1.** *I'll let you know <u>whether</u> you'll need an umbrella this weekend, right after these messages.*

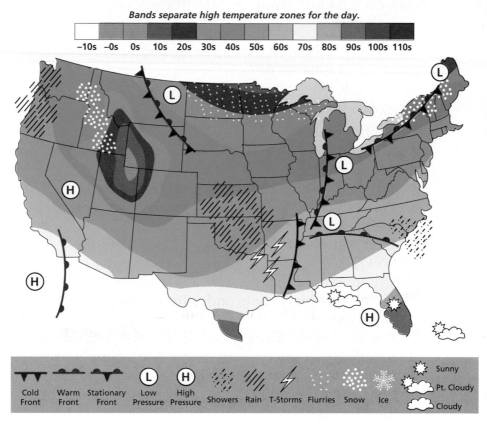

Bands separate high temperature zones for the day.

–10s –0s 0s 10s 20s 30s 40s 50s 60s 70s 80s 90s 100s 110s

 REVIEW B

Choosing Between Words Often Confused

From each pair or group in parentheses, choose the word or words that will make the sentence correct.

EXAMPLE   My parents asked my [1] (*advice, advise*) about where we should spend our vacation.
1. *advice*

Last March, my family could not decide [1] (*weather, whether*) to visit Boston or Philadelphia. Finally, we decided on Boston, the [2] (*capital, capitol*) of Massachusetts. We drove [3] (*to, too, two*) the city in three days. Even my parents could not conceal [4] (*their, there, they're*) excitement. We did not [5] (*loose, lose*) a moment. Boston [6] (*formally, formerly*) was "the hub of the universe," and we discovered that [7] (*it's, its*) still a fascinating city.

Everyone in my family [8] (*accept, except*) me had eaten lobster, and I ate my first one in Boston. I was not [9] (*altogether, all together*) certain how to eat the lobster, but my doubt did not [10] (*affect, effect*) my appetite. My parents insisted that pear yogurt was a strange [11] (*desert, dessert*) to follow lobster, but I would not [12] (*altar, alter*) my order. After the pear yogurt, I asked for a small [13] (*peace, piece*) of pie, but my father told me to be [14] (*quiet, quite*).

While in Boston, we walked up and down the streets just to [15] (*hear, here*) the strange accent of the Bostonians. [16] (*Their, There, They're*) especially noted for [17] (*their, there, they're*) pronunciation of *a*'s and *r*'s.

We had not been in Boston long before the [18] (*weather, whether*) bureau predicted a big snowstorm for the area. Since we had not taken the proper [19] (*cloths, clothes*) for snow, we decided to return home. On the way back, we were [20] (*already, all ready*) making plans for another visit to Boston.

50 Commonly Misspelled Words

As you study the following words, pay particular attention to the letters in italics. These letters generally cause the greatest difficulty in correctly spelling the words.

a*ch*e	color	fri*e*nd	r*ea*dy	ti*r*ed
ag*ai*n	cou*gh*	gu*e*ss	s*ai*d	toni*gh*t
a*l*ways	coul*d*	hal*f*	s*ays*	tri*es*
ans*w*er	c*ou*ntry	h*ou*r	sens*e*	tr*ou*ble
beli*e*ve	da*i*ly	inst*ea*d	sho*es*	*u*pon
b*ui*lt	doctor	l*ai*d	sin*ce*	*u*sing
busy	doesn't	min*u*te	special	w*ea*r
b*uy*	don't	oft*e*n	strai*gh*t	wom*e*n
ca*nn*ot	e*a*rly	*o*nce	thou*gh*	won't
can't	e*a*sy	p*ai*d	throu*gh*	*w*rite

200 Spelling Words

absence
absolutely
acceptance
accommodate
accumulate
achieve
acquire
across
advertisement
against

aisles
among
announce
anxiety
apologize
apparent
appreciation
arctic
arguing
argument

arithmetic
assistance
associate
attacked
attendance
attitude
attorney
audience
basis
beginning

benefit
bicycle
bough
bouquet
brief

brilliant
bureau
business
candidate
career

careless
carrying
ceased
ceiling
choice

college
committee
completely
conceive
conscience

conscious
control
correspondence
courteous
criticize

curiosity
decision
definite
describe
description

desirable
discipline
divine
efficiency
eighth

eliminate
embarrass
equipment
especially
exactly

excellent
execute
existence
experience
experiment

explanation
extremely
familiar
favorite
February

field
fierce
finally
foliage
foreign
fortunately
forty
fourth
genius
genuine

government
governor
grammar
guarantee
height
heir
humorous
hungrily
icicles
imaginary

immediately
independent
intelligence
interest
interpret

MECHANICS

jealous
judgment
knowledge
laboratory
leisure

license
liquor
loneliness
losing
luxury
magazine
marriage
mathematics
meant
medicine

mischief
muscle
museum
necessary
nervous
nineteen
ninety
occasion
occur
occurrence

opinion
opportunity
opposite
originally
particularly
patience
perceive
performance
permanent
personal

physical
picnic
possess
preferred
privilege
probably
professor
pursue
realize
receive

recommend
referred
religion
repetition
rhythm
safety
satisfy
scene
schedule
seize

separate
shining
similar
society
speech
strength
studying
succeed
success
surprise

suspicion
sympathy
teammates
technique
temperament

temporary
theory
thorough
tomorrow
tongue

tournament
tragedy
transferred
treasury
uncomfortable
university
unnecessary
unusually
vacuum
vague

various
veil
vicinity
villain
violence
warrior
wholly
whose
writing
yield

29 CORRECTING COMMON ERRORS

Key Language Skills Review

This chapter reviews key skills and concepts that pose special problems for writers.

- Sentence Fragments and Run-on Sentences
- Subject-Verb and Pronoun-Antecedent Agreement
- Verb Forms
- Comparison of Modifiers
- Misplaced Modifiers
- Capitalization
- Punctuation—End Marks, Commas, Quotation Marks, Apostrophes, Semicolons, and Colons
- Spelling
- Standard Usage

Most of the exercises in this chapter follow the same format as the exercises found throughout the grammar, usage, and mechanics sections. You will notice, however, that two sets of review exercises are presented in standardized test formats. These exercises are designed to provide you with practice not only in solving usage and mechanics problems but also in dealing with these kinds of problems on such tests.

▶ EXERCISE 1 **Revising Sentence Fragments**

Most of the following groups of words are sentence fragments. Revise each fragment by (1) adding a subject, (2) adding a verb, or (3) attaching the fragment to a complete sentence. You may need to change the punctuation and capitalization, too. If the word group is already a complete sentence, write *S*.

EXAMPLE **1.** Because she likes Chihuahuas.
　　　　　1. *My mother bought a book about dogs because she likes Chihuahuas.*

1. Wanted to study the history of Chihuahuas.
2. Small dogs with big, pointed ears.
3. When my mother's Chihuahuas begin their high-pitched barking.
4. Chihuahuas lived in ancient Mexico.
5. Ancient stone carvings showing that Toltecs raised Chihuahuas during the eighth or ninth century A.D.
6. Are related to dogs of the Middle East.
7. Travelers may have brought Chihuahuas with them to the Americas as companions.
8. That Chihuahuas generally score poorly on canine intelligence tests.
9. However, can be trained to assist people who are hard of hearing.
10. If you want a Chihuahua.

▶ EXERCISE 2 **Identifying and Revising Sentence Fragments**

Identify each of the following groups of words as a sentence fragment or a complete sentence. Write *F* for a fragment and *S* for a sentence. Then, revise each fragment by adding a subject or a verb or by attaching the fragment to a complete sentence before or after it. You may need to change the punctuation and capitalization, too.

EXAMPLE **1.** Juggling a fascinating hobby.
　　　　　1. *F—Juggling is a fascinating hobby.*

1. If you would like to be able to juggle.
2. You might start with a good, simple how-to book.
3. Most people can learn the basic moves.
4. Within a fairly short period of time.
5. While beginners develop a sense of how to hold one juggling bag.
6. They also practice standing in the proper, relaxed way.
7. Next must master the ability to toss one bag back and forth.
8. Then learning the right way to throw two bags.
9. Beginners often need to practice juggling with two bags for some time.
10. Before they move up to three bags.

▶ EXERCISE 3   **Revising Run-on Sentences**

Revise each of the following run-on sentences by (1) making it into two separate sentences or (2) using a comma and a coordinating conjunction. Remember to capitalize the first word of every sentence and to use the correct end mark.

EXAMPLE   **1.** Anthony uses chopsticks skillfully I have trouble with them.
    1. *Anthony uses chopsticks skillfully, but I have trouble with them.*

1. The large crane lifted the ten-ton box, it set the box on the concrete deck.
2. My dad does not know much about computers he has learned to surf the Internet.
3. Allen Say wrote *The Ink-Keeper's Apprentice* the events in the story are based on his boyhood in Japan.
4. Two robins landed on the ice in the birdbath one of them drank water from around the thawed edges.
5. Egyptian hieroglyphics may be written from left to right or from right to left, they may be written from top to bottom.
6. John is my youngest brother Levi is my oldest brother.
7. The nature preserve was beautiful some people had littered along the hiking trails.

8. Grandma believes in keeping a positive attitude, she says that thinking positively is the key to a happy life.
9. Let's see that new movie from Korea I have never seen a Korean movie.
10. All my friends like to shop for bargains at the mall, I do, too.

▶ EXERCISE 4   **Revising Run-on Sentences**

Revise each of the following run-on sentences by (1) making it into two separate sentences or (2) using a comma and a coordinating conjunction.

EXAMPLE   **1.** James Earl Jones is a famous actor he has been in movies and plays.

　　　　　1. *James Earl Jones is a famous actor. He has been in movies and plays.*

1. You may not remember seeing James Earl Jones, you would likely recognize his voice.
2. Jones provided the voice of Darth Vader in the *Star Wars* movies, Jones's deep voice helped make the character forceful and frightening.
3. Jones has a distinctive voice he has even won a medal for his vocal delivery.
4. The prize was given by the American Academy of Arts and Letters, is that the organization that gives the Academy Awards?
5. Jones's autobiography was published in 1993 it is appropriately titled *Voices and Silences.*
6. Jones was born in Mississippi in 1931, he was raised by his grandparents on a farm in Michigan.
7. His father was a prizefighter and an actor Jones decided to be an actor, too, and studied in New York City.
8. He portrayed a boxing champion in *The Great White Hope,* he starred in the Broadway production and the movie version of the play.
9. He won a Tony Award for his Broadway performance he was nominated for an Academy Award for his role in the movie.

10. Another of Jones's movies is *The Man*, in that movie he plays the United States' first African American president.

▶ EXERCISE 5 **Revising Sentence Fragments and Run-on Sentences**

Identify each of the following groups of words by writing *F* for a fragment, *R* for a run-on, and *S* for a complete sentence. Revise each fragment by (1) adding a subject, (2) adding a verb, or (3) attaching the fragment to a complete sentence. Revise each run-on by (1) making it into two separate sentences or (2) using a comma and a coordinating conjunction. You may need to change the punctuation and capitalization, too.

EXAMPLE **1.** Because my ancestors were Scandinavian.
        1. *F—I have heard many stories about Vikings because my ancestors were Scandinavian.*

1. The Viking Age lasted three centuries, it started at the end of the eighth century A.D.
2. Vikings from Scandinavian countries known today as Sweden, Denmark, and Norway.
3. Since Vikings lived along the sea, they often became boatbuilders, sailors, and explorers.
4. The influence of the Vikings was enormous Vikings developed trade routes in western Europe and the Middle East.
5. Also were skilled at fishing and farming.
6. All Vikings spoke the language called Old Norse they shared similar religious beliefs.
7. Odin was the chief god of the Vikings, Odin's son Thor was worshiped more widely.
8. After they accepted Christianity, Vikings built many wooden churches.
9. Was divided into three social classes—royal families, free citizens, and slaves.
10. Viking women held several important rights, they could own property and land, for example.

▶ EXERCISE 6 **Identifying Verbs That Agree in Number with Their Subjects**

For each of the following sentences, choose the form of the verb in parentheses that agrees with the subject.

EXAMPLE **1.** The band (*play, plays*) mostly reggae.
1. *plays*

1. Samantha and Matthew (*take, takes*) art classes at the museum.
2. (*Do, Does*) the card table and the folding chairs belong in that closet?
3. Earlene (*don't, doesn't*) know the exact time because her watch stopped.
4. Both the stalagmites and the stalactites (*was, were*) casting eerie shadows
5. Several of the other exchange students (*speak, speaks*) Portuguese.
6. Neither an emu nor an ostrich (*lay, lays*) eggs that look like that.
7. The members of the audience always (*clap, claps*) as soon as the star appears on stage.
8. Mike said that either the main herd or the stragglers (*is, are*) in the near canyon.
9. The coaches on the visiting team (*agree, agrees*) with the referee's decision.
10. Some of the fruit pies (*sell, sells*) for less than three dollars each.

▶ EXERCISE 7 **Identifying Verbs That Agree in Number with Their Subjects**

For each of the following sentences, choose the form of the verb in parentheses that agrees with the subject.

EXAMPLE **1.** (*Do, Does*) you know what a powwow is?
1. *Do*

1. Each of us in my class (*has, have*) given a report about powwows, which are ceremonies or gatherings of American Indians.

2. Dancing and feasting (*is, are*) important activities at powwows.
3. People in my family (*come, comes*) from different parts of the country to attend the Crow Fair in Montana.
4. Many of the people at the powwow (*has, have*) come here from Canada.
5. Everyone here (*know, knows*) that it is the largest powwow in North America.
6. Peoples represented at the fair (*include, includes*) the Crow, Lakota, Ojibwa, Blackfoot, and Cheyenne.
7. Only one of my relatives (*dance, dances*) all four of the main kinds of dances at powwows.
8. Both skill and practice (*go, goes*) into the Traditional, Fancy, Grass, and Jingle-dress dances.
9. Last year, all of the costumes of the Fancy dancers (*was, were*) extremely colorful.
10. Either a row of porcupine quills or a string of glass beads (*goes, go*) all the way around some of the dancers' headdresses.

▶ EXERCISE 8   **Proofreading Sentences for Correct Pronoun-Antecedent Agreement**

Most of the following sentences contain errors in pronoun-antecedent agreement. Identify each error, and give the correct pronoun. If a sentence is correct, write *C*.

EXAMPLE   **1.** Jesse and Michael enjoyed his Kwanzaa activities.
1. *his—their*

1. During Kwanzaa, December 26 through January 1, several of our friends and neighbors celebrate his or her African heritage.
2. African American families affirm traditional values and principles during their Kwanzaa activities.
3. This year, both of my sisters made storybooks as her zawadi, or Kwanzaa gifts.
4. Either Uncle Willis or Uncle Roland will bring their candles for the observance.

5. One of them also will bring their wooden candle-holder, called a *kinara*.
6. The joyful celebration of Kwanzaa has its origins in African harvest festivals.
7. Each of my parents will discuss their own individual ideas about Kwanzaa.
8. Either Lily or Charlotte mentioned in their speech that Kwanzaa was created in 1966.
9. Nobody in our family likes to miss their turn to make up dances on the sixth day of Kwanzaa.
10. Jerry and Charles will volunteer his time on the third day of Kwanzaa, when collective work is celebrated.

 EXERCISE 9

Proofreading Sentences for Correct Subject-Verb and Pronoun-Antecedent Agreement

Most of the following sentences contain agreement errors. For each error, identify the incorrect verb or pronoun, and supply the correct form. If the sentence is correct, write *C*.

EXAMPLE **1.** Every animal, including humans, need water to survive.
　　　　　1. *need—needs*

1. The human body consist mostly of water.
2. You, I, and everyone else, in fact, is about 65 percent water.
3. Everybody in my family tries to drink eight glasses of water a day.
4. "Don't Carlos usually drink more than that?" Janette asked.
5. Either Angie or Ramona said that their family usually drinks bottled water.
6. Evidence shows that water helps our bodies keep its proper temperature.
7. Ian or Calinda have studied the mineral content of our local water.
8. Industry and agriculture depend on a good water supply for its success.

9. Most of the world's fresh water is frozen in icecaps and other glaciers.
10. Erosion of land and mountains occur when water weathers soil and rock.

▶ EXERCISE 10 **Writing the Forms of Regular and Irregular Verbs**

For each of the following sentences, fill in the blank with the correct present participle, past, or past participle form of the verb given.

EXAMPLE **1.** *eat* Angela has already _____ her serving of acorn squash.

1. *eaten*

1. *install* The new shopping mall has _____ wheelchair ramps at all entrances.
2. *send* We have already _____ for a new crossword puzzle magazine.
3. *see* Have you _____ the koalas at the Australian wildlife exhibit?
4. *put* Marianna is _____ together a colorful mobile.
5. *grow* My uncle _____ the largest pumpkin in the United States this year.
6. *draw* Anthony has _____ two different self-portraits.
7. *run* Both of my stepbrothers _____ in this year's Cowtown Marathon.
8. *jump* Have the cats _____ out of the tree?
9. *write* Murasaki Shikibu of Japan _____ what may be the world's first novel.
10. *go* More than half of my friends had _____ to the May Day parade.

▶ EXERCISE 11 **Proofreading Sentences for Correct Verb Forms**

If one of the following sentences contains an incorrect past or past participle form of a verb, write the correct form. If a sentence is correct, write *C*.

EXAMPLE   **1.** Many African American women maked names for themselves during the pioneer days.
       1. *made*

1. Someone lended me a book called *Black Women of the Old West.*
2. It contains many biographies of African American women who leaded difficult but exciting lives.
3. For example, May B. Mason gone to the Yukon to mine gold during the Klondike Gold Rush.
4. Era Bell Thompson writed articles about "the wild West" for a Chicago newspaper.
5. She telled about her frontier life in *American Daughter.*
6. Our teacher has spoke highly of Dr. Susan McKinney Stewart, a pioneer physician.
7. During the 1800s, Cathy Williams wore men's clothes and served under the name William Cathy as a Buffalo Soldier in the U.S. Army.
8. I have saw a picture of Williams at work on her farm.
9. Mary Fields choosed an exciting but sometimes hard life in the West.
10. Nicknamed "Stagecoach Mary," she drived freight wagons and stagecoaches in Montana.

▶ EXERCISE 12   **Proofreading Sentences for Correct Verb Forms**

If one of the following sentences contains an incorrect past or past participle form of the verb, write the correct form. If a sentence is correct, write *C.*

EXAMPLE   **1.** When I was ten, I begun to collect stamps.
       1. *began*

1. Over the years, my collection has growed to fill nearly two binders.
2. I have went to several stamp shows.
3. At nearly every show, I seen many rare and valuable stamps.
4. I told my friend Warren that I aim to own some of those stamps one day.

5. I saw a picture of a rare two-cent stamp that cost one collector $1.1 million in 1987.
6. As you might imagine, that price setted a world record!
7. Stamps have appear in many shapes.
8. My uncle, a mail carrier, sended me a banana-shaped stamp.
9. He also has give me a book about stamp collecting.
10. It sayed that stamp collecting was already a popular hobby by the 1860s.

▶ EXERCISE 13   **Identifying Correct Pronoun Forms**

For each of the following sentences, choose the correct form of the pronoun in parentheses.

EXAMPLE   **1.** Doris and (*me, I*) would like to go to Vietnam.
        1. *I*

1. Will you take the first-aid class with (*us, we*)?
2. The captain of the debate team is (*she, her*).
3. The minister gave (*them, they*) a wedding present.
4. Ulani and (*he, him*) shouted "Aloha!" to their arriving guests.
5. Mr. Galvez saved the comics especially for (*I, me*).
6. (*They, Them*) are learning how to draw with pastels.
7. R. J. asked (*her, she*) for a Beatles CD.
8. Stan's jokes amused Martha and (*me, I*).
9. The person who called you last night was (*me, I*).
10. The principal gave (*him, he*) the key to the trophy case.

▶ EXERCISE 14   **Identifying Correct Pronoun Forms**

For each of the following sentences, choose the correct form of the pronoun in parentheses.

EXAMPLE   **1.** The guest speaker told (*us, we*) students many facts about Hispanic Americans in the arts.
        1. *us*

1. Mrs. Ramirez picked out some poems by Jimmy Santiago Baca and read (*they, them*) to us.

2. Jan and (*he, him*) agree that Barbara Carrasco's murals are outstanding.
3. Between you and (*I, me*), Gaspar Perez de Villagra's account of an early expedition to the area now called New Mexico sounds interesting.
4. (*He, Him*) wrote the first book in what is now the United States.
5. Our teacher showed (*we, us*) pictures of the work of the Puerto Rican artist Arnaldo Roche.
6. (*Who, Whom*) is your favorite artist?
7. The writings of Christina Garcia appeal to (*we, us*).
8. In Luz's opinion, however, the best writer is (*she, her*).
9. Tito Puente has recorded at least one hundred albums and has appeared in several movies; we saw (*he, him*) in *Radio Days*.
10. (*Who, Whom*) did you learn about?

▶ EXERCISE 15 **Choosing Correct Forms of Modifiers**

For each of the following sentences, choose the correct form of the modifier in parentheses.

EXAMPLE **1. Many people think that of all pets Siamese cats are the (*better, best*) ones.**
1. *best*

1. The boys thought that they were (*stronger, strongest*), but the girls beat them in the tug of war.
2. The (*simplest, simpler*) way to attract birds to a yard is by having water available for them.
3. Jovita is the (*most intelligent, intelligentest*) student in the seventh grade.
4. I worry about my grades (*least often, less often*) now that I do my homework every night.
5. Kim Lee has traveled (*farthest, farther*) on her bicycle than anyone else in class.
6. Hasn't this year's quiz-bowl team won (*more, most*) competitions than last year's team?
7. Grandfather says that this winter is the (*colder, coldest*) one he remembers.

8. Wynton Marsalis was born in the city (*more, most*) associated with jazz—New Orleans.
9. Bicyclists who wear protective headgear are injured (*least, less*) often than those who do not.
10. Louisiana has (*fewer, fewest*) wetlands than it once had.

▶ EXERCISE 16

Revising Sentences to Eliminate Double Comparisons and Double Negatives

Revise each of the following sentences to eliminate each double comparison or double negative.

EXAMPLES
1. Of the three games, the first was the least funnest.
1. *Of the three games, the first was the least fun.*
2. There are not hardly any stores near my family's ranch.
2. *There are hardly any stores near my family's ranch.*

1. The recycling center is much more busier than it used to be.
2. Sometimes even indoor water pipes freeze if they do not have no insulation around them.
3. Our dog Sammy is most happiest when the weather is cold.
4. I haven't received a birthday card from neither of my grandmothers yet.
5. Almost any circle that you draw by hand will be less rounder than one you draw with a compass.
6. Wearing sunscreen can make being in the sun more safer.
7. My cousin Giovanni is not like nobody else I know.
8. We never went nowhere during spring vacation this year.
9. That was probably the most cleverest chess move I've ever seen.
10. When I'm old enough to vote, I'm not never going to miss a chance to do so.

▶ EXERCISE 17 **Revising Sentences by Correcting the Placement of Modifiers**

Each of the following sentences contains an error in the placement of modifiers. Revise each sentence by adding or rearranging words or by doing both to correct the placement of each modifier.

EXAMPLE **1.** My grandmother and I saw a horse on the way to the movie.
  1. *On the way to the movie, my grandmother and I saw a horse.*

  1. The party was held in the park celebrating Mary's birthday.
  2. With wind-filled sails, I saw a ship approaching the harbor.
  3. The tree was struck by lightning that we had pruned.
  4. The Yamamotos enjoyed planting the iris that arrived from their Japanese relatives in a box.
  5. The softball team is from my hometown that won the district championship.
  6. Trying to steal home, the catcher tagged the runner.
  7. Jaime told Katya about the kitten playing in a happy voice.
  8. Painted bright colors, Kamal saw many houses.
  9. Hanging from a clothes rack, the drama students finally found the costumes.
  10. Recently picked from the orchard, the bowl was full of fruit.

▶ EXERCISE 18 **Identifying Correct Usage**

Choose the correct word or words in parentheses in each of the following sentences.

EXAMPLE **1.** The boys carried the recycling containers (*themselves, theirselves*).
  1. *themselves*

  1. This orange marmalade smells (*bad, badly*).
  2. In science class last week, we learned (*how come, why*) water expands when it freezes.

3. The dam (*busted, burst*) because of the rising flood waters.
4. Mario should plant (*fewer, less*) bulbs in that small flower bed.
5. This button looks (*like, as if*) it will match the material I bought for the blouse I'm making.
6. Let's (*try and, try to*) arrive at the concert early so that we can get good seats.
7. The defending champion played (*good, well*) during the chess tournament.
8. Yes, our nearest neighbor lives a long (*way, ways*) from us.
9. Those (*kind, kinds*) of fabrics were originally made in a place in India called Madras.
10. Did you share the leftover chop suey (*among, between*) the three of you?

▶ EXERCISE 19 **Identifying Correct Usage**

Choose the correct word or words in parentheses in each of the following sentences.

EXAMPLE **1.** Mrs. Lawrence is (*learning, teaching*) us about the Hohokam culture.
  1. *teaching*

1. Experts think that the Hohokam civilization (*might of, might have*) begun around 300 B.C.
2. Where did the Hohokam people (*live, live at*)?
3. The Hohokam (*use to, used to*) live in the American Southwest.
4. Hohokam farmers grew crops in a climate that was (*real, extremely*) dry.
5. The Hohokam irrigated the land by using (*alot, a lot*) of canals—more than six hundred miles of them!
6. (*Them, These*) canals sometimes changed the courses of entire rivers.
7. The Hohokam were also skilled artisans (*who's, whose*) work included jewelry, bowls, and figurines.

8. I (*can, can't*) hardly imagine what caused the culture to change so much around A.D. 1450.

9. We read (*that, where*) one excavated Hohokam site is known as Snaketown.

10. (*Their, They're*) descendants are the Papago and the Pima peoples.

▶ EXERCISE 20 **Proofreading Sentences for Correct Usage**

Each of the following sentences contains an error in English usage. Identify each error. Then, write the correct usage.

EXAMPLE **1.** If that ain't the proper first aid for heat exhaustion, what is?

1. *ain't—isn't*

1. During the track meet, we used a American Red Cross guidebook for first aid.

2. Fortunately, their was a handy section on treating heat exhaustion.

3. The day of the meet, the temperature was hotter then it had been all summer.

4. The athletes were all ready hot by the time that the races began.

5. Some of the runners should of drunk more water than they did.

6. Several runners which were not used to the high temperatures needed treatment for heat exhaustion.

7. We helped them like the first-aid guidebook instructed.

8. They soon felt alright after we took them out of the heat and helped them cool down.

9. The doctor on duty at the meet examined them and checked they're vital signs.

10. According to the doctor, even athletes in good condition must guard theirselves against heat exhaustion and heatstroke.

Grammar and Usage Test: Section 1

DIRECTIONS Read the paragraph below. For each numbered blank, select the word or group of words that best completes the sentence. Indicate your response by shading in the appropriate oval on your answer sheet.

EXAMPLE

The platypus is one of __(1)__ kinds of mammals that lay eggs.

    1. (A) to
        (B) too
        (C) two
        (D) 2

SAMPLE ANSWER   **1.**

The platypus is __(1)__ very unusual mammal. It __(2)__ external ears, __(3)__ feet are webbed, and it has thick fur. A broad tail and a fleshy bill __(4)__ to the platypus's odd appearance. Platypuses use __(5)__ bills to catch the water worms and insects that platypuses eat. Besides having a bill like a duck's, a platypus is __(6)__ like a bird than a mammal in another important way. Like a duck, the platypus __(7)__ eggs. The mother deposits __(8)__ in a nest, __(9)__ she has dug in a river bank. Platypuses live in Australia and make their nests __(10)__ burrows.

---

1. (A) an
    (B) a
    (C) the
    (D) some

2. (A) don't have no
    (B) doesn't have no
    (C) has any
    (D) has no

3. (A) its
    (B) it's
    (C) its'
    (D) their

4. (A) adds
    (B) add
    (C) added
    (D) are adding

5. (A) its
    (B) it's
    (C) they're
    (D) their

6. (A) more
    (B) most
    (C) less
    (D) least

7. (A) lays
    (B) lies
    (C) is lying
    (D) has lain

8. (A) it
    (B) they
    (C) them
    (D) their

9. (A) which
    (B) what
    (C) who
    (D) whom

10. (A) inside of
     (B) outside of
     (C) a ways from
     (D) inside

Grammar and Usage Test: Section 2

DIRECTIONS   Part or all of each of the following sentences is under-lined. Using the rules of standard written English, choose the answer that most clearly expresses the meaning of the sentence. If there is no error, choose A. Indicate your response by shading in the appropriate oval on your answer sheet.

EXAMPLE

1. The chopsticks that my aunt sent us made of bamboo .

    (A) The chopsticks that my aunt sent us made of bamboo .
    (B) The chopsticks that my aunt sent us are made of bamboo.
    (C) The chopsticks are made of bamboo, that my aunt sent us.
    (D) That my aunt sent us chopsticks made of bamboo.

SAMPLE ANSWER   1.

1. Don't buy none of that ripe fruit if you don't plan to eat it soon.

    (A) Don't buy none of that ripe fruit if you don't plan to eat it soon.
    (B) Do buy none of that ripe fruit if you don't plan to eat it soon.
    (C) Don't buy none of that ripe fruit if you do plan to eat it soon.
    (D) Don't buy any of that ripe fruit if you don't plan to eat it soon.

2. The study group meeting in the library this Wednesday?

    (A) The study group meeting in the library this Wednesday?
    (B) The study group that will be meeting in the library this Wednesday?
    (C) Is the study group meeting in the library this Wednesday?
    (D) Will the study group meeting in the library this Wednesday?

3. Some visitors to the park enjoy rock climbing others prefer kayaking.

    (A) climbing others prefer kayaking
    (B) climbing, others prefer kayaking
    (C) climbing, others, who prefer kayaking
    (D) climbing, and others prefer kayaking

4. Martin prepares the salad, Justine set the table.

    (A) prepares the salad, Justine set the table
    (B) prepares the salad, and Justine sets the table
    (C) prepared the salad and Justine sets the table
    (D) preparing the salad, and Justine set the table

5. Many Cherokee now live in Oklahoma, but this area were not their original home.

    (A) this area were not their original home
    (B) this area was not their original home
    (C) this area was not they're original home
    (D) this area were not they're original home

6. <u>Pulling weeds in the garden, a tiny toad was discovered by Ernie.</u>
   (A) Pulling weeds in the garden, a tiny toad was discovered by Ernie.
   (B) A tiny toad was discovered pulling weeds in the garden by Ernie.
   (C) While pulling weeds in the garden, a tiny toad was discovered by Ernie.
   (D) Pulling weeds in the garden, Ernie discovered a tiny toad.

7. <u>Will rehearse together for the class play.</u>
   (A) Will rehearse together for the class play.
   (B) Will be rehearsing together for the class play.
   (C) Tamara and I will rehearse together for the class play.
   (D) Because we will rehearse together for the class play.

8. Some people are <u>more afraider</u> of snakes than of any other kind of animal.
   (A) more afraider
   (B) afraider
   (C) more afraid
   (D) most afraid

9. <u>The singer waved to some people he knew in the audience from the stage.</u>
   (A) The singer waved to some people he knew in the audience from the stage.
   (B) The singer waved to some people from the stage he knew in the audience.
   (C) The singer waved to some people from the stage in the audience he knew.
   (D) The singer waved from the stage to some people he knew in the audience.

10. <u>Several important African kingdoms developed between Lake Chad and the Atlantic Ocean.</u>
    (A) Several important African kingdoms developed between Lake Chad and the Atlantic Ocean.
    (B) Several important African kingdoms that developed between Lake Chad and the Atlantic Ocean.
    (C) Several important African kingdoms between Lake Chad and the Atlantic Ocean.
    (D) Several important African kingdoms developing between Lake Chad and the Atlantic Ocean.

EXERCISE 21 **Correcting Errors in Capitalization**

The following groups of words contain errors in capitalization. Correct the errors either by changing capital letters to lowercase letters or by changing lowercase letters to capital letters. Some capital letters are already used correctly.

EXAMPLE **1.** a buddhist temple
 1. *a Buddhist temple*

1. appalachian state university
2. world history and math 101
3. tuesday, May 1
4. senator williams
5. Summer In texas
6. Thirty-Fifth avenue
7. saturn and the moon
8. a korean Restaurant
9. empire state building
10. will rogers turnpike

 EXERCISE 22 **Proofreading Sentences for Correct Capitalization**

In each of the following sentences, find the words that should be capitalized but are not. Write the words correctly.

EXAMPLE **1.** American Indians gave the name buffalo soldiers to African American troops who served in the West during the civil war.
 1. *Buffalo Soldiers, Civil War*

1. Thirteen Buffalo Soldiers won the congressional medal of honor, which is the highest military award in the United States.
2. *black frontiers: A history of African american heroes in the Old west,* by Lillian Schlissel, was published in 1995.
3. A chapter about mary fields relates the story of a woman known as Stagecoach Mary, who drove freight wagons and stagecoaches in the west.
4. One of the museums listed in the back of the book is the great plains black museum in Omaha, Nebraska.

5. The book also tells about benjamin singleton, who was born into slavery.
6. After the Civil War, he and some others bought land and founded the communities of Nicodemus and dunlap, kansas.
7. The exciting story of the cowboy Nat Love is told in his autobiography, *the life and adventures of Nat Love.*
8. bill pickett, who was of black, white, and American Indian ancestry, was one of the most famous rodeo competitors of all time.
9. Pickett's biography was published by the university of oklahoma press in 1977.
10. The businessman and gold miner Barney Ford became very wealthy and built ford's hotel on fifteenth street in denver, Colorado.

▶ EXERCISE 23 **Proofreading Sentences for the Correct Use of Commas**

For the following sentences, write each word or number that should be followed by a comma, and add the comma.

EXAMPLE **1.** The colors of the French flag are red white and blue.
1. *red, white,*

1. No the mountain dulcimer is not the same as the hammered dulcimer but both of them are stringed instruments.
2. Abraham Lincoln who was the sixteenth president of the United States died on April 15 1865.
3. If you want to knit a sweater you will need to get knitting needles yarn and a pattern.
4. After oiling the wheels on his sister's wagon Tyrel oiled the wheels on his skates and on his bicycle.
5. Running in the 10K race Nathan found that he was faster than his friends.
6. In my opinion a person should be fined if loose trash left in the back of his or her pickup truck blows out and litters the road.

7. Lupe please show us how to use the new computer program.
8. Although Cody doesn't like cats he rescued one from a tree.
9. I hope that Amy Tan my favorite author will write another book soon.
10. Many people want to conserve resources yet some of these people overlook such simple ways to conserve as turning off the water while brushing their teeth.

▶ EXERCISE 24 **Using End Marks and Commas Correctly**

The following sentences lack necessary end marks and commas. Write the word before each missing end mark or comma, and insert the correct punctuation.

EXAMPLE **1.** When will Anita Luis Martina and Sam be back from the mall
1. *Anita, Luis, Martina, mall?*

1. Wow look at the size of that alligator
2. Leaning against the mast I could feel the sails catch the wind
3. Won't these colorful flowered curtains brighten this room
4. By the way that stack of old newspapers should be recycled
5. Oil paints whether used for art projects or for home improvement should be used only in well-ventilated areas
6. Hidiko watch out for that cactus
7. Was Uncle Jesse born in Cincinnati Ohio or Louisville Kentucky
8. As far as I am concerned the most interesting parts of the lecture were about the life of W E B DuBois
9. Monday Tuesday or Wednesday will be fine for our next meeting
10. Would you like to watch a movie tonight or should I bring over the model-plane kit to work on

EXERCISE 25 **Using Semicolons and Colons Correctly**

The following sentences lack necessary semicolons and colons. Write the word or number that comes before and after the needed punctuation, and insert the correct punctuation.

EXAMPLE **1.** Elena learned Spanish and English at home she learned French and German at school.
1. *home; she*

1. They should be here before 9 30 this morning.
2. Our recycling center accepts the following materials glass, newspaper, cardboard, and aluminum cans.
3. The landscape designer planted bushes around the school last fall she will plant flowers this spring.
4. Please be at the station by 2 15 P.M.
5. The children wanted to see bears, lions, and elephants but only parrots, snakes, tortoises, and goats were on display.
6. The inspirational talk was based on Isaiah 61 1.
7. To refinish this dresser, we will need some supplies varnish remover, sandpaper, steel wool, wood stain, and polyurethane.
8. Walking is terrific exercise it improves both your stamina and your muscle tone.
9. Many children's books have beautiful illustrations some are worth having just for the art.
10. Many palaces in Europe are spectacular Linderhof in Bavaria is my favorite.

EXERCISE 26 **Punctuating and Capitalizing Quotations**

For each of the following sentences, correct any errors in capitalization, and add or change quotation marks and other marks of punctuation where needed.

EXAMPLE **1.** I learned how to play a new virtual-reality game today Pat said.
1. *"I learned how to play a new virtual-reality game today," Pat said.*

1. The most helpful chapter in my computer manual is "Trouble-shooting Tips" I explained to her.
2. Do Asian cobras look like African cobras Shawn asked.
3. I want to go to the fair after school Ivan said but my trumpet lesson is today.
4. The pilot said we are now beginning our descent into Orlando. Please fasten your seat belts and return your seats to the upright position.
5. Goodness! what a surprise Taka exclaimed
6. Did some famous person say A smile is contagious
7. Bicyclists should always wear helmets said the safety officer.
8. Was it you who said I can't eat another bite Troy asked
9. Carlos shouted, look at that dolphin near our boat!
10. During his speech at our school, the mayor said Our children are our future

▶ EXERCISE 27 **Punctuating and Capitalizing Quotations**

For each of the following sentences, correct any errors in capitalization and add quotation marks and other marks of punctuation where needed.

EXAMPLE   **1.** Sheila asked have you read about Rigoberta Menchú?
   1. *Sheila asked, "Have you read about Rigoberta Menchú?"*

1. She has lived a remarkable life Ernesto said and I admire her very much
2. Angela exclaimed yes, I know about Menchú!
3. Menchú is from Guatemala Mrs. Harper told us She won the Nobel Peace Prize in 1992.
4. I once wrote about Menchú in a poem called The Heart of a Peacemaker Gale said.
5. I think Rigoberta Menchú is a wonderful role model Carla said.
6. Menchú has tried to make life better for the peasants. Her own family is of Quiché heritage explained Mark

7. Did Stephanie say My dream is to meet Rigoberta Menchú asked Ryan

8. Yes, and I'd like to meet her too exclaimed Emilio.

9. Rose continued Menchú worked long hours on cotton and coffee plantations when she was a child.

10. Menchú's autobiography is *I . . . Rigoberta Menchú* said Mrs. Harper.

▶ EXERCISE 28 **Using Apostrophes Correctly**

Insert an apostrophe where needed in each of the following phrases. If a phrase is correct, write *C*.

EXAMPLE **1.** both boys shoes
1. *boys'*

1. somebodys lunch
2. cant play
3. Neals motorcycle
4. better than theirs
5. womens volleyball
6. too many letter *u*s
7. shouldn't worry
8. Betsy Rosss flag
9. no more *if*s
10. the bushes branches

▶ EXERCISE 29 **Correcting Spelling Errors**

Most of the following words are misspelled. If a word is spelled incorrectly, write the correct spelling. If a word is spelled correctly, write *C*.

EXAMPLE **1.** succede
1. *succeed*

1. vien
2. taxs
3. supercede
4. disallow
5. countrys
6. emptyness
7. tracable
8. stathood
9. lovelyer
10. clearest

11. wolfs
12. sheild
13. preceed
14. father-in-laws
15. improper

16. fancifuly
17. dryest
18. cluless
19. overjoied
20. skiping

▶ EXERCISE 30 **Choosing Between Words Often Confused**

From each pair of words in parentheses, choose the word or words that will make the sentence correct.

EXAMPLE **1.** The school plans to (*except, accept*) the new computer company's offer.
1. *accept*

1. Did Coach Jefferson (*advise, advice*) you to take the first-aid course?
2. My cousins and I are (*all ready, already*) to enter the marathon.
3. Sacramento has been the (*capital, capitol*) of California since 1854.
4. When garden hoses (*brake, break*), they sometimes can be mended with waterproof tape.
5. Avoid wearing (*loose, lose*) clothing when operating that equipment.
6. Many people know Mr. Perez, but I think he should be (*formerly, formally*) introduced.
7. My grandfather threw the football (*passed, past*) the trees and over the creek.
8. (*Its, It's*) a good idea to test home smoke detectors frequently to make sure that the batteries are still working.
9. One basic (*principle, principal*) of our government is the right to free speech.
10. Some domestic cats from Japan are called Japanese bobtails because of (*their, there*) very short tails.

Mechanics Test: Section 1

DIRECTIONS   Each numbered item below contains an underlined group of words. Choose the answer that shows the correct capitalization, punctuation, and spelling of the underlined part. If there is no error, choose answer D (Correct as is). Indicate your response by shading in the appropriate oval on your answer sheet.

EXAMPLE

[1]   <u>29 South Maple Street</u>

    (A)   29 south Maple Street
    (B)   29 South Maple street
    (C)   Twenty Nine South Maple Street
    (D)   Correct as is

SAMPLE ANSWER   1. Ⓐ Ⓑ Ⓒ ●

---

    29 South Maple Street
    Philadelphia, PA 19107
[1]   <u>January 15 1997</u>

    Mail-Order Sales Manager
[2]   <u>Direct Electronics, Inc.</u>
    214-C Billings Boulevard
[3]   <u>New Castle, Ken. 40050</u>

[4]   <u>Dear Sales Manager,</u>

The modem that I ordered from your company arrived [5] <u>today in peices</u>. The package was [6] <u>open and appeared</u> not to have been sealed properly. [7] <u>In addition I</u> have not yet received the game that I also ordered. Please send me a new [8] <u>modem the</u> broken modem is enclosed.

I [9] <u>appreciate you're prompt</u> attention to both of these matters.

[10] <u>Sincerely yours,</u>

Cameron Scott

1. (A) January 15, 1997
   (B) January, 15 1997
   (C) January 15th 1997
   (D) Correct as is

2. (A) direct electronics, inc.
   (B) Direct electronics, inc.
   (C) Direct Electronics, inc.
   (D) Correct as is

3. (A) New Castle Ken. 40050
   (B) New Castle, KY 40050
   (C) New Castle KY, 40050
   (D) Correct as is

4. (A) Dear sales manager,
   (B) Dear sales manager:
   (C) Dear Sales Manager:
   (D) Correct as is

5. (A) today in pieces
   (B) today in piece's
   (C) today in peaces
   (D) Correct as is

6. (A) open, and appeared
   (B) open; and appeared
   (C) open, and, appeared
   (D) Correct as is

7. (A) In addition, I
   (B) In addition i
   (C) In addition, i
   (D) Correct as is

8. (A) modem, the
   (B) modem; the
   (C) modem: the
   (D) Correct as is

9. (A) appreciate youre prompt
   (B) appreciate your, prompt
   (C) appreciate your prompt
   (D) Correct as is

10. (A) Sincerely Yours',
    (B) Sincerely your's,
    (C) Sincerely yours:
    (D) Correct as is

Mechanics Test: Section 2

DIRECTIONS Each of the following sentences contains an underlined word or group of words. Choose the answer that shows the correct capitalization, punctuation, and spelling of the underlined part. If there is no error, choose answer *D* (Correct as is). Indicate your response by shading in the appropriate oval on your answer sheet.

EXAMPLE

1. Rosie said that her cousin sent her that <u>soft colorful fabric</u> from Kenya.
   (A) soft, colorful, fabric
   (B) soft, colorful fabric
   (C) soft; colorful fabric
   (D) Correct as is

SAMPLE ANSWER 1.

1. The following people have volunteered to make <u>enchiladas, Manuel</u>, Shawn, and Anita.
   (A) enchiladas; Manuel
   (B) enchiladas. Manuel,
   (C) enchiladas: Manuel,
   (D) Correct as is

2. Our school's <u>recycling program which</u> is now three years old, has been quite successful.

   (A) recycling program, which
   (B) Recycling Program, which
   (C) recycling program; which
   (D) Correct as is

3. <u>Looking at the astronomical map in my science book I</u> spotted the constellations Orion, Taurus, and Pisces.

   (A) Looking at the astronomical map, in my science book I
   (B) Looking at the astronomical map, in my science book, I
   (C) Looking at the astronomical map in my science book, I
   (D) Correct as is

4. Donna <u>asked, "who</u> else plans to work as a baby sitter over the summer?"

   (A) asked, "Who
   (B) asked "Who
   (C) asked, Who
   (D) Correct as is

5. Angela and Wanda painted the <u>mural, and Jamal</u> attached it to the wall in the gym.

   (A) mural and Jamal
   (B) mural: and Jamal
   (C) mural, and jamal
   (D) Correct as is

6. Many television programs have closed captioning for <u>people who cant</u> hear.

   (A) people, who cant
   (B) people, who can't
   (C) people who can't
   (D) Correct as is

7. "What a great time we had at the <u>park"! Sandy</u> exclaimed, as she got in the car.

   (A) Park"! Sandy
   (B) park!" Sandy
   (C) park", Sandy
   (D) Correct as is

8. "<u>Your aunt Helen</u> certainly is a fascinating person," Carla said, "and friendly, too."

   (A) "Your Aunt Helen
   (B) "Your aunt, Helen
   (C) Your aunt Helen
   (D) Correct as is

9. "Many of us would have gone to the picnic if we had known about <u>it</u>" Alan said.
   (A) it",
   (B) it,"
   (C) it,
   (D) Correct as is

10. The Zunigas have a new <u>puppy; its</u> a cocker spaniel.
   (A) puppy; Its
   (B) puppy, its
   (C) puppy; it's
   (D) Correct as is

11. The ants <u>carried large leafs</u> across John Henry's backyard.
   (A) carryed large leafs
   (B) carryed large leaves
   (C) carried large leaves
   (D) Correct as is

12. Has the guide <u>all ready led</u> the hikers to the top of the mesa?
   (A) all ready lead
   (B) already lead
   (C) already led
   (D) Correct as is

13. If Carlos wants to play the role of Eddie in the <u>musical, he'll have too practice</u> the solos.
   (A) musical, he'll have to practice
   (B) musical; he'll have to practice
   (C) musical he'll have too practice
   (D) Correct as is

14. <u>Sara said that the big guppy in the class aquarium is going to have babies.</u>
   (A) Sara said "That the big guppy in the class aquarium is going to have babies."
   (B) Sara said "that the big guppy in the class aquarium is going to have babies."
   (C) Sara said "that the big guppy in the class aquarium is going to have babies".
   (D) Correct as is

15. On <u>October 1 1960</u> Nigeria became an independent nation.
   (A) October, 1 1960
   (B) October 1, 1960
   (C) October 1, 1960,
   (D) Correct as is

CORRECTING COMMON ERRORS

PART THREE

RESOURCES

RESOURCES

30 SPEAKING

Skills and Strategies

Effective speaking takes a little practice. Fortunately, you can learn some simple techniques that will allow you to speak confidently in almost any speaking situation. Whenever you speak, you can improve your effectiveness if you think about

- your purpose (What are you trying to say?)
- your topic (What are you speaking about?)
- your audience (Who are your listeners?)

The Communication Cycle

Communicating is a two-way process. First, a speaker communicates feelings or ideas to the listeners. Then the listeners respond to the speaker's message. This response is called *feedback.*

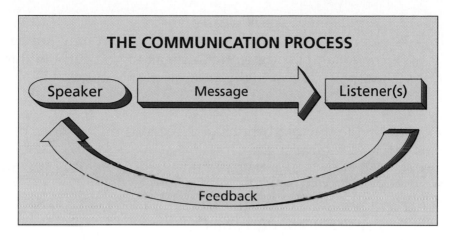

THE COMMUNICATION PROCESS

Speaker ► Message ► Listener(s)

Feedback

Speaking Informally

Impromptu Speaking

At times you will need to speak to a group of people without having time to plan what you will say. This is called an *impromptu speech.* Here are some suggestions.

1. *Think about your purpose.* (Do you want to give information to your audience? to persuade them?)
2. *Think about your topic.* (What's the main thing you need to say? If you have time, add details to explain your main ideas.)
3. *Think about your audience.* (Does what you're saying suit the time, the place, and the people that you are speaking to?)

Speaking Socially

In most social situations, you need to remember to speak clearly and politely.

Speaking on the Telephone

1. Call people at times that are convenient for them.
2. Identify yourself; then state your reason for calling.

3. Be polite and speak clearly.
4. Keep your call to a reasonable length. It may not be convenient for someone to speak to you early in the morning, late at night, or around mealtimes.

Giving Instructions or Directions

1. Divide the instructions or directions into a series of clear, logical steps.
2. Tell your listener each of the steps in the process, one at a time, in order.
3. Check to be sure your listener understands all of the instructions or directions.
4. Repeat any instructions that are not clear.

Making Social Introductions

1. Have confidence. If no one else introduces you, introduce yourself to other people.
2. When you introduce others, identify them by name.
3. When you are introducing others, it is customary to speak first to

   - a person of higher job position
   - an older person before a younger person
   - the person you know best

Speaking Formally

Preparing a Speech

A formal speech is one that you give at a specific time and place. When you give this kind of speech, you usually have the chance to prepare carefully beforehand.

Planning Your Speech

When you prepare your speech, you will need to consider your purpose for speaking. The following chart shows some common types of speeches, arranged according to their purpose.

SPEECH CONSIDERATIONS		
PURPOSE	**DESCRIPTION OF SPEECH**	**EXAMPLES OF SPEECH TITLES**
To inform	gives facts or general information or explains how to do something	Dinosaurs Once Lived in West Texas How to Take Good Snapshots
To persuade	attempts to change an opinion or attempts to get listeners to act	Why Everyone Should Recycle How Volunteering Can Make a Difference
To entertain	relates an amusing story or incident	My Most Embarrassing Moment

Considering Your Audience

When you plan your speech, you also need to consider your audience's interests.

THINKING ABOUT YOUR AUDIENCE		
QUESTIONS ABOUT AUDIENCE	**ANSWER**	**YOUR SPEECH WILL NEED**
What does the audience already know about this subject?	very little	to give background details to listeners
	a little	to give at least some background details
	a lot	to focus only on interesting points
How interested will the audience be in this subject?	very interested	to keep your listeners' interest
	only a little interested	to focus on aspects most interesting to your listeners
	uninterested	to convince your listeners that this topic is important

RESOURCES

Organizing Your Speech Notes

The most common type of speech is a speech you give using note cards. First, you prepare an outline of your main points. Next, you make note cards for each of the main points. Then, when you give your speech, you talk directly to the audience. You can refer to your note cards whenever you need to remember your main points.

Here are some suggestions for making note cards.

1. Write each main idea on a separate note card.
2. Make a special note card for anything that you might need to read word for word (such as a quotation, a series of dates, or statistics that are too difficult to memorize).
3. Include a special note card to tell you when to show a chart, diagram, graphic, drawing, model, or other visual materials.
4. Number your completed note cards to help you keep them in the correct order.

Giving Your Speech

Speaking Effectively

To give an effective speech, you'll need to use your voice and your gestures to help express your meaning to your listeners. Here are some pointers to use when you are speaking.

1. *Stand confidently.* Stand up straight and look alert. Use comfortable and appropriate movements to emphasize your words.
2. *Speak clearly.* Speak loudly enough so that everyone can hear you. Pronounce your words carefully.
3. *Look at your audience.* When you speak, look directly at your audience. Speak directly to them.
4. *Use a normal way of speaking.* Your voice gives your audience clues that help them understand what points you want to emphasize.

Speaking in Front of an Audience

It's normal to feel nervous about speaking in front of an audience. But you can use the following suggestions to help you stay in command.

1. *Be prepared.* Organize your material carefully. Practice using your note cards and any special information or visuals you plan to use during your speech.
2. *Practice your speech.* Each time you rehearse, pretend you're actually giving your speech.
3. *Remember your purpose.* Focus on what you want to tell your audience and how you want them to react instead of worrying about yourself.

Special Speaking Situations

Making Announcements

When you make an announcement, your main goal is to provide information. Follow these guidelines.

1. Write out your announcement. Be sure to include all the important facts. Add important details that will interest your listeners.
2. When it's time to give your announcement, first get your audience's attention. Then announce your message slowly and clearly.

Speaking in the Workplace

When you begin working, you will use many of the speaking skills that you now practice in the classroom. For example:

- You may work in a group to discuss information, solve problems, or make decisions.
- You may be asked to prepare and present information to a manager or to a work group.

RESOURCES

Group Discussions

Setting a Purpose

You probably work in groups in many of your classes. The goal of group discussions is to accomplish a specific purpose. This purpose may be

- to discuss and share ideas
- to cooperate in group learning
- to solve a problem
- to arrive at a group decision or to make a group recommendation

To help your group decide about your purpose, find out how much time will be allowed. Then you'll need to identify what your group will be expected to accomplish within the time allowed.

Assigning Roles

Everyone involved in a group discussion should have a specific role. Each role has special responsibilities. For example, your group may choose a chairperson to help keep the discussion moving smoothly. Someone else may be chosen as the secretary, or reporter (recorder), who has the responsibility of taking notes during the discussion.

Usually, a group establishes a plan, or outline, for the order of topics to follow in a discussion. This plan may be established by the chairperson, or sometimes the entire group may discuss and organize the plan for the discussion.

A Chairperson's Responsibilities

1. Announce the topic and establish a plan.
2. Follow the plan.
3. Encourage each member to take part.
4. Help group members stay on track. Avoid disagreements and distractions.

RESOURCES

A Secretary's or Reporter's Responsibilities

1. Take notes about important information.
2. Prepare a final report.

A Participant's Responsibilities

1. Take an active part in the discussion.
2. Ask questions and listen attentively to others.
3. Cooperate and share information.

Oral Interpretation

Oral interpretation is more like acting in a play than giving a speech. When you give an oral interpretation, you read a piece of literature expressively to your listeners. To indicate the meaning of the selection, you use facial expressions, your voice, gestures, and movements to interpret the literary work for your listeners.

Choosing a Selection

The purpose of an oral interpretation is to entertain. An oral interpretation is usually planned, so you should have enough time to select your literary piece and practice your presentation.

The material you choose for your presentation depends on several different factors, such as

- who your audience is (what their interests are and how willing they are to be an attentive audience)
- how long a presentation you plan to make (can vary greatly, from very short to very long)
- what the occasion or situation is (material suited to one occasion may not work well in another)
- how expressive an interpretation you want to give (can vary, from readings that require a lot of acting to mildly expressive pieces)

RESOURCES

Think about the kind of story you would choose to read to a group of six-year-olds during story hour. You would probably want a story with lots of action, and you would want characters whose voices and movements you could act out to amuse and entertain your young listeners.

Now think about what might be an appropriate reading for a presentation at a parent-teacher banquet near Thanksgiving. Perhaps you would select a literary work that suits the holiday coming up, or that has characters or a situation that would interest your audience. An older audience of enthusiastic parents and teachers will probably be more willing to pay attention to a longer, more serious selection than an audience of six-year-olds would.

Here are suggestions for finding a literary work for an oral interpretation.

| SELECTING AN ORAL INTERPRETATION ||
TYPE OF LITERATURE	DESCRIPTION OF POSSIBLE SELECTION
poem	a poem that tells a story, such as an epic poem
	a poem that has a speaker (using the word *I*) or a conversation between characters
	a poem that is expressive of a particular emotion
short story	a brief story, or portion of a story, that has ■ a beginning, middle, and end ■ either a narrator who tells the story (using *I*) or characters who talk to one another (using dialogue in quotation marks)
play	a short play, or one scene from a play, that has ■ a beginning, middle, and end ■ one or more characters with dialogue

You may need an introduction for your interpretation. This introduction may set the scene, tell something about the author of the piece of literature you're presenting, or give details that tell your audience about important events that have already taken place in the story.

Adapting Material

You may be able to find just the right piece of literature. It may already be the perfect length. It may have just the right number of characters, with dialogue that tells the part of the story you want to tell. But sometimes you need to shorten a short story, a long poem, or a play. This shortened version is called a *cutting*. To make a cutting, follow these suggestions.

1. Decide where the part of the story you want to use should begin and where it should end.
2. Cut out parts that don't contribute to the portion of the story you are telling.
3. From a short story, cut dialogue tags such as *she whispered sadly*. Instead, use these clues to tell you how to act out the characters' words.

Presenting an Oral Interpretation

After you've chosen a piece of literature to present, you can prepare a *reading script*. A reading script is usually typed (double-spaced or written neatly with space between each line). You can then mark this script to help you when you are reading your selection. For example, you can underline words to remind you to use special emphasis when you say them. Or you can mark a slash (/) to show where you plan to take a breath or pause briefly to create suspense. You might write a word or two or a brief note as a reminder of the emotion that you want to express when you say a character's words.

 COMPUTER NOTE: Use a word-processing program to prepare your script. You can use bold, italic, or underline formatting to show emphasis or to indicate notes to yourself. You can even change the type size.

Rehearse your presentation several different ways until you feel that you have found the most effective one.

Practice in front of your mirror. Then, try out your reading on friends, classmates, or relatives.

Use your voice to suit your meaning. Vary your body movements and your voice to show that you are portraying different characters and to show important emotions (such as fear or joy).

Review

▶ EXERCISE 1 **Speaking Socially**

For each of the situations, explain how you might handle the conversation. What would you say to be polite and to be clear?

1. You're calling to congratulate a classmate who has won a science award.
2. You've invited a new classmate to study at your house. Give directions on how to get to your house from the school.
3. You're standing in front of the school, talking to your new teacher. Your mother arrives. Introduce your mother to your teacher.
4. Explain to your classmates how to make or repair something (such as how to bake bread or repair a bicycle tire). Make sure you provide all the necessary information and give the steps in order. Repeat or summarize all necessary instructions.
5. At a baseball game, you realize that the person sitting next to you is a classmate you like but do not know well. Introduce yourself.

▶ EXERCISE 2 **Making an Announcement**

Write an announcement for an upcoming event. The event can be real, or you can make up the details. Give all the necessary information.

RESOURCES

▶ EXERCISE 3 **Preparing and Giving a Speech**

Choose a topic for a short, two- to three-minute speech to give to your English class. Think about your audience and your purpose when choosing your speech topic. Prepare note cards for your speech. Then, give your speech to the class, following the guidelines on page 830 for speaking effectively.

▶ EXERCISE 4 **Conducting a Group Discussion**

Select a group chairperson to lead a discussion on a topic your teacher assigns or one of your own choosing. Establish a plan for the discussion and assign roles. The purpose of the discussion is to make a list of the group's findings about the topic. Here are some suggestions for a topic your group might discuss.

1. activities that every community should provide for young people
2. ways to improve teacher-student relationships
3. the most important thing we can do to improve the future
4. leadership qualities and how to develop them
5. how to reduce gang violence

▶ EXERCISE 5 **Presenting an Oral Interpretation**

Select a literary work or a suitable portion of a piece of literature. Prepare a script for a three-minute oral interpretation to present to your class. Write a brief introduction telling the title and author of the selection. Present your interpretation to your class.

RESOURCES

31 LISTENING AND VIEWING

Strategies for Listening and Viewing

Listening and viewing are not as simple as they seem. You constantly hear sounds and see images of one kind or another. But you probably don't really *listen* to or *look* carefully at very many of them. Hearing and seeing just happen. But listening and viewing are active processes that require you to think about what you hear and see.

Listening with a Purpose

Keeping your purpose in mind as you listen will help you be a more effective listener. Common purposes for listening are

- for enjoyment or entertainment
- to gain information
- to understand information or an explanation
- to evaluate or form an opinion

Listening for Information

Listening for Details

When you listen for information, you need to listen for details that answer the basic *5W-How?* questions: *Who? What? When? Where? Why?* and *How?* As you listen to whoever is speaking, try to find answers for each of these questions.

Listening to Instructions

Both at school and in the workplace, careful listening is important when you are given assignments, instructions, or directions. Follow these guidelines.

1. Identify each separate step. Listen for words that tell you when each step ends and the next one begins. These words may include *first, second, third, next, then,* and *last* or *finally*.
2. Listen to the order of the steps. Take notes whenever it is necessary.
3. Imagine yourself completing each step in order.
4. Make sure you have all the instructions and understand them. Ask questions if you are unclear about any step.

Listening and Responding

Follow these guidelines to respond politely and effectively to a speaker.

1. Look at the speaker and pay attention.
2. Don't interrupt the speaker. Don't whisper, fidget, or make noises or movements that might be distracting.
3. Respect the speaker. Be tolerant of such differences as the speaker's accent, race, religion, or customs.
4. Try to understand the speaker's point of view. Know that your own point of view influences you.

RESOURCES

5. Listen to the speaker's entire message before you evaluate the speech.
6. Ask appropriate questions in a voice loud enough for the audience and the speaker to hear. In your question, use a summary or paraphrase of the speaker's point to help the speaker answer the question.
7. Use polite, effective language and gestures that are appropriate to the situation.

Using the LQ2R Method

The LQ2R study method is especially helpful when you are listening to a speaker who is giving information or instructions.

L   *Listen* carefully to information as it is being presented. Focus your attention only on the speaker, and don't allow yourself to be distracted.

Q   *Question* yourself as you listen. Make a list of questions as they occur to you.

R   *Recite* in your own words the information as it is being presented. Summarize information in your mind or jot down notes as you listen.

R   *Relisten* as the speaker concludes the presentation. The speaker may sum up, or repeat, major points of the presentation.

👉 REFERENCE NOTE: For more information about reading and study methods, see pages 877–894.

Taking Notes

You can't write down every word a speaker says. Instead, write only the key words or important phrases the speaker uses. Translate difficult terms into your own words.

👉 REFERENCE NOTE: For more about note taking, see pages 886–887.

Interviewing

An interview is a special listening situation. When you interview someone, you usually ask someone who is an expert or has special knowledge about a subject to speak to you and give you information about what he or she knows. Interviews are good sources for obtaining interesting and up-to-date information. Follow these suggestions to conduct an effective interview.

Preparing for the Interview
- Decide what information that you really want to ask about most.
- Make a list of questions to ask.
- Make an appointment for the interview. Be on time.

Conducting the Interview
- Be courteous and patient. Give the person you are interviewing time to answer each question that you ask. Respect what the person you are interviewing has to say, even if you disagree.
- Listen carefully to each answer that the person you are interviewing gives to the questions you ask. If the person gives you an answer that confuses you, or if you're not sure you understand what the person means, you may want to ask some follow-up questions to be clear about the information the person is giving you.
- It is polite to tell the person you are interviewing how you plan to use the information you are asking for. For example, if you plan to use the person's exact words in a report, it is usually best to tell the person as you begin the interview and ask permission to quote him or her directly.
- Thank the person for granting you the interview.

Following up on the Interview
- Review your notes to be sure they are clear.
- Write a summary of the interview as soon as possible.

RESOURCES

Critical Listening

When you listen critically, you think carefully about what you hear. You analyze and then evaluate the ideas being presented.

GUIDELINES FOR LISTENING CRITICALLY	
Find main ideas.	What are the most important points? Listen for clue words, such as *major, main, most important,* or similar words.
Identify significant details.	What dates, names, or facts does the speaker use to support main ideas? What kinds of examples or explanations are used to support the main ideas?
Distinguish between facts and opinions.	A *fact* is a statement that can be proved to be true. (May is the fifth month.) An *opinion* is a belief or a judgment about something. It cannot be proved to be true. (Strawberries are better than oranges.)
Note comparisons and contrasts.	Are some details compared or contrasted with others?
Understand cause and effect.	Does the speaker say or hint that some events cause others to occur? Or does the speaker suggest that some events are the result of others?
Predict outcomes and draw conclusions.	What reasonable conclusions or predictions can you make from the facts and evidence you have gathered from the speech?

 REFERENCE NOTE: For more information about interpreting and analyzing what you read, see pages 881–883.

RESOURCES

Understanding Persuasive Techniques

To get you to believe in something or to take some action, speakers may use one of the common persuasive techniques listed below. Learning to recognize these techniques can help you understand a speaker's message. It can also help you avoid being "taken in" by arguments that are not based on logic or reason.

COMMON PERSUASIVE TECHNIQUES USED BY SPEAKERS	
Bandwagon	Users of this technique urge you to "jump on the bandwagon" by suggesting that you should do or believe something because "everyone" is doing it. The idea is to make you think you're missing out if you don't join in.
Testimonial	Experts or famous people sometimes give a personal "testimony" about a product or idea. However, the person giving the testimonial may not really know much about that particular product or idea.
Emotional appeals	This technique uses words that appeal to your emotions rather than to your logic or reason.
"Plain folks"	Ordinary people (or people who pretend to be ordinary) are often used to persuade others. People tend to believe others who seem to be similar to themselves.
False cause and effect	This technique is used to suggest that because one event happened first, it caused a second event to occur. However, the two events may not actually have a cause-and-effect relationship.

Viewing Actively

You may not think about it, but much of what you see every day is *images*—pictures of someone's idea of real life. In this lesson, you'll focus on viewing images in print media: newspapers, magazines, and brochures.

Identifying Purpose and Message

Whenever you flip through magazines, newspapers, or brochures, you're viewing images that have been carefully chosen for a specific purpose or purposes. It's important to identify the image's purpose and message.

- **Some images give information.** In a brochure about a national park, a photograph shows a close-up of a woman dressed in climbing gear standing next to a cliff face. The message is clear: The park allows rock climbing.
- **Some images entertain by suggesting a story.** Although a photograph can't tell a whole story, you can imagine what happened before and after the moment it captures. A photo shows two small children and their pets. One child has a prize ribbon and a big smile. The other has no ribbon and is crying. You need no explanation.
- **Some images persuade.** Advertisers use images to associate their products with desirable qualities so that you'll go out and buy those products. If an automobile ad shows a car being driven by a man wearing a tuxedo and fine jewelry, the advertiser wants you to associate that car with wealth, luxury, and prestige. If another ad shows a truck with a full payload being driven straight up a rocky hill, the advertiser wants to persuade you that the truck is strong, rugged, and durable.

Watching for Hidden Messages

Images can arouse viewers' emotions more powerfully and immediately than words do. Thus, newspapers, magazines, and advertisers use *loaded images* that are guaranteed to trigger the reactions they want to create.

- A newspaper features on the front page a photo of a wildfire burning in a nearby forest preserve. The newspaper wants to create interest in the story and to sell more newspapers.
- A magazine shows photos of slim, attractive, young women modeling the newest fashions. The hidden message of the magazine is that the purchaser will be able to look like the models.
- An ad shows a large family celebrating a grand-mother's birthday and a young girl reading a greeting card to her. The hidden message: If you buy and send cards, you can be part of a happy family.

Viewing Images Critically

When you view images critically, you think carefully about what you see. You are aware that image makers (advertisers, political candidates, and editors) have chosen images to get you to respond in a certain way. (This is also true of the images you see on television.)

GUIDELINES FOR CRITICAL VIEWING	
Determine the image maker's purpose(s).	Is the image maker's purpose to give you information or to entertain you? to persuade you to buy a product or take an action? a combination?
See if the image communicates a message.	Look for details that answer the basic *5W-How?* questions: *Who? What? When? Where? Why? How?* Which details are important and which are unimportant?
Be aware of how the image affects your emotions.	Is it a loaded image (like birthdays, happy families, and sunrises) designed to trigger your emotions? What are the hidden messages?

RESOURCES

Review

EXERCISE 1   Listening for Information

Make up four questions similar to those that follow. Read them aloud, pausing briefly to allow your classmates time to jot down their answers. Have listeners check their answers to see how accurately they listened.

1. In the series of numbers *6—1—8—3—4*, the fourth number is ____.
2. In this list, *in—off—but—for—how*, the word beginning with *o* is ____.
3. Here is the order for pairs: first, Josh and Erika; then, Graciella and Cindy; last, Roberto and Quan. Which group is Cindy in?
4. Here are six colors: red, green, yellow, blue, purple, orange. Which color is second?

EXERCISE 2   Preparing Interview Questions

Think of an elected official, a celebrity, or an individual from history that you would like to interview. Then prepare ten questions you would like to be able to ask that person in an interview. Follow the steps for preparing for an interview on page 841.

EXERCISE 3   Listening to a Speech

Listen to a short speech presented by your teacher in class. Take brief notes. Then respond to the following questions about the speech.

1. What are the main ideas of the speech?
2. Does the speech contain details that support the main points in the speech? If so, identify several of them.
3. Can you distinguish between facts and opinions mentioned in the speech? How?
4. Does the speech contain comparisons and contrasts?

▶ EXERCISE 4   **Identifying Persuasive Techniques**

Identify the persuasive technique used in each item.

1. "Buy Yummies," says Jo Jackson, champion gymnast. "You'll start your day off right!"
2. "Everyone's joining our crusade for reforming the school system. Sign up to do your part now!"
3. "Big spenders in Washington ruin our country!"
4. Because Jim forgot to wear his lucky bowling shirt, he lost the first three games of the tournament.

▶ EXERCISE 5   **Analyzing Images**

Work with some classmates to identify the hidden message in each print ad below. Give reasons for your choice.

1. A soft drink ad shows a group of young people laughing while they play volleyball on a beach.
2. A tire advertisement shows a father driving his wife and two children at night during a terrible rainstorm.
3. A political candidate wearing jeans and a plaid shirt chats with a smiling family with farm animals and a barn in the background.
4. A clothing ad features a young man wearing a pair of jeans with the label very visible. He is surrounded by several attractive young women.

▶ EXERCISE 6   **Applying Viewing Skills**

Apply your critical viewing skills to the images in TV ads. Mute the sound and watch five ads you haven't seen before. Answer these questions for each ad.

1. Describe the images in a sentence or two. What do they tell or what story do they suggest?
2. At what point in the commercial could you tell what product was being advertised?
3. What desirable qualities do the images suggest about the product being advertised?
4. What are the hidden messages in each ad?

RESOURCES

32 THE LIBRARY/ MEDIA CENTER

Finding and Using Information

In the library or media center you can find information on many subjects. But you need to know how to find it.

The Arrangement of a Library

Every book in a library has a number and letter code, the book's *call number.* Most school libraries use the *Dewey decimal system* to assign call numbers. This number tells you how the book has been classified and where to find it.

The Dewey decimal system assigns a number to each nonfiction book according to its subject. Biographies may be placed in a section separate from other nonfiction books. They are arranged alphabetically according to the last name of the person the book is about. Two or more biographies about the same person are alphabetized according to the last name of the author. Fiction books usually are separated from nonfiction books. The Dewey decimal system groups works of fiction in alphabetical order according to their authors' last names. Two or more books written by the same author are arranged alphabetically by the first word of their titles (not counting *A, An,* or *The*).

Types of Card Catalogs

To find the book you want, find the call number in the library's card catalog. There are two types of card catalogs: the online catalog and the traditional card catalog.

The *online catalog* is stored on a computer. To find the book you want, type in the title, author, or subject of the book. The computer will display the results of the search information on the computer screen, and you can print out this information if you wish.

SEARCH RESULTS FROM ONLINE CATALOG	
Author:	Bang, Molly
Title:	Chattanooga sludge / Molly Bang.
Edition:	1st ed.
Published:	San Diego : Harcourt Brace, c1996.
Description:	1 v. (unpaged) : col. ill. ; 29 cm.
LC Call No.:	TD1061 .B36 1996
Dewey No.:	628.42 20 BAN
ISBN:	015216345X
Notes:	"A Gulliver Green book."
	John Todd attempts to clean the toxic waters of Chattanooga Creek with a Living Machine.
Subjects:	Hazardous wastes—Biodegradation—Juvenile literature.
	Sewage sludge—Juvenile literature.
	Pollution.
	Recycling (Waste).
	Environmental protection.

RESOURCES

The traditional *card catalog* is a cabinet of small drawers containing cards. These cards are arranged in alphabetical order by title, author, or subject. All books have a title card and an author card. Nonfiction books will have a third card—a subject card. You may also find a *"see"* or *"see also"* card that tells you where to find additional information on a subject.

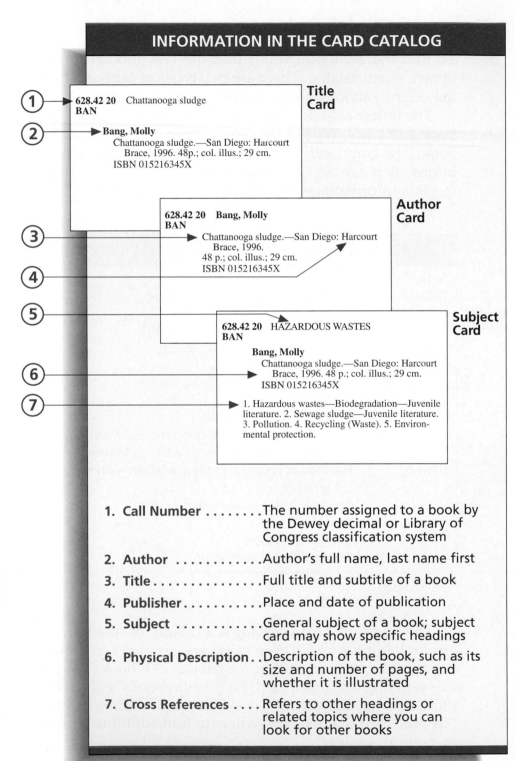

INFORMATION IN THE CARD CATALOG

Title Card

① **628.42 20** Chattanooga sludge
BAN

② **Bang, Molly**
Chattanooga sludge.—San Diego: Harcourt
Brace, 1996. 48p.; col. illus.; 29 cm.
ISBN 015216345X

Author Card

628.42 20   Bang, Molly
BAN

③ Chattanooga sludge.—San Diego: Harcourt
Brace, 1996.
④ 48 p.; col. illus.; 29 cm.
ISBN 015216345X

Subject Card

⑤ **628.42 20   HAZARDOUS WASTES**
BAN

Bang, Molly
Chattanooga sludge.—San Diego: Harcourt
⑥ Brace, 1996. 48 p.; col. illus.; 29 cm.
ISBN 015216345X

⑦ 1. Hazardous wastes—Biodegradation—Juvenile
literature. 2. Sewage sludge—Juvenile literature.
3. Pollution. 4. Recycling (Waste). 5. Environ-
mental protection.

1. **Call Number** . . . . .The number assigned to a book by
the Dewey decimal or Library of
Congress classification system

2. **Author** . . . . .Author's full name, last name first

3. **Title** . . . . .Full title and subtitle of a book

4. **Publisher** . . . . .Place and date of publication

5. **Subject** . . . . .General subject of a book; subject
card may show specific headings

6. **Physical Description** . .Description of the book, such as its
size and number of pages, and
whether it is illustrated

7. **Cross References** . . . .Refers to other headings or
related topics where you can
look for other books

Parts of a Book

Information is often easier to find if you know how to use the parts of a book effectively. The title, the table of contents, and the index are examples of the types of information that can be found in the different parts of a book.

INFORMATION FOUND IN PARTS OF A BOOK	
PART	INFORMATION
Title page	gives full title, author, publisher, and place of publication
Copyright page	gives date of first publication and of any revisions
Table of contents	lists titles of chapters or sections of the book and their starting page numbers
Appendix	provides additional information about subjects found in the book; maps and charts are sometimes found here
Glossary	in alphabetical order defines difficult or technical words found in the book
Bibliography	lists sources used to write the book; gives titles of works on related topics
Index	lists topics mentioned in the book and page numbers on which they can be found

Reference Materials

The *Readers' Guide*

The most current information on many topics is found in magazines rather than in books. To find a magazine article, use the *Readers' Guide to Periodical Literature*. The *Readers' Guide* indexes articles, poems, and stories from more than 150 magazines. In the *Readers' Guide,* magazine articles are listed alphabetically by author and by subject. These headings are printed in boldface capital letters.

Information in the *Readers' Guide* entries is abbreviated. Both the printed and online *Readers' Guides* sometimes provide abstracts of the articles.

Printed *Readers' Guide*	
(1) **SEAL, KATHY SHENKIN**	
(2) A dose of self-esteem. il *Parents* v71 P121–2 + Ja '96	(1) **Author entry**
(3) **SEALS (ANIMALS)**	(2) **Name of magazine**
Migration	
(4) North to the fish, south to the beach [elephant	(3) **Subject entry**
(5) seals; research by Brent Stewart and Robert DeLong] L. Oliwenstein. il map *Discover* v17	(4) **Title of article**
(6) p54 Ja '96	(5) **Author of article**
SEAMANSHIP	
(7) *See also*	(6) **Date of magazine**
Hands-On Power Boating (CD-ROM)	(7) **Volume number of**
SEARCH FOR EXTRATERRESTRIAL INTELLIGENCE *See* SETI (Search for Extraterrestrial Intelligence)	**magazine**
SEARCHING, ONLINE *See* Online searching	
SEATS	(8) **Subject cross-**
(8) *See also*	**reference**
Automobiles—Seats	
SEATTLE MARINERS (BASEBALL TEAM)	(9) **Page reference**
Ken Griffey Jr. signs four-year deal worth $34 million: becomes highest paid player in	
(9) baseball. il pors *Jet* v89 p57–8 F 19 '96	

Online *Readers' Guide*	
Record: 4	
AUTHOR:	Oliwenstein, Lori.
TITLE:	North to the fish, south to the beach. (elephant seals; research by Brent Stewart and Robert DeLong)
SOURCE:	Discover v. 17 (Jan. '96) p. 54 il map.
STANDARD NO:	0274-7529
DATE:	1996
RECORD TYPE:	art
CONTENTS:	feature article
SUBJECT:	Seals (Animals)—Migration.

Reference Sources

The *vertical file* is a special filing cabinet containing up-to-date materials. These materials may include newspaper clippings or government and information pamphlets.

Microforms are pages from various newspapers and magazines that are reduced to miniature size. The two most common types are *microfilm* (a roll or reel of film) and *microfiche* (a sheet of film). You view them by using a special projector to enlarge the images to a readable size.

Most libraries devote a section entirely to reference sources that contain information on many subjects.

REFERENCE SOURCES		
TYPE	**DESCRIPTION**	**EXAMPLES**
Encyclopedias	▪ multiple volumes ▪ articles arranged alphabetically by subject ▪ source for general information	*Collier's Encyclopedia* *Compton's Encyclopedia* *The World Book Multimedia Encyclopedia*™
General Biographical References	▪ information about the lives and accomplishments of outstanding people	*Current Biography* *The International Who's Who* *World Biographical Index on CD-ROM*
Atlases	▪ maps and geographical information	*Atlas of World Cultures* *National Geographic Atlas of the World*
Almanacs	▪ up-to-date information about current events, facts, statistics, and dates	*The Information Please Almanac, Atlas & Yearbook* *The World Almanac and Book of Facts*
Books of Synonyms	▪ list more interesting or more exact words to express ideas	*Roget's International Thesaurus* *Webster's New Dictionary of Synonyms*

COMPUTER NOTE: Many libraries use computers to research reference sources. Some libraries are linked to **online databases.** These databases store all types of information. Libraries that are linked to the **Internet,** an international network of computers, have access to thousands of information sources. You can search for a specific topic by typing a **keyword** or key phrase, and you can print out the information that you find.

RESOURCES

Newspapers

Most daily newspapers are divided into sections that contain a wide variety of features and types of writing. Newspaper writers write for different purposes. And readers, like you, read the newspaper for purposes of your own. The following chart shows some of the different contents that you will find in a typical daily newspaper.

WHAT'S IN A NEWSPAPER?		
WRITER'S PURPOSE/ TYPE OF WRITING	READER'S PURPOSE	READING TECHNIQUE

to inform
     news stories
     sports
	to gain knowledge or information	Ask yourself the *5W-How?* questions (page 33).

to persuade
     editorials
     comics
     reviews
     ads
	to gain knowledge, to make decisions, or to be entertained	Identify points you agree or disagree with. Find facts or reasons the writer uses.

to be creative or
     expressive
     comics
     columns
	to be entertained	Identify ways the writer interests you or gives you a new viewpoint or ideas.

Review

▶ EXERCISE 1   **Using the Parts of a Book**

Tell which part or parts of a book you would check to find the following information.

1. a list of page numbers that deal with a specific topic
2. the meaning of a technical term used often in the book
3. a list of the sources used to write the book
4. the place where the book was published
5. how many times the book has been revised

▶ EXERCISE 2 **Using the Library**

Answer the following questions to show your understanding of the information resources in the library.

1. In order, which of the following books would be shelved first: *Winter Thunder* by Mari Sandoz, or *Nisei Daughter* by Monica Sone?
2. Use the sample *Readers' Guide* entry on page 852 to find the title of an article written by Kathy Seal about self-esteem. What magazine printed this article?
3. Use the card catalog or the online catalog in your library to find a biography of a famous person. Write the book title, the author's name, and the call number.
4. Tell which reference book you might use to find the names of the countries that border Switzerland.
5. Tell which reference book might contain recent statistics on the total population of the United States.

▶ EXERCISE 3 **Exploring the Newspaper**

Using a copy of the daily newspaper from home or your library, answer the following questions.

1. Is there a special identification or title for each section of this newspaper? Explain.
2. Find an article that gives you information about a specific event in world news, sports, or entertainment. Find answers to the *5W-How?* questions (*Who? What? Where? When? Why? How?*) in the details of this article.
3. Find an editorial or a letter to the editor. Identify what the writer wants you to think or do. What facts or opinions does the writer use to try to persuade you?
4. Find a comic that you think is intended to persuade you. Find another comic that you think is intended just for fun. Explain your selection.
5. Find an advertisement or classified ad that makes you want to buy the item offered. What do you find most effective about the ad?

RESOURCES

33 THE DICTIONARY

Types and Contents

Types of Dictionaries

There are many types of dictionaries. Each type contains different kinds of information. However, all dictionaries contain certain general features.

TYPES OF DICTIONARIES		
TYPE AND EXAMPLE	NUMBER OF WORDS	NUMBER OF PAGES
Unabridged *Webster's Third International Unabridged Dictionary*	460,000	2,662
College or Abridged *Merriam-Webster's Collegiate Dictionary*, 10th ed.	160,000	1,600
School *The Lincoln Writing Dictionary*	35,000	932
Paperback *The Random House Dictionary*	74,000	1,056

A SAMPLE ENTRY

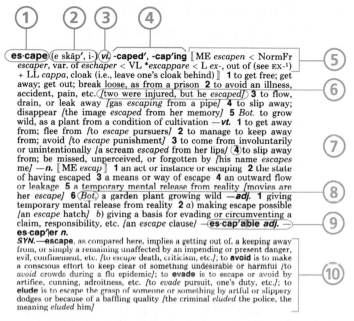

From *Webster's New World College Dictionary*, Third Edition. Copyright © 1996, 1994, 1991, 1988 by Simon & Schuster, Inc. Reprinted by permission of Macmillan USA, a Simon & Schuster Macmillan Company.

1. **Entry word.** The entry word shows the correct spelling of a word. An alternate spelling may also be shown. The entry word shows how the word should be divided into syllables, and may also show if the word should be capitalized.

COMPUTER NOTE: Programs that check spelling can be real timesavers, but they can't check homonyms.

---

2. **Pronunciation.** The pronunciation of a word is shown using accent marks, phonetic symbols, or diacritical marks. Each *phonetic symbol* represents a specific sound. *Diacritical marks* are symbols placed above letters to show how they sound.

3. **Part-of-speech labels.** These labels are usually abbreviated and show how the entry word should be used in a sentence. Some words may be used as more than one part of speech.

4. **Other forms.** Sometimes your dictionary shows spellings of plural forms of nouns, tenses of verbs, or the comparative forms of adjectives and adverbs.

5. **Etymology.** The *etymology* tells how a word (or its parts) entered the English language. The etymology also shows how the word has changed over time.

6. **Examples.** Your dictionary may demonstrate how a word may be used by giving phrases or sentences containing that word.

7. **Definitions.** If there is more than one meaning for a word, the different definitions are separated by numbers or letters.

8. **Special usage labels.** These labels identify the circumstances in which a word has a special meaning, such as *Bot.* (botany), or how it is used in special ways, such as *Slang* or *Rare.*

9. **Related word forms.** These are other forms of the entry word. For example, another form of the word might be shown that is created by adding suffixes or prefixes. Or a common phrase might be shown in which the entry word appears.

10. **Synonyms and antonyms.** Words that are similar in meaning are *synonyms.* Words that are opposite in meaning are *antonyms.* Dictionaries may list synonyms and antonyms at the end of some word entries.

Review

 EXERCISE 1   **Using the Dictionary to Check for Capitalization**

Look up the following words in a dictionary and explain when they are and are not capitalized. Your dictionary may not give capitalized uses for all the words.

1. president
2. roman
3. arctic
4. ping-pong
5. mason

▶ EXERCISE 2   **Dividing Words into Syllables**

Divide the following words into syllables. Use the same method to show syllable division that your dictionary uses.

1. habitat
2. turmoil
3. diamond
4. incomplete
5. mediterranean

▶ EXERCISE 3   **Finding Part-of-Speech Labels**

Look up each of the following words in a dictionary. Give all the parts of speech listed for each word and an example of how the word is used as each part of speech.

EXAMPLE   **1.** elastic
　　　　　1. *adj.—an elastic waistband*
　　　　　　 n.—lined with elastic

1. fall
2. interview
3. record
4. mask
5. base

▶ EXERCISE 4   **Identifying the Usage Labels of Words**

Look up the following words in a college dictionary and write the usage label or labels given for the word, if any.

1. foul
2. relief
3. grub
4. master
5. degree

▶ EXERCISE 5   **Finding Synonyms for Words**

Write all the synonyms you can think of for each of the following words. Then use a dictionary to check your list and to add to it.

1. fear
2. mix
3. enormous
4. part
5. rich

RESOURCES

34 VOCABULARY

Learning and Using New Words

You constantly learn new words from your parents and friends, from subjects you study, and from books, television, and games. You can also learn the meanings of word parts and how they are combined to form new words.

Building a Vocabulary

One good way to build your vocabulary is to start a word bank. When you see or hear a new word, write the word and its definition in a section of your notebook. Always check the definition and pronunciation of any unfamiliar words in your dictionary.

 COMPUTER NOTE: You can also create a vocabulary file on a computer. Add new words to the end of the file. Then, use the Sort command to arrange them in alphabetical order.

Using Word Parts

There are two main groups of words in English: those that cannot be divided into parts, and those that can. Words that cannot be divided into parts are called **base words.** *Hope, please,* and *round* are examples of base words.

Words that can be divided into parts, like *departure, proceed,* and *unimportant,* are made up of **word parts.** The three types of word parts are

- roots
- prefixes
- suffixes

The **root** is the main part of the word. It carries the word's core meaning. A **prefix** is a word part added before a root. A **suffix** is a word part added after a root. (Both prefixes and suffixes are known as affixes. An **affix** is any word part added to a root.) For example, in the word *disagreeable, dis–* is the prefix, *–agree–* is the root, and *–able* is the suffix.

WORD	PREFIX	ROOT	SUFFIX
biweekly	bi–	–week–	–ly
invisible	in–	–vis–	–ible
replacement	re–	–place–	–ment
predictable	pre–	–dict–	–able

Knowing the meanings of word parts can help you figure out the meanings of many unfamiliar words.

COMMONLY USED PREFIXES		
PREFIXES	MEANINGS	EXAMPLES OF PREFIXES + ROOTS
anti–	against, opposing	antisocial, antiviral
bi–	two	biannual, bicultural
co–	with, together	codefendant, coordinate
dis–	away, from, opposing	disarm, disconnect
in–	not	inappropriate, ineffective
inter–	between, among	interaction, interstate
mis–	badly, not, wrongly	misconduct, misshape

(continued)

COMMONLY USED PREFIXES *(continued)*		
PREFIXES	MEANINGS	EXAMPLES
non–	not	nonactive, nonfatal
post–	after, following	postdated, postwar
pre–	before	predawn, preview
re–	back, again	replay, restock
semi–	half, partly	semidarkness, semisweet
sub–	under, beneath	subgroup, subplot
trans–	across, beyond	transfer, transform
un–	not, reverse of	uneven, untrue

 REFERENCE NOTE: For guidelines on spelling when adding prefixes, see page 769.

COMMONLY USED SUFFIXES		
SUFFIXES	MEANINGS	EXAMPLES OF ROOTS + SUFFIXES
–able	able, likely	adaptable, changeable
–ate	become, cause	activate, invalidate
–dom	state, condition	freedom, kingdom
–en	make, become	darken, weaken
–ful	full of, characteristic of	joyful, truthful
–hood	condition, quality	childhood, sisterhood
–ion	action, condition	liberation, protection
–ize	make, cause to be	dramatize, Americanize
–ly	in a characteristic way	blandly, swiftly
–ment	result, action	enchantment, payment
–ness	quality, state	peacefulness, sadness
–or	one who	actor, editor
–ous	characterized by	joyous, murderous
–ship	condition, state	friendship, hardship
–y	condition, quality	dirty, jealousy

REFERENCE NOTE: For guidelines on spelling when adding suffixes, see pages 769–771.

Learning New Words from Context

The *context* of a word includes all the other words and sentences that surround it. These surrounding words often provide valuable clues to meaning.

USING CONTEXT CLUES	
TYPE OF CLUE	**EXPLANATION**
Definitions and Restatements	Look for words that define the term or restate it in other words. ■ The university owns a *seismograph*, a machine for measuring the force of earthquakes.
Examples	Look for examples used in context that reveal the meaning of an unfamiliar word. ■ There are many types of literary *genres*, such as novels, short stories, poems, and plays.
Synonyms	Look for clues that indicate an unfamiliar word is similar to a familiar word. ■ For a beginner, the *novice* played well.
Antonyms	Look for clues that indicate an unfamiliar word is opposite in meaning to a familiar word. ■ The speaker was *strident*, not soft-spoken.
Comparison and Contrast	Look for clues that indicate that an unfamiliar word is compared to or contrasted with an unfamiliar word or phrase. ■ A *salvo* of cheers burst, like a sudden thunderstorm, from the onlookers. ■ Unlike Sofía, who is wise and sensible, Pierce is often *fatuous*.
Cause and Effect	Look for clues that indicate an unfamiliar word is related to the cause or the result of an action, feeling, or idea. ■ Since our trip was *curtailed*, we came home early.

RESOURCES

Choosing the Right Word

Since many English words have several meanings, you must look at *all* the definitions given in the dictionary for any particular word. Always think about the context of an unfamiliar word. Then determine the definition that best fits the given context.

Dictionaries sometimes provide sample contexts to show the various meanings of a word. Compare each of the sample contexts given in the dictionary with the context of a new word to make sure you've found the meaning that fits.

Synonyms and Antonyms

Synonyms are words that have nearly the same meaning. For example, here are some pairs of synonyms: happy—glad, big—large, and beautiful—lovely. However, *antonyms* are words that have nearly the opposite meaning. For example, here are some pairs of antonyms: happy—sad, big—small, and beautiful—ugly.

When you look up a word in a dictionary, you will often find several synonyms listed. To help you distinguish between synonyms, some dictionaries give *synonym articles*—brief explanations of a word's synonyms and how they differ in meaning. Dictionaries sometimes also list antonyms at the end of an entry for a word.

EXERCISE 1   **Using Prefixes to Define Words**

For each of the following words, give the prefix used and its meaning. Give the meaning of the whole word. Use a dictionary if necessary.

1. bilingual
2. misfire
3. antilabor
4. preheat
5. nondairy

6. transatlantic
7. interdenominational
8. postgraduate
9. semiprecious
10. subnormal

▶ EXERCISE 2 **Adding Suffixes to Words**

To each of the following words add the suffix in parentheses that follows the word. Then give the meaning of each new word and its part of speech. Use a dictionary if necessary to find the meaning or the spelling of each new word. [Note: Be careful. Remember that some words change their spelling when a suffix is added.]

1. appease (–ment)
2. official (–dom)
3. like (–able)
4. civil (–ize)
5. spite (–ful)

6. state (–hood)
7. envy (–ous)
8. haste (–en)
9. grit (–y)
10. author (–ship)

▶ EXERCISE 3 **Using Context Clues**

Use context clues to choose the word or phrase that best fits the meaning of each italicized word.

a. beautiful
b. entertaining
c. considering
d. dropped sharply

e. round
f. reacting
g. myths
h. nicknames

1. Sharria spends as much time *pondering* what to wear to school as she does thinking about her homework.
2. The earth is *spherical*, like a ball.
3. Ludlow was known by various *sobriquets*, including Lumpy and Pokey.
4. Emiliano thought the tiny blue insect was *exquisite*, not hideous as his aunt believed.
5. Because the temperature *plummeted*, we decided to build a fire.

▶ EXERCISE 4   **Selecting the Correct Context**

For each sentence below, write the word from the following list that best fits the sentence. Use a dictionary to find the definition that best fits the context for each word.

flawless	intrude
caliber	eliminate
pummel	moderate
incite	envelop

1. The concert was so long that the director decided to ＿＿ two songs.
2. The dark fog seemed to ＿＿ the cottage.
3. On the field trip, the class stopped for lunch at a restaurant that had ＿＿ prices.
4. The fiery speaker was able to ＿＿ the crowd.
5. The final report of the year should be a work of high ＿＿.

35 LETTERS AND FORMS

Style and Contents

Letters are an important form of communication. Everyone likes to get letters. To receive letters, however, you usually have to write your share. It is important to learn how to write effective social and business letters. You will also find there are a few general rules you should follow when you complete printed forms.

Types of Letters

Like all other forms of communication, letters have a purpose and an intended audience.

LETTERS		
TYPE	PURPOSE	AUDIENCE
Personal	to express emotions and ideas	close friends or relatives
Social	to express appreciation or to communicate information about a specific event	close friends or social acquaintances
Business	to inform a business that you need its services, or to tell how well or badly a service was performed	a business or organization

Writing Letters

Personal Letters

A *personal letter* is often the best way to communicate, even with someone you know well. In conversations— face-to-face or on the telephone—other people or time schedules may intrude. Personal letters, however, often get their receiver's complete attention. Unlike conversations, letters last. People often save personal letters and read them many times. A friendly letter is a gesture of friendship, containing a personal message from the sender to the receiver, such as best wishes for an upcoming holiday. When you're writing a personal letter, remember to write about things that interest you and the person you're writing to.

Social Letters

Social letters are usually for a specific purpose or in response to a specific event. The most common types of social letters are thank-you letters, invitations, and letters of regret.

Thank-you Letters

You write thank-you letters when you want to thank someone for taking the time, trouble, or expense to do something for you. Thank the person, then try to add a personal note. For example, if you're thanking someone for a gift, tell why the gift is special to you.

Invitations

An invitation should include specific information about the occasion, such as the time and place and any other special details your guests might need to know (such as that everyone may bring a friend, should dress casually, or is expected to bring food).

Letters of Regret

You write a *letter of regret* when you receive an invitation to an event that you will not be able to attend. You should especially respond in writing to invitations that include the letters *R.S.V.P.* (in French, an abbreviation for "please reply").

You should always respond quickly enough so that the person who is inviting you can accurately count the number of guests to prepare for. If the planned event is very soon, you may want to telephone the person to say that you can't come. But another consideration is politeness. Even if you have telephoned to say you won't attend, it's still polite to send a follow-up letter of regret.

5455 Blackford Street
Chicago, IL 60615
March 20, 1998

Dear Felicia,

    I was so happy to receive your invitation to your birthday slumber party next Friday evening. I really would like to be there. Unfortunately, my parents had already made plans for the whole family for that night.

    Thank you very much for inviting me. I hope you have a happy birthday and a lot of fun at your party.

                Your friend,

                Bianca

RESOURCES

Business Letters

The Parts of a Business Letter

Business letters follow a particular form. There are six parts of a business letter; they are

(1) the heading
(2) the inside address
(3) the salutation
(4) the body
(5) the closing
(6) the signature

These six parts are usually arranged in one of the two most common styles used for business letters.

The *block form* places each part of the letter at the left margin of the page. A blank space is left between each paragraph in the body of the letter. Each paragraph is not indented.

The *modified block form* arranges the heading, the closing, and your signature just to the right of an imaginary line that extends down the center of the page. The middle parts of the letter all begin at the left margin. Each paragraph is indented.

Block Style

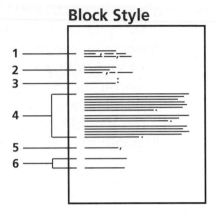

Modified Block Style

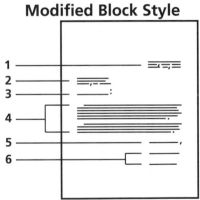

The Heading. The heading usually has three lines:

- your street address
- your city, state, and ZIP Code
- the date the letter was written

The Inside Address. The inside address gives the name and address of the person you are writing.

- If you're directing your letter to someone by name, use a courtesy title (such as *Mr., Ms., Mrs.,* or *Miss*) or a professional title (such as *Dr.* or *Professor*) in front of the person's name. After the person's name, include the person's business title (such as *Editor, Business Manager,* or *Department Chairperson*).
- If you don't have a person's name, use a business title or position title (such as *Store Manager* or *Complaints Department*).

The Salutation. The salutation is your greeting to the person you're writing.

- In a business letter, the salutation ends with a colon (such as in *Dear Mayor Williams:*). If you are writing to a specific person, use the person's name (such as *Dear Ms. Stokes*).
- If you don't have the name of a specific person, use a general salutation, such as *Dear Sir or Madam,* or *Ladies and Gentlemen.* Or, you can use a department or a position title (such as *Activity Director* or *Head of Division*), with or without the word *Dear.*

The Body. The body contains the message of your letter. Leave a blank line between paragraphs in the body of the letter.

The Closing. You should end your letter politely. There are several standard phrases that are often used to close business letters such as *Sincerely, Respectfully yours,* or *Yours truly.*

The Signature. Your signature should be handwritten in ink directly below the closing. Your name should be typed or printed neatly just below your signature.

RESOURCES

Types of Business Letters

The Request or Order Letter. In a *request letter,* you write to request a product or service. For example, you might write to an art museum to request a schedule of hours it is open and any fees that are charged. In an *order letter,* you ask for something specific, such as a free brochure advertised in a magazine. You may also need to write an order letter to ask for a product by mail that appears in a magazine or advertisement without a printed order form.

When you are writing a request or order letter, remember the following points.

1. State your request clearly.
2. If you need to receive information, enclose a stamped envelope addressed to yourself. You are asking a favor of the persons you're writing to, so it's polite not to expect them to pay for the reply.
3. Make your request long before you need whatever you are requesting. Allow the persons to whom you have sent your request enough time to fit their reply into their normal schedule.
4. If you want to order something, include all important information. For example, give the size, color, brand name, or any other specific information. If there are costs involved, add the amount carefully.

The Complaint or Adjustment Letter. When you do not receive services or products that you have reason to expect, you may wish to write a *complaint* or *adjustment letter.* Remember these points.

1. Send your letter as soon as possible.
2. Be specific in your letter. Include the following details:
   - why you are unhappy (with the product or service)
   - how you were affected (lost time or money)
   - what solution you believe will correct the problem
3. Read your letter over to make sure it's calm and courteous.

The Appreciation or Commendation Letter. In an *appreciation* or *commendation letter,* you tell someone—a specific person, a group of people, a business, or an organization—that he, she, or they did a good job with a product or service. Be specific about exactly what action or idea of this person's you are commending. For example, if your city's mayor has just proposed some new summer recreation programs that you feel teenagers need, you might want to write an appreciation letter to thank him or her for being concerned with good recreation facilities and healthful programs for the city's young people.

210 Scenic View
Minneapolis, MN 55419
March 10, 1998

Sgt. Latrice Jeffreys
Second Precinct Police Station
850 Second Avenue South
Minneapolis, MN 55402

Dear Sgt. Jeffreys:

　Thank you very much for coming to speak to our school about safety. We are aware of this issue and how much it can affect our lives. It's good to know that there are so many things we can do ourselves to keep from becoming victims of crime.

　I hope you will continue to speak to students about this very important subject. We should all know what our part is in fighting crime.

Sincerely yours,

Ingrid Johansen

Ingrid Johansen

RESOURCES

Appearance of a Business Letter

Follow these suggestions to give your letter the best possible appearance.

- Use plain, white, unlined $8\frac{1}{2}'' \times 11''$ paper.
- Type your letter if possible (single-spaced, with an extra line between paragraphs). Or, write your letter by hand, using black or blue ink.
- Leave equal margins on the sides, top, and bottom of the page.
- Use only the front of each page. If your letter is more than one page, leave a one-inch margin at the bottom of the first page, and finish the letter on the next page.

 COMPUTER NOTE: Remember to save your work every ten to fifteen minutes. Turn on the automatic Save if you have it.

Addressing an Envelope

The return address goes in the top left-hand corner of the envelope. The name and address of the person to whom the letter is written is in the center of the envelope. On the envelope for a business letter, the name and address to which the letter is being sent should exactly match the inside address of the letter.

Tama Wuliton
2703 Bryant Road
Dana Point, CA 92629

Clasprite Paperclip Company
1605 S. Noland Rd., Building 6
Borita, CA 92002

Completing Printed Forms

When you fill out a form, your purpose is to give clear, complete information. The following guidelines will help you complete all types of forms.

HOW TO FILL OUT FORMS

1. Look over the entire form before you begin.
2. Look for, and follow, special instructions (such as "Type or print" or "Use a pencil").
3. Read each item carefully.
4. Supply all the information requested. If a question does not apply to you, write "does not apply," or use either a dash or the symbol *N/A* (meaning "not applicable").
5. When you're finished, make sure nothing is left blank. Also, check for errors and correct them neatly.
6. Mail the form to the correct address or give it to the correct person.

Review

 EXERCISE 1   **Writing a Social Letter**

Write a social letter for one of the following situations, or make up one of your own.

1. A friend's mother baked you cookies for your birthday and sent you a thoughtful card.
2. You have been invited to a friend's house party but cannot attend because your grandparents will be in town for an overnight visit on the date of the party.
3. You are planning a movie-watching party at your house. Write a letter of invitation including all the information your guests would need to know.

▶ EXERCISE 2 **Writing a Business Letter**

Write a business letter for one of the situations below. Use your own return address, but make up any other information you need to write the letter. Address an envelope for your letter. Fold the letter neatly and place it into the envelope. (Do not mail the letter.)

1. Your parents said you could spend two weeks this summer at the youth camp of your choice. Write to the Circle Q Summer Camp, located at 3333 Route 1, Festus, Missouri 63028.
2. Write a letter of appreciation or commendation to an individual or organization you would like to thank or congratulate for outstanding efforts or performance.

▶ EXERCISE 3 **Completing a Form**

For each numbered blank, write what you would put in that blank if you filled out this form.

STUDENT INFORMATION FORM

NAME 1	DATE OF BIRTH 2
NICKNAME 3	PHONE # 4
ADDRESS 5	
NAME OF PARENT OR GUARDIAN 6	WORK # 7

	TEACHER	ROOM #	SUBJECT
PERIOD 0	8	9	10
PERIOD 1			
PERIOD 2			
PERIOD 3			
PERIOD 4			
PERIOD 5			
PERIOD 6			
PERIOD 7			

36 READING, STUDYING, AND TEST TAKING

Using Skills and Strategies

Good grades are almost always a sign of good reading skills and good study skills. By organizing your time and using certain reading strategies, you can improve your study habits and become a better reader. These skills will help you earn better grades with less last-minute panic before tests.

Planning a Study Routine

Plan a study schedule that will help you study successfully. When you map out a schedule, stick to it. Here are some suggestions:

1. *Know your assignments.* Write down all the assignments you have and their due dates. Be sure you understand the instructions for each assignment.
2. *Make a plan.* Break large assignments into small steps. Keep track of when you should be finished with each step.
3. *Concentrate when you study.* Set aside a time and a place to focus your attention on your assignments.

Strengthening Reading and Study Skills

Reading and Understanding

The way you read depends on what you're reading and why you are reading it. Your reading rate should match your purpose for reading. Here are some common purposes for reading.

READING RATES AND THEIR PURPOSE		
READING RATE	PURPOSE	EXAMPLE
Scanning	Reading for specific details	Looking in your math book for the page that has the explanation for solving a problem
Skimming	Reading for main points or important ideas	Looking through the chapter headings, charts, and time lines of your history book to review for a test
Reading for mastery	Reading closely to understand and remember	Reading a new chapter in your science book to plan for an in-class writing assignment

Writing to Learn

Writing can help you learn. When you write, you are forced to put your thoughts in order. Write to analyze a problem, record your observations, or work out the details of a plan. See the following chart for examples of types of writing for different purposes.

TYPE OF WRITING	PURPOSE	EXAMPLE
Freewriting	To help you focus your thoughts	Writing for ten minutes to explore plot ideas for a creative writing assignment
Autobiographies	To help you examine the meaning of important events in your life	Writing about your hopes for the future on the day of your sister's wedding
Diaries	To help you recall your impressions and express your feelings	Writing about your reactions to a speech made by a guest speaker in your history class
Journals and Learning Logs	To help you record your observations, descriptions, solutions, and questions	Jotting down notes for a biology class discussion while watching a bird building its nest
	To help you define or analyze information, or propose a solution	Listing reasons for and against a plan of action to help you decide to do it or not

Using Word-Processing Tools for Writing

A word processor or a computer word-processing program can help you plan, draft, and edit your writing. These tools can make every step of the writing process easier.

Prewriting. With a little practice, you can type quickly on a word processor. You can then rewrite your notes or ideas without having to recopy or retype them.

Writing First Drafts. You can write, revise, and rearrange your ideas as often as you want. Then you can use the printer to produce a hard copy, or printout.

Evaluating. The word processor is great for trying out different versions. Just save your original document. Then, on a copy of the document, type in your changes. If you don't like the revisions, you still have the original.

Revising. You can easily type in changes on a word processor. Then you can print a clean copy without having to rewrite or retype the unchanged portions.

Proofreading. Some word processors can check spelling or find errors in punctuation or sentence structure.

Publishing. It's simple to print a final copy with a word processor. You can even print multiple copies with your printer.

Using the SQ3R Reading Method

SQ3R is the name of a reading method that was developed by Francis Robinson, an educational psychologist. The SQ3R method includes five simple steps.

S *Survey* the entire assignment. If you're studying a chapter in a textbook, look quickly at the headings, subheadings, terms in boldface and italics, charts, outlines, illustrations, and summaries.

Q *Question* yourself. List questions that you want to be able to answer after reading the selection.

R *Read* the material carefully to find answers to your questions. Take notes as you read.

R *Recite* in your own words answers to each of the questions you wanted to be able to answer.

R *Review* the material by rereading quickly, looking over your questions, and recalling the answers.

The SQ3R method will help you read material more carefully. When you read actively, you are more likely to remember what you read.

Interpreting and Analyzing What You Read

Writers of essays, articles, and textbook chapters organize ideas and relate them to one another. If you can interpret and analyze the relationship of ideas, you will understand more of whatever you read.

Stated Main Idea.   The main idea of a passage is the most important point the writer is making. Sometimes the main idea is stated. This means the author may clearly state the main idea in one or two sentences.

Implied Main Idea.   Sometimes the main idea is not stated. There may not be one or two sentences that tell the major point the writer is making. Instead, the main idea may be implied. You may have to figure out for yourself the central idea that ties all the other ideas together.

HOW TO FIND THE MAIN IDEA

- Skim the passage. (What topic do the sentences have in common?)
- Identify the general topic. (What is the passage about?)
- Identify what the passage says about the topic. (What's the message of the passage as a whole?)
- State the meaning of the passage in your own words.
- Review the passage. (If you have correctly identified the main idea, all the other ideas will support it.)

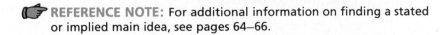 REFERENCE NOTE: For additional information on finding a stated or implied main idea, see pages 64–66.

RESOURCES

Reading to Find Relationships Among Details

Sometimes you have to work to understand the meaning of a reading passage. First, you need to understand the main idea. Then you need to look at how the details are related to the main idea and to each other.

FINDING RELATIONSHIPS AMONG DETAILS	
Identify specific details.	What details answer questions such as *Who? What? When? Where? Why?* and *How?* (*5W-How?* questions)?
Distinguish between fact and opinion.	What information can be proved true or false? What statements express a personal belief or attitude?
Identify similarities and differences.	How are the details similar to or different from one another?
Understand cause and effect.	Do earlier events affect later ones?
Identify an order of organization.	In what kind of order are the details arranged? Are they in chronological order, spatial order, order of importance, or some other pattern or order?

Reading Passage

In the story "Rikki-tikki-tavi," by Rudyard Kipling, a young English boy living in India rescues a young mongoose from drowning. Later in the story, the grateful, brave mongoose saves the lives of the boy and his parents by killing two cobras that plan to kill the humans. Kipling's story made mongooses famous.

Sample Analysis

OPINION: How did the mongoose in Kipling's story feel about humans?
ANSWER: *Rikki-tikki-tavi felt grateful to the humans for saving him. He felt brave when he was killing the cobras.*

Scientists who became interested in the mongoose proved that, just as Kipling said, mongooses could kill poisonous snakes. The mongoose is a small animal, similar to a ferret, that makes its home in Africa and some parts of Asia. Cobras and other poisonous snakes are only part of the mongoose's strange daily menu. Mongooses also feed on rodents, including rats, and insects, including wasps. A mongoose will even eat a scorpion.

Many people think that mongooses are immune to the poisonous venom of a snake. Others believe that mongooses know where to find a plant to eat that will keep a snake's venom from being harmful. But a mongoose succeeds in killing a poisonous snake only because it is faster than the snake. When a mongoose attacks a snake, it bites the snake's head and cracks the snake's skull. The mongoose then holds on to the snake's head until the snake has completely stopped struggling.

In the past, people brought mongooses to Hawaii and the West Indies, hoping that they would kill some of the rats and snakes on those islands. Instead, the mongooses hunted rare birds that were easier to catch and kill than rodents and reptiles. Because of the mongooses' unpredictable eating habits, they are allowed in the United States only for zoos and scientific research.

FACT: What is the mongoose's defense against the venom of a snake?
ANSWER: *The only defense of the mongoose is its quickness.*

DETAILS: Mongooses can be found inhabiting which two continents?
ANSWER: *Mongooses can be found in Africa and some parts of Asia.*

SIMILARITY: How is the mongoose like a ferret?
ANSWER: *The mongoose is small in size like a ferret and similar in appearance.*

CAUSE AND EFFECT: Why did the United States decide that people would not be allowed to import mongooses?
ANSWER: *Mongooses that were imported into Hawaii and the West Indies did not control pests as expected. They did not eat rats and snakes. Instead, they ate rare birds.*

RESOURCES

Applying Reasoning Skills to Your Reading

To understand what you read, you have to think about the ideas. These ideas are like clues, and you have to act like a detective to analyze evidence that you find in your reading. When you think critically, you may draw *conclusions*. *Conclusions* are decisions based on facts and evidence that are drawn from your reading.

Sometimes, thinking critically means that you must make *inferences*. *Inferences* are decisions based on evidence that is only hinted at, or implied, in what you have read. For example, when you analyze the reading passage on pages 882–883, you might draw these conclusions or inferences.

> Mongooses can survive in many different habitats. (Evidence: Mongooses are found on two continents. Also, mongooses eat all sorts of animals that live in many types of environments—deserts, mountains, or forests.)

> Mongooses prefer hunting easy prey. (Fact: When birds are available, mongooses eat them instead of snakes.)

A *valid conclusion* is firmly established by facts, evidence, or logic. An *invalid conclusion*, however, is one that is not supported by facts or logic. For example, it is invalid to conclude that mongooses are considered pests in their natural habitat. This conclusion is not consistent with facts in the reading passage. In the passage you find that the mongoose's diet in its natural environment consists mainly of animals that are considered pests by humans.

HOW TO DRAW CONCLUSIONS	
Gather all the evidence.	What facts or details have you learned about the subject?
Evaluate the evidence.	What do the facts and details tell you about the subject?
Make appropriate connections.	What can you reasonably conclude from the evidence?

Reading Graphics and Illustrations

Many times, a book or article will include visuals such as diagrams, maps, graphs, and illustrations. These visuals often make information clearer and easier to understand than if it is written out.

A paragraph filled with details is often difficult to understand. Graphics and illustrations help you understand relationships between sets of facts. For example, the pie charts below show the distribution of farm work in the United States.

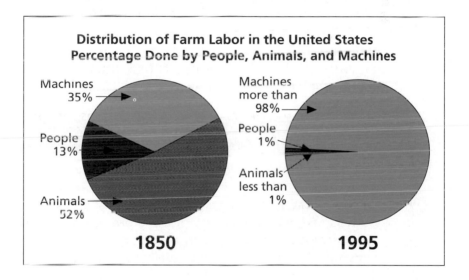

Distribution of Farm Labor in the United States
Percentage Done by People, Animals, and Machines

Machines 35%
People 13%
Animals 52%
1850

Machines more than 98%
People 1%
Animals less than 1%
1995

Looking at these graphs, you can quickly compare the overall amount of farm work performed by machines today with the amount performed by machines in 1850. Graphs like these can help you understand information more easily.

RESOURCES

Applying Study and Reading Strategies

Various study and reading strategies are simply different ways of organizing and handling information. The following are some of the most common strategies:

- taking notes
- classifying
- organizing information visually
- outlining
- paraphrasing
- summarizing
- memorizing

Taking Notes

Taking accurate notes during a reading assignment or in class is worth the extra effort. Detailed information will be recorded in your notebook, and you will be ready to study for even the most challenging test. It's much easier to review your study notes before a test than to review a whole chapter or series of chapters.

HOW TO TAKE STUDY NOTES

1. Identify and take note of the main ideas in class or your reading. These main ideas should be the headings in your notes. In class, listen for key words and phrases, such as *first, most important,* or *therefore.* These words often introduce main ideas. In a textbook, chapter headings and related subheadings usually contain key ideas.
2. Keep your notes brief. Use abbreviations and summarize material in your own words.
3. Include brief examples or details, if you can. Important examples or details can help you recall the main ideas.
4. Review your notes soon after you have written them to be sure you have included all important information.

Here's an example of careful study notes about the reading passage on pages 882–883. The notes show the main ideas as headings. Underneath these main headings are grouped important details that relate to each heading. You can see that not every detail from the passage appears in these notes. Only the most important details are listed.

Mongooses

"Rikki-tikki-tavi"

- Story written by Rudyard Kipling
- Boy in India saves mongoose from drowning
- Mongoose kills two cobras—saves boy and family
- Story made people interested in mongooses

Characteristics of mongooses

- Small and ferret like
- Live in Africa and Asia
- Eat poisonous snakes, rodents, wasps, and scorpions

Mongooses and snakes

- Mongooses not immune to snake venom
- Don't seek out special plant to counter venom
- Mongoose's advantage is quickness
- Mongoose bites snake's head and crushes its skull; holds on until snake dies
- Mongooses brought to Hawaii and West Indies to eat poisonous snakes—ate rare birds instead (thus not allowed in U.S. except for research and zoos)

Classifying

Classifying is arranging information into categories or groups. All the items that are in a category or group are related to each other. The name or description of the category shows the relationship between the various items in the group. For example, the name *sports* is the label of a category that could include various items, such as *baseball, basketball, hockey,* or *soccer.*

EXAMPLE **What do the following birds have in common?
penguins, emus, ostriches**
ANSWER **They are all birds that can't fly.**

You also use classification when you identify patterns. For example, look at the relationship between the following sequence of numbers.

What's the next number in the series?

3   6   12   24   48 _____?_____

ANSWER The first number in this series, *3*, is doubled to produce the second number, *6*. The second number is then doubled to produce the third number, *12*. This doubling goes on (*12* doubled is *24, 24* doubled is *48*). Then, to produce the next number in the series, you would double *48*. The answer is *96*.

Organizing Information Visually

Sometimes, new information is easier to understand if you organize it visually. A map, diagram, or chart is easier to understand than the same information provided in paragraph form.

For example, the passage that follows compares different poisonous snakes.

There are many kinds of venomous snakes. Rattlesnakes, for example, are found throughout the Western Hemisphere. They range from one to eight feet in length. The likelihood of a human dying as a result of a rattler's bite is low. Cottonmouths are found from Virginia to Texas. Their bite is very dangerous and may be fatal. They can reach up to five feet in length. The coral snake is smaller, ranging from one and one half to four feet in length. The coral snake, which may be found from the southern United States to South America, is very deadly. King cobras, found throughout southern Asia, may reach a length of sixteen feet. The king cobra's bite is not usually deadly. The Cape cobra, however, is very deadly. This snake reaches up to seven feet in length and is found in southern Africa. One of the largest and most deadly snakes is the black mamba. This snake reaches up to fourteen feet in length and is found in southern and central Africa. Almost all of the people who are attacked by a black mamba die if they do not receive medical treatment immediately after being bitten.

It would be very difficult to identify all the snakes and all of their differences and similarities if you just read this passage and tried to remember all the details. However, if you made a chart like the one below, you would find the information in the paragraph much easier to remember.

VENOMOUS SNAKES			
TYPE OF SNAKE	LENGTH	LIKELIHOOD OF DEATH IF BITTEN (UNTREATED)	LOCATION
rattlesnake	1–8 ft.	low	W. Hemisphere
cottonmouth	up to 5 ft.	high	Virginia to Texas
coral snake	18 in.–4 ft.	high	southern United States; North and South America
king cobra	up to 16 ft.	low	southern Asia
Cape cobra	up to 7 ft.	high	southern Africa
black mamba	up to 14 ft.	very high	southern and central Africa

RESOURCES

Outlining

An *outline* helps you organize important information. In an outline, the ideas are arranged in an order and in a pattern that makes their relationship to one another clear.

FORMAL OUTLINE FORM
I. Main Point
A. Supporting Point
1. Detail
a. Information or detail

Sometimes you might want to make a formal outline by using Roman numerals for headings and capital letters for subheadings. For taking notes in your classes, however, you might want to use a faster method. An informal outline helps organize information quickly.

INFORMAL OUTLINE FORM
Main idea
Supporting detail
Supporting detail
Supporting detail

Paraphrasing

When you *paraphrase,* you restate someone else's ideas in your own words. A paraphrase often helps explain ideas that are expressed in complicated or unfamiliar terms.

For example, the first part of President Lincoln's Gettysburg Address is "Four score and seven years ago our fathers brought forth on this continent, a new nation, conceived in Liberty, and dedicated to the proposition that all men are created equal." You might paraphrase this as "Eighty-seven years ago, our ancestors established here in America a new country that was committed to freedom and to the idea that all people are born equal."

When you write a paraphrase, it will usually be about the same length as the original. This means that you will probably not use paraphrasing for long passages of writing. However, you may sometimes be asked (usually in language arts classes) to paraphrase a short passage, such as a poem.

Here is an example of a poem and its paraphrase.

Those Winter Sundays
by Robert Hayden

Sundays too my father got up early
and put his clothes on in the blueblack cold,
then with cracked hands that ached
from labor in the weekday weather made
banked fires blaze. No one ever thanked him.

I'd wake and hear the cold splintering, breaking.
When the rooms were warm, he'd call,
And slowly I would rise and dress,
fearing the chronic angers of that house,

Speaking indifferently to him,
who had driven out the cold
and polished my good shoes as well.
What did I know, what did I know
of love's austere and lonely offices?

Here is a possible paraphrase of the poem.

The speaker in the poem is talking about his father. Each day the father would rise in the early morning, while the house was still cold, to build a fire. The father's hands were cracked and aching from his week's work. He was never thanked for his hard work.

On these cold mornings, the speaker would awake to the sounds of his father splitting wood. When the house had warmed, his father would call him downstairs. The speaker would slowly get dressed.

Unlike the house, which could be warmed, relations between the father and son remained cold and distant. The son expressed no thanks for the fires his father built or the shoes his father polished for him. The son later realizes that he was unaware of the love and commitment that motivated his father's daily routine.

Follow these guidelines when you write a paraphrase.

HOW TO PARAPHRASE

1. Read the selection carefully before you begin.
2. Be sure you understand the main idea of the selection. Look up unfamiliar words in a dictionary.
3. Determine the tone of the selection. (What is the attitude of the writer toward the subject of the selection?)
4. Identify the speaker in fictional material. (Is the poet speaking, or is it a character in the poem?)
5. Write your paraphrase in your own words. Shorten long sentences or stanzas. Use your own, familiar vocabulary, but follow the same order of events or ideas that is used in the selection.
6. Check to be sure that the ideas in your paraphrase of a selection match the ideas that are expressed in the original selection.

You also use paraphrasing when you write a research report. Make sure to cite the source of whatever you paraphrase. It's important to give credit for someone else's words or ideas.

☞ **REFERENCE NOTE:** For more about giving appropriate credit to sources when writing reports, see page 329.

Summarizing

A *summary* is a brief restatement of the main ideas expressed in a piece of writing. Like a paraphrase, a summary expresses another person's ideas in your own words. However, a summary is shorter than a paraphrase. A summary shortens the original material, presenting only the most important points.

When you summarize, you think critically about the material that you are condensing. You make decisions and draw conclusions about what to include in the summary and what to leave out.

HOW TO SUMMARIZE

1. Skim the selection you wish to summarize.
2. Read the passage again closely. This time, look for the main ideas and notice all of the details that support each main idea.
3. Write your summary in your own words. Include only the main ideas and the most important supporting points.
4. Evaluate and revise your summary, checking to see that you have covered the most important points. Make sure that the information in your summary is clearly expressed and that the person reading your summary can follow your ideas.

Here's a sample summary of the reading passage found on pages 316–317.

> The cheetah is the fastest land animal. It lives in Arabia, Africa, and parts of Asia. The cheetah's body is built more like a dog's than a cat's. Its claws are dull except for the claw on the inside of the foreleg. Cheetahs have a bad sense of smell, but they have good eyesight. A cheetah may be seven feet long from the head to the tip of the tail. Unlike most big cats, it can be easily tamed; a cheetah will even purr when it is happy. Cheetahs have been clocked at amazing speeds of up to 80 miles per hour.

Memorizing

When you take tests and quizzes, you need to memorize the information that you are to be tested on. One long effort to memorize study material the night before a test will not be very effective. Instead, you'll find that frequent, short, focused sessions are more likely to help you remember information. On the following page are some hints for memorizing effectively.

RESOURCES

HOW TO MEMORIZE	
Memorize key concepts.	Whenever possible, condense the material you need to remember.
Rehearse the material in different ways.	Copy the material by hand or recite the material out loud.
Invent memory games.	Form a word from the first letters of important terms, or make up rhymes to help you remember facts and details.

Improving Test-Taking Skills

Preparing for Different Kinds of Tests

Nervousness before a test is normal. However, you can channel the energy that comes from being nervous to help you do well on the test. Your attitude is the key.

HOW TO PREPARE FOR A TEST
Plan for success. Do everything you can to help you perform your best on the test. Identify the material to be covered on the test. Then make a plan that allows enough time to take notes, study, and review the material.
Be confident. If you have studied thoroughly, you know you are prepared. During the test, pay attention only to reading and answering the test questions.
Keep trying. Be determined to keep improving. Your efforts will help you improve your study effectiveness.

Objective questions and *essay questions* are two basic ways that your knowledge can be tested. There are specific ways to prepare for each type of test.

Objective Tests

There are many kinds of objective test questions. Some examples are multiple-choice, true/false, matching, reasoning or logic, or short-answer questions. Objective questions test you on specific information, such as names, terms, dates, or definitions. Most objective test questions have only one correct answer.

To prepare for objective tests, you will need to review specific information from your textbook and your notes. The study skills listed earlier in this chapter will help you prepare for objective tests.

HOW TO STUDY FOR OBJECTIVE TESTS

1. Identify important terms, facts, or ideas in your textbook and class notes.
2. Review the information in more than one form. For example, you may be responsible for defining literary terms. Make flashcards. Practice identifying the definition from the term, then identify the term from its definition.
3. Practice and rehearse factual information. Go over the items you have had difficulty with until you know them well.
4. If possible, briefly review all the information shortly before the actual test.

Your study strategies may be slightly different for each type of objective test. If you have to define key terms, then study using flashcards. If problem-solving questions are on the test, work out practice problems and check your answers with your textbook.

Taking Different Kinds of Objective Tests

Before you begin an objective test, quickly scan the questions. Knowing the number of items on the test helps you decide how to budget your time for each item. Here are

RESOURCES

some strategies for handling specific kinds of objective test questions.

Multiple-Choice Questions. With a multiple-choice question, you select a correct answer from a number of choices.

EXAMPLE **1.** Mongooses are effective as hunters of poisonous snakes because

A mongooses know where to find an herb that acts as an antidote for snake venom.

(B) mongooses are quicker than most snakes.

C mongooses are immune to snake venom.

D mongooses know when to find snakes sleeping.

HOW TO ANSWER MULTIPLE-CHOICE QUESTIONS	
Read the question or statement carefully.	■ Make sure you understand the key question or statement you are given before you look at the answer choices. ■ Look for words such as *not* or *always*. These words limit your choice of answers.
Read all the choices before selecting an answer.	■ Eliminate choices that you know are incorrect. This improves your chances of choosing correctly among the remainder. ■ Think carefully about the remaining choices. Select the one that makes the most sense.

True/False Questions. In a true/false question, you are asked to decide whether a certain statement is true or false.

EXAMPLE **1.** (T) F In both 1850 and 1995 in the United States, people did less farm work than machines.

RESOURCES

HOW TO ANSWER TRUE/FALSE QUESTIONS

Read the statement carefully.	■ The whole statement is false if any part of it is false.
Look for word clues.	■ Words such as *always* or *never* limit a statement. ■ A statement is true only if it is entirely and always true.

Matching Questions.   Matching questions ask you to match the items in one list with the items in another list.

> Directions: Match the name of the snake in the left-hand column with its natural home in the right-hand column.

<u>C</u> **1.** king cobra   **A** southern Africa
<u>D</u> **2.** black mamba   **B** from Virginia to Texas
<u>A</u> **3.** Cape cobra   **C** southern Asia
<u>B</u> **4.** cottonmouth   **D** central and southern Africa

HOW TO ANSWER MATCHING QUESTIONS

Read the directions carefully.	Sometimes you won't use all the items listed in one column. Other items may be used more than once.
Scan the columns.	If you match items you know first, you'll have more time to evaluate items you are less sure about.
Complete the rest of the matching.	Make your best guess on remaining items.

Reasoning or Logic Questions.   This type of question tests your reasoning abilities more than your knowledge of a particular subject. You often find reasoning or logic questions on standardized tests. You may be asked to

RESOURCES

identify the relationship between several items (usually words, pictures, or numbers).

Reasoning questions might ask you to identify a pattern in a number sequence (as in the example on page 888) or ask you to predict the next item in a sequence.

What comes next?

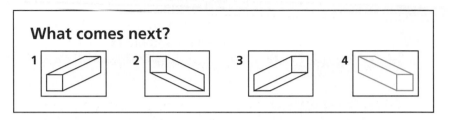

In this sequence of three drawings, the front of the block is in a different corner of the box each time. Therefore, in its final position the front of the block must be in the lower right corner of the box.

HOW TO ANSWER REASONING OR LOGIC QUESTIONS	
Be sure you understand the instructions.	Reasoning or logic questions are often multiple-choice. On some tests, however, you may need to write a word or phrase, complete a number sequence, or even draw a picture for your answer.
Analyze the relationship implied in the question.	Look at the question carefully to gather information about the relationship of the items.
Draw reasonable conclusions.	Evaluate the relationship of the items to decide your answer.

One special type of reasoning and logic question is an analogy question. In an analogy you recognize the relationship between two words and identify two other words that have a similar relationship.

EXAMPLE   **1.** Directions: Select the appropriate pair of words to complete the analogy.

GLASS : MILK :: _____

A glass : cup
B ice : iced tea
C bowl : soup
D cow : grass

In this analogy, you would express the relationship of items in the form of a sentence or question: "A *glass* is used to hold *milk.*" What other pair of words has the same relationship?

You would then test all the choices to see which one fits best. For example, to test the first choice, *A,* you would say, "Does a *glass* hold a *cup*? (No.)" For the second, you'd say, "Does *ice* hold *iced tea*? (No.)" For the third choice, you'd say, "Does a *bowl* hold *soup*? (Yes.)" Now look at the last choice, *D.* "Does a *cow* hold *grass*? (Yes, but only when the cow eats grass.)"

You now have two possibilities for answers, *C* and *D.* To choose between them, you would decide which pair of words is more like the relationship of a *glass* to the *milk* it holds. You might reason that both *milk* and *soup* are foods for humans and a *glass* and a *bowl* are both dishes. Maybe *grass* is food, but not for humans, nor is a *cow* like a *dish.* Therefore, the best choice is *C.*

Short-Answer Questions.   Short-answer questions ask for short, precise responses. Instead of choosing from among a set of choices, you write the answer yourself.

Some short-answer questions (such as labeling a map or diagram, or fill-in-the-blank questions) can be answered with one or a few words. Other types of short-answer questions require you to give a full, written response, usually one or two sentences in length.

EXAMPLE   Describe how a mongoose kills a snake.
ANSWER   *The mongoose bites the snake's head and cracks the snake's skull. The mongoose then holds on to the snake until it stops struggling.*

HOW TO RESPOND TO SHORT-ANSWER QUESTIONS

Read the question carefully.	Some questions have more than one part. You will have to include an answer to each part to receive full credit.
Plan your answer.	Briefly decide what you need to include in the answer.
Be as specific as possible in your answers.	Give a full, exact answer.
Budget your time.	Begin by answering those questions you are certain about.

Essay Tests

Essay tests measure how well you understand a subject. Essay answers are usually a paragraph or more in length.

HOW TO STUDY FOR ESSAY TESTS

1. Read assigned material carefully.
2. Make an outline of main points and important details.
3. Create your own essay questions and practice writing answers.
4. Evaluate and revise your practice answers. Check your answers by your notes and textbook. Also check the composition section of this textbook for help in writing.

Taking Essay Tests

There are certain steps you should take before you begin an essay test. Quickly scan the questions. How many questions will you need to answer? Do you need to choose from several items? Which of them do you think you can answer best? After you have determined the answers to these questions, plan how much time to spend on each essay answer. Then stay with the schedule.

Read the question carefully. You may be asked for an answer that contains several parts.

Pay attention to important terms in the question. Essay questions on tests usually require specific tasks to be accomplished in the answer. Each task is expressed with a verb. If you become familiar with the key verbs and what kind of response each one calls for, this knowledge can help you to write a more successful essay.

ESSAY TEST QUESTIONS		
KEY VERB	**TASK**	**SAMPLE QUESTION**
argue	Take a viewpoint on an issue and give reasons to support this opinion.	Argue whether or not your school should start a recycling or a landscaping project.
analyze	Take something apart to see how each part works.	Analyze the life cycle of the chicken.
compare	Point out likenesses.	Compare word processors and typewriters.
contrast	Point out differences.	Contrast Cinderella and Snow White.
define	Give specific details that make something unique.	Define the term *divisor* as it is used in math.
demonstrate	Provide examples to support a point.	Demonstrate the importance of a balanced diet to good health.

ESSAY TEST QUESTIONS *(continued)*

KEY VERB	TASK	SAMPLE QUESTION
describe	Give a picture in words.	Describe how Tom Sawyer convinces all his friends to whitewash his fence.
discuss	Examine in detail.	Discuss the term *cause and effect.*
explain	Give reasons.	Explain the need for protecting an endangered species.
identify	Point out specific characteristics.	Identify the types of clouds.
list	Give all steps in order or all details about a subject.	List the steps for opening a lock with a combination.
summarize	Give a brief overview of the main points.	Summarize the tale of Beauty and the Beast.

Take a moment to use prewriting strategies. Consider the key verbs in the question. Then jot down a few notes or an outline to help you decide what you want to say. Write notes or a rough outline on scratch paper.

Evaluate and revise as you write. You probably can't redo your whole essay, but you can edit and improve it.

QUALITIES OF A GOOD ESSAY ANSWER

- The essay is well organized.
- The main ideas and supporting points are clearly presented.
- The sentences are complete and well written.
- There are no distracting errors in spelling, punctuation, or grammar.

Review

▶ EXERCISE 1   **Choosing an Appropriate Reading Rate**

Identify the reading rate that best fits each of the following situations.

1. You are looking at a test just handed to you to decide how much time you need to allot to each section.
2. You are looking in your grammar book for the section on the proper use of a semicolon.
3. You are reading a chapter in your history book and will be tested on it in two days.
4. You are reviewing the main points of the same chapter in your history book the night before your test.
5. You are looking in a textbook chapter for the answer to a question on your review sheet.

▶ EXERCISE 2   **Applying the SQ3R Reading Method**

Use the SQ3R method while reading a textbook chapter that you need to read for a class. List at least five questions and write a brief answer to each one.

▶ EXERCISE 3   **Reading: Analyzing Details in a Passage**

Answer the following questions about the reading passage on pages 882–883.

1. Give two facts or details about mongooses (other than those noted in the sample analysis).
2. Why was the mongoose brought to Hawaii and the West Indies?
3. How did the mongoose in Kipling's story save the lives of the boy and his family?
4. What two myths about the mongoose's ability to kill poisonous snakes are discussed in the reading passage?
5. Under what conditions may a mongoose be brought into the United States?

RESOURCES

▶ EXERCISE 4 **Reading: Drawing Conclusions and Making Inferences**

Using the reading passage on pages 882–883, identify the evidence or explain the reasoning that you might use to make the following inferences or draw the following conclusions.

1. The mongoose is important for controlling the cobra population.
2. Mongooses are clever animals.
3. People in Asia and Africa probably consider the mongoose to be a very valuable member of the animal kingdom.
4. Mongooses are not timid.
5. The mongoose is able to kill almost any kind of snake in the world.

▶ EXERCISE 5 **Reading: Interpreting Graphic Information**

Using the chart on page 889, answer each of the following questions.

1. What is the longest venomous snake shown on the chart?
2. Which snake's bite would be most likely to kill you if you were left untreated after its attack?
3. Which snakes can be found somewhere in North America?
4. Which of the snakes shown on the chart is the smallest?
5. Where are king cobras found? Cape cobras?

▶ EXERCISE 6 **Analyzing Your Note-Taking Method**

Select a homework assignment in your science, social studies, or English textbook. Take study notes, following the guidelines on page 886 regarding ways to take effective study notes. Be prepared to share your notes in class and to explain how you took notes.

▶ EXERCISE 7 **Identifying Classifications**

For each of the following groups, identify the category.

1. tile, carpet, Oriental rug, linoleum
2. bed, cot, bunk, couch
3. basket, purse, suitcase, shopping bag
4. beagle, dachshund, retriever, Doberman pinscher
5. sandals, tennis shoes, hightops, boots

▶ EXERCISE 8 **Reading: Applying Visual Organization**

After reading the paragraph below, make a chart of its contents. Use your graphic to answer the numbered questions on page 906. [Hint: Your completed chart should have two columns: one labeled "Reptiles" and one labeled "Amphibians."]

> Reptiles and amphibians are two of the three classes of cold-blooded vertebrates. Reptiles and amphibians can appear to be very similar, but they are actually very different. First, reptiles are a larger class of animals than amphibians. For example, the largest reptiles, pythons and anacondas, can grow to be over thirty feet long. By contrast, the largest of the amphibians, the Japanese giant salamander, is only five feet long. Second, their appearance is different. The skin of a reptile is scaly, while an amphibian's skin is smooth and sometimes even slimy. Reptiles breathe only with their lungs. Amphibians breathe with gills when they are young and with lungs as adults. Some amphibians retain their gills and have both lungs and gills as adults. In addition, all amphibians take in oxygen through their skins. Third, their mating habits differ. Amphibians mate during rainy periods, while reptiles mate in the spring. Reptiles are born on land, while amphibians are born in water or on moist ground. Reptiles are either hatched from eggs or are born live. Amphibians always hatch from eggs.

1. How is the skin of a reptile different from the skin of an amphibian?
2. Which is a larger class of animals: reptiles or amphibians?
3. What is the difference, in feet, between the largest reptile and the largest amphibian?
4. Do reptiles breathe differently than amphibians? Explain.
5. How do reptiles and amphibians differ in their place of birth?

▶ EXERCISE 9   **Reading: Paraphrasing a Poem**

Paraphrase the following excerpt from "A Psalm of Life" by Henry Wadsworth Longfellow.

> Not enjoyment, and not sorrow,
>   Is our destined end or way;
> But to act, that each to-morrow
>   Find us farther than today.
>
>   from "A Psalm of Life"
>   by Henry Wadsworth Longfellow

▶ EXERCISE 10   **Analyzing Essay Questions**

Identify the key verb that states the specific task in each of the following essay questions. Do not write an essay response. Instead, state briefly what you would need to do to answer each question.

1. Contrast the temperaments of Rip and Dame Van Winkle in Washington Irving's "Rip Van Winkle."
2. Explain the importance of the U.S. Constitution at the time it was written.
3. Discuss the importance of setting in the poem "The Highwayman" by Alfred Noyes.
4. List the steps of the rain cycle.
5. Demonstrate the importance of imagery in the poem "Harlem" by Langston Hughes.

DIAGRAMING SENTENCES

A *sentence diagram* is a picture of how the parts of a sentence fit together. It shows how the words in the sentence are related.

Subjects and Verbs (pages 400–411)

To diagram a sentence, first find the simple subject and the simple predicate, or verb, and write them on a horizontal line. Then separate the subject and verb with a vertical line. Keep the capital letters but leave out the punctuation marks, except in cases such as *Mr.* and *July 1, 1992.*

EXAMPLE   Horses gallop.

Horses	gallop

Questions (page 407)

To diagram a question, first make the question into a statement. Then diagram the sentence. Remember that in a diagram, the subject always comes first, even if it does not come first in the sentence.

EXAMPLE   Are you going?

you	Are going

The examples on the previous page are easy because each sentence contains only a simple subject and a verb. Now look at a longer sentence.

EXAMPLE   A quiet, always popular pet is the goldfish.

To diagram the simple subject and verb of this sentence, follow these steps.

Step 1: Separate the complete subject from the complete predicate.

complete subject	complete predicate
A quiet, always popular pet	is the goldfish.

Step 2: Find the simple subject and the verb.

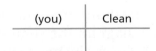

simple subject	verb
pet	is

Step 3: Draw the diagram.

pet	is

Understood Subjects (pages 415–416)

To diagram an imperative sentence, place the understood subject *you* in parentheses on the horizontal line.

EXAMPLE   Clean your room.

(you)	Clean

EXERCISE 1   Diagraming Simple Subjects and Verbs

Diagram only the simple subject and verb in each of the following sentences. Remember that simple subjects and verbs may consist of more than one word.

EXAMPLE   **1.** Gwendolyn Brooks has been the poet laureate
of Illinois.

Gwendolyn Brooks	has been

1. Angela just returned from Puerto Rico.
2. She was studying Spanish in San Juan.
3. Listen to her stories about her host family.
4. She really enjoyed her trip.
5. Have you ever been to Puerto Rico?

Peanuts reprinted by permission of United Feature Syndicate, Inc.

Compound Subjects (page 409)

To diagram a compound subject, put the subjects on parallel lines. Then put the connecting word (the conjunction) on a dotted line that joins the subject lines.

EXAMPLE   **Sharks** and **eels** can be dangerous.

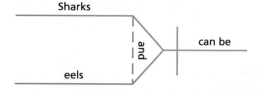

Compound Verbs (page 411)

To diagram a compound verb, put the two verbs on parallel lines. Then join them by a dotted line on which you write the connecting word.

EXAMPLE   The cowboy **swung** into the saddle and **rode** away.

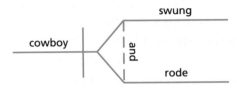

This is how a compound verb is diagramed when it has a helping verb.

EXAMPLE   Alice Walker **has written** many books and **received** several prizes for them.

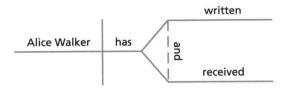

Compound Subjects and Compound Verbs
(pages 409–411)

A sentence with both a compound subject and a compound verb combines the patterns for each.

EXAMPLE   **Rosa Parks** and **Martin Luther King, Jr., saw** a problem and **did** something about it.

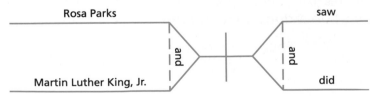

Sometimes parts of a compound subject or a compound verb are joined by correlative conjunctions, such as *both . . . and.* Correlatives are diagramed like this:

EXAMPLE   **Both** Luisa **and** Miguel can sing.

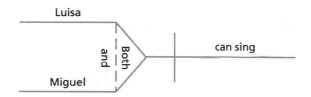

▶ EXERCISE 2   **Diagraming Compound Subjects and Compound Verbs**

Diagram the simple subjects and the verbs in the following sentences. Include the conjunctions that join the compound subjects or the compound verbs.

EXAMPLE   **1. Both Whitney Houston and Ray Charles are going on tour and cutting new albums.**

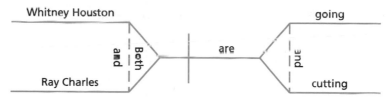

1. Everyone knows and likes Mr. Karras.
2. Hurricanes and tornadoes are frequent during the summer.
3. Julio and Rosa were frying tortillas and grating cheese for the tacos.
4. Both Jade Snow Wong and Amy Tan have written books about their childhoods in San Francisco's Chinatown.
5. Elena and I grabbed our jackets and took the bus to the mall.

Adjectives and Adverbs

Adjectives and adverbs are written on slanted lines connected to the words they modify. Notice that possessive
pronouns are diagramed in the same way adjectives are.

Adjectives (pages 434–437)

EXAMPLES **dark** room **a lively** fish **my best** friend

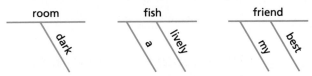

▶ EXERCISE 3 **Diagraming Sentences with Adjectives**

Diagram the subjects, verbs, and adjectives in the following sentences.

EXAMPLE **1.** A huge silver spaceship landed in the field.

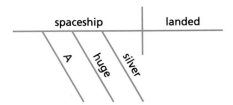

1. The horror movie will soon be finished.
2. The soft, silky kitten played with a shoelace.
3. A tall redheaded woman walked into the room.
4. The funniest television show stars Bill Cosby.
5. A weird green light shone under the door.

Adverbs (pages 454–457)

EXAMPLES walks **briskly** arrived **here late**

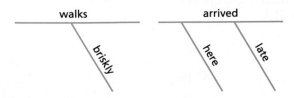

When an adverb modifies an adjective or another adverb, it is placed on a line connected to the word it modifies.

EXAMPLES   a **very happy** child   drove **rather slowly**

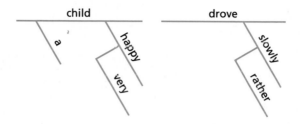

This **extremely rare** record will **almost certainly** cost a great deal.

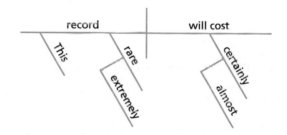

Conjunctions and Modifiers (pages 465–466)

When a modifier applies to only one part of the compound subject, it is diagramed like this:

EXAMPLE   Benjamin Davis, Sr., and **his** son worked **hard** and rose **quickly** through the military.

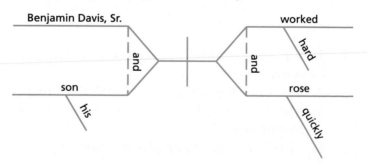

When a conjunction joins two modifiers, it is diagramed like this:

EXAMPLE The **English** and **American** musicians played **slowly** and quite **beautifully.**

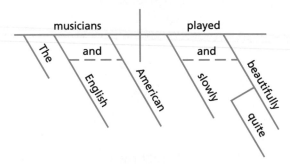

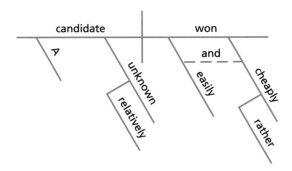

EXERCISE 4 **Diagraming Sentences with Adjectives and Adverbs**

Diagram the subjects, verbs, adjectives, and adverbs in the following sentences.

EXAMPLE **1.** A relatively unknown candidate won the election easily and rather cheaply.

1. The determined young Frederick Douglass certainly worked hard.
2. The talented actress spoke loudly and clearly.
3. Mei-Ling and her younger sister will arrive early tomorrow.
4. The best musicians always play here.
5. Generally that glue does not work very well.

Objects (pages 474–477)

Direct Objects (pages 474–475)

A direct object is diagramed on the horizontal line with the subject and verb. A vertical line separates the direct object from the verb. Notice that this vertical line does not cross the horizontal line.

EXAMPLE We like **pizza.**

Compound Direct Objects (page 475)

EXAMPLE Lizards eat **flies** and **earthworms.**

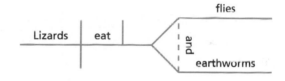

Indirect Objects (page 477)

An indirect object is diagramed on a horizontal line beneath the verb. The verb and the indirect object are joined by a slanting line.

EXAMPLE Marisol brought **me** a piñata.

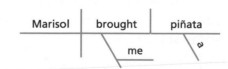

Compound Indirect Objects (page 477)

EXAMPLE   Tanya gave the **singer** and the **dancer** cues.

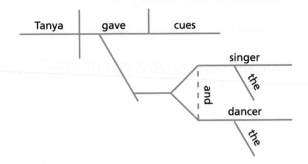

EXERCISE 5   **Diagraming Direct and Indirect Objects**

Diagram the following sentences.

EXAMPLE   **1. I gave the clerk a dollar.**

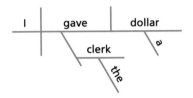

1. Several businesses bought our school computer equipment.
2. He sent the American Red Cross and Goodwill Industries his extra clothes.
3. My aunt knitted Violet and me sweaters.
4. Kim drew us a quick sketch.
5. Gerardo and Wendie are organizing the play and the refreshments.

Subject Complements (pages 480–482)

A subject complement is diagramed on the horizontal line with the subject and the verb. It comes after the verb. A line slanting toward the subject separates the subject complement from the verb.

Predicate Nominatives (pages 480–481)

EXAMPLE   Barbra Streisand is a famous **singer.**

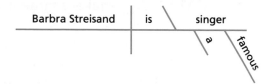

Compound Predicate Nominatives (page 481)

EXAMPLE   Clara is a **student** and a volunteer **nurse.**

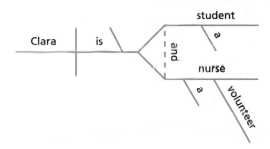

Predicate Adjectives (page 482)

EXAMPLE   She was extremely **nice.**

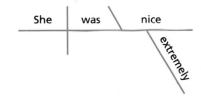

Compound Predicate Adjectives (page 482)

EXAMPLE   We were **tired** but very **happy.**

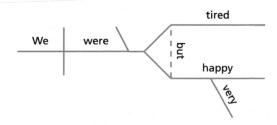

▶ EXERCISE 6   **Diagraming Sentences**

Diagram the following sentences.

EXAMPLE   **1.** The indigo snake is large and shiny.

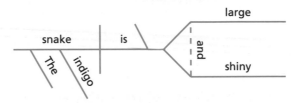

1. Turtles are reptiles.
2. Their tough bills look sharp and strong.
3. Turtles may grow very old.
4. The alligator snapper is the largest freshwater turtle.
5. Few turtles are dangerous.

Prepositional Phrases (pages 491–497)

A prepositional phrase is diagramed below the word it modifies. Write the preposition on a slanting line below the modified word. Then write the object of the preposition on a horizontal line connected to the slanting line.

Adjective Phrases (pages 493–494)

EXAMPLES   traditions **of**   gifts **from Nadine**
            the Sioux   **and Chip**

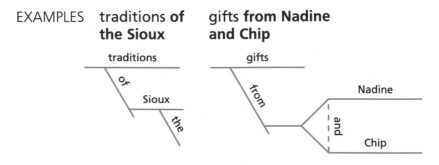

Adverb Phrases (pages 496–497)

EXAMPLES   awoke early **in the morning**

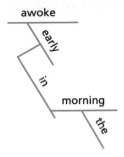

search **for the gerbil and the hamster**

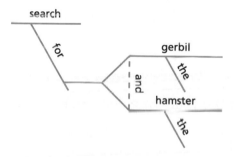

Two prepositional phrases may modify the same word.

EXAMPLE   **The tour extends across the country and around the world.**

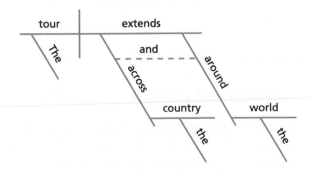

When a prepositional phrase modifies the object of another preposition, the diagram looks like this:

EXAMPLE   Richard Wright wrote one **of the books on that subject.**

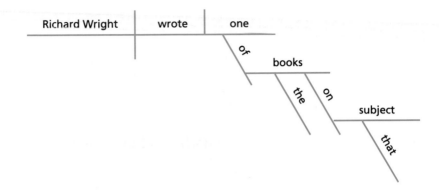

EXERCISE 7 **Diagraming Sentences with Prepositional Phrases**

Diagram the following sentences.

1. The director of that movie about the Civil War was chosen for an Academy Award.
2. A play about Cleopatra will be performed tonight.
3. Leroy practices with his band and by himself.
4. Stevie Wonder has written songs about love and freedom.
5. The scientist worked late into the night.

Subordinate Clauses (pages 516–525)

Adjective Clauses (pages 520–521)

Diagram an adjective clause by connecting it with a broken line to the word it modifies. Draw the broken line between the relative pronoun and the word that it relates to. [Note: The words *who, whom, whose, which,* and *that* are relative pronouns.] The adjective clause is diagramed below the independent clause.

EXAMPLES   The students **whose projects are selected** will attend the regional contest.

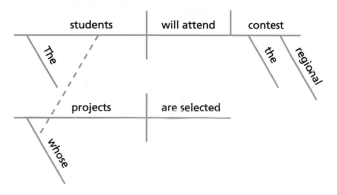

Adverb Clauses (pages 523–525)

Diagram an adverb clause by using a broken line to connect the adverb clause to the word it modifies. Place the subordinating conjunction that introduces the adverb clause on the broken line. [Note: The words *after, because, if, since, unless, when,* and *while* are common subordinating conjunctions.] The adverb clause is diagramed below the independent clause.

EXAMPLE   **If I study for two more hours,** I will finish my homework.

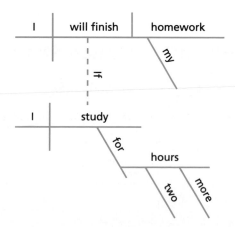

▶ EXERCISE 8   **Diagraming Sentences with Adjective Clauses and Adverb Clauses**

Diagram the following sentences.

EXAMPLE   **1. Will you stop by my house after you go to the library?**

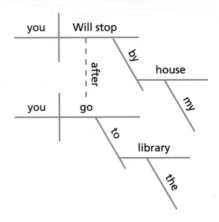

1. Proverbs are sayings that usually give advice.
2. Because the day was very hot, the cool water felt good.
3. The problem that worries us now is the pollution of underground sources of water.
4. If it does not rain tomorrow, we will visit Crater Lake.
5. Janice and Linda found some empty seats as the movie started.

The Kinds of Sentence Structure (pages 534–541)

Simple Sentences (page 534)

EXAMPLE   Ray showed us his new bike. [one independent clause]

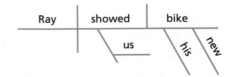

Compound Sentences (pages 536–538)

The second independent clause in a compound sentence is diagramed below the first and is joined to it by a coordinating conjunction. [The coordinating conjunctions are *and, but, for, or, nor, so,* and *yet.*]

EXAMPLE   Ossie Davis wrote the play, and Ruby Dee starred in it. [two independent clauses]

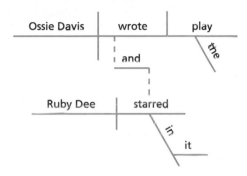

EXERCISE 9   **Diagraming Compound Sentences**

Diagram the following compound sentences.

EXAMPLE   **1.** Lucas likes that new CD, but I have not heard It.

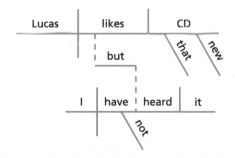

1. We went to the mall, and everyone had a good time.
2. Miriam celebrates Hanukkah, and she told our class about the holiday.
3. Luis Alvarez was an atomic scientist, but his son became a geologist.
4. Do you like basketball, or do you prefer hockey?
5. Sandy Koufax is my baseball hero, but my sister prefers Hank Aaron.

Complex Sentences (pages 540–541)

EXAMPLE   Altovise has a carving **that was made in Nigeria.**
[one independent clause and one subordinate clause]

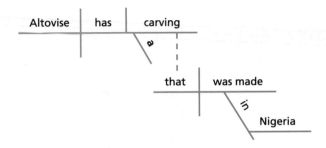

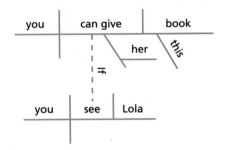

▶ EXERCISE 10   **Diagraming Complex Sentences**

Diagram the following complex sentences.

EXAMPLE   **1.** If you see Lola, you can give her this book.

1. Because my cousins live in Toledo, they took a plane to the wedding.
2. Sally Ride was the first American woman who flew in space.
3. Although Wilma Rudolph had been a very sick child, she became a top Olympic athlete.
4. All three of the children screamed as the roller coaster began its descent.
5. The amusement park that we like best offers two free rides to frequent customers.

Glossary of Terms

A

Abstract noun An abstract noun names an idea, a feeling, a quality, or a characteristic. (See page 426.)

Action verb An action verb is a verb that expresses physical or mental action. (See page 444.)

Adjective An adjective is a word that modifies a noun or a pronoun. (See page 434.)

Adjective clause An adjective clause is a subordinate clause that modifies a noun or a pronoun. (See page 520.)

Adjective phrase An adjective phrase is a prepositional phrase that modifies a noun or a pronoun. (See page 493.)

Adverb An adverb is a word that modifies a verb, an adjective, or another adverb. (See page 454.)

Adverb clause An adverb clause is a subordinate clause that is used as an adverb. (See page 523.)

Adverb phrase An adverb phrase is a prepositional phrase that modifies a verb, an adjective, or another adverb. (See page 496.)

Affix An affix is any word part added to another word or word part. (See page 861.)

Agreement Agreement refers to the correspondence, or match, between grammatical forms. For example, the number and person of a subject and verb, and the number and gender of a pronoun and its antecedent should always agree, or match. (See Chapter 20.)

Aim An aim is one of the four basic purposes, or reasons, for writing. (See pages 7 and 24.)

Antecedent An antecedent is a noun or pronoun to which a pronoun refers. (See page 428.)

Antonym An antonym is a word with the opposite meaning of another word. (See page 864.)

Appositive An appositive is a noun or a pronoun that explains or identifies another noun or pronoun. (See page 715.)

Article *A, an,* and *the* are the most commonly used adjectives and are called articles. *A* and *an* are indefinite articles. They refer to someone or something in general. *The* is a definite article. It refers to someone or something in particular. (See page 435.)

Audience An audience is the person(s) who reads or listens to what the writer or speaker says. (See page 37.)

Autobiographical incident A form of writing in which an author explores and shares the meaning of an experience that was especially important to him or her. (See Chapter 4.)

B

Base form The base form, or infinitive, is one of the four principal, or basic, parts of a verb. (See page 580.)

Body The body of a composition is one or more paragraphs that state and develop the composition's main points. (See page 107.)

Brainstorming Brainstorming is a way a writer finds ideas for writing by making a list of all thoughts about a subject without stopping to judge the ideas. (See page 29.)

Business letter A business letter is a formal letter in which a writer might request or order something, complain about or seek the correction of a problem, or express appreciation. (See page 870.)

C

Call number A call number is a number and letter code a library assigns to a book to tell how the book has been classified and where it has been placed on the shelves. (See page 848.)

Card catalog The library's card catalog is a listing of its books, magazines, CDs, and other resources. There are two kinds of catalogs. The **online catalog** is stored in a computer; the **traditional card catalog** is a set of card files stored in a cabinet. (See page 849.)

Case Case is the form of a noun or pronoun that shows its use in a sentence. (See page 606.)

Chronological order Chronological order is a way a writer arranges details in a paragraph or composition according to when events or actions take place. (See page 79.)

Clause A clause is a group of words that contains a verb and its subject and is used as a part of a sentence. (See page 516.)

Cliché A cliché is a vague and overused expression. (See page 391.)

Clustering Clustering is a way a writer finds writing ideas and gathers information by breaking a large subject into its smaller parts, using circles and lines to create a diagram of his or her thoughts. (See page 31.)

Coherence Coherence, in a paragraph or composition, means that a writer has clearly arranged and connected all ideas. (See pages 74 and 108.)

Collective noun A collective noun is singular in form but names a group of persons, animals, or things. (See page 564.)

Colloquialism A colloquialism is a casual, colorful expression used in everyday conversation. (See page 389.)

Common noun A common noun names any one of a group of persons, places, things, or ideas and is not capitalized unless it begins a sentence. (See page 424.)

Comparative degree Comparative degree is the form a modifier takes when two things are being compared. (See page 629.)

Comparing Comparing means telling how things are alike. (See page 82.)

Complement A complement is a word or group of words that completes the meaning of a verb. (See page 473.)

Complex sentence A complex sentence has one independent clause and at least one subordinate clause. (See page 540.)

Compound noun A compound noun is two or more words used together as a single noun. (See page 423.)

Compound sentence A compound sentence has two or more independent clauses and no subordinate clauses. (See pages 368 and 536.)

Compound subject A compound subject consists of two or more subjects that are joined by a connecting word and have the same verb. (See pages 366, 409, and 560.)

Compound verb A compound verb consists of two or more verbs that are joined by a connecting word and have the same subject. (See page 411.)

Conclusion (1) A conclusion restates the main idea in different words, sums up the ideas in the composition, and brings it to a definite close. (See pages 109 and 336.) **(2)** A conclusion is a decision reached by reasoning from clearly expressed facts and evidence found in a reading passage or other materials. (See page 884.)

Concrete noun A concrete noun names a person, place, or thing that can be perceived by one or more of the senses. (See page 426.)

Conflict A conflict is a situation that holds a problem or challenge for a character in a story. (See page 186.)

Conjunction A conjunction is a word that joins words or groups of words. (See page 465.)

Connotation The connotation of a word is the emotional meaning suggested by or associated with that word. (See page 390.)

Context The context of a word includes the surrounding words and the way the word is used. (See page 863.)

Contraction A contraction is a shortened form of a word, a figure, or a group of words. (See page 750.)

Contrasting Contrasting means telling how things are different from one another. (See page 82.)

Coordinating conjunction A coordinating conjunction connects words or groups of words used in the same way. *And, but, for, nor, or, so,* and *yet* are coordinating conjunctions. (See page 466.)

Correlative conjunction Correlative conjunctions are pairs of conjunctions that connect words or groups of words used in the same way. *Neither . . . nor* and *either . . . or* are examples of correlative conjunctions.

Creative writing Creative writing is writing that aims at creating literature: stories, poems, songs, and plays. (See page 7.)

D

Declarative sentence A declarative sentence makes a statement and is followed by a period. (See page 415.)

Demonstrative pronoun A demonstrative pronoun points out a person, place, thing, or idea. (See page 429.)

Denotation The denotation of a word is its direct, plainly expressed meaning—the meaning a dictionary lists. (See page 390.)

Description Description is a way a writer develops a paragraph or composition by using sensory details to describe something. (See page 77.)

Dialect A dialect is a variety of a language used by a particular group of people. Dialects of a language may differ from one another in vocabulary, grammar, and pronunciation. A dialect may be **regional** or **ethnic**. (See page 385.)

Dialogue Dialogue consists of the words that characters say in a story. (See page 194.)

Direct object A direct object is a noun or pronoun that receives the action of a transitive verb. (See page 474.)

Direct quotation A direct quotation is a person's exact words and is enclosed in quotation marks. (See page 737.)

Double negative A double negative is the use of two negative words to express one negative idea. (See page 636.)

Early plan An early plan, also called an **informal outline**, is a way for a writer to organize ideas by grouping and ordering information. (See page 100.)

End mark An end mark is punctuation placed at the end of a sentence. Periods, question marks, and exclamation points are end marks. (See page 701.)

Essay test An essay test is a test that measures how well a student understands a subject by requiring the student to express his or her understanding of that subject, in writing, in an organized way. (See page 900.)

Essential clause/Essential phrase An essential (or **restrictive**) clause or phrase is one that is necessary to the meaning of the sentence. (See page 713.)

Evaluating Evaluating is the stage in the writing process in which a writer goes over a draft, making judgments about its strengths and weaknesses in content, organization, and style. (See pages 6 and 46.)

Evaluation Evaluation is a way a writer develops a paragraph or composition by making judgments, telling what is good or bad about a subject. (See page 84.)

Example An example is a typical instance, or illustration, of an idea. (See page 69.)

Exclamatory sentence An exclamatory sentence shows excitement or expresses strong feeling and is followed by an exclamation point. (See page 416.)

Exposition *See* Informative writing.

Expressive writing Expressive writing is writing that aims at expressing a writer's feelings and thoughts. (See page 7.)

Fact A fact is a statement that can be proved true. (See page 248.)

Feedback Feedback is the listener's response to a speaker's message. (See page 826.)

Figure of speech A figure of speech is a word or a group of words that has a meaning other than what is actually said. (See page 164.)

5W-How? questions The *5W-How? questions—Who? What? Where? When? Why? How?*—are questions a writer uses to collect information about a subject. (See page 33.)

Formal outline A formal outline is a well-structured, clearly labeled writing plan. It uses letters and numbers to label main headings and subheadings, and can consist of either topics or complete sentences. (See page 101.)

Formal speech A formal speech is prepared in advance and given at a specific time and place. (See page 828.)

Freewriting Freewriting is a way of finding ideas for writing in which a writer writes whatever pops into his or her head. (See page 28.)

Helping verb A helping verb helps the main verb to express action or a state of being. (See page 451.)

Homonyms Homonyms are words that are spelled differently and that mean different things, but are pronounced alike. (See page 777.)

"How-to" process writing "How-to" process writing is a form of writing in which a writer tells a step-by-step story of how to do something. (See page 216.)

Imperative sentence An imperative sentence gives a command or makes a request and is followed by either a period or an exclamation point. (See page 415.)

Impromptu speech An impromptu speech is a short, spur-of-the-moment speech for which little or no preparation can be made. (See page 827.)

Indefinite pronoun An indefinite pronoun does not refer to a definite person, place, thing, or idea. (See page 430.)

Independent clause An independent, or **main,** clause expresses a complete thought and can stand by itself as a sentence. (See page 516.)

Indirect object An indirect object is a noun or pronoun that comes between the verb and the direct object and tells *to whom* or *for whom* the action of the verb is done. (See page 477.)

Indirect quotation An indirect quotation is a rewording of someone else's words. (See page 737.)

Inference An inference is a decision that is made based on evidence that is hinted at or implied. (See page 884.)

Infinitive An infinitive is a verbal, usually preceded by *to*, that can be used as a noun, an adjective, or an adverb. (See page 506.)

Infinitive phrase An infinitive phrase consists of an infinitive together with its modifiers and complements. (See page 508.)

Informative writing Informative writing is writing that aims at giving facts or information, or at explaining something. (See page 7.)

Intensive pronoun An intensive pronoun emphasizes a noun or another pronoun. (See page 429.)

Interjection An interjection is a word that expresses strong emotion. (See page 467.)

Interrogative pronoun An interrogative pronoun introduces a question. (See page 430.)

Interrogative sentence An interrogative sentence asks a question and is followed by a question mark. (See page 416.)

Interview An interview is a special listening situation with the specific purpose of gathering up-to-date or expert information. It usually takes place between two people. (See page 841.)

Intransitive verb An intransitive verb expresses action (or tells something about the subject) without passing the action to a receiver. (See page 446.)

Introduction An introduction begins a composition and should catch the reader's interest and present the main idea. (See page 104.)

Irregular verb An irregular verb is a verb that forms its past and past participle in some other way than by adding *–d* or *–ed* to the infinitive form. (See page 583.)

Jargon Jargon is special language that is used by a particular group of people. (See page 392.)

L

Linking verb A linking verb is a verb that expresses a state of being and links, or connects, the subject of a sentence with a word in the predicate that explains or describes the subject. (See page 447.)

List of sources A list of sources, or **Works Cited** list, tells what sources of information were used in a report. (See page 336.)

Logical order Logical order is a way of grouping ideas by what makes sense. (See page 82.)

M

Main idea A main idea is what a writer wants to say about a topic. It is the idea that a paragraph or composition is organized around. (See pages 64 and 98.)

Metaphor A metaphor is a figure of speech that compares two things directly, without using the words *like* or *as*. A metaphor says that something *is* something else. (See page 165.)

Modifier A modifier is a word, a phrase, or a clause that describes another word or limits the meaning of the word. (See page 629.)

N

Narration Narration is a way a writer develops a paragraph or composition by telling about events or actions as they change over a period of time. (See page 78.)

Nominative case The nominative case is the form a noun or a pronoun takes when it is a *subject* or a *predicate nominative*. (See page 607.)

Nonessential clause/Nonessential phrase A nonessential (or **nonrestrictive**) clause or phrase adds information that is not needed to understand the meaning of the sentence. It is set off by commas. (See page 713.)

Noun A noun is a word that names a person, place, thing, or idea. (See page 423.)

Number Number is the form of a word that indicates whether the word is singular or plural. (See page 551.)

O

Object An object receives the action of a transitive verb. (See page 446.)

Objective case The objective case is the form a noun or a pronoun takes when it is the *object* of a verb or the *object of a preposition*. (See page 611.)

Objective test An objective test consists of questions that each have only one correct answer. Objective tests may include multiple-choice, true/false, matching, or short-answer questions. (See page 895.)

Object of the preposition The noun or pronoun that ends a prepositional phrase is the object of the preposition that begins the phrase. (See page 491.)

Opinion An opinion is a belief or attitude; it cannot be proved true or false. (See page 248.)

Oral interpretation Oral interpretation is an expressive presentation of a literary work to a group of listeners. (See page 833.)

Order of importance Order of importance is a way of arranging details in a paragraph or composition according to how important the details are—most to least important, or the opposite. (See pages 84 and 160.)

Paraphrase A paraphrase is a restatement of someone's ideas in different words. (See page 890.)

Parenthetical expression A parenthetical expression is a side remark that adds information or relates ideas. (See page 718.)

Participial phrase A participial phrase consists of a participle together with its modifiers and complements. (See page 504.)

Participle A participle is a verb form that can be used as an adjective. (See page 502.)

Personal letter A personal letter is an informal letter in which a writer might thank someone for something, invite someone to a particular event or occasion, or reply to an invitation he or she has received. (See page 868.)

Personal pronoun A personal pronoun refers to the one speaking (*first person*), the one spoken to (*second person*), or the ones spoken about (*third person*). (See page 428.)

Persuasive essay A persuasive essay is a form of writing in which a writer supports an opinion and tries to persuade an audience. (See Chapter 8.)

Persuasive writing Persuasive writing is writing that aims at persuading

people to think or act in a certain way. (See page 7.)

Phrase A phrase is a group of related words that is used as a single part of speech and does not contain a verb and its subject. (See page 490.)

Plot The plot is the series of events that follow each other in a story. (See page 191.)

Positive degree Positive degree is the form a modifier takes when only one thing is being described. (See page 629.)

Possessive case The possessive case of a noun or a pronoun shows ownership or relationship. (See page 746.)

Predicate The predicate is the part of a sentence that says something about the subject. The **complete predicate** consists of all the words in the predicate that say something about the subject. The **simple predicate**, or *verb*, is the main word or group of words in the complete predicate. (See page 404.)

Predicate adjective A predicate adjective is an adjective that follows a linking verb and describes the subject of a sentence. (See page 482.)

Predicate nominative A predicate nominative is a noun or pronoun that follows a linking verb and explains or identifies the subject of a sentence. (See page 480.)

Prefix A prefix is a letter or group of letters added to the beginning of a word to create a new word with a different meaning. (See page 769.)

Preposition A preposition is a word that shows the relationship between a noun or pronoun and another word in the sentence. (See page 460.)

Prepositional phrase A prepositional phrase is a group of words beginning with a preposition and ending with a noun or a pronoun. (See pages 461 and 491.)

Prewriting Prewriting is the first stage in the writing process. In this stage, a writer thinks and plans, decides what to write about, collects ideas and details, and makes a plan for presenting ideas. (See pages 6 and 26.)

Principal parts of a verb The principal parts of a verb are a verb's four basic forms: the *base form,* the *present participle,* the *past,* and the *past participle.* (See page 580.)

Pronoun A pronoun is a word used in place of a noun or more than one noun. (See page 428.)

Proofreading Proofreading is the stage of the writing process in which a writer carefully reads a revised draft to correct mistakes in grammar, usage, and mechanics. (See pages 6 and 53.)

Proper adjective A proper adjective is formed from a proper noun and begins with a capital letter. (See page 437.)

Proper noun A proper noun names a particular person, place, thing, or idea and always begins with a capital letter. (See page 424.)

Publishing Publishing is the last stage of the writing process. In this stage, a writer makes a final, clean copy of a paper and shares it with an audience. (See pages 6 and 54.)

Purpose Purpose, or **aim,** is the reason for writing or speaking. (See pages 7, 24, and 37.)

R

Reflexive pronoun A reflexive pronoun refers to the subject and directs the action of the verb back to the subject. (See page 429.)

Regular verb A regular verb is a verb that forms its past and past participle by adding *–d* or *–ed* to the infinitive form. (See page 581.)

Relative pronoun A relative pronoun introduces a subordinate clause. (See page 431.)

Report A report is a form of writing in which a writer presents factual information that he or she has discovered through reading and asking questions about a topic. (See Chapter 10.)

Revising Revising is the stage of the writing process in which a writer goes over a draft, making changes in its content, organization, and style in order to improve it. (See pages 6 and 49.)

Run-on sentence A run-on sentence is two or more complete sentences run together as one. (See page 358.)

S

Sensory details Sensory details are words used to describe one of the five senses—sight, sound, touch, taste, and smell. (See page 69.)

Sentence A sentence is a group of words that has a subject and a verb and expresses a complete thought. (See page 398.)

Sentence fragment A sentence fragment is a group of words that looks like a sentence but does not express a complete thought. (See pages 355 and 398.)

Setting The setting is where and when a story takes place. (See page 190.)

Simile A simile is a figure of speech that compares two basically unlike things, using the words *like* or *as.* (See page 164.)

Simple sentence A simple sentence has one independent clause and no subordinate clauses. (See page 534.)

Slang Slang consists of made-up words and old words used in new ways. (See page 389.)

Spatial order Spatial order is a way of arranging details in a paragraph or composition by ordering them according to their location—from near to far, left to right, and so on. (See pages 77 and 160.)

Statement of opinion A statement of opinion is a sentence in which a writer clearly states a topic and his or her opinion about it. (See page 248.)

Stringy sentence A stringy sentence is made up of several independent clauses strung together with words like *and* or *but*. (See page 372.)

Subject The subject is the part of a sentence that tells whom or what the sentence is about. (See page 400.)

Subject complement A subject complement completes the meaning of a linking verb and identifies or describes the subject. (See page 480.)

Subordinate clause A subordinate, or **dependent,** clause does not express a complete thought and cannot stand alone as a sentence. (See page 516.)

Subordinating conjunction A subordinating conjunction begins an adverb clause and shows the relationship between the adverb clause and the word or words that the clause modifies. (See page 524.)

Suffix A suffix is a letter or group of letters added to the end of a word to create a new word with a different meaning. (See page 769.)

Summary A summary is a brief restatement of the main ideas expressed in a piece of writing. (See page 892.)

Superlative degree Superlative degree is the form a modifier takes when three or more things are being compared. (See page 629.)

Supporting sentences Supporting sentences are sentences in a paragraph or composition that give details or information to explain or prove the main idea. (See page 69.)

Syllable A syllable is a word part that can be pronounced by itself. (See page 765.)

Synonym A synonym is a word that has a meaning similar to, but not exactly the same as, another word. (See page 864.)

T

Tense The tense of a verb indicates the time of the action or the state of being expressed by the verb. (See page 592.)

Topic sentence A topic sentence is the sentence that states the main idea of a paragraph. (See page 65.)

Transitional words and phrases Transitional words and phrases connect ideas in a paragraph or composition by showing why and how ideas and details are related. (See pages 74 and 108.)

Transitive verb A transitive verb is an action verb that expresses an action directed toward a person or thing. (See page 446.)

U

Unity Unity, in a paragraph or composition, means that all the sentences or paragraphs work together as a unit to express or support one main idea. (See pages 71 and 107.)

V

Verb A verb is a word that expresses an action or a state of being. (See page 444.)

Verbal A verbal is a form of a verb used as a noun, an adjective, or an adverb. (See page 502.)

Verb phrase A verb phrase contains one main verb and one or more helping verbs. (See pages 405 and 451.)

"What if?" questions Asking "What if?" questions is a way of thinking creatively that can help a writer spark his or her imagination to explore ideas for writing. (See page 34.)

Word bank A writer's storehouse of new words or words he or she wants to use in writing. (See pages 163, 860.)

Writer's journal A writer's journal is a written record of what happens in a person's life, and how he or she feels and thinks. The journal can be a sourcebook for writing ideas. (See page 27.)

Writing Writing is the stage in the writing process in which a writer puts his or her ideas into sentences and paragraphs, following a plan for presenting the ideas. (See pages 6 and 44.)

Writing process The writing process is the series of stages or steps that a writer goes through to develop ideas and to communicate them clearly in a piece of writing. (See pages 6 and 24.)

Glossary

This glossary is a short dictionary of words found in the professional writing models in this textbook. The words are defined according to their meanings in the context of the writing models.

Pronunciation Key

Symbol	Key Words	Symbol	Key Words
a	asp, fat, parrot	b	bed, fable, dub, ebb
ā	ape, date, play, break, fail	d	dip, beadle, had, dodder
ä	ah, car, father, cot	f	fall, after, off, phone
e	elf, ten, berry	g	get, haggle, dog
ē	even, meet, money, flea, grieve	h	he, ahead, hotel
		j	joy, agile, badge
i	is, hit, mirror	k	kill, tackle, bake, coat, quick
ī	ice, bite, high, sky	l	let, yellow, ball
ō	open, tone, go, boat	m	met, camel, trim, summer
ô	all, horn, law, oar	n	not, flannel, ton
o͞o	look, pull, moor, wolf	p	put, apple, tap
o͞o	ooze, tool, crew, rule	r	red, port, dear, purr
yo͞o	use, cute, few	s	sell, castle, pass, nice
yoo	cure, globule	t	top, cattle, hat
oi	oil, point, toy	v	vat, hovel, have
ou	out, crowd, plow	w	will, always, swear, quick
u	up, cut, color, flood	y	yet, onion, yard
ʉr	urn, fur, deter, irk	z	zebra, dazzle, haze, rise
ə	a in ago	ch	chin, catcher, arch, nature
	e in agent	sh	she, cushion, dash, machine
	i in sanity	th	thin, nothing, truth
	o in comply	th	then, father, lathe
	u in focus	zh	azure, leisure, beige
ər	perhaps, murder	ŋ	ring, anger, drink

Abbreviation Key

adj.	adjective	*prep.*	preposition
adv.	adverb	*vi.*	intransitive verb
n.	noun	*vt.*	transitive verb
pl.	plural		

A

Am·ster·dam [am'stər dam'] *n.* A seaport and the official capital of the Netherlands.

ap·pren·tice [ə pren'tis] *adj.* Beginning.

ar·rest·ing [ə rest'iŋ] *adj.* Attracting immediate and full attention.

at·ta·ché [at' ə shā') *n.* A person who works for his or her own country in another country.

awed [ôd] *adj.* Feeling respect and wonder.

B

bay·o·net [bā'ə net'] *n.* A kind of blade attached to the barrel of a rifle.

bo·lo tie [bō'lō tī] *n.* A cord worn around the neck with a decorated fastener to tighten the neck loop.

braille [brāl] *n.* A system of writing used by the blind in which patterns of raised dots are felt by the fingers.

buck·skin [buk'skin'] *n.* A yellow-gray horse.

bur·dock [bʉr'däk'] *n.* A plant with large leaves and purple flowers.

butte [byo͞ot] *n.* A lone steep hill in an area of flat land.

C

cam·po [käm'pō] *n.* Spanish for rural area.

car·mine [kär'min] *adj.* Red or purplish-red.

check [chek] *vt.* To hold back.

cis·tern [sis'tərn] *n.* A large tank designed to collect rainwater for later use.

com·mo·tion [kə mō'shən] *n.* Noisy confusion.

com·pe·tent [käm'pə tənt] *adj.* Very capable; skilled.

con·fines [kän'fīns'] *n.* A fenced in or limited area.

con·sume [kən so͞om'] *vt.* To eat up.

con·quis·ta·dors [kän kēs'ta dôrz'] *n. pl.* The sixteenth-century Spanish invaders who conquered Peru, Mexico, and other parts of the Americas.

Co·pen·hag·en [kō' pən hä'gən] *n.* The capital city of Denmark.

Crazy Horse [krā'zē hôrs] *n. c.* 1842–1877. A famous chief of the Dakotas.

D

dep·re·cat·ing·ly [dep'rə kāt'iŋ lē] *adv.* In a disapproving manner.

de·scend [dē send'] *vi.* To come down.

de·scend·ant [dē sen'dənt] *n.* One who is the son, daughter, grandchild, great-grandchild, etc., of a certain person.

de·te·ri·o·rate [dē tir'ē ə rāt] *vi.* To become poorer in quality.

E

e·phem·er·al [ē fem'ər əl] *adj.* Short-lived.

e·rode [ē rōd'] *vi.* To wear away until gone.

ex·ten·sive·ly [ek sten'siv lē] *adv.* To a great extent; covering a wide variety.

F

fast [fast] *vi.* To go without food.

fa·tigue [fə tēg'] *n.* Exhaustion; weariness.

for·feit [fôr'fit] *vt.* To lose or give up something in payment for a mistake in a game.

for·mat [fôr'mat'] *n.* Form.

G

glint *vi.* To shine or reflect in brilliant flashes; gleam; glitter.

green·house [grēn′hous′] *adj.* Helping to trap the sun's rays in the earth's atmosphere, which may be causing climates all over the earth to gradually become hotter.

guf·faw [gu fô′] *vi.* To laugh loudly and roughly.

H

ha·rangue [hə raŋ′] *vt.* To address in a noisy or scolding speech.

har·assed [hə rasd′] *adj.* Troubled and busy.

ha·ven [hā′vən] *n.* A safe place.

hid·e·ous [hid′ē əs] *adj.* Horrible to see or hear about.

hu·man·oid [hyōō′mə noid] *adj.* A creature with human characteristics.

I

i·de·al·ism [ī dē′əl iz′əm] *n.* Thought based on the way one wishes things to be.

in·di·ca·tion [in′ di kā′shən] *n.* A sign; something that suggests.

in·fer·tile [in furt″l] *adj.* Not able to grow plants.

ir·i·des·cent [ir′ i des′ənt] *adj.* Showing shiny colors that change when an object is moved.

J

Ju·bi·lee [jōō′bə lē′] *n.* A cry of joy.

ju·ve·nile [jōō′və nīl′] *adj.* Immature; lacking adult skill or experience.

K

knead [nēd] *vt.* To mix and work dough or clay by folding and pressing with the hands.

L

las·so [las′ō] *n.* A long rope with a movable loop on the end for catching cattle.

M

ma·neu·ver [mə nōō′vər] *n.* A planned movement.

Ma·ya·güez [mä′yä gwes′] *n.* A western Puerto Rico seaport.

Ma·za·tlán [mä′sät län′] *n.* A seaport and resort in Mexico.

meth·ane [meth′ān′] *n.* A colorless, odorless gas given off by rotting or digested plants.

mi·nus·cule [mi nus′kyōōl′] *adj.* Very small.

N

nat·u·ral·ist [nach′ər əl ist] *n.* A person who studies nature.

Na·zi [nät′sē] *adj.* Of, by, or about the political party that controlled Germany under Hitler from 1933 to 1945.

O

ob·jec·tive·ly [əb jek′tiv lē] *adv.* Without opinion for or against.

oc·cu·pied [äk′yōō pīd] *adj.* Captured and being run by a foreign government.

or·der·ly [ôr′dər lē] *n.* A hospital or nursing home attendant.

or·ni·thol·o·gist [ôr′nə thäl′ə jist] *n.* A scientist devoted to the study of birds.

P

pad · dy [pad′ē] *n.* A rice field, partly under water.

pal · sied [pôl′zēd] *adj.* Paralyzed; often small from lack of use.

pan · o · ram · a [pan′ə ram′ə] *n.* A seemingly unlimited view of a broad area.

parch · ment [pärch′mənt] *n.* **1** A thin animal skin, usually of a sheep or a goat, prepared as a writing surface. **2** Paper treated to resemble true parchment.

par · quet [pär kā′] *n.* Flooring composed of wooden pieces, often in contrasting colors, set in a geometric pattern.

perch [purch] *n.* A freshwater fish.

per · se · cu · tion [pur′si kyōō′shən] *n.* The cruel or harsh treatment of someone for believing differently.

pre · ma · ture · ly [prē′mə toor′ lē] *adv.* Too early.

pro · ces · sion [prō sesh′ən] *n.* A group moving forward together.

prow [prou] *n.* The front part of a ship or boat.

Q

quest [kwest] *n.* A journey in search of something of value.

R

raf · ter [raf′tər] *n.* A board that helps hold up a roof.

rain · forest [rān fôr′ist] *n.* A thick, evergreen forest in a tropical area that receives rain year-round.

red-let · ter [red′ let′ər] *adj.* Designating a significant or joyous event.

re · it · er · ate [rē it′ə rāt′] *vt.* To repeat.

rem · i · nisce [rem′ə nis′] *vi.* To think and talk about memories of past events.

Re · sist · ance [ri zis′təns] *n.* The organized secret work of the people in a captured country fighting against the foreign country that has captured it.

rimed cou · plet [rīmd kup′lit] *n.* Two rhyming lines that are the same length, one written just after the other.

rouse [rouz] *vi.* To cause someone to act.

ru · pee [rōō′pē] *n.* The basic money unit of India.

S

sa · cred [sā′krid] *adj.* Holy; spiritually perfect or pure.

sage [sāj] *n.* A plant that is dried and used for seasoning; it was once believed to have healing powers.

salt flat [sôlt′ flat′] *n.* A flat area of land covered with salt from an evaporated body of water.

sau · ci · ly [sô′si lē] *adv.* In a bright, lively way.

sheep · ish · ly [shēp′ish lē] *adv.* In an embarrassed manner.

sil · ver [sil′vər] *vt.* To cover with a silvery color.

Sioux [sōō] *n.* A North American Indian people of the Northern Plains.

so · ber [sō′bər] *vt.* To make someone be serious.

soy · a [soi′ə] *n.* A plant of the pea family.

sparse [spärs] *adj.* Distributed lightly or sparingly; not dense.

spring · house [spriŋ′hous] *n.* A small building constructed over a spring or creek and traditionally used for keeping food cold.

T

te·pee [tē′ pē] *n.* A cone-shaped tent made of animal skins stretched over poles.

ter·mi·nate [tur′mə nāt′] *vt.* To put an end to.

thith·er [*thith*′ər] *adv.* Toward that destination; there.

tract [trakt] *n.* A large area of land.

trem·o·lo [trem′ə lō′] *n.* A trembling sound made by rapidly repeating the same tone.

V

ve·ran·da [və ran′də] *n.* A long, open porch.

vi·cious [vish′əs] *adj.* Intense; mean.

vi·sion [vizh′ən] *adj.* Having to do with seeing unreal, dreamlike images in the mind.

W

Wa·si·chu [wä sē′cho͞o] *n.* Lakota Sioux word for a modern non-Native American person, particularly an Anglo-American or British person.

Index

INDEX

INDEX

F

INDEX

W

Acknowledgments

For permission to reprint copyrighted material, grateful acknowledgment is made to the following sources:

Andrews and McMeel: From "Coyote Places the Stars" from *Giving Birth to Thunder, Sleeping with His Daughter: Coyote Builds North America* by Barry Lopez. Copyright © 1977 by Barry Holstun Lopez. All rights reserved.

Atheneum Books for Young Readers, an imprint of Simon & Schuster: From "Jody's Discovery" from *The Yearling* by Marjorie Kinnan Rawlings. Copyright 1938 by Marjorie Kinnan Rawlings; copyright renewed © 1966 by Norton Baskin.

Avon Books, a division of William Morrow & Company, Inc.: From *Water Girl* by Joyce Carol Thomas. Copyright © 1986 by Joyce Carol Thomas.

Broadside Press: From "Questions and Answers" by Dudley Randall from *A Capsule Course in Black Poetry Writing* by Gwendolyn Brooks, Keorapetse Kgositsile, Haki R. Madhubuti, and Dudley Randall. Copyright © 1975 by Gwendolyn Brooks Blakely, Keorapetse Kgositsile, Haki R. Madhubuti, and Dudley Randall.

Jean Caldwell: Quotation by Madeleine L'Engle from an interview with Jean Caldwell from *On Being a Writer,* edited by Bill Strickland. Copyright © 1982 by Jean Caldwell.

Carlinsky & Carlinsky, Inc.: From "Kites" by Dan Carlinsky from *Boy's Life,* May 1974. Copyright © 1974 by Dan Carlinsky.

Children's Better Health Institute, Benjamin Franklin Literary & Medical Society, Inc., Indianapolis, Indiana: From "Kachinas: Sacred Drama of the Hopis" by Lonnie Dyer from *Young World.* Copyright © 1976 by Saturday Evening Post Company.

The Christian Science Monitor: Quotation by Fairfax Cone from *The Christian Science Monitor,* March 20, 1963. Copyright © 1963 by The Christian Science Monitor.

Cobblestone Publishing, Inc., 7 School St., Peterborough, NH 03458: From "The Spaceport Mermaids" by Greg Walz-Chojnacki from *Odyssey's,* vol. 12, no. 10, October 1990. Copyright © 1990 by Cobblestone Publishing, Inc.

Doubleday, a division of Bantam Doubleday Dell Publishing Group, Inc.: From *The Diary of a Young Girl: The Definitive Edition* by Anne Frank, edited by Otto H. Frank & Mirjam Pressler, translated by Susan Massotty. Translation copyright © 1995 by Doubleday, a division of Bantam Doubleday Dell Publishing Group, Inc. From *Mighty Hard Road: The Story of Cesar Chavez* by James P. Terzian and Kathryn Cramer. Copyright © 1970 by Doubleday & Company, Inc. From *The Richer, the Poorer* by Dorothy West. Copyright © 1995 by Dorothy West. From "I'm from Out of the Beech" from *I Wish I Could Give My Son a Wild Raccoon* by Eliot Wigginton. Copyright © 1976 by Reading is Fundamental.

Dutton Signet, a division of Penguin Books, USA Inc.: From *Insets, The Creeping Conquerors and Human History* by Carson I. A. Ritchie. Copyright © 1979 by Carson I. A. Ritchie.

HarperCollins Publishers, Inc.: From *Black Elk: The Sacred Ways of a Lakota* by Wallace H. Black Elk and William S. Lyon, Ph.D. Copyright © 1990 by Wallace H. Black Elk and William S. Lyon.

HarperCollins Publishers Ltd.: From "One Day a Month, Go Without Meat" from *2 Minutes a Day for a Greener Planet* by Marjorie Lamb. Copyright © 1990 by Marjorie Lamb. Logo © 1990 by HarperCollins Publishers Ltd. Published by HarperCollins Publishers Ltd.

Henry Holt and Company, Inc.: From "A Runaway Slave" from *Chariot in the Sky: A Story of the Jubilee Singers* by Arna Bontemps. Copyright 1951 by Arna Bontemps; Copyright © 1979 by Mrs. Arna (Alberta) Bontemps.

Alfred A. Knopf, Inc.: From "Aphorisms of the Professor" from *The Physiology of Taste or Meditations on Transcendental Gastronomy* by Jean Anthelme Brillat-Savarin, translated by M.F.K. Fisher. Copyright © 1949 by The George Macy Companies, Inc.

Lion Books, Publisher, Scarsdale, NY: "Ubuhlali and Umnaka—Beaded Necklaces and Bangles" from *African Crafts*. Published by and copyright © by Lion Books, Publisher, Scarsdale, NY.

Little, Brown and Company: From *Nisei Daughter* by Monica Sone, Copyright © 1953 and renewed © 1981 by Monica Sone.

Liveright Publishing Corporation: "Those Winter Sundays" from *Angle of Ascent: New and Selected Poems* by Robert Hayden. Copyright © 1966 by Robert Hayden.

Lothrop, Lee and Shepard Books, a division of William Morrow & Co., Inc.: From "Green Dragon Pond" from *The Spring of Butterflies*, translated by He Liyi. Copyright © 1985 by William Collins Sons & Co. Ltd.

Macmillan USA, a Simon & Schuster Macmillan Company: Entry, "escape," and "Pronunciation Key" from *Webster's New World College Dictionary,* Third Edition. Copyright © 1996, 1994, 1991, 1988 by Simon & Schuster, Inc.

Margaret K. McElderry Books, an imprint of Simon & Schuster Children's Publishing Division: From *A Jar of Dreams* by Yoshiko Uchida. Copyright © 1981 by Yoshiko Uchida.

William Morrow & Company, Inc.: From "Weightless in Space" from *To Space and Back* by Sally Ride with Susan Okie. Copyright © 1986 by Sally Ride and Susan Okie. From "A Drink for Crow" from *Stories to Solve: Folktales from Around the World,* told by George W. B. Shannon. Copyright © 1985 by George W. B. Shannon.

National Dairy Board, American Dairy Farmers: Ad, "When your potassium comes with dairy calcium, you don't need a bunch." Copyright © 1990 by the National Dairy Board.

National Wildlife Federation: "Cures from the Jungle" by Whitney Hair from "Dear Ranger Rick" from *Ranger Rick* magazine, vol. 24, no. 8, August 1990. Copyright © 1990 by National Wildlife Federation. From "Meet-a-Cheetah" by Fred Johnson from *Ranger Rick* magazine, January 1969. Copyright © 1969 by National Wildlife Federation.

Newsweek, Inc.: From "A Doll Made to Order" from *Newsweek,* December 9, 1985. Copyright © 1985 by Newsweek, Inc. All rights reserved.

Orchard Books, New York: From "An Hour with Abuelo" from *An Island Like You* by Judith Ortiz Cofer. Copyright © 1995 by Judith Ortiz Cofer.

The Pushcart Press: From a quotation by Maxwell Perkins from *The Writer's Quotation Book, a literary companion,* edited by James Charlton. Copyright © 1980 by The Pushcart Press.

Marian Reiner: Haiku by Bashō from *Cricket Songs: Japanese Haiku,* translated by Harry Behn. Copyright © 1964 by Harry Behn; copyright renewed © 1992 by Prescott Behn, Pamela Behn Adam, and Peter Behn.

The Saturday Review: "The Dinner Party" by Mona Gardner from *Saturday Review,* January 21, 1942. Copyright © 1942 by SR Publications, Ltd.

School Library Journal: From a book review by Louise L. Sherman on *Number the Stars* by Louis Lowry from *School Library Journal,* vol. 35, no. 7, March 1989. Copyright © 1989 by Reed Publishing, USA.

Simon & Schuster Books for Young Readers, an imprint of Simon & Schuster Children's Publishing Division: "My Aunt" from *Meet My Folks* by Ted Hughes. Copyright © 1961, 1973 by Ted Hughes. From *Hatchet* by Gary Paulsen. Copyright © 1987 by Gary Paulsen.

Virginia Driving Hawk Sneve: "The Medicine Bag" by Virginia Driving Hawk Sneve from *Boy's Life*, 1975. Copyright © 1975 by Virginia Driving Hawk Sneve.

Gary Soto, 43 The Crescent, Berkeley, CA 94708: From "The Jacket" from *Small Faces* by Gary Soto. Copyright © 1986 by Gary Soto.

Jesse Stuart Foundation, P. O. Box 391, Ashland, KY 41114: From "What America Means to Me" by Jesse Stuart. Copyright © 1951 by Jesse Stuart and the Jesse Stuart Foundation.

Texas A & M University Press: From *Journal of an Indian Trader: Anthony Glass and the Texas Trading Frontier, 1790–1810,* edited by Dan L. Flores. Copyright © 1985 by Dan L. Flores.

Universal Press Syndicate: From "Anatidaephobia" from *The Far Side* by Gary Larson. Copyright © 1988 by Far Side Works, Inc. Dist. by Universal Press Syndicate. All rights reserved.

University of California Press: From "In the Night" from *Singing for Power: The Song Magic of the Papago Indians of Southern Arizona* by Ruth Murray Underhill. Copyright © 1938, 1966 by Ruth Murray Underhill.

University of Nebraska Press: From "Across the Big Water" from *Black Elk Speaks* by John G. Neihardt. Copyright 1932, 1959, 1972 by John G. Neihardt; copyright © 1961 by the John G. Neihardt Trust.

University of Notre Dame Press: From *Barrio Boy* by Ernesto Galarza. Copyright © 1971 by the University of Notre Dame Press.

Viking Penguin, a division of Penguin Books, USA Inc.: From "How to Eat Like a Child" from *How to Eat Like a Child* by Delia Ephron, illustrated by Edward Koren. Copyright © 1977, 1978 by Delia Ephron; illustrations copyright © 1978 by Edward Koren.

The H. W. Wilson Company: Entries "Seal, Kathy Shenkin" through "Seattle Mariners (Baseball Team)" from *Abridged Readers' Guide to Periodical Literature*, April 1996. Copyright © 1996 by the H. W. Wilson Company. Search results from *Readers' Guide to Periodical Literature*, online version, from *Readers' Guide Abstracts.* Copyright © 1983, 1984 by the H. W. Wilson Company.

PHOTO CREDITS

COVER: Ralph J. Brunke Photograph.

TABLE OF CONTENTS: vi, Nawrocki Stock Photo; vii, David Young-Wolff/PhotoEdit; viii, Archive Photos; x, SuperStock; xii, NASA; xiii, Culver Pictures, Inc.; xv(t), Ted Horowitz/The Stock Market; xv(c), HRW Photo by Russell Dian, xv(b), Bev Rehkop/Unicorn Stock Photos; xvi(t), James Balog; xvi(b), John Eastcott/YVA Momatiuk/DRK; xvii, The Granger Collection, New York; xix(tl), Mary Messenger; xix(r), UPI/Bettmann Newsphotos, xxi, Norma Morrison; xxii(both), Michael Ochs Archive; xxv(tr), Camerique; xxxii, Bob Daemmrich/The Image Works; xxxiv, HB Photo by Stephanie Maize; xxxv(l), Courtesy Dudley Randall; xxxv(r), Marc Deville/Gamma Liaison.

PART ONE: Pages 0–1, HRW Photo; 2–3(tr), Bob Daemmrich; 4(tr), Blair Seitz/Seitz & Seitz; 5(tr), Elena Rooraid/PhotoEdit; 6(tr), Marc Deville/Gamma Liaison; 7(tr), Bonnie Kamin.

CHAPTER 1: Page 21(bc), Courtesy of Dudley Randall; 27(l, br), Myrleen Ferguson/PhotoEdit; 29(tl, tc), Prettyman/PhotoEdit; 30(c), David R. Frazier/David R. Frazier Photolibrary; 33(c), HRW Photo by Ken Lax; 34(l), Lorraine Rorke/The Image Works; 34(r), Rosebush Vision/Phototake; 37(br), 38(l), David R. Frazier/David R. Frazier Photolibrary; 38(r), Ric Noyle/Visual Impact Hawaii; 40(bc), Paolo Koch/Photo Researchers, Inc.; 42, 45, 50, Nawrocki Stock Photo; 52(l), Focus on Sports; 52(r), Arnold Michlin/PhotoEdit; 52(c), Usman Khan/Greater Toledo Islamic Center.

CHAPTER 2: Page 60(bc), Smithsonian Institution; 61, Corbis-Bettmann; 62(tr), Topham/The Image Works; 64(l), Tom Bean/DRK Photo; 64(r), David Young-Wolff/PhotoEdit; 68(bc), D. Cavagnaro/DRK; 70(c), Tony Freeman/PhotoEdit; 71(cr), © 1986 Richard Howard/People Weekly/Time, Inc.; 72(c), R. Hamilton Smith/FPG; 73(bc), David R. Frazier/David R. Frazier Photolibrary; 75(r), Jim Cartier/Photo Researchers, Inc.; 75(bl), SuperStock; 76(br), Lawrence Migdale; 78(tc), Myrleen Ferguson/PhotoEdit; 83(c), Aaron Haupt/David R. Frazier Photolibrary; 85(l), Stan Osolinski/FPG; 85(r), Lee Kuhn/FPG; 87(l), Grant Heilman/Grant Heilman Photography; 87(r), Phil Schermeister/Photographers Aspen; 89(r), M. Richards/PhotoEdit.; 89(l), Reuters/Bettmann Newsphotos.

CHAPTER 3: Page 95(t), Pat and Rae Hagan/Bruce Coleman, Inc.; 95(b), Jeff Foott/Bruce Coleman, Inc.; 96, Pat and Rae Hagan/Bruce Coleman, Inc.; 97(t), Jay Freis/The Image Bank; 98(cr), Archive Photos; 99(l), David R. Frazier/David R. Frazier Photolibrary; 99(r), Tony Freeman/PhotoEdit; 101, 103, M. Richards/PhotoEdit;

105(bc), Hans Reinhard/Bruce Coleman, Inc.; 109(both), Runk/Schoenberger/Grant Heilman Photography; 111, 112(both), SuperStock.

CHAPTER 4: Page 123(cr), HRW Photo by Peter Van Steen; 124(l), Richard Hutchins/PhotoEdit; 124(r), David Young-Wolff/PhotoEdit; 125, David Young-Wolff/Tony Stone Images; 126, Courtesy Canyon Vista Middle School, Austin, Texas; 128, George D. Lepp/Comstock; 132(tc), LeRoy Grannis/Camera Press/Retna Ltd.; 134(bl), HRW Photo by Peter Van Steen; 134(bckgd), J. Stewart/Bruce Coleman, Inc.; Glenn Short/Bruce Coleman, Inc.; 139, Frank Siteman/The Picture Cube; 143, Everett Collection; 146, SuperStock.

CHAPTER 5: Page 153, James Simon/The Picture Cube; 154(t), David DeLossy/The Image Bank; 157(bc), SuperStock; 159(tr), Tony Freeman/PhotoEdit; 161(bckgd), Barry Parker/Bruce Coleman, Inc.; 161(house), Peter French/Bruce Coleman, Inc.; 162(bc), Chuck O'Rear/Westlight; 163(c), HRW Photo Library; 164(c), Gary W. Griffen/Animals, Animals; 175(cl, bl, br), HRW Photos by Eric Beggs; 176(tc), SuperStock.

CHAPTER 6: Page 185(l, r), Walt Disney Pictures/Shooting Star; 187(l, r), SuperStock; 190(l), Spectrum/Bavaria/Viesti Associates, Inc.; 190(r), S. Chester/Comstock; 194, Russ Kinne/Comstock; 199(tc), Neal and Molly Jansen/SuperStock; 200(c), SuperStock.

CHAPTER 7: Page 217(l), David R. Frazier/David R. Frazier Photolibrary; 217(r), Lawrence Migdale; 220(c), Bob Daemmrich/The Image Works; 221(c), HRW Photo by Eric Beggs; 223(tc), Camerique; 224(tl), Murray Alcosser/The Image Bank; 224(c), Robert Frerck/Odyssey, Chicago; 226(br), A. Briere/Superstock; 229(c), Rivera Collection/Superstock; 238, NASA; 239(cr), Larry Kolvoord/Viesti Associates, Inc.

CHAPTER 8: Page 248(c), Culver Pictures, Inc.; 249(bl), UPI/Bettmann Newsphotos; 249(br), Witt/Sipa-Press; 250(cr), Frank Siteman/The Picture Cube; 251(bc), Dan Helms/Duomo; 253(cr), Jack S. Grove/Tom Stack & Associates; 255(c), Eric Sander/Gamma Liaison; 257(bc), Grant Heilman Photography; 258(c), R. Azoury/Sipa-Press; 260(bc), Al Tielemans/Duomo; 264(br), UPI/Bettmann Newsphotos; 266(bc), Norma Morrison; 271(bc), Culver Pictures, Inc.; 273(c), Richard Shiell/Earth Scenes.

CHAPTER 9: Page 293, Elena Rooraid/PhotoEdit; 302(bc), HB Photo by Stephanie Maize; 304(bl), D. Cavagnaro/DRK; 304(br), John Shaw/Tom Stack & Associates; 309(bc), HRW Photo by John Langford; 312(c), Jerry Howard/Positive Images; 313(bc), UPI/Bettmann Newsphotos.

CHAPTER 10: Page 317(tc), Gunter Ziesler/Peter Arnold, Inc.; 321 (cl), Bettmann Newsphotos; 321 (cr), Gunter Ziesler/Peter Arnold, Inc.;

321(bl), NASA/Sipa-Press; 323(tl), C. Canet/
M.C.R. Communication/Gamma Liaison; 323(tc),
Brian Lovell/Nawrocki Stock Photo; 323(tr), Luca
Gavagna/Photo Researchers, Inc.; 325(cl, cr),
John Cancalosi/DRK Photo; 327(tl), SuperStock;
327(cr), Paul Conklin/PhotoEdit; 328(c), Haley/
Sipa-Press; 338(bl), Scott Camazine/Photo
Researchers, Inc.; 339, Stephen J. Krasemann/
DRK; 345(c), Charles Krebs/Allstock; 346(c),
David R. Frazier Photolibrary; 351(bl), Bev
Rehkop/Unicorn Stock Photo; 351(bc), HRW
Photo by Russell Dian; 351(br), Ted Horowitz/
The Stock Market; 353(tr), Lawrence Migdale.

CHAPTER 11: Page 355(bl), UPI/Bettmann
Newsphotos; 357(c), Richard Alan/Animals,
Animals; 361(tc), NASA/JPL Photo; 365(tc),
James Balog; 366(cl), John Eastcott/YVA
Momatiuk/DRK; 366(cr), Art Wolfe/Tony Stone
Images; 369(bl, bc, br), Lawrence Migdale;
371(br), Breck P. Kent/Animals, Animals;
374(bc), U.S. Army Photo; 377(tc), Al Grotell.

CHAPTER 12: Page 388(c), Art Wolfe/Allstock;
393(c). The Bettmann Archive; 395(tc), HRW
Photo.

CHAPTER 13: Page 399(bc), C.C. Lockwood/
DRK Photo; 403(br), UPI/Bettmann Newsphotos;
406(cr), Harriet Gans/The Image Works; 406(bl),
NPS Photo by Kepa Maly/Hawaii Volcanoes
National Park; 406(br), George Hunter/H. Arm-
strong Roberts; 410(cl), Nicholas deVore III/Pho-
tographers Aspen; 410(cr), Runk/Schoenberger/
Grant Heilman Photography; 410(bc), David
Hiser/Photographers Aspen; 417(tc), Fred Ward/
Black Star.

CHAPTER 14: Page 432(bc), Mary Messenger;
438(cr), Tom McHugh/Photo Researchers, Inc.;
438(bl), B. Thomas/H. Armstrong Roberts.

CHAPTER 15: Page 445(bc), Bob Daemmrich/
The Image Works; 451(tl) Blair Seitz/Seitz &
Seitz; 451(tr), SuperStock; 451(cl), Jeff Reed/The
Stock Shop; 453(c), Norma Morrison; 459(bc),
Herb Segars/Earth Scenes; 468(bc), Arthur Tilley/
Tony Stone Images.

CHAPTER 16: Page 476(bc), SuperStock; 483(cl),
SuperStock; 487(tl), HRW Photo by Russell Dian;
487(tr), Norma Morrison.

CHAPTER 17: Page 492(bc), Camerique; 495(tr),
Ken Yimm/UPI/Bettmann Newsphotos; 505(bl),
Culver Pictures, Inc.; 511(c), Bill Aron/PhotoEdit.

CHAPTER 18: Page 518(tl, tr, cl, c, cr), Michael
Ochs Archives/Venice, CA; 523(cl), Tony Free-
man/PhotoEdit; 526(c), Charles E. Tuttle Co. of
Tokyo, Japan.

CHAPTER 19: Page 540(c), Tony Freeman/Pho-
toEdit; 542(cl, cr), 545(bc), Culver Pictures, Inc.

CHAPTER 20: Page 553(bl), Paul Conklin;
553(bc), Jake McGuire/Washington Stock Photo,
Inc.; 553(br), Paul Conklin; 559(cr), Novosti/Sipa-
Press; 559(bl), Francois/Figaro/Gamma; 563(bc),
David Madison/Duomo; 570(c), Zheng Zhensun;
576(bc), Lisa Pomerantz/The Image Bank.

CHAPTER 21: Page 581(tr), © 1992 by Sydney
Harris; 582(br), Camerique; 601(tr), Reagan Brad-
shaw; 601(cr), Bob Daemmrich/The Image
Works.

CHAPTER 22: Page 614(cr), FPG International.

CHAPTER 23: page 633, Cameramann International, Ltd.

CHAPTER 24: Page 656(cl, c), Nawrocki Stock
Photo; 663(c), Marty Cordano/DRK Photo;
665(tc), NASA; 667(c), Renato Renolo/Gamma
Liaison.

CHAPTER 25: Page 679(tr), Bruce Asato, Honolulu Advertiser/Sipa-Press; 685(tl), Waring/The
Bettmann Archive; 685(c), Culver Pictures, Inc.;
687(br), American Museum, Bath, England/
Bridgeman Art Library, London/SuperStock.

CHAPTER 26: Page 703(cr), Brian Lanker;
705(bc), Four Square Productions, Inc.; 712(c),
Jerry Jacka; 714(c), Lewis W. Hine/Courtesy
George Eastman House; 724(tc), The Japan
National Tourist Organization, NY; 728(cr,
bl, br), Sanctuary for Animals, Westtown,
New York.

CHAPTER 27: Page 743(c), Kennedy/TexasStock;
753(bc), SuperStock.

CHAPTER 28: Page 772, S. E. Byrne/Lightwave.

Illustration Credits

Brian Battles—110, 199, 225, 227, 271, 312, 353, 359, 363, 511, 687, 743, 856

Linda Blackwell—152, 183, 204, 245, 263

Keith Bowden—70, 248, 355, 361, 387, 413, 505, 540, 663, 665, 714, 752, 768

Rondi Collette—xxii, xxvi, 518, 523, 639, 669

Jim Cummins—66

Chris Ellison—146, 168, 307, 349, 483

Richard Erickson—260, 716

Janice Fried—61, 173

Mary Jones—xxviii, xxix, 607, 770

Linda Kelen—xvii, xxvii, 68, 71, 193, 201, 212–213, 214, 215, 268, 382, 389, 391, 616, 646

Susan B. Remnitz—195, 197

Rich Lo—xii, 27, 42, 276, 278, 357, 450–451, 589

Judy Love—ix, xiv, xxxi, 10–12, 14, 16, 65, 119, 120, 240, 269, 281, 283, 284, 287, 289, 291, 509, 618

Anni Matsick—166

Yoshi Miyake—132, 377

Richard Murdock—48, 209

Precision Graphics—500, 535, 680, 685, 692, 719, 790

Preface, Inc.—9

Jack Scott—106, 318, 378

Chuck Solway—591

Troy Thomas—xi, 180–181, 182–183, 545

Nancy Tucker—67, 79, 81, 418, 498, 772

Critical Readers

The following critical readers reviewed pre-publication materials for this book:

John Algeo
University of Georgia
Athens, Georgia

Alice Bartley
Byrd Middle School
Henrico County, Virginia

Elaine A. Espindle
Peabody Veterans Memorial
High School
Peabody, Massachusetts

Merry Anne Hilty
Heskett Middle School
Bedford, Ohio

Janet Hoeltzel
Union Seventh Grade Center
Broken Arrow, Oklahoma

Rebecca Hight Miller
Westridge Middle School
Orlando, Florida

Patty Sais
Truman Middle School
Albuquerque, New Mexico

Carolyn Kavanagh
East Flagstaff Junior
High School
Flagstaff, Arizona

Jeri McInturff
Chattanooga School
for the Liberal Arts
Chattanooga, Tennessee

Martha Teague Weaver
Cullman Middle School
Cullman, Alabama

Staff Credits

Associate Director: Mescal K. Evler
Executive Editors: Kristine E. Marshall, Robert R. Hoyt
Editorial Staff: Managing Editor, Steve Welch; *Editors,* Cheryl Christian,
A. Maria Hong, Kathryn Rogers Johnson, Karen Kolar, Christy McBride,
Laura Cottam Sajbel, Patricia Saunders, Michael L. Smith, Amy Strong,
Suzanne Thompson, Katie Vignery; *Copyeditors,* Michael Neibergall,
Katherine E. Hoyt, Carrie Laing Pickett, Joseph S. Schofield IV,
Barbara Sutherland; *Editorial Coordinators,* Amanda F. Beard, Rebecca Bennett,
Susan G. Alexander, Wendy Langabeer, Marie H. Price; *Support,* Ruth A. Hooker,
Christina Barnes, Kelly Keeley, Margaret Sanchez, Raquel Sosa, Pat Stover
Permissions: Catherine J. Paré, Janet Harrington
Production: Pre-press, Beth Prevelige, Simira Davis; *Manufacturing,* Michael Roche
Design: Dick Metzger, *Art Director;* Lori Male, *Designer*
Photo Research: Peggy Cooper, *Photo Research Manager;* Jeannie Taylor,
Michael T. Smith, Sam Dudgeon, Victoria Smith, *Photo Research Team*

ISBN 0-03-050862-2

2 3 4 5 6 7 040 00 99 98 97

ELEMENTS OF

Writing

REVISED EDITION

First Course

James L. Kinneavy

John E. Warriner

HOLT, RINEHART AND **WINSTON**

Harcourt Brace & Company

Austin • New York • Orlando • Atlanta • San Francisco
Boston • Dallas • Toronto • London